CW00763454

Flann O'Brien

ACTING OUT

.

Flann O'Brien

ACTING OUT

EDITED BY

Paul Fagan and Dieter Fuchs

CORK UNIVERSITY PRESS

First published in 2022 by
Cork University Press
Boole Library
University College Cork
Cork
T12 ND89
Ireland

Library of Congress Control Number: 2022936365
Distribution in the USA: Longleaf Services, Chapel Hill, NC, USA

British Library Cataloguing in Publication Data
A CIP record for this book is available from the British Library.

ISBN: 978-1-78205-535-8

Printed by BZ Graf in Poland.
Print origination and design by Carrigboy Typesetting Services
www.carrigboy.com

Cover Image: 'Acting Out – Old Phillip Mathers', C-print on dibond, 84 x 59 cm,
edition of 20, David O'Kane, 2017 (Old Phillip Mathers performed by Edward
O'Kane). Copyright David O'Kane 2022. For further information please contact
studio.davidokane@gmail.com or visit www.davidokane.com

www.corkuniversitypress.com

Contents

Act III. Myles en scène

Act IV. Transmedial Entanglements and Interlingual Adaptations

Acknowledgements

The editors wish to express their sincere gratitude to the contributors for all their ingenuity, hard work and good-natured patience throughout the process, particularly as the volume was produced under the inordinately challenging circumstances of the Covid-19 pandemic. Further appreciation is owed to Nina Elisa Ainz, Angela Badegruber, Ruben Borg, Ciaran Byrne, Peter Chrisp, Sabine Coelsch-Foisner, Tanja Deinhamer, Christian Dupont, Katherine Ebury, Anne Fogarty, Julia Hartinger, James Hayes, Jon Haynes, Christopher Herzog, Veronika Hudetz, Flavia Iovine, Eva-Maria Kubin, Gerard Lee, Paul Lee, Val O'Donnell, Pádraig Ó Méalóid, Kurt Palm, Ondřej Pilný, Christian Raphael Resch, Arthur Riordan, Andrew Sherlock, Alan Titley, Edith Vadon, Joanna Walsh, Hugh Wilde, Michelle Witen, David Woods, Ulrike Zillinger, the RTÉ Archives, the John J. Burns Library, Boston College, and the many colleagues in the Flann O'Brien community who pitched in with their help and time throughout the process of putting this book together. Special thanks are reserved for David O'Kane for the collection's artwork and Alison Burns of Studio 10 Design for the cover design, Josette Prichard of Carrigboy for typesetting, Fionbar Lyons for indexing, Aonghus Meaney for his eagle eye in copy-editing the script, as well as to Maria O'Donovan and Mike Collins at Cork University Press for their work in bringing this volume to fruition.

In memory of Eddie O'Kane.

September 2022
Paul Fagan
Dieter Fuchs

Act V. Curtain Calls

List of Abbreviations

ABB   Myles na gCopaleen, *An Béal Bocht* (Cork: Mercier, 1999)

BM   Flann O'Brien, *The Best of Myles*, Kevin O'Nolan (ed.) (London: Harper Perennial, 2007)

CL   Myles na gCopaleen/Gopaleen, *Cruiskeen Lawn*, *The Irish Times*

CN   Flann O'Brien, *The Complete Novels: At Swim-Two-Birds, The Third Policeman, The Poor Mouth, The Hard Life, The Dalkey Archive*, Keith Donohue (introd.) (New York: Everyman's Library, 2007)

L   Flann O'Brien, *The Collected Letters of Flann O'Brien*, Maebh Long (ed.) (Victoria, TX: Dalkey Archive Press, 2018)

MBM   Flann O'Brien, *Myles Before Myles*, John Wyse Jackson (ed.) (Dublin: Lilliput, 2012)

PT   Flann O'Brien, *Plays and Teleplays*, Daniel Keith Jernigan (ed.) (Champaign: Dalkey Archive Press, 2013)

SF   Flann O'Brien, *The Short Fiction of Flann O'Brien*, Neil Murphy and Keith Hopper (eds), Jack Fennell (trans.) (Champaign: Dalkey Archive Press, 2013)

Notes on the Text

To ensure a certain consistency in the way in which reference to the author is made, we favour the name 'Brian O'Nolan' to refer to the author behind the fiction, columns, scripts and correspondence attributed variously to 'Flann O'Brien', 'Myles na gCopaleen', etc., whereas the author of specific texts may be referred to by the chosen *nom de plume*.

The *Cruiskeen Lawn* column was published in *The Irish Times* under the name 'Myles na gCopaleen' from 1940 to '52; however, the name was changed to 'Myles na Gopaleen' in the column of 9 December 1952 and this alternate spelling maintained until the column's last instalment in 1966. In this book, the spelling 'na gCopaleen' is used for columns, fiction and scripts under that name published prior to 9 December 1952 and 'na Gopaleen' for columns, fiction and scripts after this date.

References to and quotations from *Cruiskeen Lawn* are from the original instalments in *The Irish Times*, unless a particular point is being made about one of the edited collections of columns.

The lowercase 'de Selby' refers to the character in *The Third Policeman*, while the uppercase 'De Selby' refers to the character in *The Dalkey Archive*.

The spelling 'Sweeny' that O'Nolan employs in *At Swim-Two-Birds* is used throughout, except for titles by other authors that use the spelling 'Sweeney', such as William Saroyan's *Sweeney in the Trees* (as opposed to *Sweeny in the Trees*, O'Nolan's suggested alternative title for *At Swim-Two-Birds*) or Trevor Joyce's *The Poems of Sweeney Peregrine*. The spelling Finn Mac Cool that O'Nolan employs in *At Swim-Two-Birds* is used throughout.

Notes on Contributors

RICHARD BARLOW is an Associate Professor at Nanyang Technological University in Singapore and the Academic Director of the Trieste Joyce School. His articles have appeared in *Irish Studies Review*, *James Joyce Quarterly* and *Scottish Literary Review*. He is the author of *The Celtic Unconscious: Joyce and Scottish culture* (Notre Dame University Press, 2017) and *Modern Irish and Scottish Literature: Connections, contrasts, Celticisms* (forthcoming with Oxford University Press).

JOSEPH BROOKER is Professor of Modern Literature at Birkbeck, University of London. He is the author of *Joyce's Critics: Transitions in reading and culture* (2004), *Flann O'Brien* (2005), *Literature of the 1980s: After the watershed* (2010) and *Jonathan Lethem and the Galaxy of Writing* (2020).

PAUL FAGAN is a Senior Scientist at Salzburg University. He is the co-editor of *Flann O'Brien: Contesting legacies* (2014), *Flann O'Brien: Problems with authority* (2017), *Flann O'Brien: Gallows humour* (2020), *Stage Irish: Performance, identity, cultural circulation* (2021) and *Irish Modernisms: Gaps, conjectures, possibilities* (2021), as well as the founding general editor of *The Parish Review: Journal of Flann O'Brien studies* and *Production Archives*, both published by the *Open Library of Humanities*.

JACK FENNELL is a Lecturer in the School of English, Irish and Communication at the University of Limerick. He is the author of *Irish Science Fiction* (2014) and *Rough Beasts: The monstrous in Irish fiction, 1800–2000* (2019) and the editor of *A Brilliant Void: A selection of classic Irish science fiction* (2018) and *It Rose Up: A selection of lost Irish fantasy stories* (2021). He has also contributed translations of Brian O'Nolan's Irish work to *The Short Fiction of Flann O'Brien* (2013) and *Flann O'Brien: Plays and teleplays* (2013).

LISA FITZGERALD is a Performance Historian and Arts Researcher at Université Savoie Mont Blanc whose interests include nature in theatre and performance; theatre history; environmental art practice; eco-digital art; urban ecologies; and nature and technology. She is the author of *Re-Place: Irish theatre environments* (2017) and *Digital Vision and the Ecological Aesthetic* (2020).

DIETER FUCHS is Assistant Professor in Anglophone Literatures and Cultural Studies at the University of Vienna. He is the author of *Joyce und Menippos: A portrait of the artist as an old dog* (2006) and *Elizabethan Revenge Drama: Cultural representations, signifying practices and the rise of Protestant middle-class discourse* (2022).

ALANA GILLESPIE is a Lecturer at the English Department and Affiliated Researcher with the Institute for Cultural Inquiry at Utrecht University. Gillespie is completing a monograph on comedy and cultural remembrance in Brian O'Nolan's work and is working on an animated adaptation of *Rhapsody in Stephen's Green*.

S.E. GONTARSKI is Robert O. Lawton Distinguished Professor of English at Florida State University. A writer, director and filmmaker, he has published widely in twentieth-century Irish studies, modernism and performance theory, most recently *Revisioning Beckett: Samuel Beckett's decadent turn* (2018) and *Burroughs Unbound: William S. Burroughs and the performance of writing* (2021).

JOHN GREANEY is a Marie Skłodowska-Curie Fellow at Goethe University Frankfurt. He is the author of *The Distance of Irish Modernism: Memory, narrative, representation* (2022) and co-editor of *Irish Modernisms: Gaps, conjectures, possibilities* (2021).

TOBIAS W. HARRIS is an Associate Fellow at Birkbeck College, University of London. He has published in *Estudios Irlandeses*, the *James Joyce Broadsheet* and *Modernist Cultures* and is the winner of the 'Best Essay-Length Study on a Brian O'Nolan Theme (2015–16)' prize for an essay on O'Nolan and Karl Kraus published in *The Parish Review: Journal of Flann O'Brien studies*.

JOSEPH LABINE is a doctoral candidate at the University of Ottawa whose SSHRC-funded project historicises the emerging Celtic aesthetic in modernist texts. He was the 2018 Marie Tremaine Fellow, and his essay on O'Nolan's archives was published in *Moving Archives* (Wilfrid Laurier University Press, 2020), which won the 2021 Gabrielle Roy Prize. He is the managing editor of Flat Singles Press.

MAEBH LONG is a Senior Lecturer in the English Programme at the University of Waikato. She is the author of two award-winning works on Brian O'Nolan, *Assembling Flann O'Brien* (2014) and *The Collected Letters of Flann O'Brien* (2018), and is one of the general editors of *The Parish Review: Journal of Flann O'Brien studies*. She is the co-editor, with Matthew Hayward, of *New Oceania: Modernisms and modernities in the Pacific* (2020).

JOHANNA MARQUARDT is a Researcher and Lecturer with the Department of English and Linguistics at Johannes Gutenberg-Universität, Mainz. Her PhD research focuses on *Flann's Fantastic Failures: Eccentricity in the Dublin of the mid-twentieth century*. She is the co-editor of *Nationalism and the Postcolonial* (2021).

NEIL MURPHY is a Professor of English at Nanyang Technological University, Singapore. He is the author of *Irish Fiction and Postmodern Doubt* (2004) and *John Banville* (2018) and the co-editor of a special Flann O'Brien centenary issue of the *Review of Contemporary Fiction* (2011) and *The Short Fiction of Flann O'Brien* (2013). He is the co-editor (with Daniel K. Jernigan and W. Michelle Wang) of *The Routledge Companion to Death and Literature* (2021) and is currently co-editing (with W. Michelle Wang and Cheryl Julia Lee) *The Routledge Companion to Literature and Art*.

RICHARD T. MURPHY is an Associate Professor of Modern British and Irish Literature at the University of South Carolina Upstate. He has published articles on Flann O'Brien, Francis Stuart, Nuala Ní Dhomhnaill and Brinsley MacNamara.

DAVID O'KANE is an Irish artist. His short film *Babble*, which stages a multilingual conversation between Flann O'Brien, Franz Kafka and Jorge Luis Borges, won an e v + a open award (2008) from the curator Hou Hanru. His work can be seen on the covers for *Flann O'Brien: Contesting legacies* (2014), *Flann O'Brien: Problems with authority* (2017) and *Flann O'Brien: Gallows humour* (2020). Since 2019, together with his parents, Edward and Joanna O'Kane, he has held exhibitions inspired by O'Brien's literature at Salzburg University, Boston College Ireland, the Irish embassy in Berlin, Boston College's John J. Burns Library and the Alley Theatre, Strabane.

EGLANTINA REMPORT is Senior Lecturer at the School of English and American Studies, Eötvös Loránd University, Budapest. She has published on European art and the drama of the Irish Revival, including an essay on W.B. Yeats and Edward Gordon Craig in the *Irish Studies Review* (2020). She is the author of *Lady Gregory and Irish National Theatre: Art, drama, politics* (2018).

NOAM SCHIFF is a Lecturer and Researcher at Bar Ilan University, and a practising clinical psychologist. Her past research deals with the role of hell in modern Irish fiction and with the under-conceptualised relationship between the mediaeval and modern literary traditions. She is currently interested in the interconnections between modernism and psychoanalysis.

MATTHEW SWENEY is a freelance translator and editor based in the Czech Republic. He has recently co-edited *Ageing Masculinities: Alzheimer's and dementia narratives* (2022). He writes on literature and film and translates Czech poetry into English.

KERRY HIGGINS WENDT holds a PhD from Emory University. She was a graduate research assistant and postdoctoral research assistant with *The Letters of Samuel Beckett*.

PROLOGUE

Introduction

Brian O'Nolan, mask and image

PAUL FAGAN

In a quasi-autobiographical piece titled 'De Me', published in the 1964 *New Ireland* annual under the *nom de plume* of 'Myles na Gopaleen', Brian O'Nolan details the writer's dual imperatives towards self-concealment and self-multiplication:

> the compartmentation of his personality for the purpose of literary utterance ensures that the fundamental individual will not be credited with a certain way of thinking, fixed attitudes, irreversible technique of expression. No author should write under his own name nor under one permanent pen-name; a male writer should include in his impostures a female pen-name, and possibly vice versa.[1]

Under the guise of giving advice to aspiring writers, the article acknowledges O'Nolan's own status as a 'dispersed phenomenon'[2] across multiple *personae* (Myles na gCopaleen/Gopaleen, Flann O'Brien, Count O'Blather, Brother Barnabus, George Knowall, John James Doe, *et al.*), but also across diverse creative collaborations under those pseudonyms (as with Niall Montgomery, who likewise wrote under the 'Myles na gCopaleen/Gopaleen' name). Such an authorial strategy of 'compartmentation', the piece informs us, assumes a carnivalesque stance in opposition to 'every ready-made solution in the sphere of thought and world outlook'.[3] It also facilitates a negotiation of the author's canonicity on his own terms. 'Myles' is curiously, perhaps even puckishly, ahistorical in the imbalance of his programme of cross-gender pseudonyms (given the prominent cases of George Sand, George Eliot, the Bell brothers, *et al.*). Yet, the passage is noteworthy for its framing of the 'pen-name' as a

3

form of 'imposture'. Evidently, O'Nolan thinks of literary craft in terms of deceptive performance.

This late-career association of writing with imposture appears to bookend the student author's ironic aesthetic manifesto in *At Swim-Two-Birds*, O'Nolan's debut novel under the guise of 'Flann O'Brien':

> It was stated that [...] the novel was inferior to the play inasmuch as it lacked the outward accidents of illusion, frequently inducing the reader to be outwitted in a shabby fashion and caused to experience a real concern for the fortunes of illusory characters. The play was consumed in a wholesome fashion by large masses in places of public resort; the novel was self-administered in private. (*CN*, 21)

The student's mock celebration of the theatre's panoptical public consumption – in contrast to his tongue-in-cheek condemnation of the novel's masturbatory nature – and his emphasis on the production's 'outward accidents of illusion' – masks, costumes, props, lighting, movement, mimicry, as opposed to character, plot, theme – appear to announce a 'self-conscious sense of style as performance'[4] that is sustained throughout O'Nolan's career. And yet ... despite the intuition that these resonant scenes frame a consistent, even relentless, dedication to the art of artifice, the rarely cited last paragraph of 'De Me' allows the mask to slip. While withholding his biographical name, Myles makes 'a personal disclosure': he is fifty-one (this is not *quite* true); in twenty-five years has written ten books (this might be true, depending on how you count them) 'under four quite irreconcilable pen-names and on subjects absolutely unrelated' and 'an enormous mass of miscellaneous material consisting of short stories, scripts for radio and TV, contributions to newspapers and magazines, and even book reviews' (this is all true). He shares that he has lived in Dublin most of his life, but was born at 17 The Bowling Green, Strabane – and if you don't believe him, mention his name ('Myles', presumably) to his 'late mother's people, the Gormleys', at 57 Main Street and they will 'instantly take the hint and offer you a glass of malt'.[5] Having thus pulled the rug out from under any authorial pretence – even that of imposture itself – the Myles of 'De Me' endeavours to make a finer distinction: 'I am referred to locally as a [...] "Dublin gutty". I do not deserve this classification, though I sometimes condone it by acting the part; but there is definite confusion here as between *Persona* and *imago*.'[6]

At first blush, this distinction presents Myles's performances in terms of Carl Jung's psychoanalytical archetype of the *persona* – namely, as 'a kind of mask, designed on the one hand to make a definite impression upon others and on the other to conceal the true nature of the individual'.[7] By contrast, Jung theorises the *imago* as a universal unconscious prototype of *personae* that governs how the subject apprehends others. The implication is that Myles's audiences, whether on the page or the street, perceive him via the fixed stereotype of the 'Dublin gutty', rather than appreciating his artful and self-concealing simulation of this role. At the same time, Myles's choice of words situates his arsenal of masks, roles and voices within the tradition of the satirical *persona*, who gives voice to ideas, positions and values which the implied author targets for ridicule. Such conscious impostures stand in contrast to a parallel classical and medieval tradition which foregrounds *imago* as a Latin synonym for *mimesis*, an Aristotelian understanding of drama as an 'imitation of life, an image of truth'.[8] Recalling that O'Nolan adapted the Čapeks' satirical *Insect Play* for the Dublin stage, we might even be tempted to hear an echo of the biological term *imago*, which indicates the final stage of an insect's metamorphosis when it sheds its exoskeleton. Whether in the accretion of coloured gowns that change the wearer's appearance and determine their life's duration in *The Third Policeman*, Sitric Ó Sánasa's transformation into a 'hirsute' seal in *An Béal Bocht* (*CN*, 470; *ABB*, 86), or the wearing of skin as a costume in the taxidermal murder scenario of 'Two in One',[9] O'Nolan's writing pursues this metamorphic principle by recurrently transforming the relationship between characters' inner 'selves' and their 'outward accidents of illusion'.[10]

Each of these layers of meaning (biographical, performative, psycho-analytical, satirical, metamorphic) builds off the interplay of the etymologies of *imago*, meaning 'image', and *persona*, meaning 'the mask of an actor'. Through a series of interrelated examinations of his creative debts and collaborations, staged performances and modes of adaptation, *Flann O'Brien: Acting out* interrogates this complex nexus of disguise and disclosure, of simulation and authenticity, of *persona* and *imago*, that produces the unique hybrid identity of author, performer and literary character that is Brian O'Nolan, Flann O'Brien, Myles na gCopaleen, *et al.*

Masks, mimicry, modernism: O'Nolan's performative art

While he is most often celebrated for his precise, if caustic, wielding of the pen in mimicry of diverse cultural and political targets, a taste for the performative, even the outright theatrical, marks O'Nolan's work throughout his career. Indeed, his creative vocation was forged not on the page, but in the form of a phantasmagoria, when, at the age of 11, 'he and his brother Ciarán drew illustrated "films" that they projected onto the garage wall using a lens, a lamp and paraffin-soaked paper'.[11] *Blather*, an early collaborative production between Brian, Ciarán and their mutual friend Niall Sheridan, combines mock-dramatic sketches – such as 'The Bog of Allen', a travesty of the Abbey's bad-faith ruralism (*MBM*, 42–3) – with digs at the National Theatre of Ireland – as when it reports that the annual government subsidy 'is paid *on condition* the Abbey Players go to America *and remain there* for nine months of the year' as a scheme 'to prevent at all costs the further production in Dublin of *Riders to the Sea* and *Professor Tim*' (*MBM*, 143).[12] Such pieces show us that the writer's comic spirit was, in a meaningful way, theatrical and performative from the outset.

O'Nolan's most famous pseudonym was first introduced to the world in a pseudo-sincere October 1938 letter to the editor of *The Irish Times*, in which 'F. O'Brien' interjects into an epistolary debate between Sean Ó Faoláin and Frank O'Connor about whether the Abbey's 'Peasant Quality' matches their 'Ideals for an Irish Theatre': 'I do not know whether the petulant bickering which is going on in your columns, between Mr Ó Faoláin and Mr O'Connor is a private affair or whether any puling highbrow gentleman of refined tastes may take part'.[13] O'Brien's elegant, if cuttingly satirical, mock solution is to have the Abbey board invest in five hundred extras (peasants) who could occupy the stalls and laugh only when directed by O'Connor and Ó Faoláin. The ensuing epistolary scuffle, and the *Cruiskeen Lawn* column that resulted from it, are well known to O'Nolan's readers, but what is noteworthy here is the author's assumption of a satirical *persona* both to complicate the lines between public and private performance and to expose the dismissive snobbery with which, he implies, Irish cultural elites construct their imagined audiences.

Here we might recall that Myles na gCopaleen, O'Nolan's other major pseudonym and his 'most holistically conceived dramatic *persona*',[14] is a recycling of a stage-Irish figure from Dion Boucicault's *The Colleen Bawn*. From his perch 'in the gods' at *The Irish Times*, Myles regularly passed judgement on the Irish theatre scene. In February 1943, he documents his attendance at a 'frightfully boring play', throughout which the audience was 'distracted by curious rasping noises' that turned out to be 'the sound of the plot creaking';[15] in January 1957, he raises the stakes to assert the 'apocalyptic status' of the Abbey Theatre, where 'the raising of the curtain entails Revelation' – even if 'what is revealed is a flurry of very bad language'.[16] At times, Myles extended his brief to intervene directly in the running of Irish theatre's major institutions, as in his BAHAFMUSGO (Blythe and Hayes and Farren Must Go) campaign across six columns in 1952, which called for the removal of the three Abbey Theatre directors, leading to a public apology by *The Irish Times* and the disappearance of *Cruiskeen Lawn* from the newspaper's pages for nine months.[17]

While the encounter with Ó Faoláin and O'Connor shows O'Nolan advocating for the dignity of The Plain People as spectators of Irish cultural life, elsewhere Myles's frustrations with real Dublin audiences were at the root of the column's more ingenious inventions. Consider his scheme to hire out ventriloquists to project conversation on behalf of dull theatregoers 'who are very important and equally ignorant',[18] or his elegant solution to the problem of late arrivals:

> My idea is that the patron should approach his seat through a trap-door situated where he keeps his feet when seated. The patrons approach the building through a cellar and [...] mount velvet-runged ladders and reach their seats with the minimum fuss and interference. Take your stand at the back of such a theatre and watch the audience arriving. There is no door, entrance or exit of any kind. All is silence and soft light. After a time you hear a gentle click and, hey-presto, a solitary bald head has appeared in the middle of the parterre. One by one, heads appear silently throughout the vast auditorium. The usual hot-tempered wrangling about seats and ticket stubs is going on hell for leather in the cellar, but not a word of it reaches the sacred cathedral of the drayma [*sic*].[19]

At other times, the application of Myles's genius to the practicalities of theatre production provides the grounds for purely comic and joyously absurd flights of fancy – we think here, among other examples, of his 'Patent Ballet Pumps', which are fitted with 'three diminutive land mines' for ballerinas who need an extra spring in their step.[20] Whether designed for the play or its critics, the playgoers or the players, these Mylesian inventions and interventions are directed towards the pragmatics of social interaction in ways that evidence the everyday indignities and frustrations of a regular theatregoer. The columns not only display a keen awareness of the politics of contemporary Irish theatre in its social, cultural and national institutional roles, but also send up the pretensions of its playwrights, producers, critics and audiences.

By October 1941, a year into *Cruiskeen Lawn*'s run, Myles claimed to have already had 136 plays rejected by the Abbey.[21] A number of columns drop casual hints towards this fantasy 'grey canon' of unproduced work: Myles claims the Abbey will stage his English translation of Plato's *Phaedo*, set in a modern pub, in which the executioner turns to Socrates to ask, 'Well, what's your poison?'[22] In the August 1956 column 'Thoughts for a Play', Myles pitches a stage-Irish burlesque he has developed with Jimmy O'Dea and Denis Brennan called *The Four Green Fields*, in which MYLES NA GOPALEEN enters 'with a keg of potheen on his shoulder and a shillelagh in his hand', as the plot builds towards a 'weight-lifting contest [...] at a hedge pitch-and-toss school', where MOTHER MACHREE and JANEY MACK 'keep watch for peelers', accompanied by Irish traditional music and dancing courtesy of 'a chorus of leprechauns and banshees'.[23] A year later, writing about Lady Gregory and W.B. Yeats's letter to President Cosgrave offering the Abbey Theatre to the new state (an offer which was declined), he wonders what the players 'would think of being made civil servants' and his immediate response is a familiar one: 'Nice thought: I must write a play about it.'[24]

Having poked fun at the Irish theatre scene from behind the masks of Count O'Blather, F. O'Brien and Myles na gCopaleen, O'Nolan began to write for the stage in 1942, working with the Gate, Gaiety Theatre, Abbey Theatre and other Dublin companies to produce *Thirst*, *Faustus Kelly*, *Rhapsody in Stephen's Green* and *An Sgian*. In the same period, he translated Brinsley MacNamara's 1933 play *Margaret Gillan* into Irish for An Gúm. Across the course of his career, he also wrote for and appeared on 2RN and Radio Éireann and worked on projects with the BBC. He relaunched Myles na Gopaleen as a key voice of the newly founded Irish national television broadcaster Telefís Éireann with his two sitcoms *O'Dea's Yer Man* (1963–4) and *Th'Oul Lad of Kilsalaher* (September–December 1965). This writing for performance has often been neglected, even in O'Nolan studies, as inferior or 'popular' work. However, this trend is beginning to change in the aftermath of Daniel Keith Jernigan's 2013 volume of the *Plays and Teleplays*, which for the first time anthologises the Myles na gCopaleen scripts that fell out of print just as the star of Flann O'Brien's novels was rising in critical circles (*PT*, vii). Since Jernigan's collection, isolated analyses of O'Nolan's plays have hinted at their value to a fuller appreciation both of the author's *oeuvre* and of mid-twentieth-century Irish theatre, television and radio.[25] Owing both to limited travelling and working opportunities for acting and writing talent and to the easing of competitive pressure from the United Kingdom on account of the Second World War, O'Nolan's turn to the stage occurred in a period in which 'more plays were presented annually in Dublin than ever before',[26] as 'the exigencies of wartime had made Ireland attractive to Irish and English professional touring companies which in earlier days would have cast their sights elsewhere'.[27] Not only do these scripts remain to be fully reconsidered as a vital part of the author's post-novel career, but their production histories need to be explored more rigorously for what they reveal about the political contexts and cultural networks of the theatrical boom of Emergency-era Ireland.

To address these gaps, the present collection situates O'Nolan and his work within a performance network of Irish and international playwrights and practitioners, theatrical movements and theories of literary performance. The contributors uniquely overturn previous conceptualisations of O'Nolan by situating him back within his creative troupe of collaborators, producers and fellow performers and in front of his diverse audiences in public, literary, critical and theatrical contexts. Ronald J. Pelias defines performance as 'a communicative process'[28] yet one consequence of under-analysing O'Nolan's writing for stage, radio and screen has been a tendency to see him in isolation – a lonely modernist, anti-modernist or postmodernist pioneer – rather than as a figure who is shaped by social, literary, theatrical, journalistic and state networks and institutions (the Abbey, the Gate and Telefís Éireann, but also *The Irish Times* and the civil service, even the Dublin pub scene). Throughout his career, O'Nolan's work was influenced by professional and personal relationships with playwrights, producers and actors: Brinsley MacNamara, Micheál mac Liammóir, Hilton Edwards, Jimmy O'Dea and Brendan Behan, to name but a handful.[29] Lest we imagine this a closed network, we need only remember that Orson Welles launched his acting career at the Gate in a series of productions directed by Edwards in 1931, a connection that Myles na gCopaleen alludes to explicitly in 'Shows and Showers', a note he penned for the programme of the Gate Theatre's 1942 'Jack-in-the-Box' Christmas variety show at which *Thirst* was first performed.[30] As Myles's note calls for more technical experimentation on the Irish stage by imagining the mechanics of 'beautiful rain-ballets', Ireland is presented as Welles's home only a year after the triumph of *Citizen Kane*: 'It is evening at Foynes, A fairy Flying Fortress alights on the water. It is Orson Welles and his son Vic – home once more after making good. He takes a bow, and the curtain comes down amid sodden applause.'[31] To appreciate O'Nolan's work as participating in these local and international dialogues, collaborations and exchanged gazes is to advance our understanding of the author's concern with the performative, the theatrical and the illusionary across not only discursive literary genres but also within real-life encounters and relationships.[32]

A more rigorous consideration of the role of performance networks, creative collaborations and cultural institutions in O'Nolan's art draws our attention, in turn, to diverse ekphrastic relations and transmedial encounters throughout his work. Indeed, given the recurrent dismissal of his theatrical writing in previous waves of O'Nolan studies, we might be surprised to note how often critics have turned to the theatre for analogies with which to describe the innovative qualities of his novels. In his reader's report for Longmans, Green & Co., Graham Greene wrote that *At Swim-Two-Birds* filled him with 'the kind of glee one experiences when people smash china on the stage'.[33] Jorge Louis Borges links the metaleptic *mise en abyme* of *At Swim-Two-Birds* to *Hamlet*'s 'Mousetrap' scene in his 1939 review essay 'When Fiction Lives in Fiction', while Anne Clissmann likens the circular hell of *The Third Policeman* 'to that envisioned by Sartre' in *Huis Clos* (No Exit), and Keith Hopper compares both novels' crossings of narrative levels or ontological borders to Luigi Pirandello, Bertolt Brecht and Samuel Beckett's variations on modernist metatheatre.[34] In a notable recent intervention into this debate, Stefan Solomon places Martin Puchner's concept of modernist anti-theatricality into conversation with Mikhail Bakhtin's theory of novelistic discourse to argue that it is in fact O'Nolan's metafictional novels, and not his broader plays, that are aligned to the *avant-garde* anti-theatrical tradition.[35] Implicit in this line of comparative argumentation is an understanding that the anti-mimetic novel tradition in which O'Nolan is writing cannot be extracted and cordoned off from the history of metatheatre. Indeed, a closer interrogation of O'Nolan's writing and the traditions in which he is working reveals the partiality of any approach that sets strict, impermeable limits between prose, poetry, theatre, mass media and the visual arts. A central presupposition of this book is that a fuller consideration of O'Nolan's achievements needs to take into account the transformative aspects of his performative art *across* and *between* genres, media and platforms, from the celebrated novels and columns to the less-travelled terrains of his scripts, correspondence, short fiction and poetic translations.

The interplay between performance and style in O'Nolan's prose fiction exhibits both the disruptive anti-authoritarian 'acting out' of the unruly audience member and a taste for on-stage role-playing. It is worth noting, for instance, that amid the 'self-evident sham' of *At Swim-Two-Birds* (CN, 21), the authority of the petit-bourgeois uncle is exposed as fake when it is revealed he has been acting in a musical production wearing the costume of 'a policeman's hat of the papier-mâché type' (*CN*, 56).[36] The uncanny reality of the afterworld of *The Third Policeman* hinges, too, upon its strange sense of environmental and legal artifice. The police barracks has the appearance of an inartistically constructed set: 'It looked as if it were painted like an advertisement on a board on the roadside and indeed very poorly painted. It looked completely false and unconvincing. It did not seem to have any depth or breadth and looked as if it would not deceive a child' (*CN*, 265). Elsewhere, the novel anticipates Myles's needling of both the theatregoing cultured class and the uncultured 'mob' in an extended fantasy which contrasts 'the delirium of the fashionable audience inside [the La Scala Opera House] after Signor Bari had concluded his recital' with the rioting and police baton-charges outside the premises, in which 'Thousands were injured, 79 fatally'. Echoing the parodic treatment of the narrator's uncle in *At Swim-Two-Birds*, O'Nolan exploits the theatrical image here to undermine the artifice of authority with a strike below the belt, as we read how, in the ensuing melee, 'Constable Peter Coutts sustained injuries to the groin from which he is unlikely to recover' (*CN*, 255). Each novel already discloses its theatrical debts in a paratextual epigraph that initiates the reader into the text: in the epigraph from Euripides's *Heracles* that sets up the topsy-turvy world of *At Swim-Two-Birds* ('ἐξίσταται γὰρ πάντ' ἀπ' ἀλλήλων δίχα': 'for all things change, making way for each other'),[37] and in the epigraph from Shakespeare's *Julius Caesar* that introduces us to the infernal uncertainties of *The Third Policeman* ('Since the affairs of men rest still uncertain, Let's reason with the worst that may befall'; *CN*, 221).

As he assumes a remarkable variety of *personae* before distinct audiences in a vast array of cultural sites, O'Nolan explores the comic and aesthetic pleasures of masked performance. Yet, his work also interrogates the potential of performance and simulation not only to express but to *produce* identity, and the power of illusion not only to represent but to *shape* reality itself. A concern with 'the outward accidents of illusion' characterises de Selby's philosophical reflections on the 'illusory' qualities of progression, space and time (*CN*, 264, 302), indeed of any consensus about reality, as well as that novel's interrogations of the *mise en abyme* of identity ('A body with another body inside it in turn, thousands of such bodies within each other like the skins of an onion, receding to some unimaginable ultimum'; *CN*, 327). *The Third Policeman* everywhere explores the relation between *persona* and *imago*, from the de Selby scholar's many outwardly deceptive performances meant to conceal his intentions and true reactions from the policemen to the inner tension between the nameless protagonist and his soul Joe. Such a conflict between *persona* and *imago* also underpins the strange conversions of 'Mr Duffy' into 'Mr Train' in 'John Duffy's Brother' and of Murphy into Kelly in 'Two in One'. In both short stories, scenes of transformation experiment with tragic and comic form,[38] even as they emphasise the Jungian relation of the *persona* to social interactions: Duffy's anxiety centres around whether his work colleagues will interpret his metamorphosis into a train as a comic performance or as a disclosure of his true self; the murderer Murphy walks the streets 'dressed' in his victim Kelly's skin, 'receiving salutes from newsboys and other people who had known Kelly' (*SF*, 86). As O'Nolan plays on the etymology of identity as deriving from the Latin *idem* (same), his *dramatis personae* perform a range of relations between the mask and the image to explore how characters might be simultaneously the same and not the same as themselves, each other, their authors, their audiences.

Even as O'Nolan has taken centre stage in key debates of Irish studies and modernist studies over the last decade, the prominence of performance, imposture, social theatricality and literary illusion in his multi-genre project remains under-scrutinised. Consequently, his influences and debts have often been narrowed to the Irish literary sphere at the expense of his engagements with a broader range of Irish, British, European and American theatre, visual arts, radio and film. In O'Nolan studies itself, even as new work has begun to explore the place of his writing for performance in relation to his broader canon, too often, still, it reads these works evaluatively at the expense of appreciating their place within the cultural institutions, performance networks and political contexts of Emergency-era and post-war Ireland and Europe. This book aims to make significant advances to address gaps in each of these directions.

Acting out

Flann O'Brien: Acting out interrogates the roles of performance, theatricality, and illusion in O'Nolan's *oeuvre* not from a single vantage point but rather as he develops these themes through diverse positions of performance and spectatorship. The volume is the first full-length study to explore in detail the theatrical and anti-theatrical movements of O'Nolan's art in connection with romantic, melodramatic, revivalist, realist, modernist and *avant-garde* dramaturgies. In fruitful conversation with each other, the contributors cast new light on O'Nolan's pseudonyms, his collaborations and his staging of a diversity of themes (war, nationalism, gender, nonhuman bodies, posthuman identity) in genres, media, adaptations and creative receptions that vacillate between the comic and the tragic. These interventions both historicise and challenge our understanding of O'Nolan's masks by reading his novels, short fiction, columns, scripts, poetry and correspondence in diverse theatrical contexts. By not limiting themselves to his writing for performance, but by exploring the function of performativity across his multimedial, multimodal and multilingual body of work, these essays make a powerful case that if, as Richard Schechner claims, 'performances mark identities, bend time, reshape and adorn the body, and tell stories',[39] then few writers better demonstrate this shaping force and potential of the performative in literature than Brian O'Nolan.

Under the theme of 'Stage Irish', the opening section explores O'Nolan's recently published correspondence and shares new archival discoveries to situate the author more firmly within a local creative collective and to reassess more fully his writing's engagements with Irish theatrical history. Maebh Long opens the collection by analysing three acts of collaboration and possible literary theft involving O'Nolan, Niall Montgomery and Niall Sheridan which cast new critical light on the 'technique of performance plagiarism'[40] that underpins the author's broader aesthetic project. Next, Alana Gillespie explores how Myles na gCopaleen's characterisations of Irish theatregoers and his shifting positions on the role of the audience illuminate a modernist tension between a suspicion of the theatre, a fascination with its ability to 'make it new' and a concern that its innovations must also themselves becomes cliché. Reassessing the author's relationship to the stage Irish tradition, Richard Barlow reframes the influence of Dion Boucicault on O'Nolan's aesthetic through a reappraisal of the maligned author of nineteenth-century Irish melodramas as a politically charged theatrical innovator whose influence on Irish modernist writing has been critically neglected. And Dieter Fuchs takes *The Third Policeman*'s oft-overlooked epigraph from *Julius Caesar* as a launching point for reading O'Nolan's novel within the framework of Irish political restagings of the Oedipal myth, from Yeats's *Oedipus the King* to Synge's *The Playboy of the Western World*.

Even as they place O'Nolan in an Irish theatrical context and tradition, these opening essays betray an inescapable relation to the international theatrical currents that animate the local scene, from the performance theories of Konstantin Stanislavsky and Vsevelod Meyerhold (Gillespie) to the influence of Shakespeare on the Irish political imaginary (Fuchs). Building on these coordinates, the book's second section, 'O'Nolan's Globe', shifts the emphasis to the author's international theatrical contexts and debts. Joseph

LaBine devotes unprecedented scholarly attention to the correspondence between O'Nolan and American playwright William Saroyan between 1939 and '41, examining how performance, theatricality and 'play' in Saroyan and O'Nolan's letters mark the encounter between two bodies of writing with deep aesthetic and philosophical affinities. Neil Murphy advances the critical conversation regarding the resonances between the metatheatre of Pirandello's *Six Characters in Search of an Author* and the metafiction of *At Swim-Two-Birds* by expanding the horizons of the debate in two directions: first, by taking the authors' broader bodies of writing into account, in particular their short fiction; secondly, by comparatively analysing them within a distinct counter-realist tradition in European literature and theatre. Our understanding of O'Nolan's position in the European anti-realist tradition is further developed by Kerry Higgins Wendt, who considers the resonances between *At Swim-Two-Birds*'s metafictional emphasis on 'the outward accidents of illusion' and Bertolt Brecht's metatheatrical *Verfremdungseffekt* – now commonly known as the alienation, distancing or estrangement effect but first translated into English in 1936 as 'disillusion'. The comparison allows Wendt to demonstrate how O'Nolan's ironic inversions of continental theatrical theory produce a new form of metafiction, between modernism and magical realism, that engages both myth and social issues. Further interrogating questions of sociopolitical theatricality in O'Nolan's writing, Noam Schiff applies Bakhtin's theory of the carnivalesque to Mr Toole's performative pub anecdote in 'The Martyr's Crown' – which is 'better than a play' to his audience (*SF*, 76). Schiff reads the story not only as an exemplary instance of the scenes of social theatricality, hyperreal history and carefully crafted illusion that run through O'Nolan's work, but also as a carnivalesque performance of gender roles, in which religious and cultural nationalist ideals are degraded through reference to bodily functions.

Having explored the performative dimensions of O'Nolan's local and international collaborations and influences, the volume turns, in its third section 'Myles en scène', to an examination of the author's neglected writing for performance on stage in its Irish and European political contexts. Joseph Brooker investigates *Thirst*'s blending of perlocutionary effect and embodied reception to situate the play not only in line with the language performativity of O'Nolan's more celebrated novel and column writing, but also within and against the modern Irish 'performative' theatrical tradition, exemplified by Yeats and Synge. Overturning previous critical beliefs that as a playwright O'Nolan handles his source materials lightly, Tobias W. Harris closely compares *Faustus Kelly* with Goethe's four versions of *Faust* and contemporary anti-fascist continental versions of the play (by Karl Kraus, Thomas Mann, Paul Valéry and Dorothy Sayers) to demonstrate the familiarity and nuance with which O'Nolan reimagines his source text to address specific political and ideological targets, both in Europe and closer to home. Lisa FitzGerald reframes O'Nolan's full-length reworking of the Čapeks' *Insect Play* by compelling us to rethink the insect-human aesthetic of *Rhapsody in Stephen's Green* as part of a wider discourse of mechanised, posthumanist European wartime theatre. Drawing on the current nonhuman turn in literary theory, FitzGerald moves beyond anthropocentric allegorical readings of O'Nolan's play to consider its engagement with a mode of zoopoetics that grants its nonhuman dimensions a dynamic agency. Jack Fennell closes the section by casting new light on a previously darkened corner of the *oeuvre* by exploring how O'Nolan's short plays *An Sgian* and *The Handsome Carvers* evoke the precedent of the Grand Guignol theatrical movement in their representations of murderous misogyny, the civil service and Irish-language revivalist and fascist movements.

The volume's fourth section, 'Transmedial Entanglements and Interlingual Adaptations', considers diverse points of refraction through media and language in O'Nolan's writing. Paul Fagan analyses the function of the disembodied voice across O'Nolan's fiction and writing for television, reading the trope both as a modernist response both to the technologies of the gramophone, the radio and the cinematic voiceover and to an emergent posthumanist concern with the changed relation of body and soul. Picking up this theme of O'Nolan's ekphrastic art, Eglantina Remport argues that *At Swim-Two-Birds* is, in part, a pastiche of Lady Augusta Gregory's 'theatrical' collection of Celtic myths and legends *Gods and Fighting Men* (1904), a position which allows Remport to trace O'Nolan's place within both the tradition of *tableaux vivants* and the Irish modernist art scene *vis-à-vis* Mainie Jellett. Richard T. Murphy analyses O'Nolan's Irish-language translation of Brinsley MacNamara's melodramatic Ibsenite play *Margaret Gillan*, focusing on the author's struggles with the source material, the publisher and his copyeditor to explore the question of the untranslatability of the proper name. Matthew Sweney brings new archival research to bear on a close comparative analysis of Myles na gCopaleen's *Rhapsody in Stephen's Green* with its Czech source material, Karel and Josef Čapek's First World War animal satire *Ze života hmyzu*, to argue that O'Nolan's free adaptation of this material to a contemporary Irish milieu under the shadow of the Second World War is closer in spirit, tone and politics to the Čapeks' Czech original than previous English-language adaptations, such as *And So Ad Infinitum* and *The World We Live In.*

The collection's closing section, 'Curtain Calls', addresses the diverse roles O'Nolan has been made to play in his posthumous public, critical and theatrical receptions: the eccentric and the civil servant; the antiquarian and the modernist; the clown and the truth-teller; the popular entertainer and the avant-garde innovator; the local boy in the paper and the deracinated postmodernist. This focus draws on Elin Diamond's contention that drama comprises not only 'embodied acts, in specific sites, witnessed by others (and/ or the watching self)', but also all the ways in which the 'completed event' is 'remembered, misremembered, interpreted and passionately revisited across a pre-existing discursive field'.[41] On this point, Johanna Marquardt considers how the biographical author Brian O'Nolan has been 'morphed' into the image of the local jester and eccentric Myles na gCopaleen through a performative exchange of gazes in memoirs and anecdotes by colleagues, friends and family members (Tony Gray, John Ryan, Anthony Cronin, Ciarán and Micheál Ó Nualláin), many of whom were the audiences of his near-theatrical performances in Dublin pubs. S.E. Gontarski draws critical attention to a pivotal, but previously overlooked, site of O'Nolan's posthumous restaging and canonisation in the Irish journal *The Lace Curtain* in the 1970s, an important site for the redefinition of Irish modernism. Through the journal's republication of O'Nolan's sincere Irish-language poetry translations, and not his more innovative and ironised prose, alongside the newly de-pseudonymised 'Recent Irish Poetry' by his theatrical counterpart Samuel Beckett, O'Nolan's place as a modernist innovator was both shaped and concealed, subverted and misrepresented, for at least a generation. John Greaney reflects on the ways in which the recent turn towards historicist criticism in the field of Irish modernism reduces and obscures certain aspects of the internationalist modernist thought evidenced by O'Nolan's poetic use of the mask. The collection closes with a survey of stage, radio and screen productions and adaptations of O'Nolan's writing as the basis for future work on creative and performative receptions and refractions of our masked man.

ACT I

Stage Irish

I

Plagiarism and the Politics of Friendship

Brian O'Nolan, Niall Sheridan and Niall Montgomery

Maebh Long

On 4 August 1945, *Cruiskeen Lawn* featured a series of fragments whose pomposity, grandiloquence and laboured self-depreciation were typical of Myles na gCopaleen. With a delicate fatigue, Myles opens: 'Indignation at literary wrongs I leave to men born under happier stars.'[1] Myles follows with a passage outlining his indifference to public opinion and speaks on translations from the Greek accomplished before he was fifteen; he mentions grand offers made to him after his return from Germany and modestly announces that the verbal attacks made on his person do not stem from jealousy of his own simple works, but merely from his intimacy with men such as Wordsworth and Southey. In the midst of voluble declarations of prominence and humility, Myles recounts an instance in which an 'amateur performer' told a mutual friend that he deeply desired to make Myles's acquaintance, but was concerned that Myles would shun him, as the performer had penned a 'confounded severe epigram' on Myles's work – the name of which Myles discreetly redacts. Myles told the friend that if the epigram were good then its severity would be of little consequence, and asked to hear it. When the epigram was recited, Myles reacted with some amusement, as, he proclaims: 'it proved to be one which I had myself some time before written'. With this grand magnanimity in the face of flagrant plagiarism the column closes. An italicised note remains, however, to disrupt everything that came before:

> *My Excellency presents his compliments and denies on oath that he wrote the foregoing. It is the work of my uncle, Mr Samuel Taylor Coleridge and is extracted from his work, 'Biographia Literaria'. Readers must accept it as a further, scandalous example of the plagiarisms with which I am beset.*

Not a single line of the column prior to this had been the original work of Myles na gCopaleen, but had been copied verbatim, as Myles admits, from Coleridge's *Biographia Literaria; or Biographical Sketches of My Literary Life and Opinions* (1814). Behind every use of the first person was not Myles, but Coleridge and, far from the suppression of names being the diffidence of authentic realism, it was the reticence of the plagiarist.

Myles was not unfamiliar with the conjunction of plagiarism and literary predecessors. In July 1945, he had denounced intellectual fraud, demanding to know if there was 'under heaven anything more scabrous than plagiarism? Fouler? [...] to thieve ideas – to be a cut-purse trafficking in men's minds! Could sad human folly achieve greater violence?'[2] But Myles's condemnation is predicated on a particular temporal complexity, as in addition to his general censure of academic appropriation was the specific denunciation of intellectual theft by those who came before: 'That the live should steal thought from the live or even the dead, that is detestable; but that the dead should steal from the live – how very thrice detestable!' In this instance, Myles attacks Laurence Sterne for stealing his work, and some years later, in 1954, he would dismiss Charles Dickens for imitating him in 'the *minutiae* of literary technique'[3] and decry Dion Boucicault for using – and misspelling – Myles's own name in *The Colleen Bawn* (1860).[4]

In March 1954, when Myles accuses Dickens of stealing *Bleak House* (1853) from him, he writes:

> I have been reading a novel which – after vainly looking for my own name on the title page – I found had been written by Huffam [Dickens]. This work is a startling example of plagiarism, passing-off, literary assassination and unheard-of ruffianism. I will quote one of the more outrageous imitations of my style.[5]

In a beautiful logical and temporal inversion, rather than the *Cruiskeen Lawn* columns being the assemblage of many earlier writers, many earlier writers are guilty of having plagiarised Myles's work. The Coleridge extracts do not sound so recognisably like Myles because Myles is a little more than the product of fragmentary extracts; instead, the greats are all guilty of having pillaged Myles's grand texts.[6]

The *Oxford English Dictionary* notes that plagiarism derives from the classical Latin *plagiārius*, meaning a 'person who abducts the child or slave of another, kidnapper, seducer, also a literary thief'. To plagiarise is not simply to steal words or ideas but is to be involved in the theft of a person. In the case of plagiarism, we do not simply take someone's brainchild, we put it to work for us. In stealing the space of Myles's column, Coleridge is – in Myles's fancy – plagiarising him, as he is stealing Myles's words, but Coleridge is also, in a sense, kidnapping him, as he is stealing his identity. Myles is the *Cruiskeen Lawn*, in the literal sense that the character takes his existence from the column, and, on the narrative plane in which Myles can be thought to 'really' exist, Myles is figuratively the column in the way that all authors are bound up in their work. From this perspective, plagiarism is not merely the straightforward passing off of Myles's words, ideas or style, but rather the luring away of Myles's self. As such, the column of 4 August 1945 performs two forms of plagiarism – the appropriation of another's work, but also the seizure and assumption of an identity.

Alternatively, of course, and with fewer temporal convolutions, one could read Myles's lamentation of the plagiarism that besets him as an admission of guilt – that is, that Myles acknowledges that the passages had been written by Coleridge and confesses that the *Cruiskeen Lawn* columns are generally scandalous examples of plagiarism. Thus, plagiarism is acknowledged to be a habit of Myles's, and a flexibility around ideas of originality, borrowing, identity and inheritance is admitted to be a defining technique of *Cruiskeen Lawn*, as well as O'Nolan's wider *œuvre*. With this range in mind – the concealed reuse of ideas, innovative play with the notion of originality, anxieties regarding connections between identity and style – this essay engages with three events of possible plagiarism relating to Brian O'Nolan. The backdrop against which the appropriation of ideas and abduction of identity takes place is a complicated one, however, as these scenes are acted out within a space of longstanding intellectual collaboration and friendship between O'Nolan, Niall Montgomery and Niall Sheridan. Thus, this essay looks at literary alliances that become troubled by ideas, styles and identities that double and repeat as various personalities engage in a variety of forms of acting out – acting out of place, acting out a role, acting out of character and acting out someone else's script.

Brian O'Nolan, Niall Sheridan and Niall Montgomery

Brian O'Nolan (1911–66) met Niall Sheridan (1912–98) and Thomas Niall Montgomery (1915–87) at University College Dublin. O'Nolan graduated with a BA in 1932 and an MA in 1935, Sheridan graduated with a BA in 1933 and an MA in 1934, and Montgomery graduated with a BArch in 1938. O'Nolan collaborated on numerous literary projects with both; undertakings which ran from the earnest to the determinedly ridiculous. In 'Brian, Flann and Myles' in Timothy O'Keeffe's *Myles: Portraits of Brian O'Nolan*, Sheridan speaks of how he and O'Nolan worked 'hand-in-glove' on University College Dublin's (UCD's) student magazine *Comhthrom Féinne*[7] and edited their own, short-lived magazine *Blather* with Ciarán Ó Nualláin. O'Nolan based the character of Brinsley in *At Swim-Two-Birds* on Sheridan,[8] and the poem 'Ad Lesbiam', which Brinsley recites within the novel, is taken from Sheridan and Donagh MacDonagh's volume *Twenty Poems* (1934). Sheridan and O'Nolan worked with Denis Devlin on the 'All-Purpose Opening Speech', one endless sentence so devoid of meaning that it could be used on any occasion,[9] and they also, with Devlin and MacDonagh, collaborated on the Great Irish Novel that never was, *Children of Destiny*. Sheridan contributed at least one letter to the 1939 *Time's Pocket* letters frenzy that O'Nolan created in *The Irish Times*, writing under the provocative name of 'Francis O'Connor' (*L*, 35) but most importantly, Sheridan undertook the task of editing and cutting *At Swim-Two-Birds* before it was sent to Longmans. After his wedding, at which O'Nolan was best man, Sheridan went on honeymoon to Paris and while there presented a copy of *At Swim-Two-Birds* to James Joyce.

If Sheridan played a vital role in O'Nolan's first novel, Montgomery was instrumental in O'Nolan's last. Letters detail Montgomery's suggestions for changes in *The Dalkey Archive*, the majority of which O'Nolan incorporated into the final draft. Montgomery was pivotal in changing the narrative from the first to the third person, in reducing the characters' alcohol intake and in refining some of the style (*L*, 365–8). But as important as these changes are, it is Montgomery's role in *Cruiskeen Lawn* that is vital in O'Nolan's *œuvre*. Although not generally known at the time, Montgomery's involvement in the columns was not a secret – in *Niall Montgomery: Dublinman*, Christine O'Neill quotes letters from James Johnson Sweeney in 1950 and Edwin O'Connor in 1954 that praise Montgomery's *Cruiskeen Lawn* contributions.[10] In a letter to O'Keeffe in 1971, Sheridan notes that Montgomery 'worked closely with Brian in the later period of the Myles na gCopaleen column'[11] although, as we will see below, this is clearly a diminishment of Montgomery's actual contribution. More publicly, in an *Irish Times* tribute to R.M. 'Bertie' Smyllie, editor of *The Irish Times* from 1934 to '54, Terence de Vere White explains that 'Myles had a stand-in – Niall Montgomery, the cleverest and most self-effacing of his contemporaries. It would be unjust if [...] he should not have a mention in the story'.[12] Yet for many years the collaborative nature of the *Cruiskeen Lawn* venture was predominantly ignored within scholarly work; although in *No Laughing Matter: The life and times of Flann O'Brien* Anthony Cronin notes that O'Nolan used the mention of a stand-in to avoid responsibility for politically sensitive material, he implies that this was an excuse rather than a fact.[13] Keith Donohue echoes this point, but they were among the few scholars even to imply that the columns were the work of more than one individual.[14] It was not until Carol Taaffe worked on the Montgomery papers housed in the National Library that the extent of Montgomery's contribution was fully investigated.[15]

Montgomery's papers contain over 150 draft columns, dated January 1947 to February 1962, many typed on the backs of Montgomery's architectural notes or scrap office paper, or written in Montgomery's handwriting. O'Neill notes that Montgomery tended to write about 'politics and the government; partition; town planning and traffic; CIE, the ESB, and the theatre'.[16] Although Taaffe argues that 'Montgomery's pieces stand out most when O'Nolan goes through an arid phrase of producing filler material',[17] on the whole the tonal inconsistencies between O'Nolan's and Montgomery's contributions are so slight as to be unrecognisable. At times, O'Nolan edited Montgomery's versions, but they were most frequently published with few amendments. Importantly, as wide-ranging as the files in the National Library are, it seems unlikely that they represent the full contribution made by Montgomery. On 24 March 1946, Denis Devlin asked Montgomery, 'Are you still writing? or is you [your] free time still taken up with M. n. gC.?' (*L*, 173). The question suggests that Montgomery had begun to share the *Cruiskeen Lawn* task much earlier, and Montgomery's lamentation to Terence de Vere White, following O'Nolan's death and the end of the column, that he 'miss[ed] the freedom of my dear friend's shooting box!'[18] suggests engagement right up until the end.

It is also highly probable that Montgomery was not the only contributor to *Cruiskeen Lawn*. In a letter to Seán MacEntee in 1953, O'Nolan states that a

> considerable amount of of [*sic*] material appearing in *The Irish Times* under *Cruiskeen Lawn* is not written by me at all. I have two substitutes or 'stand-ins'. I personally engage in a lot of other newspaper work and when the pressure gets too high, I pass up the *Irish Times* job, mostly because that concern pays bad. (*L*, 173)

Cronin suggests that Sheridan was the second substitute and, given their work together on *Comhthrom Féinne* and *Blather*, this is a strong possibility. However, Sheridan made no recorded mention of his involvement; in the letter to O'Keeffe quoted above he mentions only Montgomery. In a 1965 letter to an individual addressed as 'Moore', an ill O'Nolan asks for help with two articles, presumably for *Cruiskeen Lawn*:

> I'm in trouble again. I've been sick since coming out of hospital a fortnight ago and tonight have to enter another hospital […]. I enclose the guts of two articles which I invite you to kick into shape to keep my series going. The material has never been published before. (*L*, 538–9)

Perhaps Moore helped him throughout the course of *Cruiskeen Lawn*, perhaps he assisted only at the end, but two things are certain – *Cruiskeen Lawn* is not the work of Brian O'Nolan alone, and Niall Montgomery was an instrumental part of O'Nolan's *Irish Times* writings.

Given the importance and influence of Sheridan and Montgomery, it is clear that collaboration long played an important role in O'Nolan's literary output. In the three instances of creative engagement between O'Nolan and the two Nialls that follow, collaboration is troubled, as it spills into something slightly less shared and somewhat more stolen. At the heart of this essay, then, is an interest in the delicate line between colluding with and conspiring against, particularly in the world of long-standing creative partnerships. This is especially fraught in the case of *Cruiskeen Lawn*, as what is being written is not simply a column or a text, but an identity, and specifically an identity that was embodied by only one of the contributors. Lurking in the background of the literary engagements of O'Nolan, Sheridan and Montgomery is the tension not only of writing, but of writing a self into being. And further complicating an already involved scene is the spectre of plagiarism. Its ghost grows stronger as the essay progresses.

In which neither Brian O'Nolan nor Niall Sheridan accuses the other of plagiarism

Although Niall Sheridan was instrumental in reworking *At Swim-Two-Birds* into the novel we recognise today, his editorial skills appear to have been less involved in O'Nolan's second novel, *The Third Policeman*. In 1971, in a short article in *Meanjin*, Sheridan reports that O'Nolan gave him the completed typescript of *The Third Policeman* to read 'in the winter of 1940 or early in

1941'.[19] In 1973, in 'Brian, Flann and Myles', he gives the same account, with the only substantial difference being the slightly earlier dates of 'January or early February of 1940'.[20]

On 17 April 1939, O'Nolan wrote to his literary agents A.M. Heath's and told Patience Ross that he supposed he 'should now see about writing another book' (*L*, 47). By 1 May he had formed some concrete ideas about the new work, and he wrote thus to Eric Gillett of Longmans:

> I have not yet done anything about another novel beyond turning over some ideas in my head. [...] I do not expect to be able to start anything until rather late in the summer and cannot see it finished until perhaps November or so. [...] Briefly, the story I have in mind opens as a very orthodox murder mystery in a rural district. The perplexed parties have recourse to the local barrack which, however, contains some very extraordinary policemen who do not confine their investigations or activities to this world or to any known planes or dimensions. Their most casual remarks create a thousand other mysteries but there will be no [question] of the difficulty or 'fireworks' of the last book. The whole point of my plan will be the perfectly logical and matter-of-fact treatment of the most brain-staggering imponderables of the policemen. I should like to do this rather carefully and spend some time on it. (*L*, 47–8)

Later letters to Ross confirm that he began writing *Hell Goes Round and Round*, which would become *The Third Policeman*, in August (*L*, 61), and by September progress was so good that he could write quite enthusiastically of the work to William Saroyan (*L*, 59–60). On 18 January 1940, O'Nolan informed Longmans that the book was completed (*L*, 67), and on 24 January he sent it to Heath's, saying:

> I enclose some evidence that I have not been idle since August last. This is meant to be a funny murder or mystery story and cannot be said to be a lot of highbrow guff like the last book. Whatever about the writing and the eccentric tone of the conversations, I think the plot is quite new and nowadays that alone is something to be slightly proud of. (*L*, 67)

In October 1939 Sheridan published a short story titled 'Matter of Life and Death' in the magazine *Esquire*. The story is set in an isolated garda barracks on the west coast of Ireland and opens thus: four gardaí are playing cards when their door is pushed open and a mud-stained stranger walks in, blinking in the light. The stranger, who is English, dramatically confesses to murdering his best friend, and the gardaí, once he has dragged their attention away from their card game, treat him kindly and gently and try to calm him with tea. The Englishman explains that he is a bachelor and that he and his only friend, a wealthy widower called Lafontaine, frequently went on holiday together. On this occasion they had travelled together to Ireland on a walking tour but were already annoyed with each other when they came to the Devil's Pool in the local mountains. As they were walking, Lafontaine kept poking the Englishman in the back with his stick, and the Englishman

> saw him as he really was for the first time in twenty years. And I knew that I hated him. I wanted to destroy his fat face and his piggy eyes and that sneering smile of his. [...] He was standing just below me, and I crashed my stick down on his skull. He fell forward on his face. Then he began to stagger to his feet. I remember how the look of surprise on his face almost made me laugh. I swung the stick again, but before I could strike him, he toppled backwards over the edge and fell into the lake.[21]

Having unburdened himself of his crime, the Englishman describes the act as 'a clear and simple case of murder', but the Sergeant gently disagrees, stating that if 'murder was as simple as it looked, myself and the boys would not be stuck here in this God-forsaken wilderness, on the edge of a quaking bog'.[22] The Sergeant begins to speak of a murder he and his companions had investigated in County Meath. They had committed themselves to the investigation and felt that they had found incontrovertible proof of guilt, but were outwitted by the lawyers for the defence, who insisted that the gardaí's evidence was circumstantial and irrelevant. The trial concluded with the murderer walking free, and as a punishment the Sergeant and his men were sent to their current isolated barracks, there to remain. Having thus been rendered loath ever again to investigate any form of murder, they gently encourage the stranger to talk himself out of his admission of guilt – to say that his friend had attacked him and then tripped over some bushes – and they allow him to walk out the door.

Within the field of O'Nolan studies this story is already of interest, but before we return to *The Third Policeman*, a pivotal scene needs to be addressed. The murderer, who remains unnamed throughout the story, has just walked through the door, and asks to make a sworn statement. The Sergeant says, with a sigh:

'Someone is after stealing your bicycle, I suppose. When was it pinched?'
He settled his cards face upwards on the table.
The stranger stared blankly at the broad expanse of the Sergeant's back,
the ruddy folds of flesh above his tunic collar. He swayed slightly on his
feet.
'I'm afraid you don't understand', he said in a low voice. 'This has
nothing to do with a bicycle. No, nothing'. [...]
'Speak up, man', the Sergeant said over his shoulder. 'You'll have to give
me an exact description. What make of bicycle was it? I suppose you
haven't the number of it'.[23]

The guards continue to play cards while the Sergeant speaks over his shoulder
to the Englishman:

'Now was it an old machine or a new one? Twenty-six or twenty-eight
inch wheels? Was there a three-speed gear on it?'
The stranger began to bang both fists on the table, scattering the
Sergeant's pile of coins.
'Will you listen', he fairly shouted. 'This is *not* about a bicycle. It's a
much more serious matter than any bicycle could be'.
The Sergeant looked at Flanagan and then at Donohue.
'I see', he said gravely. 'It's about a motor-bicycle'.[24]

So central is the concept of 'being about a bicycle' within academic and
popular work on O'Nolan that to find this scene quietly inserted into a
1939 story by O'Nolan's close friend is extremely unsettling. In an uncanny
doubling of O'Nolan's *The Third Policeman*, in Sheridan's 'Matter of Life
and Death' we are presented with a strange, isolated barracks in the Irish
countryside, a barracks associated with indefinite punishment. We are faced
with an unnamed murderer. We have a friendship between lonely men,
specifically an intimate friendship that ends in death, and a victim whose
name is strongly reminiscent of a number of academic commentators of
de Selby. We have a murder scene involving a blow to the head, we have a
rotund sergeant, we have notions of exile and strange justice. And, of course,
we have bicycles.

To return to the dates that we can confirm: O'Nolan appears to have
arrived at the idea for his novel between 17 April and 1 May, and was, by the
latter date, able to confidently describe it as an 'orthodox murder mystery in

a rural district'. In January 1940, when he sends the finished work to Heath's, he also feels comfortable in describing it as having a plot that is 'quite new'. In October 1939, Sheridan's short story was published: when we allow the necessary timespan for the story to be sent to *Esquire*, accepted, scheduled and published, it is very probable that we are looking at a commencement of April or even earlier. With a timeframe such as this, it is difficult to tell who began work on their text first. Or, more importantly, who conceived of the concept first. This is not, of course, to say that the texts have identical tone, style or plot. O'Nolan's plot, even by May, was going to hinge on 'extraordinary policemen who do not confine their investigations or activities to this world or to any known planes or dimensions', and Sheridan's stays very firmly in the real world. But, that noted, there are surely far too many similarities in these works for this simply to be a coincidence. It is perhaps instead a shared joke between friends, an idea conceivably mutually arrived upon and allowed to develop in independent ways. The odd note is not that O'Nolan wrote a novel that is always about a bicycle, and that Sheridan wrote a short story that is absolutely not. The odd note is the fact that Sheridan never mentions the resonances and possibly shared origins of their texts.

The earliest date that Sheridan gives for seeing O'Nolan's finished novel is January 1940, but he makes no mention of shared conversations about the plot. He refers with amusement to the names of the de Selby commentators but makes no reference to the fact that O'Nolan's Le Fournier is so close to his Lafontaine. His homage to O'Nolan in 'Brian, Flann and Myles' goes into much detail about his involvement with *At Swim-Two-Birds*, and yet he gives no sense that O'Nolan's second novel might have sprung from a conversation or joint idea about policemen and bicycles. There is always, of course, the whisper of suspicion that maybe this was not a case of cooperation, but of an idea taken gently by the hand and led somewhere else. But were that to be true, one would imagine that mentions of either the novel or the short story would be accompanied by some notes of anxiety or defensiveness. In an undated letter from Sheridan to Montgomery, probably written in early 1940, Sheridan refers to his 'Civic Guard' story, explaining that he is trying to turn it into a one-act play and wondering if it could be produced as a radio play with Denis Johnston.[25] On 7 September 1940, O'Nolan writes to William Saroyan and mentions this play with no sense of anything but approval: 'The other Niall (Sheridan) has written what I think is a very excellent play, also about policemen. The main characters are three policemen and a greyhound and that's not a bad start' (*L*, 92–3).

No evidence that the one-act play was performed has yet come to light, nor has the script been found, but a later, three-act adaptation that Sheridan made of his tale is available. *Seven Men and a Dog* was staged at the Abbey in 1958, with Ria Mooney producing. On 29 April 1958, a very positive review in *The Irish Times* specifically likens the play's setting to a hellish place of punishment: 'Niall Sheridan's first comedy, "Seven Men and a Dog", is set in a remote Civic Guard station, one of the "penal stations" where those who lose favour with their superiors are sent to suffer for a time or perhaps forever.'[26] The National Library contains the typescript under the title 'Seven For a Secret'. The names of some of the guards have been changed from the short story, two minor characters added – a reporter and a baron interested in lineage – and a brief mention of greyhounds in the story rounded out and embellished, but the fundamental plot is the same.

The most major minor change, if you will, is that although the dialogue within the play often draws upon the original story verbatim, it has omitted completely the dialogue about bicycles. In fact, while the opening stage set might excite the O'Nolan scholar, as it features a bicycle leaning rather prominently against a window, this is taken off stage by a young garda quite early in the first act, never to reappear. Thus, rather definitively, and for someone on the look-out for bicycle-related symbolism, rather pointedly, bicycles are removed from the play. The reporter, instead, drives a motorbike. This alteration is provocative – although bicycles and O'Nolan are now synonymous, there is little evidence to suggest that this was a defining feature of O'Nolan's *oeuvre* during his lifetime. Although the publication of *The Dalkey Archive* in 1964 introduced bicycles to O'Nolan's canon – an addition compounded by the 1965 Gate Theatre production of Hugh Leonard's adaption *The Saints Go Cycling In* – it was the posthumous issue of *The Third Policeman* that firmly blended O'Nolan with the velocipede. This is not to say that bicycles are remarkable for their absence – they are mentioned with relative, if passing, frequency in *Cruiskeen Lawn*, although 29 October 1955 saw a full column on them. In the instalment, which is entitled 'Bicyclism', Myles writes of male and female bicycles and the possibility of male bicycles becoming female bicycles in a case of dread 'gynandromorphism'.[27] In 1956, Montgomery sent a playful biographical note on O'Nolan to Jack White, the assistant editor of *The Irish Times*, in which he wrote that O'Nolan 'came to college on a black-japanned wrought iron bicycle, [and] boasted that he had become lantern-jawed from riding it in the dark without a lamp' (*L*, xi), but these kinds of associations are infrequent.

On the whole, we can infer that O'Nolan appeared neither to be preoccupied with bicycles nor distressed by their mention. Perhaps Sheridan's removal of the main point of association between his successful play and his friend's unpublished novel was accidental. Perhaps it was the deliberate removal of the reminder of their texts' shared provenance. Yet, other traces of links remain. While gardaí other than the Sergeant have little to do in the story, they take on more prominent roles in the play. One garda is called Flanagan, but Sheridan abbreviates his name to 'Flan' throughout the script. The Sergeant, intriguingly, is never given a surname, but his first name is mentioned in the text: Joe. The sexual tension between the men is retained, while the hellish space of *The Third Policeman* becomes an absurdist one in Sheridan's play, as the murderer is an author 'suffering from insomnia. Overwork. On a book of essays dealing with post-War developments in philosophical thought. Personally, I lean towards the metaphysical position of limited engagement as enunciated by Camus'.[28] When the gardaí ask him why he has turned himself in, the murderer says, with shades of the Pooka in *At Swim-Two-Birds*:

> Perhaps an obscure sense of ritual, nothing more. What does it matter? To escape or not, to live or die. Episodes in the whole meaningless charade. (<u>sardonic</u>) What really matters is ritual, abstraction, the formal pattern. Order is Hell's first law. A beginning, a middle and an end – and we all die happily ever after.[29]

We are left then, with what? With a shared idea allowed to take different courses? With a private joke kept private? With a homage that the vagaries of publishing caused to fail, as O'Nolan's novel was never released? With a collaboration that was never again referred to? With an idea that was not intended to be shared, but was? With an idea misappropriated?

In which Niall Montgomery accuses Brian O'Nolan of plagiarism

In August 1955, Uinseann MacEoin, the editor of *The Irish Architect and Contractor* (1953–64), invited Montgomery to write a monthly column, called *P.S.*, under the pseudonym 'Signwriter'. Montgomery wrote six articles, but on 14 February 1956 he wrote to MacEoin to tell him that he had decided to discontinue.[30] He wrote one final article, which was published in volume 6, no. 10 (April 1956). But before this came out, on 29 March Montgomery sent back issues of September 1955 to February 1956 to O'Nolan and suggested that O'Nolan take the job instead. O'Nolan seemed interested, and on 4 April Montgomery told MacEoin that O'Nolan would take over his role in the periodical and write as 'Signwriter'.

O'Nolan spent that summer in and out of hospital, and the matter rested until August, when a *Cruiskeen Lawn* instalment, spread over the 6th and the 7th, was published under the name 'Game of House' I and II. Montgomery read it in the newspaper and found it horribly familiar. Then he realised that the material repeated the April *P.S.* article, with paragraphs two and four of the 7 August column almost identical to his work. He wrote to O'Nolan immediately:

> The extracts you've quoted without acknowledgement today and yesterday are, as you know of course, from articles which were bought and paid for by the *Irish Architect and Contractor*. I had a word with a solicitor when I got back to town this afternoon and I wrote afterwards to MacEoin, the Editor, explaining that the publication of the stuff was not my responsibility. (*L*, 210)

O'Nolan replied on 9 August, writing on the same page: 'I don't know what above is about. I have quoted nothing from the I.A. & C. I embodied stuff about housing from typescript you sent me for C.L. and which came to light in the upheaval of the "flit"' (*L*, 210).[31]

O'Nolan did eventually manage to send something to *The Irish Architect and Contractor*, but on 22 August Montgomery wrote to O'Nolan to tell him that although O'Nolan would be paid for the article he wrote, MacEoin did not like the quality of his work and did not want to keep him on as a regular correspondent. A few days later, Montgomery wrote to the letters to the editor section of *The Irish Architect and Contractor* and sent a copy of the note to O'Nolan. MacEoin, however, erred on the side of discretion and decided not to publish it.

> I wonder how many of you noticed the wise words by my distinguished colleague, Senor na gCopaleen in the 'Irish Times', called 'Game of House'? [...] they were taken, culled, quoted in extenso verbum for verbum from the post-scriptum of my other distinguished colleague, 'Signwriter', who said exactly the same things in the same unmistakable way in the April '56 issue of the 'Contractor'. [...] Is 'Signwriter' Miles [*sic*], or vice versa? Or has Miles [*sic*] been lifting from his juniors without by-your-leave? And if so, what about the law of Copycat?[32]

We have at least two men labouring at the *Cruiskeen Lawn* columns, creating together the myth of Myles na gCopaleen, albeit a myth that only one man wraps himself in daily. For decades, O'Nolan was Myles, the *persona* that he and Montgomery wrote into being, and now – we can imagine how Montgomery felt – O'Nolan/Myles had not only taken the scripts Montgomery wrote for the *Cruiskeen Lawn*, but it seemed he was appropriating text written for an entirely different venture. It seems inevitable that the columns in the Montgomery Papers in the National Library do not represent Montgomery's full contribution to *Cruiskeen Lawn*; thus, to read gaps in that archive as indicative of periods in which Montgomery ceased to write is potentially misleading; however, it is worthy of note that after September 1955, around the time that Montgomery began the *P.S.* columns, there is a hiatus – as the archive shows it – which extended until 27 June 1956. That day sees one column penned, but this is followed by another long cessation until 31 May 1958. It is possible that these breaks indicate the period during which Montgomery worked on the 'Signwriter' column, and the period following Montgomery's accusation of plagiarism, and thus denote a reluctance on Montgomery's part to contribute to *Cruiskeen Lawn*. That said, by the end of August 1956 Montgomery and O'Nolan were working together on repairs to O'Nolan's house at 10 Belmont Avenue, and all seems well. O'Nolan and Montgomery had many disagreements over the years, but one way or another these were always resolved, and their friendship carried on.

Is this a case of plagiarism? Perhaps. It is possible, however, that O'Nolan is telling the truth: that Montgomery had written a column on the subject of housing, but not for *The Irish Architect and Contractor* but for the *Cruiskeen Lawn*. He sent it to O'Nolan, but O'Nolan never used it, and perhaps Montgomery forgot. Montgomery then published the material with MacEoin. O'Nolan, having not read *The Irish Architect and Contractor*, as Montgomery had only sent him the September to February issues, knew nothing about the material being used there. When moving house, O'Nolan found the original draft sent by Montgomery, felt relieved to have material to work from, and did what he had been doing for many years: he wrote Montgomery's ideas into *Cruiskeen Lawn*.

However, equally possible is that O'Nolan did read the April issue of the *Irish Architect and Contractor* and, being ill, distracted and in need of the money, did plagiarise Montgomery, the man whose writings he had been accustomed to adapting or inserting into his *Cruiskeen Lawn* columns. And yet, O'Nolan was a man quick to anger, and his letters rarely retreat from confrontation or the possibility of offending a recipient. The calmness of his response, its air of confusion and his request to meet with Montgomery about something else – probably the work on the house – does appear to indicate innocence of Montgomery's accusation. We are left in an ambiguous space – we either have plagiarism, or the appearance of plagiarism, in which a gift, willingly given, is mistaken for a prize that has been purloined.

Regardless, however, of whether the copying of material was accidental or intentional, the same text was published, without acknowledgement, twice – in Montgomery's *P.S.* column, and O'Nolan's *Cruiskeen Lawn* column. And yet, in his unpublished letter exposing the repeated material, Montgomery asks a question that simply and significantly blurs the lines between these articles: 'Is "Signwriter" Miles, or vice versa?' Of course, Signwriter is not Myles, as Myles was firmly embodied by O'Nolan, and O'Nolan's work for *P.S.* had been rejected by MacEoin. However, equally accurately, we can say that Signwriter *is* Myles, as Niall Montgomery was one of the assembly composing and comprising Myles na gCopaleen. For many years he quietly assisted the writing of Myles into being by providing O'Nolan with drafts. Thus, the plagiarism, if such it is, in this instance rests awkwardly on the borders of self-plagiarism, as Myles (who is O'Nolan and Montgomery) borrows material from Signwriter (who is Montgomery and – almost – O'Nolan). Montgomery's letter of complaint is also a letter marking the liminal borders of an identity and reveals a fraught instance of collaboration/ appropriation between ghostwriter and character.

In which Brian O'Nolan accuses Niall Montgomery of plagiarism

Montgomery had long desired to write his own column in *The Irish Times*. On 7 September 1957, he suggested a monthly column on Dublin architecture to Jack White, but *The Irish Times* already had someone writing on architecture. On 30 January 1961, Montgomery tried again, and suggested a weekly piece called 'The Half Nelson Column' by Persse O'Reilly. On this occasion, O'Nolan's understudy argued his case rather more aggressively by presenting himself as offering something that O'Nolan could not: authentic knowledge of his environment. That is, he argued that it was no use having O'Nolan as the voice of Dublin, as O'Nolan had 'no consistent view on the matter, no visual sense, [was] <u>not</u> a Dublinman!' (*L*, 396).

In 1964, Montgomery succeeded, and in January he began writing 'The Liberties', a column in *The Irish Times* penned under the pseudonym 'Rosemary Lane'.[33] This name linked him to Joyce, but also signalled a man whose presence had long been overrun by more prominent literary individuals: Rosemary Lane was a street in Dublin that had connected Merchant's Quay and Cook Street, but had ceased to exist when Adam and Eve's Church was built across it.[34] 'The Liberties' ran from January to March, had a brief hiatus, and then resumed in September to close, finally, in December 1964. Even though Rosemary Lane's first articles were primarily architectural in focus, their tone quickly echoed that of *Cruiskeen Lawn*. An article on 5 March mixed Irish and English and used playful asides and notes to the editor. On 7 March, spurred on by thoughtlessness, mischief, or the sense that the columns worked well together, an editor made the mistake of placing *Cruiskeen Lawn* and 'The Liberties' beside each other. The authorship of the new column became clear to O'Nolan, and on 9 March he wrote to Montgomery. Two drafts of the letter are housed in the Burns Library at Boston College, and the fact that O'Nolan wrote and retained two drafts – a practice unusual for him – is clear indication of the extent of his distress. The following is taken from the second letter, which he sent to Montgomery:

> No doubt you are anxious to know what I think of your Rosemary jazz. Apart from saying now that I have no intention of standing for it, I must express my blank amazement at this sudden parade of unsuspected cheek and ignorance. I threw the first (or thereabouts) of these pieces away after a futile attempt to negotiate incoherent drool; I thought once again another zombie had been accidentally let in. Later, when I saw 'epiphenomenon' and certain other fixtures on view, I knew where I was.[35] The painful, laboured, unblushing copying of another man's work is something (thank God) beyond my present opportunity of comment. [...] I don't want to continue this note, for I think too much of you to be provoked into saying hurtful things. Above all, I don't want to be pushed into writing to the editor inviting him to attend to his business. I have been connected with the I.T. for over 25 years and there may be people who think it is funny that I should have my own ghost at my elbow in 1964. I am personally not amused at anything that affects my livelihood. I invite you to stop this business right away. (*L*, 394–5)

On receipt of this letter Montgomery forwarded it to *The Irish Times* and wrote: 'You will note Mr O'Nolan's assertion that the publication of those articles affects his livelihood, and in the circumstances, I suggest that you suspend publication of them' (*L*, 395). Montgomery also sent a copy of this correspondence to O'Nolan, who was furious:

Your use of my letter without my permission is no doubt in line with the new presentation – the felt collar and tight trousers with the facade of [the] gentleman are now discarded. My letter would not have been so used if it had been more explicit. You should stick to architecture. [...] You were pitiable and are now contemptible. (*L*, 396)

From O'Nolan's perspective, we have an unambiguous case of plagiarism, as *Cruiskeen Lawn*'s ideas, anecdotes and style were stolen in an instance of the 'painful, laboured, unblushing copying of another man's work'. He pointedly refers to 'The Liberties' column as a zombie, a piece of undead writing desperately sustaining itself on the brains of a better writer. The difficulty with O'Nolan's position, of course, is deciding what, at this stage in *Cruiskeen Lawn*, counts as 'another man's work'. For decades Montgomery had been doing precisely that – another man's work – but at O'Nolan's request. While it is most probable that Montgomery began by doing imitations of O'Nolan's style, by 1964 the years of mutual interaction and contribution, both in *The Irish Times* and beyond it, arguably blurred the lines between original and copy. *Cruiskeen Lawn* existed for so long as the product of at least two writers – two friends – that O'Nolan's claim to sole ownership of its style becomes difficult to defend. Can Montgomery, in this situation, be accused of plagiarism? Having asked someone, for so many years, to write Myles, can you protest when he begins to become him? To harken back to the etymology of plagiarism: *can a ghostwriter be a kidnapper?*

On 13 March, Montgomery, indirectly acknowledging how much the work of Rosemary Lane read like the work of Myles na gCopaleen, asked Donal O'Donovan, assistant editor of *The Irish Times*, if he wanted to publish the remaining 'Liberties' articles as *Cruiskeen Lawn* instalments: 'That would preserve the old C.L. image intact and the only snag would be that Brian would have the mortification of seeing "drool" published over his name! (And let him have the bloody old fee, for heaven's sake)'.[36] Rather wisely, O'Donovan decided against it. On 18 March, Montgomery proposed another column called 'Fair Enough' by Donnie Brooke, but O'Donovan replied the next day to say that O'Nolan would recognise Montgomery under any name. Once you become someone's ghost, you remain known to them.

In August, Montgomery made a further attempt, this time suggesting 'Stephen Greene' as a pseudonym, but on 21 August Donal O'Donovan telephoned to say that the name had been used before.[37] For a few months at the end of the year Rosemary Lane did return, but by December she had run her course, and on 12 December Montgomery told O'Donovan that while he had enjoyed writing the columns, he was 'glad Brian is coming back: he is the man for the job – no one else has ever written with such authority, or variety or brilliance'.[38] The ghost had had his chance, but decided to return to the shadows. And perhaps there is security there: as a ghostwriter Montgomery never had to be Myles, just quietly create him for someone else.

In 1943, O'Nolan had requested a well-deserved raise from *The Irish Times*. After some reluctance on the newspaper's part, in October G.J.C. Tynan O'Mahony, the manager, had the pleasure of increasing remuneration to £1.5.0. per day, on the understanding that 'the extra 24/- you should pass on to Sir Myles na gCopaleen (The Da), who, I understand, plays a prominent part in your Jekyll and Hyde existence' (*L*, 144). Myles, and even The Da, might be the dark side of O'Nolan – although it might be more accurately put that O'Nolan was the dark side of Myles na gCopaleen – but Myles was also the shadowy side of Niall Montgomery. For many years, not quite in secret but not quite in the open, Montgomery would become Myles and through him speak of Joyce and architecture and art. A 'shooting box', as he put it, that concealed him, but also changed him. Montgomery was Myles not because of a theft, but because, after years of being asked to copy, that copy had been written into him. To put it otherwise, Montgomery had become a Sexton Blake author who one day tries to pen another detective story but realises that everything he writes is more Sexton Blake.

Where does that leave O'Nolan? Montgomery might have become a shadow Myles, but O'Nolan *was* Myles, the embodiment of the character/column. When Montgomery used the *Cruiskeen Lawn* style, he was not simply recycling an idea or repeating a style but doubling an identity. Arguably, when O'Nolan complains that the Rosemary Lane column placed his ghost at his elbow, the ghost in question is not Montgomery, but Rosemary Lane, Myles's ghostly twin. Montgomery does not haunt O'Nolan, rather, Rosemary haunts Myles. She threatens the end for Myles, as her existence not only steals a style from *Cruiskeen Lawn* but steals Montgomery away from the column. In luring away a ghostwriter, she potentially takes from O'Nolan the identity he had long been accustomed to adopting. In his *Irish Times* obituary for his friend, Montgomery wrote that O'Nolan 'could have been anything he liked: he liked to be Myles na gCopaleen'.[39] A decade later, Montgomery gave a darker twist to the same thought: O'Nolan, he writes, 'beat all his enemies, except the one who destroyed him, his own personal self, the only man in the whole city that he didn't know'.[40] O'Nolan, so long accustomed to blending with his characters, was not only concerned that Rosemary Lane might take away his income, but that Rosemary Lane might mean that Montgomery would cease to write Myles. Not only might your ghostwriter stop writing copy, but in turning this style you have honed together over the years to different ends, he might stop writing you. *Cruiskeen Lawn* had, over the years, taken breaks, either through sickness or disputes with *The Irish Times*.[41] But this appears to have been the first time that O'Nolan was worried about being unwritten. The instance of plagiarism that caused O'Nolan genuine grief was not the theft of ideas or style – the instance of plagiarism that caused real distress was hinged on the theft of himself.

2

The *Cruiskeen Lawn* Revue

Modernist (anti-)theatricality and Irish audiences

ALANA GILLESPIE

Every great dramatist realises that there is nothing involved in the drama except character. Some small concession must be made to theatre-goers, who are usually weak-minded folk, so that some plot is necessary, no matter how perfunctory or silly. Scenery, costumes, music, whiskey-bars – these are quite extraneous.

Myles na Gopaleen, *Cruiskeen Lawn*[1]

In discussion with his friend Brinsley, the student narrator of *At Swim-Two-Birds* identifies one of the superior virtues of drama as its mode of consumption:

> while the novel and the play were both pleasing intellectual exercises, the novel was inferior to the play inasmuch as it lacked the outward accidents of illusion [...]. The play was consumed in wholesome fashion by large masses in places of public resort; the novel was self-administered in private. (*CN*, 21)

Orgies and onanism aside, the student and Brinsley see the play as a 'pleasing intellectual exercise' like the novel, but only the closet drama is intended to be read and not produced; theatre is a live event, 'predicated on its own disappearance' by the end of the night.[2] As mass entertainment, modern Irish theatre clearly has a social dimension that novels lack, but the student's remarks suggest that what is good about theatre crowds is safety in numbers, social control: everybody is doing it and everybody sees each other doing it. A heterogeneous bunch any day of the week, theatre audiences differ most from readers of novels in that you can see a lot of them in one place and they can instantly affect the performance. Of course, readers also influence the success of a novel, but we do not hear them shout or applaud in unison (unless, perhaps, we are at a book launch or a book burning). It is simply different for theatre: a book can die unnoticed, but the success or failure of a play creates visceral reactions on both sides of the stage. As Myles na Gopaleen puts the matter in *Cruiskeen Lawn*, 'the audience is part of the play, a ship is useless without water setra setra setra'.[3]

The student's formula for the modern novel as 'largely a work of reference' is a creative strategy of utilitarian bricolage that is effective because it is economic to reproduce characters made by the masters who have already said everything worth saying. As we will see, either position turns on the question of successful mimesis or what makes a character believable. Myles repeats variations of this formula in *Cruiskeen Lawn*, where he also practises it. When Myles writes that 'Scenery, costumes, music' are 'extraneous', he identifies these 'outward accidents of illusion' as mere theatrical trappings, where 'theatrical' is meant in the pejorative sense of artificial, pompous, or 'put on'. But Brian O'Nolan is wildly theatrical, in a technical sense that has pragmatic value. His writing incorporates several conventions of dramatic texts, like stage directions, asides (from the safety of brackets) and dialogues. His keen awareness of the audience is almost unparalleled on the page, but not necessarily on the stage.

Faced with the question of what theatre should do, O'Nolan's complex answer (based on his various authorial *personae*'s commentary on theatre and theatre criticism) is an odd portmanteau of the views of two influential Russian theatre makers: Konstantin Stanislavsky (1863–1938) and his pupil Vsevolod Meyerhold (1879–1940). Stanislavsky and Meyerhold, like Mikhail Bakhtin, had scrutinised the consumption habits of audiences.[4] The former thought they should be ignored, while the latter considered them an essential part of a dramatic exchange and event. O'Nolan agreed audiences should be ignored but also saw them as instrumental to the performance's success, or indeed failure. As a critic, dramatist, novelist and occasional innocent bystander, O'Nolan thought and wrote a lot about audience and reader behaviour. He played to it and took advantage of it while also condemning audience tastes and bemoaning (but always acknowledging) their power in experiencing and evaluating art, whether in private or public.

Drama's 'consumption in public' provided a form of social control and a platform for elevating national consciousness throughout Europe in the late nineteenth and early twentieth centuries. Lionel Pilkington writes that the establishment of an Irish national theatre, the Abbey, in 1904 'was supposed to demonstrate that Ireland had become modern' and to serve as 'institutional proof that the country [...] now accepted the disciplinary norms of representative democracy'. *At Swim-Two-Birds* suggests that the novel is a despotic artform, created and enjoyed in private. The state does not fund such private pleasures but does support theatre in a way it never has novel writing. Theatre can contribute more to the project of cultivating national consciousness, which makes it a better investment. Pilkington explains why the theatre was suited to this project:

> Establishing a national theatre institution in Ireland [...] was not just about providing a forum for the performance of Irish plays. It was about demonstrating and normalising an idea of politics based on constitutional representation [...]. With its illuminated stage, darkened auditorium, naturalistic acting and – notionally at least – deferentially attentive audience, the theatre presented itself as a model for an ideal society.[5]

I will return to the idea of theatre as a model for an ideal society later, with some help from critic and censor Gabriel Fallon, who grandly appropriates Alexis de Tocqueville to claim that 'An audience always manages to get the theatre it deserves'.[6] Theatre has had a reputation for being the people's forum since Ancient Greece, and of course theatre's ability to fulfil the responsibility ascribed it has varied wildly both in performance and reception. Expectations about what it means to portray an ideal society on the stage diverge depending on whether one is producing, watching or reviewing a play. These differing perspectives, combined with Dublin's vivacious theatre scene, provide O'Nolan fruitful material for satirising theatre and theatricality.

Cruiskeen Lawn presents us with a grotesque revue of Irish theatre audiences (both fawning and mobbing), producers, dramatists, critics, financial backers, and so on. For O'Nolan, like Meyerhold, the theatre itself is grotesque, as it is composed of and compelled by tension between a mix of interacting opposites and consciously thrives on incongruity. By examining a selection of seven *Cruiskeen Lawn* columns written between 1943 and '55 in which Myles na Gopaleen participates in or reproduces discourses about audiences, I will demonstrate the simultaneous incongruity and integrity in his representation of audiences as diverse, powerful consumers: at once mindless mobs and (more or less) discerning individuals, simultaneously political groups seeking to shape *their* national theatre and crowds of Philistines who would not recognise art if it spat in their face. Individually, these representations are not uncommon. Even the seemingly paradoxical view of audiences as both politically empowered masses and brainless consumers of popular entertainment can be reconciled when we account for the different but symbiotic positions of audiences and producers of theatre, or more broadly, the people who make and consume imaginative works within a particular market.

Changing places: Mobs, critics and national representation

W.B. Yeats started out believing that 'in the theatre, a mob becomes a people',[7] but eventually lost some of this optimism after having heard enough from the mob when it disagreed with what it saw on the stage. *Cruiskeen Lawn* presents several examples of the players as the real mob, perhaps suggesting that Yeats's goal had been achieved. The mob became a people, and they became actors.[8]

Andreas Huyssen has argued that denigrating the popular elevates modernism and reinforces the high/low divide.[9] Helen Freshwater notes that discourses about audiences and the language used to describe them are 'laden with value judgements', especially the words that describe their behaviour and how they watch: gawking, gazing, voyeurs, impartial observers, innocent bystanders, rapt spectators, active participants, connoisseurs, and so on.[10] Butsch and Livingstone's *Meanings of Audiences* is a comparative analysis of keywords used to describe audiences and publics throughout the world. They highlight politically charged meanings behind normative definitions of audiences that are closely linked to class distinctions between masses and elites, and to ideas of democracy in the western sphere.[11] 'Terms such as crowds, mobs and masses, and multitudes, indicate the people or common folk as separate and beneath an elite'[12] – a division which was eventually made physical through architecture once the stage was raised from the audience in the seventeenth century.

Discourse defines reality, and discourses about audiences can be effective on a macro-social level in a range of contexts, including political, economic, social and religious frameworks.[13] According to Butsch and Livingstone, 'framing audiences as publics attaches Enlightenment ideas of democracy to audience activity, and sets a positive standard of an ideal audience'.[14] Societies deploy discourses about audiences to regulate the behaviour of subordinate groups like women, colonial subjects or immigrants: 'audiences imagined as superordinate tend to be praised and held up as an ideal for others who, in turn, are stereotyped as ignorant, lacking education or "taste," inherently stupid, and easily duped or manipulated'.[15] Considering some of the discourses of audiences reproduced in *Cruiskeen Lawn*, especially the comic reversals of the stereotypical roles of *national theatre* audiences and makers, will show how much his criticism of them cuts both ways.

Myles is not just a critic and a writer; he is also frequently 'just' a member of the audience. Even when he is criticising audiences, the discourses of theatre he reproduces in *Cruiskeen Lawn* demonstrate that audiences decide what a work means and whether it is commercially successful. As an author of both postmodernist metafiction and what Mary Poovey calls 'performative criticism', O'Nolan understands that 'the text achieves an identity only when it is read' or witnessed by an audience,[16] an idea that was also very clear to Stanislavsky and Meyerhold, especially in the context of national theatre, which always aims to educate and inform. But audiences sometimes take away different lessons than makers intend, a fact that has been demonstrated countless times on and off the modern Irish stage. How an audience expresses their pleasure or displeasure can make or break a play, which makes theatre audiences powerful consumers. At the same time, active spectatorship – such as clapping or rioting – is also a political means for the 'public' to engage in an almost continuous referendum on Irishness and the mimetic imperative of national theatre to represent the people accurately.

Modernist anti-theatricality and Irish audiences

While anti-theatricality has existed as long as theatre itself, Martin Puchner identifies a crucial difference in the grounds of modernist objections to the theatrical compared to previous times: reality rather than morality. Underlying O'Nolan's shifting representations of audiences is a tension surrounding the theatre and all things 'theatrical'. Puchner identifies 'anti-theatricality' as a defining characteristic of modernism. He argues that the values of modernism are explicitly defined through an attack on the theatre and traces the polemical contexts in which Walter Benjamin, Friedrich Nietzsche and Michael Fried voiced their objections to theatricality.[17] To summarise, these three thinkers reject what they regard as theatre's excessive influence on the other arts (especially the plastic arts) and share a profound suspicion of the gestural and of live actors, whom they see as getting in the way of aesthetic experience or appreciation of the work of art. For them, especially Fried, when the work of art becomes aware of the audience, it loses its self-sufficiency and integrity.[18] Theatricality, then, connotes fakery: a poor copy of the real life that twentieth-century Irish theatre producers wanted to put on the stage.

Modernism scrutinises and attacks the nature of mimesis. Since theatre depends on human actors ('no matter how estranged their acting may be') as media, people cannot be depersonalised or estranged the same as other media.[19] Objections to actorliness in modernism are not to the perceived immorality of the theatre and actors, but to the risk of what Adorno called primitive or 'aping mimesis' and, more generally, the form of mimesis in theatre 'caused by [its] uneasy position between the performing and the mimetic arts'.[20] This is relevant for national theatre audiences, who, especially in Ireland, want to see themselves on the stage. They perform their approval of or disgust for what they see on the stage in a way that affects the performance. Kathleen Heininge argues that Irish audiences have a 'particular function and identity, and they have their own ability to glean meaning, a separate facility that can work to disrupt the intentions of the authors' − but 'Actors can also be to blame for the failure [of translation] when their own representations' are based on their knowledge of dramatic expectations.[21]

Critics apply value-laden judgements to actors all the time. In describing the atmosphere in the house, as Freshwater notes, reviewers inevitably use similarly judgemental language to describe the audience's behaviour. National theatre seeks to shape the nation, and theatre critics and their editors seek to shape audience tastes. In *Cruiskeen Lawn*, O'Nolan suggests the critics may be overestimating the audience's ability to discern a good play from a bad play. Myles repeatedly complains about audiences who 'eat up' formulaic representations of Irish 'characters' or mimic ridiculous renderings of Irish speech, or who resist more thoughtful characterisation. Yet O'Nolan relies on the audience's knowledge of conventions and characters all the time. The practice informs the student's theory of literature in *At Swim-Two-Birds*, a variant of which Myles once proposed as an additional condition of an Abbey Theatre play-writing contest in 1955, since 'The best characters have already been established by the masters, so why try to better them?'[22] These characters and *personae* are so indirectly revealing because they are cleverly composed of so many 'ready-made' stereotypes and (dramatic) conventions contrived to achieve an effect. Therefore, O'Nolan's obvious impatience with Irish stereotypes on the stage is somewhat ironic as he deploys them in his own plays, but there they are either effective or completely frustrating.[23]

Echoing modern fiction writers' suspicion and awe of their theatrical counterparts, O'Nolan struggles with the inherently false nature of mimesis, but not on grounds of whether written words on a page or spoken words on a stage paint an accurate or realistic picture of life as it is. His concern is for the accuracy or believability of the language that writers use to construct that picture of life as it may be. When Myles complains of Dublin life imitating Dublin art, or of Synge releasing a 'deluge of home-made jargon all over the Abbey stage' whilst 'Lady Gregory [...] quietly knit[s] her Kiltartan',[24] he denies that the contrived language of many Abbey plays, still the dominant model for most Irish theatre, could create a believable world because no-one, let alone their authors, actually spoke such a Hiberno-English construct in daily life.

Linguistic possibility equals ontological possibility for O'Nolan: an imaginary world can exist as long as the language that constitutes it is believable enough to reflect the world that it makes. Enter J.L. Austin's theory of speech acts. Poovey contends that:

> any critical allusion to J.L. Austin's theory of performative language implicitly illuminates theorists' claims that a novel [or play] can create a 'world', for this claim implies that the language of a novel [or play] is performative: it enacts or brings into existence something that did not exist prior to the language act and that could not exist outside of language.[25]

Even though Austin believed that utterances on stage were 'hollow or void'[26] and lacked the power to *do* things with words, in the context of modern Irish theatre it is helpful to consider how language on the Irish stage actually *did* things offstage. Heininge convincingly argues that when Irish speech is represented on stage it is exactly 'the kind of [... performative] speech act' Austin describes:

> In much of drama, Austin is correct and the utterance is merely mimicry, or is relating information about a subject in varied ways, but within Irish drama, and indeed the drama of any colonised country, the very enactment of speech establishes real identity, not just stage identity, with each iteration, thus constituting the performative.[27]

Thus, writing for the stage goes beyond representing a character or type, and becomes 'the instructions for how a particular people wish to be represented, a locus for identity [wherein] the effect sought is performative'.[28] This explains why audiences sometimes had extreme reactions when they did not like what they saw or heard.

Myles finds the language of 'Synge-George Moore-Gregory-Martyn, with Yeats in the background'[29] unrealistic because it is hollow and parasitic. It is 'theatricality' in the pejorative sense used by Stanislavsky, the father of method acting, who believed that actors must ignore the audience and inhabit their side of the proscenium only.[30] Fake stage language is the linguistic equivalent of hamming it up or playing to the audience just for cheap effect or laughs. This anti-theatrical attitude relates to discourses about theatre audiences expecting to see and hear themselves in stage representations. After all, Yeats's promise to 'show the Irish people who they really were' seems like at least a tacit invitation for feedback and participation.[31]

Yeats believes that audiences could be trained and shaped, but Myles doubts this. His complaints about Dubliners speaking like Synge's peasants[32] demonstrate his pessimism about audiences' critical faculties, but also his doubts as to the Abbey playwrights' ability and credentials. As an audience member, Myles is not the 'active participant' type. He does his protesting from the safety of the newspaper; he even sees little sense in being an active reviewer. In a 1956 column he explains that it is not even necessary for theatre critics to attend the performances: reviews can be written in bed sipping sherry as long as one knows the author, the theme, the title, 'the form of the players first doing it' and 'the record of the theatre wherein produced'.[33] He continues: 'I have seen the plays. Why then spend some hours, which might engagingly be whiled away playing bézique, looking at re-shined old hat?'[34] All of the plays in question, he maintains, are Abbey plays, even if he hopes that 'there is a place in your Dublin for a play [...] wherein abides no red-toed Irish peasant, a play destitute of will and wake'.[35] But is that what audiences want? Hardly, according to Myles, who first disparages all his own plays as 'awful' before declaring that

> The Edwards-MacLiammóir combine will tell you that Dublin will not pay to look at a decent play. [...] Write a good play (if you can) and get yourself out of the theatre within a week. Write a bad, false and derivative play and be in residence for a month.
>
> There is one snag. Bad plays don't always make money.[36]

Money, markets and mobs

Regardless of theatre producers' sociocultural, civilising or cultivating mission, Dublin audiences (like most audiences) mostly wanted to be entertained and get their money's worth. In the modernist theatre, money, markets and mobs intersect. What was entertaining about the theatre often depended less on the quality of the play or the acting, and more on the quality of the audience and the 'drama' surrounding or interrupting the play. Early twentieth-century disturbances like the 1907 *Playboy* riots revealed the semantic dissonance between the Anglo-Irish playwrights' and their middle-class audiences' concepts of 'ideal' Irish identity. Their public response gave Dublin audiences the reputation of being an angry mob intent on talking back to theatre makers. But mid-century audiences also raised violent protest to national theatre produced by middle-class Irish republicans, like Seamus Byrne's *Design for a Headstone*, a prison play about a republican hunger striker's death. Its relatively successful run in the Abbey in spring 1951 was driven in part by protests on 14 April in response to supposedly blasphemous and anti-nationalist, pro-communist dialogue. Commentators praised the Dublin audiences for their spirited response, with *The Irish Times*'s 'Irishwoman's Diary' column expressing disappointment at the tameness of the Byrne disturbances relative to the 'full scale riots' that once made the Abbey such an exciting place.[37]

Bored as Dublin was with Abbey programming, a good tussle could always bring in the crowds. Theatre rowdyism, as illustrated by 'Irishwoman's Diary', was a source of local and even national pride, especially as the reputation of the Abbey spread throughout the English-speaking world.[38] The diarist positively longs for the bygone days of theatre riots, and she is relieved that 'Dublin audiences have not changed so much after all and are still capable not only of taking umbrage, but of signifying their disapproval in no uncertain manner. This kind of thing does the play no harm either, so that everybody should be happy'.[39] Byrne may not have agreed, as two IRA men demanded to speak to him after the show, but their disagreement was settled peacefully when Byrne explained what he had meant. The police were brought in the following night, and tickets for the next few nights sold out following several newspaper and word-of-mouth reports of the disturbances.

O'Nolan identifies discourses about Dublin audiences' propensity for violence in the theatre as a selling point. The spirited Dublin audience had become such a commonplace of Irish cultural remembrance that O'Nolan could parody it through a direct inversion of the trope and expect his audience to understand. In a 1949 column, Myles advises the Abbey to clarify the sign it used to tell theatregoers that they would not be admitted to the house during the play. As if to say, 'How do you like your mimesis now?' he proposes that '"Roars close at rise of curtain" might suffice as an admonition to the audience that when the curtain rises, it is the turn of those on the stage to start commotions, eat, drink and use bad language'.[40] Perhaps there is mutual influence between makers and audiences, as the players are cut from the same cloth as the people in the house.

Two weeks after Byrne's play was interrupted, Myles was claiming that 'it is now fairly common knowledge that the recent row at the Abbey Theatre was organised by the management'.[41] How widely this conspiracy theory was accepted is moot,[42] but it matters little for this column's representation of audience–theatre relations. Myles asks whether it is 'permissible to inflame public opinion to achieve financial, or even artistic objectives' and finds the answer is yes, as long as no lives are lost, because '[…] public policy should be dictated by public opinion'. This idea is inherent in *theatre for the people* and is infused with the notion of theatre as a democratic forum. In 1955, the critic Gabriel Fallon reflected on Yeats's struggle with the audience, which he had wanted to shape, but initially underestimated:

> The power of the audience in the moulding of a theatre is a power which most authors, actors and theatre-managers are inclined to under-estimate. Yeats acknowledged this power when he wrote 'We were to find ourselves in a quarrel with public opinion that compelled us against our will and the will of our players to become always more realistic, substituting dialect for verse, common speech for dialect.' This indeed was true. An audience always manages to get the theatre it deserves.[43]

In an April 1950 column, Myles complicates commitment to theatre for the people and by the people in relation to the Byrne riots with the Wildean claim that 'it is the manifest duty of organs of opinion […] to do everything possible to overcome the endemic torpor of public opinion: otherwise there will be no public opinion at all'.[44] Arbiters of opinion, like national theatres, have a mission if not a duty to shape national opinion, but part of that arrangement is that audiences must at least nod approvingly for the theatre to continue to fulfil its mission. Here then, in a rare moment of agreement with Yeats, Myles expresses the 'elite' perspective that audiences need cultural curators and notes the Abbey management's keen business acumen in recognising that crowds will stay away 'unless there is at least some prospect of a little bit of rowdyism'.[45]

Audience participation (disturbances and more) dated back to the medieval morality play and Shakespeare's time, Myles writes, but faded out, or at least became less respectable, when the architectural separation of audience from performers (much like blacking out the house after the introduction of electric lights) changed the spatial dynamics of the theatre performance by tempering audience responses. He finds it 'ludicrous [...] that the audience, far from participating in a play, may not express approval except by polite applause, or disgust otherwise than by an offended silence'.[46] But the Abbey, he adds, understands that this convention goes two ways, so instead of suffering the silence of an empty house, the management naturally, he claims, 'have a few ruffians on the pay-list' to make some scandal. This proves an effective strategy as *they* can moonlight on the stage:

> I have never seen a play in the Abbey that did not contain several ruffians, and if it is argued that these characters have their counterparts in real life, there should be a little evidence of it now and again in the shape of an Abbey patron being assisted out with a fractured ankle [...] or bloody shirt.
>
> Besides, the hard-working players are entitled once in a while to sit back on their kitchen chairs and see a play in the auditorium, and one full of the genuine Abbey characters – Guards, priests, rowdies, joxers, American visitors, *thooleramawns*, oul wans up from the country to dispute a will, patriots, Gaelic Leaguers, dressmakers, and so on.[47]

Taking the mimetic imperative of dramatic realism to its literal conclusion, O'Nolan puts the players in the house and the audience on the stage, enacting speech on the political pulpit of the Abbey stage. The actors (or the genuine article) create a disturbance, word spreads, ticket sales take off: it's a hit! Springtime for Dublin and the Abbey!

As a writer who wears his artifice on his sleeve, O'Nolan's struggle with the imperative of mimesis in the theatre turns on whether the language is realistic and the characters believable. If they are not, the performance fails. But believability and truth can be theatrical without being realistic. The 'anti-theatrical' stamp does not credibly fit his many authorial masks and *personae*, even if he attacks the theatre and writes about attacks on the theatre. O'Nolan's anti-theatricality manifests itself in critiques of playing to audience expectations without critical or creative reflection, especially where nationalist ethos is involved. These critiques also extend to bashing the theatrical behaviour of audiences in communicating those expectations. He shows that strictly adhering to ideas of national 'type' is detrimental to modern art and even to the idea of modernity. Like a true critic, O'Nolan seems to believe that some level of curatorship by experts is necessary to keep from 'debauching Dublin's slender thread of theatre taste'.[48] Ultimately, O'Nolan's treatment of audience reactions illustrates that the audience's power and taste are facts authors and producers must accept, for better or worse. Even as he critiques their tastes and points out the limits of their capacity for critical thought, he knows that audiences are the ultimate arbiters of meaning and financial success, and that the last word is theirs.

3

'That poaching scoundrel'

Brian O'Nolan and Dion Boucicault

RICHARD BARLOW

No less an authority than Fintan O'Toole has declared that Dion Boucicault's plays are 'for the most part [...] rubbish'.[1] Be that as it may, Boucicault was, as Elizabeth Cullingford has noted, 'the most popular playwright in the English-speaking world between 1840 and 1900'.[2] Boucicault was also admired by Irish dramatists such as George Bernard Shaw and Seán O'Casey.[3] Furthermore, two of Irish modernism's key figures, James Joyce and Brian O'Nolan, demonstrate a marked interest in Boucicault's works. Allusions and references to Boucicault occur in *Ulysses* and *Finnegans Wake*,[4] while one of O'Nolan's main pseudonyms, Myles na gCopaleen (and, from November 1952 onwards, Myles na Gopaleen), is taken from Boucicault's 1860 play *The Colleen Bawn; Or The Brides of Garryowen* and is adopted by O'Nolan for works in a diverse array of genres. Myles na gCopaleen, meaning 'Myles of the ponies/small horses', is used by O'Nolan as the *persona* for the *Cruiskeen Lawn* columns in *The Irish Times* (from 1940 to 1966);[5] for a column in the Manchester edition of the *Sunday Dispatch*; for a number of plays, sitcoms and short stories; and for the name of the editor of *An Béal Bocht*. The *Cruiskeen Lawn* columns also engage directly with Boucicault's work.

Boucicault and O'Nolan are connected intertextually through O'Nolan's Myles persona, but also by their similar critical receptions. While O'Nolan was long marginalised in Irish and modernist literary-critical fields as an 'apolitical humourist' or a 'virtuoso of the Irish Fact' (in Hugh Kenner's term),[6] recent decades have seen a thoroughgoing reconsideration of his place in Irish letters alongside (and often through) a reconsideration of the politics of his work. Boucicault, by the same token, was long labelled as a purveyor of sentimental and commercial stage Irishry but is undergoing a critical reappraisal for the importance of his innovations to modern Irish theatre. This reappraisal has led to a more nuanced understanding of the politics of his plays. Both Boucicault's and O'Nolan's works are increasingly read in their historical-cultural-political contexts rather than in purely aesthetic terms as exemplars of an undifferentiated, de-historicised tradition of stage Irish boozing and buffoonery.[7] In this essay, I will discuss the ongoing re-evaluation of Boucicault's place in Irish culture and reconsider O'Nolan's use of the Myles pseudonym in the light of this re-evaluation.

Boucicault, Irish drama and *The Colleen Bawn*

On the subject of why Brian O'Nolan only wrote one novel in Irish under the name Myles na gCopaleen (*An Béal Bocht*), Declan Kiberd writes: 'In the character of Myles na gCopaleen, O'Nolan rescues the buffoon from the Victorian stage and makes him articulate. The feckless clown who had once stuttered in broken English is now permitted to speak in his native tongue.'[8] However, the work of Boucicault was, in part, already an attempt to rehabilitate and reform the stage Irishman.[9] According to Cullingford, 'English dramatists created the drunken, stupid, and violent Stage Irishman; the Irish dramatist Dion Boucicault [...] reinvented him as drunken, clever, and charming'.[10] Furthermore, as Seamus Deane *et al.* have observed, 'Although Boucicault has often been misrepresented as purveying the worst kind of Irish stereotypes, his declared intention was to *abolish* stage-Irishry'.[11] A piece in *The Irish Times* for 8 November 1864 states that

> never was a country better abused by strangers than Ireland by its own dramatists. With the best and most abundant material for a true picture of national life and manners, they contented themselves with the success that is to be obtained by raising a laugh at the expense of their country. It is to their productions and not to the injustice of strangers, that we owe the disparaging estimate of the Celt which, until recently, prevailed in England. A thing of rags and tatters, of blunders and mischief-making, of noise and absurdity – a compound at best of rollicking good nature, impracticable obstinacy and effervescent courage, was the stage Irishman. If Mr Dion Boucicault did no other service, he rectified this ridiculously false impression of Irish character.[12]

Boucicault is important to Irish theatre because he attempts to modify the stage Irishman and the stage Irishwoman. I would suggest that the recalibration of our view of Boucicault's handling of stage Irishry invites us to revisit our view of O'Nolan's use of the name Myles na gCopaleen and to re-engage with the history and politics of this trope.

Previous to the establishment of Irish Literary Theatre and the Abbey Theatre, there were plays with Irish subject matter but no Irish national theatre as such.[13] Furthermore, as Christopher Morash writes, 'while almost every other aspect of Irish culture could claim an authenticating, pre-Conquest genealogy, the theatre in Ireland was not only lacking in antiquity, it was a cultural form introduced – and, to a certain extent, maintained – by the colonial administration in Ireland'.[14] Yeats and his fellow Revivalists were attempting to stage something new in Ireland, to make a clean break from previous forms of Irish theatre. Yeats's own plays, like *The Countess Cathleen*, were created as serious, high-minded, small-scale productions for 'initiated' audiences. Such works concentrated on the delivery of a mainly verbal performance (with the dialogue in highly stylised, poetic diction meant to be delivered in a ritualistic fashion, with limited action and very little in the way of frivolous 'amusement'). In the 1897 Irish Literary Theatre manifesto, Yeats, Edward Martyn and Augusta Gregory proclaimed that the new Irish drama would 'show that Ireland is not the home of buffoonery and of easy sentiment as it has been represented'.[15] Elsewhere, Yeats wrote that the new theatre in Ireland would 'expound Irish characters and ideas' and that plays would now be written as 'one writes literature, and not as one writes for the Theatre of Commerce'.[16]

Reading Boucicault's scripts provides a sense of what the Revivalist innovators were reacting against: 'buffoonery', 'easy sentiment', and the 'Theatre of Commerce'. However, Boucicault himself was a moderniser in the staging and organising of drama, introducing 'many innovations into theatre stagecraft and management, including fireproof scenery, touring companies for metropolitan productions, and royalty payments for playwrights'.[17] Despite the modern aspects of Boucicault's work, and despite Boucicault's popularity in the mid to late nineteenth century, he is sometimes excluded from the canon of modern Irish theatre. For example, Boucicault does not appear in John P. Harrington's *Modern and Contemporary Irish Drama* (2008), which includes work by Yeats, Gregory, Synge, Shaw, O'Casey, Beckett, Friel, McPherson and Carr.[18] However, Boucicault's plays are discussed by Stephen Watt in the recently published *Oxford Handbook of Modern Irish Theatre* (2016) and the volume's chronology begins in 1860 with the first production of *The Colleen Bawn*.[19] According to Nicolas Daly, the dramatic centrepiece of *The Colleen Bawn* – a scene in which the character Myles na Coppaleen dives into a pool inside a cave to save a young woman named Eily – is 'a thoroughly modern rescue, depending not just on timing, but also on all of the illusive resources of the stage: lighting to imitate moonlight, trapdoors and a small army of stagehands to facilitate the disappearance and reappearance of Myles and Eily from beneath the "waves"'.[20] In contrast, O'Nolan's 'Myles na gCopaleen' plays have a critical reputation for being dialogue heavy and low on action and spectacle, with Joseph Holloway dismissing *Faustus Kelly* as being 'all talk and no play'.[21]

Boucicault is often described as an Irish-American playwright. He was born Dionysius Lardner Boursiquot on St Stephen's Day in Dublin in 1820 and was educated at schools in Dublin and in England. The early part of his career was spent putting on plays in England. Later, he found great success in the United States, especially with the slavery-themed work *The Octoroon; or, Life in Louisiana* (1859). Boucicault came quite late to Irish material. Cullingford has discussed his identity and his turn to Irish settings and themes:

> Boucicault's Irishness, like his birth, was ambiguous. His mother's family were middle-class Protestants, as were both the candidates for his dubious paternity. He spent the first nine years of his life in Ireland, but thereafter lived in England and America, although he never lost the brogue that authenticated his playing of Irish parts. His relations with English theatre managers and critics were often hostile, but English audiences liked his plays, and he had been a successful dramatist for twenty years before he took up the subject and setting of his native land in *The Colleen Bawn* (1860), *Arrah-na-Pogue* (1864) and *The Shaughraun* (1874).[22]

After an initial run in America, Boucicault's *The Colleen Bawn* 'opened at [London's] Adelphi Theatre in September 1860 to become the biggest hit seen in London for decades; in fact, it became the first long run in the history of the English stage'.[23] The play was promoted in glowing terms in the London press, and its success was used to publicise its follow-up, *Arrah-na-Pogue*:

> **IRISH SCENERY! IRISH HOMES! IRISH HEARTS!** […] The Irish Drama was discovered by the production of the 'COLLEEN BAWN.' Until that time the Irish Character was known to the stage, in one phase only, the gay, rattling, bull-making gentleman, or the

blundering good natured clod-hopper. It was for Mr BOUCICAULT to develop its romance and pathos and to exhibit its rich humour interwoven with intensely passionate feeling.[24]

Unlike O'Nolan's theatrical output, which received mixed reviews, *The Colleen Bawn* was a massive success when it opened in Dublin. According to McFeely, the play

> was claimed by Dubliners as a long-awaited national drama of Ireland. That the play was seen to portray the nation was due to the fact that it was considered truly representative of Irish rural life, or a form of that life that was acceptable to the residents of Dublin and the Pale.[25]

As McFeely elaborates, 'While *The Colleen Bawn* is not overtly nationalistic, it can be considered to be Boucicault's first dramatic representation of an Irish cultural nationalism'.[26] However, Boucicault was more politically engaged and polemical in some of his non-dramatic work: 'Boucicault's [...] little-known pamphlet, *The Story of Ireland* (1881) [...] describes his country as "the victim of a systematic oppression and contemptuous neglect, whose story will appear to you unparalleled in the history of the world".'[27]

The plot of *The Colleen Bawn* has its basis in both literary and real events: 'Boucicault had based *The Colleen Bawn* on Gerald Griffin's novel *The Collegians*, which itself had been based on an actual murder that took place in Garryowen, just outside Limerick City, in 1819. However, Boucicault moved the setting of the play to Killarney in County Kerry.'[28] The name Myles-na-Coppaleen is also taken from the novel: 'Myles Murphy! Myles-na-coppuleen? – Myles of the ponies, is it?'[29] *The Oxford Companion to Irish Literature* provides summaries of *The Collegians* and Boucicault's theatrical adaptation:

> [*The Collegians*] tells the story of Eily O'Connor, a beautiful but untutored country girl who is murdered at the instigation of her gentleman lover Hardress Cregan, by his servant Danny Mann [...]. Rejected by the heiress Danny Chute, Hardress marries Eily but soon regrets this misalliance. Danny Mann [...] drowns her, but Cregan is tormented by guilt and finally brought to justice in a melodramatic climax [...]. In Boucicault's version the plot is given a happy ending. Myles-na-Goppaleen [*sic*] foils Danny Mann's murder attempt, and Hardress Cregan accepts the peasant girl as his bride, overcoming the class differences between them.[30]

A major difference between *The Colleen Bawn* and its source material is that no murder takes place in Boucicault's play – Eily is presumed dead and is 'resurrected'. As Eugene McNulty has discussed, this plotline has political implications:

> The play's denouement pivots on the revelation that Eily has, in fact, survived Danny Mann's murderous intentions [...]. The play subtly invites its audience to read the real-life Eily Hanley as representative of a historically wronged Ireland, and thus, to locate her resurrection and re-animation in *The Colleen Bawn* as a politically nuanced act.[31]

A London revival of *The Colleen Bawn* in 1867/8, with Boucicault playing Myles, coincided with political turbulence in Ireland and an outbreak of Fenian violence in England, including the Clerkenwell bombing of December 1867.[32] In recent decades, sections of Boucicault's work have become strongly associated with Fenianism. For example, scenes from Boucicault's politically charged *Arrah-na-Pogue*, set at the time of the 1798 United Irishmen Rising, are included in the Fenianism sub-section of 'Political Writings and Speeches 1850–1918' in *The Field Day Anthology of Irish Writing*, alongside writings by Jeremiah O'Donovan Rossa and John Devoy.[33] A song from *Arrah-na-Pogue*, 'The Wearing of the Green', has become a well-known rebel song in recent years. Furthermore, 'it has become a part of Boucicault myth that ['The Wearing of the Green'] was banned from performances of the play following the Fenian bombing of London's Clerkenwell Prison in December 1867'.[34] However, as McFeely notes, Boucicault's version of the song was never actually banned.[35]

While Boucicault and O'Nolan are comparable in their recent critical re-evaluations, which have explored the political dimensions of their art beyond their respective reputations for stage Irishry, an intertextual reading will depend upon the specific aspects of the Myles character that O'Nolan lifts from Boucicault for his *Cruiskeen Lawn* persona. In *The Colleen Bawn*, the character Myles, once a 'thriving horse-dealer',[36] has fallen on hard times and has resorted to horse rustling and unlicensed whiskey distilling: 'Who's that? – 'Tis that poaching scoundrel – that horse stealer, Myles-na-Coppaleen. Here he comes with a keg of illicit whiskey, as bould as Nebuckadezzar.'[37] Myles is described as a 'Vagabond', an 'outcast', a 'jail bird', a 'marauder' and a 'lazy, ragged fellow'.[38] Corrigan, 'A Pettifogging Attorney', knows the haunts and habits of Myles's lifestyle: 'You live like a wild beast in some cave or hole in the rocks above; by night your gun is heard shootin' the otter as they lie out on the stones, or you snare the salmon in your nets; on a cloudy night your whiskey still is going.'[39] Boucicault's Myles is the 'the main source of humour'[40] in *The Colleen Bawn*, so it is a suitable name for O'Nolan to 'poach' for the *Cruiskeen Lawn* columns.[41] That Myles is a 'poaching [...] stealer' is also appropriate, as we shall see when we consider what Maebh Long terms O'Nolan's 'performance plagiarism'.[42]

It has been claimed that Boucicault's Myles is 'the prototype of a new kind of Stage Irishman, more to be laughed with than at: affectionate, witty and canny'.[43] Despite his shady activities, and the low esteem in which he is held by some of the other characters in *The Colleen Bawn*, Myles 'proves to be the moral hero of the play'.[44] Myles saves Eily's life at the end of Act II and later relinquishes any claim he may have to Eily's hand in marriage. This leaves Eily free to marry the Anglo-Irish 'gintleman' Hardress (although this might not be such a happy ending – Hardress is a loathsome character who derides Eily throughout the play for her speech and manners and who, as a youth, 'maimed' his 'cripple' servant Danny Mann).[45] O'Nolan demonstrates a similar interest in reinterrogating, deconstructing and troubling, rather than rehearsing standard stage Irish archetypes and clichés. For example, in the *Cruiskeen Lawn* column for 28 August 1942, Myles derides Synge's 'amusing clowns' and the 'virus' of 'Playing up to the foreigner, putting up the witty celtic act, doing the lovable but erratic playboy, pretending to be morose and obsessed and thoughtful'.[46] Boucicault is not mentioned in this column. It seems that for O'Nolan, Synge is the worst offender in terms of spreading the stage Irish virus. However, Myles writes in the same column that 'This trouble probably began with Lever and Lover', referring to the nineteenth-century novelists Charles Lever and Samuel Lover.[47]

Boucicault's play ends with Eily stating that if she knew she had established herself in 'a corner' of her friend's hearts, 'there wouldn't be a girl alive happier than THE COLEEN BAWN'.[48] The script of *Arrah-na-Pogue* ends in a similarly uppercase phrase: 'Had any of ye been in my place would ye have done a ha'porth less for the man you loved than was done by ARRAH-NA-POGUE?'[49] Despite the well-documented flaws of his work (the sentimentality, the buffoonery, and so on), Boucicault does give women important roles in his plays. In the initial productions, these roles – including the character of Eily O'Connor/The Colleen Bawn – were played by Boucicault's second wife, the Scottish actor Agnes Robertson. The prominent role that Boucicault gives to women contrasts with their near-total absence in O'Nolan's plays and fiction.[50] So while Boucicault and O'Nolan share an interest in humour, in reshaping material and in re-examining and troubling standard Irish archetypes and clichés, they differ in terms of their respective degrees of interest in spectacle and in creating well-rounded female characters.

To return to the subject of Boucicault's Myles, the surname 'na Coppaleen' is part of a larger lexicon of equine imagery in *The Colleen Bawn*. The character Anne Chute, 'the Colleen Ruaidh', mentions 'coppleens' and 'mules'[51] and laments that she has bought a defective horse:

> I bought a horse at Ballinasloe fair that deceived me […] he looked well enough – deep in the chest as a pool – a-dhiol, and broad in the back, as the Gap of Dunloe – but after two days' warm work he came all to pieces, and Larry, my groom, said he'd been stuck together with glue.[52]

At another point in the action, Hardress declares that Anne is 'as wild as a coppleen'.[53] Coppleens are associated in the play with high spirits, while horses can be deceptive and unstable (pun intended). As the *persona* responsible for a host of hoaxes and textual deceptions, the character Myles na gCopaleen in *Cruiskeen Lawn* is also wholly unreliable, a multiple-trick pony.

Myles Na Coppaleen, Myles na gCopaleen and stage Irishry

The *Cruiskeen Lawn* Myles *persona* is as fragmented and inconsistent as the Colleen Ruaidh's horse, as are the attitudes and perspectives of the column itself. O'Nolan's version of the name Myles Na Coppaleen (Myles na gCopaleen) is also somewhat uneven; as Long has discussed, the 'surname, na gCopaleen, is an admixture of linguistic purity and impurity, as the correct eclipsis of "gC" is undone by the inaccurate, Anglicised "leen", which should read "lín"'.[54] However, the Anglicised "leen" is carried over from Boucicault's play. Elsewhere, Long writes that 'For his newspaper *persona*, O'Nolan adapted the name of Boucicault's Myles Na Coppaleen, thus positioning himself between stage cliché and innovative cultural commentator by embracing the brogue, poitín and easy cheer of Boucicault's Myles while simultaneously satirising and deriding him as a foolish fabrication'.[55] *Cruiskeen Lawn* contains parodies such as this:

> we are all Irish and we are in the parlour. Sweet Rosie O'Grady is pulling bottles of stout for us in the scullery. Mother Machree is in the kitchen knitting woollen shamrocks. Bould Phelim Brady is in the attic tearing the lungs out of his harp. The Colleen Bawn is below in the cellar.[56]

This passage mocks the continuation of clichés and conventions found in stage Irish theatre while appearing under the name of a character from stage Irish theatre (albeit a slightly 'reformed' stage Irish character).

O'Nolan's engagement with stage Irishry is further complicated by the merged identities of Myles-na-Coppaleen and his creator Dion Boucicault:

> In his speech to the audience after the final performance [of *The Colleen Bawn*], Boucicault played on the blurred lines between himself and the stage Irishman he portrayed, and between reality and fiction, as he would do throughout his whole career as Irish playwright: 'If I was to step out of my own characther and dhress, it would be to tell you for myself and the Colleen that we return you our best thanks ... there was amongst ye a feeling strong in favour of all that is thrue and natural. Poor Miles-na-Coppaleen wanted to be nothing more than himself, and 'tis proud I am, indeed, that he has found favour in your eyes ...'[57]

O'Nolan organised a similar blurring of role and reality in a stage Irish context at the curtain call of the *Faustus Kelly* première:

> On the opening night of his stage play *Faustus Kelly* in the Abbey Theatre in 1943, O'Nolan had an actor take his author's bow, 'dressed as the traditional stage Irishman with pipe, caubeen and cutaway coat, who did a bit of a jig and then vanished' [...], thereby reminding the audience of Myles na gCopaleen's origins.[58]

So, O'Nolan is using a pseudonym of a stage Irish character that is difficult to separate from its creator Dion Boucicault, while also engaging in onstage antics that echo and invert the merged identities of Boucicault's career. Boucicault 'step[s] out' of the character of Myles in his curtain call speech while maintaining the stage Irish mode, whereas O'Nolan has another actor take his place and dramatically escalates the stage Irish antics in his author's bow. And while Boucicault appears, O'Nolan disappears.

O'Nolan's disappearing act and his adoption of a Boucicault-inspired *nom de plume* may be seen as part of his ironic, modernist treatment of a decentred, performative notion of self or *persona*.[59] As Rónán McDonald and Julian Murphet have noted, O'Nolan's use of a variety of pseudonyms suggests 'a modernist notion of subjectivity that thwarts singular or positivistic ideas of a coherent, self-contained individual'.[60] However, Ronan Crowley has pointed out that Irish pseudonym usage also 'flourished' in the eighteenth and nineteenth centuries, as well as in the Irish Literary Revival and the twentieth-century journalistic field of which O'Nolan, or 'Myles', was a part.[61] Anticipating Joseph Brooker's comments on the need for 'a fuller engagement with history' in O'Nolan studies,[62] Crowley states that 'the frequency with which we reiterate O'Nolan's recourse to pseudonymity, singling out his practice as though it were novel or unique', is 'a critical myopia born of our underexamined and under-historicised appreciation for *noms de plume* in the Irish literary field'.[63] Crowley argues that considering the author in an Irish context

> places O'Nolan [...] in the company of fellow Irish writers whose pseudonyms largely displaced their personal names in public life [...] such as Æ (George William Russell), MacNamara (John Weldon) and Seamus O'Sullivan (James Sullivan Starkey) as well as those whose pseudonyms we no longer even recognise as concealing different birth-names – *inter alia*, Seán O'Casey (John Casey), Desmond FitzGerald (Thomas Joseph Fitzgerald).[64]

As well as aligning him with a modernist decentring of the self, O'Nolan's use of a pseudonym taken from Irish literature also signals an affiliation to a national tradition. Eamonn Hughes has claimed that O'Nolan's act of referring back

> to Dion Boucicault's *Colleen Bawn* (and further back to Gerald Griffin's *The Collegians*) [suggests] a relationship to an Irish literary tradition [...] and equally [...] a possible relationship to the readers of the *Irish Times* – still, when [O'Nolan] began to write for it, and for some time after, conservative and unionist.[65]

Since Boucicault's output is often nationalistic, there is a subtle underlying tension here. Through the adoption of a pseudonym taken from Boucicault's work, O'Nolan associates himself with a writer whose nationalism, and his connections with Fenianism, are at odds with the conservative, unionist persuasions of *The Irish Times* and its readership.

Boucicault as progenitor and plagiarist in *Cruiskeen Lawn*

In the *Cruiskeen Lawn* column for 8 June 1954, the Myles *persona* mentions that he is in Limerick. This leads him to a series of observations about Limerick itself, which he deems 'a most uneven town',[66] and about the place-name: 'I CANNOT MAKE OUT what the word Limerick (Irish *Luimneach*) really means.'[67] Myles notes that, according to 'the great lexicographer Dr Dinneen', the place-name Limerick means 'a place-name'.[68] Myles then considers the genre of poetry known as limericks, before referring to Boucicault:

> Nobody knows why limericks are so called. But while on the subject of poetry, I would like to draw attention to the work of my literary progenitor, Dion Boucicault (1822–1890) and his play 'The Colleen Bawn'. The play contains these verses:
>
>> Oh, then, if I was the emperor of Russia to command,
>> If I was Julius Caesar or Lord Lieutenant of the land,
>> I'd give up my fleet, my golden store, I'd give up my armie,
>> The horse, the rifle and the foot and the Royal Artillerie.
>> I'd give my fleet of sailing ships that range the briny seas,
>> I'd give the crown from off my head, my people on their knees.
>> A beggar I would go to bed and proudly rise at dawn
>> If by my side, all for a bride, I found the Colleen Bawn.
>
> I admit that that is not very inspiring versification, even if the title is called 'Limerick is Beautiful'.[69]

The character Myles sings this song in Act I of *The Colleen Bawn*, meaning that Boucicault himself sang it in initial productions. The play also contains the song 'Cruiskeen Lawn', which Eily (the Colleen Bawn herself) sings with Myles, Sheelah and Father Tom, after mixing a jug of punch (a '*crúiscín lán*' of 'thrue Irish liquor', hot water, sugar and lemon juice).[70]

In October of the same year, Myles returns to the subject of Boucicault and contradicts his initial position that Boucicault is his 'literary progenitor'. Alongside a piece on 'logophagy' (the practice of 'eating your own words' – appropriately enough, since Myles is now issuing a quasi-retraction of his previous comments on Boucicault),[71] Myles discusses the issue of plagiarism:

> IN THE CALENDAR of literary malpractice, where do you lave plagiarism? Personally, I take a very dim view. I feel soiled in a second-hand way in the queer example I am about to quote, for it concerns 'The Collen Bawn' [*sic*] by Dion Boucicault (1822–1890), an opera in which there is a certain character called 'Myles na Coppaleen' – couldn't even spell my name right.[72]

Myles once again brings up the subject of the song 'Limerick is Beautiful', adding unkindly 'I don't think so'[73] and once again incorporates the 'verses' above. At this point, Myles suggests that Boucicault's ballad 'Limerick is Beautiful' is a plagiarism of verses by Victor Hugo. However, Myles concedes that 'its place in history is not to be denied'.[74] While Myles is uncertain regarding the facts of the case, he has no doubt that 'one or other of them two lads was a right chancer'.[75]

In a neat reversal, and a textbook case of Mylesian 'acting out', Myles now suggests that Boucicault is not his 'progenitor' but that, in a sense, Myles is Boucicault's literary predecessor since Boucicault has supposedly stolen Myles's name for a character in an 'opera'. To borrow a phrase from *The Colleen Bawn*, Boucicault becomes the 'poaching scoundrel', not Myles. In *At Swim-Two-Birds*, the student narrator comments that 'The entire corpus of existing literature should be regarded as a limbo from which discerning authors could draw their characters as required, creating only when they failed to find a suitable existing puppet' (*CN*, 21). In keeping with this proposed aesthetic practice, O'Nolan lifts Myles na gCopaleen from *The Colleen Bawn* as a 'readymade' identity. However, in the *Cruiskeen Lawn* column, the 'queer' act of Boucicault's supposed 'literary malpractice' leaves Myles feeling 'soiled in a second-hand way' (echoing the 'second-hand' name Myles na gCopaleen/na Gopaleen). This *Cruiskeen Lawn* passage is full of possibly volitional errors – *The Colleen Bawn* is spelled wrong (ironically, given that Myles chastises Boucicault for spelling a name incorrectly) and Boucicault's play, though it contains singing and music, is hardly an 'opera' (although it was adapted as an operetta, *The Lily of Killarney*, by Julius Benedict in 1862).[76] The major 'error' – and impossibility – is that Boucicault, who has been dead since 1890, could have plagiarised from Myles, a constructed identity which only begins in 1940. A further error, which may not be intentional, concerns Boucicault's date of birth. McFeely states that Boucicault was born in 1820, not 1822 as Myles claims.[77]

That the October 1954 column playfully interacts with a column earlier in the *Cruiskeen Lawn* 'CALENDAR' is a small indication that *Cruiskeen Lawn* exists as one interconnected corpus or 'magnum opus',[78] rather than as a series of purely discrete textual units. However, that the later column contradicts and undermines the earlier column shows the modernist instability of *Cruiskeen Lawn* as a whole and the avoidance by the Myles *persona* of the assumption of a single position on any given issue. As Ute Anna Mittermaier has pointed out, 'The *Cruiskeen Lawn* columns […] were so humorous in tone and contradictory in content as to make it impossible to credit [O'Nolan] with a particular standpoint on any political or cultural matter'.[79] Like the Colleen Ruaidh's horse, perspectives in *Cruiskeen Lawn* are liable to come 'all

to pieces'. O'Nolan's use of the pseudonym Myles na gCopaleen/na Gopaleen
has similar complications and contradictions. O'Nolan is using the name of
a modified stage Irish character from the work of a playwright who worked
to put an end to the stage Irish stereotype (although Boucicault's use of the
name is received 'second-hand' from Griffin's *The Collegians*). In the act of
adopting the Myles *nom de plume*, O'Nolan is assuming an identity from the
kind of 'blarney' productions he also lambasts in the columns of *Cruiskeen
Lawn*. At the same time, he is gesturing to a form of commercial, comic Irish
theatre that was swept aside by the Revival, even as his performance as 'Myles'
should be read within a modernist culture in which the notion of singular,
coherent subjectivity is called into question. O'Nolan's use of the Myles
pseudonym should also be seen as part of a larger pattern of pseudonym usage
by other Irish writers in which national and individual identity is displaced or
decentred. Considering its appearances in *The Collegians* and *The Colleen Bawn*
as well as its function as the authorial *persona* of *Cruiskeen Lawn*, it might be
said that there never was a name quite like MYLES-NA-COPALEEN.

4

The Return of the Father and the Dispossessed Son

Shakespearean rewritings of the Oedipus myth via Synge in *The Third Policeman*

DIETER FUCHS

This essay focuses on Brian O'Nolan's rewriting of the Oedipus myth in *The Third Policeman*. It argues that the Oedipal constellation of the son dispossessed by his father serves as an archetype in O'Nolan's novel which sheds light, in turn, on the sociocultural condition of Ireland in the Free State era (1922–37) and the Irish Civil War (1922–3). In adding his own twist in this theme, O'Nolan is following a number of twentieth-century Irish writers and playwrights who framed Ireland's political condition in Oedipal terms. As Fabio Luppi has shown, the drama performed at the Abbey Theatre during the 'crucial years in the formation of the Irish State' concentrates on dysfunctional father figures who fail or refuse to assume full responsibility for what they do – both in terms of the microcosm of the nuclear family and the macrocosm of patriarchal society represented by the state apparatus.[1] Discussing W.B. Yeats's efforts to adapt Sophocles's *Oedipus Rex* for the Abbey Theatre in 1926, for instance, Robert Welch observes that:

> While this tragedy is universal in its resonances relating to guilt and wrong committed in the heat and press of events, nevertheless it spoke pointedly to a deep sense of trouble about the nature of Irish society in the aftermath of independence. [...] The Irish, it would appear, had

found some kind of release from the dominion of England, only to realise also that the freedom gained was a kind of plague, a torment of impossible choices, treacherous alliances, moral recrimination and murder.[2]

This characterisation of Ireland's 'Oedipal' fate in the aftermath of independence could double neatly as a summary of O'Nolan's novel, with its own 'torment of impossible choices, treacherous alliances, moral recrimination and murder'. As *The Third Policeman* alludes not only to the ancient Oedipus myth but also to some of its more subtle rewritings beyond Yeats, the present essay's analysis focuses on a series of intertextual references the novel makes to stage productions in which the Oedipal dilemma is acted out: J.M. Synge's *The Playboy of the Western World* and William Shakespeare's *Hamlet* and *Julius Caesar*.

Carol Taaffe characterises *The Third Policeman* as a 'resolutely apolitical piece of nonsense',[3] a non-topical or apolitical text. However, I will suggest that the intertextual nexus of Shakespeare's deeply political *Julius Caesar* – signalled as an intertext to O'Nolan's novel in *The Third Policeman*'s epigraph – evokes the revolutionary subtext of the Irish Civil War. Openly alluding to the Roman civil wars that were provoked by the assassination of the political father figure Julius Caesar at the Oedipal hand of his elective son Brutus, *The Third Policeman* debates political unrest and revolutionary upheaval in an Irish context. As Shakespeare applied Roman history as a heuristic tool to learn how to cope with the political problems of early modern England, so O'Nolan refers to Shakespeare's topical analysis of history to reflect the political situation of his own place and time. Like the mythical Oedipus, who struggles, in vain, to overcome his overpowering father, O'Nolan's Ireland is dominated by an overaged patriarchal establishment. It is ruled by father figures who prevent the young generation from taking their lives into their own hands: actual fathers, priests addressed as 'father', the pope whose name is derived from 'papa' and, until Ireland left the British Commonwealth in 1949, the king of England and his state apparatus.

James Joyce famously applied the term *paralysis* to the Irish condition of an overaged society dominated by the father figures representing the English crown and the Roman Catholic Church.[4] Oedipus may be considered an archetypal paralytic, which qualifies him in the mind of many twentieth-century Irish writers as a *persona* representing the Irish condition. As the myth goes, the Delphic oracle prophesies that Oedipus would kill his father and marry his mother, and it is owing to this prophecy that the father decides to abandon his new-born son in the woods. To guarantee the child's speedy death, the father, Laius, paralyses his offspring by pinning the baby's ankles – indeed, the name *Oedipus* is derived from the Greek word *oedema*, signifying the 'swollenness' of that character's partly lamed feet. But neither the father nor the son escapes the oracle's spell in this way: Oedipus survives, kills an old man and marries a woman from his mother's generation. When he discovers that the old man was his father and his wife his mother, he blinds himself and goes into exile. Although Oedipus wins the paternal authority struggle, the ghost of his father comes back with revenge via the culturally repressed knowledge of the past.

This constellation reflects Ireland's archetypal condition in a nutshell. From the Tudor conquest until the first half of the twentieth century, Ireland fought an Oedipal struggle against England: whenever the Irish tried to free themselves, the deputies of the father figure of the English king returned with even greater acts of repression. Rather than coming of age and contributing to the welfare of their country, the young generation are denied political agency. And rather than being encouraged to look to the future, they are forced to look back nostalgically into the allegedly better past of their country as the pre-modern 'Island of Saints and Sages'⁵ – hence the Irish Literary Revival as a *re-vival* of a romanticised Gaelic past rather than the beginning of a new future-directed life in a modernised country. Yet, even when Ireland became a Free State in 1922, in the aftermath of the 1916 Easter Rising and the War of Independence, it remained a dominion of the British Commonwealth and was bound by an oath of allegiance to the English king until the Constitution (Removal of Oath) Act 1933, with the last remaining functions of the British monarch in relation to the Irish state abolished in the Republic of Ireland Act 1948.

This history was staged by Joyce and others as one of recurrent Oedipal passivity. Yet, the Irish dilemma reflected in the classical Oedipus myth is perhaps most notably elaborated in Synge's *The Playboy of the Western World*. While *The Third Policeman*'s references to Synge have been explored by previous critics, such as Keith Hopper, these discussions have overlooked the exact relationship between the novel's intertextual allusions to *The Playboy of the Western World* and its epigraphically announced dialogue with Shakespeare. After a summary of what we know about Synge's rewriting of the Oedipus myth, this essay will show how the Shakespearean Oedipal intertextuality that serves as a rather covert structural design of *The Third Policeman* may be decoded by a more overt set of Oedipal allusions to *The Playboy of the Western World*. Hence the present essay's subtitle: 'Shakespearean rewritings of the Oedipus myth via Synge in *The Third Policeman*'.

The Playboy of the Western World

The mythical Oedipus does not know that he kills his father, and in the end both father and son turn out to be passive agents of a preordained destiny they cannot control. The protagonist of *The Playboy of the Western World*, Christy Mahon, in contrast, kills his father in a conscious act of rebellion, only to discover that the old generation refuses to die when the patriarch returns despite his severely wounded skull. To highlight the paralytic situation of an Ireland ruled by father figures representing an overaged and past-obsessed community, Christy's father is fashioned as a representative of an all-powerful establishment. Although he tries several times, in vain, to kill the old Ma(ho)n, Christy is doomed to fail in his fight for independence. Declan Kiberd frames this Oedipal struggle in colonial terms:

> In a colony, the revolt by a son against a father is a meaningless gesture, because it can have no social effect. Since the natives do not have their hands on the levers of power, such a revolt can neither refurbish nor renew social institutions. [...] When the sons of each generation rebelled, they soon saw the meaninglessness of their gesture and lapsed back into family life, as into 'a haven in a heartless world': yet it was a haven that, in every respect, reflected the disorder of the outside colonial dispensation. The compromised or broken father could provide no convincing image of authority.[6]

In her brilliant analysis of *The Playboy of the Western World*, Kelly Younger elucidates that the Irish Oedipal dilemma turns out to be aporetic in a twofold manner: 'the Irish father is also a colonised son. The Irish son, as a result, has two fathers, neither of whom he can rebel against. One is too powerful, the other too weak. Patricide, though desirable, is therefore impossible.'[7]

It is, however, not only owing to his situation as the dispossessed son that Christy may be considered an Irish Oedipus.[8] Just as his mythical counterpart marries the widowed Queen Jocasta who turns out to be his mother, Christy is supposed to marry a woman from his mother's generation. Widow Casey – who was Christy's wet-nurse, or substitute mother – is twice his age and is referred to as 'a woman of noted misbehaviour with the old and young'.[9] Like Oedipus, Christy is presented as a partly lamed person: when 'drawing off his boots' he 'holds up one of his feet, feeling his blisters and looking at it with compassion';[10] elsewhere, his father calls him 'a dunce [...] with his legs lamed under him'.[11]

When the supposedly dead father reappears to reveal that he survived the Oedipal assault, the Irish peasants let the son down like the slandered Charles

Stewart Parnell, or Jesus Christ – hence Christy's Christlike name.[12] As with Christ, who is hailed as the people's champion when he enters Jerusalem on the back of a white mule on Palm Sunday, Christy is hailed as the winning jockey of a mule race shortly before he suffers his downfall. Like Veronica, who wipes the blood and sweat from Christ's face with her veil before he is crucified, Pegeen wipes Christy's sweating face with her shawl. Pegeen's gesture occurs prior to the peasants' attempt to hang Christy in an act of self-proclaimed lynch justice, in an echo of the trial of Christ, which was likewise manipulated by the anarchic populace. Although Christy is forsaken by the people who first declared him their hero, he comes of age regarding his relationship with his father. Even if he fails in overpowering the patriarch in his first attempt, he earns respect and authority when he proves his determination to re-enact his Oedipal rebellion and splits his father's already injured skull for a second time. And this, one may argue, is the way to deal with the large-scale Oedipal struggle of Ireland with imperial Britain implied in Synge's play: rather than remaining fickle-minded like the peasants, Ireland may come of age after all. Even if it cannot overthrow the father figure of the English king at the time when *The Playboy of the Western World* was written, Ireland can resist his authority in a brave and strong-willed manner and gain political respect and agency in this way. But this goal can be only achieved through courageous deeds affecting the present and not by a capricious populace nostalgically entangled in the memory of a purportedly better past. Hence, Kiberd is certainly right to claim:

> What was written, again and again through the Irish Revival, was an *Anti-Oedipus*, which saw the ancient tale not as awful tragedy but as happy comedy. True, the children of Oedipus felt the pangs of fear and guilt which assailed the scattered offspring of Old Mahon – but Christy's comic parricide becomes the basis of a true morality, and it is his insurgency which makes History possible.[13]

And yet, although Kiberd's study focuses on the Oedipal situation of Ireland and includes a chapter on Flann O'Brien, it does not offer a discussion of the Oedipal subtext of *The Third Policeman*.

The Third Policeman

The problem of overthrowing patriarchal authority and breaking with the past recurs in *The Third Policeman*, which alludes to Synge's play in tandem with its less obvious Shakespearean intertextual deep structure. Whereas *The Playboy of the Western World* applies the Oedipal archetype to reflect on the Irish condition around 1907, *The Third Policeman* refers to this myth via Synge to analyse what has become of Ireland in the time of the Civil War. If one grants Tom Walker's reading that *The Third Policeman* is a response to the 'terror' of 'the revolutionary turmoil of the War of Independence, the Civil War and beyond',[14] then the bombing of the Big House owned by Old Mathers – as a representative of the pro-English landowning elite – serves as an allusion to the Irish Civil War from 1922 to 1923, provoked by the establishment of the Irish Free State. In this timeline, the return of the nameless narrator's ghost to haunt Divney sixteen years later occurs around 1938–9, in the immediate aftermath of the Free State era, ended by the formation of a new state (in the 1937 Constitution of Ireland) which was nevertheless still haunted by the Civil War's legacy. The narrator dies as a result of the bomb attack manipulated by Divney when he is 'nearing thirty' (*CN*, 228), so he must have been born around the time of Parnell's death in 1891. This reading is bolstered by the narrator's early childhood memories: 'My father I do not remember well but he was a strong man and did not talk much except on Saturdays when he would mention Parnell with the customers and say that Ireland was a queer country' (*CN*, 223). Sharing O'Nolan's irony, *The Third Policeman* may be thus considered 'a terrific indictment of democratic self-government, a beautiful commentary on Home Rule' (*CN*, 366).

Hopper observes that, as in Synge's play, *The Third Policeman* opens in a shebeen which at the end is run by a woman whose first name, Pegeen, is identical with that of the central female character from *The Playboy of the Western World*.[15] Like in Synge's play, the central character splits the head of a father figure with a spade. The victim's name is Old Mathers. As a conflation of 'old matters' and 'old fathers', this telling name reflects a modern Ireland paralysed by the enduring memory of the old matters and patriarchal figures of the past. Additionally, Old Mathers may be considered an intertextual echo of the name of Christy's father, 'Old Mahon'. This is a revealing name in its own right, which may be associated with the blocking character of Plautine comedy, as it is, phonologically speaking, identical with the archetypal 'old man' who represents the overaged past generation, denies the young lover the hand of his daughter and needs to be outwitted by the younger generation to regenerate a society grown old, sterile and impotent.[16] As a Plautine old man, Old Mahon refuses to share his agency with the next generation; so, at least from Divney's perspective, Old Mathers in the Big House refuses to share his wealth with the younger generation, blocking his marriage to Pegeen Meers.

Like the exhausted Christy at the beginning of *The Playboy of the Western World*, O'Nolan's nameless narrator lies down in a ditch to rest on his way to the police barracks (*CN*, 256). In both texts, the protagonist escapes the gallows by a hair's breadth. Whereas Christy suffers from sore feet and is referred to as 'lame' by his father, O'Nolan's protagonist is an amputee with a wooden leg. Although we never get to know how exactly his injury occurred, the narrator states: 'I met one night with a bad accident. I broke my left leg (or, if you like, it was broken for me) in six places and when I was well enough again to go my way, I had one leg made of wood, the left one' (*CN*, 225). We may infer from the enigmatic concession 'or, if you like, it was broken for me', that the paralytic injury was not really an accident. It might have been inflicted by somebody who, like Oedipus's father, abused the narrator's naïve and childlike disposition. Whereas the slanderous testimony of the father misrepresents Christy Mahon as a village fool in *The Playboy of the Western World*, the nameless Oedipal protagonist of *The Third Policeman* is presented from the very beginning as a hybrid of a Shakespearean 'wise fool' and a village fool in the stereotypical sense of the word, given to naïve misreadings, both of his beloved de Selby and of the world around him.

As the linearity of history comes to an abrupt standstill by way of a revolutionary outburst – the 'terror' of the Irish War of Independence and Civil War, the bomb that kills the de Selby scholar in Old Mathers's house – the post-revolutionary state needs to reinvent its collective identity as an 'imagined community' by way of a new foundational myth.[17] In American society after the US Civil War, such a foundational myth was provided by Washington Irving's Rip van Winkle, whose childlike *naiveté* reflects the situation of the American nation in its infancy.[18] While van Winkle sleeps for about twenty years before he returns to his village, the de Selby scholar is dead for sixteen years before his return to Ireland. As O'Nolan's nameless protagonist is even more infantile and ignorant, one may say that he may be considered an Irish counterpart of van Winkle and that *The Third Policeman* functions as a weird parody of a foundational myth or a foundational myth gone wrong.

The Third Policeman echoes the Oedipal constellation of *The Playboy of the Western World* to show that, although Ireland had become almost fully independent in the Free State era, the country's Oedipal dilemma had gotten even worse. Like Oedipus – who did not know his father who paralysed and abandoned him as a child – O'Nolan's nameless narrator remarks: 'my father and I were strangers' (*CN*, 223). Figuratively speaking, namelessness is a marker of a crisis or loss of identity. Rather than being dominated by the

English king as the overpowering father figure representing the pro-English establishment of pre-1907 Ireland, as in Synge's play, O'Nolan's protagonist must grow up as an orphan, and the absence of the father figure signified by Ireland's break with its semi-colonial past contributes to his loss of identity. As the Free State was independent from the United Kingdom but remained part of the British Empire, partitioned yet still bound by the oath of allegiance to the English king, opponents of the Anglo-Irish treaty considered this political construct a betrayal of the independent Irish Republic proclaimed at the 1916 Easter Rising as the seminal revolutionary event on Ireland's way to independence. A resulting crisis of patriarchal authority in the microcosm of the family and the macrocosm of the state apparatus surfaces in the revolutionary outbreak of the Irish Civil War. In a pre-revolutionary Irish society, which has been paralysed by the memory of the past, the sons suffer under the injustice inflicted by the paternal yoke but at least they could wait for their fathers' death and take their place by way of filial or lineal succession. As the new system offers a revolutionary break with the linearity of the past, however, the old fatherly prerogative has lost its authority and gives way to an anarchic power vacuum. Rather than suffering under patriarchal injustice – which paradoxically and simultaneously guarantees social stability via the son's prospect of lineal succession into the bliss of paternal omnipotence – the de Selby scholar becomes dispossessed by his father's caretaker or deputy John Divney, who usurps the patriarchal prerogative as an anarchic, 'Lord of Misrule'-like mock father-figure. In the case of the gullible son fooled by his father's caretaker, the pre-revolutionary bonds of lineage and blood have been substituted by amoral, not to say Machiavellian, power politics.

To shed light on the problems caused by the transformation of an old into a new state, O'Nolan rewrites the Oedipal conflict in terms of elective rather than lineal family relations; or, in perverted terms of the New Testamentary principle of apostolic vocation. Whereas Christ, as the Son of God, solves the Oedipal dilemma by becoming a father figure of the apostles whom he appoints by the authority of his word, Divney turns out to be an antichrist figure who, in contrast to the biblical story, succeeds in overthrowing the patriarchal system as a satanic overreacher (as Satan was the son-like archangel closest to God before his rebellion against the father deity, he may be considered a biblical variant of the classical Oedipus figure). The lack of paternal control is represented by the early death of the nameless narrator's lineal father as the actual patriarch. As such, the orphaned son – who may be considered an 'apostolic' follower of the 'false prophet' de Selby – is dispossessed by his father's deputy. As Divney usurps patriarchal authority in the same way as Satan attempts to dispossess the biblical father deity, the re-enactment of the Oedipal constellation affects not only the secular microcosm of the narrator's family life, but also the biblical macrocosm of the father deity challenged by Satan as a Christian Oedipus-figure. As the Holy Roman Catholic Church, headed by the pope as God the Father's deputy on earth, remains unmentioned in this context, it is furthermore implied that the patristic institution of the Catholic establishment fails to keep control of the increasingly anarchic Ireland in which the narrator lives. Like 'the priest's off-stage portrayal' in *The Playboy of the Western World*,[19] the Roman Catholic Church remains almost unmentioned in the afterlife of *The Third Policeman*.[20]

As a result of his usurpation of patriarchal authority, Divney ruins the shebeen family business and squanders the family heritage. However, as Divney is unscrupulously clever, he also manipulates the childlike narrator, as a representative of the Irish peasants satirised by Synge, to murder a father figure symbolising Ireland's semi-colonial past: the Big House owner Old Mathers who represents the pro-English landed gentry and the enduring paternal presence of the English king in the Free State era. In a more than obvious allusion to Synge, Old Mathers is killed with a spade: 'Not everybody knows how I killed old Phillip Mathers, smashing his jaw in with my spade' (*CN*, 223). As in *The Playboy of the Western World*, the old man with his grotesquely split skull appears for a second time. Whereas Old Mahon survives the assault, Old Mathers dies and appears to the main character in a ghostly interview. And it is only in the novel's closing pages that the reader comes to know that the main character, too, has been murdered and that his appearance as a ghost from the past drives his murderer and pseudo-father Divney out of his wits, making him die a desperate death.

Hamlet **and** Julius Caesar

At the 'end' of O'Nolan's never-ending *The Third Policeman*, the Oedipal struggle of the dispossessed son with his pseudo-fatherly usurper results in an absurd situation. The reader learns that the self-proclaimed father figure (Divney) killed his elective son (the narrator) after he had tricked him into usurping another elective father figure (Old Mathers) representing Ireland's semi-colonial past. At the same time, the reader witnesses the dispossessed son take filial revenge on his pseudo-fatherly murderer as a ghost. In this aspect, the scene echoes and inverts the constellation of *Hamlet*, the Shakespearean play which Sigmund Freud and the neo-Freudian scholar Ernest Jones consider the most important rewriting of the Oedipus myth in western literature.[21]

As a further Hamletian turn of the screw, *The Third Policeman* queers the Freudian-Oedipal constellation elaborated by Jones.[22] Rather than falling in incestuous love with his mother and revenging his father's usurped place in the family triad, the dispossessed son shares his bed with Divney as the man who, Claudius-like, usurped his father's place and assigned him the role of the dispossessed son with an antic or foolish disposition. As in the state of Denmark, there is something rotten in the Irish Free State. The Möbian cyclicality of *The Third Policeman* echoes the endless loop of *Hamlet*'s structure. Like in *The Third Policeman*, the circularity of Shakespeare's *Hamlet* is elucidated at the very end, a move which retrospectively triggers a new understanding of the text as a whole. When the dying Hamlet asks his friend Horatio to retell his tale after his death, he transforms the story of himself into a never-ending texture. As soon as Horatio ends his tale about Hamlet, the central character will ask him to retell it again, and so on *ad infinitum*.[23] *Hamlet* thus may be considered a scaffold, albeit a largely covert one, for the never-ending structural design of O'Nolan's text as a Möbius strip.

Although the Oedipal constellation presented in *Hamlet* serves as a prototype for the cyclical structural design of *The Third Policeman*, it is, however, *Julius Caesar*, and not Shakespeare's Danish play, which O'Nolan marks as an authorially confirmed intertext. Although the name of the Roman play is not mentioned, the epigraph to *The Third Policeman* turns out to be a quotation from Shakespeare's *Julius Caesar*:

> Since the affairs of men rest still uncertain,
> Let's reason with the worst that may befall.
> SHAKESPEARE (*CN*, 221)[24]

This passage is taken from the scene in which Brutus and Cassius prepare for their final battle against Antony and Octavius during the civil wars that have been set off by the assassination of Rome's imperial father figure Julius Caesar by his foster-son Brutus – another variant of the Oedipus myth. Although they are optimistic at this stage, Brutus and Cassius acknowledge the unpredictability of fate in a good Stoic manner and reckon with 'the worst that may befall'. As they will lose the battle and their lives by the play's end, they unknowingly predict their future in terms of tragic irony. Trying to keep his integrity as a truly honourable man who venerates old Roman virtues, Brutus has no chance to win his fight against the proto-Machiavellian Mark

Antony, who denounces Brutus's honour as a rhetorically skilled manipulator of the plebeians. Although he is successful in the civil war against Brutus, Mark Antony will be defeated by the even more cunning Octavius – the future Emperor Caesar Augustus.

Julius Caesar treats a revolutionary transition from republicanism to imperialism, as emphasised by the main character's flirtation with the crown.[25] Although the foster-son Brutus kills his fatherly mentor to save the old republican system, the rise of imperialist discourse cannot be stopped. The father figure has been killed, yet his memory paralyses the present and predetermines the future. Like any revolutionary movement, the assassination of Julius Caesar is followed by the anarchy of civil war. As revolutions tend to devour their children, not only Brutus, but also his antagonist Mark Antony will be defeated and leave a power vacuum to be filled by the twenty year younger Octavius – whereas the filial Brutus must die, Octavius adopts the name Caesar Augustus and celebrates himself as the legitimate 'filial' successor of Julius Caesar. Adopting the deceased patriarch's name, the self-fashioned 'son' becomes the new father figure of the Roman commonwealth.

The Third Policeman features a revolutionary movement in the opposite direction, from semi-colonial imperialist rule to a republican system. Yet, the novel may be considered a variant of the Oedipal story enacted in Shakespeare's *Julius Caesar* if one looks at the timeless dynamics of revolutionary upheavals in terms of power politics. Like Brutus, the narrator of *The Third Policeman* kills a father figure representing imperial ambition: Old Mathers, the Big House owner from the pro-English landed elite who exemplifies the 'old matters' and 'old fathers' of Ireland's semi-colonial history. As a relic and benefactor of the imperial past, Old Mathers represents the body politic of the British Empire which considered itself a successor of imperial Rome – when it reached its first climax of global extension in the Augustan Age, the king of the British Empire fashioned himself as the new Caesar Augustus, London was considered a counterpart of Rome, and so on.

As Brutus's authority is manipulated by Mark Antony's cunning, so the de Selby scholar's agency is manipulated by the parasitic Divney, who tries to profit from the narrator's Oedipal situation in a twofold manner. First, on the microcosmic level of the family. As the nameless narrator is presented as a village fool born into an Irish peasant family ruled by the pro-English state apparatus – and as he is constantly manipulated by the Mark Antony-like Divney – he recalls the fickle and child-like Roman plebeians from Shakespeare's *Julius Caesar* and the similarly unreliable Irish peasant mob from Synge's *The Playboy of the Western World*. Secondly, on the macrocosmic level of the state apparatus dominated by the ruling class of the pro-English elite representing the Caesar Augustus-like father figure of the king of the British Empire. Like the filial Brutus taking parricidal revenge on Julius Caesar's betrayal of the Roman Republic with a dagger, the unnamed narrator murders Old Mathers – a representative of the landowning class which is loyal to the Caesar Augustus-like king of the British Empire – with a spade. As the narrator unwittingly blows up Old Mathers's Big House, and himself inside it, he may be considered a parody of the IRA bombers – republican martyrs who were willing to die a Brutus-like death for what they considered an idealist mission.[26]

Like the geriatric and melancholic Saturn, the revolution devours its children.[27] Thus it is the Mark Antony-like or Claudius-like populist Divney who is killed when the nameless narrator returns as his own ghost and frightens the anarchic usurper of the paternal prerogative to death by way of post-revolutionary and post-civil war revenge. Once again, *Hamlet* comes to mind in terms of structurally inverted correspondence: in his Hamletian situation as the dispossessed son, the novel's filial narrator takes revenge on the Claudius-like pseudo-fatherly usurper by scaring him to death as his own ghost after he has met the ghost of the Hamlet Senior-like patriarch Old Mathers, whom he killed and whose property he has destroyed as a mock-IRA bomber. Divney may be considered, like Mark Antony, to be an opportunist who attempts to seize power in the post-revolutionary anarchy of the civil war but is devoured as a child of the revolution. However, his death is not brought about by Caesar's ghostly imperialist discourse, but rather by the ghost of the Brutus-like narrator, who dies as a mock-republican martyr and whose endless afterlife will be vexed by the King Hamlet and Julius Caesar-like ghost of Old Mathers in a nightmarish manner, as the unresolved 'old matters' of the past are represented by the old fathers' ghostly afterlives and revivals.

Conclusion

While its influence is not elaborated in an explicit manner – as the intertextual allusions to Synge and Shakespeare are – the Civil War subtext of *The Third Policeman*'s Oedipal drama becomes even more obvious in light of the fact that Yeats staged two post-Civil War versions of *Oedipus* at the Abbey: *Oedipus the King* in 1926 and *Purgatory* in August 1938, the second shortly before the composition of O'Nolan's novel.[28] Roche not only refers to *Purgatory* as 'the most Oedipal' of Yeats's plays, he also points out that

> In it, an Old Man [or Mahon, or Mathers?] visits the scene of a burnt-out Big House with his sixteen-year-old Son [...]. The Old Man describes almost offhandedly how he has murdered his father and burned his remains in the house; historically, the Big Houses were burned in the Civil War of 1922, the same year in which the Young Man was born.[29]

If one considers the circumstance that O'Nolan's nameless narrator bombs the Big House of Old Mathers as a father figure and accidentally kills Divney when he returns as his own ghost in a mock-Hamletian manner sixteen years after the deed, a Yeatsian influence is suggested. This echo of Yeats's *Purgatory* seems even more plausible, owing to the fact that the ghost of Hamlet's father introduces himself to his son as a poor soul trapped in purgatory and that the nameless narrator from *The Third Policeman*, son-like, returns to his pseudo-father Divney from purgatory as a ghost. As this return will recur over and over again, owing to the Möbius-strip-like cyclical structure of the text, the ghostly narrator seems to be trapped in an endless purgatorial, or even hell-like, counter-world.

Indeed, with its structural echoes of *Hamlet* and its thematic echoes of *Julius Caesar* articulated via *The Playboy of the Western World*, *The Third Policeman* implies that nothing is going to change in the long run with regard to Ireland's Oedipal passivity. Like in imperial Rome, where the patriarch Julius Caesar is replaced by his filial successor Caesar Augustus to fossilise the imperial turn of the former Roman Republic, nothing significantly new is going to happen in post-revolutionary Ireland. Even as there is a 'republican turn' away from British semi-colonial rule and the father figure of the English king, Ireland's Oedipal disposition, from O'Nolan's perspective writing in the immediate aftermath of the Free State, appears to remain largely unchanged (this is a theme he would take up with renewed and more direct force in his subsequent novel, *An Béal Bocht*). Owing to its fossilised power structures, Ireland will continue to be ruled by the memory of the dead, such as the un-resurrected Christ-figure Parnell let down by his own people (as parodied by Synge). If there is a power vacuum, this vacuum will be transitory. If there are revolutions, they will devour their own children, and nothing will change in the long run. Or, as James Joyce puts it, 'history repeats itself'[30] – an aspect which is stressed by the original title of O'Nolan's novel: *Hell Goes Round and Round*.

Hence the absence of an *Irish* Augustus-like or Messianic saviour figure in the afterworld parish of *The Third Policeman* and the cyclicality of the plot. In its Shakespearean rewritings of the Oedipus myth via Synge, *The Third*

Policeman evokes the Oedipal archetype to articulate a grim vision of Ireland's future. As history repeats itself, almost nothing is likely to change, even as a constant struggle for revolutionary turn goes on as a timeless Oedipal fight between the past and the future. To show that history repeats itself in this way, *The Third Policeman* is structured as a cyclical, *Hamlet*-like, self-perpetuating story, held together by the narrative *perpetuum mobile* of the Möbius strip. Spinning around its own axis in a never-ending way, this is the momentum to cement paralysis.

ACT II

O'Nolan's Globe

5

'Comedy Is Where You Die and They Don't Bury You Because You Can Still Walk'

William Saroyan and Brian O'Nolan's playful correspondence

Joseph LaBine

Brian O'Nolan corresponded with the American-Armenian playwright and short story writer William Saroyan from July 1939 to September 1940. Saroyan is frequently cited as having encouraged O'Nolan to write plays. This encouragement is evident in their correspondence. On 4 September 1939 Saroyan writes, 'How about a play? Write a play [...]. You could do a hell of a play' (*L*, 59). He presses the point again on 31 December 1939: 'If you find time, or if you can make time, please write a play. I'm serious. [...] I know you can do a fine kind of Irish and comic and sombre play. I hope you will give it a try' (*L*, 63). Regarding the unpublished manuscript of *The Third Policeman* he writes, on 9 June 1940, 'Please make a play of it [...] and send it out' (*L*, 77). Yet, this exclusive critical focus on Saroyan's encouragement that O'Nolan transition to writing stage plays has advanced a partial, even reductive account of the broader content of their correspondence, which ranges from war and finances to death, writing, publishing and friendship.

Early O'Nolan critic Anne Clissmann infers that 'at Saroyan's suggestion, [O'Nolan] turned to drama and wrote, in quick succession, *Faustus Kelly*, *Thirst* and *The Insect Play*'.[1] But O'Nolan's interest in theatre and performance predates Saroyan. Writing about *At Swim-Two-Birds* in March 1939, Niall Montgomery encouraged O'Nolan to 'MAKE IT INTO A PLAY' months before he met Saroyan (*L*, 45). Ciarán Ó Nualláin's biography, *Óige an Dearthár* (1973), indicates O'Nolan showed interest in plays at an early age. Some of O'Nolan's playlets appeared in *Blather* magazine, such as the 1933 satirical dramatic sketch 'The Bog of Allen' (*MBM*, 42–3). Ciarán writes that O'Nolan read *Tá na Francaigh ar Muir*, an Irish play by Cú Uladh, which Michael Nolan kept copies of in the family home. O'Nolan saw his uncle Joe Gormley rehearse the play *Tactics* at his photography studio in Strabane. *A Royal Alliance*, a play by his paternal uncle Fergus Ó Nualláin, was staged at the Abbey Theatre in 1920. Michael Nolan, a drama enthusiast, also drafted several plays throughout his life. O'Nolan saw 'almost every production of *An Comhar Drámaíochta*' (the Gaelic Drama League of Ireland, 1923–42) and 'the first production in Dublin' of Micheál mac Liammóir's 1928 play *Tóraíocht Dhiarmada agus Ghráinne* (The Pursuit of Diarmuid and Gráinne).[2]

Since Clissmann, critics have, for the most part, accepted the narrative that meeting Saroyan prompted O'Nolan to take up playwrighting; but these critics have overlooked the further ways in which O'Nolan and Saroyan influenced each other and how their writing relates aesthetically. In *No Laughing Matter: The life and times of Flann O'Brien*, Anthony Cronin quotes from the correspondence and notes that in late 1939, Saroyan borrowed 'Sweeny in the Trees', O'Nolan's preferred title for *At Swim-Two-Birds*, for one of his short plays. Saroyan was enamoured by the name Sweeny/Sweeney, claiming in his introduction to the play that 'Sweeney is one of those names art cannot resist'.[3] He began planning the play after meeting O'Nolan, and his friendship with O'Nolan connected him to Dublin's literary world: 'If no message other than the one of Sweeney in the trees had come to me in Dublin, my visit would have been all that I could ever have imagined it might be, and Flann O'Brien was no less that year than James Joyce in Dublin twenty years before.'[4] Maebh Long notes that *At Swim-Two-Birds* impressed the American author: after the war, Saroyan selected an extract from the novel entitled 'The Pooka and the Good Fairy' for inclusion in *I Wish I'd Written That* (1946), 'an anthology edited by Eugene J. Woods of texts American authors wished they had written' (*L*, 62, n. 150).[5]

Unaware that Saroyan was inspired by his visit to Dublin, some critics have doubted his admiration of *At Swim-Two-Birds*. William H. Gass, for instance, in his introduction to the Dalkey Archive Press edition of *At Swim-Two-Birds*, finds Saroyan's praise for the novel inauthentic and labels him an 'imposter'.[6] Gass's shot at Saroyan echoes the anonymous reviewer for *The*

Spectator who, in a 1935 review of *The Daring Young Man on the Flying Trapeze*, calls him 'a posturer and a poseur'.[7] However, the posturing and posing aspects of Saroyan's aesthetics suggest affinity with O'Nolan, which can be explored through their written correspondence.

Stefan Solomon convincingly suggests that the 'chain of influence was palpable' between the authors; Solomon argues that O'Nolan's stage plays demonstrate an affinity for 'the kind of eccentric, character-based drama that was the staple of someone like Saroyan' in a way that distinguishes them from the *avant-garde* modernist anti-theatre of someone like Beckett.[8] But Solomon looks specifically at how this influence played out in O'Nolan's theatrical writing, neglecting the fiction. Keith Hopper notes that Saroyan played an instrumental role in ensuring that *Story* magazine published O'Nolan's 'John Duffy's Brother' in 1941.[9] O'Nolan sent 'For Ireland Home and Beauty' to Matson under Saroyan's encouragement, and Long mentions a lost story he sent titled 'Old Iron' (*L*, 97). The co-founder and editor of *Story*, Martha Foley, writes the following biographical note: 'Flann O'Brien is a discovery of William Saroyan's, but further than that, at this moment, we know nothing except that he is not William Saroyan.'[10] Hopper's note suggests but does not pursue the possibility of exploring Saroyan's significance to O'Nolan's *oeuvre* beyond the theatrical work by acknowledging his influence on the short fiction.

In the present essay, I interpret O'Nolan and Saroyan's correspondence as a mutually influential collaboration on the aesthetics and philosophy of humour. Casting light on Saroyan's side of this collaboration – his fiction, letters and essays – reveals preoccupations with the comic, death and the afterlife, which are key aspects of O'Nolan's poetics. O'Nolan also recurrently marvels at the volume of Saroyan's written output across genres: 'I suppose you have polished off a few other plays in addition to your revue by this time, an English-Armenian Dictionary prefaced by irregular-verb paradigms and a few hundred short stories' (*L*, 52); 'do not write more stories or plays than there are printing-presses and playhouses' (*L*, 53); 'How fast are the plays and stories tumbling out of you?' (*L*, 60). At the time of their correspondence, O'Nolan commends Saroyan's enormous output, over ten short-story collections produced between 1934 and '42 at an average rate of about one hundred stories per year.[11] Saroyan's discussions of the manuscripts of *At Swim-Two-Birds* and *The Third Policeman* offer valuable insight into how O'Nolan negotiates his writing in contest between art and commercial success. And while they discuss dramatic works in their letters, both authors are primarily writers of prose fiction. The correspondence, and specifically

O'Nolan's letter to Saroyan on 7 September 1940, suggests O'Nolan took a special interest in Saroyan's fiction writing: 'I saw a very funny story of yours recently in (not necessarily a recent) issue of STORY. Don't let your tidal interest in theatre interfere with the flow in the pipe that delivers the short stories' (*L*, 91). Ideas exchanged during the correspondence relate specifically to the fiction writing of these two authors. As I will show, while writing *The Third Policeman* O'Nolan may have been inspired, in part, by Saroyan's 1939 story 'Comedy Is Where You Die and They Don't Bury You Because You Can Still Walk'. Such an exchange gives new relevance to O'Nolan's comment to Saroyan that he thinks 'the idea of a man being dead all the time is pretty new', given that 'Comedy Is Where You Die' was published before O'Nolan described the plot of *The Third Policeman* to Saroyan (*CN*, 405). But in the context of their correspondence, which was productive, this is merely one example of their collaboration: direct influence is less significant than the resonances and divergences between their poetics, especially on the comic potential of death and the afterlife. These themes are at the core of their shared philosophy of humour once it is adequately historicised through their written correspondence.

In three sections that follow, I trace a timeline for the O'Nolan–Saroyan correspondence. The first section deals with Saroyan's letters and his frustrated attempts to secure a publisher for *At Swim-Two-Birds* in the United States. The second section examines O'Nolan's explorations of the comic potential of the afterlife in *The Third Policeman* and sets up an implicit dialogue with the genre aesthetics that underpin Saroyan's 'Comedy Is Where You Die'. The third section addresses the great importance that both authors placed on selecting, exchanging and collaborating on the working titles of their works. These coordinates, with their emphasis on O'Nolan and Saroyan's fictional writing, broadly establish the importance of tracing the significance of their correspondence from its genesis until the end of O'Nolan's career and life, and then to 1967 when *The Third Policeman* was published. Limiting the timeline to the years they corresponded (1939–41), or the years that O'Nolan transitioned to writing stage plays (1940–3), gives only a partial view of what was shared.

Saroyan can't sell *Sweeny*

When the authors first met, Saroyan was on an international tour enjoying the wide reception of his recent short story collections, particularly *The Daring Young Man on the Flying Trapeze*. The book was an immediate bestseller in

1934, and Saroyan used some of the royalties to finance a trip to Europe and Armenia.[12] He visited Ireland for the first time in the spring of 1939. The visit made a lasting impression on him. The closing portion of Saroyan's 4 September 1939 letter to O'Nolan offers insight into the warmth he felt about his time in Dublin. He calls it 'That wonderful city, with the wonderful Liffey':

> I miss Dublin. Honest. I miss all the swell people I was lucky enough to meet. I miss the singing. I miss Whelan's pub at Stepaside. I miss Montgomery. How the hell is he? Is he back in Dublin? If you see him, tell him to drop me a line and let me know what's going on. [...] If you see Ruth, say hello for me. [...] You people live in a great and beautiful place. [...] With kind regards and a broken heart because I am not in Dublin. (*L*, 59)

Saroyan contacted many people in the Dublin literary scene with the help of twenty-four-year-old Niall Montgomery. (Saroyan and Montgomery had published together in issue 27 of the *transition* in 1938.) Once in Dublin, Saroyan met Montgomery and his sister Ruth Boland (née Montgomery). They introduced him to Brian O'Nolan among others. Saroyan recounted the trip in *Razzle Dazzle* (1942) in an essay about 'the play I must write about them and Dublin' that eventually became *Elmer and Lily* (1939).[13] He writes:

> In June of 1939 [...] I was in Dublin at last, going around town with the Irish poet Niall Montgomery or the Irish novelist Flann O'Brien; or driving out with these two and others to Igo Inn in Pierce Fitzgerald's wild little automobile after the announcement of 'Time, Gentlemen' in Dublin bars – going seventy miles an hour over the most wonderful streets in the world and through the most beautiful meadows; or in Kenneth Kenny's car to James Whelan's place at Stepaside, Sandyford, County Dublin, with Kenny and O'Brien.[14]

Saroyan quickly became interested in *At Swim-Two-Birds*, and his correspondence with O'Nolan began after he had returned to the United States under the shadow of impending war. The wartime context is a key concern of the letters. The war informs discussions of travel, visiting Ireland again, Ireland's neutrality, the future and whether Europe will continue to exist.

On 18 July 1939, Saroyan writes to O'Nolan that he has contacted Harcourt Brace to try and have *At Swim-Two-Birds* published in a US edition under O'Nolan's preferred title *Sweeny in the Trees*:[15]

Took your book straight away to Harcourt Brace, told them the title SWEENEY IN THE TREES. They need seven or eight days to make up their minds but let me tell you that your side of the bet is practically a dead fish. I win, you lose and SWEENEY IN THE TREES will be out in America some time this fall (this isn't positive but that's the way I talk). (*L*, 58)

Saroyan made and lost a fifty-dollar bet that the novel would be successfully published in the United States. He writes to O'Nolan again on 4 September 1939 with the update that Harcourt Brace are unwilling to publish the work: 'Well, as a predictor it looks like I'm a flop. Them rats in New York at Harcourt Brace have turned down Sweeney. The usual alibi. They just love the book but are sure it won't make money' (*L*, 58).

On 26 December 1939, Saroyan telegrams: 'wish I were in Dublin – may I use your title Sweeney in the Trees for a play I am writing – cable reply'.[16] O'Nolan's response is written on the same cable, 'Go ahead and more power to you' (*L*, 60, n. 146). On 31 December, Saroyan writes a long letter thanking O'Nolan for the title: 'When I cabled you it seemed to me I wouldn't care to finish the play unless it was Sweeney in the Trees. The title kept hanging around me ever since I heard it.' Later in the same letter he reminisces, 'I still want to write about Dublin' (*L*, 62–3). Within the dialogue established in the letters, fortified with O'Nolan's title and novel concept for his story, Saroyan's *Sweeney in the Trees* constitutes his writing about Dublin. But also, more pressingly, the play's core themes address the subservience of art to commercial concerns that determined the rejection of O'Nolan's own *Sweeny in the Trees*.

John Leggett observes that Saroyan's primary concern in *Sweeney in the Trees* is art that 'won't make money'. The play's central character Michael Sweeney despises money and regrets living in a world where 'money is worshipped'.[17] Since Sweeney does not need money himself, he creates a fake job advertisement in an effort to understand the artists, down-and-outs and various workers who need to earn a living. The play suggests art is at odds with commercial enterprise, and this theme finds an analogue in Saroyan's failure to sell O'Nolan's novels to an American publisher. The same concern underpins O'Nolan's discussion of money in his 7 September 1940 letter to Saroyan:

Gone with the Wind keeps me awake at night sometimes – I mean, the quantity of potatoes earned by the talented lady novelist. I often think I would like to be a wealthy gentleman with an eight-cylinder Ford.

Which reminds me – that 50 dollars which you sent (and shouldn't have sent at all in any circumstances) I spent exclusively on Sweep tickets here. […] My idea was that with our joint names on the tickets, something would have to happen. I was under the misapprehension that each of us would get at least £15,000. Then I could visit America. (*L*, 92)

O'Nolan's use of the word 'misapprehension', suggesting his disillusionment, is poignant: he failed to win the lottery. He had already explained his foolhardy plan in great detail to Pat Duggan of Matson and Duggan on 4 March 1940:

> I got your letter of the 24th of January last sending cheque for 50 dollars from Bill Saroyan. I should have acknowledged it months ago but couldn't think of what to do with the money. […] Now I've had an idea. I'm buying Irish Sweep tickets with it, the £30,000 to be divided between myself and Bill with maybe a cut for yourselves in the ordinary way of business. My idea is to ride in on Saroyan's luck. I'm sending half the tickets herewith for you to hold – the official receipts will follow. The race is April the fifth. I will invade America shortly after the race and have the time of my life. I hope the new play makes a lot of money for all concerned. (*L*, 70–1)

O'Nolan presents the possibility of his winning the lottery and visiting the United States as a matter of chance, dependent on 'Saroyan's luck' which, with Saroyan's publishing credits, financial success and recent Pulitzer in mind, is portrayed by O'Nolan as a commercial enterprise worth banking on. His expression 'time of my life' puns on the title of Saroyan's famous 1939 play, suggesting Saroyan titles were already loaded into his arsenal of jokes by early 1940.

O'Nolan reads Saroyan

O'Nolan read at least two of Saroyan's plays: the letters indicate he read *The Time of Your Life* (1939) and *My Heart's in the Highlands* (1939) (*L*, 68, 70). Brenda Murphy categorises *The Time of Your Life* with other American saloon plays such as Eugene O'Neill's *The Iceman Cometh*. Murphy defines the 'saloon play' as a drama that places a large cast of misfit characters in a seedy bar where they form a community whose bond is threatened by an outside character bent on enforcing his will on them.[18] This dramatic mode may illustrate further affinity between Saroyan's plays and O'Nolan's writing for performance, as this description could easily be applied to his play *Thirst*. O'Nolan and Saroyan's shared admiration of bars and pubs forms the setting for some of their dramatic output; for instance, the existing excerpt of O'Nolan's 'Untitled Play in Irish' begins in a bar with a call for '*Uisce beatha agus soda!*' (whiskey and soda).[19]

Beyond the one 'very funny' story published in *Story* magazine to which he makes allusion in his 7 September 1940 letter, Cronin claims that O'Nolan read Saroyan's *The Daring Young Man on the Flying Trapeze* collection.[20] On 14 February 1940, O'Nolan compliments Saroyan on *The Time of Your Life*:

> I do not know how you write and keep on writing those plays. I don't understand the way you make ordinary things uproarious and full of meaning and sentiment and make yourself appear saner than everybody else merely by being crazy. I've just been reading *The Time of Your Life* and I think it is what we here call the business. It is fearfully funny. There is great freshness in all your stuff. It's given me a lot of ideas but I can't use them for a while because that would be copying. (*L*, 68)

The line about 'ideas' originating in Saroyan's play is compelling. It raises questions about what influence Saroyan's writing exerted on O'Nolan, and whether he deployed any of these ideas in his own writing. His reading coincided with the composition of *The Third Policeman*. And, despite his hesitation to embrace Saroyan's influence on the basis of 'copying', he offers a tongue-in-cheek outline of a 'copying' programme in *At Swim-Two-Birds* that characters 'should be interchangeable as between one book and another' and 'existing literature should be regarded as a limbo'; authors should create only when they fail 'to find a suitable existing puppet' (*CN*, 21). O'Nolan first mentions his second novel to Saroyan in a letter on 14 February 1940:

> I've just finished another bum book. I don't think it is much good and haven't sent it anywhere yet. The only thing good about it is the plot and I've been wondering whether I could make a crazy Saroyan play out of it. When you get to the end of this book you realise that my hero or main character (he's a heel and a killer) has been dead throughout the book and that all the queer ghastly things which have been happening to him are happening in a sort of hell which he earned for the killing. [...] I think the idea of a man being dead all the time is pretty new. When you are writing about the world of the dead – and the damned – where

none of the rules and laws (not even the law of gravity) holds good, there is any amount of scope for back-chat and funny cracks. (*L*, 68–9)

An abridged version of this letter is included as an appendix to all prominent editions of *The Third Policeman*.[21] However, this edited 'Publisher's Note' removes without acknowledgement the word 'bum' before 'book' and the name 'Saroyan' before the word 'play' ('I've just finished another book [...] and I've been wondering whether I could make a crazy ... play out of it'; *CN*, 405), thus robbing the letter of vital context: Saroyan's writing is a potential source of inspiration for O'Nolan's recycling of ideas.[22]

The comic potential of the afterlife explored in *The Third Policeman* sets up an implicit dialogue with the genre aesthetics that underpin Saroyan's 1939 story 'Comedy Is Where You Die and They Don't Bury You Because You Can Still Walk'. In the story, an unnamed narrator, who is likely dead and journeying to hell, is on a train, which he thinks is headed to San Francisco. *Hell Goes Round and Round* (O'Nolan's working title for *The Third Policeman* manuscript from 1940) and the story share the idea that a main character is dead throughout the work. Saroyan also employs a concept we see in O'Nolan's novel of a narrator having an internal dialogue with his own soul. The narrator's soul, Joe, in O'Nolan's novel, is an ironic transliteration of the Irish word for confessor, *anamchara*, literally meaning 'soul friend'. Saroyan's narrator speaks to his 'heart' as a friend inside his body: 'His heart talked on, and he sat like a small child, listening, and while his heart talked, he argued with it.'[23] The narrator's heart in Saroyan's story delights in enigmatic parables, much as Joe does throughout *The Third Policeman*. The heart says to the narrator: 'Seven times the sheep have wakened and seven times it is the same afternoon. There is still light upon the earth.'[24] O'Nolan may not have read this specific Saroyan story, or seen its title, while writing *The Third Policeman*. If he did, then his comment to Saroyan that 'the idea of a man being dead all the time is pretty new' could be understood as a concession to Saroyan's doing it first in 'Comedy Is Where You Die'. Proving direct influence is difficult and perhaps not as productive, nor as vital, as showing that O'Nolan and Saroyan shared ideas about comedy, posthumous writing and death.

Saroyan critic Edward Foster places *The Daring Young Man on the Flying Trapeze* among 'the most forceful and frightening expressions of what it meant to be alive in America in the 1930s'.[25] In the collection's preface, Saroyan explicitly connects writing and death:

A writer can have one of two styles: he can write in a manner that implies that death is inevitable, or he can write in a manner that implies that death is 'not' inevitable. [...] If you write as if you believe that ultimately you and everyone else alive will be dead, there is a chance that you will write in a pretty earnest style. Otherwise you are apt to be either pompous or soft. On the other hand, in order not to be a fool, you must believe that as much as death is inevitable life is inevitable. That is, the earth is inevitable, and people and other living things on it are inevitable, but no man can remain on earth very long. You do not have to be melodramatically tragic about this. As a matter of fact, you can be as amusing as you like about it. It is really one of the basically humorous things, and it has all sorts of possibilities for laughter.[26]

Compare the end of this quotation, and notably Saroyan's phrase 'all sorts of possibilities for laughter', with O'Nolan's 14 February letter to Saroyan, in which he writes that 'When you are writing about the world of the dead – and the damned – where none of the rules and laws (not even the law of gravity) holds good, there is any amount of scope for back-chat and funny cracks' (L, 69). Both O'Nolan and Saroyan share the comic spirit of a fiction where the characters are essentially dead. We can read their conversation in the context of modernist texts that similarly explore the comic potential of a survived death or afterlife. The main example apparent to both authors would have been Paddy Dignam's appearance as a 'ghouleaten' corpse in 'brown mortuary habit' at Bloom's trial in the Circe episode of *Ulysses*.[27] Saroyan and O'Nolan discussed Joyce during Saroyan's visit to Dublin, and Saroyan telephoned Joyce and attempted to meet him in Paris.[28]

Saroyan and O'Nolan's texts embody the modernist treatment of the posthumous narrator.[29] A key recent article on this topic in O'Nolan studies is Ruben Borg's 'Reading Flann with Paul: Modernism and the trope of conversion', where Borg applies the thesis of Jean-Michel Rabaté's *The Ghosts of Modernity* (that modernism attempts to capture a haunted modernity by assuming the position of the posthumous writer) to O'Nolan's *oeuvre*. Borg argues that the narrative paradigm of living death, or death-in-life, 'recurs throughout O'Nolan's body of work'.[30] The coordinates and contexts of this critical conversation on the role of a comic portrayal of surviving death or the afterlife in literary modernism provide a productive base of knowledge for further consideration of O'Nolan's and Saroyan's aesthetics and shared philosophy of humour. Saroyan writes that writers must 'try as much as possible to be wholly alive' and 'laugh like hell'.[31] Ironically, the narrator of

The Third Policeman must die before he can begin taking pleasure in life. Once dead, he breathes 'keen, clear, abundant and intoxicating' air and notices the sky 'forever arranging and re-arranging the clouds and breathing life into the world' (*CN*, 252).

There are other productive similarities between *The Daring Young Man on the Flying Trapeze* and *The Third Policeman* concerning death and namelessness. The collection's titular story is about an unnamed writer who dies because he refuses to be anything but a writer. Borg's idea of a haunted modernity is apt here as well, since Saroyan draws an essential connection between earning a living as a modern writer and death. Saroyan's writer-narrator cannot write and live. He imagines that he is on 'a flying trapeze to some sort of eternity'.[32] The effect of this eternity is hallucinatory, as it is in *The Third Policeman*. A further resonance is found in the story 'Myself Upon the Earth', which features a peculiar exchange about a bicycle. Addressing the narrator's father during his walk to town, a farmer says, 'You will at least accept the use of my bicycle', to which the man responds:

> You ask me to mount one of those crazy contraptions? You ask me to tangle myself in that ungodly piece of junk? [...] Man was not made for such absurd inventions [...]. Man was not placed on the earth to tangle himself in junk.[33]

Like 'The Daring Young Man on the Flying Trapeze' story, the unnamed narrator of 'Myself Upon the Earth' lives only to write, in terms directly resonant with *The Third Policeman*: 'I have been nothing, or I have been walking about unalive, some indistinct shadow in a nightmare of the universe [...] without conscious articulation, without words, without language, I do not exist myself. I have no meaning, and I might just as well be dead and nameless.'[34] This of course corresponds with O'Nolan's narrator having forgotten his name, being therefore nameless, and, as the reader learns at the end of the novel, 'dead' as well (*CN*, 402).

Different models for successful comedy

O'Nolan and Saroyan's openness to copy and riff off of each other's ideas without giving credit casts new light on O'Nolan's collaborative aesthetic. O'Nolan developed and worked ideas by sharing them. In the opening essay of the present collection, Maebh Long notes an exciting connection between O'Nolan's 7 September 1940 letter to Saroyan concerning Niall Sheridan's play

Seven For a Secret, and Sheridan's story 'Matter of Life and Death' published in *Esquire* magazine in October 1939. In 1937, Niall Sheridan reviewed two of Saroyan's short story collections, *The Gay and Melancholy Flux* and *Little Children*, for *Ireland To-day*. In the first review, Sheridan noted the 'urgency and freshness' of Saroyan's prose (in his 1940 'Saint Valentine's Day' letter to Saroyan, O'Nolan commented on the 'great freshness' of *The Time of Your Life*). In his review of *Little Children*, Sheridan remarked that 'Saroyan has written something like 300 stories within the last three years, and he seems to me to be one of the most interesting contemporary prose-writers'. Long demonstrates that O'Nolan and Sheridan were both writing about policemen and bicycles around the same time and explores the complex lines between influence, collaboration and copying. O'Nolan tells Saroyan:

> Niall [Sheridan] has written what I think is a very excellent play, also about policemen. The main characters are three policemen and a greyhound and that's not a bad start. You could spend a lot of money on scenery and effects and not get anything so impressive looking on a stage. He has only submitted it just now to the theatres here but he has sent off a copy to Gross, a New York agent whom you probably know. I hope he does well with it. It's the sort of thing that could make a lot of money. It's straight, however, not in the Saroyan canon. I've not yet tried to follow your advice about making <u>my</u> policemen go on the stage. It's a grand idea but it would be very difficult to work out. (*L*, 92–3)

O'Nolan makes a number of revealing statements to Saroyan in this letter: Sheridan's play is 'straight, [and] not in the Saroyan canon'; it is 'the sort of thing that could make a lot of money'; and O'Nolan has 'not yet tried to follow [Saroyan's] advice about making [his] policeman go on stage'. In these statements, O'Nolan negotiates a space for art in the literary marketplace. The concepts he discusses are at oppositional drives: experimental comedy opposes 'straight' realism; adapting prose fiction for the stage may necessitate artistic compromises; artistic expression is in contest with financial security. O'Nolan can follow two potential paths within the context of this paradigm: he can produce a 'straight Sheridan play' or a 'crazy Saroyan play'. Yet, Saroyan offers an interesting foil for O'Nolan in this regard: he troubles these binaries as an experimental comic fiction and theatre writer who follows his muse yet nevertheless achieves popular and financial success in the United States – success that, he indicates, is possible for O'Nolan to achieve also.

Saroyan twice brings up the stateside success of Paul Vincent Carroll's *The White Steed* as an archetype of what a successful (Irish) O'Nolan play

could look like: 'The White Steed was a terrific success in N.Y.' (*L*, 59).
He opines: 'It's a great form and this country [the United States] needs and
wants plays. Paul Vincent Carroll's plays are very popular here, as you know'
(*L*, 63). Carroll's *The White Steed* also features anti-clerical themes, an Irish
setting and a Swift-like satirical tone, and these aspects of the work reveal
dimensions of how Saroyan views O'Nolan's art. The Abbey Theatre rejected
The White Steed, and the play eventually won the New York Drama Critics'
Circle Award. Carroll's work thrived in the United States away from the
scrutiny of the Irish censors. But O'Nolan raises questions about *avant-garde*
writing and commercially successful ventures, and these lie at the centre of
his correspondence with Saroyan: why is one author's comic experimental
writing successful, while another's writing fails? In recommending that
O'Nolan adapt *The Third Policeman* for the American stage, Saroyan may have
been encouraging yet another possibility for success.

The end

The correspondence stops abruptly in late 1940, but some of the ideas
discussed in the letters eventually moved into a public forum. By 1943,
O'Nolan and Saroyan were no longer writing to each other, but both were
publishing recollections about their meeting in Dublin four years previously.
In his introduction to the Faber edition of *Sweeney in the Trees*, Saroyan elevates
Flann O'Brien in 'spring of 1939' to the level of 'Joyce in Dublin twenty years
before'.[35] O'Nolan mentions Saroyan in his infamous 1943 interview with
Stanford Lee Cooper for *Time* magazine. Notoriously, the interview is filled
with inconsistencies, which include the intentional hoax of O'Nolan's claim
to have been 'bounced out of a beer hall for uncomplimentary references
to Adolf Hitler' during his trip to Germany, and his claim to have 'met and
married 18-year-old Clara Ungerland, blonde, violin-playing daughter of
a Cologne basket weaver [who] died a month later', purportedly from the
galloping consumption. And yet, the sentences describing Saroyan seem
genuine, friendly, even warm.

> William Saroyan turned up in Éire on a world tour 'to see if it actually
> was a long way to Tipperary'. O'Nolan [said he] thought that showed a
> refreshing curiosity. Saroyan told him that a better title for [his novel]
> *At Swim* would have been *Sweeney in the Trees* (one character, cursed by
> a monk, lives in the Trees). Later, Saroyan sent O'Nolan $50 for the
> suggested title.[36]

These comments speak to the quality of friendship or camaraderie that comes through in the 1939–40 letters. A convivial tone and sense of mutual good will permeates their discussion of money, agents, aesthetics and competitive boasting/humble-bragging which is doubtless also at play. The letters contain real notes of friendship: 'how the fuckin well are you?' (*L*, 52); 'I made a Novena that nothing worse than strong brandy would threaten you on the high seas' (*L*, 52); 'Now that the Yankee Clippers are running regularly between Foynes and New York, perhaps you could arrange to have a drink with me on Saturday nights?' (*L*, 53); 'please take care of yourself' (*L*, 53); 'Dein Freund' (*L*, 53), 'Comrade Brian!' (*L*, 58); 'Brian, how the hell are you?' (*L*, 59). Also 'So long, comrade. Write soon, will you? With kind regards and a broken heart' (*L*, 59); and 'Your colleague, Brian O'Nolan' (*L*, 60), which is an interesting complimentary close, in contrast to Saroyan's use of 'comrade', because it speaks to a mutual admiration and collegiality. In the last letter O'Nolan even approaches intimacy:

> Information, please. When are you reading this in the world? What time, day, room? Are you (were you last night) drunk? Who is in the same room, hall, saloon with you? Do you feel OK? Are you about to do some work on your typewriter or are you thinking of seeing a dame? Did you pass last Sunday satisfactorily? (*L*, 93)

Although O'Nolan and Saroyan pursue vastly different artistic projects after 1942, their works share aesthetic resonances *vis-à-vis* death, writing and the comic spirit. This is certainly true of Saroyan's *The Human Comedy* (1943), which is set in Ithaca, California (an obvious stand-in for Saroyan's hometown of Fresno) during the Second World War. The novel portrays various episodes in the daily lives of Homer and Ulysses Macauley. The boys' father has recently been killed and their older brother is fighting in Europe through the summer of 1942. Fourteen-year-old Homer takes a job as a telegram bike messenger. His operator is a drunkard named Grogan. The Irish surname and drinking evoke 'Grogan's public house', mentioned at several junctures in *At Swim-Two-Birds* (*CN*, 16–17, 42). Saroyan and O'Nolan's preoccupation with the bicycle is, in these novels at least, only a passing coincidence (especially when one considers O'Nolan's far more meticulous focus on bicycles in *The Third Policeman*). Yet both authors see the comedic potential in a distrust of invention. This sense permeates *The Daring Young Man* collection and resurfaces in *The Human Comedy*'s outrage at a world that values 'Machines instead of human beings!'[37] Saroyan possibly alludes to MacCruiskeen's infernal machines during Homer's interaction with the policeman who rescues Ulysses from a patent-pending steel trap. Saroyan writes: 'Homer talked to his brother. "Are you all right?" he said. "How do you get into these terrible things?" Homer looked at the ruined trap and then kicked it. "Careful there, boy," the policeman said. "That's some kind of a new invention. There's no telling what it's liable to do."'[38]

Later in his career, O'Nolan still equated Saroyan's work with his own even though he downplayed their former association. In his 27 February 1961 letter to Hester Green, O'Nolan writes:

> I met William Saroyan in Dublin a few years before the last war. He had spent several months in Germany, where several of his books had been published [...]. I never cared much for his whimsical material but it seems to have gone down very well in Germany, even with the Nazis on the ascendant. (*L*, 271)

The most common interpretation of this letter is also the most reductive, that which attributes O'Nolan's apparent rejection of Saroyan's writing to his jealousy over Saroyan's financial success. Cronin concludes that because Saroyan failed to stoke American publishers' interest in O'Nolan's novels, their correspondence fell apart. However, the context of the above letter is vital: O'Nolan is writing to Green about a proposed Rowohlt Verlag German translation of *At Swim-Two-Birds* and brings up Saroyan to make the point that his novel could do well in the German book market. The slight at Saroyan's material aside, O'Nolan still saw Saroyan's past success as a potential path for realising his own successes, even at this late stage of his career.

O'Nolan may have still been fond of Saroyan. Two years after he corresponded with Green about Saroyan, on 12 March 1963, John Ryan writes to O'Nolan to say that his 'idea of recreating the old days at Stepaside with Saroyan is very good':

> I meet [met] the man myself when we produced Dominic Behan's 'Posterity be Damned' [...]. The I.R.A. were threatening to blow up the theatre if the play went on and a horrid mob invaded the theatre on opening night. Saroyan was delighted with the entire evening. [...] I met him a few times afterwards and found him great company. (*L*, 345)

One can only speculate about the earlier conversation with O'Nolan, to which Ryan alludes. If we assume that it was in fact O'Nolan's idea to recreate the old days at Stepaside with Saroyan, to get roaring drunk and recapture the feeling of better times, the sentiment certainly complicates Cronin's impression of their friendship which terminated with O'Nolan's indifference to Saroyan's whimsical material. It personalises O'Nolan and Saroyan's relationship to an extent we may never fully understand.

In any case, Saroyan had the last word when he reviewed O'Nolan's *Stories and Plays* for *The New York Times* on 28 March 1976.[39] The essay is Saroyan's longest about O'Nolan – part book review, part overdue obituary, part biographical reminiscence. In it, Saroyan claims O'Nolan is 'outstanding and alone. Certainly, there is no shortage of writers in Ireland, but there isn't anybody remotely like him.'[40] He remembers his June 1939 visit, their discussions of Joyce, and clearly admires O'Nolan's accomplishments. Saroyan followed O'Nolan's career: he 'deeply cherished [...] the ephemeral' in *Cruiskeen Lawn* and maintained the mistaken view that O'Nolan avoided going to the United States because he had 'no care at all about the probability of [making] good, easy, abundant money'.[41] O'Nolan simply did not find an American market.

Much of O'Nolan and Saroyan's collaboration was unspoken. They were separated by war. In 1940, Saroyan refused to accept the Pulitzer Prize for *The Time of Your Life*. He was drafted into the US army in 1942. In the post-war period, his writing was less commercially successful.[42] Saroyan gambled away the remainder of his fortune and he transitioned from an experimental writer into a children's author. The two lost touch. But the O'Nolan–Saroyan correspondence remains significant to twentieth-century literature because the letters reveal how the two authors collaborated and influenced each other at the height of their creative powers.

6

Traces of Mischief

Flann O'Brien and Luigi Pirandello*

NEIL MURPHY

This essay articulates some shared genealogical patterns in the fiction of Brian O'Nolan and Luigi Pirandello, while some attention will also be directed to the latter's play *Six Characters in Search of an Author*. The genealogy in question is not necessarily a substitute for the possible presence of direct, verifiable influence in certain instances but it does form the basis for a larger, more inclusive, argument for a distinct counter-realist tradition in European literature to which both Pirandello and O'Nolan belong.

The 'Other Great Tradition'

The European counter-realist literary tradition may be discerned by identifying a specific network of unintentional associations: what Julia Kristeva calls a 'mosaic of quotations',[1] or what Steven Moore describes, in a more pointed reference to the development of the novel form, as a 'family classification'.[2] Moore sees this kind of relationship as underpinning what he terms the 'Other Great Tradition',[3] in which he traces the history of technical innovation in the novel form while repeatedly namechecking 'Flann O'Brien'.[4] Richard Kearney too includes 'O'Brien' in his 'counter-realist' tradition in Irish writing,[5] as does Rob Doyle in his 'Other Irish Tradition'.[6] Similarly, Derek Attridge situates his affect-focused analysis of contemporary experimental Irish writing against a backdrop of technically innovative Irish modernist writers (James Joyce, Samuel Beckett and O'Nolan).[7] Rüdiger

Imhof suggests, however, that 'It would be fruitless to quarrel about which of the two possible traditions – the Irish comic tradition or the international tradition of parodic literature or metaliterature – is the more appropriate one'[8] for O'Nolan, arguing that the two traditions are not at all mutually exclusive. He does acknowledge the commonplace use in Irish writing, post-O'Nolan, Joyce and Beckett, of 'the multi-faceted use of point-of-view […]; the spatialisation of narrative discourse; fragmented or split narrative; the disruption of chronology; fabulation and metafiction (including, possibly, historiographic metafiction) […] a kind of narrative shown in the process of being created'.[9] Ultimately, Imhof sees these narrative innovations as inextricably linked to 'international' rather than purely Irish trends. My consideration of the narrative interconnections between Pirandello and O'Nolan rests on similar assumptions, even if the presence of such a lineage in Irish writing is certainly distinct.

The broader European context for the counter-realist novel to which both O'Nolan and Pirandello's prose works belong has also been observed by Milan Kundera, whose conception of a European novelistic tradition places Laurence Sterne's *Tristram Shandy* (1759–67) and Denis Diderot's *Jacques le Fataliste* (1765–80) at the pinnacle of the novel's development:

> [These] are for me the two greatest novelistic works of the eighteenth century, two novels conceived as grand games. They reach heights of playfulness, of lightness, never scaled before or since. Afterwards, the novel got itself tied to the imperative of verisimilitude, to realistic settings, to chronological order.[10]

Despite Kundera's reservations about the subsequent development of the novel form, Pirandello, O'Nolan and Kundera himself, among many other writers since, offer clear evidence of the continued relevance of such a tradition both in Ireland and internationally. Contemporary authors like Alessandro Baricco, John Banville, Kevin Barry, Sara Baume, Angela Carter, Mark Z. Danielewski, Rob Doyle, Alasdair Gray, David Mitchell, Ali Smith, David Foster Wallace, Eimear McBride, Han Kang and Jeanette Winterson, among many others, extend this tradition, in which we repeatedly find: the deferral or avoidance of meaning; powerless or confounded narrators; high degrees of self-consciousness; overt intertextual play; the fragmentation of chronology and spatial order; the subversion of logical argument; technical play. Cervantes's *Don Quixote* (1605–15) and Margaret Cavendish's *The Blazing World* (1666) are usually considered among the earliest versions of the self-conscious mode that later became commonplace in twentieth-century literature, although the historical trajectory may be even deeper. Moore posits that the origins of what we call the novel can be traced back to the fourth century BC (Xenophon's *Cyropaedia*) and points to many similarities between Sterne's *Tristram Shandy*, Rabelais's *Gargantua et Pantagruel* (1532–64) and Barthélemy Aneau's *Alector, ou le coq* (1560) in terms of their 'multi-layered narrative structure'.[11] Such a genealogy suggests that the spirit of resistance to ordered narratives and parodic unmaking of one's own world are, in fact, constants of European literary history, rather than a simple aesthetic reaction to eighteenth- and nineteenth-century political and social pressures.

In the context of these variants of an innovative tradition, O'Nolan's major work is formally derived from and/or intertextually related to work by Rabelais,[12] Cervantes, Diderot, Sterne, Alfred Jarry, Pirandello, André Gide, James Branch Cabell and Aldous Huxley, not to mention a host of anti-realist Irish writers such as Jonathan Swift and James Stephens, as has been observed by many O'Nolan scholars.[13] Jorge Luis Borges, one of the first people to review *At Swim-Two-Birds*, also situates Flann O'Brien in such a rich tradition, extending backwards to *Don Quixote*, Lucius Apuleius's *The Golden Ass* and *The Thousand and One Nights*. Borges notes the long fictional inheritance of blending multiple ontological levels within the frames of fictional models, citing Schopenhauer's view that dreaming and wakefulness are the pages of a single book which we read in order to live. He concluded that books that branch into other books, like Flann O'Brien's first novel, 'help us sense this oneness' between dreaming and wakefulness, a testimony of the highest order from the author who wrote his own masterpiece, *The Garden of the Forking Paths*, just two years later.[14]

Nonetheless, while the relevance of this extended European tradition deeply resonates with O'Nolan's work, the issue of direct influence is a complex problem, not least because of the complicated publication history of Pirandello's translated stories.[15] Therefore, the focus of this essay is to draw attention to several strands of direct resonance between aspects of Pirandello's *Six Characters* and selected short stories, and O'Nolan's fiction, in an effort to demonstrate a compelling genealogy. In some cases, the distilled connections may be part of the broader tradition, or styles of writing, rather than direct allusion or influence. For example, Ondřej Pilný suggests, with respect to the possible connections between Alfred Jarry and O'Nolan, there is a 'remarkable similarity in the use of particular techniques and motifs by two outstanding innovators and [...] a certain aesthetic line may be traced in a significant amount of experimental writing in modernity'.[16]

O'Nolan, metafiction and Pirandello's *Six Characters*

O'Nolan's use of a recursive narrative structure – the novel within the novel mode, or Chinese Box, as Brian McHale has it[17] – is more immediately derived from earlier works by Huxley and Cabell, as well as from Gide's *The Counterfeiters*, than from Pirandello. Even if his use of self-reflexivity and self-parody is drawn from older origins like *Tristram Shandy*, the degree to which he pushed these technical devices reveals a spirit of subversion that often exceeds his precursors. This subversion forces the novel form into an essentially negative dialectic. As Thomas F. Shea contends, *At Swim-Two-Birds* represents 'a performance that constructs and breaks the frame of the tale, the novel flaunts its reflexive potentials, reminding us how all inscriptions refer to other words that act as traces of continually deferred meanings'.[18]

While some connections between Pirandello's *Six Characters* and O'Nolan's work will be established hereafter, the latter's presence in the general genealogical tradition of innovative literature is most compellingly felt via his fiction, rather than his drama, which largely refrained from significant engagement with metatheatrical devices. Daniel Keith Jernigan has suggested that O'Nolan's plays initially received scant critical attention in part because they had fallen out of print during the immediate upsurge in attention in the author's work in recent decades (*PT*, vii). While there is certainly substance to this claim, it is also possible that the plays were of less interest than the fiction to the postmodernist or late-modernist critics who initiated the development of a critical canon on O'Nolan's work in the 1980s and '90s. Since the plays themselves offered little to the critical debate about O'Nolan's role as an early postmodernist or fictional innovator, they attracted little initial attention. Furthermore, as Stefan Solomon has convincingly argued, the specific aesthetic logic that appears to have underpinned O'Nolan's dramatic work was inclined less towards what Martin Puchner terms the 'anti-theatrical revolution' in modernist theatre and more towards a 'characterological intensity' or 'inflated centrality of character' in the plays.[19] Solomon cites Mikhail Bakhtin's observation that drama is 'absolutely monologic' because, while it may feature 'a multitude of voices, represented in dramatic dialogue', it is nevertheless not dialogic 'because it only ever has access to one world'. By contrast, the 'novel's victory lies in its more centrifugal orchestration' of the 'cacophony of voices' of drama.[20]

With respect to O'Nolan's work, the implications of this argument are twofold. First, the focused polyphonic energy and transgressive ontological aesthetic that are so clearly deployed in *At Swim-Two-Birds* are rather more difficult to demonstrate on stage – even Pirandello, in *Six Characters*, does not cross as many ontological boundaries as O'Nolan's first novel. Furthermore, the 'inflated centrality of character' in O'Nolan's own plays is also rooted to the essential materiality of the theatricality of the actors. As I have argued elsewhere, with respect to Beckett's work, the concrete 'actuality of the stage' performance does not easily chime with the kinds of ontological disruption that one typically finds in modernist and postmodernist aesthetics.[21] O'Nolan's work for theatre clearly never sought to overcome this formal and aesthetic challenge.

Graham Greene made the connection between Pirandello's *Six Characters* and *At Swim-Two-Birds* as early as 1939 in his reader's report for the publisher Longmans Green: 'We have had books inside books before now, and characters who are given life outside their fiction, but O'Nolan takes Pirandello and Gide a long way further.'[22] It is not difficult to trace a genealogical narrative connection between *Six Characters* and *At Swim-Two-Birds*, or the 1934 O'Nolan story 'Scenes in a Novel'; both Pirandello's play and O'Nolan's fictions play with character-roles, authors and the metafictional demonstration of creative rebellion against the author (or producer) within the ontological level of the invented characters, while underpinned by the *mise en abyme* device. Neither Pirandello nor O'Nolan, of course, invented this narrative device, which has an extended literary history. Anthony Cronin names two primary antecedents to, or influences on, O'Nolan in this regard: Aldous Huxley's *Point Counter Point* (1928) and James Branch Cabell's *The Cream of the Jest* (1917).[23] While O'Nolan was certainly familiar with Branch Cabell,[24] Cronin specifically locates the point of comparison in the way that characters and fictional novelists transgress their ontological levels.[25] *The Cream of the Jest* features a fictional writer of historical romances named Felix Kennaston, who locates his plot in the fictitious country Poictesme, while the embedded narrative features a clerk named Horvendile who is in love with the heroine Ettare. But Felix too is a fictional creation, the principal character in a book by Richard Fentnor Harrowby, himself a character in a book by James Branch Cabell. Furthermore, Felix's romantic feelings for Ettare cross fictional levels in a manner similar to that found in *At Swim-Two-Birds*.

While the evidence connecting O'Nolan to Branch Cabell and Huxley is compelling, material evidence that O'Nolan actually read Pirandello is less specific and must depend to some degree on both the basis of historical probability and the presence of shared textual resonances. Daragh O'Connell argues that Pirandello was well-known to Dublin theatre audiences because The Dublin Drama League (to which the playwright Denis Johnston was connected) had produced several of Pirandello's plays during the 1920s.[26] Jernigan also points out that Denis Johnston had a great deal of success with a Pirandello-inspired metaplay, *The Old Lady Says 'No!'*,[27] and O'Nolan would certainly have been familiar with Johnston's work. Michael McLoughlin has noted that O'Nolan 'would almost certainly have been aware of the 1922 English translation of Pirandello's *Sei personaggi*, or *Six Characters*, which was used for the first Irish production of the play, at the Abbey Theatre in December 1934, a few months before' O'Nolan began *At Swim-Two-Birds*.[28] The 1922 translation was Edward Storer's, which was also used by Arthur Livingston for the first collection of Pirandello plays to appear in English.[29] McLoughlin claims that O'Nolan was interested in contemporary literature and could read Italian,[30] although there is little compelling evidence that, aside from German, he had significant language skills beyond English and Irish.

Keith Hopper has demonstrated some textual echoes between *Six Characters* and *The Third Policeman* (for example, the phrasing 'unless I'm a Dutchman' in *The Third Policeman* echoes 'or I'm a Dutchman' in *Six Characters*) and has suggested that the metanarrative similarity to Pirandello is substantial:

> The alignment between O'Brien's policeman and Pirandello's producer is quite deliberate: both characters imagine that they exert a certain control over the running of their (fictional) worlds – one polices, one produces – with the ontological irony that despite their illusions of grandeur, both are obviously just characters in a text.[31]

Hopper also makes a link between Pirandello and O'Nolan in the context of their shared metanarrative forms. Pointing to the unnamed narrator's self-conscious awareness of his textuality in *The Third Policeman*, Hopper suggests that this technique is directly inspired by 'the metatheatre of Pirandello and Bertolt Brecht, whereby the metaphors of the stage, acting and playwrighting (the ontological "real" that predetermines drama) become powerful metaphors in themselves'.[32] Hopper proceeds to suggest that O'Nolan and Pirandello (and Beckett) 'employ these metaphors to challenge the audience's perception of what is "real" and what is "fictional"'.[33]

This metanarrative technique is even more emphatic in *At Swim-Two-Birds* and *Six Characters*, particularly in the manner in which characters in both texts challenge or divert from the written script of the author, even to the degree to which sexual interaction between a female character and her fictional author is deployed as a transgressive ontological shift. In *Six*

Characters, the Stepdaughter reveals that she would try to tempt the author 'in his gloomy study' where she would spend time with him, 'on my own, all on my own, in the shadows',[34] hinting at the kind of sexual proclivity that has marked her past on the primary level of her own story. In *At Swim-Two-Birds*, Dermot Trellis, the fictional novelist created by the primary student narrator, rapes one of his fictional creations, Sheila Lamont, who gives birth to a son Orlick before Trellis subsequently kills her. In both cases, the characters stage, in different ways, acts of insurrection against the scripts and demands of their 'authors'. This rebellion is extended further in *At Swim-Two-Birds* when Orlick Trellis tries to 'write' his father to death, in his own story – a fourth fictional level. *Six Characters* and *At Swim-Two-Birds* continue to echo each other in numerous ways; for example, the deployment of Trellis's 'aestho-autogamy' theory, or the 'elimination of conception and pregnancy' (*CN*, 37)[35] as a notional construct in the origins of characters, provides a darkly comic rebuke to character formation. It also resembles Pirandello's theatrical 'characters' in *Six Characters*, which are 'timeless creations of the imagination, and so more real and consistent than the changeable realities of the Actors'.[36]

While both *Six Characters* and *At Swim-Two-Birds* embed multiple fictional levels into their narrative frames, the degree of O'Nolan's transgressions is perhaps more emphatic. The characters in Pirandello's play reflect the essential anxiety about their existence that critics most frequently associate with the epistemological uncertainty of high-modernist literature, while *At Swim-Two-Birds* instead exhibits a different response to the essential fictionality of the characters; O'Nolan's novel is more playful, more dismissive, ultimately, of the validity of characters. Or, as McLaughlin observes,

> Pirandello's six characters are forced to continue living and reliving their tragedy, the immortality assured by their connections to the fantasia immutable of their creator. O'Brien's characters cease to exist when the manuscript that gave them life is accidentally burned; they are, in the end, nothing but words.[37]

McLoughlin also rightly suggests that the characters' revolt in *At Swim-Two-Birds* is more emphatic and extreme than in *Six Characters*. This is also the case in the earlier 'Scenes in a Novel', in which the reaction of the characters to their 'author' is more incendiary than it is in *Six Characters*, leading – 'probably' – to the author's death at the hands of his characters.

This metatextual approach to handling the illusory agency of characters is intricately linked to the relative seriousness attached to the technical play in Pirandello and O'Nolan. There is always a note of frivolity in O'Nolan's observations about characters, as is apparent even in the *Cruiskeen Lawn* columns: 'The best characters have already been established by the masters, so why try to better them? New *activities* may, of course, be ascribed to them, but they must be activities in-character'.[38] Alternatively, as Pericles Lewis observes, the dominant theme of 'the illusory character of personal identity' that is so prevalent in Pirandello's stories subsequently formed the basis of some of his early plays, in particular with respect to the fascination with 'the element of self-dramatisation inherent in the roles people play in everyday life'.[39] In a sense then, there is gravity of purpose in Pirandello's deployment of metatheatrical devices, whereas O'Nolan's metafictional focus, at least in *At Swim-Two-Birds*, is devoid of any such intent.

Pirandello and O'Nolan's short fiction

The transference of theme from Pirandello's early stories to his plays is a pattern that is also evident in O'Nolan. As I and Hopper have claimed in our introduction to the *Short Fiction of Flann O'Brien*, the stories show the 'nascent stirrings of some of the artistic processes that O'Brien would later explore' in both *At Swim-Two-Birds* and *The Third Policeman* (*SF*, viii). The stories themselves exemplify the manner in which the broader innovative tradition asserts itself in the work of individual authors. O'Nolan's stories effectively take up ghostly presences in his subsequent novels, deepening the vellum of the new just as they were also marked with the presence of their own narrative inheritances. They reveal a fascination with textuality, textual play and the instability of authorial and narrative authority – all of which would become central aesthetic foundations in the longer fiction to come. It is also interesting to note that the overt metafictional strategies that one finds in the early Pirandello stories, and *Six Characters*, are largely absent from his later fiction even if, philosophically, the idea of a deeply unstable reality remains. While O'Nolan's evolution may not be quite so stark, much of the overt technical play that one finds in *At Swim-Two-Birds* certainly recedes in subsequent novels; even *The Third Policeman*, for all its wildly provocative content, is a comparatively stable narrative form, apart from the use of footnotes.

Six Characters evolved from a concept that can be traced back to the early 'Personaggi' (Characters) (1906), a short story treating the subject of an author who receives a visit from his own characters. This story was developed into

'*La Tragedia d'un Personaggio*', variously translated as 'A Character in Distress' (1938), 'A Character's Tragedy' (1994) and 'The Tragedy of a Character' (2014). There were even plans to develop these early stories into a novel titled *Sei Personaggi in Cerca d'Autore* (Six Characters in Search of an Author) which was never completed.[40] Many of Pirandello's short stories share thematic and technical interests with O'Nolan's short fiction: self-consciousness, the instability of personality, the uncertainty of meaning, the comic presentation of apparent opposites, the transformation of materiality into unlikely forms. 'A Character's Tragedy'[41] addresses almost identical concerns, and in similar metafictional terms, to 'Scenes in a Novel', which, in turn, anticipates certain aspects of *At Swim-Two-Birds*. While the earliest English translation of '*La Tragedia d'un Personaggio*' that I can locate is from 1938 and an English translation of '*Il Treno ha Fischiato*' does not appear to have been published in a major book until 1984, it is also the case that many of Pirandello's stories were translated in a series of books published in the 1930s, probably as a result of the success of *Six Characters*; earlier translations of stories also appeared in magazines, but records are scattered and fragmented. Therefore, strictly speaking, the genealogical patterns that these early stories share with O'Nolan need to be established primarily on shared narrative and aesthetics patterns.

In 'A Character's Tragedy', the narrator-author gives audience to 'the characters of future short stories' for three hours every Sunday morning, during which he takes into account their 'feelings and aspirations'. However, his characters apparently nonetheless 'go around spreading the word everywhere that [he is] extremely cruel and merciless'.[42] The characters are resistant to his plans for them and dispute his judgements, just as Carruthers McDaid and Shaun Svoolish do in 'Scenes in a Novel'. Like their counterparts in 'A Character's Tragedy', they too seek to extend the limits of the plot and the general character traits they have been assigned. In both stories, the rejection of their assigned love interests by the characters are related in similar terms. In 'Scenes in a Novel', Shaun prefers Bridie over his designated lover, Shiela (a near relative of the character Sheila Lamont in *At Swim-Two-Birds*), while Pirandello's Fileno prefers his choice, Negroni, over his assigned lover, Graziela – arguing that such an imposition is one of many crimes than can be atoned for only with blood.[43] Indeed, in 'Scenes in a Novel' O'Nolan's narrator-author Brother Barnabas ultimately pays in blood as it is strongly implied that the characters will murder him, prefiguring the fate of the attempt on Trellis's life in *At Swim-Two-Birds*.

The textual correspondence between 'A Character's Tragedy' and *At Swim-Two-Birds* also extends to that novel's aestho-autogamy theory. As earlier discussed, there are some correspondences with *Six Characters* in O'Brien's theory, but the concept is also present in 'A Character's Tragedy', in Dr Fileno's commentary on the origins of 'characters':

> There are so many ways of coming to life, sir; and you know very well that nature makes use of the human imagination as a tool for pursuing its work of creation. And anyone who is born thanks to this creative activity which has its seat in the human spirit is ordained by nature for a life that is higher than the life of those born from the mortal womb of a woman.[44]

The narrator of *At Swim-Two-Birds* offers an almost identical observation regarding the alternative birthing process of characters: 'The elimination of conception and pregnancy, however, or the reduction of the processes to the same mysterious abstraction as that of the paternal factor in the commonplace case of unexplained maternity, has been the dream of every practising psycho-eugenist the world over' (*CN*, 37).

Unlike Trellis, *et al.*, Dr Fileno is actually a character from another writer's book and is himself the author of a philosophical work entitled *The Philosophy of Distance*. In this, Dr Fileno mirrors *The Third Policeman*'s de Selby. Part of Fileno's intellectual process involves placing himself conceptually 'in the future in order to look back at the present, which he viewed as the past'.[45] In an attempt to console himself at the death of his daughter, he invented a telescope and

> convinced his mind that it should be contented to look through the larger lens, which was pointed to the future, toward the smaller one, which was pointed at the present. And so his mind looked through the 'wrong' end of the telescope, and immediately the present became small and very distant.[46]

There are echoes of de Selby's conception of the journey as hallucination here (*CN*, 263), while MacCruiskeen's magnifying glass that 'magnifies to invisibility' (*CN*, 344) also loosely resembles Fileno's theory, although the competing influence of J.W. Dunne's *An Experiment with Time* (1927), as noted by Hopper, is clearly a factor in the formulation of de Selby's philosophy.[47] In addition, the minor debate about the publishing costs of Fileno's *The Philosophy of Distance* echoes the narrator's desire to publish the costly complete edition of de Selby's work in *The Third Policeman*.

The presence of atomic-theory-inspired shape-shifting in *The Third Policemen* also bears the fingerprints of the Flann O'Brien story 'John Duffy's Brother'. Shape-shifting had, of course, long been a prominent feature of gothic literature and various mythical cycles in Europe, as with Ovid's *Metamorphoses*, and would later become a prominent feature of postmodern fiction. But as Flavia Iovine has shown, 'John Duffy's Brother' bears striking similarity to many facets of Pirandello's 1914 story '*Il Treno ha Fischiato*', translated as 'The Train Whistled'.[48] Both stories feature central figures who experience moments of transformation or transfiguration. In O'Brien's story, the character of John Duffy's brother abruptly becomes 'possessed of the strange idea that he was a train [...] long, thunderous, and immense, with white steam escaping noisily from his feet and deep-throated bellows coming rhythmically from where his funnel was' (*SF*, 56). While Pirandello's Belluca experiences a less physically material transformation, he too undergoes a momentous transfiguration of self when one evening, 'in the profound silence of the night, he heard a train whistling in the distance', that 'ripped open and carried away the misery of all [the] horrible sufferings' in his life.[49] Belluca's transfiguration subsequently involves 'roving breathlessly in the airy void of the world' on a train that 'was traveling towards [...] Florence, Bologna, Turin, Venice ...'.[50] The manner in which the story blends the motif of journey with the inner transformation felt by Belluca most closely corresponds with the imaginative life of O'Nolan's story. For example, 'now that his [Belluca's] imagination had suddenly been awakened, he could follow that moment, yes, to follow it to known and unknown cities, moors, mountains, forests, seas [...]. That same shiver, this same palpitation of time'.[51] The inner life is entangled with the motif of the train, just as it is in 'John Duffy's Brother', which concludes with a moment of resonant longing for a state that he has experienced and yet now lost: 'But to this day John Duffy's brother starts at the rumble of a train in the Liffey tunnel and stands rooted to the road when he comes suddenly on a level-crossing – silent, so to speak, upon a peak in Darien' (*SF*, 58). Both stories extensively use the motif of the train, but their true significance is more closely related to the inner lives of their central characters. While Pirandello's story is more fully developed, with a plot that more comprehensively engages with Belluca's family situation and other complex reasons for his transformation, both stories are framed against the threat of incarceration for exhibiting symptoms of mental illness, both characters are civil servants, and both mimic (although in 'John Duffy's Brother' they are actual) the sounds of trains and experience moments of intense discomfort when their 'secret' is exposed to their work colleagues.

Many of Pirandello's stories offer less direct but significant connections to the broad innovative literary tradition that frames this essay. For example, in '*Non è una Cosa Seria*' (It's Not to be Taken Seriously[52]) (1910) the character Perazzetti continually reveals an awareness of the insubstantiality of reality and the pointlessness of serious intellectual engagement: 'Strictly speaking, nothing was serious to Perazzetti. Everything depends on the importance you attach to things. If you attach importance to the most ridiculous thing, it can become deadly serious, and vice-versa, the most serious matter can become ridiculous.'[53] Similarly, several stories indicate deep reservations about the nature of reality and the possibility of truth, like '*La Signora Frola e il Signor Ponza, suo Genero*' (Mrs Frola and Mr Ponza, Her Son-in-Law) (1917),[54] which Stanley Applebaum refers to as the 'key Pirandello story about the relativity of truth'.[55] For example, the narrator at one point assures us, in terms that would not be out of place in any number of O'Nolan texts, that 'there arises in each mind the pernicious suspicion that, in any case, reality counts for no more than illusion does, and that every reality may very well be an illusion, and vice versa'.[56] Such observations are commonplace in Pirandello's stories, just as they are in O'Nolan's fiction. They are both clearly conscious of shared philosophical and aesthetic contexts, and both contribute significantly to what might be viewed as an alternative history of the European novel.

Anxiety, play and the unchartable self

For the author who wrote, via the nameless narrator of *At Swim-Two-Birds*, that the modern novel 'should be largely a work of reference' (*CN*, 21), the close textual resonances and morphological features between O'Nolan's work and others is unsurprising. That there are striking resemblances between O'Nolan and Pirandello within this extended innovative tradition – either extended family likenesses or more direct linkages – is evident, but it is also clear that they are quite distinct from each other. Pirandello more fully reflects a poetics characterised by his modernist inheritance, while O'Nolan repeatedly offers evidence that he had moved beyond the tortured self-consciousness and epistemological anxiety that is all too evident in plays like *Six Characters* and much of his Italian counterpart's fiction. This movement corresponds with McHale's characterisation of the shift from modernism to postmodernism, from a poetics dominated by epistemological concerns to one dominated by ontological concerns.[57] This shift partly explains the difference between Pirandello and O'Nolan. The correspondences between the writers are clear, but their respective responses to the nature of fiction, performance, representation, characterisation and self-consciousness significantly vary in both philosophical grounding and degrees of rebellious intensity.

In Pirandello's essay (1908; revised 1920) *L'umorismo* (On Humour), the writer's assertions about life offer clear indications of an anxiety-driven perspective:

> Life is a continuous flux which we continually try to stop, to fix in established and determined forms outside and inside ourselves because we are already fixed forms, forms that move among other immovable ones [...]. The forms in which we try to stop and fix this continuous flux are the concepts, the ideals to which we would like to conform, all the fictions we create for ourselves [...]. But within us, in what we call our soul, which is the life in us, the flux goes on, unnoticed, under the river-banks, beyond the boundaries we establish in composing a consciousness, constructing a personality for ourselves.[58]

While the essential point, that we compose self-shaping fictions of ourselves, vividly resonates with the dazzling zeal for creative construction and reconstruction that one encounters in both O'Nolan's and Pirandello's work, the latter's apparent conviction that we are more profoundly shaped by a deeper sense of the unchartable self is not at all evident in novels like *At Swim-Two-Birds* and *The Third Policeman*. In fact, rarely does one encounter such an anxiety-rich moment in Flann O'Brien. The obvious sincerity with which Pirandello uses the word 'soul' contrasts greatly with the mischievous manner that the narrator engages with the word and concept in *The Third Policeman*, when he ponders whether his own 'soul', Joe, might have a body:

> What if he *had* a body? A body with another body inside it in turn, thousands of such bodies within each other like the skins of an onion, receding to some unimaginable ultimum? [...] Who or what was the core and what monster in that world was the final uncontained colossus? God? Nothing? (*CN*, 327–8)

Here, he generates a *mise-en-abyme*-like convolution of bodily shifts, concluding in a possible negation of God that erases the ultimate grounding of the soul, rather than, like Pirandello, asserting its presence.

Despite the two authors' close narrative genealogical inheritance, their work significantly diverges in their declared allegiance to a view of the self as ultimately viable or true. O'Nolan's work occasionally reveals trace reminders of solemn self-awareness, as when the narrator of *The Third Policeman* experiences an instance of significant disquietude in which he is 'deprived of definition, position and magnitude and [his] significance was considerably diminished. Lying there, [he] felt the weariness ebbing from [him] slowly, like a tide retiring over limitless sands' but this swiftly turns to a 'feeling [that] was so pleasurable and profound that [he] sighed again a long sound of happiness' (*CN*, 327). Even when the ghosts of sincere self-reflection emerge, they are never permitted to gain traction. A persistent renegotiation of epistemological anxiety into erasure, evasion and what Fredric Jameson terms 'blank parody'[59] characterises O'Nolan's work in a way that does not quite gel with that of Pirandello. Nevertheless, their shared literary-aesthetic inheritance crucially reveals that the innovative or anti-realist tradition continually re-emerges in different contexts, generating unique responses to specific historical and literary-historical *milieux*. A persistent literary fascination throughout European history is the combination of technical innovation with an acute sense of how the imagining mind generates multiplicities rather than singularities – but this fascination does not result in a monologic approach to literary craft. Just as realism can be deployed to different ends, so too with anti-realism.

The differences between O'Nolan and Pirandello, far from undermining the validity of the anti-realist novel, in fact emphasise the diversity of focus that characterises this form of writing. Whether Rabelais or Sterne or Pirandello or O'Nolan, the tradition of intellectual scepticism, of playful reaction to the intense impositions of fixed knowledge systems, repeatedly emerges throughout the history of the novel, its forms of mischief resonating in ever-increasing cycles that echo each other, even as they appear in different guises and declare oppositional perspectives.

7

Self-Evident Shams and Accidents of Illusion

The Brechtian roots of *At Swim-Two-Birds*

KERRY HIGGINS WENDT

In *At Swim-Two-Birds*, the unnamed narrator offers his friend Brinsley 'an explanation spontaneous and unsolicited concerning [his] own work, affording an insight as to its aesthetic, its daemon, its argument, its sorrow and its joy, its darkness, its sun-twinkle clearness' (*CN*, 21). In other words, he tells Brinsley how the novel he is writing operates. Rather than presenting Brian O'Nolan's ideas about literature, or being 'instructions for [*At Swim-Two-Birds*'s] own reading', this explanation provides the rules governing the fictional world the narrator is building, a plan for the narrator's novel.[1] It draws from many sources to provide the theoretical basis for the structure of the narrator's novel, including James Joyce and T.S. Eliot, but for the manifesto's most crucial aspects, the means by which and ends for which it breaks diegetic boundaries, it draws from Bertolt Brecht's thought about alienation and illusion, social justice and consciousness, historical particularism and universalism, and narratological metalepsis. O'Nolan uniquely repurposes these scavenged ideas to build a satirical chassis for the carnival that is *At Swim-Two-Birds*. In the process, he takes aim at the three major genres – poetry, fiction and drama – and the categories of lyric, epic and dramatic, as they are elucidated by Stephen Dedalus in Joyce's *A Portrait of the Artist as a Young Man*. At the same time, he influences the magic realists who write in his wake.[2]

The 'spontaneous explanation' begins with the idea of the novel as 'a self-evident sham'. Not accidentally, he invokes the play in this explanation:

> It was stated that while the novel and the play were both pleasing
> intellectual exercises, the novel was inferior to the play inasmuch as it
> lacked the outward accidents of illusion, frequently inducing the reader
> to be outwitted in a shabby fashion and caused to experience a real
> concern for the fortunes of illusory characters. The play was consumed
> in wholesome fashion by large masses in places of public resort; the
> novel was self-administered in private. The novel, in the hands of an
> unscrupulous writer, could be despotic. In reply to an inquiry, it was
> explained that a satisfactory novel should be a self-evident sham to which
> the reader could regulate at will the degree of his credulity. (*CN*, 21)

Here, the narrator plays with the Dedalian ideas that 'the esthetic emotion'
is 'static' and that 'the feelings excited by improper art are kinetic, desire or
loathing' – that in 'proper' literature, one should not experience concern for the
characters, but rather 'static' emotions such as pity or terror.[3] The explanation
also draws quite literally on the lyric, epic and dramatic distinction.[4] For
Stephen Dedalus, lyric, epic and dramatic refer to the scope of an artist's work
– whether it speaks to and represents merely himself or others as well – with
the dramatic as the most exalted form and the lyric the least. But with a little
leeway, lyric, epic and dramatic also encapsulate the distinctions O'Nolan maps
out between the novel and the theatre – art one engages with alone and art one
consumes with others.[5] O'Nolan's narrator takes a cue from Joyce in writing
autobiographically, or lyrically, especially in his biographical reminiscences,
but he takes another cue from Stephen Dedalus in attempting the highest, or
(meta)dramatic, form of literature in the same book.

While Dedalus's ideas play an important role in the narrator's explanation,
for the theoretical material that provides *At Swim-Two-Bird*'s architectonics,
the narrator depends on Bertolt Brecht. Brecht's *Verfremdungseffekt*, now
most commonly known in English as the alienation effect or A-effect,
first appeared in print in the journal *Life and Letters To-Day* in winter 1936
– when O'Nolan was writing *At Swim-Two-Birds*. The English-speaking
world now knows Brecht's essay as 'Alienation Effects in Chinese Acting',
but it was originally published in a translation by Eric Walter White as 'The
Fourth Wall of China: An essay on the effect of disillusion in the Chinese
theatre'.[6] John Willett notes that this was the first time Brecht used the term
Verfremdungseffekt, presumably in the typescript now in the Brecht Archive,
as the essay did not appear in German until 1949.[7] In prior essays, Brecht
used the term *Entfremdung*, a more common German word with a somewhat
different, less theatrical connotation.[8]

O'Nolan's choice of the phrase 'the outward accidents of illusion' is itself no accident, for in White's 1936 translation, *Verfremdungseffekt* is translated as 'disillusion', and the translation uses the terms *illusion* and *disillusion* repeatedly – several times per paragraph in some places. While these terms have since been supplanted, in 1936 *disillusion* would have suggested a direct reference to Brecht's *Verfremdungseffekt*. Willett records that, at the time, *Verfremdungseffekt* was 'virtually a neologism, for Grimm's dictionary gives only two obscure early examples for the use of *verfremden* as a transitive verb'.[9] This and the newness of the concept may help explain White's odd early translation.

O'Nolan probably saw the essay. *Life and Letters To-Day* was established in 1928 by Desmond MacCarthy, the literary editor of *The New Statesman*, who had connections with the Bloomsbury Group.[10] The winter 1936 issue included pieces by Sergei Eisenstein, Muriel Rukeyser, Rainer Maria Rilke, William Maxwell, William Empson and Gertrude Stein, among others. It was a well-known and established literary magazine, and O'Nolan was part of a group of students that, as Niall Sheridan writes,

> formed in those years a sort of intellectual Mafia, which strongly influenced the cultural and social life of University College and controlled – through some rather dubious electoral ruses – most of the College Clubs and Societies concerned with the Arts. The editorship of [*Comhthrom Féinne*] was usually passed from one member of the group to another. It was a useful mouthpiece and entitled us to tickets for the theatres and cinemas, and also review copies of books, which could be resold for half the published price.[11]

As a member of this group, O'Nolan probably not only read the Brecht piece but also discussed it with his cohort. 'Like the rest of us,' as Niall Sheridan informs us, 'Brian read everything he could get his hands on.'[12]

Alienation, politics, history

Brecht's essay held that the stagecraft of more conventional Aristotelian drama creates an illusion that allows the audience to embed itself emotionally in a story, sympathise with the characters in terms of so-called universal values and fail to see these stories as partially determined by historical and social forces. This sympathising, Brecht argued, causes a larger kind of sociopolitical blindness. As Peter Brooker writes, 'Brecht sought to use the resources of art, in ways consistent with the tenets of dialectical materialism, to historicise and negate the commonplace and taken-for-granted, to prise open social and ideological contradictions, and so both demonstrate and provoke an awareness of the individual's place in a concrete social narrative'.[13] He wanted to use the A-effect and his other 'artistic devices [...] as means to' shake up the audience members – to break up the conventions that allow them to ingest theatre emotionally but not intellectually, and to engage their critical faculties so that they could notice and engage with a play's historical particulars.[14] Furthermore, he used these devices in a coherent, 'expressly political' theoretical and practical approach.[15]

In conventional Aristotelian drama, audiences ('large masses in places of public resort', in the words of O'Nolan's narrator) are subject to a kind of groupthink that governs the social rules of theatre attendance and dictates a willing suspension of disbelief and, therefore, a lack of critical distance. Consequently, the social blindness Brecht wants to subvert is reinforced. For Brecht, conventional western theatre lacks the 'outward accidents of illusion', or alienating devices, and the audience perceives the theatre's illusions so seamlessly as to be lulled, in Brecht's words, into 'assimilating a work of art as a whole' and 'simply identifying itself with the characters in the play'.[16] However, O'Nolan's novel effectively says that the opposite happens – that being among people in the theatre keeps one grounded in reality and being alone with a novel leads one to give in to flights of fancy – or worse, to 'self-administration in private'. For the narrator of *At Swim-Two-Birds*, a play has these alienating mechanisms conventionally, as their 'outward accidents of illusion' and the co-presence of other spectators in the auditorium already in themselves keep the audience members grounded in the reality that they are watching fiction and protect them from being swept away by pathos and caught up in the characters' emotions and fate – from being 'outwitted in a shabby fashion and caused to experience a real concern for the fortunes of illusory characters'. The narrator thus inverts Brecht's theory, as his aesthetic manifesto condemns the novel on the same grounds that Brecht condemns conventional western Aristotelian theatre and celebrates the elements of conventional drama as already employing the modes of disillusion that Brecht calls for in his 'new theatre'.

Brecht and O'Nolan's reasons for outlining how an audience works differ: the narrator of *At Swim-Two-Birds* is supposedly concerned with propriety, wholesomeness and despotism, while Brecht is concerned with sociopolitical awareness and subverting the propriety that prevents cultural and political resistance. O'Nolan's concerns are something else again. His extreme metafiction takes Brecht's ideas of alienation and illusion out of their theatrical and sociopolitical contexts to call attention to the novel's construction, to play with the rules of fictional structure, and thus to revolutionise the well-made illusionary novel by introducing the A-effect as an anti-illusionary and self-reflective device. Yet, the satirical dimensions of his metafictional project suggest that O'Nolan, too, intends to subvert propriety, what passes for 'wholesomeness' and despotism. In shifting the target of Brecht's thought to sexual mores and a more privately enacted despotism, and in adapting it for use in the novel, O'Nolan reworks the coordinates of what causes one to be 'arrested' or 'alienated' – that is, removed from one's immersion in the artwork into contemplation of its more formal aesthetic or sociopolitical dimensions. He does this via the phrase 'self-administration in private', which, in its sophomoric humour, evokes the adolescent sexuality of Lynch in Joyce's *A Portrait of the Artist as a Young Man*, writing his name on the buttocks of the Venus of Praxiteles, and Stephen Dedalus's ideas about desire and loathing as improper immersions in art. In O'Nolan's process of reworking these coordinates, Brecht's ideas about the despotism of conventional theatre and social justice become themselves estranged.

Effectively, both Brecht and O'Nolan argue for a mechanism or an alienating device to highlight a work's constructedness in order to encourage the audience's critical faculty. We see commentary on such alienating devices in the 'penultimate' ending of *At Swim-Two-Birds*, when Trellis, watching Teresa climb the stairs, notices that

> The edge of her stays, lifting her skirt in a little ridge behind her, dipped softly from side to side with the rise and the fall of her haunches as she trod the stairs. It is the function of such garments to improve the figure, to conserve corporal discursiveness, to create the illusion of a finely modulated body. If it betray its own presence when fulfilling this task, its purpose must largely fail.
>
> Ars est celare artem, muttered Trellis, doubtful as to whether he had made a pun. (*CN*, 215)

In O'Nolan's novel, implicitly compared to the 'outward accidents of illusion' of Theresa's costume, the author likewise betrays his own presence when fulfilling the task of writing his work; here, by diegetically pointing out the pun and more generally by making the metafictional devices the novel's self-reflective *raison d'être*.

Brecht wanted to adapt the *Verfremdungseffekt* he observed in Chinese theatre for use in western theatre as a tool for political critique. 'A new theatre,' he wrote, 'will need to employ disillusion among other effects if it is going to criticise society and present a historical report of social changes when these have been successfully consummated.'[17] Brecht spoke of the Marxist notion that revolution will result in a stable, equitable polity with no further need for criticism or reform, but only a need to 'present a historical report' of what changed. 'In this time of transition', Brecht declared, 'everything must be considered from the social point of view', especially, to Brecht's mind, literary characters.[18] O'Nolan took this phrase quite literally, making it a bit of theoretical scaffolding by which he could turn characters into actors – in this case, supposedly real people with actual lives in a sociopolitical sphere – paid to stand in as characters. Immediately after saying that we should not believe in characters or be deceived into feeling sympathy for them, the narrator treats characters as if they are not only real but entitled to wages and fair working conditions:

> It was undemocratic to compel characters to be uniformly good or bad or poor or rich. Each should be allowed a private life, self-determination and a decent standard of living. This would make for self-respect, contentment and better service. It would be incorrect to say that it would lead to chaos. Characters should be interchangeable as between one book and another. The entire corpus of existing literature should be regarded as a limbo from which discerning authors could draw their characters as required, creating only when they failed to find a suitable existing puppet. (*CN*, 21)

This idea of characters as actors and even as employees or labourers crosses diegetic boundaries and embodies the experience of readers sympathising with a work's characters, when literary creations indeed begin to cross over into the human realm. We should note, too, that the narrator speaks of a distinctly Marxist variety of sympathy for lower socioeconomic social strata, having to do with issues related to employment and labour rights.

Here, we must distinguish between a character strictly as written and what we might call the implied character – the imagined person the character represents. In a play, actors present an additional layer, which we might call the interpreted character. Kenneth Branagh's Hamlet differs from Daniel Day Lewis's, and these Hamlets are in turn distinct from the Hamlet in the script, the Hamlet in Shakespeare's mind, and the composite Hamlet of the audience's imagination. Especially with the proliferation of performances inherent to drama, characters can proliferate almost infinitely. O'Nolan wrings as much confusion and fun as possible from these structural and semiotic differences between plays and novels. In a novel, the lack of actors facilitates the collapse of the distinction between characters as written, entirely bound by the words on the page, and characters as fleshed out to include everything we can imagine of them – their past, future, motives, psychology, what they do in the interstices of the plot – in short, anything that is not specifically written. In Trellis's and the narrator's novels, O'Nolan turns the fleshed-out version of novelistic characters into actors who, when the curtains close and the lights go down, take off their makeup, collect their pay and head home to their families. So Furriskey, for example, is not the same person when Trellis stops writing: he goes home to Peggy and leaves his dirty work behind him.

This is not what Brecht means by treating characters as social beings, of course. 'The presentation of the human being on stage stops at the "eternal human element",' Brecht complained.

> All that happens on the stage is merely a cue for the 'eternal' answer – the inevitable, customary, natural, human answer. [...] The plot is so arranged as to contain such 'universal' situations that any man of any period or colour can express himself therein. [...] History may affect environment, but it is powerless to alter the individual.[19]

All particulars fade away in the western theatre as Brecht saw it, enabling the audience to become enmeshed with a story so generalised by the actors and the stage presentation that the characters can easily absorb the audience's projections of their own lives and concerns into a vague and generalised version of themselves.

In contrast, 'in the "historicised" theatre [...] the emphasis is laid on the strange and peculiar elements, those that demand investigation'.[20] Brecht gives the following example:

> A young girl leaves her family to take a job in a large town. [...] In the bourgeois theatre, such a situation has few possibilities: it is obviously the beginning of a story and [...] is quite general: young girls often take jobs, and in this case the audience may feel interested to know whether anything special is going to happen to her. [...] In the 'historicised' theatre [...] the emphasis is laid on the strange and peculiar elements, those that demand investigation into this every-day occurrence. What! a family is prepared to let one of its members leave its shelter so that she may become independent and earn her living on her own? Is she in

a fit state to do so? Will what she has learnt as a member of the family help her to earn her living? Can families no longer keep their children at home? Are they a burden? Was it always so[?] Is it the unalterable way of the world? Does the saying 'Ripe fruit falls from the tree' apply here? If it is a biological fact, true for all ages, that a time must come when all children claim their independence, does it always happen in the same way, for the same reasons and with the same results? Those are some of the questions which the actors must answer if they are going to present this as a unique historical occurrence and if they wish to point to it as a custom which provides a key to the whole social structure of a certain transitory period.[21]

For Brecht, even universal human elements occur in historical, material and social contexts that not only colour them but change and determine them as well. Brecht wanted audiences to notice these contexts and thus become critics and social actors themselves. Brecht wanted plays to be more historically particular and characters to be clearly subject to social forces rather than only subject to supposedly universal human emotions historically contextualised. O'Nolan used the same concepts and devices to decontextualise characters such as Sweeny and Finn Mac Cool, to strip them of particularities and to mash up genres. In the larger context of *At Swim-Two-Birds*, the fact that the 'implied characters' have working wages and outside lives draws our attention not only to the Brechtian origins of the narrator's theory but also to O'Nolan's play with ontological levels, textual boundaries and narrative metalepsis – O'Nolan's own alienating devices. But the fact that O'Nolan mashes genres suggests that he is bringing the reader's awareness not only to the novel's structure, but also to particular discourses, as opposed to Brecht's historical particulars.

The fourth wall

The fourth wall in White's translation of Brecht's title is a uniquely theatrical version of such an ontological boundary. It separates the audience from the actors and the stage and is imagined as a more-or-less physical presence located in the proscenium frame. Its analogue in the novel is the diegetic boundary between the implied reader and the narrative voice – what Gérard Genette describes as 'a boundary that is precisely the narrating [diegesis] (or the performance [mimesis]) itself: a shifting but sacred frontier between two worlds, the world in which one tells, the world of which one tells'.[22] Breaking the fourth wall began as an alienating action that shocks the audience into an awareness of their role with respect to the people on stage. Rather than simply watching the play passively and procedurally, the audience is startled into a more intellectually engaged state, which in Brechtian thought would make them more capable of sociopolitical critique. The fictional analogue of breaking the fourth wall is metalepsis. When this fictional boundary is crossed, it often looks like the evocation of the reader's experience or a representation of the reader tumbling into the book or page itself.

Alternately, we can conceive of this boundary as connecting the implied reader and the implied author through the narrative. We can see the presentation of the novel as 'a self-evident sham' and the injunction that readers 'regulate' their 'credulity' as warnings to readers that they might be outwitted in a more conventional way through irony. Wayne Booth writes that 'authors and readers achieve [irony] together'; to do so, they must reach across the invisible boundaries of the textual world and connect with each other.[23] In *At Swim-Two-Birds*, we observe the subtle irony of following the conventional mechanism of putting 'Chapter One' at the top of the novel's first page – despite the complete lack of other chapters. These rhetorical and paratextual boundary transgressions may be the more radical ones at play in *At Swim-Two-Birds*. They are, in some ways, less flashy than the metaleptic absurdity of Orlick Trellis turning the tables on Dermot Trellis, or Sweeny and Jem Casey suddenly showing up after being spoken about. Such literary fireworks have the curious effect of flattening the work and making us see it as something the author is playing with, as opposed to a world unto itself. For Genette, 'All these games, by the intensity of their effects, demonstrate the importance of the boundary they tax their ingenuity to overstep, in defiance of verisimilitude'. Such literary play bears an alienating or estranging effect. These ironic paratextual and metaleptic transgressions become the 'outward accidents of illusion' that prevent readers from 'being outwitted in a shabby fashion' – they pull readers out of identification and remind them that they are reading a novel. Genette quotes Jorge Luis Borges here to describe how this works in fiction: 'Such inversions suggest that if the characters in a story can be readers or spectators, then we, their readers or spectators, can be fictitious.'[24] In other words, they level the diegetic with reality and make readers aware of their relationship with the text.

The effect of crossing the boundary between the audience and the work – whether that boundary is the fourth wall or the page – varies greatly. For Brecht, what happens is the playwright wakes up the audience and shocks them into the knowledge that they are watching a play. For O'Nolan, what happens is a conflation of diegetic levels that depends on the logical error of mistaking actors for characters. O'Nolan removes not only his fictional version of the fourth wall – or perhaps, more accurately, the stage door – but also the diegetic boundaries that exist *within* the narrator's novel between writer and written, between Trellis and his characters. He does not, however, remove the boundary between the narrator and *his* novel about Trellis. When events cross between the narrator's life and his book, they only cross one way – from the narrator's life to his work. Thus, we have a metafiction *within* a realist novel (although realist in a very slender sense of the term).

Modernist intertextuality and interchangeability

The conceit of characters as actors who are interchangeable between plays finds its expression in the narrator's idea that literary characters should be interchangeable between books, regardless of genre. The narrator explains that one of the foundational ideas of his novel is that

> Most authors spend their time saying what has been said before – usually said much better. A wealth of references to existing works would acquaint the reader instantaneously with the nature of each character, would obviate tiresome explanations and would effectively preclude mountebanks, upstarts, thimbleriggers and persons of inferior education from an understanding of contemporary literature. (*CN*, 21–2)

The concept of the modern novel as work of reference takes a particularly mythic turn in O'Nolan's hands. O'Nolan's metafictional structure of alienating devices, combined with the idea of the modern novel as a work of reference, allows him to include Jem Casey, the working-class poet, as well as his own versions of Finn Mac Cool and Sweeny – decontextualised to the eternal/mythical element of which Brecht spoke.[25] Such use of myth and reference points us towards T.S. Eliot as another modernist author from whose work O'Nolan drew.[26] *The Waste Land* is itself a work of reference, in that it was composed of fragments from myths, religion, Jacobean drama, popular culture (compare 'Hurry up please it's time' with 'A pint of plain is your only man') and other sources in addition to original material binding those pieces together.

It is tempting to see in the narrator's idea a reference to modernists using mythical works in general, but O'Nolan's flavour is more Eliotic, as Maebh Long notes.[27] Unlike Joyce, whose Bloom stands in for Odysseus, in *The*

Waste Land Eliot lifts excerpts out of other texts wholesale, much as the narrator of *At Swim-Two-Birds* recommends lifting characters out of other texts wholesale.[28] In *At Swim-Two-Birds*, Finn is still Finn and Sweeny is still Sweeny – there are no modern analogues. But O'Nolan goes one step further than Eliot and integrates the borrowed characters into their new shared context, allowing them to interact with each other. As Long suggests, Eliot's work is more about the fragmentation, and O'Nolan's more about the assembling.

The conjunction of the 'work of reference' idea and the idea of fictional-characters-as-actors also gives rise to the Circle N Ranch episode, which enables O'Nolan to import some classic western action into the middle of Dublin, rope in some concern with labour issues and combine them with the *Táin Bó Cúailnge* (*Cattle Raid of Cooley*). Interchangeability between works of literature lays further groundwork for characters to wander from one story to another within the narrator's work, so that Sweeny can move from a character in Finn's storytelling to a character interacting with Finn, and Jem Casey can move from being talked about to suddenly appearing. Such metalepsis enables, also, the bricolage of stories and kinds of stories – of myth, press release, biographical reminiscence, excerpt and modern fiction – that characterises *At Swim-Two-Birds* as a whole.

With the exception of the frame tale, literary creation in *At Swim-Two-Birds* is largely a demonstration of the narrator's theories in action. Characters are drawn from other works, in line with the narrator's theory of the modern novel as a work of reference, and aestho-autogamy depends on the metalepsis enabled by the destruction of the boundary between Trellis and his characters and on the collapsed distinction between actor and character. Indeed, the entire plot of the narrator's work depends on such porous and broken boundaries. In twisting and recasting Brecht's theory, O'Nolan breaks it down into its component parts and demonstrates how adaptable and infinitely reconfigurable those parts are – a literary mode which the magic realists writing in O'Nolan's wake would notice and take up, especially as regards myth, cross-cultural references and functioning according to other logics.

For Dermot Trellis, writing is one part theatrical direction and one part character creation, which he achieves via two primary methods: intertextual borrowing and 'aestho-autogamy', the process through which he creates John Furriskey. In turn, there are two levels to the creation by aestho-autogamy. The first, a literal enactment, looks like this: 'Propped by pillows in his bed [...] Dermot Trellis adjusted the pimples in his forehead into a frown of deep creative import. His pencil moved slowly across the ruled paper. [...] He was engaged in the creation of John Furriskey.' In other words, Trellis sits in bed, thinks hard and writes to create his character. The suggestion is that he writes the birth notice that follows, announcing the 'birth' of Furriskey, who is 'about five feet eight inches in height, well built, dark, and clean-shaven' (*CN*, 36). About half a page of ludicrously precise description follows, demonstrating that unlike people, characters come ready-furnished with a past full of relevant details.

The second level is aestho-autogamy. Autogamy, in reference to flowers, is self-fertilisation, so aestho-autogamy is literally artistic self-fertilisation, although the birth notice Trellis writes claims aestho-autogamy is 'an operation involving neither fertilisation nor conception' (*CN*, 37). The joke, at any rate, is clear: aestho-autogamy is creation of a character through self-reflexive writing, or mental masturbation. Furriskey's creation becomes a *tour de force* in sophomoric humour, with Trellis's 'zeal and perseverance' and 'international repute in connection with his researches' essentially making him a world-renowned wanker (*CN*, 37). 'An operation involving neither fertilisation nor conception' is also a pretty good match for the Incarnation. The 'mysterious abstraction [...] of the paternal factor in the commonplace case of unexplained maternity' becomes not just a joke about illegitimacy but a reference to religious mysteries. In this way, the author is godlike, both in creating beings through quasi-sexual means and in controlling their actions. In the latter, he is both directorial and dictatorial.

If *At Swim-Two-Birds* is a demonstration of the narrator's theories in action, it is also a demonstration and lampoon of the state of modern literature at the time across the three major genres (poetry, fiction and drama) and the Dedalian subsets of lyric, epic and dramatic (in the persons of Joyce, Eliot and Brecht). Each of these he bent, twisted and adapted for use in the chassis of the narrator's novel or, in Joyce's case, for use in his own frame tale. In terms of the structural rules according to which the novel plays its game, however, Brecht's ideas resonate the most strongly. In the process of reducing Brecht's 'The Fourth Wall of China' to several 'wrong premises', O'Nolan flattened the *Verfremdungseffekt* into scaffolding for metafiction, produced some trademark O'Nolan logic and set it in motion to produce not only a wonderful comedy of fictional structure, but also a critical reflection on discourse itself and several discourses in particular.[29] By twisting Brecht's ideas and letting them act out to their logical extreme, O'Nolan created a particular kind of metafiction engaged with myth and social issues that can bring material from multiple cultures to bear on the story and that tends to operate according to its own logic, laying the groundwork for magic realist authors who wrote in his wake.

When Jorge Luis Borges reviewed *At Swim-Two-Birds*, he situated it in a tradition of 'interpolation of a fiction within another fiction', ranging from the simple 'parentheses' of the inclusion of a shorter work in a longer work in which 'the two planes – the actual and the ideal – do not mingle' to '*The Thousand and One Nights*, which doubles and dizzyingly redoubles the ramifications of a central tale into digressing tales', only to circle back on itself on night 602.[30] Borges follows the thread through the 'Mousetrap' play within *Hamlet* and its effects on our sensation of reality and fictiveness, and through other 'verbal labyrinths', only to tell us that, while *At Swim-Two-Birds* is part of this tradition, it is uniquely complex, another step in the tradition entirely: '*At Swim-Two-Birds* is not only a labyrinth – it is a discussion of the many ways to conceive of the Irish novel and a repertory of exercises in prose and verse which illustrate or parody all the styles of Ireland.'[31] But of course, Borges could not situate *At Swim-Two-Birds* in terms of what was to come afterwards, except perhaps by perspicacious implication, even prognostication. For what Borges saw in O'Nolan's novel sounds suspiciously like the magic realism of post-colonial writers, illustrating, parodying and subverting not all the styles of Ireland, but all the styles of their own colonised traditions and 'helping us to sense the oneness' of 'dreaming and wakefulness' by forcing us to 'leaf through them at random'.[32] If 'Brecht sought to use the resources of art [...] to historicise and negate the commonplace and taken-for-granted, to prise open social and ideological contradictions, and so both demonstrate and provoke an awareness of the individual's place in a concrete social narrative', then O'Nolan did something similar, but with regard to particular discourses as opposed to simply social narrative.[33]

8

A Crowning Martyr

Theatricality, spectacle and O'Nolan's carnivalesque

Noam Schiff

'The Martyr's Crown' remains one of Brian O'Nolan's most under-analysed short stories. In her review of *The Short Fiction of Flann O'Brien*, Carol Taaffe refers to the story as 'an elaborate excuse for its own punchline'.[1] Thierry Robin, one of the few critics to comment at length on 'The Martyr's Crown', directs our attention to the text's narrative layering, calling it 'a story within a story'.[2] My intention is to draw further on the significance and nature of this layering, categorising the work not as a 'story within a story', but as a gender performance within a play, aside a pantomime, within a vulgar joke, within a story. This essay thus engages questions of gender performance and sociopolitical theatricality at work within this short narrative. First, I argue that O'Nolan constructs a narrative consisting of vulgarity and of several performative literary genres to create a poetics of increasingly chaotic theatricality that turns the relationship between authenticity and farce on its head. I will then follow to illustrate how, with its narrative layering, blending of cultural and literary genres and cultivation of norm-subverting grotesque laughter, 'The Martyr's Crown' is O'Nolan's most meticulous execution of the tradition of the carnivalesque as outlined by Mikhail Bakhtin in his *Problems of Dostoevsky's Poetics*.

The short story centres on an Irish rebel's hiding-house run by a widow named Mrs Clougherty during the Irish War of Independence. On one occasion, to distract the English officers and protect the rebels in her care,

Mrs Clougherty engages in an orgy with several of the officers. The final lines disclose to the reader that the lady had fallen pregnant in the course of her sexual act of heroic martyrdom, giving birth to the first man who 'was *born* for Ireland' (*SF*, 80). The temptation to categorise this story as a dirty joke is thus initially justified by the unfolding of its plot that ends with an admittedly coarse punchline regarding the product of illegitimate sexual relations: the man who, instead of dying for Ireland, was born for it.

It is my contention that, like other works by O'Nolan, 'The Martyr's Crown' has been unjustly categorised as funny but not intellectually or thematically interesting, its intricacies written off as pegs in the mechanical utilisation of vulgarity. I contest this first impression, making instead the claim that the story's vulgarity is not its main aim, but rather is itself a peg for the substantiation of larger frames of reference, namely the story's participation in the tradition of the Irish carnivalesque.

O'Nolan's carnivalesque

The issue of O'Nolan's carnivalesque has been commented on in several studies that inform the aim of this essay. In his 1995 monograph *Flann O'Brien, Bakhtin and Menippean Satire*, M. Keith Booker describes O'Nolan's menippea in the following terms:

> Far from being confused or lacking coherence, O'Nolan's texts are informed by complex polyphonic energies to be expected of Menippean Satire. Moreover, these readings show that, contrary to popular critical perception, O'Nolan maintains a consistently experimental writing practice throughout his career [...]. O'Nolan's comedy is not gratuitous or silly but participates in important ways in his ongoing engagement with important social political and cultural issues in his contemporary Ireland.[3]

O'Nolan's important participation in the tradition of Bakhtinian carnivalesque is established in Booker's 1995 study and further pursued in key works from that decade by Kim McMullen and Keith Hopper.[4] Several recent studies elaborate on O'Nolan's carnivalesque, including Dieter Fuchs's situation of O'Nolan's carnivalesque menippea at the nexus of both the Hellenistic and Roman traditions and 'in modern and postmodern Ireland', as well as Conor Dowling's reading of the carnivalesque of *At Swim-Two-Birds* as a 'process by which one authority replaces another through the temporary institution of madness in society'.[5] The purpose of my intervention into this debate is the inclusion of 'The Martyr's Crown' within this critical tradition. Spanning only four and a half pages and to date regarded as mostly unremarkable within O'Nolan's *oeuvre*, this story contains precise and elaborate manifestations of almost all of Bakhtin's fourteen elements of the Menippean satire, making it O'Nolan's most elaborate carnivalesque endeavour.

In lieu of a list of all fourteen elements of the Menippean satire as outlined by Bakhtin and masterfully summarised in terms of their manifestation in works by O'Nolan in Booker's study,[6] I will provide a brief review of the main elements of the Menippean satire as important to my argument. To Bakhtin, the Menippean satire exhibits predominantly comic elements, and its comedy is of the nature of the carnivalesque. This means that on occasion it ignores verisimilitude, distorts scale or proportion and intermingles high with low, sacred with profane, for the purpose of philosophical experimentation and speculation. In the tradition of the Menippean satire, fantastic situations are created and alternative viewpoints are engaged. Through scandal scenes, journeys to fantastic realms, oxymoronic doubling and representations of eccentric behaviour such as irrationality, insanity and exorbitant appetite, the menippea allows for the fluid interplay and examination of contemporary social reality. The menippea displays outwardly those elements of human life that are usually unspoken, such as crude sexuality and bodily functions, elevating them to the level of high, sacred or esteemed social gestures and intermixing the high with the low. Another aspect which is crucial to this interplay of societal elements is the interchanging of genre within Menippean satire, in which different modes of verbal or textual communication blend together. For Bakhtin, a vital attribute of the menippea is its 'deliberate multi-styled and heterovoiced nature' which 'reject[s] the stylistic unity [...] of the epic, the tragedy, high rhetoric, [or] the lyric'.[7] Bakhtin outlines genre as presenting the most stable or 'eternal' manifestation of literature's development. Genre is thus inherently something that the Menippean satire strives to undo by melding different literary modes such as the Socratic dialogue, the oration, as well as tragedy, comedy and religious play.

Bakhtin lays out another primary aspect of the Menippean satire that does not make it into the list of characteristics compiled by Bakhtin and studied by Booker, but that I consider to be one of the most dominant features of O'Nolan's carnivalesque; this is the issue of the adventure hero or the adventure plot. Bakhtin describes the adventure hero as a figure through whom the carnivalesque fluidity of reality is brought to play:

> To the adventure hero anything can happen, he can become anything.
> He too is not a substance, but a pure function of adventures and
> escapades. The adventure hero is [...] not finalised [...]. The adventure
> plot [...] is precisely clothing draped over the hero, clothing which
> he can change as often as he pleases. The adventure plot relies not on
> what the hero is, not on the place he occupies in life, but more often on
> what he is not, on what (from the vantage point of the reality at hand)
> is unexpected and not predetermined. The adventure plot does not rely
> on already available and stable positions – family, social, biographical; it
> develops in spite of them.[8]

The above lines describe, with uncanny precision, the theatrical or even
farcical nature of nearly all of O'Nolan's protagonists, including that of
Toole from 'The Martyr's Crown'. The name Toole in itself can be seen as
a jest at the instrumentality of Toole's character[9] and the non-verisimilitude
of his narrative function: Toole is the precise embodiment of the Mennipean
flat character, or rather *persona*, who serves a merely textual function, being
fully subjected to the text and its meandering plot. As a Menippean parody
of the adventure hero, Toole embodies a combination of three crucial aspects
of the carnivalesque: a wilful suspension of verisimilitude alongside eccentric
behaviour, both of which participate in a third element, which Bakhtin
defines as the 'multi-styled and multi-toned nature of the menippea'.[10]

In the scene below, Toole is presented as the quintessential adventure hero
who, laying aside social norms and functioning, has the carnivalesque ability,
by dint of a paradoxical usage of social gestures, to draw his audience out of
their everyday life and into the world of adventure:

> Mr Toole had a peculiarity. He had the habit, when accompanied by
> another person, of saluting total strangers; but only if these strangers
> were of important air and costly raiment. He meant thus to make
> it known that he had friends in high places, and that he himself,
> though poor, was a person of quality fallen on evil days through some
> undisclosed sacrifice made in the interest of immutable principle early
> in life. Most of the strangers, startled out of their private thoughts,
> stammered a salutation in return. And Mr Toole was shrewd. He
> stopped at that. He said no more to his companion but by some little
> private gesture, a chuckle, a shake of the head, a smothered imprecation,
> he nearly always extracted the one question most melodious to his ear:
> *'Who was that?'* (SF, 76)

Toole's peculiar act which partakes of the social grotesque is a type of street pantomime, a display of salutations performed solely and meticulously with the body for the purpose of hailing his audiences, both witting and unwitting, out of their literally straightforward path. A 'pure function of adventures and escapades',[11] Toole, with his overstated salutation, a 'private gesture, a chuckle, a shake of the head, a smothered imprecation', engages spectators with his performance, pulling them out of the world of reality and into the world of the farce, or the 'adventure plot' – defined by Bakhtin not as a realistic local but a relational position for the functional purpose of testing out a given situation.[12] In the scene singled out, a 'young man of surpassing elegance' returns Toole's performance with the subtle social poetics of contempt:

> The young man's control was superb. There was no glare, no glance of scorn, no sign at all. He was gone, but had left in his wake so complete an impression of his contempt that even Mr Toole paled momentarily. The experience frightened Mr O'Hickey.
>
> 'Who … who was *that*?' he asked at last. (*SF*, 76–7)

Toole's adventure plot thus begins as a pantomime that is deeply Menippean in its nature. He makes alternative usage of a physical social gesture that is at the same time exaggerated, farcical and meant for failure within its social paradigm. His salutation, a societal signal communicating harmony and familiarity, is paradoxically performed to achieve estrangement and awe. This reversal of social semiotics is deeply carnivalesque in its subversive and socially divergent drive. Toole's adventure plot, moreover, as is appropriate for a work of the carnivalesque nature, quickly shifts into a different genre that will be likewise parodied, that of the epic war story.

Rewarded by the familiar question ('who was *that*?'), Toole proceeds to tell O'Hickey a story set in 1921, during the war for Irish independence. The point about Toole's story being false and performative is not a subtle one. O'Hickey is fully aware that the pantomime is only bribery, a free pre-show meant to get him to pay for the main act inside the pub. Nevertheless, he walks Toole into the pub and orders two bottles of stout, reasoning with himself that Toole, 'at his best [...] was better than a play' (*SF*, 76), thus knowingly participating in the carnivalesque adventure plot that Toole has to offer. At the outset of the war-story farce, the third-person narrator grants the reader access to O'Hickey's private response to Toole's claims: 'Mr O'Hickey nodded and said nothing. He knew that Mr Toole had never rendered military service to his country' (*SF*, 77). The admission of O'Hickey's wilful suspension of disbelief is kept for its very final lines in the earlier version of the story entitled 'For Ireland Home and Beauty', where the assertion that Toole is 'better than a play' is not at all present. These later changes in 'The Martyr's Crown' emphasise the wilful abandonment of verisimilitude and the foregrounding of diverse performative genres, two carnivalesque elements that O'Nolan purposefully chose to cultivate when revising the text.

In addition to its wilful rejection of verisimilitude and inclusion of adventure heroes and adventure plots, 'The Martyr's Crown' overtly develops other Menippean elements such as generic hybridity and narrative layering. Bakhtin explains the importance of this trait in the following terms:

> Characteristic for the menippea is a wide use of inserted genres: novellas, letters, oratorical speeches, symposia, and so on; also characteristic is a mixing of prose and poetic speech. The inserted genres are presented at various distances from the ultimate authorial position, that is, with varying degrees of parodying and objectification [...]. The presence of inserted genres reinforces the multi-styled and multi-toned nature of the menippea; what is coalescing here is a new relationship to the word as the material of literature, a relationship characteristic for the entire dialogic line of development in artistic prose.[13]

This 'multi-styled and multi-toned' Menippean element in 'The Martyr's Crown' is manifested through the story's narrative layering – the 'story within a story'[14] – which is crafted by O'Nolan to contain different diegetic levels, each satirising a different literary genre. The profuse generic hybridity of this single short story manages to contain an adventure plot, a pantomime, a war story, a gender performance, a play and a vulgar joke all wrapped up within the confines of the carnivalesque.

O'Nolan's use of framing in 'The Martyr's Crown' both deceptively reinforces the impression that the narrative is little more than a shaggy dog story, or elaborate bawdy pun, and at the same time draws attention to the text's profusion of diegetic levels. This dual function can be seen in the later insertion of two miniature framing paragraphs, consisting of two lines each, which are placed at the beginning and end of the narrative.[15] The introductory sketch sets up the story of two men walking down the street and into a pub early in the morning, while the concluding one consists of the final vulgar revelation of the story's title, an explication of the vaginal martyrdom achieved through the unfolding action. These two framing paragraphs point at the author's wilful engagement of the *fabliaux* or vulgar-joke genre through his late and purposeful framing of the narrative as a traditional pub joke that begins by two men 'walking into a pub' and ends on a comic punchline. This story's framing is addressed in Marion Quirici's essay on the frame device in O'Nolan's short fiction. While Quirici does an excellent job of defining the author's general 'metafictional framing strategies' and hyper-awareness of the frame that lends his narratives 'a definite vulnerability',[16] she finds 'The Martyr's Crown' 'illuminating for its abandonment of these conventions', calling it an unproblematic story within a story in which 'overt self-reflexivity makes no appearance'.[17] When comparing the story's versions, however, Quirici fails to mention O'Nolan's insertion of these miniature framing paragraphs into 'The Martyr's Crown' and thus to comment on the crucial alteration in framing made in the final draft of this work. My own argument is in agreement with Quirici's overall claim regarding O'Nolan's use of creatively reflexive framing devices, as I seek to position 'The Martyr's Crown' not as a counterexample to O'Nolan's art of reflexive framing, but rather as a positive illustration of this type of effect through the frame's addition to the story's principle of generic hybridity.

When classifying the generic layering of this piece therefore, we find the text is categorised as a short story, with its initial outer shell being a vulgar pub-joke. Within this frame we find the main character of the narrative Mr Toole performing a grotesquely exaggerated comedy of manners that serves as a warm-up act for a farce that his audience labels as 'better than a play', a satirical rendering of a war story in which the act of bravery and martyrdom is performed by a woman, itself constituting a Bakhtinian scandal scene. This carrousel cues in another Menippean element within the short story, orgies being of course one of the fourteen elements that Bakhtin originally lists while cataloguing this genre. This *mise en abyme* of genres contains one more level and genre of theatricality in which Mrs Clougherty, the saint, performs exaggerated acts of femininity in order to trick the British officers into her bed and out of their military duties. Clougherty's efforts are as ironically performative as Toole's pantomime of socially constructed gestures: her 'fingers' play upon the 'buttons of the satteen' as she 'puts on the guttiest voice' Toole had 'ever heard outside Moore street' and prudishly swears that there are no men at home at such an unseemly 'hour of the night' while coquettishly admitting that she wished to God there were, for how, she asks 'could the poor unfortunate woman get on without them' (*SF*, 79). This four-page narrative contains an intricate interlace of various performative genres, all of which are undershot, deflated and parodied through their interconnection within the story's plot, as well as through their oxymoronic, upside-down and therefore polyphonic-carnivalesque manifestations.

'The Martyr's Crown' is thus an elaborate incarnation of various aspects of the carnivalesque: it contains a strong comic element, which is purposefully foregrounded in the coarse joke frame of the story; it wilfully rejects verisimilitude in favour of adventure heroes and plots; it layers and hybridises genres as a method for satirising, testing and subverting different societal norms. I would now like to focus on another important aspect of the carnivalesque in 'The Martyr's Crown', which is the abundant usage of oxymoronic combinations in the story's intermixing of the high and the low, the spiritual and the earthly, the sacred and the profane.

The sacred and the profane

These combinations culminate in the character of Mrs Clougherty herself, who, from her very first mention in the story, is introduced as a figure who literally embodies the most crucial Menippean oxymoron. Though Toole refers to her as a martyr or a saint, the story constantly lowers this quasi-religious entity to the level of the earthly and the physical. Mrs Clougherty is referred to frequently as an unfortunate woman, evoking the idea of her possible work as a prostitute. Further support for the idea that Clougherty is presented as a Madonna-whore figure is that, although in the final version of the story Clougherty feigns innocence of having men in her house late at night, in an earlier version this same figure tells the officers 'there are a few men in the house certainly, why wouldn't there be' (*SF*, 143), letting them understand, whether in earnest or in play (it hardly seems to matter in this kind of narrative) that she is a prostitute.

The combination of sexual purity and promiscuity contained within the character of Clougherty ironically continues through a scene in which Toole, the adventure hero/narrator, outwardly attempts to defend her honour as a respectable woman:

> 'will I never forget Mrs Clougherty! She was certainly a marvellous figure of a woman. I never seen a woman like her to bake bread.'
> Mr O'Hickey looked up.
> 'Was she,' he said, 'was she … all right?'
> 'She was certainly nothing of the sort,' Mr Toole said loudly and sharply. 'By God, we were all thinking of other things in them days. Here was this unfortunate woman in a three-story house on her own, with some quare fellow in the middle flat, herself on the ground floor, and six blood-thirsty pultogues hiding above on the top floor, every

manjack ready to shoot his way out if there was trouble. We got feeds
there I never seen before [...]. There was one snag. We couldn't budge
out. No exercise at all – and that means only one thing ...'

'Constipation?' Mr O'Hickey suggested.

'The very man,' said Mr Toole. (*SF*, 78)

The sexual connotations of six men 'lying low' with a marvellous figure of
a woman are enough to cue in any number of obscene sexual connotations,
especially when this woman's physicality is further attached to the baking of
bread, a possible subtle jab at sexual reproduction and a foreshadowing of
coming attractions, namely, her having 'a bun in the oven'. What is interesting
here is that O'Hickey, the audience to this 'play', picks up on this innuendo
immediately and is shut down explicitly by the intradiegetic performer, who
claims chastity of thought and then continues to describe in detail a scene
that nevertheless participates clearly in every element of the grotesque and
carnivalesque. Reading Toole's description of the living arrangement, the
notion of an orgy is unquestionably evoked: this 'unfortunate woman' finds
herself in a three-story house full of men, with her on the very bottom while
the 'blood thirsty men', their manjacks at the ready, share her various 'flats'.
Toole's declaration of chastity is moreover abundant in reference to feasting,
to sex, to physical repression and, by connection, to release and even to bowel
movements. This scene checks almost every Bakhtinian box of the definition
of the carnivalesque. There is a lowering of sacred elements, a mixture of
the high with the low, as well as an emphasis and a drawing together of all
physical activity, from indigestion and copulation to physical motion and
even defecation.

An important carnivalesque element, as we have seen, according to
Bakhtin, is the lowering, the bringing down, the 'earthening' of religious
ritual. This effect is manifest throughout this short story, especially in the
scene in which, after the sexual encounter with the soldiers, Mrs Clougherty,
our Madonna-whore, forces the men to kneel in a gesture of prayer that can
no longer be read without a dimension of the grotesque, the sexual and the
profane. In this mock-religious ritual, the men are forced to genuflect before
Mrs Clougherty: whether 'Protestant, Catholic or Jewman, all hands had
to go down on the knees' (*SF*, 78) before this saintly woman. Clougherty's
grotesque bodily performance and mock-religious status is thus a crucial
embodiment of the Menippean satire that manages, through a combination
of high-with-low, to combine profanely and to reconcile different social and
religious elements: in their Bakhtinian kneeling before the Madonna-whore,
Catholic, Protestant and Jewman are grotesquely united.

The carnivalesque spectacle of this 'play' culminates in the joke's punchline that the young man who had snubbed Toole in the street is no other than the illegitimate son of Clougherty and what we can only assume to be one of several English officers who participated in this actual, as opposed to the hinted at, orgy previously discussed through the hiding arrangements. The young man who was born for Ireland is thus an ultimate figure for the Irish carnivalesque: as the illegitimate son of a possible Irish prostitute and one of several English soldiers, the seemingly polished man who snubs Toole on the street ironically becomes a figure that, to quote Bakhtin, 'is opposed to all that is finished and polished, to all pomposity'.[18] As the son of a mock-Madonna, the man functions as a fake-Messiah, a Jesus-figure born out of the least-immaculate of conceptions embodying a deflation not only of nationalistic rituals but of sociopolitical and religious ones as well. This man therefore signifies not a simply crude punchline, but a complexly crude one. In him, Bakhtin's final attribute of the menippea that is not often successfully associated with the works of O'Nolan, 'its concern with current and topical issues',[19] is fully manifested: the self-important English-Irish bastard that is the butt of this short story is, in more ways than one, a hybrid figure embodying several carnivalesque oppositions; a figure, moreover, that diffuses elements of political and religious *gravitas* through Bakhtinian laughter. In him, O'Nolan brings topical issues such as the Irish rebellion, Anglo-Irish relations and even religion and religious difference to a more basic gay level of crude, carnivalesque physicality.

Another character who furthers the theme of crude physicality is Mrs Clougherty herself. The most 'marvellous figure of a woman [...] to bake bread' (*SF*, 78), Clougherty is the saint, the martyr who is at the same time described almost exclusively in relation to physical sexuality, food or reproduction. Other than embodying a combination of the sacred and profane, Clougherty's body participates in the symbolic intermingling of high and low during birth. It becomes clear that Clougherty earned her martyr's crown by participating in an orgy and birthing an illegitimate child. Rather than a martyr's sacrificial death as an ecstatic gateway to the eternal life in the afterworld, Mrs Clougherty's all-too worldly self-sacrifice leads to what is euphemistically referred to as *la petite mort* (the little death). Through this narrative, therefore, we witness another of O'Nolan's exceptionally strong and explicit carnivalesque images: namely, a lowering of the highest and most spiritual honour. The martyr's crown that sacredly adorns a person of holy stature is usually imagined as a halo of transcendental light. The repeated foregrounding of lower bodily orifices in this story cues the important connection between its title 'The Martyr's Crown' and the lower realm of the female body that participates in the physical crowning in which this heterodiegetic narrative culminates. This degradation further represents Bakhtin's definition of the grotesque body as a body with open orifices inviting contact with the outside world:

> Contrary to modern canons, the grotesque body is not separated from the rest of the world. It is not a closed, completed unit; it is unfinished, outgrows itself, transgresses its own limits. The stress is laid on those parts of the body that are open to the outside world, that is, the parts through which the world enters the body or emerges from it, or through which the body itself goes out to meet the world. This means that the emphasis is on the apertures or the convexities, or on various ramifications and offshoots: the open mouth, the genital organs, the breasts, the phallus, the potbelly, the nose.[20]

The profane suggestion is, I would claim, that the martyr's crown is no other than that bodily orifice that was sacrificed by the mock-religious sexual and birthing acts, the open and transgressive orifice interacting with the outside world, namely, Mrs Clougherty's vagina. There can be no carnivalesque image more successful to my mind that represents this 'contact with earth as an element that swallows up and gives birth at the same time', that 'degrades, buries and sows simultaneously'[21] than a mock-martyr whose metaphorical death is copulation, who births a child and is both done and undone by this act, and who is, in fact, crowned or wreathed by the single event in the cycle of life in which that part of the human body which is traditionally seen as its lowest region physically crowns the highest point of another body. In this suggestion of the vagina as crown and open interactive orifice, O'Nolan achieves the perfect carnivalesque rendering of the mock-Bakhtinian ritual of 'crowning and uncrowning':[22] the coexistence of the high with the low, the sacred and the profane.

Conclusion

As we have seen, O'Nolan mixes genres and voices, combining diverse narrative levels that participate in different forms of the spectacle. These can be jokes, pub tales, plays, pantomimes and even social performances. He mixes high and low forms in his mock rituals and polyphonic menippea, impressively squeezing in a reference to two orgies within the space of four pages. But what conclusion can be drawn with relation to O'Nolan's carnival? What defines it and makes it unique? And, more importantly, what distinguishes its comic nature from that of regular vulgarity?

Bakhtin defines the most crucial element of the menippea as 'the fact that its bold and unrestrained use of the fantastic and adventure is internally motivated, justified by and devoted to a purely ideational and philosophical end: the creation of *extraordinary situations* for the provoking and testing of a philosophical idea'.[23] The testing of philosophical ideas is thus the true motivation behind the genre fluidity and general polyphony prevalent throughout the carnivalesque. This effect is clearly manifest in 'The Martyr's Crown', in which large-scale issues such as social etiquette, war, religion and political relations have been thoroughly carnivalised in a manner that allows them to be unpacked, explored and examined from differing angles. The 'purely ideational and philosophical end' outlined by Bakhtin is famously Socratic in its insistence on there being no fixed truths. In this regard, while Bakhtin demands 'pure philosophical ends' to Menippean satires, the purity of these ends does not connote a fixity of philosophical conclusions but rather their polyphony:

> But the most important – one could say, the decisive – expression of reduced laughter is to be found in the ultimate position of the author. This position excludes all one-sided or dogmatic seriousness and does not permit any single point of view, any single polar extreme of life or of thought, to be absolutised. All one-sided seriousness (of life and thought), all one-sided pathos is handed over to the heroes, but the author, who causes them all to collide in the 'great dialogue' of the novel, leaves that dialogue open and puts no finalising period at the end. It should be pointed out that the carnival sense of the world also knows no period, and is, in fact, hostile to any sort of *conclusive conclusion*: all endings are merely new beginnings; carnival images are reborn again and again.[24]

The figure of the author who is at once a master of 'reduced laughter' and a creator of a 'carnival sense of the world' which possesses 'a mighty life-creating and transforming power, an indestructible vitality',[25] perfectly encapsulates the philosophical-artistic drive behind the work of the mercurial author Brian O'Nolan/Flann O'Brien/Myles na gCopaleen, *et al.* This body of writing is likewise full of philosophic and literary experimentation that is 'pure' in the most Bakhtinian sense of the word, a purity partaking of polyphonic exchange, interplay and parody of different large-scale frames such as religion, nationalism or social morality. The only traditionally 'pure', fixed or clear end to be found in O'Nolan's works – and this short story is no exception – is the drive for drink which in itself is a comic mark of fluidity in the author's opus.[26] Toole, for instance, has a clear perlocutionary purpose in this narrative of un-clarity: he wants his audience to buy him a drink at the pub. In this, his goal is not all that different from that of his audience O'Hickey, who wishes to shed the yoke of the world of verisimilitude and participate in the spectacle of the carnivalesque. As one of O'Nolan's many inebriated storytellers, Toole's drunkenness is much like his audience's suspension of disbelief; namely, another dominant Dionysian element participating in O'Nolan's menippea.

Robin fittingly connects 'The Martyr's Crown' with O'Nolan's short play *Thirst* through their creation of alternative histories. Yet, what brings these narratives together for me is not only, as Robin claims, the subversion of grand narratives. The connection works on a much simpler level: they are both multi-layered narratives in which theatricality is crafted towards the ends of inebriation and in which inebriation fuels theatricality. This is an important metafictional connection, and a major element in what I would call O'Nolan's authentically carnivalesque spirit, immune to any '*conclusive conclusion*' in which 'all endings are merely new beginnings'.[27] 'Two in One' showcases the only hierarchy that is acceptable within O'Nolan's carnivalesque-infused reality: in this story, an offence is given by a lady thinking that 'her unsolicited conversation was fair exchange for a drink'. For O'Nolan, therefore, this is the real crime. One needs to pull off the narrative, to create a story that is 'fair exchange' for a drink. 'The Martyr's Crown' can therefore be seen to stand, in its entirety, for the authentic and deeply carnivalesque spirit of O'Nolan's works. His writing seeks to perpetuate an ongoing carnival of drinking in terms of dramatic, literary effect (marked by a loss of verisimilitude and a foregrounding of spectacle), but also out of a practical motivation of allowing the author to keep drinking, thereby enabling 'carnival images' to be 'reborn again and again'.[28]

Recently, Conor Dowling has pushed back against the standard Bakhtinian readings of *At Swim-Two-Birds* to argue that 'O'Nolan employs a more ambivalent and less emancipatory, celebratory or playful use of the carnivalesque in his writing'.[29] While I find Dowling's argument of the carnivalesque throughout *At Swim-Two-Birds* entirely convincing, I would like to situate the short story that is the topic of the present essay as a counterexample of O'Nolan's authentically carnivalesque spirit. A common criticism of the carnivalesque, which Dowling echoes, is that it functions as a sort of safety valve: a controlled release of inhibitions and societal regulation that are ultimately inscribed back into authoritative models of societal norms. My final claim is that O'Nolan participates in a modernist carnivalesque spirit that is impervious to such criticism, having the 'guts' (pun intended) to give in to a carnival-infused reality that lasts all year long. O'Nolan's works consist of a lowering of the high through laughter, parody and drinking that is crucially both the ends and the means for his literature and plays. 'The Martyr's Crown' is authentically carnivalesque in that it does not function as a purgatorial safety fuse, but as a self-generating, self-reflexive, ongoing carnival in which philosophical, political and social modes are found in productive polyphonic interplay.

Act III

Myles en scène

9

Dreaming After in the Dark Night

Thirst and the power of performance

Joseph Brooker

It's myself I have to trust to now, and my share of talk.

W.B. Yeats and Augusta Gregory, *The Pot of Broth*[1]

Anything can be said in this place and it will be true and will have to be believed.

Flann O'Brien, *The Third Policeman* (*CN*, 296)

It is not surprising that the revival of interest in Brian O'Nolan's work in the 2010s should have commenced with a predominance of attention to his novels. The brilliant opening salvo of fiction had left much for a new generation of critics to say. It is logical, too, that attention should steadily turn toward the rereading of *Cruiskeen Lawn*, a great mine of writing with pertinence to numerous cultural and social debates in mid-twentieth-century Ireland. In the wake of these studies, however, with the shape of O'Nolan's career becoming clearer and more fully detailed, more consideration begins to be paid to his work as a dramatist. A crucial development is the edition of *Plays and Teleplays* edited by Daniel Keith Jernigan and published by Dalkey Archive Press in 2013. From the same period, relevant critical work includes essays by Stefan Solomon, Jernigan, Maebh Long and Thierry Robin.[2] Yet this still only represents a beginning. The present essay aims to extend this nascent consideration of O'Nolan and the theatrical.

Such consideration is consonant with the attempt to think of O'Nolan's work in the context of modern Irish writing, in the period of the Revival and its aftermath.³ For theatre was not marginal but central to this creative *milieu*. The Abbey Theatre has as good a case as anywhere to be reckoned the single most important physical space in the development of Irish writing in this era. Myles na gCopaleen disparaged the Abbey, yet his most extensive play was written for it and ran there for almost two weeks in 1943. Other theatres too, like the Gate, were significant not only in fostering a native Irish art but also in bringing Irish writers and audiences into contact with European models and influences.⁴ O'Nolan's delivery of *Rhapsody in Stephen's Green* to the Gate in 1943 exemplifies this development, in adapting a Czech original to a thoroughly local idiom. Considering O'Nolan the dramatist encourages us to think of him as a figure engaged in public culture, in a necessarily collaborative artistic process; and as taking part in the crucial institutions of revivalism and, arguably, modernism in the city that he had made his own.

Faustus Kelly and *Rhapsody in Stephen's Green* were O'Nolan's most extensive ventures into theatrical writing. It is understandable that consideration of O'Nolan as dramatist should focus especially on these works. Yet his first significant work performed on stage was in fact *Thirst*, a one-act play commissioned by Hilton Edwards and performed at the Gate as part of a Christmas revue at the end of 1942. *Thirst* can make some claim to being the most successful of O'Nolan's dramatic works. Jernigan notes that this short play 'has been performed often and reproduced for both radio and television' (*PT*, x). Peter Costello and Peter van de Kamp concur that it is 'the most reliably entertaining of his plays', while Robert Tracy, editor of *Rhapsody in Stephen's Green*, also avers that it is 'Myles's most successful play'.⁵

The publication in 2018 of *The Collected Letters of Flann O'Brien* has provided more detailed evidence of the history of this play and O'Nolan's enduring regard for it. In 1956, the Gate Theatre requested a revised version of the play, along with any other shorter sketches that O'Nolan could offer, 'particularly comedy dealing with contemporary Irish life'. On 8 October 1956, Hilton Edwards personally wrote to O'Nolan asking to include *Thirst*, again emphasising the desirability of work with a contemporary setting. Writing to the Gate's Pamela Pyer, O'Nolan asserted that *Thirst* had 'been played in France and Germany, with suitable adaptations', and that while it would need 'modernisation', Robert Hennessy, the actor who had originally played the publican Mr Coulahan, would be keen to reprise the role. O'Nolan did send in a new version of *Thirst*, which has not yet been rediscovered by scholars. From his description, it is different from either of the versions published in *Plays and Teleplays*, as it features a 'Robert Emmet character', a song early in the script and a second Guard 'who stays at the door and takes no part' (*L*, 213–18). All this demonstrates, first, that Edwards and the Gate had retained a fond memory of the play and a sense of its popular potential; second, that O'Nolan himself continued to hold this short work in high enough regard to return to it and tinker with it creatively. More remarkably, in the same exchange, O'Nolan tried to persuade the Gate to stage a projected comic opera of which *Thirst* would be 'the guts of the first act' (*L*, 216). Such an opportunistic readiness to reuse material rather anticipates the recycling of parts of *The Third Policeman* in *The Dalkey Archive*. The comic opera would certainly have cast *Thirst* in a new light, but it did not transpire. *Thirst*, though, continued to come up in O'Nolan's correspondence. In January 1962 he sent the literary agent Mark Hamilton a summary of the play, describing its original production as 'a great success'. Unfavourably contrasting a 1959 BBC television production with a still more recent (January 1962) production by Telefís Éireann which 'in everybody's opinion was an uproarious triumph', he proposed the sale of the latter to a New Jersey brewery for a St Patrick's Day broadcast (*L*, 293–4).[6]

The following month O'Nolan sent Hamilton the 'camera script' of the Irish production, with an indication that 'the video tape is available' (*L*, 26). O'Nolan would continue to make reference to these broadcasts in other letters (*L*, 310, 524–5). Well into O'Nolan's last decade, the play retained a status in his mind as a viable property and dramatic prospect, while other works had been consigned to the past.

The present essay takes encouragement from this evidence of the play's endurance, in focusing on *Thirst* as a key instance of O'Nolan's work for the theatre. It argues that *Thirst* turns on the relations between language and imagination and seeks to reframe this crux with a conceptual idiom not previously applied to O'Nolan's drama, deploying the concepts of performativity and perlocutionary utterance developed by the philosopher J.L. Austin. This aspect of the play is then contextualised in a modern Irish tradition, with particular reference to W.B. Yeats and to John Millington Synge's play *The Well of the Saints* (1905).

All talk: *Thirst*

The play exists in two versions, and Jernigan states that we cannot judge which is to be considered the more authoritative. One version is slightly longer (*PT*, 139–56), but the differences between them are slight and will not be emphasised as a significant critical issue here. Reference will primarily be made to the shorter version (*PT*, 121–35), though one feature of the longer version will be highlighted later.

The play depicts an after-hours setting, in mid-winter, in a candle-lit Dublin bar. The landlord Mr Coulahan is serving alcohol late at night, illegally, to himself and two customers: Peter, and the '*hanger-on*' Jem who lurks in a corner (*PT*, 121). After a couple of pages of tavern talk, the characters are surprised by the sound of the Guards outside. They hide in darkness and silence until the Sergeant of the Guards knocks and enters. The subsequent action is ambiguous in that the Sergeant seems in no hurry to cite them for breaking a curfew. While he spends much time with his notebook, when Jem asks if he can finish his bottle of stout the Sergeant deliberately turns away from him and declares: 'What ye might do when me back is turned, is a thing I would know nothing at all about' (*PT*, 126).

Nonetheless, the primary driver of the plot is the understanding that the Sergeant will cite them for their offence – 'a breach of closed hours' (*PT*, 127) – and this legal conviction is what the publican now seeks to avoid. Mr Coulahan makes much of the idea that for him to serve a drink to the Sergeant would be a heinous offence: 'as much as my livelihood or your promotion in the force was worth', worthy of 'the gravest charges – bribery, corruption and attempted suborning of the police force' (*PT*, 126). His aim is to make this happen: to make the Sergeant take a drink, so that he will have to drop any charge against the pub itself. Mr Coulahan's strategy to this end is to describe a scene of great heat, with such conviction that the Sergeant, like others on stage, reacts as though these oppressive temperatures were real, and cannot resist drinking. The scene described is a theatre of war in the Middle East, during the First World War, when Coulahan claims to have been fighting in the British army. Coulahan's description has the desired effect. Ultimately, in the short version the Sergeant '*takes three drinks, one by one, and drinks them*' (*PT*, 135); in the longer version he

> makes a loud incoherent noise, turns slowly and deliberately, lifts the glass of stout that is beside him and drinks it off in one long appreciative draft. [...] He looks at the empty glass, puts it down smartly, on the counter and waves at MR C. to convey that a fresh round should be served. (PT, 156)

In both versions, in fractionally different terms, the Sergeant concludes the play with the request: 'Does anybody mind if I sing "The Rose of Tralee"?' (*PT*, 135, 156). The logical implication is that having taken a drink he will lose all inclination to bring charges against the public house.

One reason for *Thirst*'s relative acclaim is that it is short. Whereas Tracy states that *Faustus Kelly* 'starts well' with the interplay of Act I, then goes off in the meandering Acts II and III, *Thirst* is compact enough to complete its narrative with satisfying economy.[7] In this regard, it partakes of something of the tight structure of a joke, proceeding from exposition (or set-up), through escalation, to the pay-off of a punchline. *Thirst* is richer than such an abstract description suggests, yet it is true that it belongs with O'Nolan's broader and more popular comic works – which might include the story 'The Martyr's Crown' or some of the tales of 'The Brother' in *Cruiskeen Lawn*. While the play has subtler intellectual implications than has often been recognised, it nonetheless does not engage in the darkly philosophical speculation of *The Third Policeman*, a work written roughly three years earlier, nor of the ostentatious erudition of many of the instances of *Cruiskeen Lawn* with which it was contemporary. All this leads in turn to another reason for *Thirst*'s repute: it is rooted in materials with which O'Nolan was familiar. This is the writer who repeatedly wrote up dialogues in the Scotch House, of the kind staged in the following *Cruiskeen Lawn* column from 26 February 1951:

> And where do you think My Nabs was?
> **I cannot imagine.**
> In a certain particular place in Drumcondra that *I* know and that *you* know, stuck in the back snug with two Free State Army privates and a wumman of a certain class.
> **I see.**
> Drinking malt good-o, the four of them trying to sell somebody else's house in Clyde Road to some mad hop-off-my-thumb from the County Carlow. Country Mug is invited to make a deposit of one hundred notes in the snug there and then as a guarantee of his good faith. And do you think the celebrations stopped when the pub closed?
> **I doubt it.**[8]

Such dialogues present the artist as eavesdropper. His achievement is in the accurate rendition of speech, reflecting his intimacy with a local discursive world, which is passed on to a newspaper audience implicitly close enough to this world of speech to recognise it, but also sufficiently detached from it to find amusement.[9]

Thirst likewise starts amid the discourse of the Dublin bar. Both versions begin with conversation *in medias res*, the publican asking the rhetorical question 'And do you know why?' They proceed to the verbal abuse of absent third parties:

> MR C.: He has a brother from the County Galway that comes up every
> year for the Horse Show, a hop-off-my-thumb that you wouldn't notice
> passing you on the stairs, all dressed out in fancy riding-breeches. Last
> year he turned up in the uncle's pub beyond in Drumcondra, complete
> with fountain-pen … and cheque-book. Gave your man as his reference.
> (*He pauses ominously.*) My God, the unfortunate bloody uncle. (*He laughs
> hollowly.*) (*PT*, 122)

O'Nolan noticeably adapts his writing to the stage by adding stage directions
which slow down the movement of the conversation. Still, the rhetorical
mode is familiar to readers of his work: not only in the scurrilous, scolding
tone but even in the precise expression of contempt for a 'hop-off-my-thumb'
and his provenance in a different county of Ireland. The apparent implication
is that this unseen verbal target is a 'culchie', a member of Ireland's rural
population who is thus treated with a degree of disdain by the publican in
the nation's capital. Likewise, Jem's comment, delivered (as a stage direction
indicates) in '*a strong Dublin accent*': 'Oh, the cheque-book is the man. Manny's
the time I wished to God I had one of me own!' (*PT*, 122). Here we are not so
far from the brilliantly judged discussion of musical instruments over tea in
At Swim-Two-Birds, in which Mr Lamont declares that 'the fiddle is the man
for me' while 'Paralysis is certainly a nice cup of tea' (*CN*, 148, 157). O'Nolan's
deployment of such voices is delicate. The rendition of the conversation
of Lamont, Shanahan and Furriskey in his first novel may easily enough be
read as simple ridicule. Certainly, its prime intention is richly comic. Yet this
comedy is also intimate with its targets: as affectionate as it is mocking. In
Thirst, the deployment of local voice is done without the excessive formality
that makes *At Swim-Two-Birds*'s dialogue so finely comic. Put simply,
being staged in a bar, *Thirst* is more conventional than *At Swim-Two-Birds*'s
resituation of such speakers at a genteel tea party. The dialogue between the
drinkers in *Thirst*, prior to Mr Coulahan's great monologue, is not a matter
of outlandish exaggeration or surreal incongruity. By O'Nolan's standards,
much of it may almost be described as naturalistic. Yet it stands as an instance
of his consistent dedication to recording Dublin speech for aesthetic effect.

To a degree, here is the open secret of *Thirst*'s success: it draws on a seam
of material familiar from some of O'Nolan's finest other writings, notably
in his first novel and in *Cruiskeen Lawn*. This is also to say that it plays to his
aptitude for dialogue. The playgoer Joseph Holloway reckoned *Faustus Kelly*
'all talk and no play', but it would be redundant to accuse *Thirst* of excessive
talk.[10] Talk is of its essence, and the colour of the talk is the play's most
evident source of appeal.

Consequential effects: doing things with words

Yet something else about language in *Thirst* bears further explication. This concerns the power of words to shape perception. The narrator of *At Swim-Two-Birds* contrasts the theatre with prose narrative:

> It was stated that while the novel and the play were both pleasing intellectual exercises, the novel was inferior to the play inasmuch as it lacked the outward accidents of illusion, frequently inducing the reader to be outwitted in a shabby fashion and caused to experience a real concern for the fortunes of illusory characters. (*CN*, 21)

In referring to theatre's 'outward accidents of illusion' (*CN*, 21), he presumably means such details as characters dressed in costume, props, stage sets. A flat stage set with a painted landscape, a wooden sword, a bear costume to be worn by a human actor: in the simplifying terms just quoted, such physical items are used to foster the temporary 'illusions' of theatre. All of these, the student narrator implies, actually limit theatre's capacity to induce the suspension of disbelief: they are poor illusions, whereas those of the novel work more insidiously and effectively. (An irony unmentioned at this point of the novel is that *At Swim-Two-Birds*, far from maintaining its illusions, will go out of its way repeatedly to dismantle them and break its fictional frames.) *Thirst* itself necessarily includes some of the 'outward' illusions of theatre: the bar on stage is not really a pub (though given the number of drinks poured in the script, the bar presumably works like a real bar), the Sergeant is an actor dressed in a police uniform. In the semiotic terms offered by the nineteenth-century philosopher C.S. Peirce, such physical features may be described as 'iconic', working through a visual resemblance to their object in a way quite distinct from, for instance, the linguistic signs that make up a literary text.[11]

Yet these 'outward accidents' of illusion seem secondary, in this play, to a more profound interest in illusion, or imagination, and its relation to speech. *Thirst* turns on the capacity of spoken language to embody scenes and experiences that are not present, producing bodily effects (such as actual thirst) from thin air. It is thus a piece in which O'Nolan's textual tactics gain physical embodiment on stage, only to cede primacy once more to the word. It may be telling, in this regard, that *Thirst* has been successfully performed as a radio play, with performances on Radio Éireann in 1943, then in adaptations by H.L. Morrow in 1958 and 1964.[12] While the radio play is a distinct artistic form that would merit separate discussion, the importance of speech and, on the listener's part, imagination, to radio drama make it suggestive that *Thirst* has been adapted to this medium.[13]

The word 'performative' appears relevant, on the face of it, to any consideration of theatricality. The term has seen much use in recent academic work, thanks not least to the theoretical writings of Judith Butler, in which it has tended to emphasise the constructed and provisional character of identity.[14] Further back, the origin of the term itself is in J.L. Austin's *How To Do Things With Words*, a set of lectures given in 1955 and published in book form in 1962. (The connection between Austin's term and Butler's is not coincidental: while their emphases differ, Butler's theory of performativity is conceptually linked to Austin's before her.) Austin commences with a distinction between constative and performative speech acts. Constatives are verifiable descriptions that refer to pre-existing conditions pertaining in the world; performatives are utterances which do things, bringing a new set of conditions into being and leaving the situation in some way altered. Austin's major examples include statements like 'I do' in a marriage ceremony, or 'I name this ship the *Queen Elizabeth*'. In such performative cases, Austin writes, 'to utter the sentence (in, of course, the appropriate circumstances) is not to *describe* my doing of what I should be said in so uttering to be doing or to state that I am doing it: it is to do it'.[15] Austin describes how he has settled on the term, having briefly considered 'performatory': 'The name is derived, of course, from "perform", the usual verb with the noun "action": it indicates that the issuing of the utterance is the performing of an action – it is not normally thought of as just saying something.'[16] Austin's thinking takes us towards an understanding of language as action rather than only as information. And this intellectual move, in turn, begins to help us to describe *Thirst* as a play that is less concerned with relaying information (the 'facts' of Mr Coulahan's story) than with the use of language to bring about altered states (the 'thirst' of the title).

The kind of performatives Austin cites are heavily bound by conventional contexts. They only function or apply in pre-decided circumstances like a church on a wedding day; they can otherwise malfunction in what he calls conditions of 'infelicity'. In fact, within Austin's work another term is closer to the scenario of O'Nolan's play. This is the *perlocutionary*, which he develops in contrast to two other terms. The *locutionary* is close to the constative. The *illocutionary* describes how *in* saying something, one does something else, such as the act of ordering or protesting. But the perlocutionary, as the prefix *per* intends, suggests that *by* saying something, one causes effects. Thus: 'Saying something will often, or even normally, produce certain consequential effects upon the feelings, thoughts, or actions of the audience, or of the speaker, or of other persons: and it may be done with the design, intention, or purpose of producing them.'[17] Austin adds that 'the perlocutionary act always includes some consequences' and describes such acts as 'what we bring about or achieve *by* saying something, such as convincing, persuading, deterring, and even, say, surprising or misleading'.[18]

In this light, it is plain that *Thirst* is a study in perlocutionary discourse. Mr Coulahan's verbal portrait of the desert of what the short version of the play calls 'Messpott' or 'Messiopotamia' (*PT*, 127–8) and the longer version leaves unspecified, serves, in Austin's words, to 'produce certain consequential effects upon the feelings, thoughts, or actions of the audience', namely the Sergeant. More incidentally, the anecdote probably produces similar effects on the two customers in the bar, at whom it is ostensibly directed; but these effects are superfluous next to that achieved on the policeman, whom Coulahan coyly pretends not to be addressing at all.

But what is it about this perlocutionary performance that is compelling? It is pertinent that Coulahan's act is not merely one of persuasion, but of narration. This narrative artfully moves from a remark on the hot summer just gone in Dublin, to a memory of war in 1915 that moves through a sequence of scenes: 'the heat in the ship'; the air upon arrival, 'so thin and so hot that you wouldn't feel yourself breathing it'; the soldiers' rubber soles melting into the quayside; the march to barracks, 'the dirtiest – sweatiest – stickiest – and driest march we ever had'; the trek into the desert to fight Arabs, rubber shoes melting once more so that 'the feet began to be roasted like two joints with a fire under them' (*PT*, 127, 128, 129, 130, 132). These scenes are followed by accounts of how 'the sun began to come down on top of us'; the soldier's body dries up, with his tongue 'dry and cracked' and expanding in the heat and his eyebrows burning off; the battalion is forced to discard its water bottles as the water inside has boiled; and mental fatigue takes over to such a degree that Coulahan 'didn't know whether me head was me heels or whether I was standin' or sittin' [...] I was fallin' all over the place' (*PT*, 133, 134, 135). Coulahan's final emphasis is on the play's titular word: 'And – the – thirst!!! My God, the thirst!!!!' (*PT*, 135). In the longer version of the play, a very similar sequence of events culminates in a more sustained emphasis on that word, which is twice rendered in block capitals; and in the most notable difference between the two scripts, a final speech in which Coulahan talks not only of sand, heat and thirst but of their opposites: 'buttermilk and iced water and beer – not glasses or jugs of it but buckets and buckets, big baths and tanks full of it' (*PT*, 154–5). The speech concludes with a long, winding sentence imagining this liquid relief, the 'river of beer', as Coulahan's sensory narrative finds a recursive Joycean flow: 'until I was all like a bit of blottin'-paper – rotten with beer – rotten and soaked with beer through and through, and THROUGH roarin' mad and drenched to the skin and under it with beer' (*PT*, 155).

Through all this performance Coulahan is not, in Austin's term, trying to 'convince' the Sergeant of a truth. Rather, he is trying to bring about a state of mind by crafting a verbal narrative powerful enough to induce the suspension of disbelief – in the Sergeant, and, by extension, in the theatre audience. This verbal narrative can also be described as an invocation of verbal scenery: 'Scenery which is shown not through visual means but through a character's commentary [...]. This technique is only possible by virtue of a *convention* that is accepted by the spectator, who must imagine the place and the immediate transformation of the place as announced.'[19] The use of verbal scenery in this sense is certainly not new to O'Nolan or his era, as it was a mainstay, for instance, of Renaissance drama with its typically more minimal stage sets. Such a device is celebrated in the prologue of Shakespeare's *Henry V*, wherein the chorus proposes that the players 'On your imaginary forces work', imploring the audience to 'Piece out our imperfections with your thoughts'.[20] O'Nolan's reprisal of this traditional method marks a difference from the 'well-made play' of nineteenth-century naturalism, in that the imaginative resources of verbal scenery transcend the use of physical scenery and furniture. The specific deployment of this theatrical technique for rhetorical purposes is a noticeable feature of O'Nolan's play, with the distinction that it does not only conjure a sense of place, but a physical sensation. The state of mind that Mr Coulahan's performance induces proves intimately connected with the state of the body which gives the play its name. Coulahan's interrupted monologue is deliberately, profoundly somatic, issuing a long series of physical experiences: 'like putting your head into an oven and taking a deep breath'; the tongue 'swelled out till it nearly choked me and got as hard and dry as a big cinder'; 'like bein' grilled – except there was no gravy'; 'Our bodies dryin' up and witherin' into wrinkles like – prunes!' (*PT*, 128, 130, 133, 134). When Coulahan describes 'Every man in a lather of sweat, his clothes stickin' to his skin, and his tongue hangin' outa him lika dog's', it is appropriate that his barfly auditor Peter declares 'me own tongue's beginnin' to hang out like a dog's as well!' (*PT*, 130): the narration aims to be powerful enough to make its listeners reflect what it describes.

To vary the earlier phrase about theatre, Coulahan's narrative works not with the 'outward accidents of illusion' but with 'inward actions of illusion' in the listener's mind. This effect is paradoxical, because, unlike so many of O'Nolan's other studies in rhetoric, this one occurs on stage. In his first notable theatrical work, O'Nolan develops a mode of 'illusion' – or of the crafting of fiction – which does not rely heavily on the physical movement of actors in space (a resource that the stage, unlike the page, grants him), but is more akin to the mode of monologue, interspersed with interlocutors' interpolated responses – a literary technique that he had mastered as a columnist. To be sure, the monologue can itself be a powerful dramatic form, and the impact of Mr Coulahan's monologue perhaps points us to consider how effective the voices of *Cruiskeen Lawn*, for instance, can be in live performance – as has been shown by such performers as Eamon Morrissey and Val O'Donnell. But the central speech of *Thirst* is not only monologue, in the form of extended opinion or humour. This little play's fullest and strangest power is that it centres on the evocation of another place and time – one we cannot see, one that has no 'outward accidents' at all and almost no direct relation to what is in front of us. Mr Coulahan's act of narration here is a kind of intradiegetic performance, a narrative embedded in the broader narrative: a fictional character fictionalising at length, or at any rate (assuming that there might be truth in his story) spinning a yarn. As we have seen, what makes this narrative especially powerful is that it is not simply a sequence of narrated events but a series of perlocutionary linguistic acts attempting to bring about a sequence of bodily experiences of overheating, exhaustion and thirst in the Sergeant, rendered through such evocative rhetoric that the listener's own body is prompted to mimic them.

It is pertinent that the play minimises its own outward accidents of potential distraction, to foreground this perlocutionary performance. If we look again at the script, it is striking how the scene is pared away to a minimum. The opening stage direction states that '*The bar is lit (very badly) by two candles which are set on the counter, one of them stuck in a bottle*' (*PT*, 121). Upon the sound of the Guards outside, both candles are blown out: one of them thus, according to a stage direction, '*completely obliterating JEM*' (*PT*, 124). Reading the play on the page, it is easy to miss the fact that when the Guards first call at the door, the pub's response is to reduce itself almost to nothing:

> *There is complete silence. PETER leans over to the remaining candle and caps the flame in his hands to hide the lights. […] There is no sound at all without. Thirty seconds pass. Suddenly MR C. leaps at the candle and blows it out, leaving nothing visible save the window that is lit by the street-lamp.* (*PT*, 124)

No sound at all; thirty seconds pass; nothing visible. This reduction also temporarily reduces the play itself to nothing. In a short work, thirty seconds of complete silence is a proportionally long hiatus. This period without sound or movement is probably longer than the typical pause in Samuel Beckett's drama. And it is followed by an increase in the scene's darkness as the last candle goes out. What we can perceive here is a certain clearing of dramatic space, as those 'outward accidents of illusion' proper to the theatre are reduced almost to nothing, leaving a blank canvas on which Mr Coulahan can paint his verbal scenery. To be sure, the scene is somewhat reassembled after the Guard enters, but the *milieu* of bar-room banter has been boiled away by this act of radical reduction. Mr Coulahan's monologue needs to claim attention, to redefine the space of the stage so that the characters feel as though they are in the Middle East thirty years earlier: and O'Nolan has enough theatrical instinct to create a kind of vacancy in which that can happen.

Words alone: Irish visions

In *Thirst*, O'Nolan joins an Irish tradition of interest in the performative shaping of reality through language; a process in which verbal richness comes to create a kind of virtual world that seems as substantial as the actual world. This mode has been identified by Terry Eagleton, who proposes that 'performative rather than representational pieces of discourse' were historically characteristic of an Irish society '[where] literary realism never really took root, and where the frontier between art and politics was never exact'.[21] Eagleton traces a version of this impulse through the Irish Revival, positing a 'conflict between ideal and reality' which writers of the era handle in differing ways. Thus the poetry of Yeats sometimes seeks in idealist fashion to 'close the gap between mind and world by seeing the world as the upshot of a performative act of mind'.[22] The poet who could presume to undertake the ritual of commemorating the 1916 Easter Rising ('I write it out in a verse') had commenced his career rhapsodising that: 'The wandering earth herself may be / Only a sudden flaming word' and that 'words alone are certain good'.[23] A noteworthy archaic instance of such a performative Irish tradition is the curse. Marguerite Quintelli-Neary, in a study that identifies the presence of traditional folklore in modern Irish literature, has observed the persistence of the *geis* or magical prohibition from Irish mythology in the work of twentieth-century Irish writers including Joyce and Flann O'Brien.[24] The performative mode of the curse can be seen both in Yeats (as in the bitter poem 'The Fish') and in *At Swim-Two-Birds*, where Moling's consequential curse upon Sweeny is implicitly echoed in the verbal punishment inflicted on Dermot Trellis by acts of narration.

The enactment of this theme on stage may be different from its avowal on the poetic page, yet it remains potent. Yeats himself confronted the practicalities of theatre and continued to explore the themes of performativity and the imagination in this context. *At The Hawk's Well* (1916), one of his most celebrated pieces of minimalist drama, takes place in '*any bare space before a wall against which stands a patterned screen*', and commences:

> I call to the eye of the mind
> A well long choked up and dry
> And boughs long stripped by the wind,
> And I call to the mind's eye
> Pallor of an ivory face,
> Its lofty dissolute air,
> A man climbing up to a place
> The salt sea wind has swept bare.[25]

The play thus starts with an explicitly performative incantation: in the largely '*bare space*' of the stage, a rhetorical utterance ritually creates imaginative place and characters. The tone could hardly differ more greatly from Mr Coulahan, yet the use of verbal scenery to 'call to the eye of the mind' an otherwise absent scene is a feature that Yeats's short, vivid play shares with O'Nolan's.

Such explorations of performativity can be found elsewhere in Yeats's drama. In his 1917 play *The Cat and the Moon*, a blind beggar regains his sight by virtue of a cure consisting of an evocation of the Holy Trinity: 'In the name of the Father, the Son and the Holy Spirit I give this Blind Man sight and I make this Lame Man blessed.' The blind beggar immediately declares: 'I see it all now, the blue sky and the big ash-tree and the well and the flat stone – all as I have heard the people say – and the things the praying people put on the stone, the beads and the candles and the leaves torn out of prayer-books, and the hairpins and the buttons. It is a great sight and a blessed sight' – though he is not virtuous enough to see the saint who has blessed him.[26] Not only has a verbal formula altered the beggar's bodily condition, but his subsequent speech redoubles the performative power of rhetoric with an evocation of verbal scenery, a theatrical convention which, as we have seen, is relevant to Mr Coulahan's performance.[27] Different again in tone is *The Pot of Broth* (1904), a short play co-written by Yeats and Lady Augusta Gregory, in which a tramp deceives a couple into believing that he is making broth from nothing but a stone.[28] The Tramp makes plain to the audience, in a phrase quoted at the head of this essay, that he will have to rely on his verbal ingenuity – 'my share of talk' – to persuade the homesteaders to accept his version of reality. While his trick is achieved by inserting cabbage, onions, ham and chicken to the pot, this is occluded by his continual discourse, not merely celebrating the purported magical powers of his stone but concocting a tale of how he acquired it from 'a little old man [...] and he taking off a hareskin coat', who alternately seemed 'as small as a nut' and tall enough that 'I thought his head to be in the stars'. The Tramp goes on to sing an elaborate series of songs that he claims are the words of the village boys lovelorn for the woman of the house: at their conclusion, the man of the house declares that 'he has the poor woman bewitched'.[29] The tale staged by Yeats and Gregory bears quite a strong structural resemblance to *Thirst* in representing a man who improvises verbal effects for short-term practical impact, manoeuvring himself out of a tight spot by the power of rhetoric and linguistic performance. Hugh Kenner describes *The Pot of Broth* as an allegory of theatre itself, 'in which we see with our eyes everything the actors do and yet are hoodwinked by their rites of glory'.[30]

To be sure, these figures and instances are from diverse backgrounds. Yeats's penchant for the performative declaration that brings a state of affairs into being expresses his affectations of Anglo-Irish grandeur (a quality that he associated with Gregory and her ancestral home in Galway), while O'Nolan's equivalents (such as the global pronouncements of Sir Myles na gCopaleen) are typically the product of a mocking sensibility. Yet the common thread here is an investment in the power of language to compensate for, remake or displace the world at large; and this impulse is overdetermined by the relative poverty of Ireland, through years of agrarianism, colonial exploitation and famine, all of which Myles had already given a comic climax in *An Béal Bocht* a year before writing *Thirst*. Indeed, such performativity can be traced in *An Béal Bocht* itself, in the novel's emphasis on the formative power of language: from the 'good books' that inexorably shape 'Irish fate', to the ritual in which pupils, newly arrived at school, are uniformly renamed 'Jams O'Donnell' in a bid to induct them from an Irish to a colonial, Anglophone identity (*CN*, 425). If an ironic discrepancy between a paltry real and an inflated imaginary can be seen through much of O'Nolan's work, *Thirst* is a peculiarly explicit enactment of this dynamic, which has been too little recognised as such.

A writer pertinent to *Thirst* in this regard is John Millington Synge, who in Seamus Deane's words 'found a means to incorporate the energy of violence into the energy of speech', and in Mary C. King's estimation showed a 'sensitivity to language as action'.[31] The comparison is incongruous, in that Myles na gCopaleen could be scathing about Synge: 'That comic ghoul with his wakes and mugs of porter should be destroyed finally and forever by having a drama festival at which all his plays should be revived for the benefit of the younger people of to-day.'[32] But such disavowals of the earlier writer do not in themselves disprove a resemblance or relation. A full review of O'Nolan's relation to Synge remains to be undertaken, though Dieter Fuchs's contribution to the present volume, demonstrating the links between *The Third Policeman* and Synge's *The Playboy of the Western World*, represents one new instance of the scope of such research. In the meantime, a consideration of one of Synge's plays can further adumbrate that project and show *Thirst* in a fresh comparative light.

Synge's *The Well of the Saints* depicts a rural setting – 'Some lonely mountainous district in the east of Ireland' – where a blind married couple, the decrepit old tramps Martin and Mary Doul, are indulged by the local population into believing that they are attractive and desirable.[33] A visiting saint offers to cure their blindness with holy water. Following the Douls' recovery of their sight, both are horrified at each other's true appearance. Reunited in the third act, the couple have lost their sight again and begin once more to talk themselves into a belief in their own physical attributes. With the return of the saint, they are offered the chance of permanently renewed sight. Mary is equivocal; Martin is appalled at the prospect, smashing the vial of holy water and leading his wife away into the wilderness, in the hope of better pastures elsewhere but perhaps, in fact, to their deaths. Sight had seemed the most precious commodity that the blind couple could gain, but the saint's blessing turns out to be, in effect, a curse. Martin Doul vividly, if with apparent perversity, describes the awful prospects available to those who can see: 'For it's a raw, beastly day we do have each day, till I do be thinking it's well for the blind don't be seeing the like of them grey clouds driving on the hill, and don't be looking on people with their noses red.'[34]

What this play shares with *Thirst* is an interest in what cannot be seen but only imagined, and the curious relation of such imagined goods to physical reality. 'Illusions' are made by other means than the 'outward accidents' disdained by *At Swim-Two-Birds*'s narrator. In *Thirst*, the dark bar provides the empty space for an alternative world of light and heat to be evoked with words. In *The Well of the Saints*, the central characters on stage are – initially and finally, if not in between – unable to see the 'reality' around them that the audience, like the other characters, can. The Douls (whose name derives from the Irish for blind, '*dall*') are often referred to as 'dark', a synonym for 'blind' in Hiberno-English. The semantic connection of blindness to the literal 'darkness' of *Thirst*, the bar with its candles snuffed, is incidental yet telling, confirming the use of that darkness as a space for imagination.

A certain critical tendency to connect physical blindness and artistic vision is venerable, arguably reaching from the legend of the blind Homer to T.S. Eliot's comparison of James Joyce to Milton on the grounds that both wrote with unusual auditory flamboyance in compensation for their failing sight.[35] This tradition, whatever its critical suggestiveness, is distinct from an empirical consideration of the diverse experience of blind or partially sighted people. More concretely and locally, Einat Adar draws attention to a tradition within Irish drama of blind characters who regain their sight, and further points out that this tradition can be connected to a consideration of the issue of sight within Irish philosophy of the eighteenth century. As noted above, Yeats's *The Cat and the Moon* is one such work, which Adar also links to plays by Brian Friel and Samuel Beckett. But *The Well of the Saints* remains the canonical Irish play in which this theme is most fully explored. Adar notes that Synge's play 'contains an inherent critique of the assumption that the sighted experience of reality is superior', as the Douls 'enjoy [their] own world which is as rich and satisfactory for them as the world of the seeing'.[36]

Synge was a cosmopolitan who could refer to Mallarmé and Huysmans,[37] yet his *Well* cannot achieve its effects through rarefied textuality: like *Thirst*, *The Well of the Saints* is made for the stage. Its characters have material life for an audience most of whom are assumed to be able to see what is on stage (though new critical work in disability studies would remind us of the potentially different experiences of blind or partially sighted audience members).[38] Yet the play puts into severe question the value of such sight. The very vision that allows us to see the actors, props and sets is what is ultimately disavowed by the play's central characters, for whom sight is literally a mixed blessing.

In an aphoristic moment, Martin Doul tells the local beauty Molly Byrne that 'it's few sees anything but them is blind for a space'.[39] In such declarations, the play does not simply counterpose blindness and vision but suggests a more intricate relation between them: true vision is declared to be dependent on anterior blindness. Again, Doul talks of 'seeing you this day, seeing you, maybe, the way no man has seen you in the world'.[40] The sense is of a different register of vision, charged with unfamiliarity and fervent imagination. Ultimately, Martin Doul is content to do without external vision entirely, as his remarkable closing speech explains:

Isn't it finer sights ourselves had a while since and we sitting dark smelling the sweet beautiful smells do be rising in the warm nights and hearing the swift flying things racing in the air [...], till we'd be looking up in our own minds into a grand sky, and seeing lakes, and broadening rivers, and hills are waiting for the spade and plough.[41]

Doul's superior 'vision' – comprising 'finer sights' – derives in part from the empirical traces he receives through hearing and scent. But it transcends these sensations to evoke a whole other realm, one seemingly more desirable and fertile than that of the (fictional) real world around him. As Katharine Worth puts it, Doul has been 'holding up by the force of imagination the golden landscape he and Mary inhabit': the audience comes to perceive 'the extraordinary power they have to make a self-contained, inner world of rich possibilities'.[42]

Here the play offers a parallel to the dynamic of *Thirst*: for in that play, too, the audience is confronted with physical realities and solid bodies – the bar, the drinkers, the Sergeant – yet these are steadily, strategically demoted in favour of an alternate reality fashioned by rhetoric and intradiegetic narration creating verbal scenery. Most of Coulahan's narration, as we have seen, aims to evoke discomfort; but his closing speech in the long version of *Thirst*, with its liquid vision of 'buttermilk and iced water and beer' (*PT*, 155), is the one moment where he offers a lyrical, desirable note that might chime with Martin Doul's utopian inner flight of 'finer sights' and 'broadening rivers'.[43]

'Words alone are certain good', wrote the young Yeats; certainly, words in these two plays have rare power to reconfigure the world. Synge, with his 'deployment of language as transformative action' as King puts it, does have an interest in the performative, in Austin's primary sense.[44] After all, the single most transformative utterance in this play is the blessing of the saint, a precise instance of Austin's concept of discourse as action, which Synge writes out in Latin.[45] More generally, too, words are seen to mould reality. Before Synge's play starts, the Douls have improvised a world of words that proves superior to the physical world they actually inhabit. The audience detects an ironic discrepancy, which may be both comic and pathetic. Yet the other characters, who have convinced them of their good looks, tell each other that they have provided 'great joy and pride' by fostering this illusion.[46] A protracted, collective verbal fallacy has sustained the Douls in relative contentment: the opposite, in a sense, of the verbal evocation with which Coulahan makes the Sergeant increasingly uncomfortable. Martin Doul's evocation of the world to which he wants to take Molly Byrne – 'Let you come on now,

I'm saying, to the lands of Iveragh and the Reeks of Cork, where you won't set down the width of your two feet and not be crushing fine flowers and making sweet smells in the air'[47] – is also an ultimately unsuccessful attempt at a perlocutionary act. But what is more striking is that the Douls' powers of persuasion operate not on others (as Coulahan's do on the Sergeant) but on themselves. Rhetoric works to conjure one's own world, never mind another's. In *Thirst*, the rhetoric of verbal scenery acts as a tactical means of deceit, to achieve worldly ends. In Synge's *Well*, rhetoric is more a yarn spun across one's own inner landscape, embroidered to make an alternative vista in the face of an unforgiving visible realm.

One of Martin Doul's most vivid speeches dramatises the contrast between real and imagined worlds, as he rhetorically asks if his fate is not like

> a bad black day when I was roused up and found I was the like of the little children do be listening to the stories of an old woman, and do be dreaming after in the dark night that it's in grand houses of gold they are, with speckled horses to ride, and do be waking again, in a short while, and they destroyed with the cold, and the thatch dripping maybe, and the starved ass braying in the yard?[48]

Here Synge's dramatic action has great ironic force. For Doul's speech about rhetorical illusion and material reality is itself cast in rhetoric so baroque that it conjures a vision in itself. It is not merely physical blindness and sight that is at stake, then, but the performative power of language to reshape perception. Synge is at an advantage here, for what Yeats synaesthetically called his 'highly coloured musical language' is among the most sumptuous of its era.[49]

Conclusion

In the preface to *The Playboy of the Western World*, Synge talks of the 'richness' of peasant speech on which he purports to draw, 'as fully flavoured as a nut or apple', a quality largely unavailable to 'the modern literature of towns'.[50] O'Nolan, especially in the *persona* of Myles na gCopaleen, was in this sense a writer of the town. His language – at any rate in *Thirst* – does not purport to be beautiful in Synge's sense. It belongs to a different register: the mid-twentieth-century Dublin working- and lower-middle class, not the rural peasantry of (as *The Well of the Saints*'s stage direction indicates) 'one or more centuries ago'. Yet as we have seen, it finds its own affective force. O'Nolan in

Thirst hits on the particular seam of Irish creativity that Synge had mined and lends it an incarnation that is urban and demotic.

In this sense, *Thirst* can encourage us to view O'Nolan from a fresh angle. He emerges as closer to the imagination of the Revival than his critical reputation would suggest, maintaining its recurrent themes of performativity and imagination. Yet he also restages this tradition by his own lights. Thus, whereas the enactment of these themes in Yeats and Synge persistently takes place in a rural setting, O'Nolan's version is urban. The country peasantry and beggars who typically populate the pages of Yeats and Synge are characteristically replaced, in O'Nolan, by the Dublin 'gurrier' and barfly.[51] The high ambition characteristic of the canonical Revival writers, while certainly flavoured with their own irony, is displaced by the bathos of O'Nolan's play, concluding as it does with a frenzy for drink. By the same token, whereas in both Synge and Yeats the character invested with the authority of performative speech is a saint, in O'Nolan's play this figure is a publican. Where the saint's Latin blessing is at the heart of Synge's plot, at the heart of O'Nolan's is the publican's canny bid to corrupt the guardian of the law.

At the climax of *The Playboy of the Western World*, Synge's most emblematic line declares 'a great gap between a gallous story and a dirty deed'.[52] In a different context, *Thirst* stages such a 'gap' between story and deed. In doing so, it shows us something that Austin helps us to perceive: how a story can itself be a deed, one that makes the world anew through words. In this, Myles na gCopaleen had a little more in common with Synge than he would have admitted. He made a distinct contribution to the modern Irish dramatic tradition, by letting his own gift for language take over the stage. In this regard, the criticism of O'Nolan's drama for its verbosity misses the mark. Drawing on Austin to view language as a form of action, we can also situate O'Nolan more firmly in an Irish theatrical tradition to which he has too often appeared marginal. By the same token, we can begin to reconsider the place of drama within O'Nolan's own *oeuvre*. It emerges less as a brief, unsuccessful diversion: more, as his letters suggest, as a form in which he retained interest throughout his career, and also one that readily echoes and combines with aspects of the writing for which he remains better known.

10

'The Fausticity of Kelly'

Brian O'Nolan, Goethe and the politics of *Faustus Kelly*

TOBIAS W. HARRIS

Keith Hopper has argued that the Faustian myth is, with Joris-Karl Huysmans's *À Rebours*, the 'other dominant intertextual framework underlying the existential outcome of *The Third Policeman*'. Hopper proposes that with 'the help of Marlowe (and Goethe), *The Third Policeman* becomes a tale of a scholar who sells his soul to attain the book of knowledge'.[1] This interpretation takes 'Anti-Cartesianism' as the 'starting point' for the novel's 'Menippean satire' and closes by resolving the murder mystery of who kills the unnamed narrator: 'Descartes dunit; Descartes killed Noman.'[2] This anti-Enlightenment reading of both the Faust myth and its function in *The Third Policeman* follows the work of Frankfurt School thinkers such as Theodor Adorno, who suggests that the 'epic form' of Goethe's *Faust Part Two*, 'which calls itself a tragedy', reflects humanity's fall into a rationally administered society: 'form in the process of falling under the statute of limitations'.[3]

To support and develop Hopper's identification of *Faust* as a key intertext for *The Third Policeman*, one might compare Mephistopheles's famous words in *Faust Part One*, 'Ich bin der Geist, der stets verneint' (I am the spirit which eternally denies) with the principle of negative responses espoused by the dead Philip Mathers in the novel (*CN*, 241–7).[4] Or, widening the lens, one could relate the examples of artificial life in *Faust Part Two* (Wagner's laboratory-created homunculus and Euphorion, the hybrid offspring of Faust and Helen) to the theory of aestho-autogamy in *At Swim-Two-Birds* and its manifestation in Orlick, that novel's own hybrid offspring of characters who exist on different narratological and ontological levels.

Laying the groundwork for such a broadened understanding of the role of Faustian intertexts and resonances across O'Nolan's writing, I identify and historicise their narratological dynamics, satirical functions and political stakes in the text that most clearly advertises such a connection: *Faustus Kelly*, a three-act play written by O'Nolan in 1942 and performed for ten nights at the Abbey Theatre from January to February 1943 (*PT*, vii). Specifically, I explore the potential of the Faust myth to galvanise a reading of *Faustus Kelly* as an intertextual and satirical work which is in dialogue with both Goethe and the surge in similarly politicised Faustian works during the rise of fascism in 1930s and '40s Europe. O'Nolan's satire, I propose, comprises one strand in a web of texts which engage with the Faustian *topos* to present sceptical encounters with the themes of Enlightenment and modernity. These retellings of the Faust story include Karl Kraus's modernist montage-text *Die Dritte Walpurgisnacht* (The Third Walpurgis Night; 1933, published 1952) and Dorothy Sayers's play *The Devil to Pay* (1939); and, following O'Nolan's own contribution to the genre, Paul Valéry's short play *Mon Faust* (1946) and Thomas Mann's novel *Doktor Faustus* (1947). Read in the context of this broader European network of Second World War-era Faustian texts, *Faustus Kelly* emerges more clearly as a historically situated critique of ideological nationalist rhetoric and its attendant moral delinquency. This resituating of *Faustus Kelly* compels us to re-evaluate readings which examine O'Nolan's self-professed 'Abbey play' mainly in terms of its local Irish context.[5] My argument goes further by proposing specific local political targets for O'Nolan's satire: I demonstrate that the portrayal of Kelly parodies both the rhetoric and political programme of Fianna Fáil in the 1926–32 period and far-right Irish nationalist groups in the early 1940s. Thus, I argue that the negative Faustian thematics enacted through the final failure and false redemption of Kelly satirically associate Irish political experience with the anti-Semitic language politics of Europe's descent into totalitarianism in ways that amount to an anti-fascist gesture.

Faust and Kelly

O'Nolan studied Goethe's *Faust* when reading German for the final year of his undergraduate degree, in 1931–2. The lack of critical discussion of *Faustus Kelly* as a text which is situated in the Faust tradition may owe something to the influence of Anthony Cronin's early biographical account of this time.

In *No Laughing Matter: The life and times of Flann O'Brien*, Cronin claims that O'Nolan

> speaks of having to take it on trust that Goethe's play was a 'masterpiece'. He found *Faust* turgid, he says, when he read it at UCD [University College Dublin] but acknowledges that this may have been due to his knowledge of German being very poor. If it had improved afterwards, Myles would certainly have been the first to say so.[6]

Cronin's account is much more widely available than the source for these remarks, which he does not cite: a short article written in January 1963 by O'Nolan as 'Myles na Gopaleen' for the *RTV Guide* entitled 'The Fausticity of Kelly'. Along with a 1954 *Cruiskeen Lawn* column which I discuss below, this article is a key document for our understanding of O'Nolan's positioning of the play in relation to its sources (or at least how he represented them in later years). The full article reveals that O'Nolan's engagement with the Faust myth is more substantial than Cronin's summary suggests. He begins with a succinct but astute history of the myth. Faust, writes O'Nolan,

> first appeared (whether man or myth) in the Middle Ages, about the time of the Renaissance and the Reformation.
>
> Intrinsically, though, the legend is substantively of Jewish origin, dating back to about the beginning of the Christian era. The latter-day manifestation of Faust may be said to date from mention of him by Johann Mannel (died 1560), historian to Maximillian II: he called Faust 'a disgraceful beast and sewer of many devils'. [...] The dramatic potentiality of such a character, whether a necromancer or charlatan, was self-evident.
>
> At Frankfurt in 1587 Johan Spies published his 'Historia von D. Johann Fausten', a work reprinted many times and pirated. Similar works quickly followed but, as for drama, the pioneer was Christopher Marlowe, and his play was published in 1604.
>
> That and many other continental plays on the same theme ended with the damnation of Faust, but the advent of, first, Lessing and then Goethe led to the cleansing of the Faust legend in the interests of elevating the minds of audiences by arranging for Faust's eventual salvation.[7]

Only at this point, having taken pains to elaborate on the myth's history, does O'Nolan make the remarks Cronin cites about his first encounter with Goethe as an undergraduate:

My own first confrontation with this shady man was at U.C.D. when I took German as a subsidiary subject for an arts degree and found myself pitched headlong in Goethe's masterpiece.

I say 'masterpiece' for as such it is universally acknowledged, though I found the text pretty turgid: but then, my knowledge of German was very poor.[8]

Finally, O'Nolan situates *Faustus Kelly* in this wider tradition and emphasises its political context, taking a pot-shot at Cork politicians who are satirised by the figure of the town clerk in the play:

Many years afterwards I entered the civil service (from which I was later to escape, thank God) and for some seven years my duties as a private secretary necessitated almost daily attendance at Leinster House.

Garrulity is a feeble word to describe what I encountered in Dáil Eireann, and my innocence at the beginning may be judged from the fact that I marvelled that a certain poorly-dressed deputy could speak French so rapidly that I could not grasp his meaning.

Some weeks went by before I realised he was speaking English of the Cork intonation.

The play *Faustus Kelly* arose somehow from that Leinster House gab.[9]

O'Nolan praises the actors involved in the production and then closes his article with an ambivalent reference to negative opinions about the play: 'Many people told me afterwards in strict confidence that it was a very bad play. Maybe. I personally find Shakespeare's *King Lear* unendurable.' However, O'Nolan's admission in this article does not quite square with the archival evidence, which indicates that while he may have laboured his way through *Faust* in German, he also read it as an undergraduate in English. In 1987, two years prior to the first publication of Cronin's biography, Peter Costello and Peter van de Kamp had already presented photographic proof that O'Nolan was not constrained by the language barrier he attests to later. They printed an image of his signed copy of Lefevre's nineteenth-century English translation of *Faust Part One*, in its second edition of 1843, dated to 1932, the final year of O'Nolan's BA degree.[10]

The sense that *Faustus Kelly* is closely informed by O'Nolan's knowledge of the Faust tradition, and of the transformative moment of Goethe's *Faust*, is evidenced not only by 'The Fausticity of Kelly' but also by O'Nolan's correspondence about it at the time. *The Collected Letters of Flann O'Brien* reveals O'Nolan to be closely involved in the Dublin theatre scene. He wrote parts in *Faustus Kelly* specifically for certain Abbey players and became friends with Hilton Edwards of the Gate Theatre.[11] When pitching it to Edwards on 20 June 1942, he describes *Faustus Kelly* as paralleling the Faust theme 'closely throughout on what is meant to be an uproarious plane' (*L*, 119).

There is also evidence to suggest that O'Nolan became more proficient at German than he attests to in the 1963 article. His personal library contains some of the books bought for his undergraduate degree: a German-language edition of *Goethe's Poems* along with German editions of works by Heinrich Heine and Friedrich Schiller, all inscribed with his signature and dated to 1931.[12] The annotations indicate a rapidly developing knowledge of German in this period. In his copy of Heine's *Die Harzreise*, O'Nolan annotates the text with English translations. In his volumes of Schiller's *Wallenstein*, O'Nolan begins annotating the text with cross-references and notes written in German. It is intriguing to bear in mind that Samuel Beckett also made extensive notes on Goethe's *Faust* in the early 1930s in advance of his trip to Nazi Germany in 1936–7.[13] This was in the same year that, according to his passport stamps and a book of postcards, O'Nolan himself travelled to Germany between August and September.[14]

O'Nolan's university reading is subsequently mobilised in dozens of *Cruiskeen Lawn* columns which refer to German culture or are written partially in German, including the nine published in the 1940s which specifically reference Goethe.[15] Sometimes it is a light touch. In December 1945, Myles provides a source when the Brother asks him, 'Did you ever hear that sayin The Dead Ride Fast? / *Yes. It is from Goethe. Die Toten reiten schnell.*'[16] In May 1946, Goethe is listed in an eclectic assortment of poets Myles claims to have influenced, including the French Renaissance poets François Villon, Pierre de Ronsard, the Irish war poet Francis Ledwidge, the Austro-Hungarian modernist Rainer Maria Rilke and the Latin poet Catullus.[17] In 1948, several columns quote from the edition of *Goethe's Poems* O'Nolan purchased back in 1931. They show him deploying Goethe as an example of German literature to complicate and subvert debates which are freighted with nationalist ideology. In May he quotes Goethe's epigram '*Demut*' (Humility) and a stanza from Goethe's poem '*Rastlose Liebe*' (Restless Love) as part of a wry send-up of the commemorations of the Irish Rebellion of 1798.[18] In November, he invokes Goethe's verse in this context again, commenting on criticism of Ireland's withdrawal from the British Commonwealth in 1948 by quoting a German proverb he presents as lines from Goethe: '*Kommst du in des Königs Haus / Geh blind hinein und stumm heraus*' (Should you come into the King's house / Go blindly in and mutely out).[19] A December 1948 column about the publication of *The Pillar of Cloud* by Francis Stuart – an Irish modernist poet whose political beliefs led him to assist Nazi Germany with propaganda broadcasts during the war and who subsequently returned to the Irish academy – begins by presenting 'a good wan from the works of W.B. Goethe'. Myles combines the beginning of Goethe's poem '*In das Stammbuch von Friedrich Maximilian Moors*' (In the family album of Friedrich Maximilian Moors) with the end of W.B. Yeats's poem 'September 1913'.[20] O'Nolan consistently deploys Goethe as part of a montage strategy which subverts nationalist sentiments by generating what Catherine Flynn has described elsewhere as 'a series of overlapping identifications'; in this case between Irish and German literary history.[21]

Cruiskeen Lawn also refers to *The Tragical History of the Life and Death of Doctor Faustus* by Christopher Marlowe. Marlowe's play exists in two versions: the A-Text, published in 1604; and the substantially edited and censored B-Text, published in 1616.[22] *Doctor Faustus* was broadcast on BBC radio on 28 November 1942, just two months before *Faustus Kelly* opened.[23] In 1944, Myles discusses the Faust plays of the 'German composer Gounod Meyer – or was it Goethe Meyer' alongside 'another by Maher Lowe, the Limerick genius'. In this column, Myles says that Faust is a 'fascinating subject' and, alluding to *Faustus Kelly*, invites the placement of his own work in the tradition when he writes that he 'often thought it would make a damn good play if one changed it about a bit, give it a sort of Irish atmosphere'.[24]

As O'Nolan observes in the 1963 'Fausticity of Kelly' article, a common source for Marlowe and Goethe was the *Historia Von. D. John Fausten: dem weitbeschreyten Zauberer and Schwartzkünstleri*, a chapbook published in Frankfurt in 1587 by Johann Spies. It is 'a collection of stories rather than a history of Faust's life, a montage of episodes which shows a man who seeks knowledge and pleasure at any price'.[25] This popular edition was translated into English the same year by an unknown writer, P.F. Gent, as 'The Historie of the damnable life, and deserved death of *Doctor John Faustus*', the version which Marlowe used for his model.[26] In turn, Marlowe's own play was translated and widely performed in Europe. By the time that, as O'Nolan observes, first Lessing and then Goethe decided to work on the subject in the late eighteenth century, the Marlovian Faust had gone through a series of pantomime-like iterations, including a puppet-show.[27]

Goethe spent his entire life working on his *Faust* and left four versions of the text which bear witness to his evolving aesthetic prerogatives. The first, known as the *Urfaust*, which 'Goethe brought to Weimar in 1775, read to small circles, but never published', is 'a bourgeois tragedy in typical Storm-and-Stress fashion'. The second is *Faust: Ein Fragment*, which Goethe published as part of his collected works in 1790. In 1808 he completed *Faust Part One*, which integrates the Gretchen story that had formed the principal subject of the earlier versions into something resembling the *Faust* myth and adds scenes including the first Walpurgis Night episode.[28] In 1832, the year of Goethe's death, he published *Faust: Der Tragödie zweiter Teil in fünf Akten* (The Tragedy's Second Part in Five Acts). This vastly more complex work includes the sections which meditate on the relationship between human culture and the natural world, including the second Walpurgis Night and the closing scenes in which Faust reclaims land from the sea to build a new territory where citizens can live 'Not safely, but in free resilience'.[29]

An analysis of the plot of *Faustus Kelly* shows that it is more closely modelled on Goethe's *Faust Part One* than any other source material. In *Faust Part One* and *Faustus Kelly*, as Zuzana Neubauerová has also observed, Faust strives to win the affections of a woman named Margaret, who ultimately abandons him in disgust at his behaviour.[30] This narrative trajectory is in line with what is likely to have been O'Nolan's main textual source, the Lefevre translation of *Part One*.

Summary	*Faust Part One (Lefevre)*	*Faustus Kelly*
Man meets Mephisto	Following the 'Prelude to Faust' debate between a theatre Director, Dramatist and a Facetious Friend and then the 'Prologue in Heaven', we meet Faust in his professional context with his books in Scene I where he first summons up a 'Spirit'. Faust is interrupted by the 'brainless lad' Wagner. In Scene II, the next morning, Faust and Wagner walk amongst the people outside the town gates. Mephistopheles appears as a black poodle who follows Faust home. In Scene III the poodle transforms itself and Mephistopheles appears 'clad as a travelling student'.[31] In Scene IV Faust signs the blood pact but makes it conditional on a wager about whether he can ever be absolutely fulfilled: 'If e'er I to the moment say, / "Thou art so beauteous, rest, I pray l" / Then bind me in eternal chains'.[32]	Kelly signs the pact with the devil in the dumb-show prologue sequence and in Act I he is introduced in the public, professional setting of the urban council chamber. Kelly's behaviour is aloof from his colleagues, who either despise him or, in the case of the town clerk, act as his faithful servant. The Stranger is introduced as a newly appointed rate-collector. They have an agreement for the Stranger to help Kelly to be elected to Dáil Éireann as a T.D. (*Teachta Dála*, essentially a member of parliament), supplying 'money and votes and everything that is required' (*PT*, 57)

Summary	Faust Part One (Lefevre)	Faustus Kelly
Falls in love with a girl called Margaret	In Scene VII Faust sees the young girl called Margaret (or Gretchen) and asks Mephistopheles to help him win her heart. The rest of *Part One* revolves around their romance. Margaret is characterised by her Christian faith, and this strains her relationship with Faust when she doubts that he is 'a Christian true'.[33]	Kelly is courting the widow Margaret Crockett, a '*coarse, dowdy lady of about thirty-five*' (*PT*, 73). The Stranger has promised 'Your love for Mrs Crockett will prosper' (*PT*, 57) as part of their agreement. Margaret is a devout Christian and is suspicious of Kelly's claims to virtuousness.
Who has a jealous brother	In Scene XIX we meet Valentine, Margaret's brother, who has arrived because he has heard that her honour, previously unparalleled, has been compromised. Valentine will finally tell Margaret she is 'the strumpet of the town'.[34]	In Act II we meet Captain James Shaw, here to 'talk to [his] sister [...] about a blighter called Kelly' who has 'damaged and destroyed her fair name'. He tells Kelly: 'You have given her the reputation of a prostitute in her own town' (*PT*, 75, 78).
Man wins the duel ...	In the same scene, Valentine dies after fighting a duel with Faust, who receives demonic assistance from Mephistopheles.	In Act III, Captain Shaw is defeated in the election by Kelly, who receives demonic assistance from the Stranger.
... but loses the girl	In Scene XXIV, Margaret is shamed and imprisoned for the death of the child she bore by Faust. Margaret rejects his attempted rescue and, as she dies, is spared by God from damnation. Faust is distraught at what he has done.	Margaret is shamed and appalled by Shaw's drunkenness, who is in '*the last blibbering stages of intoxication*' and blames Kelly for it: 'You're the cause of it and you'll have to answer for it before God'. She storms out and Kelly is left '*pathetically broken*' (*PT*, 100, 101, 103).

Fig. 10.1. Comparison of plot elements in Goethe's *Faust* and *Faustus Kelly*.

This comparison reveals that much of the dramatic action of O'Nolan's version is drawn from the plot which constitutes the majority of the *Urfaust* and *Faust: Ein Fragment* texts – making up the latter half of Goethe's *Part One* – and which, Ronald Gray argues, 'has nothing essentially Faustian about it'.[35]

This subtle relationship demonstrates the predominance of Goethe's *Faust Part One* as a source text over *Faust Part Two* and the versions by Marlowe. The correspondence also highlights O'Nolan's labyrinthine approach to the interpolation of source material: the subplot which is inserted into the existing story in Goethe's *Faust Part One* becomes the main template for *Faustus Kelly*. However, O'Nolan is also clearly cognisant of the implications of the final scenes of *Faust Part Two*. At the play's close, by sparing Kelly from hell when the Stranger tears up their contract, O'Nolan also includes a form of the salvation of Faust which, as he notes in 'The Fausticity of Kelly', is pivotal in Goethe's transformation of the early modern myth.

Gray argues that not only is Faust's damnation evaded in Goethe's version but also that Goethe modifies the wager which is agreed between Faust and Mephistopheles in ways that render even the possibility of Faust's damnation uncertain. First, in the 'Prologue in Heaven' scene, there is a 'first wager' between Mephistopheles and God with the result that, 'in effect, Faust can never go wrong, never so wrong as to deserve damnation'.[36] Secondly, the wager which is subsequently agreed between Faust and Mephistopheles is different in Goethe's version:

> Traditionally, Faust merely bargained away his soul for earthly power. Goethe's Faust inserts a proviso; his soul is only to be forfeit to the devil if he ever remains satisfied with the passing moment, if he ever becomes so enamoured of such a moment that he would like it to remain his forever. [...] To make matters more difficult, Mephistopheles misunderstands Faust's proviso and continues to talk as though the legendary pact were in operation. [...] In doing this, Mephisto is acting in the role ordained for him by the Lord of pricking Faust on to further discontent, ensuring he continues to strive.[37]

If, as Gray suggests, 'striving is to be the basis on which Faust's salvation becomes possible', Mephistopheles is an accessory to Faust's redemption instead of the agent of his damnation.[38]

This transformative or redemptive version of the Faust myth would have been familiar to O'Nolan from the Irish tradition. An tAthair Peadar Ua Laoghaire's *Séadna*, an Irish-language retelling, draws on Goethe's reinvention to produce a redemptive account in which the protagonist is improved morally by his encounter with the devil (informed by a wider folk tradition of stories about outsmarting the devil which also influenced Goethe). As well as being 'explicitly referenced in *An Béal Bocht*'s satire of "na dea-leabhair"',[39]

Séadna is also source material for *Faustus Kelly*. The cautious use of 'the Stranger' to describe Mephistopheles, for example, mimics Ua Laoghaire's substitution of a more demonic moniker for his euphemism, 'the Black Man'.[40] The waves of enthusiasm for German culture in the Irish literature and literary commentary of the 1790s and 1830s had provided Ua Laoghaire and O'Nolan with several nineteenth-century Irish adaptations of Goethe's *Faust* to draw upon: from Charles Robert Maturin's *Melmoth the Wanderer* (1820) to James Clarence Mangan's 'The Thirty Flasks' (1838) – a somewhat burlesque variation on the Faust pact, set in Germany, where 'a young man, impoverished by gambling, contracts to sell his stature by inches to a sorcerer' – and the redemption of Edward Kenealy's large-scale parody *Goethe: A new pantomime* (1850), in which Goethe himself, playing 'the role of Faust', is saved from Hell by Kenealy in the guise of 'The Poet'.[41]

The ending of *Faustus Kelly* can be related directly to that of Goethe's *Faust Part Two* inasmuch as both undertake an unravelling of the foregoing dramatic action which contrives to unexpectedly redeem Faust at the last moment. In Act III of *Faustus Kelly*, Kelly receives a call to confirm that he has won the election, but his jubilation does not last. The defeat of Captain Shaw has driven him to drink and, in her disgust, Margaret blames Kelly and leaves him. Reilly, Kelly's nemesis, announces that has successfully foiled the Stranger's appointment as the town's rate collector. Not only is the Stranger out of a job, but he is also told that no one will talk to him, and he will have nowhere to live. Kelly, reneging on his side of the pact, refuses to help him. As the community closes ranks against him, the Stranger loses his earlier confidence and withers, becoming *'thoroughly scared'* (*PT*, 113). Kelly's electoral victory also unravels: we are told a guard is on his way to speak to him about 'some monkey-work', as when 'the last two boxes were opened they were full of ashes'; and a petition threatens (*PT*, 113).

The play concludes with the re-entry of the Stranger, now wearing a black robe. When his lips move, excerpts from the speech of Shawn, the town clerk, Kelly and Reilly are ventriloquised and blended *'with diabolical skill'* (*PT*, 115). When the Stranger speaks directly, he tears up the bond signed with Kelly: 'Not for any favour … in heaven or earth or hell … would I take Kelly and the others with me to where I live' (*PT*, 116). Alana Gillespie suggests that 'effective characterisation is achieved' in *Faustus Kelly* 'through accents and (character-specific) rhetoric'.[42] However, Act III, in which its characters dissolve into their accents, reverses this process. The redemption of Faust by divine intervention which O'Nolan inherits from Goethe is transfigured and posed instead as a form of perlocutionary narrative collapse:

the excesses of what Joseph Holloway condemned as 'blather and highfalutin oratory' overwhelm the Faustian archetype and induce a perverse form of redemption.[43] Adorno, addressing 'the question of whether the devil won or lost the bet' in *Faust*, regards Goethe's reworking of the 'old motif of the devil cheated' as a sign not that Faust has won the bet but that 'law itself is suspended' and, he suggests enigmatically, we witness 'the disappearance of the natural order in a different order'.[44] The new 'order' which saves Kelly is the bureaucratic labyrinth of the Irish civil service, which causes the devil to throw his hands up in defeat.

Inez Hedges, in the study *Framing Faust*, suggests that there are two main tendencies in the twentieth-century engagement with the Faust story in the wake of the ambivalence opened up by Goethe's ending to *Faust Part Two*: a negative pole represented by the motif of Faust lost in the labyrinth, 'an image of confusion, false starts and frustrating returns to the point of origin', and a positive, redemptive pole represented by the motif of the garden. As such,

> The fate of the Faustian protagonist caught in the labyrinth seems to exemplify a scepticism concerning the impulse to know and experience everything in the name of modernity. The garden or natural setting, on the other hand, offers the promise of peace and, on occasion, an escape from the 'Faustian bargain'.[45]

The formal structure of O'Nolan's conclusion takes the escape to the garden represented by Goethe's redemption of his Faust and transforms it into its negative: confusion and a return to the point of origin. The nature of Kelly's redemption proves that, as an Irish politician, he is already enmeshed in a labyrinth worse than damnation.

Faust and fascism

Goethe's Faust, and the figure of Goethe himself, became archetypal yet fluid figures who were subject to processes of revision, appropriation and counter-appropriation by successive generations. Hedges writes that in the first half of the twentieth century, Faust became enmeshed in a 'culture war' between critics who claimed Goethe's work for fascist cultural narratives and those who sought to undermine this critical narrative. The nationalist accounts of the pre-Nazi period include Houston Stewart Chamberlain's *Goethe* (1921), which 'focuses on Goethe as a "great personality"', laying the seeds for Georg Schott's overtly fascist *Goethes Faust in heutiger Schau* (Goethe's Faust in Contemporary Perspective; 1940), which 'repeatedly refers to the "Führer Faust"'.[46] These accounts share some common features, according to Karoline Kirst-Gundersen and Paul Levesque, such as Faust's 'essential Germanness, his "grand personality" (*große Persönlichkeit*) and his dedication to the "community" (*Gemeinschaft*)'.[47] In particular, drawing upon their interpretation of Faust's land reclamation project with the exhortation '*Auf freiem Grund mit freiem Volke steh'n*'[48] (On acres free among free people stand), Nazi propaganda enlisted Goethe and his Faust for the fascist cause. Kirst-Gundersen and Levesque offer an example in

> the 1937 speech, 'Goethe in unserer Zeit', delivered by Reichsjugend-führer Baldur von Schirach on the occasion of the Weimar festival of the German youth. Schirach, one of the few high-level Nazi functionaries to devote a public speech to Goethe, begins with the rousing cry: 'German, name the unmistakeably German book, it is *Faust*. Name the unmistakeably German poet, it is Goethe.'[49]

This appropriation of Faust by national socialism did not go uncontested. In 1932–3 the Hölderlin scholar Wilhelm Böhm published *Faust der Nichtfaustische* (Faust the Unfaustian) which 'discusses the discrepancy between Goethe's dramatic character Faust and the long tradition of misinterpretations of that figure which had led to a false use of the term *Faustian*'.[50] Kirst-Gundersen, Levesque and Hedges also give the example of Ernst Beutler, the director of Frankfurt's Goethe museum, who in 1941 'argues that Goethe presents Faust as a failure' and suggests that his 'sacrifice of the old couple Philemon and Baucis to accomplish his aims is Goethe's warning to the German people not to be bent on conquest'.[51]

As well as dissenting critics within Germany, writers outside of Germany who opposed the regime reappropriated the Faust theme to construct a critique of the Nazi rise to power. The prime example is Karl Kraus and his (then unpublished) 1933 work *Die Dritte Walpurgisnacht*, a putative sequel to the romantic and classical Walpurgis Night scenes in parts *One* and *Two* of Goethe's *Faust*. Edward Timms writes that from 'the title through to the final words, *Dritte Walpurgisnacht* is permeated by a sense that the "most German of events" (*das deutscheste Ereignis*) is prefigured in Faust, the "most German of poems" (*deutscheste[s] Gedicht*)'.[52] Timms observes that Kraus compares Hitler's 'feigned friendliness towards Hindenburg' to Mephistopheles's 'ravenous intimacy' (*Rabentrauchlichkeit*) and suggests that the violent events of *Faust Part*

Two prefigure Hitler's seizure of power and the crimes of his stormtroopers. On an ideological level, 'Kraus's repeated emphasis on the concept of *"Faustnaturen"* identifies the vitalism portrayed in the play as one of the ideological antecedents of fascism'.[53] His recapitulation of the Faust theme against its Nazi appropriation is combined with a documentary montage technique that quotes the Nazis against themselves. Kraus's text is built out of 'over a thousand excerpts from the political discourse of 1933, interwoven with more than two hundred literary allusions'.[54] The main objective of Kraus's satire and his use of Goethe is to expose the rhetoric of national socialism, its 'tricks' or 'snares' of intonation and the 'Mephistophelian ingenuity' by which '"sense" is turned into "nonsense" and back again'.[55]

The rhetoric of fascism in Europe held appeal for politicians of both main parties in Ireland. The best-known example is the Blueshirt movement, formed by the Army Comrades Association following Fianna Fáil's election in 1932. Under the leadership of former police commissioner Eoin O'Duffy and the tutelage of Ernest Blythe – managing director of the Abbey Theatre during the production of *Faustus Kelly* – the Blueshirts adopted the corporatism of Benito Mussolini and 'all the trappings of a fascist outfit'. They were banned after an abortive plan to march on the Dáil in August 1933, mirroring Mussolini's Blackshirts and their march on Rome in 1922.[56] In his thesis on Irish responses to fascist Italy, Mark Phelan documents how in the 1920s the Fianna Fáil party had itself borrowed heavily from Italian fascist propaganda to shape its populist messages about government frugality, rural development and a crackdown on profiteering, whilst criticising the dictatorship and Italian foreign policy. In 1929, Éamon de Valera caused outrage when he suggested that 'Fianna Fáil could be for Ireland what Fascismo was for Italy'.[57]

In 1942–3, the fascist strain in Irish politics occupied its fringes, represented by two radical Irish-language revival groups: *Ailtirí na hAiséirghe* (Architects of the Resurrection) and *Glún na Buaidhe* (The Victorious Generation). As Carol Taaffe notes, O'Nolan's brother Ciarán was involved in *Ailtirí na hAiséirghe*'s predecessor organisation and Gaelic League breakaway *Craobh na hAiséirighe* (Branch of the Resurrection).[58] The mawkishly conservative cultural politics and anti-Semitism of these extreme nationalist groups exercised O'Nolan throughout the 1940s and he wrote a grimly satirical play in Irish, *An Sgian* (The Knife) which lampoons the rivalry between the two groups (*PT*, 247–58). Taaffe cites a *Cruiskeen Lawn* column published on 15 March 1943 which compares their policies to European anti-Semitism. Myles reports listening to a street agitator from one of these small groups:

'Glún na Buaidhe', he roared, 'has its own ideas about the banks, has its own ideas about amusements, has its own ideas about dancing. There is one sort of dancing that Glún na Buaidhe will not permit and that is jazz dancing. Because jazz dancing is the product of [...] the dirty low nigger culture of America'.

Substitute jew for nigger there and you have something beautiful and modern.[59]

O'Nolan's proximity to people holding these views in both his personal and professional life is indicated by the fact that Ernest Blythe himself was also a key supporter of *Ailtirí na hAiséirghe*, helping to draft its constitution.[60] In 1947, Niall Montgomery – O'Nolan's confidant and collaborator on *Cruiskeen Lawn* – commented on an early page of O'Nolan's unpublished polemical essay about the language revival, known from one of its chapter titles as 'The Pathology of Revivalism'. Montgomery suggests making a direct comparison between national socialism and the 'Irish reaction':

I imagine there may be an analogy, though possibly a slender one, between the Irish reaction + the violence of German National Socialism (compare Nuremberg with the velocipedantic Mór-Shubhails, Jew-baiting with the wonderful notion of higher-ranked Irish officials standing at the elbows of the old English ones, the hatred for Kultur-Bolshevismus + Neue Sachlichkeit (Jewish, international, foreign) with our cultural xenophobias, the Hitlerjugend stuff, glorification of the body, etc. with the amazing T. T., virginal, cycling, open-air, kilted & non-smoking characters in Rutland Square).[61]

This remark – including Montgomery's positioning of bicycling as an Irish parallel for German fascist cultural pastimes – offers rich possibilities for a revised understanding of the significance of an anti-fascist critique and the Nazi/Gael comparison across much of O'Nolan's work.[62] For my narrower concerns here, it casts revealing light on the notable similarities I find between Kelly's rhetoric in *Faustus Kelly*, the language used by Fianna Fáil in 1926–32, the contemporary positions of the *Ailtirí na hAiséirghe* and *Glún na Buaidhe* groups and a more general emphasis on anti-Masonry and anti-Semitic rhetoric that highlights the affinities between Irish political posturing and European fascism. My analysis suggests that Kelly is something of a composite figure, designed to encompass everything O'Nolan disliked in Irish politics. As such, the play demonstrates his use of a satirical strategy which resembles the composite technique of Kraus's *Die Dritte Walpurgisnacht*.

Faust and Fianna Fáil

Kelly's political speeches in the play are never delivered at a rally or in public but always produced *extempore* and in private settings. Thus, O'Nolan emphasises the unstable nature of Kelly's rhetoric, its non-directional locutionary status and wandering referential coordinates:

> KELLY: (*Quietly.*) Margaret, are you not being a little unfair? It is perhaps true that in politics there is much that is unpleasant. But speaking for myself (*his voice rises as he unconsciously climbs into his plane of ranting*), speaking for myself, this much I will say. As an accredited deputy in the national parliament I am determined to serve my country according to my lights and to the utmost of the talents which God has given me. I am determined to strike blow after blow against the vested interest. I am determined to break – to smash – backstairs jobbery in high places. I am determined to expose – to drag into the inexorable light of day – every knave, time-server, sycophant and party camp-follower. I will meet them all and fight them. I will declare war on the Masons and the Knights. I will challenge the cheat and the money-changer. (*PT*, 97–8)

The fact that Kelly is a Catholic nationalist and political centrist ('Neither Right nor Left will save us but the middle of the road'; *PT*, 66) draws him closest to the politics of Fianna Fáil. The position supports Cronin's view – founded in his reading of 'The Fausticity of Kelly' – that O'Nolan is drawing upon the speeches he had no choice but to endure in Leinster House and all the 'agonies entailed' (*MBM*, 20) when serving as private secretary to government ministers like Seán MacEntee.[63] However, a comparison of Dáil and Seanad transcripts from the period with Kelly's speeches suggests that it is not the rhetoric of Fianna Fáil deputations in the early 1940s which O'Nolan has in his sights. In the 1940s, ministers such as MacEntee or Seán Lemass were defending Fianna Fáil's record as a party of government on matters such as shortages and unemployment assistance, rather than launching populist attacks on their opponents.[64]

Instead, Kelly uses the sort of rhetoric these same figures adopted during their earlier period in opposition mixed with the contemporary rhetoric of more radical far-right groups. O'Nolan expresses his critical view of the rising Fianna Fáil party and its main personalities in his 1955 account of the time that he ran and lost against de Valera's son Vivion for the auditorship of the Literary & Historical Society at UCD during its 1932–3 session. O'Nolan partially attributes the defeat to his recalcitrance in the face of the rise of triumphant Fianna Fáil ideology amongst the student body: 'The Fianna Fáil Party was by then firmly established, heaven on earth was at hand, and [Vivion] de Valera gained from this situation. I believed and said publicly that these politicians were unsuitable' (*MBM*, 20).

Kieran Allen, in his history of Fianna Fáil and the Irish labour movement, identifies four themes of its programme in what he calls the 'Radical Years' from 1926 to 1932, which enabled it to expand its constituency to encompass workers and nationalist intellectuals. They are:

1. '*The Banks and Financial Plunder*'
2. '*A Free Ireland means Cheap Government*'
3. '*Catholic Social Justice*'
4. '*The Appeal to Workers*'.[65]

All four themes are found in Kelly's rhetoric and speeches. Reflecting Fianna Fáil's early focus on the banks as stooges of imperialism and their accusations of a corrupt Cumann na nGaedheal tie-up with British financiers, Kelly makes continuous insinuations of corruption, 'backstairs jobbery' and hidden scandals in high places. He plans to 'say a few words about the banks' at his upcoming rallies in the second act (*PT*, 66). Whilst Fianna Fáil itself came to be known for clientelism and patronage politics, prior to de Valera's arrival in government it was Fianna Fáil figures such as MacEntee who made these attacks. Allen quotes from a 1928 election leaflet in which MacEntee suggests that:

> The banks, which have been bleeding the Irish farmer, crushing Irish industry, investing Irish money abroad, jeopardising it in British securities, want to retain the present government in office for their purposes [...]. A Fianna Fáil government would not be tied up with the old Unionist Party and the banks.[66]

The references to the influence of 'the banks' and high finance carry a strong anti-Semitic subtext which I explore in more detail shortly. The second, related theme is the demand for cheap government. Cumann na nGaedheal were accused of trying to run Ireland on 'a grand imperial scale',[67] and Kelly restates the cheap government demand in his speeches:

> Public departments must be ruthlessly pruned. Give me a free hand and I will save you a cool hundred thousand pounds in every one of them. I warrant you that if the people of this country see fit to send me to the Dáil, there will be scandals in high places. (*PT*, 66)

The theme of efficiency and outrage at the extravagance of the existing regime also links Kelly to tactics Fianna Fáil borrowed from Italian fascism. In the 1927 elections, Fianna Fáil 'made "thrift" a core principle of party propaganda', leaning on the example of Mussolini's frugal Italy as a 'comparable regime'.[68]

The theme of a corrupt government and its alternatives enters Goethe's *Faust Part Two* in Act IV, in which the rival emperor, whom Faust and Mephistopheles assist through the use of magic, is depicted redolent in his finery and making promises to his aides and archbishop of the right to 'tax, rent, levy impost' from conquered territory, declaring that 'yours be without stint / Royalties from safe-conduct, mining, salt, and mint'.[69] Faust wins the right to the coastline of the conquered territory and, in his old age, seeks to reclaim land from the sea to 'open room to live for millions / Not safely, but in free resilience'.[70] Yet these claims are ambiguous: their realisation is made doubtful by Faust's infirmity and blindness and sullied by Mephistopheles's murder of the elderly couple Philemon and Baucis on his behalf. The indistinct vision of Kelly for an Ireland freed of the yoke of an unjust government, as well as mirroring the real rhetoric of Fianna Fáil, also therefore burlesques the Faustian vision of a land free for striving, which was utilised by national socialist critics and commentators.

Allen argues that Fianna Fáil 'believed that the fusion of Catholicism and Irish nationalism could produce a unique society constructed around social justice', thus 'rejecting any imputation of communism in Fianna Fáil'. An anti-communist stance was particularly important in the face of a red scare ahead of the 1932 election in which de Valera was accused by the *United Irishman* of leading the country into 'Bolshevik servitude'.[71] Represented by figures such as Aodh De Blácam and James Devane, Catholic social conscience is a right-wing third camp position, which rejects both the excesses of Anglo-American capitalism and the evils of Soviet communism as the result of 'materialist' values, in contradistinction to the spiritual and idealist values of the Irish nation.[72] This is a significant ideological thread in Kelly's rhetoric. He peppers his speeches with references to Ireland's history as a Catholic nation that had come under foreign sway, lauding 'Niall of the Nine Hostages, who penetrated to the Alps in his efforts to spread the Gospel' (*PT*, 72), lamenting the effect of 'seven centuries of alien domination and godless misrule' (*PT*, 91) and claiming that he has chosen 'to make a few Christian principles the basis of [his] scheme of life' (*PT*, 115). When forced to quickly fabricate the Stranger's background, Kelly says that he is a 'graduate of the National University which was founded by Cardinal Newman to enable the cream

of our Catholic youth to partake of the benefits of University education'
(*PT*, 52).

Catholic social principles were taken to an extreme by the puritanical
visions of *Craobh na hAiséirghe / Ailtirí na hAiséirghe* propaganda, which
promoted the idea that a revived Ireland, drawing on the glories of its past
culture, could match and even supersede the achievements and architecture
of the Third Reich. As Taaffe notes, on 21 November 1942 *Cruiskeen Lawn*
gleefully commented on the plausibility of plans set out by *Craobh na
hAiséirghe* to replace an impure Dublin with a new capital city at Tara,
including 'a new national university, theatre and stadium; a massive "Great
National Avenue"; and a "Garden of Heroes" with a Millennium Spire-like
"Column of the Resurrection" as its centrepiece'.[73] The new Tara is presented
by Myles as the master cliché of 'revivalist absurdity': 'Cement appears out of
what cerulean ether? A blue sky. And as if by what? Magic, of course'.[74]

O'Nolan connects Kelly to these groups by having him parrot the same
nationalist clichés and, in a more sinister move, the same anti-Masonry and
anti-Semitic rhetoric used by the fascist nationalists when he declares that he
'won't be stopped by Knight or Mason' (*PT*, 67) or that he 'will challenge
the cheat and the money-changer' (*PT*, 98). In Ireland, Masonic institutions
and lodges, such as the Grand Council of Knight Masons convoked in 1923,
played a role in both republican and loyalist politics, but the Catholic Church
was and remains hostile to Masonry: joining any Masonic group has been
prohibited since Clement XII's *In Eminenti* papal bull issued on 28 April
1738.[75] Phelan finds that the anti-Masonry of Mussolini's Italy 'captured
the imagination of [Irish] commentators with a keen nose for conspiracy
closer to home. Identified with defeated unionist and surviving imperialist
sentiment, Irish Freemasonry quickly became a target of abuse.'[76] As well as
toying with anti-Semitism by castigating profiteering and 'usury', Fianna Fáil
blamed Masonry for the cost of government, trading off the perception of
the post-imperial administration as 'a Mason-dominated "old boy's club"'.[77]
Anti-Masonry sentiments at this time were firmly associated with anti-
Semite organisations across Europe. Notably, Masonry constituted part of
the tussle over Goethe's legacy between left and right when Goethe himself
came under attack for his membership of the Weimar Freemason Lodge in
Else Rost's *Goethes Faust: Eine Freimaurertragödie* (Goethe's *Faust*: A Masonic
tragedy; 1931), published by First World War general and Nazi supporter
Erich Ludendorff's anti-Semitic publishing house. The pamphlet claims that
'Goethe's *Faust*, supposedly Germany's greatest dramatic work, was in fact a
barely disguised hymn to the Freemasons' ongoing project of delivering the

world over to Jewish control'.[78] It is therefore significant that Kelly combines his anti-Masonry rhetoric with anti-Semitic remarks such as 'I will challenge the cheat and the money-changer' (*PT*, 98). Kelly's emphatic invectives against Masonry in the context of his becoming a Faustian politician subtly draw attention to this fault-line in the fascist appropriation of Goethe's *Faust*.

The fourth theme identified by Allen is 'a distinct appeal to organised workers'. Fianna Fáil argued that workers 'suffered most from foreign domination because exploitation and poverty were worse when foreign masters were in control' and therefore subordinated the trade union struggle to nationalist goals.[79] Kelly does not appeal to organised workers although his election poster, 'NOT FOR PARTY NOR PRIVILEGE BUT FOR COUNTRY AND PEOPLE – KELLY' clearly pitches his campaign as a populist appeal to the masses rather than the privileged (*PT*, 59). When confronted with Captain Shaw's '*exaggerated haw-haw English accent*' (*PT*, 68), Kelly responds with a jeremiad against 'wicked men who live in gilded palaces in England, cradled in luxury and licentious extravagance, knowing nothing and caring nothing for either the English masses, the historic and indefeasible Irish nation, the naked Negro in distant and distressed India or the New Zealand pygmy on his native shore' (*PT*, 72). He couches his attack on the wealthy in anti-imperialist terms but also privileges the Irish over the non-white colonial subject whom he dehumanises as 'naked' and 'distressed'.

O'Nolan's role in the civil service made it problematic for him to openly attack the ministers for whom he worked.[80] Yet, by having Kelly mirror the rabble-rousing rhetoric of these same figures before they had got into power and then associating Kelly with fringe groupings more contemporary to the 1940s, he is able to attack the irresponsibility of his political masters under the cover of plausible deniability. This carefully constructed cover intrudes into every detail of the play. When the Stranger is refused a ministerial sanction, the minister in question could feasibly correspond to Seán MacEntee who, as minister for local government and public health from 1941 to 1947, was O'Nolan's employer at this point. This role in defeating the devil neatly heads off any scandalous imputations that might follow from the identification of Kelly and his politics with Fianna Fáil politicians. O'Nolan suggests in a letter to John Garvin of 8 September 1952 that the then minister for finance, Seán T. O'Kelly, even assisted with 'suggestions and revisions, in an Abbey play I wrote concerned with the problem of the "unsanctioned man"' (*L*, 165). However, in subsequent accounts of the play, O'Nolan sought to reverse this masking of the play's political satire and draw out its full implications. On 3 April 1954, Myles describes it in *Cruiskeen Lawn* as 'a masterpiece, saturated with a Voltaire quality and penetrating human stupidity with a sort of ghoulish gusto'. When he comes to accounting for why so many people disliked it at the time and why 'did we all, including myself, think it so bad', Myles suggests that 'the play (though straight farce) had hurt too many people, and that sort of thing doesn't pay in this country'. He now believes that 'the work takes on a new importance by reason of life and facts catching up with it. It had an unsuspected oracular and prophetic content.'[81]

Conclusion

Faustus Kelly depicts its hero as a miniature fascist dictator-in-waiting, a parodic Hitler or Mussolini planted into the shoes of a grasping provincial politician. Kelly is a hypocritical *petit-bourgeois* figure, opportunistically relying on religious rhetoric and populist clichés drawn from the worst of the previous two decades of Irish politics, which are delivered with a frothy, undisciplined charisma arising only from his own inexhaustible self-righteousness. Kelly, as O'Nolan's repeated phrase and stage direction here suggests, is best understood as 'speaking for myself (*his voice rises as he unconsciously climbs into his plane of ranting*) speaking for myself' (*PT*, 97). He is a figure designed to concentrate in one person the corruption, prejudice and irresponsibility of Irish politics across all parties and link them uncomfortably to the wider fascist turn in European politics. By blending the radicalism of Fianna Fáil with its appeals to the authoritarian example of Mussolini and Italian fascism, and in his vitriolic anti-Masonry and anti-Semitism, Kelly resembles not only the Irish politicians who traded off these themes in the 1920s and '30s but also the hard-line Gaelic revivalists in *Ailtirí na hAiséirghe* and *Glún na Buaidhe*. In this context, the satirical message of bringing Kelly so low at the end of the play – unravelling his electoral victory and having even the devil abandon him in disgust – may be viewed as an anti-fascist gesture, the equivalent of Kraus's defiant statement after breaking his silence on the victory of Nazis in the opening line of *Die Dritte Walpurgisnacht*: '*Mir fällt zu Hitler nichts ein*' (Hitler brings nothing to my mind).[82]

What does this mean for the 'Fausticity of Kelly'? In the context of the right-wing turn in appropriations of the Faustian theme in the early twentieth century, from Oswald Spengler's 'Faustian Age' in *The Decline of the West*, vol. 2 (1922) to the avowedly national socialist appropriations of Faust afterwards, O'Nolan's failed Faust, who achieves his redemption only through a combination of incompetence and subordination to an existing bureaucratic system, becomes a scathing rebuke to the notion of '*Faustnaturen*' along the lines of Kraus's *Die Dritte Walpurgisnacht*. This interpretation aligns with the way that verse by Goethe (or lines pretending to be) is presented in *Cruiskeen Lawn*, wherein hybridising montage techniques are deployed to remind readers that there is no unifying national essence to be found in its literary figures.

Yet O'Nolan's play is also evasive and unwilling to confront these opponents directly. Through the figure of Kelly himself, *Faustus Kelly* masks its anti-fascist gestures so convincingly that they passed under the radar of one of its own targets, Ernest Blythe, who had a history of close engagement with the Irish far-right. In his letter commending the play to Blythe on 12 June 1942, O'Nolan cautiously suggests that 'there are certain political implications to it which, as a *stát-sheribhíseach*, I'm not too sure about, but possibly that could be got over' (*L*, 118). Likewise, the play's plot construction is contrived to evade charges of a frontal attack on the existing government, avoiding any negative repercussions for O'Nolan's career as a civil servant. In this light, O'Nolan's emphasis on the play's satirical significance in his column of 1954, and again in his article of 1963, is revealing. Once out of the civil service, he wishes to stake a claim for a critique that was perhaps too well hidden in the first place. In this sense, *Faustus Kelly* is a work that embodies the labyrinth that Hedges recognises as one of the Faust myth's two dominant interpretative frameworks. Like Goethe's *Faust* itself, the text is entangled by its conflicting drives and still unsure at its conclusion whether anything decisive has been said.

Adorno suggests that the salvation that Goethe affords to Faust in the final scenes of *Faust Part Two* may rely on the way he dramatically accelerates Faust's passage into senility: '[perhaps] the wager is forgotten in Faust's "extreme old age", along with all the crimes that Faust in his entanglement perpetrated or permitted'.[83] He is aware that Faust is a distinctively modern and bourgeois myth, arising quickly during the early-modern period, and, after Goethe's reinvention, entwining itself rapidly with fascism, the primary crisis of western modernity. The myth's accelerating instability as a signifier for modernity indicates the concomitant possibility of a centrifugal decomposition, and *Faustus Kelly* is a work which, for all its close correspondences to Goethe's version, enacts such a collapse of the Faust *topos* by burying it under layers of confusion and derision. Adorno's conclusion on the meaning of the final scenes of Faust might be applied to *Faustus Kelly*: as a tragedy, the play is a 'form in the process of falling under the statute of limitations. Perhaps Faust is saved because he is no longer the person who signed the pact'.[84]

11

Insect Plays

Entomological modernism, automata and the nonhuman in *Rhapsody in Stephen's Green**

LISA FITZGERALD

Myles na gCopaleen's adaptation of Karel and Josef Čapek's animal satire *Ze života hmyzu* (*From the Life of Insects* or *Pictures from the Insects' Life*) premiered in Dublin in 1943 and ran for six days; its apparent artistic and commercial failure has been widely noted in criticism ever since.[1] Responses framed *Rhapsody in Stephen's Green: The insect play* singularly as a parody of an insular Emergency-era Ireland. Yet, the use of animal imagery was widespread in occupied Europe, with plays such as Sartre's *Les Mouches* (*The Flies*), written in the same year as *Rhapsody*, conflating human and nonhuman behaviour to critique the privileged centrality of humankind in ontological and epistemological discourse. Some of the criticisms of *Rhapsody* focused on the geographically and culturally specific aspects of the play and its mean-spirited tone, whilst others felt slighted by the entomological comparison of humans with various insects such as bees and ants, particularly as insects are commonly articulated as mindless mechanical drones. This essay argues that, although there is certainly an ominous warning about the dangers of mechanical warfare in the play, there is also an acknowledgement of the non-binary nature of instinct and technology and a performance perspective on the ethics of posthumanism.

It is difficult to reconstruct how the play was produced as there is scant documentation with no photographs, set or costume design remaining.[2] But given the archival remnants that we have (such as the production notebooks), a comparative study of insect representation within the wider performance history of *Ze života hmyzu* will go some way to complicate the previous criticism of the O'Nolan version as parochial. Although O'Nolan's adaptation was indeed a disparaging mockery as is clear from the criticism, it should also be seen both within the wider context of a modernist, and mechanised, European theatre history and as a part of O'Nolan's broader vision of nonhuman instinct and technology. This comparative examination of the Paul Selver translation of the original Čapek play of 1921 and its Irish adaptation from the perspective of cultural entomology serves two purposes. First, it analyses O'Nolan's play in a continental *avant-garde* theatre and nonhuman studies context. Secondly, it argues that the conflation of insect automation and mechanical technology (in particular warfare) in early twentieth-century Europe has had a clear impact on both the Čapeks' original production and O'Nolan's adaptation and the corresponding insect aesthetic.[3] What will emerge over the course of this reading is not only the use of nonhuman nature as a metaphor or symbol for human activities in O'Nolan's play, but also an insect aesthetic with a dynamic agency in its own right.

O'Nolan's broader *oeuvre* is noted for troubling conventional narratives of the human-nonhuman binary, with examples such as people transforming into bicycles and horses through atomic exchange in *The Third Policeman*, the train metamorphosis in 'John Duffy's Brother', or the potential 'kangaroolity' of Pooka MacPhellimey's wife in *At Swim-Two-Birds* (*CN*, 104). It is therefore apt to situate O'Nolan's work within ecocentric rather than a traditionally humanist criticism. The theoretical framework that will be applied in this case will avoid the humanism that Giorgio Agamben calls 'an ironic apparatus that verifies the absence of a nature proper to *Homo*, holding him suspended between a celestial and a terrestrial nature'.[4] Within historical humanistic discourse, there are two parts that make up the human: the animal and the divine. Human animality has always been difficult to account for, in particular how it is transferred to the afterlife.[5] Humanistic man, as Rosi Braidotti argues, 'defined himself as much by what he excluded as by what he included in his rational self-representation'.[6] This essay offers a comparative reading of O'Nolan's play within the European performance history within which it was embedded in 1943 and claims that the performativity, the geographical context and the figure of the nonhuman complicates our understanding of humanism in O'Nolan's writings. The hierarchical stratification that differentiated on the basis of sex, race or class in traditional humanist discourse is challenged in the Čapeks' and O'Nolan's plays by the hybrid representations of the human-nonhuman that blur those distinctions.

The difference between the discursive use of the terms 'animal' and 'insect' should be highlighted to clarify the specific insectoid traits that illustrate their conflation with the mechanical. The physical and behavioural attributes of insects suggest that they are predisposed to the mindless mechanistic traits that were to become a central part of twentieth-century aesthetics. Whereas animals have often been individuated in representation, insects are portrayed as a collective. An entomologically sensitive or non-anthropocentric reading of the play can challenge contemporaneous appraisals of insect aesthetics. The field of cultural entomology examines the impact of insects on cultural activities.[7] Although there are many insects which feature in the plays under consideration, I have chosen three archetypal insects – bees, butterflies and beetles – that serve to highlight the essay's central thesis that insect automation counters the anthropocentric impulse. This is not to say that history is not a human story, but the aim is to broaden that anthropocentric perspective and retain the inclusivity that environmental criticism calls for. Challenging the assumed centrality of the human figure is an understandable part of a post-world-war European civilisation processing an ever-increasing mechanisation and *Rhapsody* is an integral part of that discourse.

Ze života hmyzu and entomological modernism

Ze života hmyzu is an allegorical narrative of civilisation where human conduct is likened to frequently unfavourable insect behaviour. As the machine age emerged in the late nineteenth century, iconographic renditions of the automaton (both mechanic and animalistic) appeared on the stage: *Le Papillon* (1860), *Le Roi Carotte* (1872), *Swan Lake* (1876).[8] Performing insects are not a new phenomenon, while humans have long performed as insects, embodying insects and incorporating insects in various dramatic forms.[9] Spanning the gamut from apocalyptic locust plagues to industrious beehives, insects are well-represented in western art and performance.[10] But these efforts have not often been successful in moving insects (and nonhuman nature more broadly) beyond metaphor. In many narratives, in particular with the rise of mechanisation, futurist aesthetics has featured the amalgamation of animal and machine, an example being James Ensor's *The Strange Insects* (1888) or the 1912 Russian animation *The Cameraman's Revenge* (1912). Early *avant-garde* films, such as Man Ray's *L'Étoile de Mer* (1928) and Luis Buñuel and Salvador Dali's *Un Chien Andalou* (1929) (building on Dali's surrealist manifestations of insects such as ants in his artworks), employed animal imagery (including insects) in order to hint not only at the grotesque in the animal world (a traditional fear of the 'other') but also at the natural automation that was becoming associated with seemingly unnatural mechanical warfare.

It was amid this conflation of biology and technology that Josef and Karel Čapek's collaborative play *Ze života hmyzu* was first performed in Czech at the National Theatre in Brno in February 1922 and shortly after at the National Theatre in Prague. From the outset *Ze života hmyzu* was successful. New York followed that same year and London in 1923 with forty-two performances at the Regent Theatre opening 5 May. The play features numerous nonhuman characters, with Act I (The Butterflies) featuring butterflies intent on endless physical gratification and carnal pleasure, Act II (Creepers and Crawlers) with beetles, crickets, an ichneumon fly and a parasite as lowly scavengers, bickering, stealing and generally taking advantage of others' misfortune, and Act III (The Ants) with rampaging and maniacal ants.

O'Nolan's adaptation was commissioned by Hilton Edwards and Micheál mac Liammóir and was a reworking of Paul Selver's translation of *Ze života hmyzu* for an Irish audience. Selver had translated much of the Čapeks' *oeuvre* including Karel Čapek's more renowned play *Rossumovi Univerzální Roboti* (Rossum's Universal Robots, also R.U.R.).[11] There were two English-language adaptations of Selver's translation that were performed soon after the original *Ze života hmyzu*: an American version written by Owen Davis, *The World We Live In (The Insect Comedy)*, for use at the Jolson theatre in New York in 1922 (published in 1933), and Nigel Playfair and Clifford Bax's *The Insect Play or And So Ad Infinitum* for a Regent production in London (published in 1923). The accents evident in the Selver/Playfair/Bax version are heavily emphasised, with the Tramp speaking in a thick cockney accent: 'It's a shime – it is reely.'[12] O'Nolan changed the pronunciation to emphasise particularly Irish accents. For example, where Selver's 'cockney' translation drops the first letter with expressions such as 'sling yer 'ook' or 'white-faced 'arridan', O'Nolan's uses distinctly Dublin accents such as 'me arum' for my arm.[13] The ichneumon fly in the original is replaced with a duck in the Myles na gCopaleen version. Interestingly, given the title of the adaptation, the ducks in St Stephen's Green had the dubious renown of being the reason that the 1916 Easter Rising was halted for one hour a day so they could be safely fed by the groundskeeper James Kearney. Act III (The Ants) focuses on ants whose military training and ideology infuses the final scenes with a warlike maniacal hysteria adapted in the Irish version to the warring factions of republicanism and unionism.

The cultural background and identities of various insects in *Rhapsody* is differentiated by manner, language and accent. For example, the red ants of Act II have unionist sensibilities ('we're port of the Empiere') while the green ants speak Irish and wear *fáinnes*, gold ring pins indicating willingness to speak Irish and support of a distinctly Irish culture. Mr and Mrs Beetle talk in '*an appalling Dublin accent*' (*PT*, 186). The language is more exaggerated and culturally extreme: 'Sure luckit. I seen myself wan June fourteen shifts on top of one another without a wink of slape or a bite in me mouth to kill the starvation' (*PT*, 187). The duck is described as having '*a most refined foreign accent*' and Mr and Mrs Cricket '*speak with the rawest of all possible Cork accents*' (*PT*, 192, 196). Given his criticism of Synge who 'brought forward with the utmost solemnity amusing clowns talking a sub-language of their own and bade us take them seriously',[14] the exaggerated accents in *Rhapsody* can be seen as part of O'Nolan's wider mockery of performed and widely caricatured Irish archetypal characters.

The Čapek Brothers were not unknown to Irish audiences. Selver's English version of *Ze života hmyzu* had been performed in Ireland prior to O'Nolan's adaptation: its first production is listed in *The Irish Times* in 1937 from a Dublin amateur dramatics group, the Progressive Players, at an annual drama event, Feis Maitiú. Čapek's more recognised play, *R.U.R.*, had also been performed by the Gate Theatre in May 1929 and revived in May 1931. And the Dublin University Players performed the Selver translation on the Peacock stage in June of 1942 having been given the rights, according to the 30 May 1942 instalment of 'An Irishman's Diary' in *The Irish Times*, 'through the courtesy of the Gaiety Theatre and McLiammoir-Edwards Productions'.[15] The report also states that the DU Players enlisted the help of Czech refugee Hanus Drechsler, who 'being acquainted with the original version, and, indeed, with its author, will deal with the Anglicised version'.[16] Although the poster for the Gate production at the Gaiety listed *The Insect Play* as translated and adapted by Myles na gCopaleen, he was not fluent in Czech and evidently based much of his adaptation on the available Selver translation.

Rhapsody premiered at the Gaiety Theatre in March 1943. The ethos of the mac Liammóir–Edwards partnership (who had founded the Gate Theatre Company in 1928) was to counter the folk drama of the Abbey Theatre with a 'non-representational, utopian theatre space'.[17] The Gate production emphasises the automata of the insects through music: in the production notebooks the buzzing (that is described as realistic) segues into *Flight of the Bumblebee* as the prologue closes. In the final act, The Ants, the curtain rises on Ant Hill, described in the stage directions as a '*featureless and uneven situation crowded with ever-moving ants*' (*PT*, 212). In the production notebook, the scene is described as a 'constant stream of ants' and represented in an accompanying doodle. The accompanying music is described as the 'music of machines'. The sound of the insect and the sound of machine become synonymous with a new modernity, as Deleuze and Guattari have written: 'The insect is closer, better able to make audible the truth that all becomings are molecular.'[18] These becomings to which performance can contribute, with its particular entanglement of human and nonhuman bodies, consist of 'an instantaneous zigzag', an understanding of existence as relational rather than demarcated as human and nonhuman or organic and mechanical.[19]

The conflation between the sounds of insects and machines is fascinating given the mechanisation and wartime context from which the adaptation (and the original *Ze života hmyzu*) emerged. The Emergency era ran from 1939 through to 1946 and the O'Nolan adaptation of a play that features nonhuman aesthetics reiterates that discourse on the ethics of nonhuman representation that is evident in the original 1923 play.[20] Yet, there are many modernist texts predating the Second World War, such as Kafka's *Die Verwandlung* (The Metamorphosis; 1915), which use the performative interchange between insect and man as a figure to challenge human centrality.[21] Indeed, the significant nonhuman turn in modernist literary studies in recent years has also included analyses of entomology in the modernist poetics of James Joyce and Virginia Woolf.[22] The act of representation which previously lifted the human from the mechanical or animal becomes analogous with the same base functions that mindlessly proliferate in instinctual behaviour. The music of machines towards which the insects/humans seem to gravitate is emblematic of the move towards a more instinctual (perhaps a more egalitarian) response to environmental stimuli.

The turn of the twentieth century brought a number of pronounced challenges to the discursive centrality of man, as Darwin's *On the Origin of Species* (1859) and Henri Bergson's *L'évolution créatrice* (Creative Evolution; 1907) had a profound impact on the understanding of humanity's embeddedness as opposed to pre-eminence and our place in relation to other animals and (perhaps more disappointingly) the gods.[23] The era's interest in naturalism extended to entomology, as reflections on the role of nonhuman nature led to insights into human behaviour. While Bergson focused more on the role of adaptive difference, as opposed to Darwin's progressive and linear theory of evolution, the impact of both publications and the romantic materialism that they augured had explosive reverberations on the cultural ideals of *fin-de-siècle* Europe. Entomology, along with botany and ornithology, became a way in the late nineteenth century of practising scholarship in natural history. Aquaria, glass beehives, and various models for exhibition drove a fascination for insects. Social insects, in particular, were studied to illustrate the connections between humans and their insect neighbours (if not relatives). The enfolding of natural history into cultural production was a fundamental part of both the modernist aesthetic (building on a wave of scientific and philosophical challenges to anthropocentrism) and the attempt to classify and to understand the evolutionary web from which humans emerge and from which we now cannot be disentangled.

This analysis of the European performative context for *Rhapsody* is essentially a Bergsonian reading of biotechnology that challenges the binary definitions of animal (in this case, insect or perhaps human actor/performer) and machine. Insects have replaced birds in 'becoming-molecular', Deleuze and Guattari argue, because whereas 'birds are vocal [...] insects are instrumental'.[24] Their 'chirring, rustling, buzzing, clicking, scratching, and scraping' and 'molecular vibrations' serves their worldly experience as insects where they are 'better able to make audible the truth that all becomings are molecular'.[25] Insects have a part to play in our multi-species world, not just as passive recipients of human direction, or the strange mechanical Other that haunts our base imaginations in the forms of swarms, drones, pestilence, plague. And it is important to note that becoming-animal, for Deleuze and Guattari, is not about imitation:

> For if becoming-animal does not consist in playing animal or imitating an animal, it is clear that the human being does not 'really' become an animal any more than the animal 'really' becomes something else. Becoming produces nothing other than itself. We fall into a false alternative if we say that you either imitate or you are.[26]

In thinking about becoming-animal, we cannot fall into fixed ideas of human or animal behaviours. The importance of becoming-insect lies in affinity rather than imitation; neither can one evolve into the animal (so the issues of swarming or hive mentality are not assumed). Rather, the becoming is marked by its rhizomatic multiplicities. The physical experience of performance resembles the multiplicities that Deleuze and Guattari discuss, where the unknown combinations of organism pass between and write their histories on human bodies. The materiality of performance reveals the fallaciousness of fixed binaries such as human versus animal and organic versus mechanical. Rereading *Rhapsody* from a posthumanist perspective ties O'Nolan's work to a vibrant pan-European discourse on the ethics of anthropocentrism.

Death and sex

Ze života hmyzu is an allegory heavily influenced by the work of entomologist Jean-Henri Fabre. The Brothers Čapek describe *Ze života hmyzu* as an 'Entomological Review', hinting at the scientific framework from which the idea emerged. In the Selver translation, Act I (The Butterflies) is set on a hill but in the corner there is 'a small table or bar, with high seats and coloured glass containing cold drinks and straws'.[27] Throughout the scene, the butterflies are consumed by what the lepidopterist calls the 'overture to the natural system by which Nature keeps up the balance of the population – that's what you call "playing". The male pursues the female; the female allures, avoids – selects – the eternal round of sex!'[28] *Rhapsody* differs from the Selver translation of *Ze života hmyzu* in a number of significant ways. The Čapeks' moth chrysalis is replaced with a hen's egg, and their ichneumon fly with its larva has been replaced with duck and duckling. The change O'Nolan makes from the metamorphosis of the chrysalis to the hatching of the egg is emblematic of the overall adjustments in the adaptation that render the events less utopian and more farcical. Act I of the Čapek version has butterflies whereas *Rhapsody* has wasps and initially had monkeys. The production copy of the Gate Theatre Company's *Rhapsody* (titled 'the Irish version of Čapek's *Insect Play* by Myles na gCopaleen') lists Act I as 'The Wasps' with a doodle in the margins illustrating the suggested costumes for the characters. Representation of the wasps did, however, morph into bees during the production's rehearsal. As Ondřej Pilný notes: 'The appropriate emendations, whereby bees were no longer referred to as wasps, were made in rehearsal, and as much as the typescript that was used as the prompt book does not reflect these, they duly appeared in the published version of the play edited by Tracy.'[29] The changes reflect the fluidity with which O'Nolan's adaptation was reworked during the rehearsal process.

Butterflies and bees are two very distinct types of insect: one has a light and flighty demeanour and the other is more frenzied, although more favourably communal. Basil is initially described as a wasp, whereas he is a bee in the final production copy. Even though the final decision to move from wasps to bees might seem to be a slight change, there is an associated communality in the hive behaviour of bees that makes them more readily representative of human society than the wasps. That said, the bees in *Rhapsody* are altogether more hostile, as illustrated by the Tramp's description: 'A very ferocious … baste, the bee. A very … contentious … intimidatin' … exacerbatin' animal, the bee' (*PT*, 166).

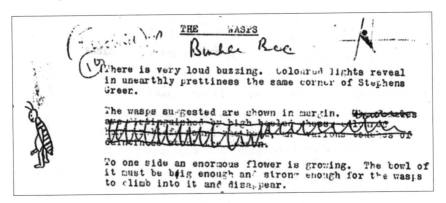

Fig. 11.1. In the production notebook the 'wasps suggested are shown in margin'.
Image courtesy of the Charles Deering McCormick Library of Special Collections,
Northwestern University Library. Copyright of the Edwards – mac Liammóir Estate.

Rather than a narrative expounding the sexual freedom of the Čapeks' butterflies, O'Nolan's bees choose between the unlikely chance of mating with the Queen or the 'sensuous delight of stinging with the rather charming death that follows' (*PT*, 173). Two bees, Cyril and Cecil, engage in a vaudeville-esque two-hander where they bemoan the lack of 'weemeen' (*PT*, 170). Realising that they have a very slim chance of mating, their conversation turns to stinging, which they describe as being 'unbearably nice' while carrying with it the inevitable penalty of death (*PT*, 171). There is a connection between the martyrdom that is considered an attractive option by the bees and the self-sacrifice that plays an integral part of the war narrative, with Cecil stating that due to conversations he has had with dying bees he has concluded that 'to die from giving our sting is to become a martyr'; it involves 'no pain' and 'death can be rather charming' (*PT*, 172). The exchange mocks the idea of martyrdom and the ideology that underpins it and seems to connect the idea of sacrifice to physical desire and, most certainly, homoeroticism. The nonhuman is conflated with the mechanical to create, in O'Nolan's work, a bee figure that equates death and sex. The unending drive for procreation and mating with the Queen is relinquished in favour of an existence that embraces pleasure over futurity. The death drive, as Lee Edelman argues, 'refers to an energy of mechanistic compulsion whose structural armature exceeds the specific object, the specific content, toward which we might feel that it impels us'.[30] Procreation is the enabling of a future and the cheating of death, through the compulsion to mirror ourselves in our children. Sex, when unhooked from procreation, is a more truthful adherence to life as it contextualises the endless postponement of procreation as Edelman reiterates: 'the deception of the societal lie that endlessly looks toward a future whose promise is always a day away'.[31] When O'Nolan's bees perform or represent that symbolic idea of sacrifice and martyrdom they are also making a choice to refute the dangerous ideology of the future.

The incident of the suicide by mutual stinging is closely followed by the entrance of the Queen, described in the stage directions as '*a superlatively erotic job*' (*PT*, 179). The death of Cyril and Cecil leaves the drone and the Queen as the last two remaining bees and, when he is too drunk on honey to respond to her advances, she commits suicide by stinging the sleeping Tramp. By contrast, in the Selver version, the life of the male insects is deemed an advantageous one with Iris saying: 'How stupid it is to be a woman. I should like to be a man – to kiss, to tempt, to overcome.'[32] Selver's female butterfly is vain and narcissistic, described by the Tramp as a 'strumpet!', a 'painted 'arlot' and a 'white-face 'arridan'.[33] The characteristics of the butterfly, its vanity and flightiness, can be assimilated into the supposed qualities of the flapper.

The conflation between insect, machine and human corresponds to the modernist decentring of the privileged role of the human body. The animality of Darwin's theory of evolution confirmed the idea of the human body as ecologically embedded. The idea of the human body as an organic machine fostered a new discourse as to the relationship between the human and nonhuman in the new, technological age of man. The possibility within modernist narratives was not just the emergence of man from within this evolutionary web but also the convergence of man and machine into the future – a vision of the *Übermensch* as envisioned by Nietzsche. The use of the figure of the parasite is also an interesting choice given the use of the Jonathan Swift quotation in both the title and the epigraph of the Selver version:

> So, Nat'ralists observe, a Flea
> Has smaller fleas that on him prey;
> And these have smaller still to bite 'em,
> And so proceed *ad infinitum*.

Although many of the insects in the play are parasitic, the parasite does not have any singular features that define the character as a specific insect. It is rather a creature that pendulates between both insect and human, embodying the negative connotations of both.

The unfavourable depiction of archetypes such as the parasite and the various insect characters is offset by the value of insects as machines. Early in the opening act of Selver's translation, the role of the lepidopterist counters

Fig. 11.2. František Roland playing the parasite in the 1922 Czech production.
Image courtesy of the Prague National Theatre Archive.

any harmonious evolution narrative by attempting to catch the butterflies as each specimen must be 'carefully killed, and then carefully pinned, and properly dried'.[34] When asked by the Tramp why he feels that he needs to do this, the lepidopterist replies: 'Love of nature.'[35] It is when the Tramp falls asleep that the butterflies begin to talk. Their main topic of conversation is sexual relations, but there is a marked difference between the tone of the conversation and that of the bees in O'Nolan's adaptation. There is a roaring twenties sense of *frisson* between the butterflies. The Tramp in Selver's version talks about the male butterfly as 'goin' 'alf balmy for them flighty things' and the female as a 'man-trap 'idden behind two silky wings'.[36] The Tramp proceeds to compare the butterflies to human society: 'Put it blunt-like – Lord Alf and Lady Rose Be'ave exactly like them insects do.'[37] The butterflies are more light-hearted than O'Nolan's bees and they certainly retain some of the sexual stereotypes of the 1920s socialite. The generational gap between the two versions is illustrated in the fact that the Selver translation seems consumed with proliferation, while the O'Nolan adaptation deals with the fallout or the failure of reproductive copulation.

Swarming (of both bees and ants) is a phenomenon that is seen primarily as negative, where the mindless interdependence that is integral to these insect colonies can often take on a darker tone. The image is one of aggression, mobility and destruction on the one hand, but of collective intelligence on the other. Discussing Maurice Maeterlinck's *The Life of the Bee* (1901) in his 2010 study *Insect Media: An archaeology of animals and technology*, Jussi Parikka contends that the 'swarm is a becoming that expresses potentialities that are always situated and yet moving'.[38] For Parikka, swarming 'happens not on the level of consciousness, human language and concepts, but as affects of murmur, whisper and a refrain that even the bees might not hear but sense in some uncanny way'.[39] Bees then possess an ability that, given the human desire for human/machine coevolution, is a feature of instinct as intelligence rather than a mindless physical compulsion.

There is certainly an argument to be made that expressionistic productions of the play fare better than more comically rendered or vaudeville versions. The beauty of the butterflies in *Ze života hmyzu* captures the era as sexually liberated, but the depiction is tinged with the shadow of mechanical warfare. In contrast, *Rhapsody* portrays the bees in a less romanticised and more pantomime style which seems to sneer rather than celebrate social gatherings (or swarming). The context within which *Ze života hmyzu* was first produced in 1921 is that of an expressionistic theatre as plays broke with the realism of the well-made play with the aim of expressing rather than representing human life. Contemporaneous works such as Eugene O'Neill's *The Hairy Ape* (1922) and Elmer Rice's *The Adding Machine* (1923) were often exaggerated, theatrical and subjective and depicted humanity's increasing anxiety of mechanistic nihilism. The 1922 Prague production of *Ze života hmyzu* was directed by acclaimed Czech director Karel Hugo Hilar, whose expressionistic work Jarka M. Burian describes as: 'a constant stylisation if not distortion of vocal and bodily expression that produced a highly dynamic, rhythmicised total presentation. Characterisation was sacrificed to artificial constructs of essential forces and ideas.'[40] The Čapeks' use of butterflies referenced the characteristic free-spirited nature of the *années folles*; a far cry from Dublin during the Emergency era. Whereas the butterflies are sexually promiscuous in the Selver translation of *Ze života hmyzu*, in *Rhapsody* the bees are more frenzied. There is certainly strong anthropocentrism evident in both adaptations. In *Rhapsody*, the stage instructions call for the bee '*females*' to be distinguished by '*high-heeled shoes, coloured handkerchiefs round the head, and various touches of daintiness about the person*' (*PT*, 168). Poesis (in the theatre sense) is helpful when discussing anthropomorphised animals such as the butterfly and the bee because it is a move away from language and its inhibiting factors. It also corresponds with the posthumanist drive to account for the voice of the nonhuman in creative work: the acknowledgment that there are other entities at play in representation.[41] Examining *Rhapsody* from the multitude of perspectives with which it is aligned is enriching for a non-anthropocentric study of animal representation/aesthetics, but more specifically it allows us to see the play from its European context. The long performance history of *Ze života hmyzu*, through its English translations and cultural adaptations, shows that O'Nolan's *Rhapsody* stems from a history of animal characters played by human bodies in theatre: a performative field that, more than O'Nolan's fiction is arguably able to achieve, foregrounds the materiality of the body and its embeddedness in the natural world.

The politics of beetle capitalism

As unlikely as it may seem, there is precedent for the use of the dung beetle in the arts, where it maintains a strong iconographic tradition (in ancient Egypt for example) of regeneration and renewal.[42] Aesop's fable 'The Eagle and the Dung Beetle', in which the dung beetle outwits and destroys the eggs of the more powerful eagle, is referenced in the Greek comedy *Lysistrata* (411 BC), where the dung beetle is labelled the midwife of the eagle. Slaves collect excrement to feed a giant dung beetle in the comedy *Peace* by Aristophanes (421 BC). But towards the end of the nineteenth century, as understanding of the complexity of smaller organisms increases with the application of advancing technology in the field of natural history, the insect becomes more closely associated with the mechanical.

Three beetles appear in the original and adapted versions of *Ze života hmyzu* and open Act II: Creepers and Crawlers. In many respects, rather than crudely misrepresenting dung beetle behaviour, the scene attempts to parody and expose human behaviour as selfish. Certainly, Jean-Henri Fabre's entomological work portrays beetles as hardworking and tenacious creatures whose mothering capacities could only be rivalled by a hymenopteran (such as a bee, wasp or ant): 'Notwithstanding their disgusting occupation, the Dung-beetles are of a very respectable standing.'[43] They are on a 'proud mission' to 'purge the soil of its filth'.[44] However, the beetles in *Ze života hmyzu* are distinctly less admirable than Fabre's characterisation, as they bicker and fight over their nest egg that amounts to a pile of dung. In Selver's translation, a pair of beetles open the scene, quarrelling:

Mʀs BEETLE: Silly swine.
Mʀ BEETLE: Fathead.
Mʀs BEETLE: Fathead yourself – mind where you're going.[45]

Reflecting the Europe from which *Ze života hmyzu* had emerged, their behaviour introduces a darker tone as the characters reveal themselves to be more materialistic opportunists than the carnally driven butterflies. The contrast between the fighting beetles and the flighty and light-headed butterflies is lessened in *Rhapsody*. After the frenzied activity of the bees in Act I, Mr and Mrs Beetle do not enter the scene arguing but seemingly working together to increase their nest-egg with Mr Beetle saying, 'An' isn't it worth puttin' yourself into a lather for – a pile of stuff that cost us the grey hairs of a lifetime to put together?' (*PT*, 186). Mr and Mrs Beetle are obsessed with their ball of dirt or capital (as the beetles themselves call it) that they have accumulated as Mr Beetle bemoans the effort that has gone into the accumulation of their life's saving: 'How we've saved and scraped and toiled and moiled to come by it.'[46] They are so impressed with their accumulated savings in *Rhapsody* that O'Nolan's Mrs Beetle goes so far as to say: 'Sure is it anny wonder some Beetles do be selling their bodies to other Beetles that does have a big pile like this?' (*PT*, 188). Again, as with the suicide by stinging of the bees, sex is used for something other than procreation, a divergent narrative when compared to the often puritanical rhetoric of Emergency-era Ireland. O'Nolan's insects are a comment on the true nature of human desire, and the use of Selver's translation of *Ze života hmyzu* as a template serves to underline the replacement of the human figure with that of the insect as a commentary on increasing mechanisation.

In both the Selver translation and O'Nolan's adaptation, fearing that their dung will be stolen and eager to begin new piles, the beetles decide to bury the nest egg. While Mr Beetle exits looking for a suitable hole to bury the ball of dung, Mrs Beetle finds what is termed the lair of an Ichneumon fly in *Ze života hmyzu* and a nest in *Rhapsody*. In her absence, Strange Beetle enters and steals the ball of dung. In the Selver translation, when confronted by the Tramp who claims that the ball of capital smells, Strange Beetle counters: 'Capital don't smell – Off you go, me precious – this way, my little all, my nest-egg, my capital.'[47] Led to believe (by the Tramp) that her husband has left with the 'savings', Mrs Beetle exits. In Fabre's entomological work, the tenacity of the dung beetle is admired in an incident where a ball of dung is stolen: 'The Dung-beetle does not allow himself to be cast down by this piece of ill-luck: he rubs his cheeks, spreads his antennae, sniffs the air and flies to the nearest heap to begin all over again. I admire and envy this cast of character.'[48] In *Rhapsody*, there is the same tone and admiration for the work ethic if not the dubious choices of the dung beetle:

> TRAMP: (Musing.) Well begob can you beat that! The bloody bees do spend the time blathering out of them but your men the beetles is all for work, gatherin' up all classes of muck and dirt an' rollin' it into big balls, balls that would take the sight out of yer eyes with the smell that's off them. (*PT*, 191)

The scene plays out as a critique of capitalism and the selfishness and insularity it engenders. When compared to the flighty butterflies in the Selver version, the Tramp acknowledges that the beetles work hard, 'But these 'ere beetles – lumme, They *do* work, anyway!'[49] He is in the throes of extravagance with his well-earned pile of dirt: 'Smell it, woman, lick it, taste it! It's ours!'[50] When the pile is stolen by the Strange Beetle in *Rhapsody*, the Tramp again notes that there is an odour, and the Strange Beetle counters: 'Who ever heard of a smell being off a life's savins. Sure all this stuff is me capital. It's grand stuff, I'm a happy man, it does me heart good to feel it and see it' (*PT*, 190). When Mr Beetle hears that the pile of dirt has been stolen, he is more interested in its recovery than his wife's welfare. In both versions his capital takes precedence over his wife. In the Selver translation he calls out: 'They've killed me, they've done me in. Who cares about my wife? It's my pile they've taken',[51] whereas in *Rhapsody*, 'They've stolen me savins, me capital, they've stolen me investments, me pile! I'm ruined, ruined, where was that bloody bitch of a wife of mine?' (*PT*, 196).

In both the Selver translation and O'Nolan's adaptation of *Ze života hmyzu*, the beetles are portrayed as selfish, conniving and greedy. The characters are dehumanised, yet their compulsion to hoard is used to represent human greed. There are differing versions of the beetle characters in various productions, as Stephen Johnson notes:

> the appearance of the Dung Beetles in the Broadway production emphasised their comic *personae*. The designers made them into oversized burlesque comics. By contrast, the Czech Dung Beetle seemed more obviously a social caricature. While the Dung Beetle's portrayal incorporated humour, the design emphasised the long, grasping fingers and oversized jaw and might best be compared to a political cartoon.[52]

Fig. 11.3. Josef Čapek's original beetle costume sketch.
Image courtesy of the Prague National Theatre Archive.

This demarcation between the comic Broadway production and the Czech version as a political cartoon underlines the differentiation between the pantomime-style of characters played for laughs as they perform realistic human actions and the more expressionistic butterflies of the original Czech production. The pantomime characterisation of insects (such as those found in O'Nolan's adaptation), while successful, can be more easily dismissed by an audience than the piece performed as political satire, which the audience would more readily accept as a performance that has a moral lesson to impart.

The original audiences for *Ze života hmyzu* were confronted with what Jennifer Sheppard describes as an 'uncompromising condemnation of humankind'.[53] This was not a light-hearted animal fable, but a dark vision of society overrun with human creatures driven by base instinct. Even as it presents an ecological vision for collective living, in the play itself individuals suffer as they scramble for survival and the fabric of social living is picked apart by those acting in their own self-interest. Building on Bergson, by way of Elisabeth Grosz, Parikka argues that animal instinct should be seen as a tool that gives more direct access to one's environment than intelligence: 'the instinct approach points to an understanding of technics as affects, as relations that are concretely felt by the participants in a systematic means of participation'.[54] This biotechnological view of nonhuman nature categorises instinct as something more than the simple conflation of automation and mindlessness. The beginning of the Second World War marked the end of modernism (or of high modernism at least), and in *Rhapsody* we can see a challenge to the essentialism and reductionism that many saw as endemic in the modernist aesthetic. But is the Čapek original a modernist text and the O'Nolan version a postmodernist text? In many ways the separation is stylistic. Whereas the Čapek version hinges on the experimental radicalism of high modernism, O'Nolan's is self-consciously farcical. *Ze života hmyzu* predicts a future of the automated insect/machine and the increasing suspicion that its ties with humankind are more than tenuous. The Irish adaptation, written a generation later, similarly mocks the social mannerisms that attempt to conceal the instinctual intelligence that suffuses human behaviour. In O'Nolan's adaptation, these themes are distinguishable in that the moral response of the Tramp to this insectoid/mechanical behaviour is more extreme. The original play is a moral commentary on war where humans are reduced (or overcome) by innate insectoid behaviour. It is framed as a human morality tale narrated by the human rather than the insect characters. Sheppard points out that 'the morals are explicitly drawn by a lone human figure, a tramp, who observes the insects and comments on their behaviour'.[55] Critics maintain that humans still frame the behaviour from within their own (seemingly objective) moral standpoint in the play. In fact, the Tramp's opinion of the insects, and – as this is an allegory – by extension humankind, is darker in the O'Nolan version, for example in the response to the warring ants willing to sacrifice all:

> TRAMP: [...] Them buggers is all mad. Down the road we have a dead beetle with his dirty bloody guts stickin' out of him and all classes of bees and bluebottles tryin' to ate him – a dirty useless-lookin' sight. And these lads here wants to die for that. (*PT*, 226)

The Selver translation below could be read as a more measured but also more morally ambiguous response to the violence:

TRAMP: It does yer good to see 'em pass,
        Prepared to shed their blood –
        And jest for 'alf a yard o'mud,
        Between two blades o' grass.[56]

Neither the humans nor the insects fare well as the play progresses. *Ze života hmyzu* emerged from a discourse around insect aesthetics that combined natural automata with the mechanical age. Most notably, this connection surfaces in the increased mechanisation of war.[57] The impact of the widespread use of mechanical warfare during the course of both the First and Second World Wars reverberated throughout Europe. The adaption of the play for Emergency-era Ireland illustrates that insect/mechanic conflation as something that was profoundly modern, in that the use of insects in cultural and artistic processes betrays the role of insects, not only as metaphorical animal others, but as creatures with characteristics that are strangely mechanical. On the spectrum of human versus machine, insects were assumed to be very much on the side of the machine. They were driven by animal instinct but fitted with the tools and features that border on the robotic. As Parikka argues, 'the watershed question related to intelligence versus repeatable actions resided at the core of the age of technology: what actions would be automatised and hence transformed into a machine, and what are unique to the intelligent human being'.[58]

Conclusion

Ze života hmyzu, its translations and adaptations, including *Rhapsody*, follow Agamben's argument that for the 'totalitarianisms of the twentieth century', the end result 'for a humanity that has become animal again' is 'the taking on of biological life itself as the supreme political (or rather impolitical) task'.[59] Humanism, in the wake of the techno-charged tragedies of global warfare, could not continue on its anthropocentric course, the route of world-making that overextended mankind beyond Uexküll's *Umwelten*.[60] The use of animal characters in performance has cultural resonances for many of these changes. For Agamben, 'the total humanisation of the animal coincides with a total animalisation of man'.[61] The conflation between the two augurs a discourse of posthumanism where our collective spaces host a convergence of human, nonhuman and mechanical bodies.[62] Using humour as a theatrical and narrative device, *Ze života hmyzu* and *Rhapsody* are powerful allegories for a change in the representation of humanity as the centralising and omnipotent figurehead.

To discount the complexity of the insect in a cultural entomological realignment of *Ze života hmyzu* is to simplify cultural representations of insects. This is a disservice to a complex relationship between aesthetics and meaning. The biological and instinctual tools with which insects are equipped for survival suggest a new means or method for organisation that could be represented in the arts. As Parikka insists, rather than seeing insect behaviour as 'closed loops of automatic behavior', we should see 'instincts functioning as intensities – prelinguistic modes of intertwining the body with its surroundings'.[63] This new interpretation of insect behaviour moves the idea of instinct from 'automated reflex-(re)action' to a 'tendency' or 'potentiality' that flourishes in its difference rather than linearity.[64] In a tradition of representation in which the bee has been used to represent the value of collective understanding and teamwork, the choice of archetypal insects in the Čapek/O'Nolan plays speaks to their value or presence within a human-oriented framework. The very different choices that are made, the exchange of butterflies for bees for example, illustrate the different functions and energies that the character of the insect brings to *Ze života hmyzu* and *Rhapsody*.

The key to reading these plays as animal satire is to appreciate the complexity inherent in both insect and human behaviour and its corresponding aesthetic. To reduce the productions to symbolism is to do them a disservice and deny the very liveliness that is a part of the theatrical process. As Deleuze and Guattari write, 'to break the becoming-animal all that is needed is to extract a segment from it, to abstract one of its moments, to fail to take into account its internal speeds and slownesses, to arrest the circulation of affects'.[65] This action severs the complex relations between actors, and what remains are the 'imaginary resemblances between terms, or symbolic analogies between relations'.[66] This is neither a light-hearted nor a simplistic comedy. O'Nolan developed work that conflated the animal, mechanics and the human imaginary to critique an idea of anthropocentric exceptionalism that is self-serving and exploitative. *Rhapsody* is a performative narrative that expounds O'Nolan's handling of the discourse surrounding the damaging fallout of anthropocentric exceptionalism. This essay argues that *Rhapsody* plays a significant role in O'Nolan's broader canon because it points to the representation of the nonhuman not as a facetious and glib shorthand or metaphor for the worst excesses of humanity, but as a realisation that human behaviour cannot be decontextualised from the instinctual and animalistic/ materialistic underpinning from which it emerges.

12

Thunderous Anger and Cold Showers

Grand Guignol in Myles na gCopaleen's
An Sgian and *The Handsome Carvers*

JACK FENNELL

On St Stephen's Day, 1944, the Gaelic Theatre Guild (*Compántas Amharclainne na Gaedhilge*) began its initial week-long run of its festive variety show *Geamaí na Nodlag* (Christmas Capers) at the Peacock Theatre – owned by, and situated within, the Abbey Theatre. The show proved so popular that it was continued for another week, the first time in twenty-one years that an Irish-language production's run had been extended.[1] In fact, *Geamaí na Nodlag* would have been renewed for a third week, had the theatre not already been reserved for a performance by the Insurance Institute of Ireland Dramatic Society.[2] Towards the end of the second week, the Guild asked *The Irish Press* to apologise on their behalf 'to the hundreds of persons who could not find room in the Peacock Theatre during the past two weeks'. The *Irish Press* theatre critic concluded from the show's remarkable success that 'The problem of entertainment through Irish has been solved by this group in the only way in which it could be solved: giving as good and better than the English-speaking groups'.[3] By public demand, *Geamaí na Nodlag* was granted an additional run at the Peacock from 19 February 1945, adding some new items to the original programme.[4]

The item most frequently referenced in newspaper reviews from the time is Con Ó Liatháin's *Huntin', Fishin', Shootin'*, but the show also included a one-act sketch by Brian O'Nolan, as Myles na gCopaleen, called *An Sgian* (The Knife). While na gCopaleen is mentioned in a handful of articles, reviewers at the time tended to ignore *An Sgian*, or else gloss over it as vaguely as possible. An *Irish Press* review from the show's opening week describes *An Sgian* as 'Myles Na gCopaleen's satirical slant on some of our youth movements';[5] later, an Irish-language review of the February run promises that the sketch 'will knock a laugh out of the gloomiest person under the light of the sun, especially because the Guild is mocking ourselves here'.[6] While the English review avoids naming the targets of the sketch, the Irish-language article tries to frame it as a work of good-natured self-deprecation. The likely reason for this hesitancy and diplomacy is that *An Sgian* is actually an attack on two fascist organisations, *Ailtirí na hAiséirghe* (Architects of the Resurrection) and *Glún na Buaidhe* (The Victorious Generation). As Carol Taaffe succinctly puts it, the *Ailtirí* and *Glún na Buaidhe* 'shared an unhealthy brand of right-wing exclusivist nationalism, as well as a bitter rivalry'. Initially treating these organisations with amused disdain in his *Cruiskeen Lawn* columns, O'Nolan became increasingly worried about their long-term goals from early 1943 onwards.[7]

A particularly interesting aspect of the composition and production history of *An Sgian* is that O'Nolan wrote an undated English-language sketch, *The Handsome Carvers*, based on the same premise, but with noticeable differences.[8] Here, I will compare and contrast these works with an eye to genre and psychology, as well as to their language and gender politics.[9]

An Sgian opens in the middle of a spat between Tadhg and his wife Peig. Peig is a member of *Glún na Buaidhe* and intends to host a committee meeting in their house on Thursday. Tadhg is a member of *Ailtirí na hAiséirghe* and he holds *Glún na Buaidhe* in contempt. They bicker about their respective group allegiances until Tadhg finally loses his cool, takes a carving knife from a box, chases Peig around the stage with it and stabs her to death. Afterwards, he finds and reads a letter which explains that the carving knife was a wedding present from Tadhg's former colleagues at the Gaelic League.

The Handsome Carvers presents the conflict between husband and wife in less light-hearted manner: the room is bare, the unnamed wife is crying and the husband, now named Peter Dunleary, is drunk, *'ranging around the room, like a caged beast'*, having pawned all their belongings to buy drink (*PT*, 261). When the wife snaps and suggests that he pawn their wedding gifts too, he loses his mind completely and pulls a carving knife from a drawer. He chases her around the stage and raises the knife, poising to strike, before the lights black out and the curtain falls. Act II is a prologue to what we have just seen. We are transported to a gathering of civil servants in a hotel function room, where Peter is presented with a gift of a cutlery set by his colleagues on the occasion of his engagement. After some drunken speechifying by two 'gentlemen' present, he gratefully accepts the gift of 'the handsome carvers' and confesses that this occasion is the first time he has ever taken whiskey. The curtain falls as he proposes to have another one, and the other civil servants sing a round of 'For He's a Jolly Good Fellow' (*PT*, 264).

Daniel Keith Jernigan considers *An Sgian* to be the more accomplished of the two plays. Whereas *An Sgian* expands upon language politics O'Nolan had already tackled in his newspaper column, thus adding 'an intriguing addition to his perspective on the issue', Jernigan feels that *The Handsome Carvers* 'reads suspiciously like a skit written for the Abstinence League' (*PT*, xv). A straightforward comparison between the two supports this judgement to a large extent.

As Louis de Paor describes, the domestic row in *An Sgian* is a satirical comment on the violent fascist rhetoric of *Ailtirí na hAiséirghe* and *Glún na Buaidhe*, as summed up in their parent organisation *Craobh na hAiséirghe's* motto, '*Téid focal le gaoth, ach téid buille le cnámh*' (Words go with the wind, but a blow strikes the bone).[10] Rather than being an allegory for the groups' mutual animosity, Tadhg and Peig's fight draws upon that animosity directly. Central to the fight is the issue of custodianship and authenticity, with each of them effectively trying to 'out-Irish' the other and assert ownership over the language and culture they fetishise. *An Sgian* begins in the middle of an argument over how each of them learned to speak Irish: Tadhg claims to have taught Peig all the Irish she knows; she scoffs at this assertion and derides his Irish lessons, which seem to have been more appropriate for children than adults (*PT*, 251–2). From here, their spat becomes ever more hyperbolic. When the fight reaches its murderous climax, the 'victory' of one side over the other accomplishes nothing but tragedy: after killing Peig and discovering the letter, Tadhg seems to be so overwhelmed by horror that he cannot countenance what he has done, dissociating from the scene and instead correcting the letter's grammar, as if in a trance (*PT*, 257). As de Paor points out, 'That [Tadhg] is mistaken in his amendment only adds to the vicious irony of the situation'.[11]

In *The Handsome Carvers*, by contrast, there are no political inferences to be drawn at all, unless we read something into Peter's '*prim, "cultured" voice*' (*PT*, 264), or the fact that his name is 'Dunleary' – from Dún Laoghaire, formerly a major connecting port to Great Britain. These characteristics might indicate that Peter is a 'West Brit', but such an interpretation adds little to a political reading of the story. Rather, this posh characterisation serves the dramatic irony, as does the first speaker's description of Peter as 'courteous', 'considerate' and 'gentlemanly' in Act II (*PT*, 262–3) – since at this point, we already know that Peter is going to end up a violent alcoholic, because of an addiction born at this very gathering. As the target of the joke shifts from political extremists to civil servants, however, the trenchant allegorical reading of *An Sgian* is lost.[12] Judging from the stage directions, it is quite possible that O'Nolan never intended for *The Handsome Carvers* to be staged at all, or perhaps intended it simply as a writing exercise, or as a rough draft of a short screenplay. At the end of Act I, he specifies that the transition from one act to the next should take place '*as quickly as possible*', and that transition is punctuated by an abrupt black-out (*PT*, 262), as though he is trying to emulate a cinematic scene-to-scene progression. During this brief blackout, the bare domestic setting has to change to a crowded hotel function room, and in the new scene, Peter is supposed to suddenly look '*younger and cleaner*' (*PT*, 262). A similar 'cut to black' happens in *An Sgian*, though without the logistical complexity (*PT*, 252).

This is what makes one of the key differences between the two plays so interesting: in *An Sgian*, Peig's murder happens onstage, but in *The Handsome Carvers*, the 'cut to black' happens just as Peter raises the knife, and the act is merely suggested. Without knowing the precise date of *The Handsome Carvers*'s composition, I suspect that the success of *An Sgian* as part of the *Geamaí na Nodlag* show may have prompted O'Nolan to try to broaden the sketch's appeal – hence the shift to English and the absence of any specific political references that might unnerve prospective reviewers. However, the omission of the deathblow in *The Handsome Carvers* calls attention to its inclusion in *An Sgian* and invites discussion as to why O'Nolan saw fit to write such a violent and potentially controversial skit for a Christmas variety show. One possible explanation emerges when we consider the popularity of *Grand Guignol* theatre, and its related genres, among the Irish theatregoing public.

Grand Guignol in Ireland

Le Théâtre du Grand-Guignol (The Theatre of the Great Puppet) initially specialised in two minor genres – *Moeurs populaire* (popular manners) and *Fait divers* (news items), which were both naturalist in outlook. The former were single-act slices-of-life focusing on 'the lowest strata of society', often 'static [and] undramatic' in their presentation, while the latter were adapted from short notices in newspapers – usually brief, sensationalist accounts of 'little robberies, muggings, rape, a lover burned with acid by his mistress, etc'.[13] When Max Maurey took over as director of the theatre in 1898, he emphasised the second aspect of the Grand Guignol's remit, jettisoning the low-key naturalism and focusing on the horror. After staging numerous plays by André de Lorde, the Grand Guignol's 'house style' was further refined with anticipation and suspense, and the theatre settled into a pattern of alternating between horror and farce.[14] It was, of course, the horror for which the Grand Guignol would become better known, and by the mid-twentieth century, the term 'Grand Guignol' itself came to stand for a particular kind of horror fiction.

The usual themes of Grand Guignol are crime, death and insanity. Because the stage of the original theatre was quite small, the scenery tended to be simple, and the action was usually confined to one setting – most often a drawing room, a prison cell, an operating room or a cell in a mental hospital. The realistic detail and the 'moral detachment from the theme' were derived from the theatre's naturalist roots, but this naturalism was combined with a generous helping of melodrama; the stage design, meanwhile, strove 'to combine verisimilitude and atmosphere'.[15] In 'classic' Grand Guignol, the supernatural was rarely invoked to prompt the audience's fear, but ghosts and science-fictional *Frankenstein*-style reanimations did make occasional appearances.[16] Grand Guignol plays also made extensive use of lighting effects, partly to create atmosphere and partly to conceal imperfections in the painted backdrops. Sound effects were equally prominent, as were retractable blades and various formulae for fake blood.[17] No matter how extreme the Grand Guignol's horrors got, though, they were always 'well within the accepted norms of society': in France, the villains of these plays could get away with all kinds of grisly deeds onstage, but when the villain was executed by guillotine in a 1921 performance, this *mise en scène* prompted demonstrations outside the theatre until the directors agreed to drop the curtain at the moment of beheading.[18] In terms of staging, Grand Guignol had a 'modular' structure in common with American vaudeville shows: each brief segment was self-contained and could be replaced or moved around from week to week, depending on how well audiences responded to it.[19]

Though this theatrical formula enjoyed great popularity in the interwar period in France, the attempts to bring the Grand Guignol theatre performances to Italy, Britain, Canada and America were only modestly successful and not long-lived.[20] If theatre reviews and notices are anything to go by, however, Irish audiences and critics responded well to this material and exhibited a healthy appetite for Grand Guignol-inspired plays through the 1920s and '30s. A commentator for the *Cork Examiner* linked this appreciation to the violence of the Civil War, noting that 'the crack of a rifle during the night and the whirr of the machine-gun have become familiar sounds' in the twenty-six counties, and that 'people can grow accustomed to gunfire – just as eels are said to grow accustomed to being skinned, but the educational process is not pleasant'. The same commentator, like so many others since, also worries about the psychological effects of gruesome entertainments:

> Some persons like to be thrilled and willingly pay for the luxury, if luxury it be. The Grand Guignol plays; the melodrama in which poison, daggers, red fire, and revolvers pursue the heroine to the end of the last act, or gruesome tragedy in which most, if not all of the players expire uttering maledictions, usually find admirers and supporters. [...] One may hope that crude and flatulent melodrama will be sufficient to satisfy the taste of the rising generation, and that such thrills as the stage supplies will be sufficient for those who, if wise, would cultivate moderation in such matters.[21]

If we accept, for the sake of argument, that the violence of the early twentieth century may have increased the popularity of violent entertainment, it should be noted that there was a pre-existing enthusiasm for such material. Shortly after John Millington Synge's death in 1909, for example, James Joyce made arrangements for *Riders to the Sea* to be translated into Italian and performed by Alfredo Sainati's Italian Grand Guignol Company.[22] Over the next decades, the public's appreciation for macabre dramas and 'thrillers' became evident from the volume of reviews, festival programmes and specialist productions dedicated to these genres.

A theatre reviewer for the *Freeman's Journal*, describing a performance of Mary Roberts Rinehart's *The Bat* at the Gaiety in 1923, wrote in glowing terms that the play constituted 'the nearest approach we have yet had to the plays of the Grand Guignol'.[23] The following May, the *Irish Times* reviewer who went to a performance of John Willard's *The Cat and the Canary* opined: 'The play is so extraordinary that it will probably replace politics and gas strike discomforts as matter for Dublin conversations this week.'[24] In 1928, the *Belfast News-Letter* announced 'Grand Guignol Fails', noting that Grand Guignol-style plays were failing to draw substantial audiences in London and positing that such material had lost much of its novelty.[25] In the Free State, by contrast, the first-season programme for Dún Laoghaire's new Civic Theatre in 1929 specifically included Grand Guignol pieces;[26] later, a drama festival in 1933 promised in its press releases that it would boast a 'balanced' programme, by necessity including 'a "thriller" of the Grand Guignol order'.[27] This appreciation for macabre theatre was not confined to the cities, either – an English company with the apposite name of The Grand Guignol Players toured rural Ireland in 1932.[28]

Irish playwrights and theatre companies soon started to write and stage Grand Guignol-style material themselves. Notable among these were the Gaelic Players, who translated a number of plays into Irish and performed them on a recurring basis, including André de Lorde's *Au Téléphone* in 1926[29] and *The End of the Book* by American playwright Henry Myers in 1930.[30] Lord Dunsany's *A Night at an Inn*, featuring an enigmatic cult and numerous on-stage murders, was presented by the Dublin University Dramatic Society in 1928[31] and staged again as a 'curtain-raiser' for a longer comic play in 1932.[32] Other original short pieces containing horrid murders and melodrama were written about Dublin's criminal underworld,[33] and those written in similar idioms, no matter how vague the comparison, were often described as 'Grand Guignol' or 'belonging to the Grand Guignol tradition', such as Wicklow playwright Vivian Connell's controversial *The Nineteenth Hole of Europe* (1943), which is set in a Europe ravaged by plague.[34]

As mentioned previously, the Grand-Guignol Theatre did not fare very well outside of its native Paris. Their planned ten-week season in New York in the autumn of 1923 barely lasted for seven, due to a miscalculation in their choice of material. Fearing prosecution or public outrage, the company deliberately chose 'weaker' scripts that would not offend American sensibilities. As John M. Callahan notes, the critics who went to the opening performances were disappointed, and theatregoers who otherwise would have gone to see the show decided not to bother after reading the lukewarm reviews; by the time the Grand-Guignol realised its mistake and started staging stronger pieces, it was too late to correct the public perception. New York audiences did not find the Grand-Guignol scary at all – in fact, they laughed.[35] More precisely, they laughed at the parts at which they were not supposed to laugh. A Grand-Guignol programme typically consisted of six short sketches, alternating back and forth between horror and farce to induce a 'whiplash' effect in the audience, an arrangement known as 'hot and cold showers'.[36] As demonstrated by the New York reaction, it was an arrangement that could very easily go awry. In the case of *An Sgian*, however, a domestic fight culminating in the wife's violent death is presented comically, and the few critics who reviewed it (however circumspect their descriptions of the subject matter) seemed to enjoy it; given the fact that the sketch was retained for the show's 1945 rerun, we can infer that audiences responded well to it too. If the variety-show structure of *Geamaí na Nodlag* echoed that of the classic Grand Guignol Theatre, *An Sgian* boiled the Parisian hot-and-cold sequence down to a condensed mixture of comedy and horror.

Born in 1911, O'Nolan would have been far too young to be allowed to see such macabre plays during the first wave of their popularity in Ireland; it is thus safe to assume that at the time he started writing, he would have been more familiar with the term 'Grand Guignol' as a descriptor than as the name of a subgenre. It is clear, however, that his dramaturgical instincts pointed in the direction of the Grand Guignol. For one thing, he believed that the theatre should present a dramatic reality rather than a naturalistic one. Taaffe points out that early in his writing career O'Nolan was annoyed at what he perceived to be snobbery on the part of the Abbey Theatre and its fixation with 'Peasant Quality' actors and actresses, his counterargument being that authenticity did not necessitate quotidian realism; he believed that the Irish theatrical scene needed 'a transfusion of contemporary European drama'.[37]

More obviously, as Sean Pryor points out, O'Nolan's 'comedy thrives on what seem to be immoralities – brutal murders, grotesque violence, systematic oppression, rape, theft [and] adultery', which certainly lend themselves to Grand Guignol drama. However, Pryor also argues that in O'Nolan's works, such acts are often carried out by 'inevitably evil' characters, who lack autonomy because each one is 'less like an ethical subject than a personification. [...] Call every boy Jams O'Donnell and he will by vocation be Jams O'Donnell.'[38] This issue of moral culpability becomes much more complex in other works, such as the sketches under consideration here, in which characters seem frustrated by their responsibilities as moral agents and are looking for excuses to abandon them.

Rage and release

Both sketches considered here are variations on the same grim joke – a husband kills his wife in a rage, using a knife that had been given to him as a wedding gift by his former colleagues. As *The Handsome Carvers* is not dated, it is difficult to tell which version came first, but it is clear that O'Nolan had been pondering the premise for a number of months at least. An allusion to the set-up of both sketches appears in the middle of a June 1944 *Cruiskeen*

Lawn farce, wherein Sir Myles na gCopaleen (the da) returns to public life when solicitors exhume him, months after his apparent death, in order to clarify vague phraseology in his will. After his exhumation, which sees him 'alive and well', Sir Myles is entertained to supper at the United Services Club by *Ailtirí na hAiséirghe*, who present him with 'a handsome wallet of carvers'. His none-too-impressed widow, who has married Sir Myles's wastrel cousin Sir Hosis in the interim, is presented with 'a handsome six-day clock'.[39] The episode calls to mind de Paor's belief that some of the satire of *An Sgian* is secretly directed at O'Nolan's own family: his father had been presented with a wedding gift of a decorative plate by colleagues from the Gaelic League, and his brother Ciarán was a member of both *Ailtirí na hAiséirghe* and *Glún na Buaidhe*.[40]

There is also the possibility that O'Nolan was inspired by a real-life case when writing the sketches. In *The Handsome Carvers*, the two unnamed speakers among the civil servants appear to be based on real people – see the stage direction that the first gentleman should preferably have '*a strong Cork accent*' (*PT*, 262), while the second fellow has a '*loud, toneless voice, flat Dublin accent*' and is repeatedly late to work (*PT*, 263) – so it is, perhaps, not too much of a stretch to suppose that O'Nolan might have had a specific incident in mind. A cursory search of the newspaper archives from the time reveals that there were numerous cases of manslaughter as a result of 'provocation' through the 1930s and early 1940s: these included a soldier of the First Irish-Speaking Battalion who bayonetted a fellow private for talking about him behind his back,[41] and a shopkeeper in Ballinasloe who stabbed his wife to death because she had been 'tormenting' him.[42]

We need not expend too much energy looking for a specific real-life inspiration, though, because there are ample precedents within O'Nolan's own literary output. In his 1932 short story '*Eachta an Fhir Ólta: CEOL!*' (The Tale of the Drunkard: MUSIC!), an otherwise 'inoffensive' man murders two of his neighbours with his 'lovely knife' after being driven to insanity by their incessant use of gramophones and radios at all hours of the day and night.[43] In 'Two in One', the frustrated taxidermist Murphy bludgeons his tyrannical boss to death after reaching the end of his tether, telling us that 'On this occasion something within me snapped. I was sure I could hear the snap' (*SF*, 85). In *The Third Policeman*, the narrator – a somewhat naïve young man and an amateur scholar – seems to lose control of himself when his partner-in-crime, John Divney, orders him to finish off old Mathers, whom they have mugged on a country road:

I went forward mechanically, swung the spade over my shoulder and smashed the blade of it with all my strength against the protruding chin. I felt and almost heard the fabric of his skull crumple up crisply like an empty eggshell. I do not know how often I struck him after that but I did not stop until I was tired. (*CN*, 232)

In O'Nolan's imagination, loss of self-control leads directly to violence in the majority of cases. In another short story, 'John Duffy's Brother', the eponymous character suffers an unexplained psychotic break (during which he believes himself to be a train), and upon returning to normal, he immediately starts to panic that he may have behaved violently while in this altered state of mind: 'So far as he could recall he had killed no one, shouted no bad language, broken no windows' (*SF*, 58). The potential for violent crime, or at least antisocial behaviour, is always present in O'Nolan's characters, requiring only a momentary lapse in one's vigilance and self-restraint.

Keith Hopper notes that O'Nolan's use of violence begins as parody, 'but quite often his initial intention gets derailed by his fascination with the act of violence itself'; these violent scenes become 'self-publicising vignettes independent from the network of associations from which they sprang'. The setting of *An Béal Bocht* is 'a world where violent rage becomes the only outlet for expression available, usually fuelled by copious amounts of alcohol'.⁴⁴ O'Nolan does not replicate the exact details of any legal cases or incidents, but he revisits the concept of diminished responsibility numerous times and seems fascinated by the cathartic 'release' implied in the triumph of one's emotions over one's self-control.

In *An Sgian*, O'Nolan initially seems to parody this infantile linkage between anger and potency. At one point in the proceedings, Tadhg produces the *Aiséirghe* newspaper, most of which he claims to have written himself; full of pride, he tells Peig to 'Look at the ANGER in the poetry! Red, thunderous anger, I'm telling you!' Peig responds by producing the *Glún na Buaidhe* magazine, *Indiu*, and tells him, 'If it's anger you want, read what's on the front page there. You've never read the like of it' (*PT*, 254–5). However, as Hopper observes in O'Nolan's other works, such parody quickly gives way to an uncomfortably real episode of violence: for all his protestations and appeals to heaven for succour, Tadhg actually wants to give in to his violent impulses and allow his anger to take over.

It is no surprise that the 'provocation' in *An Sgian* occurs in the context of a marital row. As Maebh Long notes, in *Cruiskeen Lawn* 'Myles's Dublin man treats his marriage as a battleground of hostility and violence', and women are generally seen as 'a burden and a nuisance'.[45] In *The Handsome Carvers*, Peter's wife is an almost-voiceless victim, but in *An Sgian*, Peig is as hot-tempered as her husband and deliberately tries to needle him. She makes a point of telling him that she is not afraid of him; she impersonates him mockingly and dismisses his orders for her to shut up (*PT*, 251–2). She repeatedly mocks his loudness, at one point sarcastically asking him to speak up; when he threatens her and warns that he will kill any member of her faction who enters the house, she answers back, 'You? You couldn't frighten the cat. Ho, ho, ho. Fee fi fo fum!' (*PT*, 252). She responds to his claim that the *Ailtirí* are 'waking up' the country: 'That fine talk of yours isn't all lies – I know one little Ailtire who wakes me up plenty' (*PT*, 254). The ambiguity of this line seems calculated to annoy him: she could be mockingly referring to his stentorian manner, or possibly hinting at having cuckolded him with a member of his own organisation.

As Long notes, in O'Nolan's work the idealised, saintly, long-suffering image of Irish womanhood is treated sarcastically. This attitude is particularly apparent in the short story 'The Martyr's Crown',[46] while in *The Third Policeman* women are portrayed as 'impediments to comfort [...] and even what seems soft in them is hard'.[47] His depiction of the wife in *The Handsome Carvers* is more sympathetic, but she is barely present as a character at all; the only dialogue she has is a hysterical scream buried in the stage directions: 'There's a couple of wedding presents left – why don't you pawn them too?' (*PT*, 261). The fact that she does not have a name places her, perhaps, in the company of the protagonists of *At Swim-Two-Birds* and *The Third Policeman*, but her namelessness is also, more pointedly, in keeping with O'Nolan's tendency to elide individual identity in his portrayals of women.[48] In both plays we see his tendency to attack 'the myth of the home as a quiet refuge', calling attention to domestic violence and drudgery, as well as the hypocrisy of drawing a veil over these things in the public sphere.[49]

Conclusion

Both sketches were produced at the tail-end of the 'Emergency'. In spite of Irish officialdom's attempts to appear neutral, they could not prevent news of Nazi barbarity from reaching Irish shores, nor could they keep the Irish people ignorant of the scale of human casualties worldwide. If war normalises violence enough to allow people to laugh at it, it is little surprise that a sketch about a man murdering his wife was included in a Christmas variety show in 1944 and early 1945. That both characters were members of fringe fascist movements may have added to the light-hearted tone, coding them as 'acceptable' targets of violence and mockery.

The success of *Geamaí na Nodlag* may have prompted O'Nolan to broaden the appeal of the sketch by writing a version in English, without any political content that might prove controversial or else require familiarity with the targets being satirised. This would have been a shrewd decision on O'Nolan's part: as demonstrated by the fate of the Grand Guignol in New York, disappointed or nonplussed reviews could scupper a show's run. Furthermore, *The Handsome Carvers* emulates some of the structure of a screenplay, suggesting that O'Nolan may have seen the Christmas show's resounding success as an opportunity to expand into film or television, as he would try with his 1960s teleplays that he submitted to Telefís Éireann: *The Boy from Ballytearim, Flight, The Time Freddie Retired, The Dead Spit of Kelly, The Man with Four Legs* and *A Moving Tale*.

What both scripts have in common, however, is an unnerving reliance on a main character's loss of control over his violent impulses. While temporary losses of sanity occur with notable frequency in O'Nolan's work, as in 'John Duffy's Brother' and *The Third Policeman*, one is more likely to come across characters with pent-up anger and frustration, who finally act out those emotions in a momentary lapse of self-control. His killers are more often guilty of manslaughter than premeditated murder. Tadhg from *An Sgian* is a perfect example of this tendency, and it is strongly implied in the text that his barely restrained rage has been encouraged by his membership of a fascist organisation.

Peter Dunleary from *The Handsome Carvers* fits the mould less obviously, but his 'prim, cultured' demeanour may communicate his self-discipline as much as it indicates his social class and economic background. There is a hint that his co-workers are unconsciously aware of a violent temper lurking beneath Peter's calm exterior: the Second Gentleman confesses that he was marked late to work eighteen times the previous year, and when summoned to a meeting with Peter to explain himself, felt terribly nervous and expected 'to have the face chawed off me' (*PT*, 263). The laughter that accompanies his anecdote may be straightforward mirth, but it might also be knowing or wry amusement on the part of civil servants who know what Peter is capable of.

De Paor's observation that the satire of *An Sgian* is at least partly directed at O'Nolan's own family leads to some unsavoury conclusions about the writer's attitude to his own life. As we have seen, a lot of O'Nolan's work depicts violence or conflict within a domestic setting, and what begins as a parody of violence often descends into an unnerving exploration of it. This is not to suggest that there is a one-to-one correspondence between the depicted actions and author's private life: though we can draw some unpalatable conclusions from the fact that Peig 'brings it on herself' in *An Sgian*, the sketch can be read as (mostly) comedy because it targets a pair of deeply unpleasant people. Tadhg is hardly meant to serve as a stand-in for O'Nolan himself, unless the character is an expression of extreme self-loathing.

The Handsome Carvers, on the other hand, is subtitled *A Tragedy in Two Acts*, suggesting that the comedic distance of the previous sketch has been lessened in favour of dramatic irony and tragic effect. Here, the killing happens quickly and is presented in a distressing manner; the satire, rather, is directed at the civil service. The presentation of the knives happens in a *'cheap hotel'*, where a *'greasy waiter is endlessly pulling bottles of stout in the corner'*; the two Gentlemen are described as *'pompous'*, and the First Gentleman speaks in *'absurdly stilted and remote jargon'*; it is clear that all those present (except for Peter Dunleary) are already drunk (*PT*, 262). These details, combined with the fecklessness of the Second Gentleman, speak to a frustration on O'Nolan's part towards his own civil service post, and it is telling that Peter's alcoholism and violence towards his wife are indirectly blamed on the behaviour of his co-workers.

In the final analysis, in these sketches O'Nolan fashions two distinct Grand Guignol vignettes from the same premise, and the difference lies in where the horror is located. In *An Sgian*, we see a husband murder his wife in a fit of rage after being nagged once too often, but the audiences and critics who saw it performed on stage felt distanced enough from the characters to derive some enjoyment from the spectacle; it is still a horrific act, but the comedic treatment and unpleasantness of the characters and their affiliations keep it at arm's length, allowing audience and author alike to conceive of the death in an abstract sense. *The Handsome Carvers*, however, is a 'private' horror show for the author himself, a meditation on the toll his stultifying job may yet take on himself and his family.

Act IV

Transmedial Entanglements and Interlingual Adaptations

13

Voices Off

Brian O'Nolan, posthumanism and cinematic disembodiment

Paul Fagan

As a tale of metamorphosis, it is fitting that Brian O'Nolan's 'Two in One' was itself constantly transformed. The potboiler murder plot began as a *Cruiskeen Lawn* column, then morphed into a radio play, a short story, a theatre script and, finally, in 1962, a teleplay intended for the recently founded Telefís Éireann.[1] For many critics, this final script, retitled *The Dead Spit of Kelly*, reveals O'Nolan's struggles in adapting his prose to this visual medium. Anne Clissmann contends that he 'had no very clear idea of the resources of the television camera',[2] while Anthony Cronin insists that O'Nolan's late teleplays 'are certainly not explorations of the medium (he did not even possess a television set)'.[3] Indeed, the translation of first-person narration to television results in an opening dialogue between the taxidermist Burke (Murphy in the original story) and an unnecessary new character, Pat, who provides clumsy exposition. Throughout Part 1, an inelegant use of dramatic asides gives the viewer insights into Burke's thoughts. However, O'Nolan finds his feet in Part 2, which consists of a single, sustained close-up of Burke's face in a bar as his voiceover relays the inner dilemma. In the background, the script advises, customers *'are talking but no sound is heard from them'* (PT, 396). The art of this proposed shot is its thematic relation to the directly preceding and following scenes, in which we have witnessed Burke murder his boss Kelly and will see him enact his deranged plan to skin his victim and wear his epidermis to conceal his murderous act. The next time we see Burke, in Part 3, the voiceover remains the same, but his face is that of the corpse: '*in appearance the dead spit of Kelly*' (*PT*, 400). While the camera's eye maintains its contemplation of Burke's new outer form, the soundtrack grants us access to his inner thoughts.

As written, these scenes exploit the voiceover's disjunction of film and soundtrack to interrupt the cinematic gaze's standard organisation of subject and object, surface and depth, appearance and reality. In some ways, the importance of this device to the script's relation of medium, theme and effect allows for the shortcomings of Part 1. While the use of the voiceover technique throughout could have tidied up some of that scene's expositional devices, O'Nolan makes a creative decision only to exploit the voiceover after the murder – standardly at first in Part 2, then more radically in Part 3 – to formalise the ontological shift that occurs once Burke assumes the mantle of Kelly's dead skin and *becomes* his victim. The relationship between accident and essence is vexed, even under the camera's scrutiny, through the soundtrack's disembodied voice.

Recent years have seen a series of studies that document the importance of media technologies such as the phonograph, gramophone, radio, film and television to a strand of modernist writing that is distinguished by 'an uncannily disembodied vocality'.[4] Yet, to date, O'Nolan has not been acknowledged for his significant position in this particular modernist mode, which 'holds the body apart from its voice rather than uniting them',[5] despite the prevalence of disembodied voices in his writing. Immediately, the Good Fairy in *At Swim-Two-Birds* and the soul Joe in *The Third Policeman* come to mind. While I will return to these examples, I begin with *The Dead Spit of Kelly* because I claim, in part, that the disembodied voice in O'Nolan's *oeuvre* needs to be read in the context of 'the modern experience of technologies of the voice'.[6] From its first iteration in *Cruiskeen Lawn*, 'Two in One' was conceived in terms of its adaptability and thematic suitability to technologies of sight and sound, as 'a work of art in the modern American sense'.[7] Myles na Gopaleen claims that the BBC are after this 'play' and conveys the story's 'outrageous' suitability to 'modern' cinematic sensibilities by analogising it with a man 'who likes to rig up gramophones to play records of the masterpieces – *backwards*', thereby creating a 'very queer and ghostly' effect in which 'time and rhythm are unimpaired but the message is quite dissimilar'.[8] This 'queer and ghostly' image of a technologically disrupted relation of body and voice recurs throughout O'Nolan's writing as an effect of, and a commentary on, a certain twentieth-century mode of thinking the human that is both modernist and specifically posthuman in its imagination.

O'Nolan and the posthuman imaginary

In her pioneering 1999 study, N. Katherine Hayles asks *How We Became Posthuman* in the twentieth century and develops three interrelated narratives in response:

1. Information lost its body – from the Turing Test through Norbert Wiener's 1950s cybernetics theories about the possibility of telegraphing human beings and Hans Moravec's futurist speculations on downloading human consciousness into computers, '"intelligence" [became] a property of the formal manipulation of symbols rather than enaction in the human lifeworld'. Thus 'human identity' was reconceived as 'essentially an informational pattern rather than an embodied enaction' and a future was imagined for the human voice, mind or spirit in which the body would no longer be a necessity.[9]

2. The cyborg, a cybernetic organism comprising feedback between organic and integrated biomechatronic body parts, 'was created as a technological artefact and cultural icon'.[10]

3. Previous conceptual boundaries between the 'human' and the 'machine' began to break down, so that 'a historically specific construction called the human' gave way 'to a different construction called the posthuman'.[11]

By these discursive moves, the self is reduced to sequences or patterns of symbols, as verbal performance is detached from embodied experience.

A 'common theme' of posthuman cultural expression is 'the union of the human with the intelligent machine'.[12] In *The Short Fiction of Flann O'Brien*, Keith Hopper and Neil Murphy speculatively attribute to O'Nolan the story 'Naval Control', published under the name John Shamus O'Donnell in *Amazing Stories Quarterly* in 1932. While we remain unsure whether the story is his,[13] what interests me is the perception of an O'Nolan-esque quality to this tale of an Irish mad scientist who creates a robotic double of the narrator's deceased wife. The attribution suggests that a posthuman imagination and a cyborgian subjectivity are immediately recognisable qualities of O'Nolan's work. Indeed, Jack Fennell has demonstrated 'the frequent appearances of science fiction tropes and plots' across O'Nolan's novels, short fiction and columns.[14] Of course, the example *par excellence* is the 'monstrous exchange of tissue for metal' in the human–bicycle hybrids of *The Third Policeman* and *The Dalkey Archive* (*CN*, 684), which, Amanda Duncan reflects, in their 'indeterminacies between human and machine' express an 'unsettling ontological decentering of human autonomy'.[15] Yet, we may also think, here, of O'Nolan's short story 'John Duffy's Brother', in which the protagonist comes to believe that he is a train, or the *Cruiskeen Lawn* column in which we read about Remington, who has a typewriter inserted into his chest to produce reams of typo-laden copy.[16] While these human–machine hybrids are familiar to us as key motifs of O'Nolan's writing, here I wish to draw attention to the more specific ways in which the author explores this posthuman image through the figure of the bodiless voice.

By situating O'Nolan's writing more explicitly in its proximity to these material and discursive mechanisations of the 'human', I am joining a critical conversation that interrogates his poetics at the nexus of modernist, cyborgian and posthuman vantages. Led by recent work from Amanda Duncan, Jack Fennell, Ruben Borg, Maebh Long and Joseph Brooker, among others,[17] this focus has emerged in tandem with a broader trend of biopolitical readings that consider the function of corporeality and embodiment in O'Nolan's aesthetic project.[18] Rather than a fashionable turn in O'Nolan studies, I conceive these interrelated debates as deeply rooted extensions of the concerns with mind–body dualism that have been a cornerstone of the field since Clissmann's pioneering reading of *At Swim-Two-Birds* as a novel about 'the interrelationship of *caro* and *spiritus*, or imagination (mind-spirit) and reality (body-world)'.[19] Clissmann's analysis places that text's engagement with a non-essential relation between body and voice into a series of discursive contexts that predate and are independent of mass media technologies – from the religious rhetoric of the soul's independence from the body to the Cartesian theory of mind–body dualism, from the ghost story's disembodied revenants to the theatre's many 'voiceless bodies and bodiless voices'.[20] And yet, as Eamonn Hughes observes, 'the contention between modernity and tradition' in O'Nolan's writing is manifested not only in a pre-modern idiom of the disembodied spirit, pneuma, or soul, but also in a 'fascination with steam trains, gramophones, cinema'[21] and all manner of technological phantasmagoria. I agree and contend that O'Nolan's depiction of twentieth-century subjectivity attends specifically to the encounter between these vitalistic and religious rhetorics and modern technologies.

Hayles's writing on posthuman disembodiment is germane to a study of these images in O'Nolan's fiction and scripts, I propose, because O'Nolan shares her apprehensions about an ontologically and ethically suspect fantasy of disembodied immortality that is sustained by a presupposition of a non-essential relation between mental life and embodiment. Significantly, Hayles calls on posthumanism 'to counter this cybernetic fantasy by emphasising the co-implication of the virtual and the material'.[22] In his monograph *Fantasies of Self-Mourning: Modernism, the posthuman and the finite*, Borg demonstrates that the modernist response to an emergent posthumanism is to challenge these concepts by 'insisting on the ideological pitfalls of models of subjectivity that flirt with disembodiment'.[23] Borg's study draws our attention to the modernist/posthumanist co-implication of the material and the virtual in *The Third Policeman*, 'Two in One' and 'John Duffy's Brother' by situating these works as part of a wider network of similarly themed modernist texts (from Virginia Woolf's *Orlando* to Samuel Beckett's *Trilogy*) which stage scenes of impossibly transgressed limits – between human and machine, between life and death – in ways that problematise 'naïve fantasies of disembodiment, of [...] freedom from flesh, and triumph over materiality'.[24] In O'Nolan's work, the motif of disembodiment is recurrently linked to engagements with technological mediation in which image and soundscape, body and voice, are placed out of joint.

Drawing from this debate and developing its interpretations of O'Nolan's engagements with modernist and posthuman imaginaries, I propose that the recurrent *topos* of the bodiless voice in his novels and scripts can be read profitably as:

1. *posthumanist*, in Hayles's conception, in its awareness that a new relation between the human and the machine has emerged in the twentieth century that has consequences for the concepts of life, soul, identity, matter and afterlife, yet which cannot be adequately engaged by recourse to a renewed Cartesian dualism; and
2. *modernist*, in the sense that Borg advances, in its attempts to rethink the terms of this debate through representations of a form of *embodied virtuality* – a merging of soul and machine – through a curious but insistent representation of the *materiality* of the disembodied voice.

To narrow my focus in relation to this expansive theme, I will concentrate here on O'Nolan's handling of the disembodied voice in its relation to the imaginaries of the phonograph, gramophone, radio, film and television, with their attendant fantasies and anxieties concerning the voice's technologically disembodied immortality.

Phonograph, gramophone, radio, film

Adam. J. Engel traces the modernist 'anticipation and fear of disembodiment' back to 'the technological advancements of the late nineteenth century, including the phonograph'.[25] The literary trope of the disembodied voice thus undergoes a significant transformation as it moves from the nineteenth-century gothic to twentieth-century modernist writing. Where, in the former, the spectral voice captures a hauntological liminality between life and death, body and spirit, presence and absence, the modernist turn reflects on the ways in which a distinctly mechanical rupture of voice and body (through the telephone, phonograph, gramophone, radio broadcasts, film, etc.) changes again the self's relation to, and experience of, time, space, death, absence and presence. A key presupposition of my argument is that O'Nolan perceives this mechanical disembodiment of the voice to be at once *a source of anxiety*, in its mutual degradations of the body and the spirit, and *a source of comedy*, in its transformations of both life and afterlife into mechanised and mediated simulations of their previous forms.

O'Nolan is not the first Irish modernist to find this situation darkly comic. In James Joyce's *Ulysses*, Leopold Bloom imagines the posthumous and posthuman possibilities of the gramophone while walking through Glasnevin cemetery:

> Besides how could you remember everybody? Eyes, walk, voice. Well, the voice, yes: gramophone. Have a gramophone in every grave or keep it in the house. After dinner on a Sunday. Put on poor old greatgrandfather. Kraahraark! Hellohellohello amawfullyglad kraark awfullygladaseeagain hellohello amarawf kopthsth. Remind you of the voice like the photograph reminds you of the face.[26]

Elsewhere, Beckett's *Krapp's Last Tape* offers a paradigmatic image of the ways in which voice recordings may rupture our temporal experience of subjectivity and condemn us to an uncomfortable, even humiliating disembodied afterlife.

A 1932 Irish-language short story announces O'Nolan's early engagement with the theme of the increased difficulty of telling the embodied human voice from its mechanical simulation or iteration. In '*Eachta an Fhir Ólta: CEOL*', published in *The Irish Press*, a man is driven mad to the point of murder when he confuses a phonograph record with a human voice.[27] These thematic interests extend to the radio in the *Blather* articles dedicated to 'the Blather Pirate Station, 2BL', whose live radio programme consists almost exclusively of broadcast gramophone recordings. Chapter 3 of *An Béal Bocht* mechanises the novel's satirical confusion between human and animal, as a Dublin folklorist gathers evidence of 'the folklore of our ancients and our ancestors […] when both he and the instrument were hidden in the end of a cabin and both of them listening intently' (*CN*, 431–2). Even though the sounds he records on the *gramafón* are of a drunken pig, he is awarded a degree because of the 'lore which he had stored away in the hearing-machine that night' (*CN*, 433).[28] In *Cruiskeen Lawn*, Myles characterises the transformation of schoolchildren into automatons through the rote memorialisation and regurgitation of facts for the school inspector as changing them, essentially, into gramophones: 'A person who cannot reel off thousands of facts from memory is scarcely a person at all.'[29]

O'Nolan's reflections on the twentieth-century mechanics of disembodiment are thematised through his foregrounding of the gramophone and radio as phenomena that both mechanise and dislocate the relationship between body and voice. Yet, the medium of film is the most paradigmatic of a specifically modernist articulation of this posthuman *topos*. In O'Nolan's lifetime, Dublin cinemas projected images of the robot Maria in Fritz Lang's *Metropolis*, Gort from *The Day the Earth Stood Still*, and the cyborg of *The Colossus of New York*.[30] However, there is something posthuman about the cinematic apparatus and event themselves, in excess of such science-fictional images, in their very transformation of human life into machine-operated phantasmagoria via an imperfectly concealed rupture between image and sound, body and voice.[31]

O'Nolan's engagement with film is well-established. *Blather* engages in extended 'parodies of Hollywood cinema',[32] while Myles regularly passes judgement on the films he endures on his trips to the cinema.[33] His report on his excursion to see the 1953 remake of *Quo Vadis* is mostly taken up with a long and detailed history of the technological evolution of the medium, from Leonardo da Vinci through Thomas A. Edison's attempt to adapt 'the cylindrical records of the gramophone he had invented' to 'make motion pictures', to Auguste and Louis Lumière's invention of the 'magic box'.[34] As such a long-view history reveals, the enduring success of classic cinema's sound-on-film technique and its dominance in the present day can conceal to twenty-first-century viewers how prominent the disjunction between projection and soundtrack would have been to cinema audiences in the 1920s and '30s, from the live musical accompaniment of the silent era to the 'synchronisable phonograph mechanism' that enabled the first sound film, 1927's *The Jazz Singer*.[35] Thus, before it is brought in line through the cinematic realist technique – and especially in the work of modernist film experimenters who pursued the aesthetic and philosophical potential of this disjunction of image and sound[36] – cinema's emergence marks a distinctly posthuman moment, in which the 'disembodied sound of [...] a "voice" that is not rooted in any clearly locatable subject' is 'disconcerting to those who follow [...] seemingly straightforward assumptions about the relation between speech and the human body, between voice and selfhood'.[37]

In O'Nolan's fiction, an engagement with cinema's technological imaginary foregrounds a thematic dislocation of time and a fragmentation of the embodied self. In the Myles na gCopaleen short story 'Time and Drink in Dublin',[38] an alcoholic bender that leads to 'a comic disruption of all temporal coordinates'[39] is launched by a discussion of Billy Wilder's *The Lost Weekend*. In *The Third Policeman*, de Selby's theory that 'Human existence' is 'a succession of static experiences each infinitely brief' is founded on his failure 'to grasp the principle of the cinematograph' when he studies 'some old cinematograph films [...] patiently picture by picture' (*CN*, 263). Yaeli Greenblatt has shown how recurrent close-ups on teeth in O'Nolan's writing foreground an uncanny effect in which 'bodies are at constant risk of becoming external to the self'[40] – not coincidentally, Sergeant Puck comments to the de Selby scholar that it is in the cinematograph that 'you see the fine teeth they do have in Amurikey' (*CN*, 272). Not only in his late-career teleplays but even from his early novel writing, O'Nolan draws on cinematic technologies and imaginaries to thematise a distinctly modernist and posthuman figuration of subjectivity.

The voice and the frame

In examining the relation between film and the disembodied voice in O'Nolan's fiction, I am interested in what Mary Ann Doane identifies as the 'radical otherness' of the free-floating cinematic voiceover.[41] Doane highlights the disembodied voiceover's simultaneous connection to and disconnectedness from the screen's frame and shows that this visual limit is, in fact, established through its constant transgression by cinema's free-floating voices. For Doane, the key to the cinematic voiceover's credibility is the impossibility of thinking a voice without a body. She argues that 'Techniques of sound recording tend to confirm the cinema's function as a *mise en scène* of bodies', even as those cinematic bodies are rendered fantasmatic rather than material.[42] Allan Casebier adds that the fantasmatic cinematic body 'authorises and sustains certain relationships between sound and image' upon which cinematic verisimilitude rests: 'Instead of using sound recording and sound editing to emphasise the separateness of visuals and sound in our experience of film', realist films 'make it *seem* as if the sounds and the visuals belong to a body',[43] even as this seeming relation is a pure construction of the medium, in which fragmentary pieces of film and sound are edited together to create the illusion of unity and sequence.

Michel Chion draws our attention not only to distinctions between homodiegetic and heterodiegetic elements of film sound, but also to the question of whether and how the voice is connected to the body in the filmic illusion of simultaneity, focusing specifically on the liminal 'offscreen' voice of a body that 'has just left the image but continues to be there [...] *neither entirely inside nor clearly outside* the frame'.[44] Chion's argument builds on the distinction that Doane develops between the voiceover and the voice-off, which

> refers to instances in which we hear the voice of a character who is not visible within the frame. Yet the film establishes, by means of previous shots or other contextual determinants, the character's 'presence' in the space of the scene, in the diegesis. He/she is 'just over there', 'just beyond the frameline', in a space which 'exists' but which the camera does not choose to show. The traditional use of voice-off constitutes a denial of the frame as a limit.[45]

Of course, the voice-off is also a theatrical device, which similarly both denies and reaffirms the stage's limit, and this too can be a relevant coordinate for interrogating the notable prominence of the voice-off technique in O'Nolan's fiction. Yet, it is my wager that the fantasmatic body of the silver screen is ultimately the more significant reference point for O'Nolan's disembodied voice than the actor's material body hiding in the wings.

Several scenes in *At Swim-Two-Birds* employ the voice-off technique for comic effect, but also to establish a relation between in- and off-frame in the narrative situation.[46] An early scene with Finn Mac Cool establishes a traditional construction of 'truth' which requires an identifiable relation of voice to body.

> Good for telling, said Conán.
> Who is it? said Finn.
> It is I, said Conán.
> I believe it for truth, said Finn. (*CN*, 15)

As Jarrett Walker underlines, 'the oratorical tradition [...] treated the body as a container of the voice, serving primarily to make the text present in the space of performance'.[47] However, a comic effect of the narrative situation of O'Nolan's Finn Mac Cool scene is the mythological character's inability to identify or distinguish between the voices that speak to him. As the authenticity and authority of the direct voice of oral or bardic tradition, with its connotations of authenticity and presence, is subjected to ridicule, it is replaced by the new posthuman cultural logic of mass mediation in which the mechanically disembodied voice comes to speak 'with an authority that the embodied voice lacks'.[48]

As part of the novel's project to document the shift, under technologies of mass reproduction, from the mythical authority of the embodied voice to the posthuman authority of the disembodied voice, it is notable that the uncle's interventions into the student author's biographical reminiscences often take the form of the voice-off. Consider the framing of the novel's opening scene, in which the uncle berates his nephew over breakfast:

> He got up from the table and went out to the hall, sending back his voice to annoy me in his absence.
> Tell me this, did you press my Sunday trousers?
> I forgot, I said.
> What?
> I forgot, I shouted. (*CN*, 8)

The uncle's voice-offs are explicitly related to mass cultural technologies of mediation and disembodiment in the sixth part of the narrator's biographical reminiscences, where he relates: 'I heard the loud voice of my uncle from the hallway intermixed with another voice that was not known to me at all' (*CN*, 89). The uncle and Mr Corcoran, both members of the Rathmines and Rathgar Operatic Society, enter carrying a gramophone. The conflict between the soul and the mechanical voice is made explicit in the scene as the two men discuss the catechism – a term which, etymologically, means 'to teach by word of mouth' (from *katá*, 'down' + *ēkhéō*, 'to echo, sound, or resound') – before comically attempting to wrangle a voice from the machine (*CN*, 91–2). From the outset of the novel, it is established that the narrator's bedroom is his sanctum that allows him refuge from his uncle's surveillance: 'Whether in or out, I always kept the door of my bedroom locked. This made my movements a matter of some secrecy' (*CN*, 6). Yet in the gramophone episode, even when the narrator escapes to his bedroom 'the thin music came upon [his] ear, thinner and hollower through the intervening doors' (*CN*, 93): once mechanically disembodied, the voice of surveillant authority becomes omnipresent.[49]

This theme of the suspect modern authority of the technologically disembodied voice is further developed in the scene in which the Voice in the

Cloud informs the newly formed character Furriskey of his role in Trellis's novel:

> It was pointed out to him by the voice that he was by vocation a voluptuary concerned only with the ravishing and destruction of the fair sex. [...] At the conclusion of the interview, the voice administered a number of stern warnings as to the penalties which would befall him should he deviate, even in the secrecy of his own thought, from his mission of debauchery. (*CN*, 48)

Several well-known binaries are rehearsed here, most notably the supremacy of the elevated voice (as it relates to the soul or mind) over the degraded body (as manifested in Furriskey's carnal tasks). The scene figures the tyrannical relationship between the author-god (the Voice in the Cloud) and its creations,[50] even as it echoes several scenarios unique to alienated modern life, such as the loudspeaker on the factory floor, or the loss of presence enacted through the radio or the gramophone – indeed, the whole scene might be a play on the gramophone label 'His Master's Voice' as much as it is a riff on the God of the Book of Genesis, who speaks the world into being ('In the beginning was the Word').

In the novel's scheme, then, the voice-off and the voiceover are mostly reserved for figures of suspect authority: Finn Mac Cool, the uncle, Trellis, the authorial Voice in the Cloud. While we must primarily appraise these authorial and patriarchal voices in a literary context, I suggest that comparing their representation to the cinematic voice-off and voiceover techniques can reveal their specific functions in O'Nolan's text. For Lilya Kaganovsky, 'The disembodied voice relies on sound cinema's ability to produce the effect of "truth" through the disengagement of voice from body', as the free-floating voice, 'unanchored to a specific body, takes on the attributes of omniscience and omnipotence'.[51] Elsewhere, Doane claims that 'It is precisely because the [cinematic voiceover] is not localisable, because it cannot be yoked to a body, that it is capable of interpreting the image, producing its truth. Disembodied, lacking any specification in space or time, the voice-over is [...] beyond criticism.'[52] Beyond merely giving the character his orders, the authorial Voice in the Cloud – a figuration of the voice of the omniscient narrator – claims an inorganic gaze that enables an omniscient surveillance of even 'the secrecy of [Furriskey's] own thought' (*CN*, 48). The authority of the disembodied voice comes from the fact that it is extricated from the systems of surveillance it articulates, 'for how can one monitor a voice that does not emerge from a locatable body?'.[53] Furriskey will come to echo and endorse this authority with his later declaration that 'The voice was the first [...]. The voice was Number One. Anything that came after was only an imitation of the voice' (*CN*, 148).

Clearly, in *At Swim-Two-Birds*, the disembodied voice is embedded in discourses of truth, and in dynamics of power and surveillance. Yet, significantly, these functions are ironised in O'Nolan's text through two counter-discursive approaches. The first is the mode of the self-disclosing hoax, which both stages and reveals a certain imposture to challenge the uncritical discursive connection between the disembodied voice and 'truth'. Indeed, the 'truth' or 'authenticity' of the disembodied voice is disturbed recurrently in a chorus of false voices that speak throughout O'Nolan's work, from *Cruiskeen Lawn*'s escort service for dull-witted theatregoers, in which strategically placed ventriloquists help the client to engage in sparkling conversation,[54] to the mismatch of voice and appearance that is played out in *The Dead Spit of Kelly* (the principle is borne out on a grander scale in O'Nolan's diverse pseudonyms and satirical *personae*). In *At Swim-Two-Birds*, the discursive connection between the voice and 'truth' is broken when the student author takes to his bed for three months and covers for his absence in university through a convenient ruse: 'Alexander, who had chosen a scheme of studies similar to my own, answered with my voice at lecture roll-calls' (*CN*, 40). The second, more carnivalesque, approach O'Nolan takes in the novel is to rematerialise the disembodied voice of authority. The authority of the uncle's disembodied voice is undermined in the gramophone scene, for instance, through the narrator's close-ups on his body: 'My uncle, his back to me, also moved his head authoritatively, exercising a roll of fat which he was accustomed to wear at the back of his collar, so that it paled and reddened in the beat of the music' (*CN*, 92). In a similar way, the authorial Voice in the Cloud is undercut by the fact that the material transcript of its instructions to Furriskey has been 'lost beyond retrieval' by the student author (*CN*, 46). Both approaches, in concert, advance a key dimension of O'Nolan's aesthetic project, which Long identifies as the destabilisation of 'the apparent authenticity of the voice'.[55]

Embodied virtuality

The first voice we hear in *The Third Policeman* is that of the narrator's father, as, again, the voice-off technique introduces the theme of a voice that both transgresses and establishes the frame:

studying in the kitchen at night I could hear him through the thin door to the shop talking there from his seat under the oil-lamp for hours on end to Mick the sheepdog. Always it was only the drone of his voice I heard, never the separate bits of words. (*CN*, 223–4)[56]

As in other key scenes in the *oeuvre*, the voice in *The Third Policeman* is disembodied, but here, consequently, it is *less* clear as a channel of meaning. Thierry Robin notes that

> language in *The Third Policeman* is [...] often presented as unintelligible noise, from the narrator's father's voice, which sounds like a drone, in which the separate bits of words cannot be made out, to Old Mathers's final words, whose meaning oscillates between 'I do not care for celery' and 'I left my glasses in the scullery'.[57]

Rather than establishing authenticity, identity and truth, in *The Third Policeman* the disembodied voice takes on the function of anxiogenic self-Othering – an instance of dislocation between speech and subjectivity, truth and its source – and foregrounds a posthuman understanding of the multiple, dispersed and decentred self. This theme had been explored in *At Swim-Two-Birds*; for instance, when, following his 'first steps in life', we are told that the sound of Furriskey's own 'voice startled him. It had the accent and intonation usually associated with the Dublin lower or working classes' (CN, 46). In *The Third Policeman*, however, this theme is framed in increasingly cyborgian terms.

When the de Selby scholar attempts to speak, at one juncture, he relates: 'Words spilled out of me as if they were produced by machinery. My voice, tremulous at first, grew hard and loud and filled the room. [...] I am sure that most of it was meaningless' (*CN*, 241). This mechanised dislocation of the voice is a source of uncanny, even abject, horror for the de Selby scholar, which moves him 'beyond classical constructions of subject–object boundaries'.[58] Consider his recoil at the unintelligible 'unearthly voice' produced by MacCruiskeen's mangle, which can 'stretch a ray [of light] until it becomes sound':

> it disturbed me in a way that could only be done by something momentous and diabolical. [...] What happened eventually was not a shout but a shrill scream, a sound not unlike the call of rats yet far shriller than any sound which could be made by man or animal. (*CN*, 317)

This mechanically accelerated confusion of human and nonhuman limits 'throws into question one of the central ways in which human beings [...] defined themselves against animals and objects', namely through a rigid distinction between the human rational voice and nonhuman instinctual or automated sound.[59] Moreover, the connection of the novel's mechanisation of the voice with its interwoven themes of posthumousness and posthumanity figures O'Nolan's participation in what Engel identifies as a 'uniquely modernist anxiety', which asks: 'Can a being that inhabits the liminal space between two Worlds – life and death, embodiment and disembodiment – communicate meaning?'[60] As I have endeavoured to show in the present essay, these questions were significantly complicated by the technologies of the gramophone and cinematograph. And as I have worked here to argue, where the rubber really hits the road in O'Nolan's marshalling of these topoi and themes is in a complex insistence upon the co-implication of the virtual and the material in these disembodied voices in ways which respond, with significant reservations, to emergent posthuman fantasies of disembodiment.

The Good Fairy of *At Swim-Two-Birds* declares to the Pooka, 'I have no body' and describes themself later to Orlick as being 'like a point in Euclid [...] position but no magnitude' (*CN*, 144). And yet, the Good Fairy's every utterance is strangely spatialised and localised:

> That time you spoke, said the Pooka, it is of course a secret where your voice came from?
> When I spoke last, said the Good Fairy, I was kneeling in the cup of your navel but it is bad country and I am there no longer. (*CN*, 103)

As Long observes, the Good Fairy 'perfectly embodies, or rather, disembodies' a certain 'paradoxical formlessness' which

> enables him to be all forms, and as a result he is located undecidably between the masculine and the feminine, the embodied and the disembodied [...]. Thus, while technically without a body, the Good Fairy is continually referred to as sitting, pointing, holding cards and threatening to vomit. He is all-seeing and all-pervasive, and yet without front or face.[61]

This is a bodiless voice that is shown impossibly, even absurdly, to engage in embodied consumption – when the Pooka asks the Good Fairy where they keep their pipe, the response is: 'It is cigarettes I smoke' (*CN*, 103).

This same state of embodied virtuality holds for the de Selby scholar's soul Joe, who functions as his inner voice in *The Third Policeman* in a way that 'attacks the notion of a singular subject'.[62] As Jennika Baines observes: 'Joe notices the bandage on the neck of Mathers and the wooden leg of the man building the scaffold. This implies that Joe might even have eyes of his own, existing behind or within the eyes of the narrator.'[63] The narrator imagines Joe's bodiless voice as slimy, or perhaps rough like a cat's tongue, or maybe even scaly: '*That's not very logical – or complimentary either,* [Joe] said suddenly [...] *By God I won't be called scaly*' (*CN*, 327). Lying in bed, the narrator

> heard Joe murmuring some contented incoherency. His voice was near me yet did not seem to come from the accustomed place within. I thought that he must be lying beside me in the bed, and I kept my hands carefully at my sides in case I should accidentally touch him. (*CN*, 327)

The de Selby scholar's reflection on the corporality of Joe's disembodied voice draws him towards the precipice of a *mise en abyme* of souls and bodies in which a clear distinction between life and its material embodiment becomes unthinkable:

> A body with another body inside it in turn, thousands of such bodies within each other like the skins of an onion, receding to some unimaginable ultimatum? Was I in turn merely a link in a vast sequence of imponderable beings, the world I knew merely the interior of the being whose inner voice I myself was? (*CN*, 327)

In the later scene in which the narrator is about to be hanged, the immaterial soul Joe reveals how he aspires, in death, to achieve a form of embodied materiality:

> *I do not know, or do not remember, what happens to the like of me in these circumstances. Sometimes I think that perhaps I might become part of ... the world, if you understand me?*
> I know.
> *I mean – the wind, you know. Part of that. Or the spirit of the scenery in some beautiful place like the Lakes of Killarney, the inside meaning of it if you understand me.*
> I do.
> *Or perhaps something to do with the sea.* [...] *A big wave in mid-ocean, for instance, it is a very lonely and spiritual thing. Part of that.*
> I understand you.
> *Or the smell of a flower, even.* (*CN*, 368)

Such scenes demonstrate that the disembodied voice, in O'Nolan's writing, is not merely a series of language patterns or algorithmic information, but it is also a *mise en scène* of fantasmatic bodies comparable, I suggest, in a non-trivial way to the cinematic voices Doane describes. If the voice in O'Nolan's writing is represented as a vital and vitalistic force – as spirit, soul, pneuma – its existence in the fictional world is always embodied, even if fantasmatically. Through this impossible figure of a disembodied voice *which is nevertheless embodied*, O'Nolan expresses a comic ridicule of the Cartesian roots of humanism, but also a profound modernist reservation regarding a certain posthuman imaginary which celebrates, and ascribes authority and truth to, an envisioned technological dematerialisation of life itself.

Conclusion

Once we open up the critical lens beyond commonplaces about the inferiority of O'Nolan's late-career writing for the screen, a series of fascinating questions come into view. How do these scripts relate and respond to the history of Irish modernist broadcasting, from W.B. Yeats's 1931–8 BBC radio talks and poetry readings to the Irish 'radio modernism' of James Plunkett, or Denis Johnston's work as a television and radio producer for the BBC, whose meta-medial and 'self-referential metafictional broadcasts' Jeremy Lakoff compares to *At Swim-Two-Birds*?[64] How might they be profitably read in contrast to and comparison with, for instance, Beckett's *Film* or his own television writing (*Eh Joe, Ghost Trio, …but the clouds…, Quad, Nacht und Träume*), which exhibit a fascination with the camera's roaming eye *vis-à-vis* a series of impossibly related and ruptured bodies, spaces, silences and spectral voices? How might they be understood in relation to the notable function of the gramophone in Lennox Robinson's plays?[65] Whether the topic is the significance of mass-media technologies in modernist interrogations of the relationship between the material and the virtual, or the overlooked role of radio and television in twentieth-century Irish writing, O'Nolan's writing for broadcast should be a significant part of the conversation.

I began with the position that while O'Nolan's teleplays evidence some uncertainty with the medium, they demonstrate an interest in the form's possibilities for exploring the rupture between body and voice, a key concern of his writing across genres. Even as '*Only rudimentary camera cues are given*' in his scripts, as '*Generally this task is left to the producer*' (*PT*, 287), notable attention is paid to the disembodied voice. In the author's note for *The Dead Spit of*

Kelly we read: '*There is only one important character, BURKE. The part naturally calls for a good player but particularly one whose voice and accent are unmistakeable, because some of his utterances (By way of thought.) are heard on the sound track while he proceeds on the screen in dumb show*' (PT, 387). Similarly, *The Man with Four Legs: A true tale of terror* opens with a five-minute '*dumb show*' in which Mr O'Brien's '*voice is heard on the sound track*' (PT, 361). *The Boy from Ballytearim* begins with a voiceover ('*The VOICE is heard, off*'; PT, 289) reading the eponymous poem from *Songs of the Glens of Antrim* by Moira O'Neill, as the camera considers Peter and Anne in silence before the ensuing scene turns to focus on their bodily complaints (back pains, boils on the elbow, bad blood).

It has been my argument that these concerns are not merely an attempt to come to terms with the formal aspects of a new medium but are indices of a thoroughgoing interest in the posthuman, mechanically disembodied voice that is manifested across O'Nolan's body of writing. Often, these media are exploited to express the quintessentially O'Nolan-esque metafictional and metaleptic transgression of the narrative frame and the dislocation of a dispersed subjectivity. At the outset of his career, the 'objects' of *Blather*'s 2BL radio station 'are two-fold, even manifold', but primarily they are 'to jam and jam and jam' the nation's official radio station 2RN (*MBM*, 131). The very last letter in *The Collected Letters of Flann O'Brien* discusses the projected Telefís Éireann sitcom about *The Dalkey Archive*'s Sergeant Fottrell, as O'Nolan himself is almost literally on his deathbed. The 15 March 1966 letter describes his situation to Gunnar Rugheimer of Telefís Éireann in explicitly embodied terms:

> For your letter of 9 March regarding Sergeant Fottrell I say thanks very much. This idea (as I conceived it) excited me and was well into the first of the short plays ... when PLONK! I got very sick. I am still far from the land but one feature – vomiting several times every day – seems to have eased up. (*L*, 556)

He continues, turning from his own corporeal ailments to his, ultimately unrealised, plans for the programme, and back to the limitations of his own body:

> Later, when the Sergeant's personality and tongue form a countrywide treasure, the Sergeant may well take a hand in interfering with other people's programmes and ultimately could become the unofficial voice of T.E. [Telefís Éireann]. He would make his remarkable views known

on Nelson, the Budget, Decimals … anything of cultural import; he transcends all his situations. [...] Meanwhile I'm once again entering hospital for blood transfusions and other boons. (*L*, 557)

In this final letter, O'Nolan points tantalisingly to an awareness of how he can finally make the medium of television bend to his own aesthetic project by having the voice of his protagonist transcend the screen's frame.

14

Theatre and the Visual Arts

Brian O'Nolan and Lady Gregory

Eglantina Remport

This essay examines the interconnected nature of the verbal and the visual arts in Brian O'Nolan's *At Swim-Two-Birds* (1939) and Lady Augusta Gregory's *Cuchulain of Muirthemne* (1902) and *Gods and Fighting Men* (1904), as well as in both authors' writing for performance. The aims of investigating these works inter-relationally and intermedially are manifold. In the first instance, I mean to establish the various lines of mythological, antiquarian and revivalist influence that run between these authors, which have been variously ignored or hinted at in previous works of O'Nolan studies. However, I wish also to argue that the connection between O'Nolan and Gregory is more substantial than this still, in so far as they are mutually indebted to a specific pictorial tradition that can be observed in the immediate influence of Edward Bulwer-Lytton's *The Last Days of Pompeii* (1834) on Gregory's *tableaux vivants*, but which reaches back, ultimately, to an ekphrastic literary tradition that has its origins in the historical period of Miguel de Cervantes Saavedra's *El ingenioso hidalgo don Quixote de la Mancha* (1605/1615), a text which influences both O'Nolan's and Gregory's use of Irish mythological material and Celtic legends, albeit in different ways. Despite their obvious surface differences, the works of O'Nolan and Gregory owe much of their special pictorial character to their shared interest in a unique interplay between theatre, literature and the visual arts that has been in operation for centuries.

Given the terms of the investigation, the essay is divided into three sections: one that discusses the connection between fiction and the *tableaux vivants*; one that considers the pictorial tradition in relation to the theatre;

and one that examines the *picaresque* as ekphrastic literature. In the concluding part, I read *At Swim-Two-Birds* in the context of the Irish modernist visual arts scene of O'Nolan's day, as exemplified by Mainie Jellett's abstract and cubist representations of Celtic and Christian themes. Such intermedial examinations are new to O'Nolan studies; for this reason, the essay draws primarily on methods used in theatre studies, specifically in that of theatre historiography.

O'Nolan, Gregory and Victorian ekphrastic literature

As regards the diverse Irish literary sources that influenced O'Nolan when composing *At Swim-Two-Birds*, Declan Kiberd identifies the *Fiannaíocht* and the *Buile Suibhne*, Carol Taaffe writes about Standish Hayes O'Grady's *Silva Gadelica* and the *Acallamh na Senórach*, Maebh Long mentions the medieval Irish voyage tale, the *Immram*, and Michael McAteer traces the novel's debts to Samuel Ferguson's *Congal: A poem in five books*.[1] Drawing on Cathal G. Ó hÁinle's article on the Fionn and the *Buile Suibhne* legends in *At Swim-Two-Birds*, Louis de Paor investigates further O'Nolan's engagement with O'Grady's *Silva Gadelica* and J.G. O'Keeffe's 1913 bilingual edition of *Buile Suibhne*, stressing that O'Nolan was trying to negotiate between Irish revivalist and European modernist movements.[2] Ó hÁinle, Taaffe and de Paor offer detailed analyses of O'Nolan's interest in the literature of the Irish Literary Revival and in medieval Irish-language poetry, an interest that evolved in a significant way during O'Nolan's studentship at University College Dublin.[3] De Paor draws attention to the fact that O'Nolan singled out O'Grady's *Silva Gadelica* as a source of reference in an *Irish Times* column published under the byline 'Flann O'Brien' to commemorate the twenty-fifth anniversary of O'Grady's death, in which O'Nolan discusses O'Grady's (mis)translation of Old Irish Poetry.[4] One author missing from this list of influences on O'Nolan's work with the Irish myths and legends is the *grande dame* of the Irish Revival: Lady Augusta Gregory.

Kiberd draws attention to a possible connection between *At Swim-Two-Birds* and Gregory's collection of the Finn Mac Cool legend in *Gods and Fighting Men*.[5] O'Nolan's familiarity with Gregory's work is indeed evidenced in a number of *Cruiskeen Lawn* columns that make reference to her life and writing; for instance, in the 16 August 1943 column, Myles na gCopaleen peruses his old copy of *Gods and Fighting Men*, expressing his amusement at Gregory's characterisation of Finn Mac Cool as 'not naughty'.[6] O'Nolan further contends that having read 'everything in print about her', Gregory 'emerged as a person who liked irony', someone who 'invented a language of her own [...] for the ideas she tried to present or rehash'.[7] 'Rehash' is perhaps too strong a judgement here, given the complexity of Gregory's antiquarian work during the late 1890s, but it is true that she used old manuscript materials for her compilation of Celtic legends, one of which was O'Grady's collection *Silva Gadelica*, a source O'Nolan also used for *At Swim-Two-Birds*. Indicating the seriousness with which she went about the process of collecting the ancient sources, Gregory dedicates a whole chapter to the Celtic material in her autobiography, *Seventy Years*.[8] Amongst the material she consulted were works by Ernst Windish, Kuno Meyer, Marie Henri d'Arbois de Jubainville, Eugene O'Curry, Douglas Hyde, Whitley Stokes, Eleanor Hull, as well as *Silva Gadelica*.[9] Eugene O'Curry's *Lectures on the Manuscript Material of Ancient Irish History* – a book based on a series of talks he had given in 1855 and 1856 at Cardinal John Henry Newman's Catholic University – is testament to the extraordinary stylistic and generic diversity of the medieval material. Gregory herself recounts some of the obstacles in her way when creating coherent stories out of the fragmented manuscript material: the tales existed in various versions and formats and in a number of different manuscripts.[10] O'Curry's *Lectures*, too, highlight this fact: some of the transcribed manuscripts were in the form of poems; some of them abounded in narrative descriptions; while some others were conversational throughout the legend.[11] Out of this fragmented material, Gregory aimed to create coherent stories, while at the same time trying to maintain the authorial and generic diversity of the source material.

The connection runs deeper, however, than Gregory and O'Nolan's shared source materials in *Gods and Fighting Men* and *At Swim-Two-Birds*. O'Nolan seems to be ridiculing the antiquarian methods of revivalist authors such as O'Grady, O'Curry and Gregory herself. As a student of Irish literature, O'Nolan was aware of the generic and authorial diversity within the medieval texts with which revivalists were attempting to preserve the Celtic heritage of Ireland. During his student years, O'Nolan learned about the difficulties that arose from the fact that the old tales existed in fragments and in various manuscripts; that a tale often had more than one beginning and more than one ending; and that the narratives were treated distinctly in different manuscripts. O'Nolan plays with this fragmentation and multiplicity in *At Swim-Two-Birds*: the narrative has 'three openings' (*CN*, 5) and numerous conclusions; there are a number of narrators, each with its distinct narrative voice; there is an instance of a manuscript being mislaid, remembered and summarised; there are stories embedded within the main story of the novel;

and a wide variety of styles are used from *oratio recta* to *oratio obliqua* and beyond. Moreover, O'Nolan seems to mock the very concept that Gregory had chosen to adopt when assembling the legends, in which she draws together the fragmented materials so as to create biographies of Setanta/ Cuchulain and Finn Mac Cool.[12] This so-to-say 'biographical approach' was unlike those of her literary precursors O'Curry and the O'Gradys, who used essentially historical frameworks.[13] In an ironically resonant move, *At Swim-Two-Birds* begins with two births, those of Dermot Trellis and Furriskey, who is born through a process called 'aestho-autogamy', defined in the novel as 'producing a living mammal from an operation involving neither fertilisation nor conception' (*CN*, 37). Much has been written about this process: it has been linked to a wide range of notions from masturbation to eugenics, from economic materialism to creative writing.[14] Here, I should like to emphasise how aestho-autogamy reveals the author's critical stance on the pseudo-scientific language used in nineteenth-century versions of the old legends, such as Standish James O'Grady's *History of Ireland* (1878–80), and his mockery of the mode of birth of the main Celtic hero, Cuchulain, in Gregory's *Cuchulain of Muirthemne*.[15]

The endings of the mythological tales also follow a certain biographical logic: *Cuchulain of Muirthemne* ends with the death of the title hero Cuchulain, and *Gods and Fighting Men* ends with the death of Finn Mac Cool. Finn's death is accentuated by his son, the 'great' Oisin's elaborate lament on the lost world of the Fianna.[16] In a similar manner, O'Nolan's novel ends with the death of the 'poor German [...] who made each aspect of his life a thing of triads' (*CN*, 217). Of course, he is only a subsidiary character in the novel but, as Keith Hopper argues, the three 'good-byes' that signify the German's suicide (*CN*, 217) not only conclude the narrative of his life but also form a 'triadic closure' appropriate to the 'triadic structure' initiated in the opening pages of *At Swim-Two-Birds*.[17] O'Nolan makes surreptitious use of the number three throughout *At Swim-Two-Birds*, providing further links with the medieval Celtic material as gathered by mythographers during the Irish Literary Revival, as numbers three and seven were considered to be magical numbers in the old tales. Speaking of the number three, both Deirdre and Naoise's tale in Gregory's *Cuchulain of Muirthemne* and Diarmuid and Grania's story in *Gods and Fighting Men* are based on a love triangle: one between Deirdre, Naoise and Conchubar, high king of Ireland; the other between Diarmuid, Grania and Finn, king of Almhuin.

Besides their biographical character, Gregory's collections differ from those of her predecessors and contemporaries in another way: they were written to be used by the emerging dramatic movement in Ireland.[18] For this reason, the narratives in her collections of myths were often written in the form of dialogues, a form of narration generally not found in O'Curry's *Lectures*, Standish Hayes O'Grady's *Silva Gadelica* or Standish James O'Grady's *History of Ireland*.[19] Furthermore, desiring success in the world of the theatre, Gregory wrote the main narratives of *Cuchulain of Muirthemne* and *Gods and Fighting Men* as a series of *tableaux vivants*.[20] She was following a fashionable literary trend in this regard. While the *tableaux vivants* are mainly identified today with static and silent scenes in theatre, during the nineteenth century the idea of the *tableau vivant* was broader, sometimes involving narrative and movement intended as a 'living picture'. An acquaintance of Gregory's, Edward Bulwer-Lytton, made a name for himself in London by writing fictional works that used the format of the *tableaux*, works that became some of the most popular in the century. Bulwer-Lytton's novels consisted of a series of short chapters, each describing movement and involving dialogue, the overall effect of which was to create a *tableau*, a 'living picture'.

The theatrical nature of Bulwer-Lytton's *The Last Days of Pompeii* is evident, despite the long descriptive passages that provide the readers with pictures of the customs, manners, architecture and the general way of living in the Roman Empire. From the gladiators' battle to the catastrophic eruption of Mount Vesuvius that destroyed the city of Pompeii, the love stories of Glaucus, Ione, Arcabes and Nydia are narrated in a series of short chapters, each functioning as a theatrical scene. After its first publication in a three-volume format in 1834, Bulwer-Lytton's novel soon caught the attention of theatre managers and stage directors. Jeffrey Richards notes that two London theatres premiered their respective adaptations of *The Last Days of Pompeii* soon after its publication: the Adelphi Theatre in 1834 and the Royal Victoria in 1835.[21] The novel continued to enjoy success throughout the century, with the Queen's Theatre in London putting on a new adaptation in January 1872. Richard notes that the playwrights J.B. Buckstone, Edward Fitzball and John Oxenford, who were involved in these productions, aimed to retain as much as possible of Bulwer-Lytton's original dialogues.[22] On the other side of the Atlantic, Louisa H. Medina's American version, titled *The Last Days*, was performed in the Bowery Theater in New York in February 1835.[23] An Italian translation was even staged at the Scala as Errico Petrella's *Jone, ossia L'ultimo giorno di Pompei* in 1858. Petrella's *Jone* was one of the musical adaptations that included Victorin de Joncières's *Le dernier jour de Pompéi* (1869), George Fox's *Nydia* (1892) and Marziano Perosi's *Pompei* (1912).[24] Critics were generally delighted with the plays and their pictorial quality: the reviewer of *The Times* commented on the beautiful *tableaux* that were used at the Queen's Theatre in London, drawing attention to the masterful work of famous scene-painter Charles Marshall.[25]

Bulwer-Lytton himself referred to *The Last Days of Pompeii* as a painting, a portrait of Pompeii and its people before the tragic eruption of Mount Vesuvius in the first century, 'when Rome was at its proudest and most gigantic eminence of unbridled luxury and unrivalled power'.[26] Indeed, Bulwer-Lytton began writing the novel after visiting the ruins of Pompeii near Naples and seeing Russian artist Karl Briullov's monumental historical canvas *The Last Days of Pompeii* (1830–3) in Milan, and Giovanni Pacini's opera *L'ultimo giorno di Pompei* in the Scala in the early 1830s. Briullov's monumental historical painting of the ancient tragedy showed striking similarity to Alessandro Sanquirico's stage picture for the production of Pacini's opera at the Scala, which suggests that Sanquirico's designs made a strong impression on the Russian painter. Drawing on the German playwright and theoretician Gotthold Ephraim Lessing's proposition that a play was effectively a 'living painting', Victorian theatre practitioners advanced far in their use of the theatrical *tableau*.[27] Such interconnectedness between the verbal and the visual arts was not uncommon in the nineteenth century, as testified by the composition history of *The Last Days of Pompeii* itself.[28]

Gregory would have been aware of Bulwer-Lytton's classic, given its popularity and the intense public debate around the intertwined nature of the sister arts at the time. Additionally, Bulwer-Lytton was a personal acquaintance from the imperial circles of Britain and Ireland. Gregory's husband, Sir William Gregory, was governor of Ceylon when Bulwer-Lytton's son Edward Robert served as viceroy and governor general of India (1875/6–80). While viceroy of India, it was Edward Robert Bulwer-Lytton who declared Queen Victoria the empress of India in Delhi in 1877. Closer to home, Edward Bulwer-Lytton's granddaughter Elizabeth and her husband Gerald Balfour, chief secretary for Ireland (1895–1900), were seriously involved in the Irish Literary Revival. Lionel Pilkington notes that Balfour administered an amendment to the Local Government Bill that created the legal framework for the establishment of the Irish Literary Theatre in 1899, a forerunner of the Abbey Theatre that opened in Dublin in December 1904 under the directorship of Yeats, Synge and Gregory.[29]

As for O'Nolan and his knowledge of the famous story of the last days of Pompeii: in the *Cruiskeen Lawn* column for 5 September 1961, Myles na gCopaleen mentions that he had recently been to see *The Last Days of Pompeii*, most likely the 1959 film adaptation of Bulwer-Lytton's novel, directed by

Mario Bonnard and Sergio Leone. There were other movie adaptations of the novel screened in Dublin during O'Nolan's lifetime: Carmine Gallone and Amleto Palermi's 1926 silent film adaptation, played in the Sackville Picture House in 1927; and Ernest B. Schoedsack and Merian C. Cooper's spectacular movie screened at the Pavilion in 1936. These adaptations granted Irish movie-goers familiarity with the storyline of Bulwer-Lytton's novel during the early to mid-twentieth century; even those who had not read the original work, possibly including O'Nolan among their number.

O'Nolan, Gregory and the *tableau vivant*

Gregory connected the disjointed narratives to facilitate the 'acting out' of the legends on the theatre stage – hence the overuse of dialogues in her two collections of Celtic stories. Each scene functioned as a nineteenth-century *tableau vivant*, waiting to be 'acted out' on stage. Dramatist friends of hers were inspired: Synge wrote his moving masterpiece *Deirdre of the Sorrows* (posthumously produced at the Abbey Theatre in 1910), and Yeats set out on a long journey to write *Deirdre* (1906/08) and the Cuchulain cycle of plays (1904–39). In fact, *tableaux vivants* were widely used by dramatists and social activists of the Irish Revival. Maria Tymoczko and Catherine Morris have convincingly demonstrated the influence of this form of theatre on the emerging drama scene in Ireland.[30] Morris examines in detail the political uses of the *tableau* by the Gaelic League, the *Inghinidhe na hÉireann* and those involved in the 1898 commemorations of the 1798 United Irishmen rebellion. Yeats himself considered his *The Countess Cathleen* a series of *tableaux vivants*, and many short plays from the early period of the Abbey made use of the fashionable pictorial trend.[31] For that matter, many of Gregory's own plays took inspiration from the pictorial roots of Victorian theatre, something that was recognised by her contemporaries, as a review from D.P. Moran's newspaper *The Leader* attests. The reviewer called her *Twenty-Five* a 'perfect genre picture', a 'Connaught idyll'.[32] Aiming for theatrical realism, Gregory was inspired by the works of famous nineteenth-century realist painters, such as Jean-François Millet, and she took to those old masters whose work carried a certain realist trait, including those of Jan Vermeer van Delft, Jan Steen, Jan van Eyck, Hans Memling, Diego Velázquez and Rembrandt. She had studied their works during her *Grand Tours* of museums and galleries of continental Europe that she and her husband undertook in the 1880s.[33] Her one-acters, from *Spreading the News* (1904) to *Hyacinth Halvey* (1906) and *The*

Workhouse Ward (1908), were testimonies of her interest in the realist tradition of paintings and in the theatrical use of the realist *tableau*. Similar to Bulwer-Lytton, who was inspired to start working on *The Last Days of Pompeii* after seeing Karl Briullov's historical canvas of the same title in Milan, Gregory used her extensive knowledge of European painting in her work as dramatist of the Abbey Theatre. Despite the differences in styles that inspired them as writers, Bulwer-Lytton and Gregory had a shared interest in ekphrastic literature: Bulwer-Lytton's propensity towards monumentalism is not present in Gregory's short, intimate and private plays that were inspired by the works of Millet, Steen, Vermeer and Velázquez, whose scenes were closer to the Irish experience than Briullov's sketch of the eruption of Mount Vesuvius.

Gregory's indebtedness to the *tableaux* tradition left a clear mark on the theatre of her time and it has reverberated in Irish theatre ever since, most notably in the drama of Beckett, McPherson, McDonagh – and O'Nolan. Drawing on Victorian interpretations of Lessing's dictum, Gregory considered the stage a 'living picture', a speaking work of art. This suited her style of drama for it required little emphasis to be placed upon action – almost all physical action was transferred to the characters' dialogues. (Notoriously, Joseph Holloway dismissed O'Nolan's *Faustus Kelly* in similar terms as 'all talk and no play'.[34]) For instance, in *The Workhouse Ward*, Mike McInerney and Michael Miskell only *talk* about rooting up potatoes, devouring cabbage, stealing eggs, hiding from dogs rushing out to bite them. In real life, they are confined to their workhouse beds as they are unable (and unwilling) to leave the wretched place to bring action back into their lives. This kind of 'static theatre' was characteristic of many of Gregory's plays, including *The Bogie Men* (1912), *Coats* (1910) and *The Rising of the Moon* (1907). Her influence on Beckett's minimalist theatre has now been well documented by Emilie Morin and Anthony Roche.[35] Besides *Waiting for Godot* and *Endgame*, however, Gregory's legacy can be felt in a whole range of other twentieth-century Irish plays: Yeats's *Purgatory*, Conor McPherson's *The Weir*, Martin McDonagh's Aran trilogy and his *The Beauty Queen of Leenane*, as well as Frank McGuinness's *Observe the Sons of Ulster Marching Towards the Somme* and Marie Jones's *Stones in His Pockets*. Some of O'Nolan's plays also display the influence of Gregory's minimalist theatre.

O'Nolan's *The Dead Spit of Kelly* and *An Sgian* (translated by Jack Fennell as *The Knife* in 2013), for instance, bridge the gap between Gregory's and Beckett's theatres. *An Sgian* brings to mind *The Workhouse Ward*, itself a re-write of Douglas Hyde's *Teach na mBocht* (1902), translated by Gregory as *The Poorhouse* (1903). Janet Egleson Dunleavy and Gareth W. Dunleavy draw a connection between Hyde's early comedies (especially *Pleusgadh na Bulgóide*) and O'Nolan's 'bilingual satires'.[36] Dunleavy and Dunleavy, however, focus only on the language aspect of Hyde's influence on O'Nolan and pay no attention to the dramatic aspect of Hyde's work for the theatre. *The Poorhouse*, when rewritten as *The Workhouse Ward*, takes on a whole new life. In Gregory's play, Mike McInerney and Michael Miskell have an argument until the visit of Mike's sister, Mrs Donohoe, who offers her brother a way out of his dire situation at the ward. With the double prospect of being subject to serious physical work and losing his life-long friend, Mike declines his sister's offer. Mrs Donohoe having taken her leave, the play ends in a pillow fight between Mike and Michael, who throw all kinds of insults at one another, while looking content to stay together on the ward of the workhouse.[37] Ann Saddlemyer has uncovered *The Worked-Out Ward, a Sinn Féin Allegory*, a political satire of Gregory's from 1918. Saddlemyer writes that this play is 'a metamorphosis of [the] cantankerous pauper[s]', turning the two Michaels into John Dillon, MP, and Stephen Gwynn, MP, and Mrs Donohoe into Ireland herself in the figure of Kathleen ni Houlihan.[38] In the play, Gregory gave voice to her dissatisfaction that, through the squandering of Irish nationalist politicians, Home Rule had become an improbability by 1918.[39] Saddlemyer argues that in *The Worked-Out Ward*, the playwright describes the political impasse 'partially [as] the result of leaders caring more for their own political histories than for the future welfare of shabby Kathleen Ni Houlihan'.[40]

O'Nolan, too, puts a political spin on *The Workhouse Ward*, turning it against Douglas Hyde and the Gaelic League. Much in the manner of Gregory's comedies, *An Sgian* features two arguing characters – the married couple Tadhg and Peig. They argue because Peig has arranged the next meeting of *Glún na Buaidhe* to take place in their home against the wishes of her husband. In the climactic moment of the play, Tadhg, fuming at his wife over the decision, stabs her with a knife. Rather ironically, the murder weapon turns out to be the same knife that Tadhg and Peig had received as a wedding present from the Central Branch of the Gaelic League (*PT*, 257). As Jennika Baines observes, there is a murderous streak in O'Nolan's writings – it is evident in this play as well.[41] Such a streak, however, is absent from Gregory's literary work – there is 'only' a pillow fight at the end of *The Workhouse Ward*, and *The Worked-Out Ward* ends with Dillonnell and Gwynerney seizing *The Freeman's Journal* and *The Irish Times* to throw at one another. Contrary to this, O'Nolan's play is a bloodshot satire on the constant bickering between the Gaelic League and its breakaway organisations,

Craobh na hAiséin and *Glún na Buaidhe*, during the early 1940s. Each of these organisations was interested in advancing the cause of the Irish language but there were continuous disagreements amongst the parties as to the ways in which the use of the language should be advanced, which seemed to mire the prospects of them working together for the common goal. O'Nolan saw the workings of *Conradh na Gaeilge* and its disagreements with its splinter groups through the experiences of his own brother, Ciarán Ó Nualláin, who was a member of *Glún na Buaidhe* and editor of its journal/newspaper *Inniú* when it was founded in 1943. With *An Sgian*, O'Nolan took one of Gregory's most popular plays, *The Workhouse Ward*, and gave it a thematic twist to align its plot more closely to the ongoing debate about the Irish language in the first few decades of the Irish Free State. Additionally, O'Nolan's *An Sgian* reconnects not only to Gregory's 'static theatre' but also to the tradition of the political *tableau vivant* that was popular with the Gaelic League and *Inghinidhe na hÉireann* at the time of the foundation of the Abbey Theatre.

O'Nolan, Cervantes and the modern art debate in Ireland

Sinéad Garrigan Mattar remarks that in compiling *Cuchulain of Muirthemne* and *Gods and Fighting Men*, Gregory aimed to emulate Miguel de Cervantes Saavedra's *Don Quijote*,[42] a novel which has also been widely compared to *At Swim-Two-Birds*, especially its more metafictional second volume.[43] Garrigan Mattar's comments reinforce the ekphrastic character of Gregory's compilations. As a young woman, she had read Cervantes's novel, which would serve as a literary reference all through her life.[44] Additionally, a copy of Charles Jarvis's translation from 1742 (in a 1756 edition) was in Sir William Gregory's library in Coole Park.[45] Ana María G. Laguna categorises Cervantes's writing as belonging to 'ekphrastic literature', stating that 'the visuality of Cervantes's narrative technique is unanimously recognised' by scholars of Spanish literature.[46] She further claims that in Cervantes's time, painting was one of the 'great topics of conversation', with 'Spain maintaining a reverence for Flemish art well into the sixteenth century'.[47] While the paintings of Jan van Eyck and Hans Memling were 'well known and appreciated', writes Laguna, 'Italian references caught up with Flemish ones in Spanish art under Charles V's forty-year reign (1516–56)'.[48] This development reinforced what she calls a 'cultural symbiosis' between Flemish and Italian art in Spain, a 'unique cultural co-existence' of two noticeably different styles of drawing and colouring.[49] This renewed appreciation of painting impacted on Cervantes's way of thinking and, as a result, his way of writing. Laguna notes that 'critics have uncovered in Cervantes's writing a *museum of words*, a vast corpus of pictorial allusions to well-known pieces of Renaissance art'.[50] Indeed, Helena Percas de Ponseti, Frederick A. de Armas and Alicia R. Zuese have unravelled the impact of Italian art on Cervantes's drama and fiction, in particular on *El cerco de Numancia* (*c*.1582) and *Don Quijote*.[51] Gregory may not have been aware of the particulars of Cervantes's interest in art, or that he meticulously studied painting when in Rome, but she would have recognised the pictorial qualities of *Don Quijote*. All the more so as during her *Grand Tours* of European art Gregory had studied the works of Raphael, Botticelli, van Eyck, Memling and Dürer in Italy and the Low Countries, and she was familiar with Velázquez's canvases painted under the influence of Flemish Renaissance art.[52]

Helen H. Reed records that *Don Quijote* abounds in what is called *quadro de costumbres*, with each station of Don Quijote and Sancho Panza's epic journey functioning as a 'pictorial *tableau*', a genre picture of Spain's Golden Age.[53] In these *tableaux*, Don Quijote and Sancho Panza become actors themselves, 'acting out' various roles as they proceed with their journey through mid-Spain.[54] Cory A. Reed, and later Melanie Henry, elucidate that Cervantes had been known for 'novelising his drama' and 'dramatising his fiction', indicating the writer's way of thinking about the interconnection between fiction and the theatre, and, further, painting.[55] Signalling a life-long interest in the theatre, Cervantes brought out *Ocho comedias, ocho entemeses nuevos* (Eight new comedies, eight new farces) in 1615, between the publication of Part I and Part II of *Don Quijote*. Cervantes's drama can be compared to that of Félix Lope de Vega y Carpio (1562–1635), the father of Spanish theatre, in honesty of sentiment and smartness of thought. Bulwer-Lytton's contemporary T.S. Munden, who concealed himself under the pseudonym 'M', believed Cervantes's drama to be akin to his fiction in that it mocked the theatre of his time 'in the same manner as his Don Quixote was designed to parody the equally popular romances of chivalry'.[56] Cervantes dedicated his *Ocho comedias, ocho entemeses nuevos* and Part II of *Don Quijote* to his patron, Pedro Fernández de Castro y Andrade, Count of Lemos, in the hope that the count would finance Cervantes's next visit to the Apennine Peninsula to study Italian painting.[57] Short as these *entremeses* were, they were written to entertain the audience between longer acts and scenes.[58] Acted out in front of a painted background or the curtain that separated the stage from the audience, they occasionally looked like 'living pictures', genre pictures of Spanish life.[59] This seventeenth-century form of entertainment sometimes resembled *quadros de costumbres* and could be perceived as forerunners of the pictorial tradition of the French *entr'act tableau*, popularised during the late eighteenth and the nineteenth centuries, first in France and then in Britain.

What Cervantes's epic and Gregory's legends have in common in the context of intermedial discussions on art and literature/drama is their ekphrastic character. In its obscure relation to these works and traditions, pictorialism is a feature also of O'Nolan's *At Swim-Two-Birds*, albeit in a more modern form. At the time of the novel's composition, there was a cultural debate in Ireland on the state of modern Irish painting, involving members of the Irish Academy of Letters, the Dublin Painters' Society, the Royal Hibernian Academy, the Academy of Christian Art and the Dublin Municipal Gallery of Modern Art. Síghle Bhreathnach-Lynch writes that the debate revolved around the following question: what *was* modern Irish art? Was it the case that only 'paintings of cottages, bog, sea, mountains and a hardy peasantry engaged in tasks associated with rural life provided [the] easily identifiable visual codes of Southern Ireland'?[60] For there was what Bhreathnach-Lynch calls 'a kaleidoscopic diversity of trends of artists' within the Irish school of painting, from painters of rural life to artists whose work reflected the various modernist trends of emerging continental European schools.[61]

The *Twelve Irish Artists* exhibition of 1940 reflected some of these debates and 'the taste of Irish patrons of art', with nine artists exhibiting pictures depicting the blissfulness of Irish country life.[62] The traditionalist world of Leo Whelan, Seán Keating, Dermod O'Brien, Frank McKelvy and Maurice MacGonigal, however, was soon challenged by the abstract vision of Irish disciples of the modernist school of continental painting: Evie Hone and Mainie Jellett. Hone and Jellett had studied in Paris under André Lhote and Albert Gleizes, friends and fellows of famous French-Belorussian artist Marc Chagall (1887–1985). The two Irish artists had exhibited at shows of *Abstraction-Création*, a modernist breakaway group of *Cercle et carré* founded in 1929.[63] M. Llüisa Faxedas observes the gender diversity of both groups, making the point that women artists were welcome and encouraged to join these new organisations.[64] There was no such gender diversity among the artists of the *Twelve Irish Artists* exhibition of 1940. One of the reasons for this, Mary Cosgrove remarks, was that Jellett's 'public debates and educational programs spearheaded discontent with the Royal Hibernian Academy's control of the nation's fine art'.[65] In October 1935, she went on the radio for a public debate with Dermod O'Brien, president of the Royal Hibernian Academy and contributor to the *Twelve Irish Artists* exhibition.[66] Gregory was an important precursor to Jellett in this regard because she was a woman who was at the forefront in promoting European art in Ireland. This enthusiasm was evident in the impressive collection of artworks amassed by the Gregory family at their residence in Coole Park in County Galway. Gregory's own commitment to the cultural value of painting was seen in her long-drawn campaign for public funding to support the housing of Hugh Lane's art collection that he bequeathed to the city of Dublin, on condition that the municipal authorities provided a suitable location for the gallery. Lane's was a major collection of French impressionist paintings that would not only have added immensely to the cultural capital of Dublin, but would also have been beneficial to students of painting in the city.[67] Gregory played a central role in the campaign to secure a suitable location for her nephew's invaluable collection in Dublin.

The legacy of the Hugh Lane controversy reverberated in Jellett's debate with O'Brien in the 1930s, concerned as Jellett was with the significance and the direction of art during the first decades of Irish independence. Over time she gathered a substantial number of followers within the Irish art world, amongst them collector Ernie O'Malley. As in the case of the works of Jack B. Yeats, O'Malley appreciated Jellett's colour palette and her cubist modes of expression – the way 'modernist technique [...] allie[d] itself to an Irish content' in works like *Mise Éire* (1940), her take on Patrick Pearse's famous poem from 1912.[68] Before her death in 1944, Jellett painted a number of pictures that fused Celtic and Christian subject matter with continental abstraction in design, for instance her *Pietà* (1940) and *The Virgin of Éire* (1943).

O'Nolan himself followed these debates on art with some enthusiasm, as evidenced by references to Mainie Jellett in *Cruiskeen Lawn*.[69] In 1944, the year of Jellett's death, Dublin held a Loan Exhibition of Modern Continental Painting, sampling impressionist, post-impressionist and cubist works by Claude Monet, Édouard Manet, Henri Matisse and Pablo Picasso. Having seen the exhibition, O'Nolan felt compelled to write a series of articles on it in *The Irish Times*, including a response to a review by Patrick Kavanagh.[70] At the end of the run, O'Nolan writes an instalment in which Myles na gCopaleen makes the following comments on individualism and modern art:

> my painting must inevitably exhibit the same characteristics – under my own control and use of light, pigment, canvas, form, texture, colour, chroma, value, sense, line, impasto and chiaroscuro. These . . . events are . . . organised to produce not merely a symbol, a décor, but a . . . sort of legendary organism which is to be appreciated and can only be judged in terms of itself.[71]

Of course, not all modern art was to his liking, but the fact that he invested time and effort into commenting on the exhibition and wrote so lyrically and knowingly about painting suggests that O'Nolan was knowledgeable about art and was aware of contemporary debates. This is witnessed in the *Cruiskeen Lawn* columns, in which Myles references controversial French artist Georges Rouault, who was championed by Jellett. Karen Brown observes that both Hone and Jellett took leading roles in the 'Rouault Row' of 1942, which started with the Municipal Gallery of Art's refusal to accept the French painter's *Christ and the Soldier* (1927).[72] It was Jellett who led the petition for the acceptance on behalf of the Friends of the National Collections of Ireland, the same organisation that was behind the Loan Exhibition of Modern Continental Painting in 1944.[73] The row was another example of the shadow cast by the Hugh Lane controversy in Irish art, a controversy in which Gregory had expended much energy earlier in the century. Typical of his judgements on painting, Myles na gCopaleen was ambivalent about the merits of Rouault's work: he applauded the artist's rejection of 'the reverence and formalism that are traditional in treating sacred themes' but criticised him for his 'terrible paroxysm of brutality'.[74]

From the point of view of O'Nolan's ekphrastic writing in *At Swim-Two-Birds*, it is significant that he references in his work some of the main artistic events and rows of the late 1930s and early 1940s. Clair Wills writes that with the outbreak of the Second World War in 1939, numerous artists fled England and continental Europe to seek refuge in Ireland, bringing with them their own unique artistic vision which would influence the Irish cultural scene and those debates on the merits of modern art.[75] 'This influx of talent and energy,' writes Wills, 'could not fail to have some effect.'[76] Several one-man shows were organised, exhibiting new artistic talent fostered in England and continental Europe and challenging at the same time the somewhat fossilised views of the Royal Hibernian Academy. As Wills points out, the artistic debate soon entered a new phrase with questions being asked about the origins of artistic influences: should Irish art be influenced by 'native' and 'local' or by 'foreign' and 'European' views?[77] Somewhat sarcastically but rather insightfully Myles concludes: 'modern art tends to surround itself with "difficulties"'.[78]

One of the recurring themes in O'Nolan criticism today is the writer's attitude towards this cultural debate on modernism/modernity and traditionalism/tradition in the Ireland of the 1930s–40s. Whether it is his eventual acceptance of self-censorship, his resourceful use of farce and satire, his ingenious choices for dramatic themes or his originality in reinventing old medieval Irish-language materials, criticism today focuses on O'Nolan's response to this tension between the traditional and the modern in the Ireland of his times.[79] Kim McCullen puts it bluntly when discussing O'Nolan's 1939 novel:

> *At Swim-Two-Birds* deconstructs various efforts to inscribe 'Ireland' within the literary languages of the Celtic Revival, realism and modernism, as well as within the state-subsidised discourse of post-independence cultural nationalism, even as it voices the heteroglossia of mid-twentieth-century Ireland. Its postmodern narrative strategies – dizzying intertextuality, interpenetrating frame tales, interanimated discourses and reflexivity – expose the limits of received definitions to assert an Ireland that [is] self-conscious, plural, historically-reticulated and in constant dialogue with its past.[80]

Undeniably, *At Swim-Two-Birds* is a literary reflection on the long-standing cultural and political debate over the representation of the Irish experience. Gregory Dobbins argues that, because of this, the novel should be read within the context of Éamon de Valera's drafting of *Bunreacht na hÉireann* between 1935 and '37.[81] The novel should indeed be evaluated within this context of historical and social change but it should also be given merit as a piece of (post)modernist fiction that bears witness to those debates on the state of Irish theatre and painting during the 1930s.

Jellett's comparative example is significant in this regard: both Jellett's paintings and O'Nolan's *At Swim-Two-Birds* are situated somewhere between abstraction and figuration. While Gregory's mythical narratives could never stand accused of abstraction, their *tableau vivant* aspect grants them a pictorial quality that is testimony to the importance of painting to her work as a whole, particularly her dramas for the Abbey Theatre. Of course, O'Nolan's novel does not abound in *tableaux vivants*, as did Cervantes's fiction or Gregory's collection of legends, but its structure does resemble the compositional schemes of contemporary art works (even painted *tableaux*), revealing the ekphrastic character of its narrative. Bruce Arnold notes that Jellett would build her pictures 'from a central "eye" or "heart" in arcs of colour' held together 'by the rhythm of line and shape'.[82] Arnold's words would be apt to describe the compositional scheme of *At Swim-Two-Birds*. According to Jellett's compositional scheme, the story of mad King Sweeny would serve as the 'eye' or 'heart' around which the other stories circulate, including that of Shanahan, Furriskey and Lamont; that of the Pooka MacPhellimey and the

Lamonts; that of Dermot and Orlick Trellis; that of Brinsley and the student narrator; that of Slug, Shorty and the Good Fairy; that of Byrne, Kerrigan and the student narrator and, ultimately, that of legendary Irish character Finn Mac Cool. Should each storyline be annexed to its own colour, the various subplots would create a vibrant picture of concentric storylines, one not dissimilar to Jellett's abstract paintings from the 1930s: *Abstract* (1930), *Composition* (1932), *Abstract Composition* (1935). On O'Nolan's own canvas of fiction, centring on the 'eye' or 'heart' of the story of mad King Sweeny, the various concentric lines would exist in an irregular-looking yet incredibly regular and carefully designed fashion. This would create a colourful canvas of storylines, in front of which O'Nolan's 1939 novel could be easily 'acted out', like the storylines of a contemporary play. No wonder that Niall Montgomery suggested to O'Nolan to consider the dramatisation of the novel.[83]

15

Cad é atá in ainm?

Maighréad Gilion by Brian O'Nolan and *Mairéad Gillan* by 'Brian Ó Nualláin'

RICHARD T. MURPHY

In a 1938 letter to James Montgomery, Niall's father and the first Irish film censor, Brian O'Nolan claimed to have approached An Gúm for a contract to translate James Stephens's *The Crock of Gold*. The offer was refused, according to O'Nolan, because Stephens thought that 'nobody could do justice to his work'. 'He is probably right as far as the usual Gaelic writers are concerned,' O'Nolan writes, 'but I would like to have a shot at it. I did in fact translate a few passages as "samples" for the Gúm + found it very difficult but it is a pleasing intellectual exercise.' His closing hint that Montgomery might 'bully Stephens by post' (*L*, 20–1) on his behalf was ultimately ineffective – a shame, given the affinity between the early novels of Flann O'Brien and Stephens's novel.[1] Yet, the letter indicates that O'Nolan had ambitions to do 'very difficult' translation work into Irish, particularly of a work that had influenced his own writing.

It may seem odd, then, that the only Irish translation he did have published – and the only one under the name Brian Ó Nualláin – was of a realistic if melodramatic Ibsenite tragedy featuring a powerful female title character: Brinsley MacNamara's 1933 play *Margaret Gillan*. The translation was completed in manuscript in 1943 as *Maighréad Gilion* but not published until ten years later – with significant editorial changes – under the altered title *Mairéad Gillan*. Both scripts offer generally faithful, even unimaginative translations, neither literal nor libertine. They were typed and printed in the roman type O'Nolan did not prefer, the modernised spelling he disliked and the indication of lenition with an 'h' that he despised.[2] The script itself seems to stand out from O'Nolan's anarchic column-writing and ebullient playwriting from the period in terms of its genre, its themes and its uncharacteristically workmanlike execution.

And yet, a comparative analysis of the translation's two versions, a consideration of an uncollected *Cruiskeen Lawn* column written about the experience, and a closer inspection of the written correspondence between the key creative labourers involved reveal two characteristically Mylesian themes to be at play: the incommensurability between languages and the fraught relationship between name and identity. Three dynamics are key to a fuller appreciation of how precisely these thematics shaped O'Nolan's approach to, and troubles with, the translation: the wrangling between translator and publisher about the proper rendering of the play's title; the unexplained interval between the manuscript and publication; the uncredited work of a second translator/editor. Furthermore, the plot of MacNamara's play itself hinges on proper and improper naming, official titles versus public monikers and conflicts between birthright and legally documented identities. The differences between the manuscript he wrote and the play that was published, which Myles na Gopaleen would disavow in a 1953 *Cruiskeen Lawn* column, reflect his lifelong disdain for the official, standardised Irish demanded by An Gúm and state publications. Seemingly an anomaly with a questionable place in his *oeuvre*, then, *Maighréad Gilion/Mairéad Gillan* ends up instantiating the themes and issues that permeate it: authorship and authority, name and identity, the translatable and the incommensurate.

MacNamara's play

Set in the small County Meath town of Croane at the end of the nineteenth century, *Margaret Gillan* returns to the grim territory of MacNamara's 1918 novel *The Valley of the Squinting Windows*: a small-town, pre-independence Irish midlands paralysed by the grudges, loveless May–December marriages and malicious gossip of MacNamara's Garradrimna. Margaret Gillan, a 'still handsome woman of about thirty-seven', has inherited the small shop she had run with her recently deceased husband, Peter. She discovers that Peter's will names as trustee and executor John Briody, the owner of the adjoining, much more successful shop and Margaret's love from her teens. The will stipulates that if she remarries – if she ceases to remain Margaret Gillan – the shop will be passed to Briody, or to her seventeen-year-old daughter Esther once she turns twenty-one years of age. Margaret vows to break the 'spancel' that is, according to the old, manipulative Master, 'a magnificent will, superbly drawn. Not a loophole in it'.[3] The key provisions of Gillan's will, we infer, are motivated by his jealousy towards his wife's love for Briody, yet they also codify larger themes of inter-generational sexual policing determined by familial economics and the legal mechanisms by which the language of the dead controls the fates of the living. When Briody forgives the mortgage and begins to visit the shop on friendly terms, however, Margaret briefly dreams that they might finally marry, until she realises that Briody has been courting Esther, who reluctantly consents – just as her mother had nineteen years before to Gillan – in order to secure the finances of the family. Over the next year, Margaret, with the help of her lieutenant Michael Taafe, turns her frustration towards ruining Briody's shop, while Briody and Esther are living next door. Knowing her shop will soon pass to Esther, Margaret plans to offer to exchange her now-prosperous shop for Briody's and to marry the much younger Michael, whom she entices on the mercenary grounds that when the two again defeat Briody in business, he'll be 'the biggest man in Croane in no time. You could walk on them all!'[4] After Esther dies in pregnancy, however, Margaret rules over both shops – Margaret Gillan's Number One and Number Two – but, with her rage at Briody unsatisfied by ruining him, she stabs him to death with a breadknife, fulfilling her prophecy that the people of Croane will 'remember Margaret Gillan always … and what became of her'.[5]

MacNamara's play itself offers rich grounds for critical examination. Analysis might be undertaken of the psychoanalytic displacements of desire (there are even more than a few hints that Esther may be Briody's biological daughter and, after the engagement, Briody calls Margaret 'mother'), the citations of *Medea* (Margaret says she had to kill Esther to hurt John), the inverted Oedipal scenario, or the influence of *Hedda Gabler* as a likely intertext. This essay does not attempt to explore all those avenues, but instead to focus on the themes of naming implicit in the translations themselves and in O'Nolan's refusal to adopt the reader's recommended title because 'the title of the drama is woven into' the theme and action of the play (*L*, 137).

Margaret Gillan's productions and reception

While MacNamara's plays in general have not received sustained critical attention, *Margaret Gillan* was widely known and respected in the 1930s. It premiered at the Abbey in July 1933 for a successful week-long engagement directed by Arthur Shields. Quidnunc reports in the 'Irishman's Diary' that 'although many people who saw it did not like the play, it was a tremendous success from the box-office viewpoint, and it might easily have extended that success for another week if the arrangements at the Abbey did not prevent its continuance';[6] and, indeed, it was staged for another week in mid-September, in a production directed by Lennox Robinson.[7] In a December 1933 retrospective of what they characterised as a 'Lean Year for Irish Drama', the *Irish Times* drama correspondent claimed that 'the only [...] play of any importance' staged that year, besides Lennox Robinson's *Drama at Inish*, had been *Margaret Gillan*. In the review, MacNamara's play is described in mixed terms:

> [It is] a strange, involved study of character, in which the darker side of life is always uppermost. The central character is filled with an obsessive hatred that is not far removed from insanity, and the others are all either fools or knaves. [...] The idea was powerful enough, if sordid, but it was expressed with an obscurity which made the play difficult to follow.[8]

The criticism that the play was 'expressed with [...] obscurity' is curious in a piece that otherwise blames Robinson and George Shiels's offerings that year for lack of ambition and for characters that are '"stage Irishmen" of the twentieth-century style'. This critical ambivalence, at least in *The Irish Times*, tilted in MacNamara's favour in June 1934, when the Irish Academy of Letters (of which MacNamara was one of twenty-five founding members, twenty-four of them men) awarded the play the Casement prize for the best Irish play of 1932–3.

Even closer to O'Nolan's orbit, *The Irish Times* related on 4 December 1934 that the University College Dublin (UCD) Dramatic Society 'gave an interesting private production' of *Margaret Gillan* 'before an invited company'.[9] A longer notice, published on 10 December, reported that MacNamara attended the production and said afterwards 'that the conception of the play by the director [Liam Mac Réamoinn] was nearer to his own than any he had yet seen'.[10] Although there is no record of O'Nolan's attendance at the production, in this period he was revising his MA thesis at UCD and working on *Comhthrom Féinne* and *Blather* with his UCD collaborators.[11] The UCD production ran at the Peacock for a week in 1935 and received praise in *The Irish Times*, with particular admiration for the lead actor, Moya Devlin, who would be a regular Abbey player throughout the decade.[12] Two years later, it was produced at the Abbey with the UCD principals, with Devlin in the lead and Cyril Cusack as Michael Taafe, with the UCD alumnus

Liam Mac Réamoinn reprising his role as director.[13] In the same year, the advisory board of the Belfast Playhouse released suggestions for Irish plays to be produced 'headed by Brinsley MacNamara's "Margaret Gillan"', in a list that included plays by Teresa Deevy, Denis Johnston, Lennox Robinson, T.C. Murray, George Shiels, Peadar O'Donnell, W.B. Yeats and J.M. Synge (*Tinker's Wedding*, which had not been produced in Dublin).[14] The play was sufficiently well known by this time that *The Irish Times* printed a cartoonist's rendition of the *dramatis personae*, captioned: 'Our Cartoonist sees *Margaret Gillan* at the Abbey Theatre.'[15]

Why this play at this time?

Despite its contemporary prestige, it remains odd that O'Nolan would devote his scarce time in the spring of 1943, when he was involved in the productions of both *Faustus Kelly* and *Rhapsody in Stephen's Green*, to translating a play so different in genre, tone and subject to these works and indeed to all of his other writing. Grisly murders are not rare in O'Nolan's work, to be sure, but even in *An Sgian* (The Knife), in which a husband murders his wife with the titular prop, it is in the context of a short satire on Gaelic League factionalism and pedantry.[16] Anthony Cronin informs us that O'Nolan and MacNamara would become friendly regulars in the Smyllie gang at the Palace Bar as early as 1938, but he makes mention neither of *Margaret Gillan* nor of O'Nolan's translation.[17] O'Nolan's own accounts present two slightly different origin stories. His first reference is in a letter of November 1946 to the Department of Finance protesting that it had ruled him 'barred from promotion because of [his] newspaper work' and other spare-time literary activities. O'Nolan charges that 'the State itself connives at [the] delinquency' of literary side-gigs, claiming that he 'was asked to translate a play into Irish for the Gúm, which [he] did' (*L*, 151). However, in a *Cruiskeen Lawn* column from Halloween 1953, the year the translation was finally published – technically not by An Gúm but by Oifig an tSoláthair – he gave a different account of the genesis: 'In some year such as 1939, I had a conversation with my friend, Mr Brinsley MacNamara, and we agreed that I should translate his fine tragedy, *Margaret Gillan*, into Irish; there was some "money" in it for myself.'[18]

The manuscript at the John J. Burns Library at Boston College, titled *Maighréad Gilion* and signed, 'By B O'Nolan, 4 Avoca Ter., Blackrock, 29/3/43',[19] establishes that O'Nolan completed the translation just after the short run of *Rhapsody in Stephen's Green*, which opened at the Gaiety on 22 March but closed, according to Daniel Keith Jernigan, after only five days

(*PT*, xi). This leaves us to speculate on the reason he might have thrown himself into the task at that busy time. Was he riding out a streak of hopeful productivity? Or turning to a dramatic form more amenable to Dublin audiences after an indifferent reception to his own plays? In any case, the fact that he did complete and submit for editorial review the translation of a respected play two days after the run of *Rhapsody in Stephen's Green* requires us to qualify the judgement of both Jernigan (*PT*, xi) and Anne Clissmann that the failure of the latter play 'put an end' to O'Nolan's 'theatrical ambitions' for more than a decade.[20]

The length of time between O'Nolan's completion of the translation and its publication is even more curious given that two Irish translations of earlier MacNamara plays had been published in 1944: *The Glorious Uncertainty* (1923), as *An Tnúth Cráidhte* by Mícheál Ó Siochfhradha, and *Look at the Heffernans!* (1926), as *Dearc ar na hIfearnánaigh!* by Mícheál Ó hAndún.[21] Moreover, despite the mixed success of *Faustus Kelly* and *Rhapsody in Stephen's Green*, it seems likely that O'Nolan's credibility as a stage-dramatist was at its peak in 1943. One might speculate that O'Nolan pushed for the translation's publication after being retired from the civil service in February of 1953, when he was more than typically hard up, but for the same reason, his ability to influence an arm of the state like Oifig an tSoláthair presumably would have been compromised. As for its production, Padraic O'Farrell states in *The Burning of Brinsley MacNamara* that *Mairéad Gillan* was broadcast by Radio Éireann,[22] but he does not supply a date.[23]

Translator versus editor

In his 1953 *Cruiskeen Lawn* column on the subject, Myles refers to 'locutions' made by the editor in the published text of which he (Myles) 'took a poor enough view'.[24] These alterations and insertions to O'Nolan's own work appear to fall into a few related but distinct categories. The first group amounts to copy-editing items that were either errors born of carelessness on O'Nolan's part or idiosyncratic usages that diverged from standardised definitions. An example of the former appears when the editor changes O'Nolan's '*annso amach*' to express the futurity in Margaret's line, 'that's how it'll have to be soon'[25] with '*amach anseo*'.[26] Hewing to more standard definitions, the editor changes O'Nolan's description of Michael Taafe as '*fear óg cíocrach lághach*' – 'an eager, pleasant young man' in MacNamara's original – to '*fear óg lághach aigeanta*'.[27] The last adjective means 'lively' or 'cheerful' but without the connotation, inappropriate for Taafe, of greed as in 'eager (for food, etc.)' that is conveyed in O'Nolan's choice of '*cíocrach*'.²⁸ Similarly, when Margaret speaks 'impulsively', O'Nolan's '*go ráscánta*' – which Ó Dónaill defines as 'Waggish, facetious; irresponsible in speech'²⁹ – changes to the more officially accurate '*go taodach*' – a variant of '*taghdach*' that Ó Dónaill defines as 'Fitful, impulsive, quick-tempered'.³⁰

Other changes evince the editor's efforts to make O'Nolan's more literal rendering of the syntax of MacNamara's English take advantage of the syntactical possibilities of Irish. However, while the results often yield more idiomatic Irish, they also domesticate the translation and eradicate lexical and syntactical *Béarlachais*. This dynamic is demonstrated by the editor's notable preference for copula forms. For instance, when Margaret tells Michael that 'It would be ridiculous for [him] to think of the like'³¹ of entertaining designs on Rose, O'Nolan renders this line as '*Bheadh sé leamh agat go fírinneach smaoineamh ar a leithéid*'³² and the editor as '*Ba shuarach an mhaise duit smaoineamh ar a leithéid*'.³³ Elsewhere, O'Nolan's Maistir patronisingly tells Maighréad '*níl sé furasta agat*',³⁴ while the editor has '*ní furasta duitse*'.³⁵ Margaret's grudging admiration for the will as 'Far-sighted, no doubt'³⁶ is rendered as '*Tá sé faid bhreathnuigh* ['-*nuigh*' copy-edited to '-*theach*'] *gan amhras*' in O'Nolan's manuscript,³⁷ and as '*Ba faid-bhreathnaitheach an mhaise dó é gan amhras*' in the final publication.³⁸ And Margaret's jealous observation to Rose that she 'seem[s] to have a great opinion of him, anyway!'³⁹ is '*Ar chaoi ar bith, tá meas mór agat féin air!*' in O'Nolan's manuscript,⁴⁰ but '*Is léir go bhfuil an-mheas agat féin air!*' in the published form.⁴¹ The editor's impulse to use the copula whenever possible, even, in one case, overrides his maintenance of verbal and tense parallelism. When Margaret asks Michael, 'Was the market any good to us today?',⁴² both translations have '*An raibh aon mhaitheas dúinn sa mhargadh inniu?*', but O'Nolan renders Michael's reply of 'No, not much' in the same syntax as the question, '*Ní raibh morán*',⁴³ whereas the editor uses the present copula, '*Ní morán é*'.⁴⁴ Yet, even as the editor 'Gaelicises' O'Nolan's script, he overlooks some possibilities for stretching the expressive potential of Irish and even dulls MacNamara's diction. The Master is called an 'ibex' and a 'fiend',⁴⁵ both of which the published version translates as the more general '*an diabhal sin*'. The former instance sheds the connotation of sexual predation, a prominent theme in the play, that the low-frequency 'ibex' has in English.

Other choices speak to the translation's de-Anglicisation of the play's setting, characters and references. A measure of the pomposity of the Master is his habit of quoting from Shakespeare, but only once in the published play is there an attempt at translation – where '"Take him for all and all", as the Bard says'⁴⁶ is translated as '*Dá mbeadh fear ar phingin ba fear é!*'⁴⁷ – the other two instances are simply omitted. This omission likely had little to do with debates earlier in the century among Gaelic revivalists about the wisdom of translating the Bard;[48] instead, Shakespeare is not to be heard from in the English-free house style of An Gúm. However, O'Nolan left the two other quotations stand in English, with the Master pedantically citing '*an Bard Sasanach*'. At other points, the editor risks accuracy in replacing O'Nolan's lazy literalism with forced idiomatic *blas*. O'Nolan renders MacNamara's 'no matter what you do'[49] as '*is cuma cad a dheineann tú*',[50] which the editor transforms to '*dá gcuirfeá do shúil ar chipín*', a common enough idiom in Irish that Ó Dónaill includes it in his definition of '*cipín*', but with the slightly different meaning of 'Try as you may'.[51] Despite the affront to dramatic realism in setting an Irish-speaking community in the late-nineteenth-century Irish midlands, O'Nolan's manuscript does allow that any such community would be peppered with the kinds of *Béarlachais* that characterise the Gaeltacht speech which O'Nolan would have heard in his youth. For example, the manuscript refers to Ó Bruadair as the '*trustaoi*', whereas the published text has '*ina iontaobhaí ar an tiomna*'.[52] *Margaret Gillan* has 'John Brody, the Trustee'.[53] Margaret's first line refers to 'the travellers', and O'Nolan's '*trabhlaleirí*' becomes '*taistealaithe*' in the published version. When Margaret scolds the bibulous Master with the line 'You never saw anything but through the bottom of a decanter',[54] O'Nolan preserves the Anglicism (and the pun on 'bottom') with '*Ní fhaca tú riamh faic acht a raibh le feicsint* [*sic*] *tríd tóin an dacantar*', which the editor flattens into '*Ní fhaca tú faic ach a raibh fágtha sa buidéal*' (You never saw anything but what was left in the bottle).[55] While O'Nolan's translation is less inventive or interventionist, it acknowledges the borrowings common to contemporary *caint na ndaoine*. Imagining an Irish-speaking town in the Irish midlands – set before the foundation of the Meath Gaeltacht – in which Shakespeare is familiar to its bilingual inhabitants embraces the earlier dream of progressive language revivalists; deleting the English, scraps as well as gems, rejects it.

A more significant sacrifice of thematic resonance to indifferent translation appears at the end of Act I, when the 'fairly dense' Briody is surprised, absurdly, that Margaret should be enraged by his marrying Esther. He asks the Master why she should hate him 'when we're all more or less one now', a creepy phrasing that the Master repeats in shock. O'Nolan offers '*nuair is cleamhnaithe sinn anois*' (when we're relations by marriage now), a neutral statement of fact which leaves out the intimation that the marriage is actual or spiritual incest, or that John sees Esther as a replacement for, or translation of, the Margaret of nineteen years before. Two other alterations reflect opposing associations between the play and MacNamara's biography. When Briody complains about his loss of custom, he states, 'Sure it's like a regular boycott',[56] for which O'Nolan gives '*Shílfeá gurb amhlaidh atá na daoine im choinne*' (you'd think it's the way the people are set against me).[57] Perhaps O'Nolan again wanted to avoid a *béarlachas* like '*baghcat*', but it removes a word with great resonance in a play MacNamara dedicated to the memory of his father, who famously suffered a boycott of his school by irate villagers who assumed he had had a role in his son's writing of *The Valley of the Squinting Windows*. Another translation intervention encourages that very connection. Whereas MacNamara's Master explains he has free time to cause mischief 'ever since [he] retired from slavery',[58] O'Nolan makes a rare addition: '*Ón lá a chuas ar pinsin ó dhaorbhroid na scoile.*' Identifying him as a former schoolmaster who saw his job as 'dire bondage'[59] could suggest a resemblance between MacNamara's father and the meddling, amoral Master, which the author surely did not intend. Perhaps adding in the school ('*scoil*') merely makes the former occupation of a man titled the Master harmlessly explicit; perhaps O'Nolan was compensating for dropping the earlier allusion to MacNamara's life.

Proper naming

Beyond such editorial intervention, competing notions of what was at stake in conceptions of translation equivalence come to the fore in the problem of proper names and titles, a main theme in MacNamara's play and the primary sticking point between O'Nolan and his editors. Myles even resorts to the Master's reference to bondage in his vague recollection of his servitude as a translator in his 1953 column on 'discovering' the curious play apparently written by himself.

> This experience of slavery comes back to me when I look again at a preposterous correspondence with some native-speaking Gael in the Department of Education, who took great exception to my translation of the title to 'Mairéad Gillan' [...]. The unnamed savant said that the correct titles was 'Mairéad Ní Ghilleáin' – i.e., 'Miss Margaret Gillan'. I stated the situation in one-syllable words, but it took me about three months to win my simple point.[60]

The archive of his correspondence tells a slightly more complicated story. On 10 May 1943, O'Nolan responded to Seán Mac Lellan of the Department of Education objecting to the manuscript reader's suggestion that the title character's name should be 'Maighréad Ní Ghilleáin' instead of O'Nolan's 'Maighréad Gilion':

> If the name '(O) Gilleán' is used, I don't see any way around it except
> to call the woman 'Maighréad Bean Uí Ghilleáin', and obviously that
> would not make sense as a title. I don't see any solution but to use some
> 'non-Irish' version like 'Gilion'. The importance of this point is that the
> title of the drama is woven into it. (*L*, 137)

This letter apparently did not satisfy the reader, so O'Nolan sent back seven
accurate, if pedantic, enumerations. Point 3 asserts that '"Maighréad Ní
Ghilleáin" doesn't mean "Mrs Margaret Gillan"; it means "Miss Margaret
Gillan"'. Point 4 makes the gratuitous clarification that 'therefore your reader
is completely deranged' in favouring the 'Ní Ghilleán' surname. Points 5 and
6 again claim that 'if it is thought necessary to use an "Irish" [note quotation
marks] surname', he must use the Bean Uí Ghilleán form 'as the title of the
drama, something which, of course, would not do'. Point 7 concludes, 'It
is necessary, therefore, to use a different "non-Irish" surname.' He closes,
'That's precisely what I intend to do. If your reader can solve the difficulty
I've mentioned, I cannot. The title of the play cannot be changed' (*L*, 138). He
repeats this insistence in a terse cover letter a month later, in May 1943: 'the
author is unwilling to change the title of the play' (*L*, 140).

His use of the word 'author' (*an t-údar*) rather than 'translator' (*an
t-aistritheoir* or some equivalent) may have been posturing, but it also suggests
that he wanted to protect MacNamara's work from a drastic title change.
While 'Maighréad Ní Ghilleáin' is simply inaccurate, *Mairéad Bean Uí Ghilleán*
'of course would not do' because it would reverse MacNamara's deliberate
decision to omit her married title and would be tantamount to styling Ibsen's
play *Mrs Hedda Tesman*.[61] But whereas Ibsen explained that his 'intention in
giving it this name was to indicate that Hedda as a personality is to be regarded
rather as her father's daughter than her husband's wife',[62] MacNamara has
Margaret retain and take ownership of the name in defiance of Peter's attempt
to control her from beyond the grave. O'Nolan recognised this and insisted
that the name function as a unique identifier rather than as a descriptor with
reference to her husband. Indeed, her maiden name is never mentioned, and
she refers to herself only as Margaret Gillan as an assertion of individual
identity. When the shop assistant Rose tells her that the townspeople now
call the shop 'Margaret Gillan's' and asks whether she is thinking of changing
it, Margaret exclaims, 'By changing my own name, is it? Not at all!'[63]

The manuscript peremptorily raises and dispatches the question of the
names in a translator's note:

Níl gealú na n-ainmneacha acht sealadach agus meastar nach n-oireann na leaganacha cirte Gaedhilge i gcomhnuí – eg., O Bruiadeadha, Lionaide &c.

Fós níl iarracht déanta an Béarla a aistriú go glan díreach [asterisk added: 'in áiteacha'] ar a shon go bhfuil sé riachtanach línte atá ion-labhartha a thabhairt do na h-aisteoirí, ní atá níos tábhachtaí ná cruinneas asitrithe.

(There is no clarifying of the names but occasionally and when it's thought the correct Gaelic version does not fit in equivalence, eg., O Bruiadeadha, Lionaide &c.

Furthermore, no attempt is made to translate the English literally because it is necessary for the translator to provide speakable lines, something more important than exact accuracy of translation.)[64]

Elsewhere, O'Nolan is consistent with MacNamara's own practice in listing Margaret's daughter's surname as Gillan in the list of characters, despite the fact that she marries, and in any case she is not referred to by either surname in the course of the play. Yet, if O'Nolan took the path of least resistance in translating most of the text, he was firm in his rejection of the manuscript reader's recommendation that the play's title and name of the main character be styled in Irish. His refusal to 'translate' Margaret Gillan's surname foregrounds and scrutinises both a main theme of the play as well as the vexed concept of equivalency, which had been the default, untheorised practice of An Gúm. The implicit ideological frame here is one in which Anglicisation, even colonisation, can be reversed or undone by effortless translation 'back' into Irish, whether of proper names or of texts in English, as long as they are composed by 'those Anglo-Irish writers whose sympathies were national'.[65] O'Nolan's small but stubborn rebuke to this notion aims to activate through translation potential meaning only latent or muted in the source text, and it corresponds with earlier progressive revivalists' desire for translation to be 'a catalyst to the shaping of Irish as a twentieth-century literary language'.[66]

In *Assembling Flann O'Brien*, Maebh Long re-presents Evelyn O'Nolan's concerns about the transcription of the Irish names to English equivalents in Patrick Power's *The Poor Mouth*, asking, 'Why, in a text so engaged [...] with the treatment of the Irish language, would the translation present proper names according to English spellings?'[67] To develop this point, Long cites Jacques Derrida's explanation of the resistance that proper names pose to translation itself: proper names 'are taken to be untranslatable because they have no [...] conceptualisable and common meaning; they only have [...] a unique referent'.[68] Derrida adds that versions of names in different languages do not constitute translation because these are adaptations 'in transcription or pronunciation'; as such, 'Londres is not a translation of London',[69] just as 'Mairéad' is not a translation of 'Margaret'. But if, as Derrida writes, proper names 'designate individuals who do not refer to any common concept'[70] and, therefore, in Long's words, 'do not mark a particular category',[71] the case is not the same for titles such as Miss or Mrs, which *do* have a conceptualisable meaning: Mrs does not designate a person the way 'Margaret' does, as an essentially arbitrary baptism; it describes her as a member of the category of married woman. The fact that Irish – or at least the official Irish O'Nolan was instructed to use – offers no possibility of naming an individual woman without simultaneously describing her relationship either to her father (Ní) or husband (Bean Uí) leaves the translator of 'Margaret Gillan' with an insoluble problem that the An Gúm reader, the 'native Gael' Mac Lellan, thinking in English but prescribing in Irish, missed.

The uninflected 'Gillan' interrupts the play as a linguistic anomaly even more as the surnames of the other two female characters in the play do receive Gaelicised 'translations': Rose Leonard becomes Róise Ní Leannáin and Ellen Ledwidge becomes Eilís Ní Léadús. That O'Nolan otherwise followed An Gúm convention to the extent of completely changing the first names of Ellen and Esther (to Eilís and Treasa) because they lack common cognates in Irish throws his retention of the not-quite-not-Irish name Gillan into sharp relief.

This detachment of the surname from reference to her husband is one aspect of the original that O'Nolan's translation amplifies, replacing 'Mrs Gillan' with translatable Irish common nouns. Indeed, I would suggest that the choice is an improvement that makes the best case for not consigning the translation to journeyman's work. The opening scene throws these erasures into sharp contrast with Margaret's insistence on using proper titles. When Rose, the shop assistant, refers to 'John Briody' in the opening scene, Margaret objects, '*John* Briody! Would you never learn to say *Mr* Brody?'[72] (In O'Nolan's translation this is rendered 'Mac Uí Bhruadair', *sans* italics). Four times in MacNamara's play, Michael addresses her as Mrs Gillan, which O'Nolan replaces with '*a mhaistreas*'.[73] The Master, who has most at stake in maintaining the spancel to her husband's will, calls her 'Mrs Gillan' nine times, but O'Nolan replaces three of these with '*a bhean a' tí*',[74] two with '*a bhean mhódhúil*' (gentle woman),[75] another two with nothing at all,[76] one with '*a bhean chléibh*' (dear woman)[77] – and only a single time with '*a Bhean Ghillan*',[78] which itself omits the 'Uí' before the surname.

As a translation, *Mairéad Gillan* fits the description that O'Nolan gave himself in a 10 January 1944 letter to Patrick Cannon: 'both busy and lazy'

(*L*, 145). In most of it, he dutifully supplies the dull equivalencies that characterise so many of the state-sponsored translations he disdained. And yet, he busily champions the independent 'Gillan', which, unlike the play and the other surnames in it, refuses to be translated back into Irish and thus exists as a kind of defamiliarised linguistic orphan. Moreover, precisely because the name is haunted by the absence of its available Irish version, its 'original' even, Gillan, not Gilion, turned out to be just the 'non-Irish' name O'Nolan had demanded.

16

'A play with two titles and several authors is a rather unusual event'

Rhapsody in Stephen's Green by Myles na gCopaleen and *Ze života hmyzu* by the Brothers Čapek*

MATTHEW SWENEY

A PLAY with two titles and several authors is a rather unusual event and, from that point of view, *Rhapsody in Stephen's Green* or *The Insect Play*, presented at the Gaiety Theatre last night by the Edwards-MacLiammoir Company was interesting. But, I am still wondering if William Shakespeare, the Czech brothers Capek and Myles na gCopaleen, with a dash of Jimmy O'Dea and Harry O'Donovan, is a digestible dish.

T.W., '*The Insect Play* at The Gaiety'[1]

There is probably nobody still living who attended Myles na gCopaleen's *Rhapsody in Stephen's Green: The insect play*, Brian O'Nolan's adaptation of Josef and Karel Čapek's *Ze života hmyzu*,[2] presented at the Gaiety Theatre in Dublin by Micheál mac Liammóir and Hilton Edwards' Gate Company from 22–27 March 1943. There are some sources that say the play was a failure – notably, poet and biographer Anthony Cronin (who was fourteen when it was staged).[3] But contemporary reviewers uniformly praised the production values and the acting and debated the politics – which would have been the goal of the Gate Company to produce it in the first place. Hilton Edwards himself was pleased, signing a letter to O'Nolan afterwards 'With you to the death. Yours ever, Hilton, The Producer of the Insect Play' (*L* 127, n. 165). The play may have had its run cut short due to protests about using boy actors as the ants and thus exposing them to the adult themes in the play.[4] Furthermore, the Gate Company had supervised a Dublin University Players' week-long run of the *Insect Play* (not the na gCopaleen version) from 1 to 6 June 1942 at the Peacock which had reportedly sold out, so that may have affected audience numbers.[5] In any case, *Rhapsody in Stephen's Green* ran for a week: not such a bad run, and likely anybody in Dublin who wanted to see it would have seen it.

Rather than argue about the play's reception, I would like to point out some of the layers of this palimpsest of multiple titles and multiple authors. I plan to show that the play is not a failed farce, but instead

1. a topical revival of a play by the Čapek Brothers, one of whom (Karel) had been recently lost to the Nazi occupation, the other of whom (Josef) was still interned in a concentration camp;

2. a great translation, closer in dialogue and spirit to the original than any English translation staged before it; and

3. a searing commentary on Irish neutrality and de Valera during the Irish Emergency, produced by two Englishmen in Dublin.

As a coda to my research, I will focus on a discovery which may seem tangential, but I think it adds ammunition to my reading of *Rhapsody in Stephen's Green*.

Of course, an essay can have three beginnings, so perhaps one should start instead with the first title of the play, 'Rhapsody in Stephen's Green' ... and Isaac Bickerstaff. Not the Isaac Bickerstaff of Swift's invention, but the Irish playwright Isaac Bickerstaff, born a generation after the Dean (1733–1812?) and author of a 1763 tome titled *Stephen's-Green: A rhapsody exhibiting the characters of the belles, beaux, bucks, bloods, flashes, fribbles, jemmies, jesssamies, &c. of all ranks and professions, that frequent the beau-walk*. Where O'Nolan came across the book or reference to the book is anyone's guess, but its very existence explains the dual title of na gCopaleen's version, and in addition to the title there are a few similarities. Bickerstaff describes how the strollers of the park 'flutter up and down, like so many Butterflies' on the first page proper;[6] there is coarse (even unprintable – gaps are left) language used; there are Cork jokes; and the curmudgeonly observer could easily be our superannuated Tramp some 200 years later. His description sounds Nolanesque: 'In his younger Days he travelled much; but for the last forty Years of his Life, has lived a Citizen of the World in *Dublin*.'⁷ Bickerstaff's text is neither a play nor a rhapsody, but an excoriation – mostly against the seven deadly sins as personified by the citizens of Dublin, who are given pseudonyms ('Alderman GUZZLE', 'Lady UPSTART', etc.) but who at the time may have been easily identified by Dublin locals. And last but not least, a note to Joyce scholars: it is also very likely the earliest Irish text to use the word 'metempsychosis'....⁸

Now to the second title, 'The Insect Play' by the Brothers Čapek. Hilton Edwards was not satisfied with the English text of the play and wrote to O'Nolan in July 1942 (immediately after the sold-out performances by the Dublin University Players in conjunction with the Gate) to commission an 'Irish' version for the Dublin stage:

> For a long time I have wanted to produce Capek's 'Insect Play' for which I have the rights. I have not produced it because I don't like the only version available in English. I believe it is not so much a translation as an adaptation for the English theatre. I think it cumbersome and it aims at an English colloquial quality which it misses; and which even if achieved would render the version ineffective for Ireland. I am in rather a quandary. I have got to do this play sometime, but I don't want to do this version.
>
> What about an Irish version with a tramp speaking as an Irishman would and with various insects speaking as Irish insects and not as cockneys? It is much more than a matter of accent, as the original play is in Czech. [...] What about the plain people of Ireland, or why not Miles [*sic*] himself? [...] You have hit a terrific theatre medium because there are characters expressing themselves through dialogue. (*L*, 122–3)

Edwards was right to be dissatisfied: what is not widely known is that in 1942, the 'translation' of the 'Insect Play' available in print in English – Paul Selver's 1923 translation *The Insect Play (And So Ad Infinitum)* – was a corrupted text, Bowdlerised with omissions and substitutions (including the ending).⁹ Myles na gCopaleen's *Rhapsody in Stephen's Green* is in fact not just a matter of a free 'adaptation' of the Čapeks' play but it is an entirely new, imaginative reworking of the play, fixing the holes in the only English translation available to the public at the time and updating the politics from 1922 to 1942. O'Nolan brought what had been a topical play in 1922 back to life another war and generation later by changing the locale in time and space to contemporary Dublin, invigorating the dialogue and still managing to offend certain parties that they are no better than the bugs that crawl on the ground, or under it.¹⁰

Rhapsody in Stephen's Green is not a minor work of comedy but a major work of translation and a topical satire on the Irish Emergency in the 1940s, and O'Nolan managed it in two months (August–September 1942).

I would like to put the play back into the perspective of the events of 1942–3 and to briefly compare it to the published English translation available at the time and to the Czech original. In many important ways, O'Nolan's translation is better than the 'official' English one known to the theatre-going community, and as such it is also an important contribution to the history of the English-language staging of the play (with some Irish thrown in).

The World We Live In

First, the political context in 1942–3. Needful to say, as it is not much glossed on in Robert Tracy's 1994 edition of *Rhapsody in Stephen's Green*, the world was at war, but not Ireland. At that time, the Čapek Brothers were synonymous with Czechoslovakia and its fate. If you look up Karel Čapek, you will probably read that he died of pulmonary oedema in December 1938, at the age of forty-eight. If you ask a Czech about the cause of his death, they will say it was the Nazis. His death is seen by Czechs as the epitomic loss of the nation's leading intellectual before fascism, just as Alfons Mucha's death after Nazi 'questioning' in July 1939 was seen as the loss of the nation's leading artist.

As the most famous Czech writer of his day, an outspoken public defender of democracy, long-term president of the Czechoslovak PEN Club and a leading European intellectual, Karel Čapek was a Gestapo target and knew that in the case of imminent invasion he would be detained and probably tortured. He was already a target of the pro-Hitler factions in Czechoslovakia in the months leading up to his death, and his premature demise from 'exhaustion' was a blow to Czechoslovakia – and reported as such in December 1938 in *The Irish Times*: '[Čapek's] death at the age of 48 is a loss to his own country; it is no less a loss to the whole world.' *The Insect Play* is also mentioned by name in the obituary: 'In *The Life of the Insects (And So Ad Infinitum)*, the lesson of the dangers threatening humanity was repeated.'[11]

While Ireland may have been neutral, war was the topic of the day, and not even 'Flann O'Brien' could escape it. John Garvin writes about the party O'Nolan had upon the publication of *At Swim-Two-Birds*, in a pub where R.M. 'Bertie' Smyllie fulminates about 'the rape of Czechoslovakia and the lunatic exultation on the power-crazed Führer's face as he gazed from an eminence upon the beauties of Prague. I noticed that Brian had grown silent, withdrawn into himself behind a toothy grimace.'[12] What is more, one of O'Nolan's close university friends, Charlie Donnelly, had left to fight in the Spanish Civil War against fascism and lost his life.[13]

The Brother: Josef Čapek not only designed stage settings and costumes, but also published plays, poems and novels (it was he who suggested the word 'robot' for the automatons of *R.U.R.*), and was also one of Czechoslovakia's foremost painters, accomplished in many styles. He suffered the fate his brother would have had he not died: at the time of the performance of *Rhapsody in Stephen's Green* at the Gaiety, he was being held in the Sachsenhausen concentration camp. Like his brother Karel, Josef was a Czech patriot, and his last displayed works were defiantly patriotic, allegorical canvases.[14] He was taken prisoner by the Nazis on 1 September 1939 and transported to a series of concentration camps: Dachau, Buchenwald, Sachsenhausen and finally to Bergen-Belsen in February 1945, where he later contracted typhus and, according to witnesses, died shortly before the camp was liberated. The date of his death and the location of his remains are unknown. There is a symbolic gravestone located at the cemetery in Vyšehrad, Prague in the section reserved for national artists and heroes.

To adapt and stage a play by the Brothers Čapek during the Second World War was in itself a political statement. In September 1938, both Čapeks were signatories to a manifesto by Czech authors published in the world's newspapers – including *The Irish Times* – condemning the Munich Agreement, warning 'Let nobody forget that, after us, the same fate would befall other nations and countries'.[15] Karel Čapek's last two plays, *Bílá nemoc* (*The White Plague* or *The White Scourge*, also known as *Power and Glory*, 1937) and *Matka* (*The Mother*, 1938), have powerful anti-fascist messages about the wartime sacrifices one must make in order to preserve democracy.

Edwards and mac Liammóir were not the first, nor the last, to stage Čapek plays during the war. *The Mother* was played at the Gaiety in 1939.[16] *The White Plague – An Sciursal Bán –* was produced in Irish in Galway in 1941; the Czechoslovak government-in-exile ambassador wrote a letter of commendation to the producer. *The Insect Play* was also produced at the Father Mathew Hall Feis in Dublin, just prior to the war, in 1937.[17] There was an English performance at the Theatre Royal in Workington in March 1938; photos from the production show the actors in Act III giving fascist salutes.[18] There was a May–June 1939 BBC television production with Maire O'Neill reprising her role of Mrs Beetle from the original London production of 1923, a few months before television broadcasting was shut down due to the war.[19] And *The Irish Times* reported that the new Mask Theatre in Belfast was to open with 'The Insect Play' as its first production in June 1944.[20]

March 1943 was after the Battle of Britain, after the Blitz, less than a year before the Baby Blitz. Both producers of the Gate, mac Liammóir and Edwards, were English by birth. I cannot see how an audience in March of 1943 would have found, in Cronin's words, 'the thrust of the satire, if satire it was, obscure'.[21] O'Nolan's 1942 Gate Christmas play *Thirst* also mentions war (in 'Messpot'): the irony of the lack of Irish conscription in the present war would not have been lost on theatregoers.

Ze života hmyzu and *And So Ad Infinitum ...*

The Czech original is a lively satire of human society and its foibles, especially in the post-war situation of Europe in the 1920s. It is divided into a prologue, three acts and an epilogue. As Tracy points out in his introduction to *Rhapsody in Stephen's Green*, the Brothers Čapek stated they wrote the play as three one-act plays with bookends, rather than one play made up of three acts. Each act is concerned with a different group of insects. The prologue, epilogue and entre-actes feature a human tramp, likely a war veteran, who stumbles upon the various types of insects in the woods. His role is that of a Greek chorus, though one extremely hungover and confused, sometimes mistaking insects for people.

The structure of the play, however, is not random. The three acts (in English, 'Butterflies – Creepers and Crawlers – The Ants') represent three physical levels of being for insects (above ground – ground level – underground); and metaphorically, three social levels of being for humans: the upper class – the middle class – the lower classes. Similarly, the satirical effect of the acts upon a middle- to upper-class audience is one that is meant to gradually build from Act I, amusement – Act II, mild indignation – Act III, outrage.[22]

The first act is a send-up of empty-headed dilettantes: the butterfly women are 1920s flappers, the men effete poets. In Act II ('Looters' in the Czech original), dung beetles and their obsession with their all-important dung ball symbolise the middle class, as do crickets who are looking for a home, and a pupa who is about to emerge: the themes are capital, property, children. Where there is capital there is theft: the 'looters' of the act's title arrive and steal the ball of dung (the couple's life savings), the house is taken over by illegal squatters, the pupa is eaten by another insect. Act I about the idle class in the Roaring Twenties is somewhat funny, Act II is more savage, but these two have all been but prologue to Act III – The Ants. Here the Čapek Brothers' subject is war, the military-industrial complex, the ability to sway the masses to support their country's agenda by their own blood in times of war. The play was written just after the end of World War One. The jingoism of the dialogue is the result of direct quotations from leaders of the day, on all sides: democracies, dictatorships and monarchies alike.

It is likely that it was Act III which prompted Hilton Edwards to ask O'Nolan to rework the Čapek Brothers' play, to comment on the state of war in 1942–3. The ants in the original are 'a democracy' – 'the biggest democracy', a world superpower 'fighting the battle of peace', wanting 'to rule the world' for 'freedom'. (If this sounds familiar, the sure sign of good satire is its agelessness.) At the same time, the Czech text was topical again; the speech explaining why the ants are going to war against the yellow ants over the patch of grass between the birch tree and the pine tree uses language similar to that which Hitler would use when talking about Czechoslovakia: 'This land is in the historical, vital, industrial, sacred and military interest of our state, thus according to law it is just.'[23]

There are several serious problems with the Čapeks' play in the English translation in print at that time – namely: poor dialogue, Bowdlerisation and a changed ending. Comparison with the original Czech shows that O'Nolan had managed to 'fix' the mistakes in his adaptation: *Rhapsody in Stephen's Green* is brimming with lively dialogue, the coarseness of the original has been retained and the ending is more akin to the original than the English translation. Edwards and O'Nolan may have felt the flaws in the English translation and fixed them intuitively, but there are references to O'Nolan seeking help for his adaptation. If not access to the original Czech, he may have had access to a good English and/or German translation, and to people familiar with the play as performed in Czech and German. O'Nolan concerned himself with translation and adaptation from the very beginning of his literary career. It is not often noted that in *At Swim-Two-Birds*, his translations from *Buile Suibhne* (his title for the book was 'Sweeny in the Trees') are superior to the existing translations at the time.[24]

First, a little information about the complicated publication history of *The Insect Play* in English. Unfortunately, the two mainstays of translation – fidelity to the original and poetry in the target language – were not kept tightly by the English translators/adaptors of the Čapeks' play. The Czech original, *Ze života hmyzu*, was translated and performed as *And So Ad Infinitum* on the London stage. *And So Ad Infinitum* was translated by Paul Selver, as adapted by Nigel Playfair and Clifford Bax. Selver was the premier Czech-to-English translator of his day, also having translated *An Anthology of Modern Bohemian Poetry* and Jaroslav Hašek's *The Good Soldier Schweik*, as well as the Čapeks' *R.U.R.* However, the case of *Schweik* is a travesty of translation: it is so heavily Bowdlerised, that only about one-third of this classic of modern world literature was translated by Selver (Book 4 is missing entirely), leaving no clue to the sauciness of the original. While *The Good Soldier Schweik* may have been too risqué for print in English at the time, this is not true of *The Insect Play*. One can only presume that self-censorship or prudishness intervened.

Selver's fair translation existed prior to Bax and Playfair's adaptation; it was also used as the basis for the American adaptation of the play by Owen Davis, called *The World We Live In*. This is a more faithful adaptation of the play than the London version, a fact which perhaps is responsible for its longer run: III performances of *The World We Live In* in New York opening in 1922 *versus* forty-two of *And So Ad Infinitum* in London opening in 1923, despite a stellar cast including John Gielgud, Elsa Lanchester, Maire O'Neill and Claude Rains. Selver's fair translation, on which both adaptations were based, was not published, however, until 1950.[25] Owen Davis's American adaptation was not published until 1957.[26] Thus the only edition available to the public in English in 1942 would have been the Oxford text of the adaptation by Bax and Playfair.

Edwards and mac Liammóir had been considering a production of the play as early as in their second season, in 1929.[27] And since Edwards had ties to theatre in London and New York, it would not have been out of the question for him to have obtained copies of the Davis adaptation and/or Selver's original translation at some point since the 1920s. Walter Moore's biography of the physicist Erwin Schrödinger states that 'Myles consulted Erwin for advice about his adaptation of *The Insect Play*'.[28] And *The Irish Times* mentions an amateur production in Dublin in the summer of 1942:

> through the courtesy of the Gaiety Theatre and McLiammoir-Edwards Productions, Dublin University Players have been given the rights of the Capeks' 'Insect Play' [...] the D.U. Players have the services of a Czech producer, Mr Hanus Drechsler. It will be interesting to see how Mr Drechsler, being acquainted with the original version, and indeed with its author, will deal with the Anglicised version.[29]

Whether young Hanuš Drechsler, a Jewish refugee originally from Pilsen, was a producer or knew the Čapeks is debatable.[30] What is not debatable is that mac Liammóir and Edwards had optioned the play already, had involved a Czech speaker with the production and were aware that it needed revisions to work on the contemporary Irish stage.

Sure luckit. You took the words outa me mouth

Na gCopaleen's prologue has nothing to do with the Čapek Brothers' prologue – theirs features a tramp as well, but also an academic chasing butterflies. Na gCopaleen's Tramp discourses on bees instead. The forest has changed to Stephen's Green – and so too the fauna of the Green who populate the play. What is interesting here is that the Selver/Bax-Playfair English prologue is much shorter than the Czech original and serves to introduce Act I, rather than the themes of the play itself. O'Nolan's prologue diverts considerably from the English prologue, first in setting the play in a park and putting a park keeper in the place of the Lepidopterist (*PT*, 161–4), and secondly in doubling the length of the English version by inserting lines about work and having a home (*PT*, 166), themes which will turn up later in his play, more in line with the length and function of the Czech original which was significantly cut in the English prologue.

> TRAMP: [...] What a man like me wants is ... family allowances ... yeh know ... family allowances ... and plenty of free insurances, d'yeh understhand me. (*He is becoming more and more maudlin.*) An' house-buildin' facilities for gettin' married. (*PT*, 166)

O'Nolan's position within the government made him intimate with the realities of Emergency-era family life; a letter from him dated 13 June 1940 to the Secretary, Department of the Taoiseach, is an official remonstrance that the matter of family allowances 'is one of urgency' (*L*, 83–4). That letter is probably the limit of what he could do in his official capacity – however his literary alter ego could do more, and the na gCopaleen *Rhapsody* reflects the de Valera Emergency years just as much as his earlier play *Faustus Kelly*.

In the original's Act I, 'Butterflies', the Brothers Čapek satirise the idle class: poets and society debutantes. It is almost a parody of Oscar Wilde, for these are unwitty dandies. In Czech, the dialogue is full of untranslatable puns, and the juxtaposition of the butterflies' flirty chatter about oviposition and the bitter reality of the males being eaten by birds is funny. The English translation however falls flat, with lame rhymes ('She came in the blue spring weather,/As gay as foxglove is;/And our two hearts rhymed together,/And our lips were one in a kiss') and *non sequiturs* (the Czech original has one of the female butterflies ask one of the male butterflies to grunt in order to impress her with his baritone voice – in the Selver/Playfair-Bax version, she tells him 'Say "ninety-nine".').[31] Rather than recreate this empty banter, na gCopaleen replaces the butterflies with bees and makes them English: Cyril, Cecil and Basil, three upper-class bees who long to meet (and mate) the Queen.[32] Although completely different from the original, na gCopaleen succeeds in making the first act both witty in and of itself. At the same time, he adds an English, apiarian element which you would not find natively in Ireland – i.e. the idea of a queen, and the monarchy:

> CECIL: (*Seriously*) I should really like to see the Queen. Just for a short time, you knaow. And alone.

The idea of mating or even meeting with the Queen, though mathematically improbable,[33] is slightly more possible in the insect world than in the human world, and the coarseness of the idea is akin to the Menippean satire of the Čapek original.[34]

Act II in Selver's version is the act most faithful to the Czech original. Accordingly, here na gCopaleen sticks fairly close to Selver's adaptation. The only place where Selver's version is not faithful to the Czech is in terms of language. To give a small but characteristic example, the act opens with the Tramp, as always, and then voices are heard offstage. In the English version, the dialogue is as follows:

> MR BEETLE [and not 'dung' beetle – even his name has been sanitised]: What yer getting at?
> MRS BEETLE: Me?
> MR BEETLE: Yes, you – you lump of rubbish.
> MRS BEETLE: Silly swine.
> MR BEETLE: Fathead.
> MRS BEETLE: Fathead yourself – mind where you're going.
> MR BEETLE: It's all right, isn't it?[35]

The opening of the act in the Czech original gives the audience ample time to refamiliarise themselves with married life:

> MALE VOICE: Sleep well last night? ['*Jak to valíš?* – a pun which doesn't translate well into English: literally, 'How are you rolling', which means

'How's it going?' but is easily misheard as '*váliš*', which would mean
'How is it you're sleeping around?']
FEMALE VOICE: Me?
MALE VOICE: You!
FEMALE VOICE: Me??
MALE VOICE: You!!
FEMALE VOICE: Me??
MALE VOICE: You!!! You idiot!
FEMALE VOICE: Peasant!
MALE VOICE: Lout!
FEMALE VOICE: Boor!
MALE VOICE: Slut! Hussy!
FEMALE VOICE: Shit beetle!
MALE VOICE: Watch yourself with that ball! Be careful!
FEMALE VOICE: Easy, now![36]

The jealousy and the vindictiveness of the name-calling in the original is
missing in the English translation, which is a pity, as the voices introduce the
avaricious, capitalistic characters who are about to roll in from the wings with
their gigantic ball of dung. In O'Nolan's version, the dialogue is coarser than
the English translation, more akin to the Czech: when Mr Beetle is looking
for his wife, the Tramp comments: 'You don't mean to stand there and tell
me you get into bed with that?' (*PT*, 195). The dung beetles are obsessed with
their ball of dung, their capital. Where the English translation reads 'smell it
old woman, – pinch it – feel the weight of it' na gCopaleen comes in with:
'Smell it, woman, lick it, taste it!' (*PT*, 188).

By far the biggest diversion from the Czech text in the Selver/Bax-Playfair
English translation is the epilogue. In the original, the stage is pitch black, the
Tramp is fighting with something, echoes of voices from other characters in
the play are heard, including, more and more strongly, the voice of the pupa,
who is being born. The light increases, the creature emerging from the pupa
is seen to be a mayfly, which as we know only lives a few hours before dying.
The Tramp renews his losing battle against Death, and two snails slither by
and laugh at him. 'That wath funny' one lisps. 'Life ith thweet' lisps the other.
A Woodcutter comes across the Tramp's dead body. He meets a neighbour
woman who is taking her sister's baby to be baptised. The cycle of life and
death continues.

In the English version, the mayfly of the original has been turned into
a moth, the Tramp's battle with Death is not so existential (in the English

version, we think that it is only in his head; in the original, he seems to be fighting with a real, though invisible, force), there is a woodcutter, woman and baby to be baptised, but they leave the stage and are replaced by schoolchildren who end the play by singing 'As I went down to Shrewsbury Town'.

Na gCopaleen rightly dismisses this crazy *non sequitur* to what has taken place over the last hour and has his tramp eaten when trying to save the egg from being devoured by a gang of insects formed from characters in various acts throughout the play. He's found by the park keeper, a boy and girl walk by talking about marriage, the keeper finds the hatched eggshell and so the cycle of life and death continues (*PT*, 240–6). Na gCopaleen's epilogue, though vastly different, is truer to the original text in intent and spirit.

Flann at war: Rhapsody in green and orange and red and purple

While there may be justification for not translating the rawness of some of the dialogue onto the London stage in 1923, there can be no justification for smoothing the biting and bitter anti-war criticism out of Act III 'The Ants'. For example, here is a monologue in the original by the Tramp, who has been swept up in the furore of war hysteria:

TRAMP: To arms! To arms! For the route among the blades
is in jeopardy! Do you hear me? The pass from one blade to the other,
the expanse of ground from grass to grass, your sacred right,
the greatest interest of the state, the greatest question in the world today,
is at stake! Ants, to arms!
How could we live, if the land between two weeds
belonged to someone else?! If a foreigner carried ant bundles
through there to another anthill?
One hundred thousand lives for two blades of grass
are too few! I was in the war, you!
Now that's insect work! Dig that trench,
shovel that clay, hurray!, the firing line is advancing,
hump across the mounds of corpses, fixed bayonets,
fifty thousand dead, just so's you could occupy
twenty paces of latrines. Hurrah! To arms!

It's for the allies, it's the heritage of your history,
what is more, it's freedom for the homeland, what is more, it's world
domination,
what is more, it's two blades of grass! Such a huge thing
can only be managed by the supreme sacrifice! To arms! To arms![37]

By changing the scale of the battlefield to the ant world, the bitter reality of
human trench warfare is laid bare. Unfortunately, the English version turns a
deadly call to arms into a mocking description, rendered in the rhythm of a
drinking song (I quote in full):

> TRAMP: It does yer good to see 'em pass,
> Prepared to shed their blood –
> And jest for 'alf a yard o' mud,
> Between two blades o' grass.
>
> It does yer good to see 'em all
> So 'andsome and so spry.
> They're not afraid to up and die –
> They've 'eard the Nation's call.
>
> It makes you think o' them old scenes
> With star-shells over 'ead,
> The night we left a thousand dead –
> And captured two latrines.
>
> Now, fellers, dig yerselves right in,
> And stay there till you bust.
> Them Yellers wants yer yard o' dust.
> And don't you let 'em win.[38]

This trite version of the speech is rightly omitted by na gCopaleen. Instead,
he emphasises the distinctions between ants: in the original, the ostensibly
black ants are at war with the yellow ants, after having defeated the grey ants.
In *Rhapsody in Stephen's Green*, with its Dublin setting, na gCopaleen invents
ants which are predictably green and orange. The green ants have crossed the
border into the orange lands to retrieve a dead bug which they need for food.
The orange ants are quick to go to war, on territorial principles:

CHIEF ENGINEER: Ond because thon porties hov tacken down the flag of the Good Awnts and poot up some other flag.

2ND ENGINEER: Ond because they're not loyal, d'ye see.

CHIEF ENGINEER: They'll do what thon awnt over in Rome tals them.

2ND ENGINEER: Ond thot's whey they all tok Latin.

CHIEF ENGINEER: A dad longuage.

2ND ENGINEER: Ond they want to mack us tok Latin too.

CHIEF ENGINEER: Ond hov it taught in the schools.

2ND ENGINEER: Ond hav it shoved down the wee awnts nacks.

(*PT*, 216)

The red ants from across the way (this is 1943, remember) are also at war, and they want more from the orange ants in taxes; this is refused by the orange ants and so they go to war against them. In the confusion of battle ('Do you know what I'm goin' to tell you, you're makin' my head go round worse than anny feed of malt ever did. I'm dizzy!'; *PT*, 214), the inferior forces of the green ants somehow come out on top, only to start fighting each other in factions over whether one speaks Latin or not. In the end, the Irish-speaking green ants win, with a proclamation from their emperor that from now on the whole world will speak Irish only, at which point the Tramp crushes them to death with his feet: 'You … dirty … bloody … lousy … little bastard of an insect. Ouwathat!' (*PT*, 239). Featuring orange ant slogans such as 'The Awnt State will feight ond the Awnt State wull be rieght!' (*PT*, 215), O'Nolan himself was aware of the 'political commentary in the last act which may be unsuitable for the times' (*L*, 125–6).[39] With an ultimatum from the green ants 'Signed by Deevil … Deevil so-ond-so (*PT*, 223)', it was not a coincidence that the attack on the play was led by *The Irish Press*, the 'organ of the Fianna Fáil party'.[40] As Tracy points out, the green ant emperor is a 'thinly disguised Éamon de Valera', and the orange and red ant invasion reflect real fears of the British army crossing over the border.[41] However in 1943, nobody in Ireland would have been able to stomp de Valera out.

And so in fact there are two wars going on in 1943: the ant war on the Irish stage, and the world war in the theatres outside. O'Nolan's play restores the topicality and the venom of the original, showing that, unfortunately, while the whole world is at war, the factions on the Emerald Isle are just fighting over the same two blades of grass.

There is a cogent comment by the *Bell*'s reviewer regarding the politics of the Čapeks' play and why it had not been revived lately:

My copy of the Paul Selver translation is dated 1923, and several impressions, or depressions, appeared after that: but none, I fancy, after 1935. That marks the end of the vogue – for the very natural reason that the Spanish War revived all that the Capeks mocked – enthusiasm, courage, faith, hope, and everything else that the world is now once again dying for and living on.[42]

However cogent, the reviewer was wrong, for the play had been republished and revived, several times, leading up to and during the Second World War.[43] Why? Partly because of solidarity with the fate of Czechoslovakia and the fate of the Čapeks. Mac Liammóir and Edwards staged a Czech play in 1943 with O'Nolan's help to take a side against fascism and protest neutrality – exactly what the Czech writers urged in their manifesto – the neutrality that did not work for Neville Chamberlain. While millions of lives are being lost, na gCopaleen's Tramp puts a button into the Red Cross charity chest. The change of focus to Ireland in Act III by Edwards and O'Nolan incorporates this shift in attitudes, for it shows how the internecine squabbles of the Irish pale against the global turmoil in which Ireland proclaimed neutrality ('I'd die meself of course, if I'd any reason to. I'd give me life this minute for a pint of porter and often risked me life for less. But a dead beetle!'), raging on outside the insect world of Ireland in the bigger world, where there *are* things worth fighting for – a turmoil which proved fatal to the play's original authors. I read na gCopaleen's play as a Second World War reinterpretation of human behaviour: if fighting is in our nature, one group of ants ever against another, then we should choose our fight. Ridicule – whether against our 'uncle' Dev or rival 'awnt' – can be more than an indigestible dish: it can be a weapon wielded by artists, a 'chastening rod'.

Coda

I own Micheál mac Liammóir and Hilton Edwards's copy of *The Poetry and Prose of William Blake*, inscribed in Edwards's hand with their names and 'Dublin: August 1939'.[44] On the flyleaf before the rear cover board is written what I would call a meditation. It starts with the title and page number of Blake's poem 'Auguries of Innocence' and then it reads like this:

> There's nothing wholly evil
> There's nothing wholly good
> There's nothing wholly anything
> That does not come from God

~~If~~ God created evil then
As God created Good
Who dares then against an evil man
To raise a chastening rod
                    H.E. Sept. '43

Six months after *Rhapsody in Stephen's Green* was opened and closed in Dublin, Edwards is reading Blake and writing a meditation on God, good and evil, and the courage to chastise an evil man. I see Edwards's inspired choice of O'Nolan to rewrite *Ze života hmyzu* as him daring to raise a chastening rod – against Hitler, against de Valera, against the 'Deevil' (or devil) era and the complacency of the neutral Irish in the Second World War.

ACT V

Curtain Calls

17

Morphed into Myles

An eccentric performance in the field of cultural production*

Johanna Marquardt

Brian O'Nolan's use of pseudonyms is a well-established feature in O'Nolan studies. Since its inaugural conference in 2011, the International Flann O'Brien Society[1] has attempted to re-evaluate the usage of the proper name and pseudonyms in the critical field. So far, new perspectives have emerged, but given O'Nolan's diverse, and at times inconsistent, performances under a variety of masks, an all-purpose formula seems out of the question, perhaps even undesirable. There is a growing tendency to use the pseudonyms belonging to the texts under which they were published if the 'character-authors', rather than the empirical author, are the intended referent, such as 'Myles na gCopaleen'.[2] Yet, volumes of criticism still largely use 'Flann O'Brien' as a signpost even if they deal with texts published under various pseudonyms or the empirical author Brian O'Nolan and his contexts.

Recognising these unresolved issues, the strategies and effects of O'Nolan's pseudonymity have received growing critical attention.[3] Adrian Oțoiu, in a brave attempt to come to terms with the messy ontologies behind the names, has proposed that O'Nolan's critics draw a distinction between autonym and Fernando Pessoa's term heteronym, the former being a pseudonym that refers to the empirical author, the latter being a pseudonym that refers to a performed or inhabited identity with a distinct biography and personality other than the empirical author's.[4] In this framework, Oțoiu argues, 'Myles na gCopaleen' is a heteronym that functions differently from the autonym 'Flann

O'Brien'.[5] John Greaney notes the recent critical turn in O'Nolan studies away from a postmodern emphasis on the slipperiness of the pseudonym to a more historicist and new modernist focus, in which '"Brian O'Nolan" has increasingly served, if not somewhat reductively, as the authorial agent when referencing this *oeuvre*, thereby [...] facilitating the possibility of [the diverse *personae's*] comparison within a holistic structure'.[6] More recently, Scott Eric Hamilton has asserted 'the need to be able to refer to each individual persona both in their own right and as a part of a network of actors with an influential relationship with the biographical individual', pointing to 'the intersections of influence or points of deviation between the personas of O'Nolan as they destabilise lines of genre, text, and authorial authority'.[7] By focusing on the broader twentieth-century Irish literary and journalistic fields rather than the individual author, Ronan Crowley has shown that O'Nolan's strategies of pseudonymity and masking are far from unique in Irish revivalist, modernist and journalistic contexts.[8]

Academic problems with naming are due in part to the ontological and referential issues created by O'Nolan's pseudonyms, but also to the traditions of naming we have inherited from previous waves of O'Nolan scholarship. 'Flann O'Brien' was established as the most impactful moniker in literary criticism early on, most prominently by Anne Clissmann's pioneering 1975 monograph *Flann O'Brien: A critical introduction to his writings*. But upon closer inspection, the status and function of the eponymous character-author is precarious: despite the promise of an introduction to his writings, the volume opens with a biographical chapter. This biography begins by introducing first 'Myles na gCopaleen' and then 'Flann O'Brien'; 'Brian O'Nolan' is first introduced through the false biography of the *Time* magazine hoax.[9] This initial reluctance to refer to the literary agent by the name of the empirical author, to privilege an anecdotal reiteration of O'Nolan's identity games over an analytical mode, counteracts the establishment of a system, no matter how tentative.

While Clissmann's *Flann O'Brien* stands out as the solitary monograph dedicated to a scholarly analysis of the author in this period, most writing in the first wave of O'Nolan studies is explicitly biographical and memoirist in nature. In these memoirs, the hierarchy and usage of O'Nolan's various names works differently again from academic studies, favouring 'Myles' to refer to the empirical author Brian O'Nolan. In his contribution to *Myles: Portraits of Brian O'Nolan* (1973), Jack White uses 'Myles' almost exclusively,[10] as does John Ryan in the 'The Incomparable Myles' chapter of his memoir *Remembering How We Stood: Bohemian Dublin at the mid-century* (1975).[11] This practice is continued by Tony Gray in the chapter 'Myles and Company' in *Mr Smyllie, Sir* (1991), an account of the life and times of the prominent and eccentric *Irish Times* editor R.M. 'Bertie' Smyllie.[12] Brian's brother Ciarán Ó Nualláin chose to include Myles na gCopaleen as the only name in the title of his 1973 memoir *Óige an Dearthár .i. Myles na gCopaleen* (The Youth of the Brother i.e. Myles na gCopaleen),[13] a practice which was continued by Brian's youngest brother, the artist Micheál Ó Nualláin, who also chose to include the pseudonym in the title of his 2011 collection of anecdotes *The Brother (Myles).*[14]

What can be observed in such biographical and memoirist writings is the process by which '"Myles" supplanted Flann O'Brien, even, in important externals at least, Brian O'Nolan. [...] The fate of the licensed jester had befallen him' and he 'became [his audience's] creation'.[15] This quotation from Anthony Cronin's *Dead as Doornails: Bohemian Dublin in the fifties and sixties* (1976) neatly captures two recurring issues surrounding memoirs on O'Nolan. First, there is a pervasive sense of failure and nostalgia, even melancholia, most obvious perhaps in the overall dramaturgy of Cronin's own *No Laughing Matter: The life and times of Flann O'Brien* (1989), the most widely received memoir on O'Nolan, which morbidly follows its subject's descent from 'The Brilliant Beginning' to 'The Close'.[16] Secondly, the pseudonym 'Myles' takes precedence over Brian as a proper name and is appropriated by his audience. By these means, issues of authority but also of authenticity and referentiality are complicated.

The patterns of naming in these memoirs are significant to the posthumous reception and evaluation of O'Nolan's life and works. Their continued circulation and influence perpetuate the creation of a semi-fictional character caught up in a complicated web of ontological issues intentionally and accidentally spun by various storytellers, performances and audiences. This essay engages with the establishment of the eccentric character 'Myles' in the field of cultural production and its implications for the relationship between authors, texts and their readerships. At stake is a greater critical understanding of the precise ways in which Myles 'became a mythical figure in which were mixed characteristics borrowed from the experiences of a typical Dublin man – and occasionally of O'Nolan himself – and a mass of unbelievable, extravagant features'.[17] For this investigation, extracts from memoirs by Gray, White, Ryan and Micheál Ó Nualláin are analysed regarding their treatment of 'Brian O'Nolan' and 'Myles na gCopaleen'.[18] These texts avoid the term 'biography', with its aspirations to factuality, and prefer the more personal connotations of the term 'memoir'. In fact, these memoirs are a pastiche of genres, comprising biographic sketches, summaries of and extracts from O'Nolan's own fictional and journalistic writings, anecdotes and characterisations. The term 'memoir' reduces expectations of objective factual accuracy and stresses the personal, subjective character of the narrative. Yet, at the same time, the authors are careful to point out any lapses of memories or doubts regarding sources, contradicting, in a way, the generic label they chose for their texts. This is the first in a line of contradictions which pepper the passage from Brian O'Nolan to the collaborative character 'Myles'.

Out of the genres constituting these pastiche texts called memoirs, anecdotes are the most enduring and ubiquitous. The reasons for their prevalence seem obvious: first, they are entertaining because they showcase O'Nolan's intellect or vicious sense of humour, the attributes on which he built his career as a writer. Secondly, they spare their narrators the cumbersome and ultimately impossible task to summarise O'Nolan's life and the spirit of his works based purely on either biographical data or primary literary material, by rather exemplifying certain aspects which are made to characterise the person. By creating types, rather than rounded characters which might more closely resemble the real, multi-faceted and mutable personalities they represent, this formal feature pushes the supposedly referential memoir further into the realm of fiction. At the same time, the plentiful iterations of the same one-dimensional character remain framed or shot through with biographic sketches, stressing their dedication to factuality. By hovering between referentiality and fictionality, the memoirs suspend their subject in an ontological limbo. They strengthen the perception that 'Myles', with all his antics, refers to O'Nolan and create what may well be called a semi-fictional biographical character.

When viewed through the lens of eccentricity, a critical concept advanced by the work of Rainer Emig, O'Nolan's performances as 'Myles', their written recordings by his contemporary audiences and the contradictions they incur, point to larger issues pertaining to the working principles of culture itself.[19] Emig identifies an exchange of gazes between the eccentric and their audiences as constitutive of eccentricity: both exert a certain agency, but lacking a direct verbal exchange, their perspectives remain irreconcilable. For their audiences, eccentrics are strange but not threatening, different but not wholly other, interesting but neither in terms of ideals nor competition. They are often thought influential in hindsight but were never powerful in a direct way in their lifetime.[20] Eccentrics therefore inhabit an ambiguous space between otherness and ideal. In the past, eccentricity has been largely dismissed as a critical concept, or embraced only when studies remained anecdotal rather than analytical, shunning conceptualisation or structural model; 'individualism, anachronism and lack of subversive potential', Emig posits, are the reasons for the reluctance of critical and cultural theory to engage with the concept. When analysed more closely and diachronically, however, these supposed weaknesses provide a useful counterpart to neater but somewhat reductive centre-periphery models of culture because they enter 'the messy realms of human practice'.[21] As such, they can account for cultural shifts without postulating norms. O'Nolan, the civil servant and satirist, prodigy and failure, who is often remembered but remains enigmatic, promises to be an interesting case study.

After introducing how O'Nolan entered the field of cultural production of mid-twentieth-century Dublin and reflecting on the working principles of this field by employing Pierre Bourdieu's theory of the field of cultural production,[22] I analyse the memoirs from this field which contributed to the metamorphosis of Brian O'Nolan into the eccentric hybrid character 'Myles'. In conclusion, I point to the wider-ranging implications of Emig's critical concept of eccentricity for studies of literary and cultural production by assessing metacritically the shaping effect of these early memoirs on O'Nolan studies.

Brian O'Nolan's performance in the literary and journalistic fields

The attribution of the name 'Myles' to the person of Brian O'Nolan in memoirs and anecdotes from the journalistic field seems understandable, 'Myles' being quite certainly connected to Myles na gCopaleen, the character-author of *Cruiskeen Lawn*. 'Myles' is preferred to 'Brian' or 'Flann' in the recollections of White and Gray, who were journalists writing for *The Irish Times*. Ryan, who also opts to refer to O'Nolan as 'Myles', was a contributor, editor and publisher with *The Bell* and *Envoy*, critical literary periodicals in 1940s and '50s Dublin to which O'Nolan contributed writing. A considerable overlap between literary and journalistic writing accounts for his use of the largely journalistic pseudonym. That Micheál and Ciarán Ó Nualláin should single out that particular name for the titles of books whose primary intention is to commemorate their brother Brian, however, enhances the impression introduced by Cronin that Myles had supplanted Brian, even in the (admittedly publicised) private realm of the family.

Because many writers in mid-twentieth-century Dublin worked for newspapers in order to make a living, the literary and journalistic fields shared many agents.[23] In the case of *The Irish Times*, a key factor in this overlap was the paper's 'legendary editor' Smyllie, who had 'cultivated literary and artistic associations from early in his career' and, together with Alec Newman, introduced the Saturday book page.[24] Smyllie was himself a renowned eccentric figure, 'a vivid sight, even for Dublin, as he pedalled on his bicycle to the office wearing a huge green sombrero, a voluminous cloak about his rotund figure with his portable typewriter hanging from the bar of his machine'.[25] Both the literary and journalistic fields had publicly accessible meeting places: for *The Irish Times*, this was the Palace Bar and later the Pearl Bar, both on Fleet Street; for the literary scene, especially the literary periodicals *The Bell* and *Envoy*, it was McDaid's pub just off Grafton Street.[26] The story of how O'Nolan entered the journalistic field through his encounter with Smyllie – the beginning of his metamorphosis into 'Myles' – in one of these public houses is recounted in various memoirs.[27] What varies is the degree of detail in which the process is presented, and there are minor but clearly identifiable discrepancies regarding the time frame between Niall Sheridan's, White's and Gray's accounts but no actual contradictions.[28]

Smyllie's interest in O'Nolan is invariably attributed to the series of 'Letters to the Editor' hoaxes that the author staged with Niall Sheridan, Niall Montgomery and others between 1938 and '40, under pseudonyms such as 'Lir O'Connor', 'Luna O'Connor', 'Whit Cassidy', 'Judy Clifford', 'Hilda Upshott' and 'Velvet-Texture', and in which he was suspected of posing, among others, as Frank O'Connor. Sheridan took O'Nolan to the Palace Bar, where Smyllie '[held] court among his cronies',[29] and they quickly struck a deal. According to Gray, who provides the most fleshed-out version of events, Smyllie had previously used his contacts to learn as much about O'Nolan as possible and had commissioned an article from 'Flann O'Brien' before announcing that there would be a column.[30] Gray's *Mr Smyllie, Sir* dedicates a chapter to 'Recruitment and Training'[31] in which a variety of budding journalists undergo an initiation process similar to O'Nolan's. In another chapter, Gray describes the general working principle of 'The Palace Bar Crowd',[32] a congregation which corresponds to that depicted in Alan Reeve's famous 1940 caricature *Dublin Culture* which is reprinted in the centre pages of Ryan's memoir. According to Gray, 'by a generally understood and widely accepted convention', a place in Smyllie's vicinity was kept vacant so that supplicants could approach him with a drink and a project.[33] It must have been a similar setting in which Sheridan introduced O'Nolan to the editor.

In 'The Field of Cultural Production', Bourdieu disputes the mode of analysis

which tends to foreground the individual, or the visible interactions
between individuals, at the expense of the structural relations [...]
between social positions that are both occupied and manipulated by
social agents which may be isolated individuals, groups or institutions.[34]

O'Nolan's and Smyllie's performances should therefore not be considered
individually and in isolation, but rather should be understood to be indicative
of the structure of the field and the habitus of its agents (by habitus, Bourdieu
means 'a subjective but not individual system of internalised structures,
schemes of perception, conception and action common to all members of
the same group or class'[35]). That their deal would have appeared 'haphazard,
completely casual'[36] seems essential to the performance aesthetics of the
field and should be taken into consideration as well. O'Nolan's and Smyllie's
performances were likely well prepared and, at least in the case of the latter,
well-rehearsed, yet they were to appear casual and improvised in their public
forum. This display of cool self-confidence in a public, social setting is an
expression of the habitus of agents in the literary and journalistic fields,
both of which were very much domains of masculinity in mid-twentieth-
century Dublin. While it is clear that writers want to be published, asking
for assurances belies their confidence in their field. Because there are no
assurances, writers inhabit the most precarious positions in the field, while
arguably being the most essential agents in it, having to prove themselves
time and again in often overlapping professional and social arenas. At the same
time, the decision-making power resides with the brokers of their wares, the
editors, who do not, however, possess the financial capital themselves but
are answerable to a board of executives. A performance of self-confidence is
therefore necessary for both types of agents. Moreover, because the field of
cultural production operates on inverted economic principles, meaning that
a writer can lose literary prestige through gaining financial success, financial
security could be seen as a double-edged sword.

This wilfully casual deal with Smyllie is the first of Myles's performances
to be narrativised and memorialised in the many surviving anecdotes.
Conceptualising these anecdotes as theatrical performances is prompted by
the fact that Myles is clearly being watched and is playing to an audience. In
some cases, his pub performances would at least in part consist of the rehearsal
of jokes which would later be published in *Cruiskeen Lawn*, as Gray, Cronin
and Mícheál Ó Nualláin confirm,[37] even as Mícheál suggests that 'He [Brian]
wouldn't be like that really'.[38] This sense of public performance concurs
with Cronin's description of the pub rehearsal: 'he was always pleased if you

adverted to something that had been in [the column], but it must have torn his guts out over the years'.[39] While Ó Nualláin and Cronin may have different reasons for doing so, the fact that they both doubt O'Nolan's sincerity or the authenticity of his interactions in these sites supports an interpretation of O'Nolan's behaviour in public as a performance necessitated and shaped by the rules of the field. Indeed, this sense of Myles as not only a *nom de plume* or a self-fashioned character, but as a theatrical performer in Dublin's literary, journalistic and social fields shapes later criticism in subtle but pervasive ways, for instance when John Wyse Jackson claims that 'Myles na gCopaleen was not just another pseudonym: he would become the greatest fictional artefact that O'Nolan ever created. Myles might be the "writer" of *Cruiskeen Lawn*, but he is also the main actor in it'.[40]

Terence Brown attributes these performances to the frustrating stagnation of late 1940s and early 1950s Dublin, in which 'eccentricity, showmanship and bravado [...] would distract both public and writer from the serious business of his art'.[41] The abundance of entertaining anecdotes about eccentric writers from the time corroborates that thesis, Patrick Kavanagh and Brendan Behan being only two in a long line of examples.[42] The fact that these scenes and narratives were recorded for posterity hints at the symbolic value that was attached to them. The proliferation of anecdotes also means that O'Nolan was not a special case but rather that these performances are indicative of a prevailing habitus: far from being seen as an expression of individualism, eccentricity is part of the habitus in the field of cultural production in mid-twentieth-century Dublin. The recording, reworking and reiteration of such performances – in other words, the self-fictionalisation and commodification of the field – are ingrained in its structure, turning authors into fictions, agents into products.

Mylesian memoirs

These characteristics are common to all of the memoirs under analysis: centralising the *persona* 'Myles', typifying his character as an eccentric, reading his behaviour summarily as theatrical performance and creating anachronisms through acts of remembrance that nostalgically or melancholically dwell on the past. Eccentric performance is, then, a crucial component of these memoirs, recorded in anecdotal form. In combination with biographic sketches and various intertexts, they form a complex pastiche which is brought to bear on O'Nolan.

Gray's *Mr Smyllie, Sir* introduces O'Nolan's journalistic *persona* as 'Myles and Company'

> because Myles was not one character but many, all of them angry, intolerant, irascible, extremely critical of the Establishment, violently opposed to pretension in any shape or form, and all very, very funny.
>
> Above all he was Myles na Gopaleen [...] of *The Irish Times*, the first humorous columnist in the Irish language. But he was also Flann O'Brien, now well known in the UK and the USA as the author of *At Swim-Two-Birds* and *The Third Policeman*, two extravaganzas which have become classics in their genre. He was in addition the notorious Brother Barnabas of the UCD [University College Dublin] college magazine, *Comhthrom Féinne* ('Fair Play'), who in time became a character as full and as complete and as eccentric as Myles himself.[43]

Eccentricity is explicitly identified as a quintessential attribute of 'Myles', the hierarchically privileged *persona* to whom all the other characters, *personae* and proper names are subordinated and compared (he is Myles 'Above all'). Notably, the title 'Myles and Company' frames Myles's actions and writings as theatrical performances: Myles is eponymous and appears as the leader of a theatrical troupe, comprised of O'Nolan's other *personae*. While Gray reads all of the *personae* alike as fictional characters, he paradoxically also attributes them to Myles rather than to O'Nolan, underpinning the established hierarchy and, in part, contributing to the ill-defined status of the pseudonym in the first wave of O'Nolan criticism. A few lines later, Gray actually goes on to explain that 'In private life he was Brian O'Nolan, a civil servant', attributing 'Brian O'Nolan' as a role performed by 'Myles', the 'he' of this claim. This formulation also presents his job as a civil servant, which is anything but private, as his private life, further cementing the idea of an entirely public figure. The summary judgement 'all very, very funny' equates O'Nolan's behaviour in public with his writing, interpreting his actions in each sphere as comic performances.

In using the phrase 'now well known' with regard to Flann O'Brien's fame, Gray points to the fact that the success of *The Third Policeman* was posthumous and, as such, did nothing to further its author's career while alive. *The Hard Life* and *The Dalkey Archive* did not come to prominence, which is presumably why they are left out of this overview. And the 1960 reprint of *At Swim-Two-Birds* came much too late to shift power relations between 'Flann' and 'Myles' in favour of the former. A touch of melancholia seems to linger about the author whose fame came late: 'Flann', the literary *avant-gardist*, should have been the star, but he is ultimately considered a failure in his own lifetime; 'Myles', the clown for the masses, stole his limelight. This assessment is shared by most of O'Nolan's chroniclers and is especially prominent in Cronin's biography. It arguably points to the perverse power relations in Bourdieu's field of cultural production of which the literary and journalistic sub-fields form a part: while literature possesses more cultural capital and its producers are held in high esteem, economic capital favours journalistic mass production, and writers, who need money to survive, are caught in the double bind between literary kudos and worldly existence.

In the title of Timothy O'Keeffe's 1973 edited volume *Myles: Portraits of Brian O'Nolan*, 'Myles' is again eponymous. This time, however, 'Myles' is recognisable as the product of a creative process; 'Brian O'Nolan' is the real historic person represented by 'Myles', the artifice. The title also stresses the collaborative principle which is at work: Myles is not one but several portraits. The metaphor of portraiture again points to construction, seeking to capture a subject but ultimately producing a stylised version of it. Ian Ó Caoimh argues that there is a comparable ironic distance between the actual subject and its representation in Ciarán Ó Nualláin's portrait of his brother 'Myles' in *Óige an Dearthár*, which subtly echoes the pseudo-biographic writings of Bónapárt Ó Cúnasa's memoir *An Béal Bocht* that is supposedly edited by 'Myles na gCopaleen'.[44]

The chapters of *Myles: Portraits of Brian O'Nolan* refer to their subject as the contributors see fit. O'Nolan's brother Kevin chooses 'Brian' for 'The First Furlongs'; Sheridan, his college friend, also opts for 'Brian', as does John Garvin who was acquainted with him through the civil service. White, like Gray a journalist who worked for *The Irish Times*, uses the name 'Myles' throughout. Given that *Myles: Portraits of Brian O'Nolan* is from Martin, Brian & O'Keeffe, a London-based publishing company, it is curious that the book seems to be aimed at a decidedly Dublin audience. A British or international readership would have required the name 'Flann O'Brien' in the title, one imagines, if it were to take an interest in the book. It was in Dublin where Myles's fame superseded that of the novelist and letters-to-the-editor writer Flann O'Brien, primarily to readers of *Cruiskeen Lawn*, as well as to the audiences of his Dublin stage plays (*Faustus Kelly*, *Thirst*, *Rhapsody in Stephen's Green*), Telefís Éireann sitcoms (*O'Dea's Yer Man*, *Th'Oul Lad of Kilsalaher*), and the various advertising campaigns to which his 'name' had been attached (Guinness & Co., Odearest Mattresses, Hospital Sweepstakes)[45] – but also, and importantly, as a notorious character-about-town. The use of the name

'Myles' for the person whom a *Cruiskeen Lawn* reader and the inscribed reader of *Myles: Portraits of Brian O'Nolan* might have met in the street, or indeed in a public house, underlines the difference in quality between the author's names and *personae*: 'Flann O'Brien' is not written about by authors other than O'Nolan as though he had an existence outside that of his own authorial voice. 'Myles', however, about whom O'Nolan himself had written as a character and not simply employed as a pseudonym,[46] is also the protagonist of highly stylised narratives by writers other than O'Nolan.

Within the volume *Myles: Portraits of Brian O'Nolan*, White's and Sheridan's headings present a little play on sequences: while Sheridan's chapter carries the title 'Brian, Flann and Myles', White's sequence runs 'Myles, Flann and Brian'. The juxtaposition of the two titles challenges the reader to infer what might be the organising principle. The former might be read as a temporal sequence, the latter as a Russian-doll-model of the character-author in which Myles is the public figure, Flann the figure of the publishing and academic fields and Brian the private man. They can represent hierarchies in which either Myles or Brian are most prominent. Or one can view Myles as the outcome of a process.

Drawing out the full complexity of these relations, White's contribution begins thus:

> Myles na Gopaleen sprang fully-grown from the brain of Brian O'Nolan in the autumn of the year 1940; and for about a quarter of a century his 'Cruiskeen Lawn' appeared, with erratic regularity, in *The Irish Times*. No other writer in his class, so far as I know, has produced a daily newspaper column: certainly no other has written in this form so much of his best, his most original, and his most influential work. The influence of Myles was pervasive precisely because his writings appeared in this ephemeral form. Through the columns of the newspaper which was read by most literate Dubliners, the work of Myles na Gopaleen was able to irrigate their minds and their speech.[47]

While establishing a relationship between 'Myles na gCopaleen' and 'Brian O'Nolan', the opening words in fact constitute an intertextual allusion to Flann O'Brien's *At Swim-Two-Birds*. The character Furriskey comes into the world through the process termed 'aestho-autogamy' (*CN*, 37), which requires only one person, an author, for the creation of a new being, a fictional character. In extending the points of biographical reference not only beyond the margins of the text, but also beyond the realm of the biographical itself – and into the realm of the fictional – such recurrent intertextual references are, so to speak, the *modus operandi* of eccentricity (from Greek *ekkentros*, 'out of the centre'). In White's turn of phrase, agency is accorded to Myles rather than to O'Nolan, and the authorship of *Cruiskeen Lawn* is also attributed to him. Like Zeus's daughter Athena, who crawled from her father's head after he had devoured her mother for fear of a challenge to his power – or, indeed, like Trellis's characters in *At Swim-Two-Birds* – Myles appears to be outside of the control of his maker, whose biography increasingly deviates from its centre. The oxymoron 'erratic regularity' likewise points to a lack of control and a certain eccentricity. The theatrical immediacy of Myles's not-quite-regular interactions with his responsive audiences is also foregrounded in White's praise of Myles's influence on his readership, and he later states that Myles came to interpret 'instant reaction as influence, or even power'[48] as he increasingly 'tried to mobilise readers'.[49]

In his memoirs *Remembering How We Stood*, Ryan titles his chapter on O'Nolan 'The Incomparable Myles'.[50] This text, too, is filled with intertextual references: the volume's title stems from Valentin Iremonger's poem 'Clear View in Summer',[51] which looks back with a sense of foreboding on the halcyon days before the state of 'Emergency' in Ireland during the Second World War and establishes a note of melancholia.[52] Within this nostalgic framework, the chapter's title refers to Patrick Kavanagh's recollection, following O'Nolan's death, of the first Bloomsday celebrations, and his abiding memory of 'the incomparable Myles pissing on Sandymount Strand'.[53] These intertextual references at the paratextual thresholds of the volume and of the chapter establish notes of nostalgia and melancholia, the former harking back to a time of promise and opportunity for the young writer O'Nolan, the latter pointing out his incomparable loss (albeit in somewhat ironic terms). 'The Incomparable Myles', then, is a perfect subject for Ryan's thematic and tonal purposes here, given that, as Emig argues, eccentrics are inherently anachronistic and nostalgic in their function as markers

> of the good old bad old days when certain privileged individuals were granted the right to behave slightly outside the norm, and society regarded their antics as amusing and perhaps even enriching, without, however, feeling provoked into debating or tempted to copy them.[54]

As a further explicitly intertextual feature, and like all chapters in *Remembering How We Stood*, 'The Incomparable Myles' opens with an epigraph, here taken from *The Third Policeman*. As with the allusion to *At Swim-Two-Birds* that opened White's text, in choosing an intertextual echo so intricately connected to Flann O'Brien, the text in fact digresses from its subject Myles. The quotation is a rendition of de Selby's characteristically ludicrous and austere concept of life as a hallucination caused by being condemned to walk a tightrope or perish (*CN*, 304–5). The tone this extract sets for the chapter, while humorous, is reminiscent of the dark undertones of O'Nolan's writings and appears ironically to undermine the supposed purpose of the memoir genre from the outset: rather than capturing or portraying life, it renders the memoir's very subject matter as an illusion. Ryan thereafter introduces his subject as 'Brian O'Nolan' in an even more direct contravention of the chapter's title and states that he 'was three divinely humorous *personae* in one'.[55] Unlike Gray, Ryan attributes the *personae* to O'Nolan rather than Myles. However, here, O'Nolan is put on a par with his *personae*. Only a few lines later, Ryan states that 'Hereinafter he will be referred to, by me, simply as Myles',[56] privileging the pseudonym. This turn to refer to the empirical author by the name of the character-author is performed even after Ryan notes that Myles na gCopaleen is himself also an intertextual reference, namely to Dion Boucicault's blundering rogue and staple Victorian stage Irishman in *The Colleen Bawn*.

When Ryan's text finally arrives at the proper description of Myles, it does so only to compare him to the genius of Joyce, which would become a well-worn tradition in O'Nolan criticism:[57]

> [Myles's] knowledge of languages and the complexities and idiocies of semantics [...] was as deep and widespread as Joyce's. Indeed, the existence of Myles explodes any theory that Joyce's appearance on the Irish literary scene was a unique event, never to be in any way repeated [...]. Myles allowed that Joyce had a keener ear for dialogue than he.[58]

To title the chapter 'The Incomparable Myles' and then to make a direct comparison between Myles and Joyce shows that Ryan's main structuring principle is highly ironic. The passage defeats its own purpose by relativising Myles's qualities rather than making them stand out beyond comparison, and indeed marking them as inferior to Joyce's. In pointing to other authors, in the figures of Iremonger, Kavanagh and Joyce, to situate the 'Incomparable Myles', Ryan's memoir establishes intertextual distraction as an organising principle and thus constitutes a further instance of the contradictions which are defining characteristics of the memoirs which attempt to portray the untraceable figure of 'Brian O'Nolan' *aka* 'Myles'. Rather than capturing Brian O'Nolan, these memoirs assemble a pastiche that circles him while at the same time ironically creating a distance to the subject they try to represent.

Myles as an example of the eccentricity of culture

To complete the array of Mylesian memoirs for this essay, *The Brother (Myles)* by Micheál Ó Nualláin offers an anecdote titled 'No Room at the Inn'[59] which places his brother, under the name of 'Myles na Gopaleen', in a troupe of 'well-known Dublin characters'.[60] What marks them as 'characters' is that each of them is barred from one pub or the other, making it impossible for them to find anywhere to drink together as a group. Why exactly they are barred is left to the reader's imagination. What emerges from this scene is a sense of divergent perspective: the characters are excluded from certain social practices, however not entirely but only in certain places. The text presents their plight as comic rather than tragic, and their exclusion from pubs is treated as the consequence of minor slips in *decorum* rather than as indicative of truly menacing criminal tendencies. They are seen and presented not as wholly other but as marginal and eccentric. These eccentrics in turn gaze past how they may be perceived and concentrate on telling tales of the good old days. A sense of anachronism and melancholia is attributed to this group of 'well-known Dublin characters', who ironically mourn the loss of 'characters' in Dublin in their time, even as they themselves fill the very void they bemoan. The exchange of gazes which is only possible because the eccentrics are not othered and thus excluded from all communication causes an oscillation of perspective which lends the situation its irony.

Close analyses of these memoirs show up contradictions, ironies and paradoxes surrounding eccentrics. They do not, however, explain them away as typical of a particular context because that is precisely what they are not perceived as. Viewed through the lens of eccentricity, they instead point to larger issues of cultural dynamics. For the field of cultural production in Dublin at the mid-twentieth century, however, they are even more interesting because eccentric characters abounded yet retained their attraction as oddities.

There is, then, more to eccentricity than a verbal brushing aside of behaviours and attitudes society cannot readily make sense of. Eccentrics linger at the margins of culture because of their ambiguous status as strange but not threatening, different but not other, interesting but neither as ideals nor as competition. By considering both the eccentrics' and their audiences' perspectives as an exchange of gazes, and by allowing for what seems contradictory, eccentricity structures perceptions of culture and is able to account for shifts without first assuming fixed positions. From their ambiguous position, eccentrics influence without executing power.

While it is 'Myles' who is labelled as eccentric, a slight change of focus shows that the memoirs themselves are as eccentric as the character they create: seeking to capture eccentricity, they are structured by it. They are necessarily anachronistic because they commemorate personalities and events past; with melancholy, they resuscitate dead contemporaries. In a Dublin context they have even continued to do so, not only in the preservation of the memoirs, but in orally transmitted anecdotes. They are different in that they seek to capture life but fictionalise it by assembling and narrativising an intertextual pastiche, thus transgressing genre boundaries. Because fiction may be referential and constructedness is considered a given in biography, however, they are not wholly other. They are dismissed as anecdotal entertainment rather than authoritative scholarship – for instance, in Keith Hopper's influential call in the mid-1990s for a new wave of O'Nolan scholarship that turns away from an earlier 'indigenous school of Irish criticism', which he characterises as 'insular', 'invariably folksy and anecdotal, and often lacking in critical acumen'[61] – but they did undoubtedly influence a certain discourse on O'Nolan.

Brian O'Nolan, who was morphed into the 'licensed jester',[62] the eccentric Myles, inhabits this ambiguous space between otherness and ideal: part deviant, part bourgeois; part canonical, part failure. The men who wrote his life accord his writings and *personae* with an influence they are at the same time reluctant to associate with their author. The attribution of agency and authorship to Myles rather than O'Nolan in the memoirs works in the same way. O'Nolan's opinions, hidden as they were behind various masks, are forever doubted and read as theatrical roles and performances by his chroniclers; at the same time, his real public presence and visibility to a Dublin audience and the memoirs' choice of the 'Myles' pseudonym to represent a biographical subject work to fossilise the conflation of man and mask. An approach to the biographical subject is constantly deferred by intertextual deflections which, while professing to unmask the man, distract attention away from him and collaboratively create another highly stylised and narrativised character whose referent remains ambiguous. Contradictions, ironies and deflections become integral in the divergent perspectives of the eccentric and his audience, troubling the sense of priority of the man over the mask. In biographical writings therefore, O'Nolan's public performances, complemented by a perpetuation of his own identity games, have distracted from the man as much as they have shaped his representation.

18

Sweeny Among the Moderns

Brian Ó Nualláin, Samuel Beckett and *Lace Curtain* Irish modernism*

S.E. Gontarski

Lacking traditions one must make them; having traditions one must break through them.

Brian Coffey, autumn 1973[1]

This particular state, Ireland, is no longer young [...]. It is time we grew up, forgot about Cathleen and all her hang-ups and hangovers. Time to forget about the Celts, time to face the reality that Irish unification may never happen, and it does not matter much anyway. Time to embrace a post-nationalist Ireland in a post nation-state Europe.

Dennis Kennedy, October 2010[2]

The recent critical effort to resituate Brian Ó Nualláin in the canon of Irish modernism has been led, in part, by a series of new comparative readings of Ó Nualláin's and Samuel Beckett's early novels, and, to a lesser extent, their writing for theatre.[3] The present essay offers a different slant of light on these conversations, by turning to the republication and reception of Ó Nualláin's poetry translations and Beckett's writing about poetry in the 1970s Irish journal *The Lace Curtain*. This is a previously neglected site of Ó Nualláin's posthumous reception and canonisation, in a pivotal moment for the redefinition of Irish modernism, which gives us a new vantage on the ways in which Ó Nualláin has been made to perform, variously, the roles of 'antiquarian' and 'modernist' in different critical waves. Yet, even as the journal chooses to foreground different aspects of Ó Nualláin's and Beckett's relationships to tradition and modernity in poetry, a return to this juncture in the authors' divergent trajectories in the critical history of Irish modernism also reveals their shared taste for self-concealing pseudonyms, performative hoaxes and deflationary comedy to burlesque certain 'lace curtain' Irish pretensions.

In August of 1934, *The Bookman*, a distinguished London monthly, published an essay called, innocently enough, 'Recent Irish Poetry'.[4] It turned out to be a provocative, even pugnacious assault on Ireland's literary patrimony, its national, artistic endowment, if not on nationalism itself. It drew a line in the turf for the relatively new, post-colonial Irish Free State; delineated what the essay's author saw as a parochial preoccupation with place; established alternatives – rather antitheses – to a received nationalist narrative; and challenged its ethos and aesthetics. Terence Brown summarises the issues in general terms thus: 'the 1930s would certainly give the cultural historian apparently sufficient ground for concluding that modernism and post-colonial nationalism [...] are antithetical in their particular manifestations'.[5] J.C.C. Mays concurs: 'the thesis of the Revival [which] focused on the myth and folklore of the Irish countryside produced an antithetical interest in the modern urban world'.[6] The line that marked out that divide between the 'Irish countryside' and 'the modern urban world' was the one delineated in 'Recent Irish Poetry', written by one 'Andrew Belis', pseudonym, it turned out, of recent Trinity College alumnus and acolyte of James Joyce, Samuel Beckett. Outlined in 'Recent Irish Poetry', in a brash, even superior tone, is a set of reservations, something of an argument for what will come to be called modernism. It segregates Irish writers, at least Irish poets of the 1930s, on either side of that marshy, shifting boundary: parochial, bog-bound on one side and urban-cosmopolitan on the other, a demarcation between western and eastern, between archipelago and continent, between Romantic and modernist, perhaps, and finally between homebodies and exiles.

But Beckett's *demesne* is neither so easily geographical nor national, and so not overtly binary. The pseudonymous author proposes as his principle of individuation or segregation (which he applies consistently) the degree to which Irish writers are aware of 'the breakdown of the object', a theme in the fore of his own critical and creative efforts. He accuses the majority of Irish poets, those whom he calls 'antiquarians', of 'delivering with the altitudinous complacency of the Victorian Gaels the Ossianic goods' and further condemns their mysticism – what he calls the 'iridescence of themes' of such poetic luminaries as George Russell (Æ), James Stephens, Austin Clarke and William Butler Yeats. Among those approved, on the other hand, are, most notably, friends. Denis Devlin is one of the few who is 'aware of the vacuum which exists between the perceiver and the thing perceived',[7] and Thomas MacGreevy is praised for his 'vision without the dip'[8] – that is, insights without aid of a candle. Beckett thus ridicules *The Candle of Vision* (1918),[9] Russell's essays on Celtic mysticism to which Miss Carriage will allude in Beckett's *Murphy* shortly thereafter[10] and in which narrative, the narrator acknowledges, the eponymous Murphy shares Neary's fear to 'fall among Gaels'.[11]

'Recent Irish Poetry' was reprinted in the 1970s in *The Lace Curtain: A magazine of poetry and criticism*, a publication committed to an aggressive rethinking of Irish poetry and so of Irish modernism and cosmopolitanism. In a retrospective essay on the journal and its associated New Writers' Press, Trevor Joyce, one of the founders of both publishing ventures, noted of the Beckett reprint, 'This was, to the best of my knowledge, the first time he allowed his piece on Devlin to come out under his own name'.[12] Joyce's memory fails some here as he seems to confuse the essays reprinted in *The Lace Curtain* nos. 3 and 4, since the Belis/Beckett effort in issue 4 featured Devlin so little, and Joyce continues his misremembering: 'It had originally appeared anonymously in *The Bookman* in the 1930s'[13] – well, 'pseudonymously' anyway.

Trevor Joyce was one of the stalwarts of this post-colonial redefinition of Irish modernism, if not Irish nationalism, and he was considered, in some respects, the poetic heir to Brian Coffey. He offered his own treatment or redrafting of the received Irish literary patrimony with his translation or reworking of the *Buile Suibhne*, edited by his *Lace Curtain* cohort Michael Smith and published in 1976 by their New Writers' Press as *The Poems of Sweeney Peregrine: A working of the corrupt Irish text*.[14] As the subtitle suggests, the translation offers a satirical reworking of the tale, particularly 'The Man of the Wood' segment. It thus shares characteristics with the Finn Mac Cool rendering of *Buile Suibhne*, itself redrafted as St Ronan's curse on Sweeny-Trellis in Orlick's assault on his own patrimony in *At Swim-Two-Birds* (*CN*, 170–1). Such rerenderings of Irish myth were not uncommon – Niall Montgomery's play *The Winter Man* is also based on *Buile Suibhne*, and Beckett's own lampoon of the Cuchulain legend in *Murphy* is a further case in point. The fourth number of *The Lace Curtain*, then, took a decidedly defiant stand against the Celtic Twilight, even out-Becketting Beckett's 1934 attack, into which Flann O'Brien's antiquarian lampoon, his own *working of the corrupt Irish text*, might have nestled nicely had the editors chosen to use it and so to champion his creative modernity directly. Instead, they chose to publish representative examples of Brian Ó Nualláin's translations from Old Irish poetry, a choice which, juxtaposed with Beckett's republished essay establishing stark distinctions between antiquarian and modernist poetry, may have helped to delimit Ó Nualláin's place in such rethinking rather than to celebrate him as one of the notable figures within this second wave or second generation of Irish modernism.

The Lace Curtain republication of 'Recent Irish Poetry', now under Beckett's own name,[15] was simultaneously something of a repatriation as well, suggesting at least a post-war or post-Nobel *rapprochement* between the apostate Beckett and his homeland, as Smith and Joyce used Beckett's stinging critique of certain forms of hermetic Irishness to develop and legitimise their own realignments. The 1934 essay was then embraced in an attempt to carve out a native Irish modernism and simultaneously to introduce the Irish reading public to more non-Irish writing, Beckett, perhaps, straddling those categories.

As early as its second issue (spring 1970), Smith and Joyce took the 'criticism' subtitle of their journal's title seriously and opened their 'Editorial' with a look behind the genteel 'lace curtain' of Irish literary respectability: 'The awarding of the Nobel Prize to Samuel Beckett affords the Irish literary Establishment another occasion for publishing the lie that Ireland is an incorrigibly literary country and that Dublin is an *internationally important* centre of literary activity.'[16] The editors dispute that 'lie' on the grounds that the nation's most internationally prominent writers fled the land of their birth in order to develop creatively. They confront the political issues of the day directly, moreover, noting that 'Mr [Charles] Haughey's tax concessions are irrelevant to the Irish artist who must work full time at some mundane livelihood job or else never earn enough to be taxed anyway',[17] and they offer two salient examples:

> It was only through an almost miraculous moral tenacity and integrity that such writers as Patrick Kavanagh[18] and Brian O Nualain [*sic*] (Flann O'Brien) survived (even if somewhat scarred).[19] [Both had been closely associated with John Ryan's pre-*Lace Curtain* journal, *Envoy: A review of literature and art*, 1949–51.[20]] Their survival was their own individual achievement; they were wise enough and great enough not to care for the plaudits and 'respect' of uncivilised and hypocritical 'educated' Dublin society. *The Lace Curtain* salutes the living spirit of these two

great writers [both dead by then, we might add, Ó Nualláin on April
Fool's Day in 1966, Kavanagh a year later], and while it admires the
work of Mr Beckett, it should have been happy – and now especially
since he hardly needs the money – to see him – like Mr Sartre, reject
that soiled prize.[21]

In the following issue, no. 3, Michael Smith offers a longish editorial/
review contrasting 'Irish Poetry and Penguin Verse'. In his 1995 retrospective
essay, Joyce calls this editorial 'a rebarbative attack on Brendan Kennelly's
Penguin Book of Irish Verse',[22] a collection that maintains 'a nostalgic backward
look', according to Smith.[23] Much of the editorial half of the review is an
all-out attack on the patriarch of Irish poetry, Yeats, and Smith suggests
that 'Even a superficial look at the Literary Revival reveals Yeats as the
arch-manipulator, encouraging here, criticising there, always suppressing,
hoisting, punishing'.[24] In a gesture of inclusion if not appropriation,
perhaps, Kennelly includes a single Beckett poem translated from the French
and retitled generically as 'Poem' (i.e., 'I would like my love to die') and a
single poem, 'The Colours of Love', by Devlin, who, Kennelly says (in the
'Contents' but not in the 'Introduction') 'Deserves more attention'[25]; both
are poems of failed love. Smith's editorial, then, retraces the battle lines set
out in Beckett's 1934 essay on Irish poetry, Kennelly subsuming it all under
a grand metanarrative of native Irish myth around which Irish poetry (and,
by implication, the Irish themselves) is seen to be unified and so defined. And
Smith lays out Kennelly's biases (while deflecting his own): 'In all the reviews
of the anthology I have read, none has failed to comment on the ludicrously
unjustified preponderance of space allotted to Frank O'Connor [twenty-two
poems and whom Kennelly calls 'Ireland's Ezra Pound'[26]], James Clarence
Mangan [of 'Dark Rosaleen' fame, eighteen poems[27]] and Sir Samuel
Ferguson [of *Lays of the Western Gael* (1865) fame, eleven poems]', translators,
real or fake, all.[28] None of Ó Nualláin's poetic translations are included in
Kennelly, however.

   Smith's pointed response to Kennelly's highly influential, defining
anthology is taken up more fully in *The Lace Curtain*'s subsequent issue that
reprints Beckett's review of Devlin's poems, *Intercessions*, in which Beckett
praises Devlin for creating a poetry 'free to be derided (or not) on its own
terms and not in those terms of the politicians, antiquaries (*Geleerte*) [*sic*,
exhausted or depleted] and zealots'.[29] Beckett is here used as something of
a counterweight to Kennelly's grand narrative of Irish aesthetics and so,
presumably, against a principle of political unity.[30] The poetically inclined

Good Fairy in *At Swim-Two-Birds* might also have been enlisted to counter Kennelly's emphasis on 'antiquaries', as he favours not exhausted 'antiquaries' but cosmopolitans and expresses poetic preferences for 'the works of Mr Eliot and Mr Lewis and Mr Devlin' (*CN*, 117). Within Kennelly's structure, moreover, in something of a canonisation, almost all of translations of Irish poetry or song from Old or Middle Irish are those of the prolific Frank O'Connor, to whose preponderance in this anthology Smith repeatedly objects.

The expanded issue, no. 4 (summer 1971) – now edited by Smith with Brain Coffey acting as assistant editor, Joyce having abandoned his direct editorial function to concentrate on writing his own poetry – returns to the battle as it takes on the look of a Beckett tribute with a portrait of Ireland's latest Nobel laureate dominating its cover. The opening 'Editorial' resumes the direct assault on received literary wisdom: 'Conventionally, the tradition of Modern Irish Poetry is described as having its source and existence in W.B. Yeats and his survivors in the Twilight.'[31] The counterexample that follows immediately thereafter is a suite of Beckett poems reprinted from his first poetry collection, *Echo's Bones and Other Precipitates* (Europa Press, 1935),[32] suggesting the sort of poetry Beckett was writing as he was simultaneously castigating his homeland's poetic patrimony: 'Alba', 'Serena I', 'Da Tagte Es', 'Malacoda' and 'Gnome'.[33] The issue reprints as well two more of Beckett's early essays, the aforementioned 'Recent Irish Poetry' and 'Humanistic Quietism',[34] the latter a brief appraisal of MacGreevy's *Poems* of 1934,[35] written originally for *The Dublin Magazine* and signed simply S.B. The MacGreevy review opens with the now-famous incantation, 'All poetry, as discriminated from the various paradigms of prosody, is prayer', an acknowledgement at least of, if not a tribute, perhaps, to MacGreevy's piety.[36] Beckett's praise for MacGreevy is even more direct in 'Recent Irish Poetry' where he deems his work 'the most important contribution to post-War Irish poetry'.[37] In his summation of the period Mervyn Wall would note: 'these urban poets, Coffey, Devlin and Beckett, had no wish to write of battles long ago, nor were they mesmerised by the Irish countryside. "I hate scenery" was a constant saying of Devlin's'.[38] In such a context, Estragon's injunction in *Waiting for Godot* takes on political import: 'You and your landscapes! Tell me about the worms!'[39]

Issue no. 4 further features two essays by Niall Montgomery, the second of which is what appears to be a belated tribute to or a gesture of recuperation for Brian Ó Nualláin. The tribute reprints Montgomery's obituary for Ó Nualláin, 'An Aristophanic Sorcerer', from *The Irish Times* of 2 April 1966, the day after Ó Nualláin's death.[40] The reprint comes complete with an editing curiosity that may have been intended to recall the metatextuality of *At Swim-Two-Birds* if it were not simply a transcription blunder noticed too late in the publishing process to be corrected. Rather than correct the error, the editors compound it by leaving about a quarter of the page blank to signal it, then add a footnote to call attention to it thus: '[Lines 1 & 2 on the next page should be ignored]'.[41] Those now inadvertently highlighted lines 'on the next page' announce prematurely Montgomery's suggested epitaph, Ó Nualláin's 'description of his earliest and brightest *persona*, Brother Barnabas'. Those redundant opening 'Lines [...] on the next page' now precede Ó Nualláin's *pieta* of twenty years earlier and so devalue his heartfelt tribute 'To a man grieved by the death of a sister's unborn child'.[42] Such typographical gamesmanship might have suggested a gesture worthy of Flann O'Brien (or Brother Barnabas) while also offering a nod of approval to Beckett's *Watt* (which, with *At Swim-Two-Birds*, both Anthony Cronin and Montgomery consider not only distinctly Irish, but Dublin novels) if it did not so severely undercut Montgomery's point about Ó Nualláin's compassion.[43]

As Montgomery notes at the essay's opening: 'Brian Ó Nualláin was a fantastic and wonderful fellow and to say *nach mbeidh a leitheid aris ann* is putting it mildly; there was never the like of him, certainly not in UCD [University College Dublin] in the 'thirties, where he descended, like a shower of paratroopers, deploying a myriad of pseudonymous personalities in the interests of pure destruction.'[44] Montgomery's Irishism, '*nach mbeidh a leitheid aris ann*' (or, *Ní bheidh a leithéid arís ann*), is not only a staple of Irish obituaries; it recurs throughout *An Béal Bocht*. 'Most dazzling,' Montgomery continues,

> was his consistent presentation of uncommon ideas as common sense: the delirium on which he imposed order was very real to him – he hypnotised a generation into believing that it [presumably the 'delirium'] was Ireland. Maybe it was, then.
>
> His satire, when he was young, seemed to spring up not out of bitterness but from helpless, disbelieving enjoyment of the perverse fantasy of conventional behaviour.[45]

If the unacknowledged republication of Montgomery's *Irish Times* obituary of 1966 was a gesture to embrace Ó Nualláin among the writers of a new Irish modernism, the choice of representative work is something less than a compelling argument, limited, presumably, by the journal's emphasis on the genre of poetry. That is, the issue prints another side of

Ó Nualláin: neither satires nor the 'pure destruction' cited by Montgomery or even the *Buile Suibhne* translations and recastings prominently on display in *At Swim-Two-Birds* to which Montgomery refers, but three tender, even sentimental translations from Old Irish. Isolated thus, the poems or airs – since they are decidedly song-like – would likely bring an approving nod from those 'antiquarians' of the Celtic Twilight, Brendan Kennelly included, but belong to a mode that Beckett excoriates in his essay, republished in the same issue. The '*Three Poems from the Irish*', translated by one 'Myles na gCopaleen',[46] include the love poem 'Aoibhinn, A Leabhráin, Do Thriall'[47] (To the Lady with a Book), the nature lyric 'Domfarcai fidbaidæ fál' (A hedge [of trees] before [surrounded or fenced] me)[48] and, the most famous of them (which appears in the first volume of the *Field Day Anthology*, there not in Ó Nualláin's translation, however), the song 'Scél lem dúib' (Brief Account; or rather 'Here's a song').[49] These three 'Myles na gCopaleen' translations were originally published in *The Irish Times*, in three separate *Cruiskeen Lawn* columns in 1941,[50] and first published as a triptych in a 1944 collection published by *The Irish Times* called *Poems from Ireland*, edited by Donagh MacDonagh with a preface by the paper's editor R.M. Smyllie.[51] The first and third of these translations were reprinted in 1958 in MacDonagh and Lennox Robinson's *The Oxford Book of Irish Verse*, under the name 'Brian O'Nolan', and again in the *A Flann O'Brien Reader* in 1978, hard upon their appearance in *The Lace Curtain*.[52] Ó Nualláin's translation of 'Scél Lem Dúib' was broadcast on RTÉ on 12 November 1977 as part of the show *The Pleasures of Gaelic Poetry*. In 1984, it was made available on audio cassette by RTÉ for education purposes.[53] 'Scél Lem Dúib (A Ninth Century Irish Poem)' is cited in full by J.C.C. Mays in Rüdiger Imhof's *Alive-Alive O! Flann O'Brien's At Swim-Two-Birds* (1985).[54] All three translations reappear in *Myles Before Myles: A selection of the earlier writings of Brian O'Nolan* (1988) in what editor John Wyse Jackson calls a '(perhaps) complete collection of O'Nolan's published verse translations' (*MBM*, 253, 259–61). The poems were selected for publication in *The Lace Curtain* by Ó Nualláin's widow, Evelyn, a note tells us.

Montgomery ends his tribute with a look backwards to Ó Nualláin's UCD days: 'last evening [this marks the moment four years earlier since the piece is republished unaltered (except for the transcription blunder cited above) from *The Irish Times* of 1966] the posters said "Death of Famous Irish Writer" and there was snow in April for a man who did his M.A. thesis on nature in Irish poetry'. In his tribute to Ó Nualláin shortly after his death, John Montague, in his 1967 collection *A Chosen Light* (MacGibbon & Kee), also offers a translation of one of Sweeny's laments from the *Buile Suibhne* in a poem entitled 'Sweetness (from the Irish)' and subtitled 'I. M. Flann O'Brien, who skipped it' (suggesting that this lament is excluded from *At Swim-Two-Birds*). A prose introduction to the poem evokes the novel by locating Sweeny at 'the church of Swim-Two-Birds, opposite Clonmacnoise' and Montague's tribute ends, without irony, in prayer:

> O hear me, Christ
> Without stain, never
> Let me be severed
> Oh Christ, from your sweetness![55]

And yet, even as they seem out of character if not out of place in so politically charged a journal, these poems invoke books and writing and come out of a tradition of monkish meditation and song, essentially prayer – like all good poetry, according to Beckett in 'Humanistic Quietism'[56] – and they are not Frank O'Connor's translations.

Perhaps a more appropriate entry for *The Lace Curtain* – at least one more in keeping with Montgomery's assessment and the politics of the journal, although it is not poetry *per se* – might have been Ó Nualláin's treatment of 'antiquarians', of Irish nostalgia for its past: the Sea Cat episode from his Gaeltacht novel *An Béal Bocht* (although only available in Irish until Patrick C. Power's English translation *The Poor Mouth* two years later, in 1973), a satire of cosmopolitan urbanites getting in touch with their authentic Irish roots. Of the Dublin folklorist, one of the Dublin *Gaeilgeoirí*, we are reminded that: '*Thuig sé go mbíonn an dea-Ghaeilge deacair agus an Ghaeilge is fearr beagnach dothuigthe*' (*ABB*, 36) ('He understood that good Gaelic is difficult but that the best Gaelic of all is well-nigh unintelligible'; *CN*, 433). The Sea Cat herself, moreover, gave off 'an ancient smell of putridity which set the skin of [Bónapárt's] nose humming and dancing' (*CN*, 453). Eminent historian Dennis Kennedy opened his lecture at Trinity College Dublin in October of 2010 by invoking the Sea Cat encounter: 'Bonaparte O'Coonassa, wandering among the rocks of Donegal, feels menaced by something evil pursuing him. He smells it and hears it snorting and barking, and then he sees it – "a large quadruped – a great hairy object, grey haired with prickly red eyes".'[57] For Kennedy:

> The people of Ireland, like O'Coonassa, it seems, are being pursued and terrified by a creature, possibly of their own imagining – and it is Ireland, 'the pleasant little land which is our own' as O'Brien has it.

And that, it seems to me, is Ireland in a nutshell, a nightmare hangover resulting from too much bad history and an obsession with the physical island itself. History, like alcohol, is highly intoxicating, and bad history, like bad drink, can cause serious hangovers. Nationalism is one of these. It can leave those who have over-indulged incapable of thinking clearly, possessed of strange notions, in a general state of hostility towards any who do not share their views.[58]

Kennedy goes on to note that 'One British commentator and writer, the gloomy Dean Inge of St Paul's, acidly described a nation as "a society united by a common delusion about its ancestry and by a common hatred of its neighbours". He was probably thinking of Germany, but the definition applied as aptly to Ireland.'[59] Kennedy's essay would have fit neatly into *The Lace Curtain* campaign, particularly the issue of 1971, and might serve as a companion piece to Beckett's critique of 1934. But this is not the Ó Nualláin that *The Lace Curtain* foregrounds at this pivotal moment in the formation of the Irish modernist sensibility.

Writing in *The Irish Times* on the centenary of Ó Nualláin's birth, Fintan O'Toole extends the comparison and draws a direct parallel to Beckett thus:

> The ancient smell of putridity that emanates from this half-comic, half-terrifying embodiment of Ireland is not unrelated to the stink of 'history's ancient faeces' that, according to the narrator of Samuel Beckett's *First Love* (written five years after *The Poor Mouth* in 1946) largely constitutes 'the charm of our country'. If Beckett and O'Brien shared a great deal besides their belief that something was rotten in the state of Ireland, the overwhelming difference between them is that Beckett, like the majority of their literary contemporaries, managed to flee from the Sea-cat. O'Brien, almost alone among the great writers of 20th century Ireland, fell into its clutches. He stayed in Ireland and paid a fearful price in frustration and neglect.[60]

Beckett, too, might have yielded to the Sea Cat and paid that 'fearful price'. As the typescript for *Murphy* was floundering and being rejected by a sequence of publishers, he toured Germany and wrote to Mary Manning on 18 January 1937: 'No, I have not written at all and have no plans. Mother writes why don't I contribute to the papers, I write at least as well as the Irishman Diarist.' That 'An Irishman's Diary' was written mostly by then-*Irish Times* editor R.M. 'Bertie' Smyllie, who soon after would become interested in a series of letters to the paper's editor from Brian Ó Nualláin (with Montgomery and Niall Sheridan) that would develop into the *Cruiskeen Lawn* column, the first instalment appearing in October of 1940. And Beckett would comment in the letter to Manning on something of the strange smell of Ireland: 'I know the smell you describe. The decay ingredient you omit, what you get in a cemetery. You like it because it is associated with your innocence. I dislike it for the same reason. It is part of the home poison. A swamp smell.'[61]

Much of what Beckett and Ó Nualláin shared – 'swamp smell' or 'The ancient smell of putridity' aside – is apparent in their first published novels: *Murphy* was Beckett's novel of flight, although his past pursues him into and throughout London; *At Swim-Two-Birds* was Flann O'Brien's novel of imaginative flight but physical resignation. Both, as John P. Harrington notes, share 'a parodic deflation of the contemporary power of Celtic myth – for O'Brien the Finn legend of the Leinster cycle as for Beckett the Cuchulain legend of the Ulster cycle'.[62] They were published within a year of each other; James Joyce read and loved both, quoting portions of *Murphy* by heart and recommending them to Paris bookseller Adrienne Monnier in 1940.[63] According to another Irish poet and civil servant, Mervyn Wall, in an interview with Smith in *The Lace Curtain* no. 4, 'Some Questions about the Thirties', '[James] Joyce was delighted with *At Swim-Two-Birds* and sent a copy to O'Nolan to be autographed'.[64] In one of the curiosities of modernist literature, stores of both *Murphy* and *At Swim-Two-Birds* would be destroyed in the blitz of 1940. And Ó Nualláin could be as sharp a critic of the antiquarians as Beckett or Smith, as invoked, for instance, in Shanahan's assessment of Finn Mac Cool's Sweeny tale in *At Swim-Two-Birds*:

> Now take that stuff your man was giving us a while ago [...] about the green hills and the bloody swords and the bird giving out the pay from the top of the tree. Now that's good stuff, it's bloody nice. [...] You can't beat it, of course, [...] the real old stuff of the native land, you know, stuff that brought scholars to our shore when your men on the other side were on the flat of their bellies before the calf of gold with a sheepskin around their man. It's the stuff that put our country where she stands today, Mr Furriskey, and I'd have my tongue out of my head by the bloody roots before I'd be heard saying a word against it. (*CN*, 72)

Of the original publication of 'Recent Irish Poetry', Devlin had written to MacGreevy on 31 August 1934 that Beckett's essay had 'raised a storm' and that 'It appears that Yeats was furious; it appears that Austin Clark [...] will pursue Sam to his grave; it appears Seamas [for Seumas] O'Sullivan thought he might have been mentioned at least'; while Higgins was 'glad he got off so lightly',[65] Beckett cheekily admiring 'the sweet smell of dung' in Higgins's poetry. The reissue of 'Recent Irish Poetry' in *The Lace Curtain*, on the other hand, generated no such response and even went unmentioned in subsequent editorials. *The Lace Curtain* translations did little to enhance Ó Nualláin's reputation, even as the 1970s saw his work reprinted in important literary magazines like *Antaeus* – issues 16 and 19, both of 1975, reprinting excerpts from *The Poor Mouth* (1973) – although the editors misidentify one of Flann O'Brien's books as *The Salkey Archive*.[66] The Irish return to Beckett in the 1970s, on the other hand, did effect, or at least sped, his repatriation. In 1984 he was elected to the Aosdána as Saoi, a Charles Haughey created honorific, a state-sponsored association, with stipend, of some 250 Irish artists (200 at the time), poets Anthony Cronin (Haughey's culture advisor), John Montague and Trevor Joyce among them. The repatriation culminated, or was completed perhaps, just weeks before Beckett's death in 1989, as Montague, after a poetry reading in Paris, visited the infirm Beckett and solicited from him a contribution to *The Great Book of Ireland*, a monumental project, finally completed and published in 1991. The volume includes some 143 poets in the single, handcrafted volume now held at University College Cork. Beckett's contribution written in his shaky, failing hand directly onto velum was a poem he had written originally on the occasion of the death of his father, 'Da Tagte Es', reprising thereby his contribution to *The Lace Curtain* no. 4 and doing so, as it turned out, on the eve of his own death. Montague's recollection of the scene is his own farewell, not surrogate:

> The scroll will not stay put. Baffled, Beckett wrestles with the vellum, whilst I set up the small black ink bottle, with the skinny nib to dip in it. Finally, I have to hold down the curling corners, as he strives to write what may be his last lines [...]. The lines are not new: he has chosen a quatrain written after his father's death, and the implications for his own demise, so long attended, are all too clear.
>
>> Redeem the surrogate goodbyes
>> the sheet astream in your hand
>> who have no more for the land
>> and the glass unmisted above your eyes.
>
> The sheet is not astream, but bucking and bounding, and his hands are shaking. Twice he has to stroke out lines, but he still goes on, with that

near ferocity I associate with him, until the four lines are copied, in the centre of a page. He looks at me, I look down to check, and murmur appropriate approval. He rolls the vellum, and with due ceremony hands it over to me, with the carton. Then, with a gesture of finality, he sweeps the lot, ink bottle, long black pen and spare pages of vellum, into the wastepaper bin.[67]

For Beckett, both exiled and at home in Paris, the gesture may have again been some compensation for the paternal goodbye undelivered in person, the farewell scene revisioned, the sentiment disguised in a foreign tongue. For Ireland, as a new millennium approached, Beckett, it appears, received a death-bed redemption as an Irish poet, despite the ambiguities of 'no more for the land'. His attitude may have been best summed up, however, in the 'Addenda' to *Watt*: 'for all the good that frequent departures out of Ireland had done him, he might just as well stayed there'.[68] Beckett returns to the sentiment in his first radio play of 1957, *All That Fall*, as Maddy Rooney notes: 'It is suicide to be abroad. But what is it to be at home, Mr Tyler, what is it to be at home? A lingering dissolution.'[69] Others had heeded such advice to their detriment.

Montgomery, Dublin architect and friend to artists, Beckett and Ó Nualláin not the least among them, and in whose house the two met in 1939 just after the publication of *At Swim-Two-Birds* (but of which Beckett is reported to have said of their discussion of James Joyce that the meeting 'is better forgotten'[70]), wrote one of the earliest appreciations, what he, like Molloy, Moran and Malone calls a 'report', on Beckett's fiction for *New World Writing* no. 5 in 1954.[71] The title, 'No Symbols Where None Intended', cites the closing lines of *Watt*, which Montgomery calls 'the definitive Irish peasant novel', and further writes that it 'is accurate Dublin, as first noticed by Joyce [that is, James in this case], and subsequently orchestrated in *At Swim-Two-Birds*, by Flann O'Brien, a homebased exile whose only other points of community with Beckett are bicycles, scatology and plenary literary powers'.[72] To this list we might add a distaste for provincialism, nationalism and theocracy coupled with an embrace of at least certain forms of worldliness if not cosmopolitanism. Both had treated Ireland's mythic patrimony with something short of respect in major novels written only a year apart. Both at least acknowledged the climate of parochial Irish censorship in those novels as well, the dissolute narrator of *At Swim-Two-Birds* secreting all mention of questionable subjects: 'Hastily I covered such sheets as contained references to the forbidden question of the sexual relations' (*CN*, 89). In *Murphy*, Beckett's narrator retreats into metaphor and is yet more direct: 'Murphy knew what that meant. No more music [i.e. sex with Celia]. The phrase is chosen with care, lest the filthy censors should lack an occasion to commit their filthy synecdoche.'[73] And the narrator describes Celia's kiss as 'the slow-motion osmosis of love's spittle', then adds, 'the above passage is carefully calculated to deprave the cultivated [i.e. lace curtain] reader'.[74] As Donal Ó Drisceoil notes in the *Irish Examiner*:

> Censorship in Ireland, which was largely overturned 50 years ago, meant the public couldn't easily get their eyes on work by our best writers, making it a badge of honour. [...] The mere suggestion of homosexuality, promiscuity or prostitution was enough to ban a book. Most of the leading writers of modern fiction fell victim, leading cynics to dub the Irish Register of Prohibited Publications 'The Everyman's Guide to the Modern Classics'.[75]

What Beckett tried to take on in 1934, in personal retribution in some respects, was something like home-grown modernism, a category just shy of home-grown *avant-gardism*, and into which he tried to fit MacGreevy even as the category seems gerrymandered and exclusionary. In 1970, the ideological and aesthetic contrasts between *The Penguin Book of Irish Verse* and the literary journal *The Lace Curtain* reignited the issues, the latter rearmed with the award to Ireland of its third Nobel Prize for Literature creating something like duelling laureates between the latter two, the neo or belated romantic, Yeats, and the neo or belated modernist, Beckett (Shaw more often than not deemed something of a West Brit). Into that climate of renewed laureateship with Beckett's Nobel award in 1969, a spate of posthumous Ó Nualláin publications and republications followed: Patrick C. Power's translation of *The Poor Mouth* and the Viking Press's publication of *Stories and Plays*, both in 1973; the Penguin Group and Viking Press (in the Richard Seaver imprint) followed with reissues of two of Flann O'Brien's most important novels, *At Swim-Two-Birds* (originally 1939 Longmans, then 1950–51–52 Pantheon, rereleased 1961 and 1968, and reissued in 1975 by Penguin) and *The Third Policeman* (1967), both Plume editions in 1976, and followed up with a major anthology, *The Flann O'Brien Reader*, edited by Stephen Jones in 1978. Ó Nualláin's reputation would spike amid this flurry of publication, peaking about 1986, falling off considerably shortly thereafter, however. Beckett's and Joyce's reputations would continue to rise as Ó Nualláin's, after periods of stagnation, is on the ascent as well. Ó Nualláin remains, however, in a league with (or in league with) Beckett and Joyce once we attend to his mastery of deflationary comedy, his narrative dislocations and his assaults on certain forms of 'lace curtain' Irish pretensions. All three had rapier wit and a tendency towards parody and hoax, Beckett in his faux Trinity College lecture in French to the Modern Languages Society on 'Le Concentrisme' (1930),[76] the closing letters of complaint to 'Mr Germs Choice', often attributed to Joyce himself but written evidently by Vladimir Dixon (with Joyce's oversight) for *Our Exagmination Round His Factification for Incamination of Work in Progress* (1929), and Ó Nualláin, writing as Brother Barnabus, as early as the short-lived, six-issue UCD journal *Blather* (August 1934–January 1935) and the series of letters to *The Irish Times* that developed into the *Cruiskeen Lawn* column. For a time, Joyce was left out in the cold, at least by the lace curtain Irish, because of the perceived decadence, indelicacies and continental qualities of his most Dublin novel, *Ulysses*, and Beckett likewise (if he was more aggressively anti-lace curtain than Joyce, Beckett was as decidedly decadent, and Francophile to boot), while the bilingual Ó Nualláin was never fully in because of his European, cosmopolitan-infused modernity and never fully out as a stay-at-home writer and a civil servant from an Irish-speaking home still flirting with antiquarian Ireland. As such work evinces a resistance to what Beckett has called, in reference to Joyce in 1929, 'the neatness of identifications',[77] aesthetics and techniques suited neither to nationalist nor émigré aesthetics, critical and theoretical interest in Ó Nualláin has been regenerated within a renewed and recalculated context of Irish modernism. If such neitherness, something of a Hibernian hybridity, a '*neither/nor-but-both-at-once*' status,[78] had previously excluded or marginalised him from certain formulations of the Irish modernist canon, it now affords him an indisputable place at its centre.

19

The Richness of the Mask

Modernist thought and historicist criticism

JOHN GREANEY

This essay addresses the problems that Brian O'Nolan's various masks and shifting pseudonyms pose to historicist criticism of the Flann O'Brien/ Myles na gCopaleen/Brian O'Nolan corpus.[1] Given the difference between the author's pseudonymous creations and the singularity of the respective literatures to which they are attached, it is perhaps too convenient to suggest that O'Nolan 'did not really hide himself behind these various masks [...] and that the illusion was fairly transparent',[2] and thus that these literary works can be explained with recourse to his biographical, historical and social existence. In the essay that opens the present collection, Maebh Long has demonstrated that the Flann O'Brien/Myles na gCopaleen corpus does not always correspond to the individual body of the man who, for various reasons, needed to claim the identity of those pseudonyms. Indicating that the inspiration for *The Third Policeman* might not have been 'original' but born from direct plagiarism, Long's findings complicate understandings of it as a work authored individually by Brian O'Nolan,[3] thus adding to the now accepted appreciations that *At Swim-Two-Birds* and *Cruiskeen Lawn* were respectively authored by collaborations led by O'Nolan.

Recent and emerging criticism has already seen the delivery of some timely research on the topic of O'Nolan's pseudonyms. Adrian Oțoiu specifies in detail the particularity of each of the pseudonyms and how they differentiate. The premises of this essay rest on Oțoiu's groundwork, particularly the insistence that there are 'significant differences among these names'.[4] As Oțoiu suggests, 'Some are meant for usage in the public sphere (distinct from the cultural one); some are mere fictional façades, with no trace of a purported identity behind them; some point to complex identities, either competing [with] that of the flesh-and-blood author, or inhabiting the fictional space'.[5] Responding to the difficulty of categorising this corpus and its chief writer, Rónán McDonald and Julian Murphet, in their introduction to *Flann O'Brien & Modernism*, present a dual approach for tackling this problem. They suggest that O'Nolan's multiple identities can be conceptualised with recourse to a historicist lens founded on methodological nationalism and with comparative reference to 'the international pantheon of modernism'.[6] More an aim than an achievement of *Flann O'Brien & Modernism*, McDonald and Murphet's dual approach – situating O'Nolan at the nexus of localised historicism and international modernism – offers substantial, though not always compatible, opportunities for theorising the issue of pseudonymity as it pertains to this corpus. Following the first strand of this approach, Ronan Crowley, in an essay in *Flann O'Brien: Problems with authority*, has substantiated McDonald and Murphet's claim that O'Nolan's play with pseudonymity has 'precursors in an Irish tradition of self-concealment or self-invention'; deftly demonstrated, Crowley manifests O'Nolan's use of pseudonyms as related to authorial practice particular to the Irish Revival.[7] Less established in *Flann O'Brien & Modernism*, and elsewhere, is the full extent to which concepts prevalent to international modernism, and thus modernist thought, impact theorisations of the pseudonyms. The framework of Irish modernism, though perhaps apposite as a critical lens for tackling this problem, also involves a negotiation of the radicality of modernist thought as it might pertain here. To give full consideration to the difficulties that O'Nolan's masks pose to historicist criticism, and how that problem can be defined within modernist coordinates, 'modernism' needs to be relieved of the weight of an 'Irish' anchor.

This essay explores the extent to which correlates in modernist literature and thought impact theorisations of the issue of O'Nolan's masks. In turn, it assesses the extent to which modernist thought is compatible with methodological nationalism and the tenets of historicist criticism for theorising the relationship between O'Nolan and the mask. I begin by considering the motive for O'Nolan's masks in relation to Niall Montgomery's obituary for O'Nolan and Walter Benjamin's theorisation of 'the destructive character'. Comparison is then drawn between Nietzsche's thinking on the role and importance of the mask for 'profound' things or individuals and Yeats's thinking on the mask with some tendencies which are particular to O'Nolan criticism currently. I conclude by outlining how the textual forms and modernist tendencies of this corpus lend productively to conceptualising the problems of pseudonymity and the mask. In such terms, my argument seeks to highlight the *richness* of a unique problem with which criticism of the Flann O'Brien/Myles na gCopaleen/Brian O'Nolan *oeuvre* must deal; a problem that historicist criticism often invalidates given its particular methodologies and modes of investigation. Ultimately, then, my argument reconsiders the idea that Brian O'Nolan evidently hides behind the masks of the various pseudonyms and aims to establish broader theoretical and critical coordinates for thinking about issues of the mask and the pseudonym as it concerns this body of work.

The destructive character

In his *Irish Times* obituary for O'Nolan, Montgomery gives an account of the writer which resonates with Benjamin's description of 'the destructive character', a concept which is related here to elaborate the stakes of Montgomery's tribute to O'Nolan and his pseudonymous activity. From the outset, the terms of Benjamin's destructive character – that anonymous persona intent on the destruction of bourgeois values and liberation from subjectification and which 'knows only one watchword: make room; only one activity: clearing away'[8] – are tacit in Montgomery's account which outlines the anarchic and insurrectionary impulses that constituted much of the O'Nolan/O'Brien/na gCopaleen corpus. Casting O'Nolan in the plural, Montgomery writes that 'he descended, like a shower of paratroopers, deploying a myriad of pseudonymous personalities in the interests of pure destruction'.[9] And through this multiplicity of paratroopers and pseudonyms, as Montgomery continues, 'most dazzling was his consistent presentation of uncommon ideas as common sense: the delirium on which he imposed order was very real to him – he hypnotised a generation into believing that it was Ireland'.[10] As he dons the pseudonym in the interest of pure destruction and establishing the uncommon as common, O'Nolan resembles Benjamin's destructive character who 'rejuvenates in clearing away the traces of our own age' and 'cheers because everything cleared away means to the destroyer a complete reduction, indeed eradication, of his own condition'.[11] Thus, O'Nolan's Ireland, to recast it in Benjamin's words, 'is simplified when tested for its worthiness of destruction'.[12] And for Montgomery, as for Benjamin, such disruption and destruction is dependent on, and attained through, the erasure of the subject, which in the case of O'Nolan is readily achieved through the array of pseudonyms. As the empty *persona* allows for an ever-greater reach of subversion, O'Nolan's destructive pursuits and plural and vacuous identities are co-dependent. It is, then, not difficult to see the importance of the many masks to an understanding of the anarchic and insurrectionist energies of the O'Nolan/O'Brien/na gCopaleen corpus. As Benjamin suggests of its necessary lack of identity, the destructive character, in its endeavours to distort received cultural wisdoms and to reduce 'what exists [...] to rubble', 'sees nothing permanent' and 'tolerates misunderstanding'; and 'for this very reason, he sees ways everywhere, he always positions himself at a crossroads'.[13] Indeed, we find an echo of this position in *The Third Policeman:* as the narrator says to Sergeant Pluck in a seeming metacommentary on the pseudonym, 'Do you recall that you told me I was not here at all because I had no name and that my personality was invisible to the law?' (*CN*, 309). Thought in these terms – disbanding with fixity, permanence and being understood – the pseudonym enables the various and wide targets of the O'Nolan/O'Brien/na gCopaleen corpus: from the convention of the novel to the multiple disappointments and hypocrisies of Free State culture and beyond. Moreover, to link the issue of the mask to Benjamin's discussion of the loss of aura in the age of mass culture: 'the technique of reproduction detaches the reproduced object from the domain of tradition. By making many reproductions it substitutes a plurality of copies for a unique existence'. This process of mass technological reproduction results, for Benjamin, 'in a tremendous shattering of tradition which is the obverse of the contemporary crisis and renewal of mankind'.[14] In such terms, the destructive character, as well as the reproduction of the author that occurs with the mask, delights in the obfuscation of authenticity, intention and originality. O'Nolan's pseudonymous play, then, when thought through Montgomery's and Benjamin's accounts regarding the specific relationship between the pseudonyms and such anarchic literary efforts, derives less from an identity crisis caused by his culture than it does from a strategic effort to rattle the very roots of that culture.

Preceding and anticipating Benjamin, Nietzsche and Yeats respectively meditate on the fate of such mask wearers through their conceptualisations of the relationship between the mask and the individual. In *Beyond Good and Evil*, Nietzsche ponders what remains of the individual after the mask has been donned. In a much-quoted aphorism on the concealment of shame and goodness in *Beyond Good and Evil*, Nietzsche writes that 'Everything profound loves the mask; the profoundest things of all hate even image and parable'.[15] With this axiom, Nietzsche discusses the agency involved in the cultivation of a mask by the individual who has something either shameful or good to conceal; 'there are occurrences of so delicate a description that one does well to bury them', he writes.[16] The necessity of such a creation lies in the fact that, for Nietzsche, both histories of shame and benevolence need to be cultivated and protected so as to remain instructive and continuously productive. Moving beyond the control and ownership of the mask by its cultivator, Nietzsche introduces the idea that the mask is also cultivated from without and is thus a creation which proliferates beyond the control of the individual. He writes:

> Such a hidden man, who instinctively uses speech for silence and concealment and is inexhaustible in evading communication, *wants* a mask of him to roam the heads and hearts of his friends in his stead, and he makes sure that it does so; and supposing he does not want it, he will come to see that a mask is there in spite of that – and that that is a good thing. Every profound spirit needs a mask: more, around every profound spirit a mask is continually growing, thanks to the constantly false, that is to say *shallow* interpretation of every word he gives, every step he takes, every sign of life he gives.[17]

Thus, even if the profound individual or thing does not want to cultivate or wear a mask, or if the individual who has cultivated a mask and at a later point would like to discard it, it is not always possible to do so. Profundity necessarily entails the constitution of a mask, thus creating the enigma of the profound thing's origin and putting the shame and the goodness (or the good and evil) which precedes it beyond representation. The mask, then, is not just a product of the person, but a product of the work this person produces; and, like the work produced, the meaning of the mask proliferates beyond the control of the individual who produces the work. A potential danger of the mask is that the wearer becomes permanently lost behind its visage as it multiplies in meaning.

The mask

W.B. Yeats stands out as perhaps the most prominent example of the mask wearers and cultivators in modern literature, and one who addresses the issue in his work. In a manner reminiscent of Benjamin and Nietzsche, Yeats probes the enigma of the mask in his autobiographical writings. He writes that all happiness depends on having the energy to assume the mask of some other self; that all joyous or creative life is a rebirth as something not oneself, something created in a moment and perpetually renewed. We put on a grotesque or solemn painted face to hide us from the terrors of judgement, invent an imaginative Saturnalia where one forgets reality, a game like that of a child, where one loses the infinite pain of self-realisation.[18]

Donning the mask, then, the writer undergoes a transformation, or a 'rebirth', 'as something not oneself', and so the mask wearer escapes subjectification.[19] And crucially, as a result of this process, the mask takes precedence over, and obscures, the subject, a circumstance which Yeats outlines in his poem 'The Mask': 'It was the mask engaged your mind / And after set your heart to beat / Not what's behind.'[20] Thus, the mask roams and entices the interest of the public sphere, and not the individual behind it. Like Benjamin and Nietzsche, then, Yeats posits an insurmountable and irreducible distance between the mask and the biography of its wearer because the mask has no memory and is perpetually renewed from moment to moment both by its readers and the work of its fabricator(s). Criticism on Yeats's work has remained alive to this facet of his poetic practice. Moving away from a binary approach to Yeats's life and corpus – exemplified in 'the man and the mask' methodology deployed by Louis MacNeice and Richard Ellmann[21] – recent work has affirmed multiplicities and variations, as well as inconsistencies, of identity stemming from the mask.[22] I argue that a similar critical turn is required for that other prominent man-of-many-masks in the canon of Irish literary modernism, Brian O'Nolan.

A fundamental difference between these two mask cultivators is that the latter's critics are immediately and always faced with the question of his pseudonyms – Flann O'Brien, Myles na gCopaleen – given that he steadfastly published under these names and others. Yeats's readers can always treat his masks as an eccentricity of a poet and writer who can also be understood as having heavily indulged in the spinning and weaving of autobiography. The same is not the case for O'Nolan, though that is not to say that critics have discovered anything less about his life than Yeats's. In doing so, criticism has often set aside the logic of the mask – the tool in both Nietzsche and Yeats's terms that is used to destroy personal memory so as to make literature happen – to go from the mask to the life, and thus generate the biography and historical circumstances so as to explain the literature. As a result, and as is a standard feature of historicist literary criticism, the life and times of O'Nolan are often used as critical tools to explicate various aspects of the output attached to his name(s). It is as such that Daniel Keith Jernigan can suggest that 'It was also during his UCD [University College Dublin] days that O'Nolan first began experimenting with pseudonymous *alter egos*, most famously as Brother Barnabas in the student publication *Comhthrom Féinne*'.[23] Though very likely a truism, such trends have led to the suggestion that the image of O'Nolan as a 'diffident individual skirting behind the masks of Flann, Myles and their various associates' is 'more a creation of his readers than his work'; and that 'it is [...] questionable how important these individual identities are in themselves'.[24] This appreciation of the profundity, or lack thereof, of O'Nolan's many masks is symptomatic of some criticism of the O'Nolan corpus today; as in the above example, a tendency has developed to limit the play of the masks and pseudonyms so as to understand the motivations (and shame) of O'Nolan. In this sense, various critical assessments of this body of work correspond to what Heather Love identifies as a dominant practice in literary studies currently: 'what is occurring in much of the recent work at the intersection of sociology and literature is a turn away from the singularity and richness of individual texts and a concomitant refusal of the ethical charisma of the literary translator or messenger'.[25]

There are two obvious reasons for this trend in Brian O'Nolan/ Flann O'Brien/Myles na gCopaleen criticism. The first: the problem of pseudonymity. The significance of each pseudonym in how it differs and how it functions in relation to Brian O'Nolan's biography and *persona* is difficult to unravel. It is thus unsurprising that criticism has sought a homogenising or a one-caters-for-all approach. The second reason, and which is important and particular to this essay: the influence of new historicist and cultural materialist methodologies is evident in this phenomenon. Both modes of historical investigation have, in recent years, moved away from the reading strategies developed by Stephen Greenblatt and Raymond Williams respectively; that is to say, new historicism and cultural materialism, broadly speaking, have read texts as a series of cultural documents which reveal the distribution of ideology and power in the respective period under analysis. In recent years, the focus on ideology and power has dwindled, but the reading strategies of these approaches have remained; they have a stronghold in literary criticism currently and are often deployed to piece together the life and times of the writer under investigation. The influence of this is clear in the wealth of criticism that has emerged on the O'Nolan corpus over the last decade. A feature, on occasion, of such criticism, however, is that it often works against the mask and pseudonymity to reveal Brian O'Nolan as the authorial agent.

For example, Giordano Vintaloro has recently suggested, regarding the pseudonyms, that 'The ambiguity was created by the author himself, to be sure, and he was almost delighted that many failed to recognise him as the man behind Myles or Flann. But once we are certain that the author is dead – and we are – there is no point in keeping up this distinction.'[26] As such, the recommendation comes that 'it is time for literary criticism to make a step further and speak of Brian O'Nolan, the author'.[27] Though only recently prescribed, the sentiments of this dictum have tacitly been operative for some time. The results, however, of this annulation of the significance and difference of the individual pseudonyms have in some cases led to the situation in which Flann O'Brien, having been made equal to Myles na gCopaleen and Brian O'Nolan, has been cited as a novelist, a journalist and an almost political correspondent by critics slightly less accustomed to the histrionics and hoax-playing of pseudonymous writers of fiction. It has as such been suggested that 'the chronicles are part and parcel of Flann O'Brien's literary imagination and cannot be separated from his so-called major work [...] the very structure and themes of *Cruiskeen Lawn* cannot be ignored as they are integral to Flann O'Brien's satirical genius'.[28] And elsewhere, 'Flann O'Brien estimated there were 1,200 licensed dance halls in the 26 counties, accounting for perhaps 5,000 dances annually, but he suggested there were another 5,000 unlicensed'; and that 'Flann O'Brien suggested an Irish bank, in the sense of a banking concern dedicated to furthering the interest of Ireland, did not exist'.[29] What is particularly destabilising for historical verisimilitude in making Myles na gCopaleen and Flann O'Brien equal to Brian O'Nolan is that the journalism cited might not even be verifiable – Paul Fagan's work on the hoax in modern Irish literature is timely in this respect.[30]

In many ways, what this problem represents is the paradox of literary criticism turning upon itself. The suggestion that O'Nolan's reticent image is 'more a creation of his readers than his work'[31] underscores what Nietzsche describes as the potentiality of the mask to proliferate through the work of the reader; to quote Nietzsche again: 'around every profound spirit a mask is continually growing, thanks to the constantly false, that is to say *shallow* interpretation of every word he gives'.[32] Leaving Nietzsche's ill-fated designation of literary criticism aside for the moment, the idea that O'Nolan is a 'diffident individual skirting behind his masks',[33] rather than diminishing the significance of the mask, actually reinforces the logic of the mask as it occurs in both Nietzsche and Yeats's terms. As Nietzsche suggests: 'Such a hidden man, who instinctively uses speech for silence and concealment [...] is inexhaustible in evading communication';[34] or as Yeats writes: 'It was the mask engaged your mind, / And after set your heart to beat, / Not what's behind.'[35] In this sense, it is '[un]questionable how important these individual identities or masks are in themselves'.[36] Rather than revealing Brian O'Nolan as hidden behind them, the various masks and pseudonyms which are attached to his name function differently to obscure any holistic identity which can be attributed to his name whilst also confounding the use of his biography as an equalising critical tool.

The understanding of this body of writing as modernist, and textual, is significant to this issue, and contextualising the question of the mask within that philosophical landscape provides an alternative framework for its conceptualisation. The fragmentary and radically symbolic forms which are a respective feature of Flann O'Brien's novels and some of Myles na gCopaleen's journalism establish these texts as hermeneutic enigmas which resist easy classification and identification with a stable author figure. It is as such that the extent of Montgomery and Sheridan's contributions to the Flann O'Brien and Myles na gCopaleen corpus are beyond precise accumulation because, as well as not knowing with precision the scope of their involvement, the radical symbolism of the writing destroys the trace of the author. Roland Barthes is particularly attuned to this dilemma concerning the relationship between the writer and the radically symbolic text and offers a theorisation of it in 'From Work to Text'. He writes that the text

> can be read without the guarantee of its father, the restitution of the inter-text paradoxically abolishing any legacy. It is not that the Author may not 'come back' in the Text, in his text, but he then does so as a 'guest'. If he is a novelist, he is inscribed in the novel like one of his characters, figured in the carpet; no longer privileged, paternal, aletheological, his inscription is ludic. He becomes, as it were, a paper-author: his life is no longer the origin of his fictions but a fiction contributing to his work; there is a reversion of the work on to the life (and no longer the contrary).[37]

Indeed, *At Swim-Two-Birds* anticipates Barthes's meditation as two of its narrators become involved in the stories they are telling: Dermot Trellis famously features in his characters' story, and the student narrator saves Trellis from death by reconciling with his uncle. If Barthes's logic of the text is accepted, then the author proceeds the text as much as they precede it. In such terms, the identity of the mask and the pseudonym is as much constituted by the texts as by the writer who attaches the pseudonym to the text. And thus, as each new critical reading proliferates the meaning of the text, the identity of the pseudonym is invested with further and different meaning. In these terms, as Barthes suggests, the word 'bio-graphy re-acquires a strong etymological sense' given that the act of writing becomes the act of creating a life as text; it is as such that the works of Marcel Proust or Jean Genet respectively 'allow' their lives to be read as text where text, as Barthes describes, is 'structured, but off-centered and without closure'.[38] Thus, rather than O'Nolan lurking in the shadows or hiding behind these pseudonyms, it is the pseudonyms which continually give O'Nolan his identity, thus making the name 'Brian O'Nolan' another mask, the final pseudonym, which is constituted and developed by this corpus.

The pathos of distance

What is also disrupted is an analysis of the ethical distance or proximity – or what Jean Michel Rabaté, with recourse to Nietzsche, describes as the pathos of distance of modernist writers – at which Brian O'Nolan stands to his work, its construction and its subject matter. For Rabaté, the 'leveling out' and 'sameness' of modernity, as well as the 'irremediable flatness overcoming the world',[39] outlined with reference to Nietzsche and Henry James respectively, prompted modernist artists to engage their pathos of distance. As Rabaté suggests, 'The awareness of a contradiction between egalitarianism and elitism cause pain and discomfort felt acutely by the main modernists; it fed again their own pathos of distance.'[40] In such terms, Rabaté can analyse and outline Alfred Jarry's 'hard', and thus distant, French modernism and William Magee's softer, and more syncretic, Irish modernism, to take two starkly contrasting examples from *The Pathos of Distance*. No wonder, then, that Rabaté does not include Brian O'Nolan/Flann O'Brien/Myles na gCopaleen within his analysis of Irish modernism. Undoubtedly, the influence of Nietzsche, a key feature of Rabaté's analysis, is not as clear with O'Nolan as it is in the cases of Yeats, Joyce and Beckett. More problematic for such analysis, however, is the consistent definition of the distance and/or proximity of Brian O'Nolan/Flann O'Brien/Myles na gCopaleen's output to its subject matter. While Flann O'Brien's *At Swim-Two-Birds* and *The Third Policeman* are overtly oblique and thus distant, in relation to an implied subject matter which might concern the masses, Flann O'Brien, between the writing of these two novels, in a letter to the editor of *The Irish Times* in October 1938, intervenes into an issue more particular to the masses – the direction of Irish theatre – and thus manifests his proximity to some of their concerns. Thus, 'Flann O'Brien' simultaneously manifests both a hard, male modernism with *At Swim-Two-Birds* and *The Third Policeman*, as well as the massification and flattening of the role of the writer with his letters to the editor. Regarding the latter, as Benjamin writes:

> With the increasing extension of the press, which kept placing new political, religious, scientific, professional and local organs before the readers, an increasing number of readers became writers [...]. It began with the daily press opening to its readers space for 'letters to the editor'. [...] Thus, the distinction between author and public is about to lose its basic character.[41]

In contrast, while Myles na gCopaleen repeatedly professed himself as one of The Plain People of Ireland in *Cruiskeen Lawn*, the column, on occasion, features moments of exalted elitism in translation. Quoting Horace in the original Greek on 28 January 1956,[42] Myles captions an episode of a visit to hospital with the line 'I will not wholly die; much will escape the Goddess of the Dead: through future praise I will grow ever fresh',[43] thus manifesting his position beyond The Plain People of Ireland. Or, as Catherine Flynn has astutely demonstrated, *Cruiskeen Lawn* creates for itself a paradoxical role, both conservative and experimental, as it displays the polyvalent power of the traditional Irish language while undermining any identity associated with it,[44] and thus ventures a series of innovatory identifications 'in a newly "liberal" *Irish Times*'.[45] Moreover, notwithstanding the paradoxical and contradictory distances and proximities to subject matter manifested within the same pseudonym, the fact that exploitations of the comic journal, the newspaper article and column, short fiction, the novel, the play, radio drama and the teleplay emerge across both different and the same pseudonyms during and after O'Nolan's life disrupt the possibility of consolidating his ethics and pathos of distance. Rabaté's approach in *The Pathos of Distance* relies on inventive biographical reading, often in terms of a link to Nietzsche, which then aids the explication and exploration of the respective artwork or theory under analysis and thus the ethics of distance of the modernist artist in question. Because of the destructive character of the pseudonyms, and their marked difference from each other and Brian O'Nolan, Brian O'Nolan's/Flann O'Brien's/Myles na gCopaleen's relationship to modernity and modern society is always oscillating between different levels of proximity and distance, and thus beyond critical homogenisation.

Conclusion

As I have endeavoured to demonstrate, contradictions arise when Flann O'Brien, Myles na gCopaleen and Brian O'Nolan are made equivalent to each other or the biography of Brian O'Nolan, the man, is treated as the historical predecessor of all the texts attached to his name. The temptation to minimise this issue will always remain, especially as criticism itself becomes more and more distant. Yet, the problem of the mask as it is posed by this corpus is unique and rich and demands continued consideration rather than hasty classification. There is no easy solution to this problem, but it is this in itself which ensures that Brian O'Nolan/Flann O'Brien/Myles na gCopaleen criticism has a long, complex and healthy future. And it is as well for these reasons that the O'Nolan/O'Brien/na gCopaleen *oeuvre* will always resist the determinism of historicist approaches that seek to explicate it via the self-evidence of the empirically lived world. As such, historicist and materialist approaches that are not tailored to the specifics of this corpus, of which the mask is a key feature, will always allow for their own deconstruction. Historicism and materialism need to be self-reflexive, and thus engage with theory and the specifics of modernist thinking, when deployed in the analysis of this corpus.

20

Productions and Adaptations of Brian O'Nolan's Works

for Stage, Radio, Screen*

Paul Fagan

*F*lann O'Brien: Acting out has foregrounded the themes of illusion, masking and collaborative performance in Brian O'Nolan's writing. The contributors have broken new ground in the field by examining the author's prose, columns, poems, letters, translations and scripts within diverse historical and twentieth-century Irish, British, European and international theatrical and medial contexts. Yet, significant scholarship remains to be undertaken regarding actual productions and adaptations of O'Nolan's work for stage, radio and screen.

Building on the advances made in these essays, future criticism might profitably move beyond O'Nolan's scripts themselves to a more rigorous analysis of the material, economic and institutional dimensions of their production histories. Following Sabine Coelsch-Foisner's guidelines for such work, critics might reconstruct specific productions and adaptations of O'Nolan's writing through their paratheatrical, genetic and semiophoric archival traces: production images, director's notes, costume designs, lighting plans, scripts, promotional materials, programmes, fliers, musical accompaniment, newspaper coverage, theatregoers' diaries, blogs, social media posts and comments, etc.[1] In the same spirit, the collaborative dimensions of O'Nolan's art that have been emphasised in the present book might be extended to accommodate more expansive ideas of creative labour and its significance, which recognise technical, mechanical, operational and organisational labourers as cultural actors.[2] Such studies might consider what the material and digital records of performances of O'Nolan's work reveal about the historical situatedness, economic conditions, power relations and gender/race/class dynamics of cultural institutions and their repertoires. Elsewhere, critics might profitably consider productions, adaptations and translations of O'Nolan's works in André Lefevere's terms as 'refractions' that are distorted for reception across historical, cultural and linguistic boundaries in ways that reveal new dimensions of the texts in their diverse sites of production, reception and recreation.[3]

This concluding essay bridges the advances made by the present collection (regarding the performative and collaborative dimensions of O'Nolan's writing) and this future work (on actual productions and adaptations of the *oeuvre*) by providing a basic working inventory of key productions and adaptations of O'Nolan's work for stage, radio and screen. It begins with productions of O'Nolan's scripts and then turns to stage, radio and film adaptations of his fiction and columns, and finishes with an overview of O'Nolan bioplays and anthology shows. As with the volume as a whole, the intention is not to be comprehensive or exhaustive – no doubt the information here will be supplemented and corrected by subsequent scholars – but rather to provide the community with some fundamental coordinates for this next step in O'Nolan studies.

O'Nolan's scripts

Thirst

Thirst premiered as part of Hilton Edwards and Micheál mac Liammóir's 'Jack-in-the-Box' Christmas variety show at the Gate Theatre, Dublin, 26 December 1942. The variety show included: mac Liammóir's performance as 'La Veranda', an imitation of Carmen Miranda; Edwards as Cardinal Wolsey in an excerpt from Shakespeare's *Henry VIII*; Betty Chancellor as Daisy Belle and a lioness in the Dublin zoo; Christopher Casson playing songs with a harp; Meriel Moore as Myrrhina in Oscar Wilde's unfinished play *La Sainte Courtisane*, with music by Delius; ballads from Colm O'Lochlainn's *Irish Street Ballads*, including 'Finnegan's Wake'; A.A. Milne's 'The Old Sailor'; Mairin Fenning's rendition of Tyrell Pine's 'Snow in the Air'; an adaptation of Hans Christian Andersen's 'The Little Match Girl'. 'Myles na gCopaleen' also penned an original note for the 'Jack-in-the-Box' programme called 'Shows and Showers'.[4] The variety show ran for eight weeks, and owing to its popularity 'special performances had to be staged on two Sundays during the run'.⁵ The production was revived in March 1943 for a special performance at the Theatre Royal organised by *The Irish Times* for 'One thousand officers and men of the Defence Forces stationed in Dublin'.⁶

Thirst was directed by Edwards with set design by Molly MacEwen and costume design by mac Liammóir and Patrick Perrott. Robert Hennessy played Mr C. alongside Liam Gaffney (Sergeant), William Fassbender (Jim) and Sean Colleary (Peter). Reviews singled out Hennessy for praise (R.M. Fox in the *Evening Mail* wrote that his performance 'as a publican deserves a bouquet'), although *The Irish Times* noted that Gaffney 'distinguished himself by knocking back a pint of plain in one draft'.⁷ Edwards later reflected:

> Correctly directed and well played, I personally regard *Thirst* as a little masterpiece of theatrical comedy. It gives great acting opportunities and was always received rapturously: hence the numerous revivals. [...] Hennessy [...] gave what was perhaps his finest performance as the loquacious bartender, on whose shoulders rested the entire burden of the play which, incidentally, requires the most careful grading to ensure that the trap is sprung, and the *denouement* arrived at at precisely the right moment.⁸

A favourite of amateur performance troupes in need of a short engaging production, *Thirst* has been revived more times than space here allows to detail. It was staged by the Dublin University Players in autumn 1943 starring Roy Bradford, Peter Mortished and John Bateman, and Jimmy O'Dea is reported to have included a variation on *Thirst*'s central conceit in his Gaiety revue show around this time.⁹ Subsequent productions include lunchtime shows staged at Druid Lane Theatre, Galway (premiered 12 March 1980) and by the Cork Theatre Company at the Ivernia Theatre (July 1984, directed by Garvin McGrath and starring Donnacha Crowley as Mr C.), and performances in Dublin by Plough Players (premiered 14 August 1992) and Poor Relations (premiered 17 October 1992). The Cork Theatre Company adaptation mixed passages from across O'Nolan's work into the script, with a customer in the pub (whom reviewer Mark Hennessy described as being dressed like 'a misplaced teddy boy') reciting Lamont's cure for blackheads from *At Swim-Two-Birds*, and the Sergeant reciting the 'atomic theory' passage from *The Third Policeman*.¹⁰ A notable version by Rough Magic premiered at Trinity College Dublin Theatre, 10 September 1984, starring Stanley Townsend (Mr C.) and Arthur Riordan (Sergeant), with Rory Murray and Anne Byrne as the pub's clientele. The production was 'spiced with mood piano music' by

Helene Montague, including the *Pink Panther* theme,[11] and was revived for performance at the International Flann O'Brien Symposium in Dublin, April 1986.

The play has often been performed as part of a double with another short. It was paired with Lady Gregory's *The Rising of the Moon* in a Trinity College Dublin production by the Dublin University Players that ran 7–11 November 1977. Drybread Theatre premiered a double-bill of *Thirst* and *Gibber* by Robert Lee at the An Béal Bocht pub, Charlemont Street, on 1 October 1990 for the Dublin Theatre Festival (twelve performances). The cast featured Don Foley as Mr C. alongside Martin Dunne, Brent Hearne and the director Paul Lee. The set exploited a 'pub within a pub idea (constructed by the proprietor [of An Béal Bocht], Mick Gleeson)'.[12] Liverpool Irish Literary Theatre (LILT) performed *Thirst* in a triple-bill with O'Nolan's *The Dead Spit of Kelly* and Lord Dunsany's *The Glittering Gate* at ARGEkultur Salzburg on 19 July 2017, as part of the fourth International Flann O'Brien Conference, starring Gerry Smyth (Mr C.), David Llewellyn (Sergeant), Isaac Nixon (Peter) and Jade Thomson (Julia [Jem in original]).

Thirst was adapted for radio by H.L. Morrow and broadcast on Radio Éireann (RÉ) on 14 November 1958. A version for television was aired by the British Broadcasting Corporation (BBC) on 1 April 1959 under the title *After Hours*. It was produced by Barbara Burnham, with designs by Stanley Dorfman, and starred J.G. Devlin (Mr C.), P.G. Stephens (Sergeant), Wilfrid Brambell (Peter) and Shay Gorman (Jem). Alana Gillespie has shown that the script for *After Hours* contains five pages of new dialogue not included in any known version of *Thirst*, in which 'the Sergeant tells his own story of thirst' concerning 'a violent encounter on the job which left him badly injured and unable to drink liquid while he recovered in hospital'.[13] The teleplay's authors are identified as 'Brian Nolan' and 'Larry Morrow', so it is conceivable that Morrow wrote these additional lines and scenarios, although this remains speculation. A half-hour television adaptation aired on Telefís Éireann (TÉ) in the broadcaster's first week in 1961. It was produced by Shelah Richards, with designs by Wm. F. McCrow, and starred Danny Cummins (Mr C.), Geoffrey Golden (Sergeant), Brendan Cauldwell (Jem) and Seamus Healy (Peter). A 4 January 1962 *Irish Press* review was critical of the TÉ production, 'while on the same day the *Irish Independent* called it a "gem"' (*L*, 525, n. 347).

Faustus Kelly

The first production of *Faustus Kelly*, directed by Frank Dermody, premiered at the Abbey Theatre, Dublin, 25 January 1943. The original cast included

F.J. McCormack (Kelly), Liam Redmond [Liam Mac Réamoinn] (Mr Strange) and Cyril Cusack (Town Clerk), alongside Fred Johnson (Cullen), Michael J. Dolan (Reilly), Brian O'Higgins (Shawn Kilshaughraun), Denis O'Dea (Hoop), Ria Mooney (Mrs Crockett), Eileen Crowe (Hannah) and Gerard Healy (Capt. Shaw). Michael Clarke designed the sets with Udolphus Wright as stage manager. According to the programme notes, an orchestra performed the following selections: *Overture: La damnation de Faust (The Damnation of Faust) – Hungarian March,* by Hector Berlioz; Irish Airs: 'It is not the tear', *arr.* Dorothy Clifton, 'Down by the Salley Gardens', *arr.* Herbert Hughes, 'Suite of Airs', *arr.* Julia Gray; 'The King's Cave', *arr.* Frederick May; 'Two Songs – Wiegenlied and Feldeinsamkeit' and 'Excerpt – Trio in E Flat, Op. 40' by Johannes Brahms.[14]

The Carlow Little Theatre Society chose *Faustus Kelly* as its Tostal production in 1956. Two decades later, a production premiered at the Peacock Theatre on 22 May 1978, starring Eamon Morrissey as Kelly (in a 'crumpled pinstriped suit with baggy pants'[15]) and directed by Patrick Laffan, whose direction was 'full of "business" with hats, chairs, papers and sound effects'.[16] The cast included Derek Chapman (The Devil), Godfrey Quigley (The Begrudger) and Stephen Brennan (Town Clerk) – whose performance reviewers almost universally singled out for praise – alongside May Cluskey, Paul Murphy, John Molloy, Geoffrey Golden, Frank Mellis and Fedelma Cullen. The amateur Rathangan Players Drama Group staged a production of *Faustus Kelly* on 11 March 1983 as part of the Tipperary Drama Festival. 1988 saw two productions: one by the Strand Players, which premiered at the Hawk's Well Theatre, Sligo, 20 July 1988, and another that ran at the Edinburgh Festival Fringe, Bedlam Theatre, Edinburgh, from 12 to 17 August 1988, produced by Tania Cheston and starring Stephen Hogan as Kelly. The set of the latter was covered in 'kitsch-green' shamrock wallpaper[17] and the production was favourably reviewed in *The Irish Times* as a 'revolutionary achievement', directed 'with sympathy, intellect and laughter' by Conall Morrison and performed with 'frenetic exhibitions of lucidly logical lunacy, as Mephistopheles magnificently degenerates from her (it is "her", being the work of a superbly disciplined performance by a masculine-appearing Lisa Baraitser) stoical and sinister silences'.[18]

Faustus Kelly was adapted for radio by H.L. Morrow and a version produced by Frank Dermody was broadcast on RÉ on 31 January 1960. G.A. Olden wrote of the broadcast:

It was good fun to hear again Myles na Gopaleen's satirical study of Irish public life [...], although the radio performance couldn't possibly match the original Abbey production [...]. A number of purely visual comic effects [...] suffered in the transition – one remembers in particular the county councillor's sheepish return after his angry exit in somebody else's hat. The preliminary deed-signing, too, done in dumb show on the stage, has now to be conveyed in explicit dialogue, and, as far as I can remember, there have been changes in the closing passages of the last act. What came through splendidly in Larry Morrow's adaptation was the authentic flavour of a rural council meeting – its glorious inconsequence [...] and the speed with which the suspicions of political opponents are aroused.[19]

Morrow's radio adaptation was rerecorded with a new cast and producer (Sean Cotter), and broadcast on RÉ on 21 August 1966. Dick Walsh writes that the players 'made a fine job of this play with Tomas Studley, as Kelly, overdoing the sleveen whine a little maybe, but Niall Tóibín making a splendid piece of pompous ignorance out of the Town Clerk'.[20]

Rhapsody in Stephen's Green

Rhapsody in Stephen's Green, Myles na gCopaleen's adaptation (and significant rewrite) of Karel and Josef Čapek's *Ze života hmyzu* (From the Life of Insects), was produced by Edwards-mac Liammóir Gate Theatre Productions and premiered at the Gaiety Theatre, Dublin, 22 March 1943, with twenty-eight parts. The play ran for one week with the following cast: Robert Hennessy (Tramp), Sally Travers (Mrs Beetle), Meriel Moore (Mrs Cricket), A. James Neylin (Young Man), Valentin Iremonger (Slattery), Liam Gaffney (Visitor/ Parasite/Messenger Ant), William Fassbender (Keeper/Mr Beetle/Blind Ant), Betty Chancellor (Queen Bee), Cecil Monson (Basil Bee), J. Winter (Mr Cricket/Chief Engineer Ant), Tyrell Pine (Strange Beetle), Jean St Claire (Voice of the Egg), Rosalind Halligan (Lady in Green), Norman Barrs (Cecil Bee/Cross-Channel Ant), Patricia Kennedy (Girl Student), Alexis Milne (Duckling), Robert Dawson (Young Bee), Sean Colleary (2nd Engineer Ant), Antony Walsh (Cyril Bee/Politician Ant), P.P. Maguire (Duck), Stephen King (Drone Bee). The production also included nine children acting 'by permission of Miss Ursula White': Eileen Ashe, Collette Redmond, Tony Mathews, Teddy Lucas, Ita McManus, Deirdre King, Dolores Lucas, Peggy Kennedy and Maeve Kennedy. Edwards directed and served as lighting designer, mac

Liammóir and Perrott designed the costumes with Dodie Higgins (hats), with settings by Molly McEwen and choreography by Sara Payne.

Ondřej Pilný notes that O'Nolan collaborated with Edwards on the script, sending him drafts and incorporating his feedback: 'O'Nolan included drawings of his ideas of the insects (now lost) in the margins of the typescript, Edwards sketched his own vision of the ants on the back of the letter, wearing gas masks and military helmets in a clear allusion to the world war that was going on at the time.'[21] Moreover, O'Nolan is reported to have consulted the physicist Erwin Schrödinger on the script,[22] and it was Niall Montgomery who wrote much of the first draft of the first act which originally featured monkeys,[23] before Edwards suggested rewriting the first act with wasps (which were subsequently changed into bees in rehearsal).[24] Indeed, Edwards continued to make changes to O'Nolan's script throughout the rehearsal process:

> The Gate prompt book shows that Edwards's cuts [...] mostly affected the more verbose passages, such as some of the Drone's Shakespearean speeches in Act I, and much of the discussion of Ulster unionist politics and militant propaganda by the Chief Engineer, the 2nd Engineer and the Politician in Act III. [...] Edwards was clearly working towards the most effective way of staging the war scenes, which shifted the emphasis somewhat from language to non-verbal action.[25]

Perhaps owing to the fact that the script remained unpublished until 1994,[26] as well as to the scale of the production, there have been no major subsequent productions of *Rhapsody in Stephen's Green*. There is, however, a forthcoming animated film by Alana Gillespie and Henk-Jan Vinke (Imperial Finch Films), animated by Katharina Galland and Michel Lichtenbarg and starring John D. Ruddy, Eoghan mac Giolla Bhrighde, Rosemary Orr, Paul Treanor, Andrew Graeme McClay and Cillian Leneghan. A trailer for the film was released in 2015, and audio for the film was memorably recorded at the closing of the 2017 International Flann O'Brien Society Conference in Salzburg, with the assembled delegates directed by Gillespie to provide the sound of the insects' death rattles.[27]

An Sgian

Myles na gCopaleen's short play *An Sgian* was produced by the Irish Theatre Guild as part of the Gaelic Theatre Guild's Irish-language variety programme *Geamaí na Nodlag* (Christmas Capers) and premiered at the Peacock Theatre on 26 December 1944. Praising the full programme as 'something really new in Irish', *The Irish Times* favourably mentioned

> the satire in Myles na gCopaleen's '*An Sgian*' and Con Liathain's 'Huntin', Shootin', Fishin' [...], the reverence of Seamus de Bhilmot's '*A Mhiorbhuilt Féin*', and the comedy in Michael O Cinneide's translation from the Spanish and Michael O Siochfhradha's '*Ce h-é sin amuigh?*'. In '*Thíos Cois na Tragha*' Mairin Ni Shuilleabhain wove song and music neatly into a stage scene. The '*Putog na Nodlag*' and verse-speaking in Irish were Ursula de Faoite's arrangement.[28]

The show's run was extended by a week owing to its popularity and revived at the Peacock from 19 February 1945, with some new items added to the original programme.[29] After Louis de Paor recovered the script in 2001 from among the Flann O'Brien Papers, held by the John J. Burns Library, Boston College, a rehearsed reading of *An Sgian* was presented at the Town Hall Theatre, Galway, on 31 March 2002.[30]

Radio and television scripts

A fifteen-minute Myles na gCopaleen piece 'A Letter from Dublin' was broadcast on BBC's Third Programme on 12 August 1952.[31] An Irish-language script 'Cuimhne Ar An Athair Eoghan Ua Gramhna' among the Flann O'Brien Papers at the John J. Burns Library is marked as being 'likely for Radio Eireann broadcast, probably 1954'. Na Gopaleen's radio script *Something in the Air: A drama of the skies* was broadcast for twenty minutes on RÉ on 16 January 1959; an adapted version of the script for television is collected in *Plays and Teleplays* under the name *Flight*. On 26 September 1955, O'Nolan sent the script for *The Boy from Ballytearim* to Sam Hanna Bell, director of drama for BBC Belfast, who rejected it (*L*, 195–6, 198). O'Nolan sent a copy to Hilton Edwards in 1961, who was then head of drama at TÉ (*L*, 276) and to the director of drama, Ulster Television, on 8 August 1962 (*L*, 309). To my knowledge, the script was never produced on stage, radio or television. In fact, I can find no record in O'Nolan's correspondence, contemporary TV listings, or the Raidió Teilifís Éireann (RTÉ) archives that any of his teleplay scripts – *The Man with Four Legs* (Edwards's rejection letter is published in *L*, 297), *Flight*, *The Boy from Ballytearim*, *The Time Freddie Retired*, *The Dead Spit of Kelly* – were ever actually produced or aired, despite critical claims to the contrary.[32] Indeed, in a letter to Gunnar Rugheimer, controller of programmes at TÉ, in June 1966, Evelyn O'Nolan writes: 'I have a couple of short plays which he wrote for television, but which were never produced.'[33]

What certainly was produced and aired on TÉ were O'Nolan's two sitcoms *O'Dea's Yer Man* (1963–4) and *Th'Oul Lad of Kilsalaher* (September–December 1965). O'Nolan produced twenty-four scripts for *O'Dea's Yer Man* over the next year, initially with a high degree of script doctoring by producer and director James Plunkett, who turned the monologues that O'Nolan had written for O'Dea into dialogues and enhanced the role of Ignatius that would be played by David Kelly.[34] Each episode consists of a fifteen-minute dialogue in which the signalman and the porter in a railway signal box discuss diverse themes, generally intergenerational issues that contrast 1960s Ireland with 'the auld times', such as changing gender roles, new technologies and the Irish language question.[35] O'Dea's 1963 Gaiety Theatre performance of Harry O'Donovan's 'Gay Summer Revue' *We're Joking of Course* included 'additional material by Myles na Gopaleen' in the form of O'Dea and Kelly on stage performing a scene from *O'Dea's Yer Man*.[36]

Th'Oul Lad of Kilsalaher, directed by Jim Fitzgerald, is a series of fifteen dialogues between Dubliner Marie-Thérèse (Máire Hastings), nicknamed 'Puddiner', and her uncle Andy (Danny Cummins), renamed Hughie a few episodes into the run, in their kitchen. O'Nolan originally pitched Maureen Potter and Eamon Kelly in the lead roles, and the title *A Shanachy's Shenanigans*, to the show's producer Aindrias Ó Gallchóir, writing that while *O'Dea's Yer Man* was 'too sedentary [...], the new series will have more resilience and bounce, even some crazy music making' (*L*, 509–10). When the show was discontinued on 20 December 1965, O'Nolan reflected to Fitzgerald that Cummins's 'personality and face could not withstand the penetration of the TV camera' but that Hastings was 'always in command of her role' and she had 'a bright future, on and off television' (*L*, 551). In the same letter, O'Nolan pitched his TV series *The Detectional Fastidiosities of Sergeant Fottrell*, which would consist of 'short plays of 20/25 min. duration, each with a sharp if preposterous plot' (*L*, 551). O'Nolan died four months later, and the series was never realised.

Adaptations of O'Nolan's early novels

At Swim-Two-Birds

Eileen Battersby notes that 'By the late 1960s, three writers were working on stage adaptations of *At Swim-Two-Birds*, all with an eye to the Abbey stage.

The version which earned the approval of the writer's widow, Evelyn, was by Dublin writer Audrey Welsh.'[37] The first production of Welsh's adaptation – which reportedly did not use 'a single word that isn't in the text'[38] – was directed by Alan Simpson and premiered at the Abbey Theatre, Peacock Stage, Dublin, 12 February 1970 with the following cast: Eamon Keane (Bran [name given to the novel's unnamed narrator]/Tracy), Micheál Ó Briain (Finn/Uncle/Trellis), Patrick Laffan (Brinsley/Furriskey), Pat Layde (Jem Casey), Joan O'Hara (Peggy/Teresa/Maidservant/Sheila Lamont), Des Cave (Kelly/Lamont/Shorty Andrews), Peadar Lamb (Sweeny/Corcoran), Vincent Dowling (Shanahan/Slug Willard/Donaghy), John Olohan (Dona Ferentes) and Bernard Collins (Timothy Danaos). According to the programme, the cow was provided courtesy of Mitchelstown Creameries. Puppeteer and ventriloquist Eugene Lambert (of *Wanderly Wagon* fame) ventriloquised the roles of the Cow, the Good Fairy and the Pooka, who took the form of a puppet operated by Judy Lambert. John Ryan's settings were 'a mixture of *Art Nouveau* and ancient Celtic motifs' and were 'supplemented by slide projection, designed by Bob Fanning the caricaturist',[39] with musical accompaniment from a string quartet which played mainly Mozart, lighting design by Leslie Scott, and costumes by Lyn Avery. The production returned to the Abbey stage for a two-week run in June 1970 without Eugene Lambert, who was replaced by Kathleen Barrington (Good Fairy) and Aiden Grennell (Pooka). A production of Welsh's stage adaptation directed by Lou Stein premiered on 10 April 1979 as the first performance of the fringe pub theatre The Gate in Notting Hill, London. Maeve Binchy's *Irish Times* review praised the performances of John Quinn (in three roles), Seamus Crowe (Pooka) and Treasa Ni Fhatharta (Sheila Lamont), who also appeared 'heavily disguised in space gear' as the Good Fairy.[40] A new production of Welsh's adaptation ran for three weeks in November 1981 at the Peacock, Dublin, starring its director Eamon Morrissey alongside Kevin McHugh, Tom Hickey, May Cluskey and Emmet Bergin.

The next major stage adaptation of *At Swim-Two-Birds* was developed by Jon Haynes and David Woods for the Ridiculusmus theatre company. Haynes and Woods recall their initial difficulties in getting permissions for a new version:

> MLR who control the rights to Flann O'Brien's stuff wouldn't authorise a new adaptation. They were happy with the existing one written by Audrey Welsh for the Abbey at least 20 years earlier and we had to do that. The way around it – the Welsh one was a dull literary reading of

the novel – was that it required a cast of 40 and impossible technical demands for small-scale touring. So we were given the go-ahead for an adaptation of the adaptation and proceeded with our new adaptation regardless.[41]

The Ridiculusmus production of *At Swim-Two-Birds* premiered at Battersea Arts Centre in 1994, starring Haynes (Uncle/Jem Casey/Finn/Trellis) and Woods (Sheila Lamont/Sweeny/Shanahan) performing alongside Angus Barr (Fellermelad/Furriskey) and Helen Trew (Pooka/Orlick).[42] Ridiculusmus toured the UK and Ireland throughout 1995 with an emended cast of Haynes (now also playing Red Kiersay/Antony Lamont/Orlick), Woods (now also playing Tracy/Corcoran/Brinsley) and Pete McCabe (taking over the roles of Fellermelad/Furriskey/Pooka). Jocelyn Clarke, who would adapt the novel for stage over a decade later, favourably reviewed the production's appearance at the 1995 Kilkenny Arts Week, singling out its 'energetic recreation of the book's scatological and sophomoric obsessions'.[43]

With the restrictions on performing the Welsh version loosened, two major adaptations were staged in subsequent decades. Alex Johnston's adaptation premiered at the Abbey Theatre, Peacock Stage, on 29 July 1998 with the following cast: Ronan Leahy (Student/Lamont), Mick Nolan (Uncle/Trellis), Brendan Conroy (Corcoran/Jem Casey), Kevin Hely (Shorty Andrews/Small Man in a Coat/Moling), Niall Ó Sioradáin (Slug Willard/ Christian Brother/St Ronan), Catherine Walsh (Teresa/Cow/Newsreader/ Hag/Good Fairy), Robert Price (Orlick/Linchehaun/Lover), Anto Nolan (Kelly/Shanahan), Tony Flynn (Sweeny/Verney Wright), Ned Dennehy (Pooka), Johnny Murphy (Finn), Karl Shiels (Brinsley/Furriskey), Maeve Coogan (Peggy/Lover/Prostitute). Reviewer Gerry Colgan noted that 'familiar characters fill the stage from the off', yet:

> A difficulty on stage is that they are never really integrated as a group, as if the fact of their visibility inhibits the imaginative leap required. The creative lunacy of the book is reduced to a series of set-pieces – many of them very funny, others less so – which lack the harmony of a creative whole. [...] Jimmy Fay's direction, with Johanna Connor's flexible set and Trevor Dawson's lighting design, gets the right Dublin feel.[44]

Blue Raincoat Theatre Company premiered Jocelyn Clarke's stage adaptation *At Swim Two Birds* (2009) (with the hyphens dropped from the title) at The Factory Performance Space, Sligo, 3 November 2009, before touring Ireland in February 2010 and touring internationally in 2011. Clarke's adaptation 'structures the play as a series of biographical reminiscences, extracts from the book and occasional TV interviews'.[45] In the production (directed by Niall Henry, with lighting by Michael Cummins and sound design by Joe Hunt):

> The centre of the auditorium is filled with a thrust stage. To its left and right are the normal paraphernalia that one expects to be hidden away in the wings: lights, costume rails, microphones, and so on. At the back of the auditorium is a proscenium arch, with a melodramatic red velvet curtain covering it. [...] it seems as if we've been transported to a slightly grotty nineteenth-century music hall, designed with characteristic wit by Jaimie Vartan. As the actors arrive on stage, it quickly becomes obvious that the novel's exploration of fiction has been re-imagined as an exploration of the theatrical. Whereas O'Brien thought of his narrator as the author of three different stories, Clarke [...] present[s] the narrator as a playwright/director/ringmaster with three different dramas to put on. As the play begins, the narrator (played by Sandra O'Malley) summons his characters to the stage – with the roles shared out between [John] Carty, [Kellie] Hughes, [Ciaran] McCauley and [Fiona] McGeown. These characters burst clumsily through the curtains, stumbling to the front of the stage in ill-fitting costumes, delivering their lines in accents that veer from the shaky to the overconfident. It's as if an under-prepared (and largely untalented) troupe of actors has suddenly found itself in the mortifying predicament of being confronted unexpectedly with an audience. And the results are extraordinarily funny.[46]

Under this conceit, the characters are presented 'like an increasingly stressed bunch of actors and stagehands, leaping in and out of their different costumes in a desperate (and occasionally unsuccessful) attempt to deliver their next line at the appropriate time', using 'fast-paced physical and vocal transformations to move from one part to the next'.[47] Chris McCormack singles out a striking transition between characters:

> O'Malley as the Pooka MacPhellimey is pacing confidently towards the audience, fedora firmly resting on her head. As the clown music thumps louder, and MacPhellimey approaches the front of the stage, O'Malley removes the hat and produces a red clown nose to indicate her switch to the reserved Orlick. It is a moment of instant transformation that

is presented directly to the audience. As she lowers the hat, and the stern facial expression of the Pooka is replaced by the timid courtesy of Orlick, O'Malley demonstrates her immense ability to command body language and movement in a way that defines character and consciousness.[48]

The 1990s saw several staged public readings of *At Swim-Two-Birds*. Austrian theatre director Kurt Palm arranged a seventeen-hour reading of *In Schwimmen-Zwei-Vögel*, Harry Rowohlt's 1989 German translation of *At Swim-Two-Birds*, in Vienna in 1991. The director recalls: 'There was a lot of alcohol involved [...]. We had beds on the stage so people could stay overnight.'[49] Palm produced the first German-language stage adaptation of the novel at the Sargfabrik, Vienna, in the same year (29 August–14 September 1991), starring Rowohlt as Finn Mac Cool and the voice of the Good Fairy.[50] Rowohlt is well-known in the German-speaking world for his captivating live readings from his own German-language translations of O'Nolan, some of which have been released as audiobooks. To mark the sixtieth anniversary of the book's publication, Joe Kennedy organised an eight-hour reading of *At Swim-Two-Birds* on 3 October 1999, which took place on a 1947 double-decker bus travelling from Davy Byrnes pub to Dalkey and back, with stops in 'numerous pubs either mentioned by O'Brien or closely associated with the author'.[51] Extracts from the Ringsend cowboys scene were read by Labour Party leader Ruairi Quinn at Paddy Cullen's in Ballsbridge and by party colleague Liz McManus at the Sorrento in Dalkey, with other excerpts read by Shay Healy, Brendan Balfe, Brendan Conroy and the St Patrick's Dramatic Society.

Eric Ewens's radio adaptation of Welsh's stage play was broadcast on BBC Radio 3 on 26 August 1979. The radio play was directed by Ronald Mason and starred Niall Buggy as Myles (the name given to the novel's unnamed narrator in this production), alongside Patrick McAlinney (Uncle), Patrick Magee (Pooka), Jim Norton (Brinsley), Donal McCann (Furriskey), Allan McClelland (Jesuit/Sweeny), Tom McCabe (Orlick), Kevin Flood (Shanahan), Kate Binchy (Fairy), Sean Barrett (Tipster/Lamont) David Blake Kelly (Conán/Moling), Denys Hawthorne (Finn/Trellis), Harry Webster (Kelly/Casey), Alan Barry (Ronan/Corcoran), Wesley Murphy (Byrne/Tracy) and Elizabeth Morgan (Cow). A two-hour radio adaptation of the novel by Ewens starring the RTÉ Players (Patrick Dawson, Eamon Keane, Gerald Fitzmahony, Brendan Cauldwell, Conor Farrington, Des Nealon) and directed again by Mason was broadcast on RTÉ Radio 1 on New Year's Day

1982. Mason describes Ewens's decision to introduce a third-person narrator to the adaptation, noting that while a television adaptation would be 'confined by the essentially anti-filmic device of a narrator [...], Eric used the narrator device tremendously effectively on radio, so that the structure of the original work was preserved' to let the audience know that 'Myles was writing a novel in which the characters took over [...] and were taking part in a drama'.[52] The adaptation was broadcast in stereo, owing to the 'huge number of aural scene changes, which rise to a crescendo of sound mixes with the courtroom scene'.[53]

Despite Brendan Gleeson's widely reported frustrations in realising his *At Swim-Two-Birds* film project,[54] the novel has only been brought to the screen once, in a German-language adaptation by Kurt Palm (director and screenplay), filmed in Austria. *In Schwimmen-Zwei-Vögel* was produced by Markus Fischer for Fischer Film, with cinematography by Wolfgang Lehner, editing by Karina Ressler and music by Chrono Popp. Many of the cast returned from Palm's staged versions, including Werner Wultsch as Bran (the name is taken over from Welsh's stage adaptation) and Rowohlt reprising his stage roles. The film premiered in Vienna, November 1997, before being screened in Berlin and at both the 1998 Dublin Film Festival and the 1998 Galway Film Fleadh. Palm acknowledges David Lynch[55] and Bertolt Brecht[56] as influences on the visual style and artistic ethos of the adaptation. He discussed the process of adapting O'Nolan's novel to the screen in a conversation with Eileen Battersby:

> 'I don't like the end of the novel,' he says, so he has had some fun with it as well as making other changes, such as presenting the Red Swan Hotel in a more isolated country setting and dispensing with the university sequences. Palm has deliberately imposed a narrative structure on a novel which does not have one. 'Of course this was needed – it's only when you come to do something on screen you see the things you can't use. You can't always take an image that works very well on the page. There are things I liked that I couldn't use. [...] But [...] the book is really about rejecting the rigidity of art and I think that comes across well.'[57]

The Third Policeman

O'Nolan discussed turning *The Third Policeman* into a stage play on several occasions after the novel's rejection, notably in correspondence with Ernest Blythe of the Abbey and Hilton Edwards of the Gate in June 1942 (*L*, 118–19).

Niall Montgomery contended in 1950 that O'Nolan had in fact written 'a dramatic adaptation of [the novel], "Bás i-nÉirinn"' (L, 118, n. 141), although the adaptation never materialised, and no further evidence that O'Nolan in fact penned the script has since transpired.

Eamon Morrissey was the first to adapt *The Third Policeman* for the stage in a Dublin Comedy Theatre production that premiered at the Gate Theatre, Dublin, 30 September 1974 as part of the Dublin Theatre Festival.[58] Morrissey directed a cast of Niall O'Brien (Hero), Arthur O'Sullivan (Pluck), Dermot Tuohy (MacCruiskeen), Edward Byrne (Mathers), Frank Kelly (Divney) and Catherine Byrne 'making a brief and wordless appearance as a female bicycle'.[59] Robert Heade's set was designed to be 'flexible' and 'mobile' and was 'made out of what appeared to be a stack of rustic fencing'.[60] Eileen Long's wardrobe drew comment from a number of critics: Robert Somerset's de Selby was presented onstage in 'the stock image of the looney intellectual, straight from the mad academies of Vienna',[61] or 'like something out of a Disney cartoon',[62] while Robert Carrickford's Finnucane appeared 'like a peg-legged Darby O'Gill'.[63] Regarding the adaptation itself, Charles Lewsen's review observed that Morrissey 'has not kept the dialogues between the hero and his soul, nor found a theatrical device to match the footnotes [...]. In effect, he has not attempted a surreal form for the surreal content; nevertheless, with complete clarity and with great zest he conveys the mad story'.[64] Elsewhere, Desmond Rushe asserted that Morrissey had performed a 'workmanlike job' as adaptor and director, but 'those who look for genuine Flann O'Brien are likely to be let down', attributing the problem to the original text's fantastical and surreal qualities, as 'a work of this nature defies translation to the stage'.[65] John Boland was less generous regarding the production's straight take on the novel's 'lunatic' spirit: 'It's almost impossible to translate fantasy into visual terms, but Mr Morrissey makes a particularly poor fist of it.'[66] Emmanuel Kehoe echoes this critique and adds that the adaptation gets much of the novel's tone wrong by playing its 'cruel' and 'frightening' moments (such as the opening murder, or 'the horror of the police station') for laughs.[67]

Ken Campbell's 1980 adaptation of *The Third Policeman* (which he also directed) amped up the surrealism and spectacle. The production played at the ICA theatre from 26 February to 15 March as part of the 'A Sense of Ireland' festival, and starred Mitch Davies (A Man With Neither Name Nor Bicycle), Richard Hope (MacCruiskeen), Arthur Kohn (Pluck), Bunny Reed, Oengus Macnamara, Barclay Johnson, Chris De-Piss, Brian Calloway and Vanda Goodenoughski, with a four-piece band led by Camilla Saunders who also played on frying pans and wine glasses.[68] The stage was adorned with mirrors and 'flashing tubes of light'.[69] The actors wore distorted false buck teeth, which Campbell claimed was an attempt to conceal the fact that they did not have Irish accents: 'There's a lot of talk about teeth in the book, so I got a dentist to make false teeth that go over your own. And the whole business of trying to keep your teeth in unified the accents.'[70]

Ridiculusmus adapted *The Third Policeman* for the stage in a promenade show that was first performed as a five-hander at Aras na nGael, London in 1992, starring Kevin Henshall (Yer Man), Jon Haynes (Mathers/Finnucane/ O'Corky), David Woods (Divney/Pluck), Lucy Cuthbertson (MacCruiskeen/ Pegeen) and Angus Barr (Soul/de Selby). The show toured in repertory in four-hander and three-hander versions until 1997.[71] Haynes recalls: 'We devised it in each other's living rooms and bedrooms, which is why two wardrobes ended up as important parts of the set, with characters disappearing into them to go to Eternity, and the interview between O'Corky and Yer Man at the end of the story taking place inside one.'[72] The promenade production is remembered for its audience interactivity, as punters who turned up with bicycle lamps were given a free glass of 'The Wrastler' stout and lighting effects were created by the audience's bicycle lamps. The audience were held at gunpoint to look on the floor for the black box and made to go through a doorway into the police station for the next scene.[73] At the final performance at the Black Box in Galway in 1997, Haynes, as Inspector O'Corky, drove a Nissan Micra onto the stage. There was a one-off revival of the show in a pub in Manor House, as part of a planned retrospective of Ridiculusmus's work in London in 2001 – Haynes notes that his 'lung collapsed on the first day of this extravaganza and several of the shows were cancelled', but *The Third Policeman* went ahead with Aidan McCann stepping in to replace him in the three-hander version with David Woods and Pete McCabe.[74]

Two separate adaptations of *The Third Policeman* were staged in 2006–7. The first, produced by the Pembroke Players, was performed at the ADC Theatre, Cambridge, from 22–25 February 2006. Directed by Henry Eliot and produced by Nell Pearce-Higgins, with lighting design by Stuart Cuthbertson, the production starred Helen Cripps as Flann O'Brien (the novel's unnamed narrator) alongside Jonathan Lis (Pluck), Nina Flitman (MacCruiskeen), Frank Paul (Mathers/O'Corky/Fox), James Kinman (Divney/Finnucane/Gilhaney/O'Feersa) and Rebecca Pitt (Pegeen). The Blue Raincoat Theatre Company premiered Jocelyn Clarke's new stage adaptation of the novel at The Factory Performance Space, Sligo, 16 October 2007. Directed by Niall Henry, the production featured 'a giant book, positioned centre stage, which Jamie Vartan's design [...] rendered as both a dais for the performance and an oracle to be consulted' for de Selby's writing.[75] In a memorable scene, a bicycle was elevated high up on the back wall of the performance space on which the protagonist makes his escape. Sara Keating's *Irish Times* review noted that the play's 'Multiple entrances, exits and journeys across the stage' were 'fluidly choreographed with a slow expressionistic physicality, while Michael Cummins's unsettling mood-setting lights' – including a starlit backdrop of bulbs that flickered to signify eternity – 'and Joe Hunt's portentous circus score [lent] an extra ominous edge to the actors' marionette-like movements'.[76] Sandra O'Malley starred as the barefoot Man With No Name, supported by Fiona McGeown (O'Corky), Ciaran McCauley (Mathers/Fox), John Carty (Pluck/Divney/MacCruiskeen), Kellie Hughes (Joe/Pegeen/O'Feersa) and Patrick Curley (Finnucane/Gilhaney). As part of their thirtieth anniversary commemorations, Blue Raincoat posted a video of O'Malley discussing the production alongside film footage of performances.[77]

Most recently, Bill Scott wrote and directed an adaptation of *The Third Policeman* for outdoor performance in a Miracle Theatre production that toured the UK as a four-hander in the summer of 2017. Hannah Stephens played the nameless de Selby scholar alongside Benjamin Dyson (Pluck), Ben Kernow (Divney/MacCruiskeen) and Catherine Lake (Mathers/Finnucane/ Mrs Gilhaney/O'Feersa/Fox). Scott reflected that when adapting *The Third Policeman* he got 'a very strong sense that Flann O'Brien must have originally conceived it as a play. For all its complex and profound ideas, it has a simple structure and a small number of vivid characters, with most of the memorable lines written as dialogue that cries out to be spoken aloud.'[78]

A noticeable trend in stage adaptations of *The Third Policeman* is the incorporation of musical performance in genres ranging from vaudeville to opera. *De Eeuwige Fietser*, a Dutch-language production from the theatre company Orkater (produced by Marc van Warmerdam and Linda Lodeizen), premiered at De Lantaren, Rotterdam, on 17 November 1988, and toured until February 1989. The play was translated from *The Third Policeman* by Casper Hendriks and adapted for the stage by Aat Ceelen, who also directed and starred as the unnamed protagonist alongside Michiel Romeyn (MacCruiskeen). The set, designed by Pat van Hemelrijck (who also played Pluck) was built out of salvaged waste materials and junk objects, including a sloping steel plate, bicycle parts, telephones and garbage cans. Thijs van der Poll performed music on stage on harmonium, saxophone, mandolin and flute, with the policemen singing harmonies in choir. In July 2003, a production premiered at the Galway Arts Festival in which Stephen Rea narrated excerpts from *The Third Policeman*, while acoustic guitarist Colin

Reid performed a specially composed suite, *Quintet No. 2*. The show was revived for an Irish tour in 2011–12 with Rea again and an expanded musical accompaniment: Colin Reid (piano), Neil Martin (cello), Becky Joslin (cello), Niamh Crowley (violin).

The twenty-first century saw a series of full musical adaptations of *The Third Policeman*, beginning with the German-language *Der dritte Polizist*, adapted by Christopher Blenkinsop and Carsten Dane. The show premiered at Theater im Haus der Kunst, Munich (a museum exhibition room converted into a stage) in 2002 under the artistic direction of Dieter Dorn and with a cast including Alfred Kleinheinz, Helmut Stange, Hermann Beyer, Richard Beek, Arnulf Schumacher and Thomas Holtzmann, with Carsten Dane on piano. Rather than an American gold watch, the protagonist goes to the police station to report the loss of his cassette tape. The voice of Joe was piped through an old tube radio. As the play progressed, three large tea chests were pushed aside as different elements of a makeshift 'music machine' were gradually added to the stage, including a table as bellows, bicycles as bell players, organ pipes on rough-hewn wooden beams, winches and a long musical ball track.[79] Ergo Phizmiz's *The Third Policeman: An electronic neuropera vaudeville machine* premiered at Tête à Tête: The Opera Festival, Riverside Studios, Hammersmith, London in August 2011, followed by a tour of the UK and the Netherlands. Phizmiz published a detailed testimony about the process of writing, rehearsing, staging and touring the play in the first issue of *The Parish Review: Journal of Flann O'Brien studies*.[80] The following year, *Der dritte Polizist*, a German-language opera by Florian Bramböck (with libretto by Doris Happl and musical direction by Hansjörg Sofka), was performed at the Tiroler Landestheater, Innsbruck. The opera gives O'Nolan's unnamed protagonist a name (Joe Mulrooney, played by Matthias Wölbitsch) and changes the gender of his soul to female (Josephine, die Seele, played by Renate Fankhauser).

Eric Ewens's radio adaptation of *The Third Policeman* was broadcast on BBC Radio 4's 'A Book at Bedtime' in ten parts, premiering 11 June 1979. It was produced by Northern Irish author Maurice Leitch and read by Patrick Magee. There was also a radio adaptation, produced by Rewind for Comedy Bookcase on BBC Radio 2 and first broadcast 3 February 1993, in which Les Dennis read extracts from the novel.

An Béal Bocht

Addressing the UCD Literary and Historical Society in 1944, Abbey managing director Ernest Blythe blamed the dearth of Irish-language theatre on a lack both of actors who could play the parts and suitable contemporary literature written in Irish, but singled out Myles na gCopaleen's 'magnificent' *An Béal Bocht* as an exception.[81] However, it would be over two decades before Seán Ó Briain wrote the first stage adaptation of the novel, which he also directed in a UCD Gaelic Players production that premiered at the Damer Hall, Dublin, 31 January 1967, starring Bearnard Mac Donncha (Bónapárt), Breandán Ó Murchú (An Sean Duine Liath) and an ensemble cast from An Cumann Gaelach, UCD. The play won the Universities Gaelic Drama Festival in Galway, where it played in the Taibhdhearc theatre on 5 February.

Ó Briain's adaptation was produced by the Abbey, where it played for four nights, opening 26 July 1967, as the first show to be staged on the new Peacock Stage. Frank Dermody directed (under the name Proinnsias Mac Diarmada) with set design by Peadar Lamb (as Peadar Ó Luain), music by Eamonn Ó Gallchobhair and choreography by Bernadette Keogh. It starred Sean Mac Philib (Bónapárt), Micheál Ó Briain (An Sean Duine Liath), Máire Ní Dhomhnaill (An Mháthair), Eamon Ó Ceallacháin [Eamon Kelly] (An Piscín Piaclach), Micheál Ó hAonghusa (Máirtín Ó Bánasa), Sean Mac Carthaigh (Sitric), Harry Brogan (Fear an tSiopa), Padraig de Buis (Maoldún Ó Pónasa/An Cigire Gallda), Cladhbh Mac Oireachtaigh (Placeman/An Dochtúir Gearmánach), Bernadette Nic Chionnaith (Nábla), Domhnall Ó Coiligh (Aimhirgean Ó Lúnasa), Micheál Ó Conghaile (Michelangelo), Seamus Ó hEili (Ferdinand), Seosamh Ó Dubhlainn (Jams O'Donnell I), Eamon Guaillí (Jams O'Donnell II) and a large ensemble cast.[82] The reviews were largely negative, with Sean Page accusing the Peacock production of transforming O'Nolan's 'grotesque humour' into a 'topical pantomime' and turning his 'satire into a romp' in which the novel's parody of Irish revivalism and nativism is 'played straight', so that 'the production makes a point quite opposite to the one intended by the writer'.[83] The play was abruptly withdrawn by the Abbey on 1 August following a disagreement between Evelyn O'Nolan and Dolmen Press, owing to 'a misunderstanding about the actual version' of the novel which had been used for the stage adaptation.[84] In short, there was a sense that the production had made substantial unauthorised changes to Ó Briain's approved adaptation and Evelyn O'Nolan asserted that, as she was the sole executrix of her husband's estate, Heath & Co. and Dolmen Press had illegally granted permission for the production without her signature or approval.

In November 1970, Ó Briain wrote to Evelyn O'Nolan about a proposed production of his adaptation by Cork's Compántas Chorchaí. In the letter, he waives any claim to performance rights for the production and insists his adaptation is 'based on the original edition of the book as published by An Preas Naisiunta and NOT on the later Dolmen edition'.[85] With Evelyn O'Nolan's permission, the adaption was revived in March 1971 in Cork – first in the Everyman Theatre and then in the Little Theatre – before playing at An Taibhdhearc, Galway, 9–16 May. The Galway performance featured three actors playing Bónapárt (Ó Briain himself, Maoilíosa Stafford and Sean Ó Coistealbha) alongside Coiril Ó Mathúna (An Sean Duine Liath), Máire Stafford (Máthair), Seán Stafford (Máirtín Ó Bánasa), Ciarán Ó Maoldúin (Michelangelo), Michael Ó Maolallaigh (Sitric/Maoldún Ó Pónasa/Aimhirgean Ó Lúnasa), Seán Mac Íomhar (Feardanand), Róisin Ní Dhuigneáin (Nábla) and a large ensemble cast, including fifteen 'schoolchildren and neighbours'.[86] In October 1974, Tomás Mac Anna, artistic director of the Abbey, wrote to Evelyn O'Nolan, acknowledging the difficulties with the 1967 Peacock run and asking to produce *An Béal Bocht* again as the Abbey's Christmas presentation. Ó Briain's adaptation was once again staged by the Abbey Theatre in the Peacock in January 1975, this time with a much smaller cast in a production co-directed by Tomás Mac Anna and Micheál Ó Colgáin. Micheál Ó Briain and Máire Ní Dhomhnaill reprised their 1967 roles as An Sean Duine Liath and An Mháthair, respectively, with MacDara Ó Fatharta taking over the part of Bónapárt alongside an ensemble cast taking up the rest of the roles (Eamon Ó Ceallaigh [Eamon Kelly], Peadar Ó Luain [Peadar Lamb], Áine Ní Mhuirí, Bill Foley, Brian Ó Muirí, Raymond Hardie). The reviews of this revival were generally much more positive than the 1967 run, with Ó Briain's adaptation and especially the cast singled out for praise, although *Irish Times* reviewer Dominic Ó Riordan protested both the long passages read directly from the book and the introduction of 'song and dance to lighten the scholastic approach'.[87]

Dry Bread Theatre Company/Priory Productions produced both an English-language stage adaptation of *The Poor Mouth* (the title of Patrick C. Power's English-language translation of *An Béal Bocht*) in 1989 and an Irish-language stage adaptation of *An Béal Bocht* in 1991. *The Poor Mouth* was adapted for the stage by Paul Lee and premiered at An Béal Bocht, Dublin, June 1989, as part of the 1989 Dublin Theatre Festival, before touring Ireland and the UK and winning the Guardian Critics Choice Award at the Edinburgh Festival 1991. The play was a two-hander starring Paul Lee (Ould Grey Fella) and Patrick J. Brady (Bonaparte), who looked, per Francine Cunningham's review, 'suitably pale and scrawny in a sackcloth nappy – a sort of Robinson Crusoe of the western isles'.[88] The play was directed by Ronan Smith with designs by Bláithín Sheerin, with Ambrose the Pig represented by a wooden cut-out. The show was revived in Irish three times: first, in 1991 as *An Béal Bocht* with Mick Lally and Macdara Ó Fátharta (An Béal Bocht, Dublin, 15–30 April 1991); secondly, by the Abbey with Peadar Lamb and Dónall Farmer at an international theatre show in Luxemburg; and, thirdly, by the Project Theatre, starring Farmer (An Sean Duine Liath) and Ó Fátharta (Bónapárt) and including the use of puppetry, in a production that premiered 5 August 1994 before touring Ireland. The Irish-language version was recorded and broadcast on RTÉ radio with Lally and Ó Fátharta. Several other actors played parts in productions of this adaptation over the following years including Frank O'Sullivan, Jack Lynch and Gerard Lee.[89]

An Béal Bocht was adapted for the stage and directed by Darach Mac Con Iomaire in a production that premiered at An Taibhdhearc in April 2004, starring Marc Mac Lochlainn and Darach Ó Dubháin, with set design by Dara McGee, costume design by Breege Fahy and puppet design and construction by Carmel Balfe and Tom Meskall. In 2009, Bríd Ó Gallchóir wrote and directed a new stage adaptation of the novel that was produced by Aisling Ghéar with translations by Conor Blaney and set design by Niall Rea. It premiered at Cultúrlann McAdam Ó Fiaich, Belfast, 6 November, with the following cast: Tony Devlin (Bónapárt), Mary Ryan (Máthair/Sitric Ó Sánasa), Donncha Crowley (An Máistir Scoile/An Sean Duine Liath/Athair Bhónapart), Melanie Clark-Pullen (An Cigire/Garda/Máirtín Ó Cúnasa/Nábla O'Donnell/Uachtarán Chonradh na Gaeilge). *Le pleure-misère*, Clara Simpson's French-language stage adaptation from André Verrier and Alain Le Berre's translation, played at the Théâtre des Marronniers à Lyon in 2012, with lighting by Xavier Davoust, costumes by Sophie Bouillaux-Rynne, scenography by Fanny Gamet and direction by Georges-Antoine Labaye. The adaptation is a two-hander that plays in a bar setting, with Gilles Fisseau relating the story and Davóg Rynne singing Irish airs and providing musical accompaniment on the bodhrán.[90]

The Poor Mouth, the third of Jocelyn Clarke's stage adaptations of O'Nolan's novels for Blue Raincoat, premiered at The Factory Performance Space, Sligo, 25 October 2011. The production was directed by Niall Henry with the following cast: Sandra O'Malley (Bonapart), Ciaran McCauley (Policeman/Old Grey Fellow), John Carty (Pig/Policeman/Ferdinand/Inspector/Gaeilgeoir), Kellie Hughes (Mother/Sitric/Michelangelo O'Coonassa) and Bob Kelly (Gentleman/Inspector/Máirtín Ó Bánasa/Osborne O'Loonassa). Seona Mac Réamoinn praised the 'subtly choreographed ensemble movement' with which the 'energetic cast' morphed 'into a medley of characters, animals, chunks of landscape', and favourably reviewed both Joe

Hunt's soundscape and Jamie Vartan's 'simple' stage design, which included 'an off-kilter map of Ireland on the floor'.[91] The production toured to the Project Arts Centre November in 2012 and the Tron and the Traverse theatres in Scotland in June 2013.

An extract from *An Béal Bocht* was read by Seán Ó Síothcháin on RÉ, 26 September 1946. A fuller production, *An Béal Bocht: Droch scéal ar an droch shaol*, was adapted for radio by Proinsias Mac Aonghusa and broadcast on RÉ, December 1957–January 1958 (rebroadcast 1961). In 1981, Maurice Leitch produced a radio adaptation of *The Poor Mouth* read by Patrick Magee and broadcast in eleven parts on BBC Radio 4. *An Béal Bocht* was broadcast in three parts on RTÉ radio, on 27–29 November 1983. Following on the success of Colmán Ó Raghallaigh, Breandán Ó Conaire and John McCloskey's 2012 graphic novel adaptation, Tom Collins wrote and directed the 33-minute animated short film *An Béal Bocht* (Nerve Productions, 2018), with animation by McCloskey and Pádraig O'Grady, starring Owen McDonnell (O'Cunasa), Donncha Crowley (Old Grey Fellow) and Tommy Tiernan (Martin O'Bannasa).

The late novels

The Dalkey Archive

O'Nolan's late novels have not been adapted as often as his earlier, more celebrated works. However, one of the most significant stage adaptations of his writing is Hugh Leonard's *When the Saints Go Cycling In*, adapted from *The Dalkey Archive*. The correspondence between the authors reveals O'Nolan's involvement in the adaptation at the early conceptual stage – suggesting plots, characters and motifs that might be left intact, cut or altered, vetting Leonard's proposed changes and rearrangements.[92] As their communication continues, we see Leonard slightly taken aback at O'Nolan's tendency towards self-censorship, yet Leonard holds firm to win out on most of his creative choices. The final script includes several significant changes to O'Nolan's novel, including a different ending, which O'Nolan conceded is an improvement on the original.

When the Saints Go Cycling In premiered at the Gate Theatre, Dublin, on 27 September 1965, produced by Gemini Productions in association with Dublin Theatre Festival and directed by Denis Carey, with set design by Alan Pleass. The following cast played at the premiere: Bill Golding (Mick), Newton Blick (De Selby) (Blick 'died suddenly on 13 October, during the run, and was replaced by Joe Lynch' (L, 528, n. 351)), Ronnie Walsh (Joyce), Martin Dempsey (Fottrell), Máire Hastings (Mary), Edward Byrne (Cobble),

Fred Johnson (Augustine), Charles Roberts (Hackett), Isobel Couser (Laverty), Desmond Perry (Crewett). The play was revived by the Gate on 14 February 1984, under the shortened title *The Saints Go Cycling In*, with some revisions to the original script by Leonard himself.[93] This revival was directed by Patrick Laffan, with settings by Alpho O'Reilly and lighting by Albert Cassells, and starred Barry McGovern as Joyce alongside Garrett Keogh (Mick), Aiden Grennell (De Selby) and Jim Bartley (Hackett). Martin Dempsey revived his role as Sergeant Fottrell from the original production. Leonard also adapted the play for radio, in a production that was broadcast on RTÉ Radio 1 on 22 September 1987, featuring Dempsey, as ever, in the role of the Sergeant, alongside Ronnie Walsh and Garvan McGrath. Kurt Palm directed the first German-language stage performance of *When the Saints Go Cycling In*, which premiered in the Alte Reithalle, Vienna on 19 June 1995, starring Martin Puntigam (Fottrell), with costumes by Renato Uz and scenography by Ursula Hübner (set designer on Palm's film adaptation of *At Swim-Two-Birds*), who has posted images of the production in her online archive.[94]

Hull Truck Theatre Company's production of Alan McClelland's adaptation of *The Dalkey Archive* (under the title of O'Nolan's book) toured internationally in 1978–9, including performances at the Bush Theatre, London, the Project Arts Centre, Dublin, the Studio Theatre, Birmingham and the Long Wharf Theatre, New Haven. The production was directed by Mike Bradwell with a cast of Arthur Kelly (Mick), John Blanchard (Joyce), Susie Kelly (Mary), Howard Lew Lewis (Fottrell), Steve Novak (Nemo Crabbe/Augustine) and Oengus MacNamara (whose father, Desmond MacNamara, designed the original jacket cover for the novel), with McClelland in the role of De Selby. Reviews note the musicality of the production; for instance, when Sergeant Fottrell 'mentions the Irish worship' of bicycles, 'the cast breaks into "Master McGrath"', while at another juncture Joyce 'sings and dances' to the ballad 'Finnegan's Wake'.[95] Despite praising the production's 'impeccable sets, costumes and props' – and singling out its staging of the play's 'loquacious bicycles' – Maev Kennedy criticises the adaptation as too deferential to the source material, resulting in a two-and-a-half-hour runtime that drags when Joyce, De Selby or Fottrell are not on stage.[96] Reviewing the run at the Bush Theatre, R.B. Marriott likewise finds the parts of the play without Joyce to be 'tedious', given over to unremarkable 'Irish self-wallowing, off-hand philosophising, and religious comment'.[97] Michael Coveney, by contrast, lauds the decision to have the action 'gravitate around the bar in the Colza hotel' and praises the 'brown atmosphere' created through Gemma Jackson's design as being 'conducive to the strange matter of dialogue between the regulars'.[98]

The Hard Life

Pat Layde's stage adaptation of *The Hard Life* played at the eighteenth Dublin Theatre Festival in September 1976 before premiering on 7 October at the Peacock Theatre, Dublin in a version directed and 'edited' by Alan Simpson. Layde himself played Collopy, alongside Eamon Morrissey (Manus), Philip O'Sullivan (Finbarr), Raymond Hardie (Fahrt), Derek Chapman (Pope) and Micheál Ó hAonghusa (Cardinal Baldini). In a mixed review that treats the play and its source material as a thinly spread 'lavatory joke', Ken Gray singles out Wendy Shea's costumes for praise and applauds 'the ingenious and imaginative ideas' with which Simpson exploits the limited space to elevate the material[99] – including, Con Houlihan writes elsewhere, 'a set so high in part that one was alarmed at the absence of a safety net'.[100] In the *Irish Independent*, Tony Hennigan noted that Collopy's audience with the Pope was 'played with all the macabre of the "Nighttown" sequence of *Ulysses*'.[101] A revival of Layde's adaptation premiered at the Abbey on 6 February 1986 under Patrick Laffan's direction, with Philip O'Sullivan switching to playing the older brother Manus alongside Malcolm Douglas (Finbarr), Philip O'Flynn (Collopy), Eamon Kelly (Fahrt), Eileen Colgan (Annie), Kathleen Barrington (Crotty) and May Cluskey (Claffery). Anne Clissmann contributed a note to the programme. David Nowlan's negative review of the 1986 production echoed Gray's previous evaluation of the material itself, dismissing it as 'a lavatorial load of nonsense' and insisting that the novel 'just doesn't work as a piece of theatre'.[102]

Kerry (Lee) Crabbe attempted to overcome this problem by mixing his adaptation of *The Hard Life* with material from *Cruiskeen Lawn* (such as 'The Catechism of Cliché') in a production for Tricycle Theatre that played in London in September–October 1985 under the title *Flann O'Brien's Hard Life – or, Na Gopaleens Wake*. Crabbe acknowledges that *The Hard Life* is 'not the most satisfactory of the books' and received permission to use O'Nolan's 'brilliant newspaper columns to change the shape of it and beef it up a lot',[103] as well as material from *The Third Policeman* (including the erotic encounter with the bicycle). Terry Stoller describes the premise:

> Flann [...] enters the theatre, voices a protest [against the adaptation and Crabbe himself], but winds up watching a play about his younger self based on his novel. [...] Along with a fellow [drinker], the Plain Man [...], Flann is at a bar raised above the action, looking down on the story [...]. Towards the end of the play, Flann is raised up high above the stage in a fantasy scene in which he is playing Pope Pius X.[104]

Rodney Ford provided the stage design, which comprised 'a Gargantuan bar counter which opens out to reveal a tuppence-coloured domestic interior'[105] and a steel wire network above the stage for Manus's high-wire walking scenes. Mike Bradwell directed a cast which included Dermot Crowley (Flann O'Brien), John Joyce (Plain Man), Paul Boyle (Finbarr), Killian McKenna (Manus), David Blake Kelly (Collopy), Howard Lew Lewis (Fahrt) and Heather Tobias (Annie). In her *Irish Times* review of the adaptation's January–February 1986 revival in the same theatre (but now with Deborah Bestwick as director, Des Nealon as the Plain Man, David Blake Kelly as Collopy and Kate Binchy as Annie), Maeve Binchy reflects that 'Myles na Gopaleen would surely have found it worthy of ironic comment [...] that, twenty years after his death, his book *The Hard Life* would be turned into two different plays and performed simultaneously in London and Dublin'.[106] Binchy's positive review notes that the production was 'much helped by some initial adverse publicity in the form of a protest that the poster was stage Irish and made stereotype and caricature out of Irishmen as drunkards'.[107]

A radio production of *The Hard Life*, read by Brendan Cauldwell, was broadcast by RTÉ Radio 1 in ten-minute instalments through March and April 1984, and a German-language adaptation for radio was broadcast on the South German Radio station from 19 to 26 August of the same year.

Slattery's Sago Saga

The Performance Corporation's production of Arthur Riordan's adaptation, and completion, of O'Nolan's unfinished novel *Slattery's Sago Saga* premiered at Rathfarnham Castle, Dublin, on 16 July 2010. The characters meta-theatrically reference the fact that O'Nolan's source material for Riordan's adaptation was unfinished – with the writer Imelda trying to keep the plot moving on her typewriter despite running out of source material – as they become aware of their status as fictional characters.[108] Harvey O'Brien singles out the direction, designs and performances for praise:

> Director Jo Mangan keeps the energy levels up with lots of cartoony criss-crossing of the small space. Niamh Lunny's costumes are a hoot, from MacPherson's heavy woollen tartan to Imelda's Day-Glo go-go girl hair and dress. [Louis] Lovett is great fun in his four distinctly different roles [Billy Colum/Eustace Baggeley/Aloysius Foley/Ned Hoolihan] [...]. [Clare] Barrett is suitably loathsome and terrifying as [Crawford] MacPherson, [Malcolm] Adams a gentle anchor as the hapless [Tim] Hartigan, [Darragh] Kelly completely at ease [as Sarsfield Slattery] savouring the best of O'Brien's convoluted syntax with a welcome

grin that's always just a shade too wide, and [Lisa] Lambe, when her character [Imelda] finally fully enters proceedings, is, as ever, seemingly born to this type of tone – able to strike a pose with just the right degree of exaggeration to be funny and yet hold the moment.[109]

The show was performed in the round on site at Rathfarnham Castle, beginning outside the venue with a character pulling up to the house in a car, with the audience then following the actor into a large living room inside the castle where the main action was played.

Columns and short fiction

O'Nolan wrote to the Department of Finance on 13 November 1946: 'Quite recently Radio Éireann asked me, in repeated letters, to do a radio feature based on the newspaper work [...]. I refused because I could not find the time, but I eventually agreed to hand over a mass of my existing material so that they could get somebody else to work on it' (*L*, 151). While it is unclear what came of this exchange, the *Cruiskeen Lawn* column was adapted for radio on several occasions both during and after O'Nolan's lifetime. A reading from 'The Brother' was broadcast on RÉ on Christmas Day, 1943;[110] David Kelly's readings of 'The Brother-in-Law' and 'The Holiday' were broadcast on the RTÉ programme *My Choice* in 1975; an extract from *The Hair of the Dogma* and a reading of 'The Workman's Friend' were broadcast on the RTÉ programme *Ballads and Bits* on 7 October 1983; and 'Christmas Cheer from the *Cruiskeen Lawn*' was broadcast on RTÉ Radio on 23 and 26 December 1984. In *The Best of Myles* (BBC Radio 4, 26 May 1980), Jim Norton read five selections from *Cruiskeen Lawn* (including 'The Brother', 'The Plain People of Ireland' and 'Keats and Chapman') which had been adapted for radio by Eric Ewens and produced by Maurice Leitch.

The first major adaptation of the column for the stage was the two-hour Myles na gCopaleen revue *Cruiskeen Lawn*, adapted by Fergus Linehan and directed by Barry Cassin, which premiered at the Eblana Theatre (situated in the basement of Busáras, Dublin's central bus station) on 21 March 1972. The show featured stage design by Paul Funge and starred an ensemble cast of Eamon Morrissey, Máire Hastings, Jimmy Bartley and Robert Carrickford, with Des Nealon as Myles himself. The adaptation included scenarios from 'The Brother', 'The Da', 'The Steam-Man', 'The Catechism of Cliché', 'Keats and Chapman', 'The Plain People of Ireland', 'How to Write a Play for the Abbey' and several 'District Court' scenes, as well as some original song interludes devised by Noel Kelehan not adapted from Myles, such as a song about the building in Trinity College Park. The show took place during an unofficial strike by 800 shift workers in the Electricity Supply Board, who were seeking regrading and pay increases, and continued with special gaslights, reportedly provided by the actor Carrickford.

Maureen White and Mary Durkan's stage adaptation of *The Best of Myles* was produced by Toronto's Nightwood Theatre, Canada's oldest professional women's theatre, and performed at the Rhubarb Festival in November 1980.[111] James Hayes adapted selected *Cruiskeen Lawn* columns for his one-man stage show *A Horde of Unemployed Ventriloquists*, which played at the National Theatre, London, in 1981 with a set that reproduced the front page of *The Irish Times*. The show opened with Myles's attempt to bribe his way into the presidency of WAAMA and included selections from 'The Brother' (for which Hayes donned an old mac and a peaked cap), 'Keats and Chapman', 'Bookhandling', 'Patent Ballet Pumps', 'For Steam Men' (during which Hayes wore his own father's CIE badge) and the ventriloquist 'Escort Service'. Hayes toured the show for several years, including performances at the 1984 Edinburgh Festival, the Gate Theatre Club, Dublin in 1984, and at the Royal Shakespeare Company's black box theatre The Other Place, Stratford-Upon-Avon, in January 1994. *The Bother with the Brother*, a one-man show starring Aidan Jordan which Val O'Donnell adapted from 'The Brother' pieces in *Cruiskeen Lawn*, was presented at Bewley's Café Theatre in October 2011 as part of O'Nolan's centenary celebrations and ran for three weeks. Gerry Smyth's two-man show *The Brother* debuted in Charlie P's, Vienna, at the first night of the 2011 inaugural International Flann O'Brien Society Conference and was subsequently performed in Trieste, Lille, Liverpool, Aberdeen, and at a six-night run at the Edinburgh Free Fringe Festival in August 2012. The play starred Smyth and David Llewellyn, and was directed by Andrew Sherlock, who has written on the challenge of striking the right combination of linguistic dexterity and physicality in adapting O'Nolan's column for the stage.[112] While the play was adapted from *Cruiskeen Lawn*, it ended with Smyth's 'Plain Man' and Llewellyn's put-upon patron singing a version of 'The Workman's Friend' from *At Swim-Two-Birds*.[113]

O'Nolan's short fiction has likewise been adapted for stage, radio and film. In his own lifetime, 'Their Funniest Stories: "John Duffy's Brother", by Flan [*sic*] O'Brien' aired on RÉ as an hour-long programme on 15 March 1940, while O'Nolan's correspondence suggests that he adapted 'Two in One' as a radio play (*L*, 181, n. 63) and as the stage script/teleplay *The Dead Spit of Kelly*. Gerard Lee's one-man adaptation of 'Two in One', titled *The Living Spit of Kelly*, accompanied by cellist Vivienne Long, served as the

curtain-raiser for Gerry Stembridge's *Daniel's Hands* at the City Arts Centre
in April 1994. Mikel Murfi and Mark O'Halloran performed a dramatic
reading of 'John Duffy's Brother' at Università Roma Tre and O'Halloran
performed a dramatic reading of 'Two in One' at the Fiddler's Elbow, Rome,
both as part of the 2013 International Flann O'Brien Society Conference. A
full recording of LILT's 2017 one-man stage adaptation of *The Dead Spit of
Kelly* (adapted by Gerry Smyth, directed by David Llewllyn, performed by
Thomas Galashan) is available online.[114] Park Films have produced two film
adaptations of O'Nolan's short fiction: *John Duffy's Brother* (2006), adapted
for the screen by Eoghan Nolan and directed by Mikel Murfi, starring Mark
O'Halloran and narrated by Michael Gambon, and *The Martyr's Crown* (2007),
directed by Rory Bresnihan and starring David Kelly, Brian Cox and Alan
Devlin. A film adaptation of 'Two in One', adapted for the screen by Johnny
Ferguson under the title *The Dead Spit of Kelly*, is currently slated as being in
pre-production, to be directed by Iain Softley and starring Jason Isaacs, Jessica
Barden and Colin Morgan.

Anthology shows and bioplays

A notable strand of O'Nolan adaptation is the anthology or variety show
comprising short excerpts from his columns and novels. Maeve Binchy, for
instance, observed the prevalence of Myles anthology shows on the London
stage in the mid-1980s at the same time as 'the radio producers in the BBC
[were] having a renewed attack of Myles fever'.[115] Around St Patrick's Day
1985 she noted three separate productions: *RTÉ Players Flann O'Brien Show*,
scripted and presented by Brendan Caldwell and Brendan O'Duill at the
Tricycle Theatre; *Yer Man and the Brother*, a sixty-minute one-man anthology
sketch show by Tom McCabe (also at the Tricycle, before touring London
theatres throughout 1986; the original production premiered at Walpole Hall
on 10 August 1984),[116] which included an adaptation of the short story 'Two in
One' alongside selections from the novels and columns; and Hayes's *A Horde
of Unemployed Ventriloquists*, at the Irish Club in Eaton Square. Binchy reflects:
'It would be very hard to live in London today and not know about Myles.'[117]

The anthology template was pioneered by John Ryan, who produced and
arranged *An Evening with Myles na gCopaleen*, which premiered 8 September
1968 at the Abbey Theatre. The first part of the show consisted of adaptations
from *The Best of Myles* (including sketches based on excerpts from 'The
Brother' and 'The Catechism of Cliché') performed by Ryan, Ronnie Walsh
and Seán Mac Réamoinn, alongside Irish-language columns delivered by

Mac Réamoinn and Niall Tóibín; the second part of the show staged 'the Bicycle Syndrome sequence' from *The Third Policeman* starring Pat Layde and Michael Hennessy.[118] Eamon Morrissey established this anthology format as a theatrical standard for O'Nolan adaptations with his one-man-show *The Brother*, which he adapted from excerpts of *Cruiskeen Lawn*, *At Swim-Two-Birds*, *The Third Policeman*, 'The Martyr's Crown' and 'Two in One' and which he performed while working through a steady supply of balls of malt and pints of porter. Morrissey's show was first performed at the Abbey Theatre, Peacock Stage, Dublin, on 18 February 1974, directed by Gerry Sullivan, with lighting by Robert Carrickford. Alongside Morrissey's adaptation and performance, critics praised Sullivan's set design for the play's pub setting; made of 'old wood and tinted glass',[119] it was hailed as a 'jewel' which 'combined the best-loved features of all the best-loved old bars' of Dublin.[120] Morrissey adapted *The Brother* for television in a 1975 production by Little Bird and RTÉ, which was directed by Declan Lowney and produced by Jane Doolan, with Morrissey reprising his ensemble roles and Karl O'Neill playing 'The Hand'. Morrissey toured *The Brother* throughout the world over the next four decades and would write other stage shows using different excerpts from across O'Nolan's works, including *And the Brother Too*, which premiered at the Tricycle Theatre in 1999.

Val O'Donnell has written about Morrissey's influence on the O'Nolan anthology shows he devised for the stage.[121] O'Donnell's *Time, Gentlemen, Pleaaase!*, which draws from both the novels and columns, was presented by the Dublin Shakespeare Society at Theatre @36, Dublin, in 2006 and revived in 2007. O'Donnell's latest anthology show, *Flann's Yer Only Man*, intersperses information about O'Nolan's life with material from the columns and novels. It was performed at over twenty-five venues around Ireland between 2013 and 2017 – including the Listowel Writers' Week festival in 2013 and the Smock Alley Theatre, Dublin, in May 2017 – and at the Shakespeare, Salzburg in July 2017, as part of the fourth International Flann O'Brien Conference. The enduring popularity of the O'Nolan anthology show for Irish theatres was demonstrated by the success of *Thirst (and other bits of Flann)*, which was developed by and starred Garret Lombard, Aaron Monaghan, Rory Nolan and Marty Rea, and performed at the Peacock Theatre, Dublin, in December 2018.

The RTÉ programme *Anthology: The worlds of Flann O'Brien* was the first anthology adaptation of O'Nolan's works for television, broadcast on 18 November 1970 under the direction of Aindrias Ó Gallchóir. Devised for television and presented by Niall Sheridan, the show featured studio dramatisations from *At Swim-Two-Birds*, *The Third Policeman* and *Cruiskeen Lawn* performed by Niall Tóibín, Martin Dempsey, David Kelly, Arthur O'Sullivan, Chris Curran, Des Perry, John Molloy, Derry Power, Jim Bartley and Eamon Morrissey. *40 Myles On: A night of Irish comedy* (produced by AnneMarie Naughton for Park Films, 2007) was a filmed live performance at Vicar Street, Dublin to mark the fortieth anniversary of O'Nolan's death. The performance placed comedy stand-up (Tommy Tiernan, John Lynn) alongside an ensemble cast (Barry Murphy, Kevin Gildea, Aiden Jordan, Jack Lynch, Eamonn Hunt, Ciaran Taylor, Tomás Ó Súilleabháin) that performed excerpts from and sketches based on *Cruiskeen Lawn*, including 'The Catechism of Cliché' and 'Bores', with Jon Kenny from d'Unbelievables as the Sergeant in an abridged version of *Thirst*, and author Patrick McCabe performing scenes from *The Third Policeman*. The broadcast version includes filmed segments of David Kelly reading from *Cruiskeen Lawn*.

Eamonn Morrissey's ten-part radio series *Myles Apart*, which dramatically staged excerpts from across O'Nolan's novels and columns, was broadcast on RTÉ, first in six parts from 4 March to 7 April 1979 and then in four parts from 18 May to 8 June 1980. The framing device for the programme is a dialogue between Myles, Yer Man and The Plain People of Ireland, which sets up the readings from the novels and cuts them off, often through abrupt interruptions. The approach allows for a good deal of fluidity between the works, as Myles enters into dialogues with characters from the Flann O'Brien novels such as Jem Casey and Sergeant Pluck. *The Cruiskeen Lawn* (BBC Radio 4, broadcast in two parts, 13 and 20 August 1997), adapted for radio by Owen Dudley Edwards and produced by David Batchelor, dramatised extracts from O'Nolan's fiction and columns (including *At Swim-Two-Birds* and Myles's description of his face's beauty from *Cruiskeen Lawn*), performed by voice actors Dan Reardon, Gerry O'Brien, Brendan Cauldwell, Jonathan White, Luke Griffin, Malcolm Douglas and Deirdre Monaghan.[122]

The template of mixing readings from the author's work with narrated biography has been followed in several television and radio productions. *Flann O'Brien: Man of parts*, a television profile of the author which was broadcast on RTÉ on 20 March 1977, included dramatisations, of approximately ten minutes each, of *At Swim-Two-Birds* and *The Hard Life*. For the radio, *Discords of Good Humour: A portrait of Brian O'Nolan*, written and narrated by Aidan Higgins (BBC Radio 3, 13 October 1981, produced by Maurice Leitch) featured readings from *The Poor Mouth*, *The Third Policeman* and *The Best of Myles* by Jim Norton alongside the voices of Ciarán Ó Nualláin, Kevin

O'Nolan (Caoimhín Ó Nualláin), Liam Redmond (Liam Mac Réamoinn), Barbara Redmond, Ben Kiely, Timothy O'Keeffe, John Ryan, Arthur Power and Anthony Cronin.[123] Maurice Sweeney's documentary *Flann O'Brien: The lives of Brian* is narrated by Brendan Gleeson, and mixes biographical documentary with talking heads (Anthony Cronin, Tommy Tiernan, Micheál Ó Nualláin, Carol Taaffe) and fictional sketches featuring O'Nolan's *personae*, starring Tom Hickey (Myles na gCopaleen), Dermot O'Hara (Flann O'Brien/Brian O'Nolan) and Maurice O'Donoghue (voice of Flann O'Brien). Annie Caulfield's radio play *Your Only Man* (31 August 2008) imagines a meeting between the biographical Brian O'Nolan (Ardal O'Hanlon) and his *personae* Flann O'Brien (Dermot Crowley) and Myles na gCopaleen (Dara Ó Briain) on the day he was asked to leave his civil service post, with Pauline McLynn as Evelyn O'Nolan/Miss Fahy and Lloyd Hutchinson playing the rest of the roles. David O'Kane's multilingual 2008 short film *Babble* depicts Flann O'Brien, Franz Kafka and Jorge Luis Borges conversing through quotations from their literature in their native tongues.

In 2016, the Irish-language broadcaster TG4 aired *Flann O'Brien: An béal saibhir*, a documentary, directed by Brian Reddin, on O'Nolan and his works that combines dramatic readings and interviews with Irish-language scholars. Cleverality's 2017 radio docudrama *Bones of Contention: Flann O'Brien*, written by Marc-Ivan O'Gorman and produced by Eoin O'Kelly for Lyric FM, tweaks the formula by mixing assessments of the writer from Louis de Paor, Julian Gough, Patrick McCabe, Blindboy Boatclub, Eamon Morrissey, David McSavage, Tommy Tiernan and Ardal O'Hanlon 'with a suitably twisty plot that sees a local newspaper reporter, George Knowall (another O'Nolan pen-name), attempt a *Citizen Kane*-style precis after the writer's death, in 1966'.[124] This fantastical use of O'Nolan or his *personae* as characters in historical or fictional situations is realised on the stage in Arthur Riordan and Bell Helicopter's Rough Magic musical satire *Improbable Frequency* (premiered at the O'Reilly Theatre, Dublin, 27 September 2004), in which 'Myles na gCopaleen' (played by Darragh Kelly) appears as a character alongside Erwin Schrödinger in 1941 Dublin, and in Gerry Smyth's *Will the Real Flann O'Brien …? A life in five scenes* (performed at Divadlo Na Prádle, Prague, on 18 September 2015 as part of the third International Flann O'Brien Society Conference), in which the biographical O'Nolan encounters comically exaggerated versions of historical literary figures (Ernie O'Malley, James Joyce, Samuel Beckett) as well as his own critics.

Epilogue

Until the present volume, the theatrical debts and performative qualities of O'Nolan's broader aesthetic may have been neglected in O'Nolan studies due to the critical marginalisation of his writing for performance. Yet, as this overview has shown, the performative, dramatic and theatrical qualities of his art have long been evidenced by productions, adaptations and creative receptions of his writing for the stage, radio and screen. In their diversity of approaches to the material, these productions demonstrate the potential that O'Nolan's writing carries in diverse sites of performance and contexts of reception – may they, like other aspects of his cultural and critical legacy, be oft revived.

Notes

Introduction

1 Myles na Gopaleen, 'De Me', *New Ireland: Magazine of the New Ireland Society of the Queen's University of Belfast*, no. 2, March 1964, pp. 41–2.

2 Catherine Flynn, 'Everybody Here Is under Arrest: Translation and politics in *Cruiskeen Lawn*', in Ruben Borg and Paul Fagan (eds), *Flann O'Brien: Gallows humour* (Cork: Cork University Press, 2020), p. 9.

3 Mikhail Bakhtin, *Rabelais and His World*, Hélène Iswolsky (trans.) (Bloomington: Indiana University Press, 1984), p. 3.

4 Thomas F. Shea, *Flann O'Brien's Exorbitant Novels* (Lewisburg: Bucknell University Press, 1992), p. 12.

5 na Gopaleen, 'De Me', p. 42.

6 Ibid.

7 Carl G. Jung, 'Anima and Animus', in Shelley Saguaro (ed.), *Psychoanalysis and Woman: A reader* (New York: New York University Press, 2000), p. 161.

8 Gregory A. Staley, *Seneca and the Idea of Tragedy* (Oxford: Oxford University Press, 2010), p. 52. For the medieval concept of *imago* as *mimesis*, see Brigitte Bedos-Rezak, *When Ego Was Imago: Signs of identity in the Middle Ages* (Leiden: Brill, 2011), p. 172. 'Mimesis' in the sense of imitation (*imitatio*) shares the same Latin root (*imitari*) as 'image' (*imago*).

9 Yaeli Greenblatt, '"the tattered cloak of his perished skin": The body as costume in 'Two in One', *At Swim-Two-Birds* and *The Third Policeman*', in Borg and Fagan (eds), *Flann O'Brien: Gallows humour*, pp. 131–45.

10 For more on O'Nolan's engagement with the Ovidian topos of metamorphosis, see Paul Fagan, '"I've got you under my skin": "John Duffy's Brother", "Two in One" and the confessions of Narcissus', in Ruben Borg, Paul Fagan and Werner Huber (eds), *Flann O'Brien: Contesting legacies* (Cork: Cork University Press, 2014), pp. 60–75; and Noam Schiff, '"the situation had become deplorably fluid": Alcohol, alchemy and Brian O'Nolan's metamorphoses', in Borg and Fagan (eds), *Flann O'Brien: Gallows humour*, pp. 116–30.

11 Maebh Long, 'Flann O'Brien: Man of (many) letters, man of many masks', *The Irish Times*, 26 April 2018, https://www.irishtimes.com/culture/books/flann-o-brien-man-of-many-letters-man-of-many-masks-1.3475060.

12 The precursor to the Abbey, the Irish National Theatre Society, premiered J.M. Synge's *Riders to the Sea* at the Molesworth Hall in February 1904. Following its Abbey premiere on 20 January 1906, *Riders to the Sea* remained a staple of the theatre's stage and touring repertoire for decades, including an extensive American tour in 1932–3. George Shiels's three-act romantic comedy *Professor Tim* premiered in the Abbey on 14 September 1925 and was subsequently either staged or toured by the Abbey every year until 1939 (with gaps only in 1935 and 1937), with a number of American dates between 1931 and '33.

13 Flann O'Brien, 'Ideals for an Irish Theatre', *The Irish Times*, 15 October 1938, p. 7.

14 Keith Hopper, *Flann O'Brien: A portrait of the artist as a young post-modernist* (Cork: Cork University Press, 1995), p. 35.

15 *CL*, 26 February 1943, p. 3.

16 *CL*, 2 January 1957, p. 6.

17 *CL*, 25 January 1952, p. 4; 26 January 1952, p. 9; 28 January 1952, p. 4; 30 January 1952, p. 4; 1 February 1952, p. 6; 4 February 1952, p. 6. The apology is issued in *The Irish Times*, 5 March 1952, p. 3. See Catherine O. Ahearn, '"Where you bin, bud?": Myles na gCopaleen's disappearing act', in Borg and Fagan (eds), *Flann O'Brien: Gallows humour*, p. 109.

18 *CL*, 8 December 1941, p. 2.

19 *CL*, 19 September 1941, p. 2.

20 *CL*, 8 December 1941, p. 2.

21 *CL*, 15 October 1941, p. 2.

22 *CL*, 12 October 1944, p. 3.

23 *CL*, 28 August 1956, p. 8.

24 *CL*, 10 September 1957, p. 6.

25 See, for instance, Amy Nejezchleb, 'O'Brien's Your Man: Myles, modernity and Irish national television', in Jennika Baines (ed.), *'Is it about a bicycle?' Flann O'Brien in the twenty-first century* (Dublin: Four Courts Press, 2011), pp. 98–111; Stefan Solomon, '"The outward accidents of illusion": O'Brien and the theatrical', in Julian Murphet, Rónán McDonald and Sascha Morrell (eds), *Flann O'Brien & Modernism* (London: Bloomsbury, 2014), pp. 41–54; Thierry Robin, 'Tall Tales or "Petites Histoires": History and the void in "The Martyr's Crown" and *Thirst*', in Borg, Fagan and Huber (eds), *Flann O'Brien: Contesting legacies*, pp. 76–92; Daniel Keith Jernigan, '"Simulato Ergo Est": Brian O'Nolan's metaperformative simulations', *New Hibernia Review*, vol. 21, no. 1, spring 2016, pp. 87–104; Maebh Long, '"No more drunk, truculent, witty, celtic, dark, desperate, amorous paddies!": Brian O'Nolan and the Irish stereotype', in Ruben Borg, Paul Fagan and John McCourt (eds), *Flann O'Brien: Problems with authority* (Cork: Cork University Press, 2017), pp. 34–53; Schiff, '"the situation had become deplorably fluid"', pp. 124–8; Ondřej Pilný, 'The Brothers Čapek at the Gate: *R.U.R.* and *The Insect Play*', in Ondřej Pilný, Ruud van den Beuken and Ian R. Walsh (eds), *Cultural Convergence: The Dublin Gate Theatre, 1928–1960* (Cham: Palgrave Macmillan, 2021), pp. 141–73.

26 Clair Wills, *That Neutral Island: A history of Ireland during the Second World War* (London: Faber & Faber, 2007), p. 305.

27 Terence Brown, *Ireland: A social and cultural history 1922–2002* (London: Harper Perennial, 2004), p. 167. My thanks to Tobias W. Harris for bringing these contexts and sources to my attention – see his doctoral thesis *Dublin's Dadaist: Brian O'Nolan, the European avant-garde and Irish cultural production* (Birkbeck College, University of London, 2020), pp. 152–3, and the 2020 podcast he hosted with Joseph Brooker, *Upstaging Ireland: The theatre of Flann O'Brien*, https://soundcloud.com/birkbeck-podcasts/upstaging-ireland-the-theatre-of-flann-obrien.

28 Ronald J. Pelias, *Performance Studies: The interpretation of aesthetic texts* (New York: St Martin's Press, 1992), p. 15.

29 In 'Behan, Master of Language', an obituary piece published in *The Sunday Telegraph*, 22 March 1964, Flann O'Brien asserts that Behan 'was, in fact, much more a player than a playwright'. See Paul Fagan, 'Secret Scriptures: Brendan Behan in the *Cruiskeen Lawn*', in John McCourt (ed.), *Reading Brendan Behan* (Cork: Cork University Press, 2019), pp. 183–4.

30 Welles first appeared in the Edwards-directed production of *Jew Süss*, Ashley Dukes's adaptation of Lion Feuchtwanger's novel, which ran from 13 to 31 October 1931, and starred in and directed numerous plays in Dublin theatres throughout 1931–2.

31 'Shows and Showers' in the 1942 *Jack-in-the-Box* programme notes, p. 5 (McCormick, Northwestern University).

32 The time is ripe for re-evaluating O'Nolan's role in this performance network given the recent publication of a number of significant critical studies of the Gate Theatre. As well as Pilný, van den Beuken and Walsh (eds), *Cultural Convergence*, see David Clare, Des Lally and Patrick Lonergan (eds), *The Gate Theatre, Dublin: Inspiration and craft* (Oxford: Peter Lang, 2018); Ruud van den Beuken, *Avant-Garde Nationalism at the Dublin Gate Theatre, 1928–1940* (New York: Syracuse University Press, 2021); and Marguérite Corporaal and Ruud van den Beuken (eds), *A Stage of Emancipation: Change and progress at the Dublin Gate Theatre* (Oxford: Oxford University Press, 2021).

33 Graham Greene, Reader's Report on *At Swim-Two-Birds* for Longmans, Green & Co., reprinted in Rüdiger Imhof (ed.), *Alive-Alive O! Flann O'Brien's At Swim-Two-Birds* (Dublin: Wolfhound Press, 1985), p. 41.

34 Jorge Luis Borges, 'When Fiction Lives in Fiction', in *Selected Non-Fictions*, Eliot Weinberger (ed.) (New York: Penguin, 1999), pp. 160–2; Anne Clissmann, *Flann O'Brien: A critical introduction to his writings* (Dublin: Gill & Macmillan, 1975), p. 354; Keith Hopper, *Flann O'Brien: A portrait of the artist as a young post-modernist*, 2nd edn, J. Hillis Miller (foreword) (Cork: Cork University Press, 2009), pp. 93–4, 110.

35 Solomon, 'O'Brien and the theatrical', pp. 41–54.

36 See Conor Dowling, 'Carnival and Class Consciousness: Bakhtin and the Free State in *At Swim-Two-Birds*', in Borg and Fagan (eds), *Flann O'Brien: Gallows humour*, p. 55.

37 For a detailed discussion of the Euripides epigraph to *At Swim-Two-Birds*, see Tobias W. Harris and Joseph LaBine, 'John Garvin and Brian O'Nolan in Civil Service: Bureaucratic, Joycean modernism', *The Parish Review: Journal of Flann O'Brien studies*, vol. 6, no. 1, spring 2022, pp. 5–8.

38 For a discussion of comic and tragic form in 'John Duffy's Brother', see Ruben Borg, *Fantasies of Self-Mourning: Modernism, the posthuman and the finite* (Leiden and Boston: Brill | Rodopi, 2019), pp. 161–4.

39 Richard Schechner, *Performance Studies: An introduction* (London: Routledge, 2002), p. 22.

40 Maebh Long, *Assembling Flann O'Brien* (London: Bloomsbury, 2014), p. 3.

41 Elin Diamond, 'Introduction', in Elin Diamond (ed.), *Performance and Cultural Politics* (New York: Routledge, 1996), p. 1.

1. Plagiarism and the Politics of Friendship

1 *CL*, 4 August 1945, p. 3.

2 *CL*, 20 July 1945, p. 3.

3 *CL*, 3 March 1954, p. 4.

4 *CL*, 2 October 1954, p. 2.

5 *CL*, 3 March 1954, p. 4.

6 The use of Coleridge in the August 1945 column is particularly apt, as Coleridge has long been associated with unacknowledged borrowings: in particular, *Biographia Literaria* was described by De Quincey as a '"barefaced" plagiarism' of Schelling. Qtd in Tilar J. Mazzeo, *Plagiarism and Literary Property in the Romantic Period* (Philadelphia: University of Pennsylvania Press, 2004), p. 23.

7 Niall Sheridan, 'Brian, Flann and Myles', in Timothy O'Keeffe (ed.), *Myles: Portraits of Brian O'Nolan* (London: Martin, Brian & O'Keeffe, 1973), p. 35.

8 The character's name Brinsley is a reference to the playwright Richard Brinsley Sheridan.

9 Ibid., pp. 40–1.

10 Niall Montgomery, *Niall Montgomery: Dublinman – Selected writings*, Christine O'Neil (ed.) (Dublin: Ashfield Press, 2015), p. 93. For the letters themselves see James Johnson Sweeney to Montgomery, 1 December 1950, National Library of Ireland, Niall Montgomery Papers

(hereafter NLI NMP) 50,118.26.22, and Edwin O'Connor to Montgomery, NLI NMP MS 50,118.26.41.

11 Sheridan to Timothy O'Keeffe, 24 November 1971, Folder 8.1, 1993.002, Timothy O'Keeffe Papers 1948–82, McFarlin Library, the University of Tulsa.

12 Terence de Vere White, 'Smyllie and His People', *The Irish Times*, 14 June 1984, p. 12.

13 Anthony Cronin, *No Laughing Matter: The life and times of Flann O'Brien* (New York: Fromm International, 1998), pp. 181–2.

14 Keith Donohue, *The Irish Anatomist: A study of Flann O'Brien* (Dublin: Maunsel, 2002), p. 8.

15 Carol Taaffe, *Ireland Through the Looking-Glass: Flann O'Brien, Myles na gCopaleen and Irish cultural debate* (Cork: Cork University Press, 2008), pp. 163–6.

16 Montgomery, *Dublinman*, p. 93.

17 Taaffe, *Ireland Through the Looking-Glass*, p. 163.

18 Montgomery to Terence de Vere White, 16 August 1968, NLI NMP 50,118.22.5.

19 Niall Sheridan, 'Brian O'Nolan: A postscript', *Meanjin*, vol. 30, no. 2, 1971, p. 240.

20 Sheridan, 'Brian, Flann and Myles', p. 51.

21 Niall Sheridan, 'Matter of Life and Death', *Esquire*, October 1939, p. 110.

22 Ibid.

23 Ibid., p. 97.

24 Ibid.

25 Sheridan to Montgomery, n.d., NLI NMP 50,118/26/2.

26 M.K., 'Seven Men and a Dog', *The Irish Times*, 29 April 1958, p. 8.

27 *CL*, 29 October 1955, p. 10.

28 Niall Sheridan, 'Seven for a Secret', The National Library of Ireland, MS 29,491, p. 82.

29 Ibid., p. 87.

30 Correspondence between Niall Montgomery and Uinseann MacEoin, NLI NMP 50,118.23.30.

31 The 'flit' refers to the move from 81 Merrion Avenue to 10 Belmont Avenue.

32 Montgomery to *The Irish Architect and Contractor*, LTE, unpublished, *c.* 27 August 1956, NLI NMP 50,118.23.30.

33 See Montgomery, *Dublinman*, pp. 94–7.

34 See John Doherty, 'Memory Lane', Letters to the Editor, *The Irish Times*, 15 September 2017, p. 15.

35 Rosemary Lane, 'The Liberties', *The Irish Times*, 28 January 1964, p. 8.

36 Montgomery to O'Donovan, 13 March 1964, NLI NMP 50,118.6.2.

37 O'Donovan to Montgomery, telephone message, 12 August 1964, NLI NMP 50,118.6.3.

38 Montgomery to O'Donovan, NLI NMP 50,118.6.3. Rosemary Lane remained a regular correspondent in the letters pages. Her initials were also used to sign an article entitled 'Cocktails and Liqueurs and All' that Donal O'Donovan asked Montgomery to write in 1964 but which did not appear in *The Irish Times* until 29 July 1969.

39 Niall Montgomery, 'An Aristophanic Sorcerer', *The Irish Times*, 2 April 1966, p. 7.

40 Niall Montgomery, *The New Republic*, vol. 178, no. 7, 18 February 1978, p. 34.

41 See Catherine O. Ahearn, '"Where you bin, bud?" Myles na gCopaleen's disappearing act', in Ruben Borg and Paul Fagan (eds), *Flann O'Brien: Gallows humour* (Cork: Cork University Press, 2020), pp. 97–115.

2. The *Cruiskeen Lawn* Revue

1 *CL*, 25 February 1955, p. 6.

2 Peggy Phelan, *Mourning Sex: Performing public memories* (London: Routledge, 1997), p. 2.

3 *CL*, 4 October 1954, p. 4.

4 Dick McCaw, *Bakhtin and Theatre: Dialogues with Stanislavsky, Meyerhold and Grotowski* (London: Routledge, 2016), p. 7. This reduction of Bakhtin's work mentions Stanislavsky, but not Meyerhold.

5 Lionel Pilkington, *Theatre & Ireland* (Basingstoke: Palgrave Macmillan, 2010), p. 5.

6 Gabriel Fallon, 'The Future of the Irish Theatre', *Studies: An Irish quarterly review*, vol. 44, no. 173, 1955, p. 94.

7 W.B. Yeats, 'The Irish Literary Theatre' (1899), in *Uncollected Prose of W.B. Yeats, Vol. 2: Reviews, articles and other miscellaneous prose*, J.P. Frayne and C. Johnson (eds) (London: Macmillan, 1975), p. 141.

8 See Pilkington on Matthew Arnold's description of the Irish people as an apt description of the actor, *Theatre & Ireland*, p. 5.

9 Andreas Huyssen, 'Mass Culture as a Woman: Modernism's other', in Tania Modleski (ed.), *Studies in Entertainment: Critical approaches to mass culture* (Bloomington: Indiana University Press, 1986), pp. 188–207.

10 Helen Freshwater, *Theatre and Audience* (London: Palgrave Macmillan, 2009), pp. 2–3.

11 Richard Butsch and Sonia Livingstone, 'Introduction: "Translating" audience, provincializing Europe', in Richard Butsch and Sonia Livingstone (eds), *Meanings of Audiences: Comparative discourses* (London: Routledge, 2014), p. 9.

12 Ibid. See also Jeffrey Schnapp and Mathew Tiews (eds), *Crowds* (Stanford: Stanford University Press, 2006).

13 Butsch and Livingstone, 'Introduction', p. 9.

14 Ibid.

15 Ibid.

16 Mary Poovey, 'Creative Criticism: Adaptation, performative writing and the problem of objectivity', *Narrative*, vol. 8, no. 2, May 2000, p. 126.

17 Martin Puchner, *Stage Fright: Modernism, anti-theatricality and drama* (Baltimore: Johns Hopkins University Press, 2002), pp. 3–6.

18 Ibid., p. 3.

19 Ibid., p. 5.

20 Ibid., pp. 4–5.

21 Kathleen Heininge, *Buffoonery in Irish Drama: Staging twentieth-century post-colonial stereotypes* (New York: Peter Lang), p. 89.

22 *CL*, 25 February 1955, p. 6.

23 See Maebh Long, '"No more drunk, truculent, witty, celtic, dark, desperate, amorous paddies!": Brian O'Nolan and the Irish stereotype', in Ruben Borg, Paul Fagan and John McCourt (eds), *Flann O'Brien: Problems with authority* (Cork: Cork University Press, 2017), pp. 34–53.

24 *CL*, 4 October 1954, p. 4.

25 Poovey, 'Creative Criticism', p. 123. Poovey provides a fascinating overview of how narratives have been defined over the years as either dramatic, objective or critical, noting that by the 1850s it had become a 'critical commonplace that novels should be praised as "dramatic" when they "showed" their action or created a "world"' (ibid., p. 112).

26 J.L. Austin, *How to Do Things with Words* (Cambridge: Harvard University Press, 1975), p. 22.

27 Heininge, *Buffoonery in Irish Drama*, p. 121.

28 Ibid.

29 *CL*, 4 October 1954, p. 4.

30 McCaw, *Bakhtin and Theatre*, p. 7.

31 Adrian Frazier, qtd in Heininge, *Buffoonery in Irish Drama*, p. 8.

32 *CL*, 28 August 1942, p. 3.

33 *CL*, 27 August 1956, p. 6.

34 Ibid.

35 Ibid.

36 *CL*, 30 March 1951, p. 4.

37 Candida, 'An Irishwoman's Diary', *The Irish Times*, 28 April 1950, p. 5.

38 For example, in America, Irish immigrants were apparently mobilised to riot on opening nights of Synge, O'Casey and others, in a public performance of national identity and outrage.

39 Candida, 'An Irishwoman's Diary', *The Irish Times*, 28 April 1950, p. 5.

40 *CL*, 20 May 1949, p. 4.

41 *CL*, 24 April 1950, p. 3.

42 Robert Hogan writes that an 'ultra-right-wing Catholic organisation staged a demonstration' and the protest, with no popular support, dwindled. Robert Hogan, *After the Irish Renaissance* (Minneapolis: University of Minnesota Press, 1967), p. 75.

43 Fallon, 'The Future of the Irish Theatre', p. 94. Yeats, *Dramatis Personae,* p. 180, qtd in Fallon, ibid.

44 *CL*, 24 April 1950, p. 3.

45 Ibid.

46 Ibid.

47 Ibid.

48 *CL*, 30 March 1951, p. 4.

3. 'That poaching scoundrel'

1 Fintan O'Toole, 'Making a Botch of Boucicault', *The Irish Times*, 28 July 1990, p. 5.

2 Elizabeth Butler Cullingford, 'National Identities in Performance: The stage Englishman of Boucicault's Irish drama', *Theatre Journal*, vol. 49, no. 3, October 1997, p. 290.

3 Robert Welch (ed.), *The Oxford Companion to Irish Literature* (Oxford: Oxford University Press, 2001), p. 57.

4 See Richard Barlow, 'Dion Boucicault, *Arrah-na-Pogue* and Stage Irishry in *Finnegans Wake*', in Paul Fagan, Dieter Fuchs and Tamara Radak (eds), *Stage Irish: Performance, identity, cultural circulation*, *Irish Studies in Europe*, vol. 10 (Trier: Wissenschaftlicher Verlag Trier, 2021), pp. 73–85.

5 O'Nolan was not the first to use a Boucicault-derived pen-name in *The Irish Times*. One reader uses the name 'Myles na Coppaleen' in 1864, asking the newspaper 'to advocate the reduction of the prices of admission to the Theatre Royal' to 'enable many hard-working artisans to witness the performance of *Arrah na Pogue*'. Myles na Coppaleen, 'The Rate of Admission to the Theatre Royal', Letters to the Editor, *The Irish Times*, 8 November 1864, p. 3.

6 Hugh Kenner, *A Colder Eye: The modern Irish writers* (Baltimore: Johns Hopkins University Press, 1989), p. 10.

7 For recent considerations of O'Nolan's work in contexts such as the Irish Civil War, biopolitics and international politics, see Ruben Borg, Paul Fagan and Werner Huber (eds), *Flann O'Brien: Contesting legacies* (Cork: Cork University Press, 2014); Ruben Borg, Paul Fagan, and John McCourt (eds), *Flann O'Brien: Problems with authority* (Cork: Cork University Press, 2017); and Ruben Borg and Paul Fagan (eds), *Flann O'Brien: Gallows humour* (Cork: Cork University Press, 2020).

8 Declan Kiberd, *Inventing Ireland: The literature of a modern nation* (London: Vintage, 1996), pp. 497–8.

9 Boucicault's plays frequently include loan words from 'the native tongue' and distinctly Hiberno-English terms.

10 Cullingford, 'National Identities in Performance', p. 287.

11 Seamus Deane, *et al.* (eds), *The Field Day Anthology of Irish Writing Volume II* (Derry: Field Day Publications, 1991), p. 234.

12 Anon., 'Theatre Royal – *Arrah na Pogue*', *The Irish Times*, 8 November 1864, p. 3.

13 However, Boucicault's Irish plays were received in Ireland as the appearance of a 'long-awaited national drama'. Deirdre McFeely, *Dion Boucicault: Irish identity on stage* (Cambridge: Cambridge University Press, 2012), p. 28.

14 Christopher Morash, *A History of Irish Theatre, 1601–2000* (Cambridge: Cambridge University Press, 2002), p. 13.

15 Augusta Gregory, *Our Irish Theatre* (Gerrards Cross: Colin Smythe, 1972), p. 20.

16 W.B. Yeats qtd in Stephen Watt, 'Late Nineteenth-Century Irish Theatre: Before the Abbey – and beyond', in Shaun Richards (ed.), *The Cambridge Companion to Twentieth-Century Irish Drama* (Cambridge: Cambridge University Press, 2004), p. 19.

17 Welch (ed.), *The Oxford Companion*, p. 57.

18 John P. Harrington (ed.), *Modern and Contemporary Irish Drama: Backgrounds and criticism*, 2nd edn (New York: W.W. Norton & Company, 2008).

19 See Stephen Watt, 'The Inheritance of Melodrama', in Nicholas Grene and Chris Morash (eds), *The Oxford Handbook of Modern Irish Theatre* (Oxford: Oxford University Press, 2016), pp. 9–23, and Nicholas Grene and Chris Morash, 'Modern Irish Theatre: A chronology', in ibid., pp. xxvi–xxx.

20 Nicholas Daly, 'The Many Lives of the Colleen Bawn: Pastoral suspense', *Journal of Victorian Culture*, vol. 12, no. 1, spring 2007, p. 13. According to Daly, 'Peter Brooks showed some years ago that melodrama is a theatrical mode that arises alongside the advent of the political modernity of the French Revolution, and subsequent critics have refined and adapted [...] that theory in a number of ways, suggesting, for example, that it is the social modernity of the city that melodrama captures and perhaps even assimilates, or that it provides a form of public sphere for an emergent consumer culture' (ibid., pp. 12–13). In the case of *The Colleen Bawn*, 'modernity arrives cloaked in a version of pastoral' (ibid., p. 14).

21 Qtd in Anthony Cronin, *No Laughing Matter: The life and times of Flann O'Brien* (London: Grafton, 1989), p. 134.

22 Cullingford, 'National Identities in Performance', p. 290.

23 McFeely, *Dion Boucicault*, p. 21. Discussing the play's impact in London, Daly notes that 'the public rushed to buy sheet music – Colleen Bawn galops, quadrilles, polkas and waltzes – that they could play at home on the piano; they wore red "Colleen-Bawn cloaks" inspired by Eily's costume; and they had to deal with the traffic jams generated by hundreds of "Colleen cabs" lined up in the Strand. In short, [...] this "sensation drama" was rapidly assimilated into the cultural bloodstream of the city' (ibid., p. 5).

24 Playbill for *Arrah-na-Pogue*, Dublin, 10 November 1864. See McFeely, *Dion Boucicault*, p. 35.

25 Ibid., p. 28.

26 Ibid., p. 22. Boucicault also produced a play titled *Robert Emmet* at the McVicker's Theatre, Chicago in 1884. However, it appears that Boucicault was not the main author of this play (see ibid., p. 139).

27 Cullingford, 'National Identities in Performance', p. 291.

28 McFeely, *Dion Boucicault*, p. 16. The murdered woman's name was Ellen Scanlan, née Hanley. She was killed by her husband John Scanlan's servant Stephen Sullivan in 1819 on a boat crossing the River Shannon. Scanlan was charged with murder and found guilty (despite being defended by Daniel O'Connell). Sullivan was also found guilty of murder.

Both men were sentenced to death by hanging. The story is also the basis for Michael James Whitty's 'The Poor Man's Daughter', in *Tales of Irish Life: Illustrative of the manners, customs and condition of the people* (London: J. Robins & Co., 1824), and a number of other plays, such as *Eily O'Connor, or, The Foster Brother* (1831) by J.T. Haines. See Eugene McNulty, 'The Cultural Afterlife of the Colleen Bawn Murder: From crime scene to law scene', *New Hibernia Review*, vol. 20, no. 2, summer 2016, pp. 98–114, and Judith Flanders, *The Invention of Murder: How the Victorians revelled in death and detection* (London: Harper Press, 2011).

29 Gerald Griffin, *The Collegians* (London: Atlantic, 2008), p. 65.

30 Welch (ed.), *The Oxford Companion*, p. 106.

31 McNulty, 'The Cultural Afterlife', p. 107.

32 See McFeely, *Dion Boucicault*, pp. 21–4.

33 See Deane, *et al.* (eds), *The Field Day Anthology*, pp. 234–8.

34 McFeely, *Dion Boucicault*, p. 30. See Welch (ed.), *The Oxford Companion*, p. 22, for an example of this myth.

35 McFeely, *Dion Boucicault*, p. 30.

36 Dion Boucicault, *The Colleen Bawn; Or, The Brides of Garryowen*, in George Rowell (ed.), *Nineteenth-Century Plays* (London: Oxford University Press, 1953), pp. 173–231; Act I, Scene II.

37 Ibid., Act I, Scene II.

38 Ibid., Act III, Scene V; Act I, Scene II.

39 Ibid., Act I, Scene II.

40 McFeely, *Dion Boucicault*, p. 16.

41 Ute Anna Mittermaier, 'In Search of Mr Love; Or, the internationalist credentials of 'Myles before Myles', in Borg, Fagan and Huber (eds), *Flann O'Brien: Contesting Legacies*, pp. 95–7.

42 Maebh Long, *Assembling Flann O'Brien* (London: Bloomsbury, 2014), p. 3.

43 Welch (ed.), *The Oxford Companion*, p. 385.

44 McFeely, *Dion Boucicault*, p. 16.

45 Boucicault, *Colleen Bawn*, Act I, Scene I.

46 *CL*, 28 August 1942, p. 3.

47 Ibid.

48 Boucicault, *Colleen Bawn*, Act III, Scene V.

49 Dion Boucicault, *Arrah-na-Pogue; Or, the Wicklow wedding*, in Julia M. Wright (ed.), *Irish Literature 1750–1900* (New York: Blackwell, 2008), pp. 438–76; Act III, Scene III.

50 According to Thomas Jackson Rice, 'marriage, sexual life and women in general seem to be sources of high anxiety for the protagonists in O'Nolan's novels and apparently sources of anxiety for their author as well. There is not a single remotely convincing portrayal of a female character in all these works'. Thomas Jackson Rice, 'Brian O'Nolan: Misogynist or "ould Mary Anne"?', in Borg, Fagan and Huber (eds), *Flann O'Brien: Contesting Legacies*, p. 197.

51 Boucicault, *Colleen Bawn*, Act I, Scene I.

52 Ibid., Act I, Scene I.

53 Ibid., Act I, Scene I.

54 Maebh Long, 'Absolute Nonabsolute Singularity: Jacques Derrida, Myles na gCopaleen and fragmentation', in Birgit Mara Kaiser (ed.), *Singularity and Transnational Poetics* (London: Routledge, 2015), pp. 103–4.

55 Maebh Long, '"No more drunk, truculent, witty, celtic, dark, desperate, amorous paddies!": Brian O'Nolan and the Irish stereotype', in Borg, Fagan and McCourt (eds), *Flann O'Brien: Problems with authority*, pp. 40–1.

56 *CL*, 8 December 1950, p. 5.

57 McFeely, *Dion Boucicault*, pp. 26–7.

58 Long, 'Absolute', p. 104.

59 For a discussion of O'Nolan as an 'ironic modernist', see Stephen Abblitt, 'The Ghost of "Poor Jimmy Joyce": A portrait of the artist as a reluctant modernist', in Julian Murphet, Rónán McDonald and Sascha Morrell (eds), *Flann O'Brien & Modernism* (London: Bloomsbury, 2014), pp. 55–66.

60 Rónán McDonald and Julian Murphet, 'Introduction', in ibid., p. 1.

61 Ronan Crowley, 'Phwat's in a nam? Brian O'Nolan as a late revivalist', in Borg, Fagan and McCourt (eds), *Flann O'Brien: Problems with authority*, p. 122. Perhaps James Clarence Mangan (aka, The Man in the Cloak, Drechsler, Hi-Hum, Terrae Filius, Herr Hoppandgoön Baugstrauter and Herr Popandoön Tutchemupp) is exemplary in this regard. See Sinéad Sturgeon, *Essays on James Clarence Mangan: The man in the cloak* (Basingstoke: Palgrave Macmillan, 2014). In the eighteenth century, Jonathan Swift published works under names such as Lemuel Gulliver, Isaac Bickerstaff and M.B. Drapier.

62 Joseph Brooker comments that 'what would prolong Flann O'Brien studies further is a fuller engagement with history. Not so much in the broad strokes of, say, nationalism and revisionism, important though they are, but in more close-grained attention to specific moments, places and institutions'. Joseph Brooker, *'Acting Out: The fourth international Flann O'Brien conference* at the University of Salzburg', Birkbeck, University of London English and Humanities blog, 25 July 2017, http://blogs.bbk.ac.uk/english/2017/07/25/314.

63 Crowley, 'Phwat's in a nam?', p. 120.

64 Ibid., p. 123.

65 Eamonn Hughes, 'Flann O'Brien's *At Swim-Two-Birds* in the Age of Mechanical Reproduction', in Edwina Keown and Carol Taaffe (eds), *Irish Modernism: Origins, contexts, publics* (Bern: Peter Lang, 2010), p. 113.

66 *CL*, 8 June 1954, p. 4.

67 Ibid.

68 Ibid.

69 Ibid.

70 Boucicault, *Colleen Bawn*, Act I, Scene III.

71 *CL*, 2 October 1954, p. 4.

72 Ibid.

73 Ibid.

74 Ibid.

75 Ibid.

76 See Welch (ed.), *The Oxford Companion*, p. 106.

77 See McFeely, *Dion Boucicault*, p. 5.

78 Ruben Borg, Paul Fagan and Werner Huber, 'Editors' Introduction', in Borg, Fagan and Huber, *Flann O'Brien: Contesting Legacies*, p. 5.

79 Mittermaier, 'In Search of Mr Love', p. 96. It is also worth noting that '"Myles" was a construct of at least two writers – of Brian O'Nolan *in primis*, but also of his friend Niall Montgomery'. John McCourt, 'Myles na gCopaleen: A portrait of the artist as a Joyce scholar', in Borg, Fagan and Huber (eds), *Flann O'Brien: Contesting legacies*, p. 113.

4. The Return of the Father and the Dispossessed Son

1 Fabio Luppi, *Fathers and Sons at the Abbey Theatre (1904–1938): A new perspective on the study of Irish drama* (Irvine: Brown Walker, 2018), p. xiii.

2 Robert Welch, *The Abbey Theatre 1899–1999: Form and pressure* (Oxford: Oxford University Press, 1999), p. 101. According to Anthony Roche, Yeats planned to stage his post-

Sophoclean version of *Oedipus the King* after the opening of the Abbey Theatre and discussed this plan with Synge in December 1906. A later version of Yeats's *Oedipus* was performed at the Abbey in 1926. Referring to the troubles of the Irish Civil War in this 'post-Civil War' version, Yeats includes the line 'Does he think he has suffered wrong from me in these present troubles?' Anthony Roche, 'Oedipus at the Abbey', *Classic Ireland*, no. 8, 2001, pp. 102–10.

3   Carol Taaffe, *Ireland Through the Looking-Glass: Flann O'Brien, Myles na gCopaleen and Irish cultural debate* (Cork: Cork University Press, 2008), p. 65.

4   See James Joyce, 'The Sisters', in *Dubliners*, Hans Walter Gabler and Walter Hettche (eds) (New York: Garland, 1993), pp. 165–74; James Joyce, *Ulysses*, Hans Walter Gabler (ed.) (New York: Vintage, 1986), p. 17.

5   See James Joyce, 'Ireland: Island of saints and sages', in *James Joyce: Occasional, critical and political writing*, Kevin Barry (ed.) (Oxford: Oxford University Press, 2002), pp. 108–26.

6   Declan Kiberd, *Inventing Ireland: The literature of the modern nation* (London: Vintage, 1996), pp. 380–1.

7   Kelly Younger, 'Irish Antigones: Burying the colonial symptom', *Colloquy: Text, theory, critique*, no. 11, 2006, p. 152.

8   Other treatments of the Oedipal dimension of *The Playboy of the Western World* include Mary Rose Sullivan, 'Synge, Sophocles and the Un-Making of Myth', *Modern Drama*, vol. 12, no. 3, 1969, pp. 242–53; Stanley Sultan, 'A Joycean Look at *The Playboy of the Western World*', in Maurice Harmon (ed.), *The Celtic Master: Being contributions to the first James Joyce symposium in Dublin* (Dublin: Dolmen Press, 1969), pp. 45–55; Nicholas Grene, *Synge: A critical study of the plays* (London: Macmillan, 1975), p. 133; Warren Akin IV, '"I Just Riz the Loy": The Oedipal dimensions of *The Playboy of the Western World*', *South Atlantic Bulletin*, vol. 45, no. 4, 1980, pp. 55–65; Roche, 'Oedipus at the Abbey', pp. 102–10; Younger, 'Irish Antigones', p. 152; Bradley W. Buchanan, *Oedipus Against Freud: Myth and the end(s) of humanism in twentieth-century British literature* (Toronto: University of Toronto Press, 2010), p. 107; Michael Lloyd, 'Playboy of the Ancient World? Synge and the classics', *Classics Ireland*, no. 18, 2011, pp. 54–5; Gabriel Sunday Bámgbóṣé, 'Naturalist Aesthetics in John Millington Synge's *Riders to the Sea* and *The Playboy of the Western World*', *Humanicus*, no. 8, 2013, pp. 16–17; and Luppi, *Fathers and Sons at the Abbey Theatre*, p. 67.

9   J.M. Synge, *The Playboy of the Western World*, in *Collected Works, Vol. 4: Plays, Book 2*, Ann Saddlemyer (ed.) (London: Oxford University Press, 1968), pp. 103, 101. See Roche, 'Oedipus at the Abbey', *passim*, and Akin, '"I Just Riz the Loy"', p. 57.

10 Synge, *Playboy*, p. 79.

11 Ibid., p. 137.

12 See Sultan, 'A Joycean Look'; and Hugh H. MacLean, 'The Hero as Playboy', *University of Kansas City Review*, no. 21, 1954, pp. 9–19. The Jungian approach to culture considers Jesus to be a variant of the Oedipal archetype, as elucidated by Gerhard Vinnai, *Jesus und Oedipus: Zur psychoanalyse der religion* (Fischer: Frankfurt am Main, 1999). According to Hans Walter Gabler, Joyce fashions Parnell as a Jesus-figure. Hans Walter Gabler, 'The Christmas Dinner Scene, Parnell's Death and the Genesis of *A Portrait of the Artist as a Young Man*', *James Joyce Quarterly*, vol. 13, no. 1, 1975, pp. 27–39. Concomitantly, Buchanan argues that Yeats fashions Parnell as a counterpart of Oedipus; *Oedipus Against Freud*, pp. 95–6.

13 Kiberd, *Inventing Ireland*, p. 388.

14 Tom Walker, '"A True Story": *The Third Policeman* and the writing of terror', in Ruben Borg, Paul Fagan and Werner Huber (eds), *Flann O'Brien: Contesting legacies* (Cork: Cork University Press, 2014), p. 129.

15 Keith Hopper, *Flann O'Brien: A portrait of the artist a young post-modernist*, 2nd edn, J. Hillis Miller (foreword) (Cork: Cork University Press, 2009), pp. 79, 187.

16 See Buchanan, who also elaborates on the phonological quality of the name 'Mahon' with regard to Christy: 'Christy's last name, pronounced "Man", implies that he is a microcosm of humanity (as well as a Christ figure)' (*Oedipus Against Freud*, p. 107).

17 See Benedict Anderson, *Imagined Communities: Reflections on the origin and spread of nationalism* (London: Verso, 2006).

18 Washington Irving, 'Rip van Winkle', in *The Legend of Sleepy Hollow and Other Stories* (New York: Penguin, 1978), pp. 32–49.

19 Paul Michael Levitt, 'Fathers and Sons in Synge's *The Playboy of the Western World*', *The Explicator*, vol. 66, no. 1, 2007, p. 19, n. 8.

20 The 'fat man with a red face and a black suit' who tells the narrator's father 'that there was no doubt where she [the deceased mother] was' in the novel's opening pages, and who reappears after the father's death, is the only overt reference to a priest's voice in *The Third Policeman* (*CN*, p. 224).

21 Ernest Jones, 'The Oedipus-Complex as an Explanation of Hamlet's Mystery: A study in motive', *American Journal of Psychology*, no. 21, 1910, pp. 72–113.

22 Regarding the queer subtext of *The Third Policeman*, see Hopper, *Flann O'Brien*, pp. 75–84, and Andrea Bobotis, 'Queering Knowledge in Flann O'Brien's *The Third Policeman*', *Irish University Review*, vol. 32, no. 2, autumn/winter 2002, pp. 242–58.

23 See Terence Hawkes, 'Telmah', in Patricia Parker and Geoffrey Hartmann (eds), *Shakespeare and the Question of Theory* (New York: Methuen, 1985), pp. 310–32.

24 *Julius Caesar* 5.1.95–6. Jeffrey Mathewes offers a brief outline of some of the central intertextual analogies in 'The Manichaean Body in *The Third Policeman*: or why Joe's skin is scaly', *The Scriptorium: Flann O'Brien*, 2005, p. 2.

25 'I thrice presented him a kingly crown, / Which he did thrice refuse' (3.2.97–8).

26 Although R.W. Maslen focuses on the outbreak of the Second World War and the discovery of the atomic bomb, his reading of *The Third Policeman* as a 'bomb shell' may be also applied to the Civil War where Big Houses were destroyed and bombs were used to blow people up. R.W. Maslen, 'Flann O'Brien's Bombshells: *At Swim-Two-Birds* and *The Third Policeman*', *New Hibernia Review*, vol. 10, no. 4, 2006, p. 99.

27 See Raymond Klibansky, Erwin Panofsky and Fritz Saxl, *Saturn und Melancholie: Studien zur geschichte der naturphilosophie und medizin, der religion und der kunst*, 3rd edn (Frankfurt: Suhrkamp, 1998). As Saturn castrates his father with a scythe and eats his own children to avoid being overthrown by his son in a similar way to how he overthrew his own father, it is relevant that Christy Mahon, armed with a spade, fights against old Mahon armed with a scythe (Synge, *Playboy*, p. 103). In a Catholic context, the personification of death is an old man armed with a scythe. See Luppi, *Fathers and Sons at the Abbey Theatre*, pp. 65–7.

28 Michael McAteer notes the implicit influence of Yeats's *The Herne's Egg* (published 1938) on *At Swim-Two-Birds* in 'Law and Violence in Ferguson's *Congal*, Yeats's *The Herne's Egg* and O'Brien's *At Swim-Two-Birds*', in Ruben Borg and Paul Fagan (eds), *Flann O'Brien: Gallows humour* (Cork: Cork University Press, 2020), pp. 197–216.

29 Roche, 'Oedipus at the Abbey', p. 109.

30 Frank Budgen, *James Joyce and the Making of "Ulysses" and Other Writings* (Oxford: Oxford University Press, 1972), p. 17.

5. 'Comedy Is Where You Die and They Don't Bury You Because You Can Still Walk'

1 Anne Clissmann, *Flann O'Brien: A critical introduction to his writings* (New York: Barnes & Noble Books, 1975), p. 23.

2 See Ciarán Ó Nualláin, *The Early Years of Brian O'Nolan* (Dublin: Lilliput, 1998), pp. 26, 34, 55, 56.

3 William Saroyan, 'Note on *Sweeney in the Trees*', in *Three Plays: The Beautiful People, Sweeney in the Trees, and Across the Board on To-morrow Morning* (London: Faber & Faber, 1943), p. 57.

4 Ibid., p. 58.

5 See Quidnunc, 'An Irishman's Diary', *The Irish Times*, 30 April 1947, p. 5.

6 Flann O'Brien, *At Swim-Two-Birds*, William H. Gass (ed.) (Normal: Dalkey Archive Press, 1998), pp. xii–xiii.

7 Anon., 'Current Literature', review of *The Daring Young Man on the Flying Trapeze*, by William Saroyan, *The Spectator*, 1 February 1935, n.p.

8 Stefan Solomon, '"The outward accidents of illusion": O'Brien and the theatrical', in Julian Murphet, Rónán McDonald and Sascha Morrell (eds), *Flann O'Brien & Modernism* (London: Bloomsbury, 2014), pp. 41–2.

9 Keith Hopper, 'Coming Off the Rails: The strange case of "John Duffy's Brother"', in Ruben Borg, Paul Fagan and Werner Huber (eds), *Flann O'Brien: Contesting legacies* (Cork: Cork University Press, 2014), p. 234, n. 11.

10 Martha Foley, *The Story of STORY Magazine* (New York: W.W. Norton & Company, 1980), p. 268.

11 See Niall Sheridan, 'Review of *The Metamorphosis*, by Franz Kafka, and *The Gay and Melancholy Flux*, by William Saroyan', *Ireland To-day*, vol. 2, no. 5, May 1937, pp. 89–90; and see 'Mixed Quartette', review of *Little Children*, by William Saroyan, *Brynhild*, by H.G. Wells, *Castle Bran*, by K.F. Tegart, and *Fortune Must Follow*, by D.G. Waring, *Ireland To-day*, vol. 2, no. 12, December 1937, pp. 86–7. For a list of Saroyan's published short story collections, see Edward Halsey Foster, 'Saroyan, William', *American National Biography Online*, 2000, American National Biography Online.

12 Ibid.

13 William Saroyan, *Razzle Dazzle* (New York: Harcourt Brace & Company, 1942), p. 4.

14 Ibid., p. 3. O'Nolan and his friends read Saroyan's essay about their time together in Dublin. In his contributor notes to a 1943 issue of *Furioso*, Montgomery claimed to be part of 'a group of young brilliant Irish writers which includes Brian O'Nolan (Flann O'Brien) and Niall Sheridan [...] see Saroyan's *Razzle Dazzle*'. Donagh MacDonagh and James Johnson Sweeney published in the same issue. In his poem 'Philomel's Wake', Montgomery laments not only Joyce's death in 1941 but also that he was never awarded a Nobel Prize. Joyce is the male Philomel figure. The title of the poem also sounds like *Finnegans Wake*, and the reference to 'analivious Dedalus' cements the Joycean allusion. See Niall Montgomery, 'Philomel's Wake', *Furioso – A Magazine of Poetry*, vol. 2, no. 1, 1943, p. 11.

15 O'Nolan frequently writes to his agent and publishers that he prefers 'SWEENY IN THE TREES' to the *At Swim-Two-Birds* title (*L*, 12, 16, 55–6).

16 Saroyan, telegram, 26 December 1939. Brian O'Nolan Papers, Special Collections Research Centre, Morris Library, Southern Illinois University Carbondale, Box 3.1. Dashes added for clarity.

17 Saroyan, 'Note', p. 65.

18 Brenda Murphy, '*The Iceman Cometh* in Context: An American saloon trilogy', *The Eugene O'Neill Review*, no. 26, 2004, p. 215.

19 See the carbon copy of Act III, Act IV and part of Act V of a play in Irish, title unknown, thirty-two pages. Housed at John J. Burns Library, Boston College, Flann O'Brien Papers, MS.1997.027, box 4 folder 15.

20 Anthony Cronin, *No Laughing Matter: The life and times of Flann O'Brien* (London: Grafton, 1989), p. 107.

21 See, for instance, the MacGibbon & Kee and the Harper Perennial Modern Classics editions of *The Third Policeman*.

22 The phrase 'crazy Saroyan play' registers a different sense than O'Nolan's conception of a crazy play. O'Nolan's use of 'bum' also yields two meanings: the word could mean a dissolute loafer (American usage), like the character John Divney, or buttocks (Irish usage), or both.

23 William Saroyan, 'Comedy Is Where You Die and They Don't Bury You Because You Can Still Walk', in *Peace: It's wonderful* (New York: Modern Age Books, 1939), pp. 125–6.

24 Ibid., p. 125.

25 Edward Halsey Foster, *William Saroyan* (Boise: Boise State University, 1984), p. 5.

26 William Saroyan, *The Daring Young Man on the Flying Trapeze and Other Stories* (New York: Harcourt Brace, 1934), p. 12.

27 James Joyce, *Ulysses* (London: Penguin, 2000), pp. 597–8.

28 Saroyan, 'Note', pp. 58–9. Saroyan connects Joyce with Flann O'Brien. In 1941, he records, 'From Dublin I returned to London [...]. From London I took an airplane to Paris. I went to a publishing house near Notre-Dame and the next thing I knew I was on the telephone talking to James Joyce [...]. I didn't want to meet James Joyce or anybody else by appointment. That is like asking somebody to breathe next Tuesday at two-thirty. I had met him in Dublin – in Flann O'Brien anyhow' (ibid., pp. 58–9).

29 Other examples of similar narrative modes are Pirandello's *The Late Mattia Pascal*, Joyce's *Finnegans Wake*, and in an American and non-comic context, Faulkner's *As I Lay Dying*.

30 Ruben Borg, 'Reading Flann with Paul: Modernism and the trope of conversion', in Ruben Borg, Paul Fagan and John McCourt (eds), *Flann O'Brien: Problems with authority* (Cork: Cork University Press, 2017), pp. 220–1. Borg reads the Sir Myles columns in *Cruiskeen Lawn*, 'Two in One' and *The Dalkey Archive* as well as *The Third Policeman* as examples of these paradigms.

31 Saroyan, *Daring Young Man*, pp. 12–13.

32 Ibid., p. 22.

33 Ibid., p. 62.

34 Ibid., p. 63.

35 Saroyan, 'Note on *Sweeney in the Trees*', in *Three Plays: The Beautiful People, Sweeney in the Trees, and Across the Board on To-morrow Morning* (London: Faber & Faber, 1943), p. 58.

36 Anon. [Stanford Lee Cooper], 'Eire's Columnist', *Time*, 23 August 1943, pp. 90, 92.

37 William Saroyan, *The Human Comedy* (New York: Harcourt Brace, 1943), p. 30.

38 Ibid., p. 92.

39 See William Saroyan, 'Stories and Plays', review of *Stories and Plays* by Flann O'Brien, *The New York Times*, 28 March 1976.

40 Ibid.

41 Ibid.

42 See Foster, 'Saroyan, William'.

6. Traces of Mischief

* Thanks are owed to Flavia Iovine for alerting me to echoes between Flann O'Brien's 'John Duffy's Brother' and Pirandello's 'A Train Whistled ...', in her paper 'Visual Metamorphoses in "John Duffy's Brother": An example of textual analysis', delivered at *Metamorphoses: III international Flann O'Brien conference*, Charles University, Prague, 16–19 September 2015, available at: https://www.academia.edu/19575367/Visual_Metamorphoses_in_John_Duffys_Brother_an_example_of_textual_analysis?auto=download.

1 Julia Kristeva, 'Word, Dialogue and Novel', in *Desire in Language: A semiotic approach to literature and art*, Leon S. Roudiez (ed.), Thomas Gora, Alice Jardine and Leon S. Roudiez (trans.) (New York: Columbia University Press, 1980), p. 66.

2 Steven Moore, *The Novel: An alternative history – beginnings to 1600* (New York: Continuum, 2010), p. 5.

3 Ibid., p. 3.

4 Two volumes of a projected three-volume set have been published: ibid., and *The Novel: An alternative history – 1600–1800* (London: Bloomsbury, 2013). Volume three is apparently in process.

5 'My purpose is to indicate how their writing becomes self-reflexive as it explores fundamental tensions between imagination and memory, narration and history, self and language. In short, I propose to show how these authors share, with Joyce and Beckett, the basic modernist project of transforming the traditional narrative of quest into a critical narrative of self-questioning.' Richard Kearney, *Transitions: Narratives in Irish culture* (Dublin: Wolfhound Press, 1988), p. 83.

6 Rob Doyle defines his tradition as containing 'startling talents, oddities, subversives and transgressors', *The Other Irish Tradition: An anthology* (McLean: Dalkey Archive Press, 2018), p. 11.

7 Derek Attridge, 'Modernism, Formal Innovation and Affect in some Contemporary Irish Novels', in Alex Houen (ed.), *Affect and Literature* (Cambridge: Cambridge University Press, 2019), pp. 252–4.

8 Rüdiger Imhof, 'Introduction', in Rüdiger Imhof (ed.), *Alive-Alive O! Flann O'Brien's At Swim-Two-Birds* (Dublin: Wolfhound, 1985), p. 23.

9 Rüdiger Imhof, 'How it is on the Fringes of Irish Fiction', *Irish University Review*, vol. 22, no. 1, spring/summer 1992, p. 153.

10 Milan Kundera, *The Art of the Novel*, Linda Asher (trans.) (New York: Perennial Classics, 2003), p. 15.

11 Moore, *Beginnings to 1600*, p. 342.

12 O'Nolan was familiar enough with Rabelais to favourably contrast him with Joyce in the special James Joyce issue of *Envoy* that he guest-edited: 'True humour needs this background urgency, Rabelais is funny, but his [Joyce's] stuff cloys. His stuff lacks tragedy.' Brian Nolan, 'Editorial Note: A bash in the tunnel', *Envoy*, April 1951, p. 11.

13 This 'alternative history' also closely corresponds with M. Keith Booker's situation of O'Nolan's work in an anti-Enlightenment Menippean tradition in his *Flann O'Brien, Bakhtin and Menippean Satire* (New York: Syracuse University Press, 1995), while Hopper, José Lanters and Dieter Fuchs also consider O'Nolan's work in terms of Menippean satire. Keith Hopper, *Flann O'Brien: A portrait of the artist as a young post-modernist*, 2nd edn, J. Hillis Miller (foreword) (Cork: Cork University Press, 2009), pp. 193–228; José Lanters, *Unauthorized Versions: Irish Menippean satire, 1919–1952* (Washington: Catholic University of America Press, 2000); Dieter Fuchs, '*The Dalkey Archive*: A Menippean satire against authority', in Ruben Borg, Paul Fagan and John McCourt (eds), *Flann O'Brien: Problems with authority* (Cork: Cork University Press, 2017), pp. 230–41.

14 Jorge Luis Borges, 'When Fiction Lives in Fiction', in *Selected Non-Fictions*, Eliot Weinberger (ed.) (New York: Penguin, 1999), pp. 160–2.

15 While many of Pirandello's stories were translated into English and published in various book-length collections, and in numerous editions, between 1932 and '59, many other translations were published from 1924 onwards in magazines and journals such as *The Golden Book Magazine*, *The Fortnightly Review*, *The Spectator*, *The Listener* and *Esquire*, among many others. For a listing of a broad selection of stories translated into English, see 'Translations of the Short Stories', in Luigi Pirandello, *Luigi Pirandello: Short stories*, Frederick May (ed. and trans.) (London: Oxford University Press, 1965). This is far from a comprehensive list of translated stories which, to my knowledge, has not been assembled.

16 Ondřej Pilný, '"Did you put charcoal adroitly in the vent?": Brian O'Nolan and pataphysics', in Ruben Borg, Paul Fagan and Werner Huber (eds), *Flann O'Brien: Contesting legacies* (Cork: Cork University Press, 2014), p. 159.

17 Brian McHale, *Postmodernist Fiction* (London: Routledge, 2001), p. 112.

18 Thomas F. Shea, 'Patrick McGinley's Impressions of Flann O'Brien: *The Devil's Diary* and *At Swim-Two-Birds*', *Twentieth Century Literature*, vol. 40, no. 2, summer 1994, p. 278.

19 Stefan Solomon, '"The outward accidents of illusion": O'Brien and the theatrical', in Julian Murphet, Rónán McDonald and Sascha Morrell (eds), *Flann O'Brien & Modernism* (London: Bloomsbury, 2014), pp. 41–54; in reference to Martin Puchner, *Stage Fright: Modernism, anti-theatricality and drama* (Baltimore: Johns Hopkins University Press, 2002).

20 Solomon, 'O'Brien and the theatrical', pp. 42–3.

21 Neil Murphy, 'Beckett and the Stage Image: Toward a poetics of postmodern performance', in Daniel K. Jernigan (ed.), *Drama and the Postmodern: Assessing the limits of metatheatre* (Amherst: Cambria Press, 2008), p. 353.

22 Graham Greene, 'Proof-Reader's Report on *At Swim-Two-Birds* for Longmans Green Ltd., 1939', qtd in *A Flann O'Brien Reader*, Stephen Jones (ed.) (New York: Viking, 1978), p. 31.

23 Anthony Cronin, *No Laughing Matter: The life and times of Flann O'Brien* (New York: Fromm International, 1998), p. 83.

24 In addition to Cronin's claim, and the fact that Cabell was referred to as 'James Joyce Cabell' in *Cruiskeen Lawn* (Cronin, *No Laughing Matter*, p. 83), a copy of Cabell's *Jurgen* is listed in the inventory of Brian O'Nolan's Library in Boston College – to which the story 'Naval Control' makes an oblique reference, as discussed in the 'Editor's Note' to *Appendix II: Naval Control*, in *SF*, pp. 148–9.

25 Cronin, *No Laughing Matter*, pp. 83–4.

26 Daragh O'Connell, 'Pirandello and Joyce say Yes! in Denis Johnston's *The Old Lady Says No!*', *Pirandello Studies*, no. 27, 2007, p. 77.

27 Daniel Keith Jernigan, '"*Simulat Ergo Est*": Brian O'Nolan's metaperformative simulations', *New Hibernia Review*, vol. 20, no. 1, spring/earrach 2016, p. 89.

28 Michael McLoughlin, 'At Swim Six Characters or Two Birds in Search of an Author: Fiction, metafiction and reality in Pirandello and Flann O'Brien', *Yearbook of the Society for Pirandello Studies*, no. 12, 1992, p. 25.

29 This translation was the one included in Luigi Pirandello, *Three Plays* (New York: Dutton, 1922).

30 McLoughlin, 'At Swim Six Characters', p. 25.

31 Hopper, *Flann O'Brien*, p. 110.

32 Ibid., p. 93.

33 Ibid., p. 94.

34 Luigi Pirandello, *Three Plays*, Robert Rietty, Noel Creegan, John Linstrum and Julian Mitchell (trans.) (London: Methuen, 1993), pp. 124–5.

35 An earlier variation of the 'aestho-autogamy' theory is also evident in 'Scenes in a Novel', according to Germán Asensio Peral, who cites the following passage from the story as evidence that O'Nolan had the same concept in mind, without explicitly naming it: 'Carruthers McDaid is a man I created one night when I had swallowed nine stouts and felt vaguely blasphemous. I gave him a good but worn-out mother and an industrious father, and coolly negativing fifty years of eugenics, made him a worthless scoundrel, a betrayer of women and a secret drinker.' *SF*, p. 50, and qtd in Germán Asensio Peral, 'The Origins of Flann O'Brien's *At Swim-Two-Birds*', *ES Revista de Filología Inglesa*, no. 36, 2015, p. 53.

36 Pirandello, *Three Plays*, p. 75.

37 McLoughlin, 'At Swim Six Characters', p. 30.

38 *CL*, 25 February 1955, p. 7.

39 Pericles Lewis, 'Six Characters in Search of an Author', *The Modernist Lab at Yale University*, https://campuspress.yale.edu/modernismlab/six-characters-in-search-of-an-author/.

40 Guido Davico Bonino, 'Introduction', in Luigi Pirandello, *Sei Personaggi in cerca d'autore*, Einaudi Tascabili, Classici 118 (Torino: Einaudi, 1993), pp. viii–x.

41 I work with the 1994 translation in this essay, 'A Character's Tragedy', in Luigi Pirandello, *Eleven Short Stories*, Stanley Applebaum (ed. and trans.) (New York: Dover Publications, 1994), pp. 144–57.

42 Ibid., p. 145.

43 Ibid., p. 155.

44 Ibid., p. 153.

45 Ibid., p. 149.

46 Ibid., p. 151.

47 J.W. Dunne suggested that 'Nothing stays fixed to be looked at. Everything is in a state of flux […]. That you enter houses without passing through walls is, of course, one of the most commonplace of happenings in a four-dimensional world' (qtd in Hopper, *Flann O'Brien*, p. 198).

48 Iovine, 'Visual Metamorphoses'. '*Il treno ha fischiato*' was translated as 'The Train Whistled …' by Giovanni R. Bussino, for *Tales of Madness: A selection from Luigi Pirandello's short stories for a year* (Brookline Village: Dante University of America Press, 1984), pp. 99–105.

49 The silence here reminds one of the protagonist being struck silent at the close of 'John Duffy's Brother'. For the significance of 'silence' as a recurring motif in earlier studies of postmodernism, see Ihab Hassan, *The Literature of Silence: Henry Miller and Samuel Beckett* (New York: Alfred A. Knopf, 1967) and George Steiner, *Language and Silence: Essays on language, literature and the inhuman* (New York: Atheneum, 1967). The significance of silence in modern Irish writing is the subject of Michael McAteer (ed.), *Silence in Modern Irish Literature* (Leiden: Brill, 2017). More directly relevant to this essay, see Keith Hopper, '"Silent, so to speak": Flann O'Brien and the sense of an ending', in ibid., pp. 177–87.

50 Pirandello, 'The Train Whistled …', p. 104.

51 Ibid.

52 '*Non è una cosa seria*' was first translated into English as 'It's Nothing Serious' by Arthur and Henrie Mayne and included in the collection *Better Think Twice About It!* (London: John Lane, 1933). I cite the translation by Stanley Applebaum, 'It's Not To Be Taken Seriously', collected in Pirandello, *Eleven Short Stories*.

53 Ibid., p. 125.

54 Pirandello, '*La signora Frola e il signor Ponza, suo genero*' was first translated into English as 'Mrs Frola and Her Son-in-Law, Mr Ponza' by Violet M. Sanders and included in the collection *Quattro Novelle* (London: Harrap, 1939). I cite the translation by Stanley Applebaum collected in Pirandello, *Eleven Short Stories*.

55 Stanley Applebaum, 'Introduction: The Man and His Work', in Pirandello, *Eleven Short Stories*, p. xviii.

56 Luigi Pirandello, 'Mrs Frola and Mr Ponza, Her Son-in-Law' in ibid., p. 173.

57 McHale, *Postmodernist Fiction*.

58 Qtd in Marilena De Chiara, 'Life is a Succession of Habits: Pirandello's *Umorismo* and Beckett's *Proust*', *Pirandello Studies*, no. 29, 2009, p. 40.

59 Fredric Jameson criticises postmodern parody as 'blank parody' because he views it to lack political agency. Parody-as-satire, for him, has been replaced in postmodernism by pastiche: 'Pastiche is, like parody, the imitation of a peculiar or unique, idiosyncratic style, the wearing of a linguistic mask, speech in a dead language. But it is a neutral practice of such mimicry, without any of parody's ulterior motives, amputated of the satiric impulse, devoid of laughter.' Fredric Jameson, *Postmodernism, or, the Cultural Logic of Late Capitalism* (Durham: Duke University Press, 1991), p. 17.

7. Self-Evident Shams and Accidents of Illusion

1 Susan Stewart, *Nonsense: Aspects of intertexuality in folklore and literature* (Baltimore: Johns Hopkins University Press, 1979), p. 94, qtd in Keith Hopper, *Flann O'Brien: A portrait of the artist as a young post-modernist*, 2nd edn, J. Hillis Miller (foreword) (Cork: Cork University Press, 2009), p. 218.

2 This essay draws extensively from my dissertation 'The Epigraphic Character: Fiction and metafiction in the twentieth-century novel', PhD diss. (Emory University, 2011) and from a conference paper I presented on 'Flann O'Brien and the Accidents of Illusion: The novel as self-evident sham and Bertolt Brecht's alienation effect' at *Problems with Authority: The II international Flann O'Brien conference* in Rome, June 2013, and at Southern ACIS in March 2013.

3 James Joyce, *A Portrait of the Artist as a Young Man: Text, criticism and notes*, ed. Chester G. Anderson (New York: Penguin Books, 1968), p. 205.

4 'The image, it is clear, must be set between the mind of senses of the artist himself and the mind or sense of others. [...] art necessarily divides itself into three forms progressing from one to the next. [...] the lyrical [...] wherein the artist presents his image in immediate relation to himself; the epical [...] wherein he presents his image in immediate relation to himself and to others; the dramatic [...] wherein he presents his image in immediate relation to others.' Ibid., pp. 214–15.

5 For further commentary on this 'solemn drool', as O'Nolan put it, see *CL*, 18 June 1947, p. 4.

6 Bertolt Brecht, 'The Fourth Wall of China: An essay on the effect of disillusion in the Chinese theatre', Eric Walter White (trans.), *Life and Letters To-Day*, vol. 15, no. 6, winter 1936, pp. 116–23; see also Bertolt Brecht, 'Alienation Effects in Chinese Acting', in *Brecht on Theatre: The development of an aesthetic*, John Willett (ed. and trans.) (New York: Farrar, Straus & Giroux, 2001), pp. 91–9.

7 See Willett's annotation in Brecht, *Brecht on Theatre*, p. 99, n.

8 See Willett's annotation in Brecht, *Brecht on Theatre*, pp. 76–7, n., 99, n. There is a long history of genetic scholarship in Brecht studies tracing the development of such ideas as *Verfremdungseffekt* through an extensive body of notes, drafts and publications, in multiple versions both in German and in translation. Willett notes that, while 'Brecht had already been feeling his way towards some such formula', the new term was 'virtually a neologism' with strong theatrical roots in the ideas of Viktor Shklovsky. The new term marks a turning point in Brecht's thought. For more on the development of this concept in Brecht's work, see Anthony Squiers, *An Introduction to the Social and Political Philosophy of Bertolt Brecht: Revolution and aesthetics* (Amsterdam: Rodopi, 2014); Douglas Robinson, *Estrangement and the Somatics of Literature: Tolstoy, Shklovsky, Brecht* (Baltimore: Johns Hopkins University Press, 2008); John J. White, *Bertolt Brecht's Dramatic Theory* (Rochester: Camden House, 2004); and Peter Brooker, 'Key Words in Brecht's Theory and Practice of Theatre', in Peter Thomson and Glendyr Sacks (eds), *The Cambridge Companion to Brecht* (New York: Cambridge University Press, 1994), pp. 209–24.

9 See Willett's annotation in Brecht, *Brecht on Theatre*, p. 99, n.

10 Michael Patrick Gillespie, 'Life and Letters', in Alvin Sullivan (ed.), *British Literary Magazines: The modern age, 1914–1984* (New York: Greenwood Press, 1986).

11 Niall Sheridan, 'Brian, Flann and Myles: The springtime of genius', in Timothy O'Keeffe (ed.), *Myles: Portraits of Brian O'Nolan* (London: Martin, Brian & O'Keeffe, 1973), p. 35.

12 Ibid., p. 39.

13 Brooker, 'Key Words in Brecht's Theory and Practice of Theatre', p. 186.

14 Ibid.

15 Ibid.

16 Brecht, 'Alienation Effects', p. 91. 'Regarding a work of art as a whole' and 'identifying themselves with the dramatic *personae*' in White's translation, respectively (Brecht, 'Fourth Wall of China', p. 116).

17 Brecht, 'Fourth Wall of China', p. 123.

18 Ibid.

19 Ibid., pp. 121–2.

20 Ibid., p. 122.

21 Ibid.

22 Gérard Genette, *Narrative Discourse: An essay in method*, Jane E. Lewin (trans.) (Ithaca: Cornell University Press, 1980), p. 236.

23 Wayne Booth, *A Rhetoric of Irony* (Chicago: University of Chicago Press, 1974), p. xiv. Booth distinguishes between the implied author and the actual author in *The Rhetoric of Fiction*. A similar distinction exists between the implied and actual reader.

24 Jorge Luis Borges, *Other Inquisitions, 1937–1952*, R. Simms (trans.) (Austin: University of Texas Press, 1964), p. 46, qtd in Genette, *Narrative Discourse*, p. 236.

25 See John Foley, 'The Historical Origins of Flann O'Brien's Jem Casey', *Notes and Queries*, vol. 52, no. 1, March 2005, pp. 97–9.

26 Niall Sheridan notes that, in the intellectual university crowd O'Nolan spent his time with, 'Eliot was a big influence' ('Brian, Flann and Myles', p. 39).

27 'The fragments that *At Swim-Two-Birds* has shored against its ruins share with Eliot's *The Waste Land* a radical aesthetics, structural experimentation, unconventional chronology, skepticism towards a coherent identity, varied quotation and allusion, uncertain narrative frames, contaminated planes of reality and a tendency to do everybody in different voices.' Long does follow this with a discussion of important differences in Eliot's and O'Nolan's contexts and aims, but the strong similarities remain. Maebh Long, *Assembling Flann O'Brien* (London: Bloomsbury, 2014), pp. 9–11.

28 The ending of *At Swim-Two-Birds* is another reference to Eliot, with 'good-bye, good-bye, good-bye' echoing the final line of *The Waste Land*: 'Shantih, shantih, shantih'.

29 Hugh Kenner, *A Colder Eye: The modern Irish writers* (New York: Knopf, 1983), pp. 253–4.

30 Jorge Luis Borges, 'When Fiction Lives in Fiction', in *Selected Non-Fictions* (New York: Penguin, 1999), p. 160.

31 Ibid., pp. 161–2.

32 Ibid., p. 162.

33 Brooker, 'Key Words in Brecht's Theory and Practice of Theatre', p. 186.

8. A Crowning Martyr

1 Carol Taaffe, rev. of *The Short Fiction of Flann O'Brien*, *The Parish Review: Journal of Flann O'Brien studies*, vol. 2, no. 1, fall 2013, p. 67.

2 Thierry Robin, 'Tall Tales or "Petites Histoires": History and the void in "The Martyr's Crown" and *Thirst*', in Ruben Borg, Paul Fagan and Werner Huber (eds), *Flann O'Brien: Contesting legacies* (Cork: Cork University Press, 2014), p. 79.

3 M. Keith Booker, *Flann O'Brien, Bakhtin and Menippean Satire* (New York: Syracuse University Press, 1995), p. 7.

4 Kim McMullen, 'Culture as Colloquy: Flann O'Brien's postmodern dialogue with Irish tradition', *NOVEL: A Forum on Fiction*, vol. 27, no. 1, autumn 1993, p. 64; Keith Hopper, *Flann O'Brien: A portrait of the artist as a young post-modernist*, 2nd edn, J. Hillis Miller (foreword) (Cork: Cork University Press, 2009), pp. 32, 169–71.

5 Dieter Fuchs, '*The Dalkey Archive*: A Menippean satire against authority', in Ruben Borg, Paul Fagan and John McCourt (eds), *Flann O'Brien: Problems with authority* (Cork:

Cork University Press, 2017), p. 233; Conor Dowling, 'Carnival and Class Consciousness: Bakhtin and the Free State in *At Swim-Two-Birds*', in Ruben Borg and Paul Fagan (eds), *Flann O'Brien: Gallows humour* (Cork: Cork University Press, 2020), p. 54.

6 Booker, *Flann O'Brien, Bakhtin and Menippean Satire*, p. 143.

7 Mikhail Bakhtin, *Problems of Dostoevsky's Poetics*, trans. and ed. Caryl Emerson (Minneapolis: Minnesota University Press, 1984), p. 108.

8 Ibid., pp. 102–4.

9 Thierry Robin comments upon the '*instrumental* ambiguity' of Toole's name in 'Tall Tales', p. 83.

10 Bakhtin, *Problems of Dostoevsky's Poetics*, p. 108.

11 Ibid., p. 102.

12 As per Bakhtin's definition, 'the adventure plot is combined with the posing of profound and acute problems; and it is, in addition, placed wholly at the service of the idea. It places a person in extraordinary positions that expose and provoke him, it connects him and makes him collide with other people under unusual and unexpected conditions precisely for the purpose of testing the idea and the man of the idea'. *Problems of Dostoevsky's Poetics*, p. 105.

13 Ibid., p. 118.

14 Robin, 'Tall Tales', p. 79.

15 In an earlier version entitled 'For Ireland Home and Beauty', the contents of the mini paragraphs are either omitted or embedded within a larger block of text. This is also true for earlier manuscripts of the story that are housed in the John J. Burns Library, Boston College, Flann O'Brien Papers, MS.1997.027. When finalising the story, O'Nolan therefore purposefully chose to frame it ostensibly within the traditional 'start' and 'end' cues of the dirty joke genre. A study of these changes reveals that O'Nolan sacrifices dramatic effect and even a metafictional comment to foreground this dirty-joke frame in the final version to this story. His participation in this comic tradition, as well as the generic hybridity that stemmed from this choice, should therefore be seen as important conscious decisions.

16 Marion Quirici, '(Probably Posthumous): The frame device in Brian O'Nolan's short fiction', in Borg, Fagan and Huber (eds), *Flann O'Brien: Contesting legacies*, p. 46.

17 Ibid., p. 55.

18 Mikhail Bakhtin, *Rabelais and His World*, trans. Hélène Iswolsky (Bloomington: Indiana University Press, 1984), p. 3.

19 Bakhtin, *Problems of Dostoevsky's Poetics*, p. 118.

20 Bakhtin, *Rabelais and His World*, p. 26.

21 Ibid., p. 21.

22 Ibid., p. 23.

23 Bakhtin, *Problems of Dostoevsky's Poetics*, p. 114.

24 Ibid., p. 165.

25 Ibid., p. 107.

26 For an elaboration on the transformative role of inebriation in O'Nolan's *oeuvre* in which drink is an agent for the non-fixture of identity politics and philosophical concepts, see Noam Schiff, '"the situation had become deplorably fluid": Alcohol, alchemy and Brian O'Nolan's metamorphoses', in Borg and Fagan (eds), *Flann O'Brien: Gallows humour*, pp. 116–30.

27 Bakhtin, *Problems of Dostoevsky's Poetics*, p. 165.

28 Ibid.

29 Dowling, 'Carnival and Class Consciousness', p. 52.

9. **Dreaming After in the Dark Night**

1   W.B. Yeats and Lady Augusta Gregory, *The Pot of Broth*, in *The Collected Plays of W.B. Yeats* (London: Macmillan, 1952), p. 93.

2   Stefan Solomon, '"The outward accidents of illusion": O'Brien and the theatrical', in Julian Murphet, Rónán McDonald and Sascha Morrell (eds), *Flann O'Brien & Modernism* (London: Bloomsbury, 2014), pp. 41–54; Daniel Keith Jernigan, '"Simulat Ergo Est": Brian O'Nolan's metaperformative simulations', *New Hibernia Review*, vol. 20, no. 1, spring/earrach 2016, pp. 87–104; Maebh Long, '"No more drunk, truculent, witty, celtic, dark, desperate, amorous paddies!": Brian O'Nolan and the Irish stereotype', in Ruben Borg, Paul Fagan and John McCourt (eds), *Flann O'Brien: Problems with authority* (Cork: Cork University Press, 2017), pp. 34–53; and Thierry Robin, 'Tall Tales or "Petites Histoires": History and the void in "The Martyr's Crown" and *Thirst*', in Ruben Borg, Paul Fagan and Werner Huber (eds), *Flann O'Brien: Contesting legacies* (Cork: Cork University Press, 2014), pp. 76–92.

3   A significant essay in this regard is Ronan Crowley, 'Phwat's in a Nam? Brian O'Nolan as a late revivalist', in Borg, Fagan and McCourt (eds), *Flann O'Brien: Problems with authority*, pp. 119–35.

4   On the history of the Gate Theatre see David Clare, Des Lally and Patrick Lonergan (eds), *The Gate Theatre, Dublin: Inspiration and craft* (Oxford: Peter Lang 2018); and Ondřej Pilný, Ruud van den Beuken and Ian R. Walsh (eds), *Cultural Convergence: The Dublin Gate Theatre, 1928–1960* (London: Palgrave, 2020).

5   Peter Costello and Peter van de Kamp, *Flann O'Brien: An illustrated biography* (London: Bloomsbury, 1987), p. 82; Robert Tracy, 'Introduction', in Flann O'Brien, *Rhapsody in Stephen's Green*, Robert Tracy (ed.) (Dublin: Lilliput, 1994), p. 6.

6   The BBC version aired on television on 1 April 1959, from 19:30 to 20:00, under the title *After Hours*, with writing credit given to Larry Morrow (who also worked on the radio adaptation) as well as Brian Nolan. See Alana Gillespie, 'Pipes Aloft: *After Hours* and "Shows and Showers"', *The Parish Review: Journal of Flann O'Brien studies*, vol. 5, no. 2, fall 2021, pp. 1–6.

7   Tracy, 'Introduction', p. 6.

8   *CL*, 26 February 1951, p. 4.

9   For more commentary on this aspect of O'Nolan's writing see Joseph Brooker, 'Myles' Tones', in Jennika Baines (ed.), *'Is it about a bicycle?' Flann O'Brien in the twenty-first century* (Dublin: Four Courts Press, 2011), p. 18; and Maria Kager, '*Lamhd Láftar* and Bad Language: Bilingual cognition in *Cruiskeen Lawn*', in Borg, Fagan and McCourt (eds), *Flann O'Brien: Problems with authority*, p. 69.

10 Joseph Holloway, qtd in Anthony Cronin, *No Laughing Matter: The life and times of Flann O'Brien* (London: Grafton, 1989), p. 134.

11 See Terence Hawkes, *Structuralism and Semiotics* (London: Methuen, 1977), pp. 128–9; and Keir Elam, *The Semiotics of Theatre and Drama* (London: Methuen, 1980), pp. 22–3.

12 For more details about radio performances of *Thirst*, see Paul Fagan's essay 'Productions and Adaptations of Brian O'Nolan's Works for Stage, Radio, Screen' in the present volume.

13 On the role of auditory imagination in radio drama see for instance Ian Rodger, *Radio Drama* (London: Macmillan, 1982); and Steven Connor, 'Art, Radio and Alibi', http://stevenconnor.com/artradio.html.

14 See Judith Butler, *Gender Trouble: Feminism and the subversion of identity* (London: Routledge, 1990), and *Bodies That Matter: On the discursive limits of 'sex'* (London: Routledge, 1993).

15 J.L. Austin, *How to Do Things with Words* (Oxford: Oxford University Press, 1962), p. 6.

16 Ibid., pp. 6–7.

17 Ibid., p. 101.

18 Ibid., pp. 107, 109.

19 Patrice Pavis, *Dictionary of the Theatre: Terms, concepts and analysis*, Christine Shantz (trans.) (Toronto: University of Toronto Press, 1998), p. 431.

20 William Shakespeare, *The Complete Works of William Shakespeare*, John Dover Wilson (ed.) (London: Octopus Books, 1984), p. 459.

21 Terry Eagleton, *Figures of Dissent* (London: Verso, 2003), p. 9.

22 Terry Eagleton, *Heathcliff and the Great Hunger: Studies in Irish culture* (London: Verso, 1995), pp. 310–11.

23 W.B. Yeats, *Collected Poems*, Augustine Martin (ed.) (London: Vintage, 1990), pp. 178, 5–6.

24 See Marguerite Quintelli-Neary, *Folklore and the Fantastic in Twelve Modern Irish Novels* (Westport: Greenwood, 1997), pp. 83–97, and especially, on the *geis*, pp. 89–90, 93.

25 W.B. Yeats, *At The Hawk's Well*, in *Collected Plays*, pp. 207–8.

26 W.B. Yeats, *The Cat and the Moon*, in *Collected Plays*, p. 468.

27 For a brief discussion of this play in the context of the theme of blindness in Irish drama see Einat Adar, 'From Irish Philosophy to Irish Theatre: The blind (wo)man made to see', *Estudios Irlandeses*, no. 12, 2017, p. 5.

28 R.F. Foster, *W.B. Yeats: A Life. I: The Apprentice Mage 1865–1914* (Oxford: Oxford University Press, 1997), p. 250, dates the play's co-authorship to 1901.

29 Yeats and Gregory, *The Pot of Broth*, in Yeats, *Collected Plays*, pp. 93, 97–101.

30 Hugh Kenner, *A Colder Eye: The modern Irish writers* (New York: Knopf, 1983), p. 43.

31 Seamus Deane, *Strange Country: Modernity and nationhood in Irish writing since 1790* (Oxford: Clarendon, 1997), p. 142; Mary C. King, 'J.M. Synge, "National" Drama and the Post-Protestant Imagination', in Shaun Richards (ed.), *The Cambridge Companion to Twentieth-Century Irish Drama* (Cambridge: Cambridge University Press, 2004), p. 79.

32 *CL*, 28 August 1942, p. 3.

33 J.M. Synge, *The Playboy of the Western World and Other Plays*, Ann Saddlemyer (ed.) (Oxford: Oxford University Press, 1995), p. 57.

34 Ibid., p. 74.

35 T.S. Eliot, 'Milton I', in *Selected Prose*, Frank Kermode (ed.) (London: Faber, 1975), pp. 262–3.

36 Adar, 'From Irish Philosophy to Irish Theatre', p. 5.

37 Synge, *The Playboy of the Western World and Other Plays*, p. 96.

38 See for instance Kirsty Johnston, *Disability Theatre and Modern Drama: Recasting modernism* (London: Bloomsbury Methuen Drama, 2016); and Benjamin Whitburn and Rod Michalko, 'Blindness/sightedness: Disability studies and the defiance of di-vision', in Nick Watson and Simo Vehmaas (eds), *The Routledge Handbook of Disability Studies* (New York: Routledge, 2019), pp. 219–33.

39 Synge, *The Playboy of the Western World and Other Plays*, p. 79.

40 Ibid.

41 Ibid., p. 90.

42 Katharine Worth, 'Drama of the Interior', in Ronald Ayling (ed.), *J.M. Synge: Four plays – a casebook* (Basingstoke: Macmillan, 1992), pp. 112, 113.

43 Synge, *The Playboy of the Western World and Other Plays*, p. 90.

44 King, 'J.M. Synge', p. 81.

45 Synge, *The Playboy of the Western World and Other Plays*, p. 68.

46 Ibid.

47 Ibid., p. 79.

48 Ibid., p. 77.

49 W.B. Yeats, 'Programme Note', in Ayling (ed.), *J.M. Synge*, p. 102.

50 Synge, *The Playboy of the Western World and Other Plays*, p. 96.

51 The distinction between O'Nolan on one hand, and Yeats and Synge on the other, described here is plain. It should be added, though, that the Irish Revival as a whole was broader than those towering figures, and its drama sometimes took urban as well as rural settings. In the post-independence era of the Abbey Theatre, the canonical example of this is Sean O'Casey, who corresponded with O'Nolan in 1943 (*L*, pp. 114–17). Before 1922, the Abbey's urban dramatists are less well-known and influential, but they include the Belfast-born St John Greer Ervine, who served as the Abbey's general manager, and W.F. Casey, whose comedy *The Suburban Groove* (1908) led the critic Andrew E. Malone to describe him as 'the only playwright who attempted to study the people of Dublin's suburbs in the theatre'. See Andrew E. Malone, 'The Rise of the Realistic Movement', in Lennox Robinson (ed.), *The Irish Theatre: Lectures delivered during the Abbey Theatre Festival held in Dublin in August 1938* (New York: Haskell House, 1971 [1939]), p. 99. For a comprehensive study of this field see Elizabeth Mannion, *The Urban Plays of the Early Abbey Theatre: Beyond O'Casey* (New York: Syracuse University Press, 2014). O'Nolan himself would continue – for instance in *Cruiskeen Lawn* – to emphasise the notion that the Abbey was primarily a site for peasant drama, but a fuller study of O'Nolan's relations with the Irish Revival could take more account of the aspects highlighted by Mannion, as well as the canonical figures on which the present essay has focused.

52 Synge, *The Playboy of the Western World and Other Plays*, p. 144.

10. 'The Fausticity of Kelly'

1 Keith Hopper, *Flann O'Brien: A Portrait of the artist as a young post-modernist*, 2nd edn, J. Hillis Miller (foreword) (Cork: Cork University Press, 2009), p. 84.

2 Ibid., pp. 227–8.

3 Theodor W. Adorno, 'On the Final Scene of *Faust*', in *Notes to Literature*, 2 vols, Shierry Weber Nicholsen (trans.) (New York: Columbia University Press, 1991), vol. 1, p. 119. First published as '*Zur Schlussszene des Faust*', *Akzente*, no. 6, 1959, pp. 567–75.

4 Johann Wolfgang von Goethe, *Faust: A Norton critical edition*, 2nd edn, Walter Arndt (trans.), Cyrus Hamlin (ed.) (New York: Norton, 2001), p. 37 (l. 1338). Hereafter referenced by line number.

5 O'Nolan describes *Faustus Kelly* as written 'for the Abbey' or an 'Abbey play' in letters to Michael Walsh on 31 May 1942 and Hilton Edwards on 20 June 1942 (*L*, pp. 118–19). Carol Taaffe argues that in *Faustus Kelly*, O'Nolan is 'struggling into the motley of the Abbey comedy', in *Ireland Through the Looking-Glass: Flann O'Brien, Myles na gCopaleen and Irish cultural debate* (Cork: Cork University Press, 2008), p. 178. Maebh Long suggests that *Faustus Kelly*'s regional accents 'fell afoul' of a confusion with 'stage brogue' in her essay, '"No more drunk, truculent, witty, celtic, dark, desperate, amorous paddies!": Brian O'Nolan and the Irish stereotype', in Ruben Borg, Paul Fagan and John McCourt (eds), *Flann O'Brien: Problems with authority* (Cork: Cork University Press, 2017), p. 43.

6 Anthony Cronin, *No Laughing Matter: The life and times of Flann O'Brien* (New York: Fromm International, 1998), p. 69. The same account is repeated on p. 133.

7 Myles na Gopaleen, 'The Fausticity of Kelly', *RTV Guide*, 25 January 1963, pp. 12–13.

8 Ibid., p. 13.

9 Ibid.

10 There is an image of the signed copy, dated to 1932, in Peter Costello and Peter van de Kamp, *Flann O'Brien: An illustrated biography* (London: Bloomsbury, 1987), p. 46.

11 Letter to Ernest Blythe of 22 August 1942 (*L*, p. 124); letters to Hilton Edwards, October to November 1942 (*L*, pp. 125–8).

12 Catherine Ahearn and Adam Winstanley, 'An Inventory of Brian O'Nolan's Library at Boston College', *The Parish Review: Journal of Flann O'Brien studies*, vol. 2, no. 1, fall 2013, pp. 50, 56.

13 Dirk Van Hulle, 'Samuel Beckett's "Faust" Notes', *Samuel Beckett Today/Aujourd'hui*, no. 16, 2006, pp. 283–97.

14 John J. Burns Library, Boston College, Flann O'Brien Papers, MS.1997.027, box 24.

15 *CL*, 28 November 1944, p. 3; *CL*, 5 January 1948, p. 4; *CL*, 15 March 1950, p. 4; *CL*, 20 December 1945, p. 4; *CL*, 10 November 1945, p. 3; *CL*, 22 December 1948, p. 5; *CL*, 29 August 1949, p. 4; *CL*, 29 November 1948, p. 2; *CL*, 5 November 1948, p. 4.

16 *CL*, 20 December 1945, p. 4.

17 *CL*, 15 May 1946, p. 4.

18 Goethe, *Goethe's Poems*, pp. 132, 41.

19 *CL*, 29 November 1948, p. 2.

20 *CL*, 22 December 1948, p. 5, citing from *Goethe's Poems*, p. 1, and W.B. Yeats, *The Poems*, Daniel Albright (ed.) (London: Everyman, 1992), p. 159: '*Es hat der Autor, wenn er schreibt / So etwas Gewisses, das ihn treibt / Den Trieb hatt auch der Alexander / Und all die Helden mit einander* – / All that delirium of the brave – / Romantic Ireland's dead and gone, / It's with O'Leary in the grave!'

21 Catherine Flynn, '"the half-said thing": *Cruiskeen Lawn*, Japan and the Second World War', in Borg, Fagan and McCourt (eds), *Flann O'Brien: Problems with authority*, pp. 85–6.

22 Christopher Marlowe, *Doctor Faustus and Other Plays*, David Bevington and Eric Rasmussen (eds) (Oxford: Oxford University Press, 2008), see 'Note on the Texts', pp. xxv–xxviii.

23 Anon., 'Radio Programmes', *The Irish Press*, 28 November 1942, p. 2.

24 *CL*, 28 November 1944, p. 3.

25 Klaus L. Berghahn, 'Georg Johann Faust: The myth and its history', in Reinhold Grimm and Jost Hermand (eds), *Our Faust? Roots and ramifications of a modern German myth* (Madison: University of Wisconsin Press, 1987), p. 8.

26 Christopher Marlowe, *Dr Faustus*, 2nd edn, Roma Gill (ed.) (London: Methuen, 1989), p. 8.

27 Berghahn, 'Georg Johann Faust', p. 10.

28 Ibid., pp. 16–17.

29 Goethe, *Faust: A Norton critical edition*, l. 11564.

30 Zuzana Neubauerová, 'An Analysis of Selected Plays by Flann O'Brien', unpublished doctoral thesis, Univerzita Palackého of Olomouci, 2015, p. 18, www.theses.cz/id/pzjjsh/Thesis_Neub.pdf.

31 *Goethe's Faust: Translated into English verse*, 2nd edn, George Lefevre (trans.) (London: D. Nutt, 1843), p. 50.

32 Ibid., p. 64.

33 Ibid., p. 153.

34 Ibid., p. 171.

35 Ronald Gray, *Goethe: A critical introduction* (Cambridge: Cambridge University Press, 1967), p. 129.

36 Ibid., p. 134.

37 Ibid., pp. 137–8.

38 Ibid., p. 139.

39 Ian Ó Caoimh, 'The Ideal and the Ironic: Incongruous Irelands in *An Béal Bocht*, *No Laughing Matter* and Ciarán Ó Nualláin's *Óige an Dearthár*', in Borg, Fagan and McCourt (eds), *Flann O'Brien: Problems with authority*, p. 154.

40 Peter O'Leary, *Shiana* (Dublin: The Irish Book Company, 1916), p. 6.

41 Patrick O'Neill, 'The Reception of German Literature in Ireland 1750–1850: Part 2', *Studia Hibernica*, no. 17/18, 1977/8, pp. 104, 101.

42 Alana Gillespie, review of *Flann O'Brien: Plays and teleplays*, Daniel Keith Jernigan (ed.), *The Parish Review: Journal of Flann O'Brien studies*, vol. 2, no. 2, spring 2014, p. 32.

43 Joseph Holloway, *Joseph Holloway's Irish Theatre*, 3 vols, Robert Hogan and Michael J. O'Neill (eds) (Dixon: Proscenium, 1999), vol. 3, p. 83.

44 Adorno, 'On the Final Scene of *Faust*', pp. 118–19.

45 Inez Hedges, *Framing Faust: Twentieth-century cultural struggles* (Carbondale: Southern Illinois University Press, 2005), p. 193.

46 Houston Stewart Chamberlain, *Goethe*, 3rd edn (Munich: F. Bruckmann, 1921); Georg Schott, *Goethes Faust in heutiger Schau* (Stuttgart: Tazzelwurm Verlag, 1940); qtd in Hedges, *Framing Faust*, p. 48.

47 Karoline Kirst-Gundersen and Paul Levesque, '"Faust im Braunhemd": Germanistik and fascism', in Grimm and Hermand (eds), *Our Faust?*, p. 154.

48 Goethe, *Faust: A Norton critical edition*, l. 11580.

49 Baldur von Schirach, *Goethe an uns – Ewige Gedanken des großen Deutchen* (Munich/Berlin, 1938), qtd in Kirst-Gundersen and Levesque, 'Faust im Braunhemd', p. 158.

50 Ibid., p. 164.

51 Ernst Beutler, 'Goethes Faust, ein Deutsches Gedicht', in Gerhard Fricke, Franz Koch and Lemens Lugowski (eds), *Von Deutscher Art in Sprache und Dichtung*, vol. 4 (Stuttgart: W. Kohlhammer Verlag, 1941), pp. 279–80; qtd in Hedges, *Framing Faust*, p. 50.

52 Karl Kraus, 'Warum Die Fackel Nicht Erscheint', *Die Fackel*, no. 890–905, July 1934, p. 81, qtd and trans. in Edward Timms, *Karl Kraus: Apocalyptic Satirist, Vol. II: The post-war crisis and the rise of the swastika* (New Haven: Yale University Press, 2005), p. 503.

53 Ibid., p. 504.

54 Ibid., p. 496.

55 Ibid., p. 500, alluding to alluding to Goethe, *Faust: A Norton critical edition*, l. 1976.

56 Kieran Allen, *Fianna Fáil and Irish Labour: 1926 to the present* (London: Pluto, 1997), p. 52.

57 Mark Phelan, 'Irish Responses to Fascist Italy, 1919–1932', PhD thesis, NUI Galway, 2013, http://hdl.handle.net/10379/3401, pp. 119–226. De Valera's remarks are cited on p. 223, referring to their original publication in *Anglo-Celt*, 21 September 1929, as cited in Brian Reynolds, *The Formation and Development of Fianna Fáil, 1926–32*, PhD thesis, Trinity College Dublin, 1976, p. 177.

58 Taaffe, *Ireland Through the Looking-Glass*, p. 115.

59 Ibid., citing *CL*, 15 March 1943, p. 3.

60 R.M. Douglas, 'Ailtiri na hAiséirghe: Ireland's fascist new order', *History Ireland*, vol. 17, no. 5, September–October 2009, p. 44.

61 Brian O'Nolan, '"The Pathology of Revivalism" annotated and corrected carbon copy, undated', John J. Burns Library, Boston College, Flann O'Brien Papers, MS.1997.027, box 2, folder 43, p. 2.

62 Eamon Hughes offers one such reading in his essay 'Flann O'Brien's *At Swim-Two-Birds* in the Age of Mechanical Reproduction', in Edwina Keown and Carol Taaffe (eds), *Irish Modernism: Origins, contexts, publics* (Bern: Peter Lang, 2010), pp. 111–28.

63 Cronin records that on 18 August 1941 O'Nolan became private secretary to Seán MacEntee in the Ministry of Local Government. Cronin, *No Laughing Matter*, p. 120.

64 See, for example, 'Private Deputies' Business. – Annulment of Unemployment Assistance (Employment Period) Order—Motion', 20 March 1941, https://www.oireachtas.ie/en/debates/debate/dail/1941-03-20/15/.

65 Allen, *Fianna Fáil and Irish Labour*, pp. 21–4.

66 Ibid., p. 22; citing Fianna Fáil, *North Dublin Election Leaflet 1928*, O'Brien Collection, National Library of Ireland.

67 Ibid., p. 22.

68 Phelan, 'Irish Responses to Fascist Italy', p. 205.

69 Goethe, *Faust: A Norton critical edition*, l. 10497–8.

70 Ibid., l. 11563–4.

71 Phelan, 'Irish Responses to Fascist Italy', pp. 23, 52.

72 Such as Aodh de Blacam, 'What Do We Owe the Abbey?', *Irish Monthly*, no. 63, July 1935, pp. 199–200, and James Devane, 'Is an Irish Culture Possible?', *Ireland To-day*, vol. 1, no. 5, October 1936, p. 23. See Taaffe, *Ireland Through the Looking-Glass*, p. 46 for a discussion of the Catholic social critics.

73 Description of plans in Douglas, 'Ailtiri na hAiséirghe', p. 42.

74 Taaffe, *Ireland Through the Looking-Glass*, p. 115 and *CL*, 21 November 1942, p. 3.

75 Charles H. Lyttle, 'Historical Bases of Rome's Conflict with Freemasonry', *Church History*, vol. 9, no. 1, 1940, p. 3.

76 Phelan, 'Irish Responses to Fascist Italy', p. 206.

77 Ibid., p. 205.

78 Kirst-Gundersen and Levesque, 'Faust im Braunhemd', p. 157.

79 Allen, *Fianna Fáil and Irish Labour*, p. 24.

80 For more on this topic, see the special issue of *The Parish Review: Journal of Flann O'Brien studies*, vol. 6, no. 1, spring 2022, dedicated to 'Brian O'Nolan and the Civil Service', guest edited by Jonathan Foster and Elliott Mills.

81 *CL*, 3 April 1954, p. 10.

82 Kraus, 'Warum Die Fackel Nicht Erscheint', p. 2.

83 Adorno, 'On the Final Scene of *Faust*', p. 119.

84 Ibid.

11. Insect Plays

* This research was supported by a grant from the *Stratégie d'attractivité durable, Région Bretagne*.

1 *The Irish Press*, reviewing *Rhapsody in Stephen's Green*, wrote that the Čapek Brothers would 'have been amazed to find their translator and adaptor using their work […] to sneer at the people of Ireland' and that 'cheap jokes about motherhood are not worthy of any civilisation'. 'The Insect Play at the Gaiety', *The Irish Press*, 23 March 1943, p. 3. The *Evening Herald* wrote that they were 'saddened by Myles na gCopaleen's tampering with such an ingenious work'. '"Insect Play" at the Gaiety', *Evening Herald*, 23 March 1943, p. 2. O'Nolan's own paper, *The Irish Times*, was, understandably, supportive, calling it a 'brilliant adaptation'; 'An Irishman's Diary', *The Irish Times*, 24 March 1943, p. 3. Maxwell Sweeney commented that O'Nolan's version combines the satire of the original with the 'elements of farce'; 'Entomology in Eire', *The Irish Times*, 27 March 1943, p. 4. More recently, Rüdiger Imhof described the play as 'a bit of a dud'. Rüdiger Imhof, 'O'Brien's Bees Have Little Buzz and No Sting', *The Irish Times*, 24 January 1995, p. 12. A more detailed analysis of the critical reception of the play can be found in Ondřej Pilný, 'The Brothers Čapek at the Gate: *R.U.R.* and *The Insect Play*', in Ondřej Pilný, Ruud van den Beuken and Ian R. Walsh (eds), *Cultural Convergence: The Dublin Gate Theatre, 1928–1960* (Cham: Palgrave Macmillan, 2021), pp. 141–73.

2 The production notebooks are held in the Dublin Gate Theatre Archive at the Charles Deering McCormick Library of Special Collections, Northwestern University Library.

3 It is worth noting that Deleuze and Guattari have differentiated between animals that have been tainted by their interaction with humans (oedipal and state animals) and truly wild (or what they call demonic) animals who offer humanity the opportunity for becoming-animal. Gilles Deleuze and Felix Guattari, *A Thousand Plateaus: Capitalism and schizophrenia*, Brian Massumi (trans.) (London: Continuum, 2004), p. 265.

4 Giorgio Agamben, *The Open: Man and animal*, Kevin Attell (trans.) (Stanford: Stanford University Press, 2004), p. 29.

5 Agamben also notes the complex relationship in the humanist classifications of animals such as in Carl Linnaeus's taxon of Anthropomorpha in the first edition of *Systema Naturae* (1735) which included both humans and apes (ibid., p. 23).

6 Rosi Braidotti, 'The Critical Posthumanities; or, is medianatures to naturecultures as *Zoe* is to *Bios*?', *Cultural Politics*, vol. 12, no. 3, 2016, p. 381.

7 There is also a growing field of work in animal studies and posthumanism countering anthropocentric readings of work depicting, representing or otherwise aestheticising the nonhuman, with theorists such as Donna Haraway, Cary Wolfe and Rosi Braidotti complicating narratives of human exceptionalism. For further reading see Donna Haraway, *When Species Meet* (Minneapolis: University of Minnesota Press, 2008); Cary Wolfe, 'From Dead Meat to Glow-in-the-Dark Bunnies: Seeing "the animal question" in contemporary art', in S.I. Dobrin and S. Morey (eds), *Ecosee: Image, rhetoric, nature* (Albany: Suny Press, 2009), pp. 129–51; and Rosi Braidotti, *The Posthuman* (Malden: Polity Press, 2013).

8 For an extensive discussion of the automaton in performance, see Jane Goodall's 'Transferred Agencies: Performance and the fear of automatism', *Theatre Journal*, vol. 49, no. 4, 1997, pp. 441–53.

9 For example, flea circuses have entertained for centuries and, in the eighteenth century, entomologists/performers featured or performed as various types of insects including Gustavus Katterfelto (otherwise known as Doctor Caterpillar) and Thomas Wildman with his iconic bee beard. For an expansive analysis of these performers, and the gender implication for the emergence of the queen rather than the king bee, see Deirdre Coleman, 'Entertaining Entomology: Insects and insect performers in the eighteenth century', *Eighteenth-Century Life*, no. 30, 2006, pp. 107–34.

10 An interesting exploration of the use of insects (in early modern literature) and scale is Joseph Campana's 'The Bee and the Sovereign: Political entomology and the problem of scale', *Shakespeare Studies*, no. 41, 2013, pp. 94–113.

11 Selver's translation, which was adapted for the Regent by Nigel Playfair and Clifford Bax, will be used throughout the essay. The edition referenced will be Karel and Josef Čapek, *R.U.R. and The Insect Play (And so Ad Finitum)*, Paul Selver (trans.), Nigel Playfair and Clifford Bax (adapt.) (Oxford: Oxford University Press, 1961).

12 Ibid., p. 109.

13 Ibid., p. 127; *PT*, p. 184.

14 *CL*, 28 August 1942, p. 3.

15 Quidnunc, 'An Irishman's Diary', *The Irish Times*, 30 May 1942, p. 2.

16 Ibid.

17 Chris Morash and Shawn Richards, *Mapping Irish Theatre: Theories of space and place* (London: Cambridge University Press, 2013), p. 24.

18 Deleuze and Guattari, *A Thousand Plateaus*, p. 340.

19 Ibid., p. 307.

20 For analysis of animals in Irish literature see Kathryn J. Kirkpatrick and Borbála Faragó (eds), *Animals in Irish Literature and Culture* (Basingstoke: Palgrave Macmillan, 2015) and Maud Ellmann, '*Ulysses*: Changing into an animal', *Field Day Review*, no. 2, 2006, pp. 74–93.

21 The term 'zoopoetics' was first coined by Jacques Derrida in '*L'animal que donc je suis*', when speaking of 'Kafka's vast zoopoetics'. 'The animal,' he writes, 'is a word, it is an appellation that men have instituted, a name they have given themselves the right and the authority to give to the living other.' Jacques Derrida, *The Animal That Therefore I Am (More to Follow)*, David Wills (trans.), *Critical Inquiry*, vol. 28, no. 2, winter 2002, pp. 374, 392. It is worth

noting that Deleuze and Guattari see the idea of 'Becoming-animal, becoming-molecular, becoming-inhuman' as a part of Kafka's work. They also claim that in Kafka 'it is impossible to separate the erection of a great paranoid bureaucratic machine from the installation of little schizo machines of becoming-dog or becoming-beetle' (*A Thousand Plateaus*, p. 3).

22 See Rachel Murray, 'Beelines: Joyce's apian aesthetics', *Humanities*, vol. 6, no. 2, 2017, https://doi.org/10.3390/h6020042; Benjamin Bagocius, 'Queer Entomology: Virginia Woolf's butterflies', *Modernism/modernity*, vol. 24, no. 4, 2017, pp. 723–50.

23 Other publications of note that impacted on the decentralisation of humankind was Friedrich Nietzsche, *The Birth of Tragedy*, Shaun Whiteside (trans.) (London: Penguin, 2003); and Sigmund Freud, *The Interpretation of Dreams*, 3rd edn, A.A. Brill (trans.) (New York: The Macmillan Company, 1913).

24 Deleuze and Guattari, *A Thousand Plateaus*, p. 340.

25 Ibid.

26 Ibid., p. 238.

27 *Insect Play* (Selver trans.), p. 112.

28 Ibid., p. 110.

29 Pilný, 'The Brothers Čapek at the Gate', p. 157.

30 Lee Edelman, 'The Future Is Kid Stuff: Queer theory, disidentification and the death drive', *Narrative*, vol. 6, no. 1, January 1998, p. 26.

31 Ibid., p. 29.

32 *Insect Play* (Selver trans.), p. 118.

33 Ibid., p. 127.

34 Ibid., p. 110.

35 Ibid.

36 Ibid., p. 125.

37 Ibid., p. 126.

38 Jussi Parikka, *Insect Media: An archaeology of animals and technology* (Minneapolis: University of Minnesota Press, 2010), p. 49.

39 Ibid., p. 50.

40 Jarka M. Burian, 'K.H. Hilar and the Early Twentieth-Century Czech Theatre', *Theatre Journal*, vol. 34, no. 1, 1982, p. 64.

41 The answer to the binary opposition that exists between humanism and anti-humanism, according to Rosi Braidotti, is posthumanism, specifically post-anthropocentric posthumanism which avoids the sentimentality of humanistic values. See Braidotti, *The Posthuman*.

42 Historical representation portrays Khepri, the Egyptian God as a dung beetle.

43 Jean-Henri Fabre, *The Sacred Beetle and Others*, Alexander Teixeira de Mattos (trans.) (New York: Dodd, Mead & Company, 1918), p. viii.

44 Ibid., p. 3.

45 *Insect Play* (Selver trans.), p. 130.

46 Ibid., p. 131.

47 Ibid., p. 133.

48 Fabre, *The Sacred Beetle*, p. 36.

49 *Insect Play* (Selver trans.), p. 134.

50 Ibid., p. 131.

51 Ibid., p. 139.

52 Stephen Johnson, 'The Integration of Theatre History and Theatre Practice in the University: A case study using *Ze života hmyzu* (*From the Life of Insects*) by Karel and Josef Čapek', *Theatre Topics*, vol. 4, no. 2, 1994, p. 197.

53 Jennifer Sheppard, 'How the "Vixen" Lost Its Mores: Gesture and music in Janáček's animal opera', *Cambridge Opera Journal*, vol. 22, no. 2, 2010, p. 152.

54 Parikka, *Insect Media*, p. 22.

55 Sheppard, 'How the "Vixen" Lost Its Mores', p. 152.

56 *Insect Play* (Selver trans.), 162.

57 Another Czech production, an opera called *Příhody lišky Bystroušky* (The Cunning Little Vixen) by Leoš Janáček premiered in 1924 at the National Theatre Brno and featured various animals, including insects. In fact, a later production staged at the Prague National Theatre in 1925 featured Josef Čapek as designer.

58 Parikka, *Insect Media*, p. 22.

59 Agamben, *The Open*, p. 76.

60 For an analysis of Uexküll's theory of *umwelten* in O'Nolan's work (specifically 'John Duffy's Brother'), see Dirk Van Hulle, '"widening out the mind": Flann O'Brien's "wide mind" between Joyce's "mental life" and Beckett's "deep within"', in Ruben Borg, Paul Fagan and John McCourt (eds), *Flann O'Brien: Problems with authority* (Cork: Cork University Press, 2017), pp. 105–18.

61 Agamben, *The Open*, p. 77.

62 For an analysis of the application of Agamben's theory of bare life to *An Béal Bocht*, see Maebh Long, 'The Trial of Jams O'Donnell: *An Béal Bocht* and the force of law', in Ruben Borg, Paul Fagan and Werner Huber, *Flann O'Brien: Contesting legacies* (Cork: Cork University Press, 2014), pp. 181–94.

63 Parikka, *Insect Media*, p. 24.

64 Ibid.

65 Deleuze and Guattari, *A Thousand Plateaus*, p. 260.

66 Ibid.

12. Thunderous Anger and Cold Showers

1   Anon., 'Pantomimes a Triumph for Irish Talent', *Sunday Independent*, 31 December 1944, p. 2.

2   Anon., 'Music and Drama: Show that made history', *Evening Herald*, 6 January 1945, p. 2.

3   Anon., 'Theatre and Film Review', *The Irish Press*, 8 January 1945, p. 2.

4   Anon., 'Theatre, Film Reviews', *The Irish Press*, 29 January 1945, p. 2.

5   Anon., 'Gaelic Pantomime Best Show of All', *The Irish Press*, 28 December 1944, p. 3.

6   'Bainfidh "An Sgian" le Myles na gCopaleen […] gáire as an duine is gruamdha da bhfuil fé luighe na gréine, go mór mór toisc go bhfuil an Compantas ag magadh fúinn féin annseo'. 'An-Ghreann Sa Pheacóig', *The Irish Press*, 20 February 1945, p. 4.

7   Carol Taaffe, *Ireland Through the Looking-Glass: Flann O'Brien, Myles na gCopaleen and Irish cultural debate* (Cork: Cork University Press, 2008), p. 115.

8   For convenience's sake, I will be quoting from the English version of *An Sgian* collected in Daniel Keith Jernigan's *Flann O'Brien: Collected plays and teleplays* (2013), rather than the original Irish script. As I translated that piece for the collection, any misinterpretations or mistaken emphases are my own.

9   The implications of transnational archival research (given that the little-known sketch was discovered among O'Nolan's papers in Boston College, rather than in Ireland) – particularly for scholarship that has tended to frame his work in terms of national identity or belonging – are outside the scope of this particular essay. For a dynamic interrogation of this issue, see Joseph LaBine's essay 'Myles na gCopaleen's "An Sgian": A Knife in the back of Irish archivists', in Linda M. Morra (ed.), *Moving Archives* (Waterloo, ON: Wilfrid Laurier University Press, 2020).

10 Louis de Paor, 'Twisting the Knife', *The Irish Times*, 29 March 2002, p. 12.

11 Ibid.

12 In the *Handsome Carvers*'s defence, I would argue that it is better structured than *An Sgian*. In the latter, we are supposed to accept that Tadhg does not realise the knife's provenance until he reads the letter that came with it – apparently for the first time – after killing Peig, despite the fact that the knife is a wedding present from an organisation to which he is deeply committed. In *The Handsome Carvers*, the audience actually sees the set of knives being presented to Peter on stage; thus, it does not matter whether or not he remembers where they come from, because the audience is not relying on him alone to supply that information. *The Handsome Carvers* succeeds by presenting the plot in reverse: had it been presented as a straightforward sequential narrative, it would lack a meaningful ending, and the sense of a heavy-handed morality fable would only be emphasised.

13 František Deák, 'Théâtre du Grand Guignol', *The Drama Review*, vol. 18, no. 1, March 1974, p. 35.

14 Ibid., pp. 36–7.

15 Ibid., p. 39.

16 Ibid., p. 41.

17 Ibid., p. 40.

18 Ibid., p. 43.

19 Mel Gordon, *Theatre of Fear and Horror: The grisly spectacle of the Grand Guignol of Paris, 1898–1962* (Port Townsend: Feral House, 2016), p. 14.

20 Deák, 'Théâtre du Grand Guignol', pp. 38–9.

21 Anon., 'Thrills', *Cork Examiner*, 31 August 1922, p. 4.

22 Joan Fitzgerald, 'James Joyce's Italian Translation of *Riders to the Sea*', in Jacqueline Genet and Richard Allen Cave (eds), *Perspectives of Irish Drama and Theatre: Irish literary studies*, no. 33 (Gerrards Cross: Colin Smythe, 1991), p. 95.

23 Anon., 'After Grand Guignol: "The Bat" provides thrills at the Gaiety', *Freeman's Journal*, 4 September 1923, p. 4.

24 Anon., 'Dublin Theatres: "The Cat and the Canary"', *The Irish Times*, 27 May 1924, p. 6.

25 Anon., 'Grand Guignol Fails', *Belfast News-Letter*, 28 May 1928, p. 10.

26 Anon., 'Dun Laoghaire's Civic Theatre', *Irish Independent*, 24 August 1929, p. 10.

27 Anon., 'Dramatic Festival', *The Irish Press*, 26 May 1933, p. 9.

28 Anon., 'A Treat for Carrick-on-Shannon', *Leitrim Observer*, 9 January 1932, p. 4.

29 Anon., 'Grand Guignol in Irish: New play at the Abbey Theatre', *The Irish Times*, 12 January 1926, p. 9.

30 Anon., 'Gaelic Plays at the Peacock Theatre', *The Irish Times*, 26 May 1930, p. 4.

31 Anon., 'Two Plays, Presented By Amateurs', *Irish Independent*, 31 January 1928, p. 6.

32 Anon., 'New Comedy at the Abbey Theatre', *Evening Herald*, 8 November 1932, p. 6.

33 Anon., 'Grand Guignol at the Abbey: One-act sketch of Dublin "Underworld"', *The Irish Times*, 17 July 1928, p. 4.

34 Anon., 'Wicklow Man's Play', *Irish Independent*, 17 May 1946, p. 4.

35 John M. Callahan, 'The Grand-Guignol in New York City, October–November 1923: Violence fails to draw an audience', in Arthur Gewitz and James J. Kolb (eds), *Art, Glitter and Glitz: Mainstream playwrights and popular theatre in 1920s America* (Westport: Praeger, 2004), pp. 159–60.

36 Gordon, *Theatre of Fear and Horror*, p. 60.

37 Taaffe, *Ireland Through the Looking-Glass*, p. 26.

38 Sean Pryor, 'Making Evil, With Flann O'Brien', in Rónán McDonald, Julian Murphet and Sascha Morrell (eds), *Flann O'Brien & Modernism* (London: Bloomsbury, 2014), p. 16.

39 *CL*, 13 June 1944, p. 3.

40 De Paor, 'Twisting the Knife', p. 12.

41 Anon., 'Soldier Dead in Barracks: Manslaughter verdict – sentence of 18 months in jail', *The Irish Times*, 14 June 1934, p. 5.

42 Anon., 'Stabbed to Death: Galway murder charge; husband accused of killing wife', *The Irish Times*, 28 April 1936, p. 2.

43 Brian Ó Nualláin, 'Eachta an Fhir Ólta: CEOL!', *The Irish Press*, 24 August 1932, p. 4. Translated as 'The Tale of the Drunkard: MUSIC!' by Jack Fennell in *SF*, pp. 35–7; previously translated as 'The Narrative of the Inebriated Man' by Breandán Ó Conaire in *MBM*, pp. 173–5.

44 Keith Hopper, *Flann O'Brien: A portrait of the artist as a young post-modernist* (Cork: Cork University Press, 2009), p. 63.

45 Maebh Long, *Assembling Flann O'Brien* (London: Bloomsbury, 2014), p. 158.

46 Ibid., pp. 154–5.

47 Ibid., p. 91.

48 Ibid., pp. 166–7.

49 Ibid., pp. 163–4.

13. Voices Off

1 A year before its publication in *The Bell*, Myles na Gopaleen laid out the plot of 'Two in One' in the *Cruiskeen Lawn* column 'The Perfect Crime'; *CL*, 26 May 1953, p. 6. Maebh Long notes that O'Nolan's correspondence suggests that he next adapted the plot as a radio play (*L*, 181, n. 63). The short story was published as Myles na Gopaleen, 'Two in One', *The Bell*, vol. 19, no. 8, July 1954, pp. 30–4. For the stage script see Sarah Poutch, 'Flann O'Brien and *The Dead Spit of Kelly*', *Archives and Special Collections – James Hardiman Library*, 8 November 2010, http://nuigarchives.blogspot.com/2010/11/flann-obrien-and-dead-spit-of-kelly.html. For the teleplay, see *PT*, pp. 385–413.

2 Anne Clissmann, *Flann O'Brien: A critical introduction to his writings* (Dublin: Gill & Macmillan, 1975), p. 338.

3 Anthony Cronin, *No Laughing Matter: The life and times of Flann O'Brien* (New York: Fromm, 1989), p. 222.

4 Steven Connor, 'Echo's Bones: Myth, modernity and the vocalic uncanny', in Michael Bell and Peter Poellner (eds), *Myth and the Making of Modernity: The problem of grounding in early twentieth-century literature* (Amsterdam: Rodopi, 1998), p. 214. For examples of the recent critical interest paid to modernist media, see, for instance, Matthew Feldman, Erik Tönning and Henry Mead (eds), *Broadcasting in the Modernist Era* (London: Bloomsbury, 2014) and Chris Forster, *Modernism and Its Media* (London: Bloomsbury, 2021).

5 Connor, 'Echo's Bones', p. 214.

6 Ibid., p. 213.

7 *CL*, 'The Perfect Crime', 26 May 1953, p. 6.

8 Ibid.

9 N. Katherine Hayles, *How We Became Posthuman: Virtual bodies in cybernetics, literature and informatics* (Chicago: The University of Chicago Press, 1999), pp. xi, xii.

10 Ibid., p. 2.

11 Ibid.

12 Ibid.

13 Jack Fennell makes the argument for attributing the story to O'Nolan in 'The Case for John Shamus O'Donnell', *Journey Planet*, no. 43, 2018, pp. 28–38.

14 Jack Fennell, 'Myles in Space: Science fiction and *Cruiskeen Lawn*', *The Parish Review: Journal of Flann O'Brien studies*, vol. 3, no. 1, fall 2014, p. 64. See also Jack Fennell, 'Irelands Enough

and Time: Brian O'Nolan's science fiction', in Ruben Borg, Paul Fagan and Werner Huber (eds), *Flann O'Brien: Contesting legacies* (Cork: Cork University Press, 2014), pp. 33–45.

15 Amanda Duncan, 'Communing with Machines: The bicycle as a figure of symbolic transgression in the posthumanist novels of Samuel Beckett and Flann O'Brien', in Jeremy Withers and Daniel P. Shea (eds), *Culture on Two Wheels: The bicycle in literature and film* (Lincoln: University of Nebraska Press, 2016), p. 166.

16 *CL*, 7 December 1942, p. 3. See Maebh Long, 'Is It About a Typewriter? Brian O'Nolan and technologies of inscription', *The Parish Review: Journal of Flann O'Brien studies*, vol. 4, no. 2, spring 2020, pp. 4–5.

17 Ruben Borg, *Fantasies of Self-Mourning: Modernism, the posthuman and the finite* (Leiden and Boston: Brill|Rodopi, 2019); Duncan, 'Communing with Machines', pp. 152–70; Joseph Brooker, 'Do Bicycles Dream of Atomic Sheep? Forms of the fantastic in Flann O'Brien and Philip K. Dick', *The Parish Review: Journal of Flann O'Brien studies*, vol. 4, no. 2, spring 2020, pp. 1–23; Long, 'Is It About a Typewriter?', pp. 1–16.

18 See the biopolitical focus of the essays in Ruben Borg and Paul Fagan (eds), *Flann O'Brien: Gallows humour* (Cork: Cork University Press, 2020).

19 Clissmann, p. 144. For a recent analysis of how O'Nolan's writing problematises the strict Cartesian dualism between the *res cogitans* and the *res extensa*, see Dirk Van Hulle, '"widening out the mind": Flann O'Brien's "wide mind" between Joyce's "mental life" and Beckett's "deep within"', in Ruben Borg, Paul Fagan and John McCourt (eds), *Flann O'Brien: Problems with authority* (Cork: Cork University Press, 2017), pp. 105–18.

20 On bodiless voices in the theatre see, for instance, Jarrett Walker, 'Voiceless Bodies and Bodiless Voices: The drama of human perception in *Coriolanus*', *Shakespeare Quarterly*, vol. 43, no. 2, summer 1992, pp. 170–85; and Sarah Balkin, *Spectral Characters: Genre and materiality on the modern stage* (Ann Arbor: University of Michigan Press, 2019).

21 Eamonn Hughes, 'Flann O'Brien's *At Swim-Two-Birds* in the Age of Mechanical Reproduction', in Edwina Keown and Carol Taaffe (eds), *Irish Modernism: Origins, contexts, publics* (Oxford: Peter Lang, 2009), p. 119.

22 Borg, *Fantasies of Self-Mourning*, p. 6, n. 6.

23 Ibid.

24 Ibid., p. 11.

25 Adam J. Engel, 'Talking Heads: Bodiless voices in *Heart of Darkness*, "The Hollow Men" and the First World War', *Conradiana*, vol. 45, no. 3, fall 2013, p. 21.

26 James Joyce, *Ulysses*, Jeri Johnson (introd. and ed.) (Oxford: Oxford University Press, 1998), p. 109.

27 A variation on a scene of madness communicated through a gramophone is played out in *CL*, 6 April 1942, p. 2.

28 See Long, 'Is It About a Typewriter?', p. 9.

29 *CL*, 19 December 1941, p. 4. Elsewhere, Myles endorses using gramophone records as material for a slow fire owing to their high level of petroleum (*CL*, 20 May 1942, p. 2); expresses confusion at the mangled words coming from his gramophone player, such as 'the lost roe-hose of some mare' [*sic*] (*CL*, 9 December 1942, p. 3); derides the piano as 'a defective gramophone that cannot produce vocal[s]' (*CL*, 11 April 1944, p. 3); and claims to never listen to records but only to speed-read them directly off their surface (*CL*, 15 May 1944, p. 3).

30 *Metropolis*, directed by Fritz Lang (Berlin: Universum Film, 1927), was screened in the Olympia, Dublin by the Irish Film Society in March 1943; *The Day the Earth Stood Still*, directed by Robert Wise (Los Angeles, CA: 20th Century Fox, 1951) was screened in the Pavilion (Dún Laoghaire) in March 1952; *The Colossus of New York*, directed by Eugène

Lourié (Los Angeles, CA: Paramount, 1958) was screened in the Adelphi, Dublin in April 1960.

31 For William Brown, posthumanism is 'better understood as a framework through which to consider all cinema, rather than as a set of qualities that pertain to a specific body of contemporary films' in the science-fiction genre. William Brown, 'From DelGuat to ScarJo', in Michael Hauskeller, Curtis D. Carbonell and Thomas D. Philbeck (eds), *The Palgrave Handbook of Posthumanism in Film and Television* (New York: Palgrave Macmillan, 2015), p. 16.

32 Joseph Brooker, *Flann O'Brien* (Tavistock: Northcote House, 2005), p. 95. For examples, see *BM*, pp. 95, 108–10.

33 As a small sample, Myles discusses Charlie Chaplin and *Fantasia*, directed by Samuel Armstrong *et al.* (Burbank, CA: Walt Disney Productions, 1940) in *CL*, 8 May 1942, p. 3; *Gone with the Wind*, directed by Victor Fleming (Culver City, CA: Selznick International Pictures, 1939) in *CL*, 30 October 1942, p. 3; and *The Rising of the Moon*, directed by John Ford (Burbank, CA: Warner Bros., 1957) in *CL*, 14 May 1956, p. 6.

34 *CL*, 'The Tragic Box', 28 May 1953, p. 5.

35 Richard S. James, 'Avant-Garde Sound-on-Film Techniques and Their Relationship to Electro-Acoustic Music', *The Musical Quarterly*, vol. 72, no. 1, 1986, p. 75.

36 Sergei Eisenstein, Vsevolod Pudovkin and Grigori Alexandrov's 1928 'Sound Manifesto' insisted on 'distinct, non-synchronisation [of sound] with the visual image' so that cinematic sound may be 'treated as a new montage element'. Sergei Eisenstein, Vsevolod Pudovkin and Grigori Alexandrov, 'A Statement on Sound (USSR, 1928)', in Scott MacKenzie (ed.), *Film Manifestos and Global Cinema Cultures: A critical anthology* (Berkeley: University of California Press, 2014), p. 567.

37 Gina Bloom, *Voice in Motion: Staging gender, shaping sound in early modern England* (Philadelphia: University of Pennsylvania Press, 2007), p. 167.

38 Myles na gCopaleen, 'Drink and Time in Dublin', *Irish Writing*, no. 1, 1946, pp. 71–7.

39 Sam Dickson, '"No Unauthorised Boozing": Brian O'Nolan and the thirsty muse', in Julian Murphet, Rónán McDonald and Sascha Morrell (eds), *Flann O'Brien & Modernism* (London: Bloomsbury, 2014), p. 165.

40 Yaeli Greenblatt, '"the tattered cloak of his perished skin": The body as costume in "Two in One"', *At Swim-Two-Birds* and *The Third Policeman*', in Borg and Fagan (eds), *Flann O'Brien: Gallows humour*, p. 139.

41 Mary Ann Doane, 'The Voice in the Cinema: The articulation of body and space', *Yale French Studies*, no. 60, *Cinema/Sound*, 1980, p. 42.

42 Ibid., p. 37.

43 Allan Casebier, *Film and Phenomenology: Towards a realist theory of cinematic representation* (Cambridge: Cambridge University Press, 1991), p. 92.

44 Michael Chion, *The Voice in Cinema*, trans. Claudia Gorbman (New York: Columbia University Press, 1999), p. 4 (emphasis in original).

45 Doane, 'The Voice in the Cinema', p. 37.

46 See, for instance, the 'invisible' voice of Kelly in the pub scene (*CN*, p. 35).

47 Jarrett Walker, 'Voiceless Bodies and Bodiless Voices', p. 170.

48 Lilya Kaganovsky, *The Voice of Technology: Soviet cinema's transition to sound, 1928–1935* (Bloomington: Indiana University Press, 2018), p. 204.

49 For a reading of the gramophone in *At Swim-Two-Birds* as a mechanised figure of the intergenerational 'cultural stress' of the Free State era 'that belies the post-war peace', see Zan Cammack, *Ireland's Gramophones: Material culture, memory and trauma in Irish modernism* (Clemson: Clemson University Press, 2021), pp. 16, 151–64.

50 The theme of the tyrannical or despotic author-god is treated at length in Keith Hopper, *Flann O'Brien: A portrait of the artist as a young post-modernist*, 2nd edn, J. Hillis Miller (foreword) (Cork: Cork University Press, 2009).

51 Kaganovsky, *The Voice of Technology*, p. 204.

52 Doane, 'The Voice in the Cinema', p. 42.

53 Bloom, *Voice in Motion*, p. 167.

54 *CL*, 8 December 1941, p. 2.

55 Maebh Long, *Assembling Flann O'Brien* (London: Bloomsbury, 2014), p. 193.

56 A few pages later, the voice-off technique is further emphasised when the narrator notes hearing the pub customers' 'voices through the thin door' (*CN*, p. 227).

57 Thierry Robin, 'Representation as a Hollow Form, or the Paradoxical Magic of Idiocy and Skepticism in Flann O'Brien's Works', *The Review of Contemporary Fiction*, vol. 31, no. 3, fall 2011, p. 40.

58 Hyewon Shin, 'Voice and Vision in Oshii Mamoru's *Ghost in the Shell*: Beyond Cartesian optics', *Animation*, vol. 6, no. 7, 2011, p. 7.

59 Bloom, *Voice in Motion*, p. 161.

60 Engel, 'Talking Heads', p. 21.

61 Long, *Assembling*, pp. 45–6.

62 Jennika Baines, '"Un-Understandable Mystery": Catholic faith and revelation in *The Third Policeman*', *The Review of Contemporary Fiction*, vol. 31, no. 3, fall 2011, p. 83.

63 Ibid.

64 See Emilie Morin, 'W.B. Yeats and Broadcasting, 1924–1965', *Historical Journal of Film, Radio and Television*, vol. 35, no. 1, 2015, pp. 145–75; Damien Keane, 'Time Made Audible: Irish stations and radio modernism', in Kathryn Conrad, Cóilín Parsons and Julie McCormick Weng (eds), *Science, Technology and Irish Modernism* (New York: Syracuse University Press, 2019), pp. 330–45; Jeremy Lakoff, 'Broadcatastrophe! Denis Johnston's radio drama and the aesthetics of *Working It Out*', in ibid., pp. 161–4.

65 Cammack, *Ireland's Gramophones*, pp. 131–64.

14. Theatre and the Visual Arts

1 Declan Kiberd, *Irish Classics* (Cambridge: Harvard University Press, 2001), pp. 504 and 506; Carol Taaffe, *Ireland Through the Looking-Glass: Flann O'Brien, Myles na gCopaleen and Irish cultural debate* (Cork: Cork University Press, 2008), pp. 41 and 38; Maebh Long, *Assembling Flann O'Brien* (London: Bloomsbury, 2014), p. 114; Michael McAteer, 'Law and Violence in Ferguson's *Congal*, Yeats's *The Herne's Egg* and O'Brien's *At Swim-Two-Birds*', in Ruben Borg and Paul Fagan (eds), *Flann O'Brien: Gallows humour* (Cork: Cork University Press, 2020), pp. 197–216.

2 Louis de Paor, '"a scholar manqué"? Further notes on Brian Ó Nualláin's engagement with early Irish literature', in Ruben Borg, Paul Fagan and John McCourt (eds), *Flann O'Brien: Problems with authority* (Cork: Cork University Press, 2017), pp. 194–7.

3 Cathal G. Ó hÁinle, 'Fionn and Suibhne in *At Swim-Two-Birds*', *Hermathena*, no. 142, 1987, pp. 11–49; Taaffe, *Ireland Through the Looking-Glass*, pp. 37–49; de Paor, '"a scholar manqué"?', pp. 192–202.

4 de Paor, '"a scholar manqué"?', pp. 189 and 194–5.

5 Kiberd, *Irish Classics*, p. 506.

6 *CL*, 16 August 1943, p. 3; 10 September 1957, p. 6; 11 September 1957, p. 6. For Myles's other references to Lady Gregory, see *CL*, 7 May 1943, p. 3; 12 October 1944, p. 3; 16 August 1946, p. 4 (where she is part of an elaborate Keats and Chapman routine); 9 May 1947, p. 4; 4 October 1954, p. 4; 6 April 1960, p. 8.

7   *CL*, 10 September 1957, p. 6.
8   Lady Augusta Gregory, *Seventy Years: Being the autobiography of Lady Gregory* (Gerrards Cross: Colin Smythe, 1974), p. 391.
9   Ibid., pp. 390–9; Lady Augusta Gregory, *Cuchulain of Muirthemne: The story of the men of the red branch of Ulster* (Gerrards Cross: Colin Smythe, 1975), pp. 271–2. For *Silva Gadelica*, see Gregory, *Seventy Years*, p. 404; Lady Augusta Gregory, *Gods and Fighting Men* (Gerrards Cross: Colin Smythe, 1970), p. 8.
10 Gregory, *Seventy Years*, pp. 390–9.
11 See Eugene O'Curry, *Lectures on the Manuscript Material of Ancient Irish History* (Dublin: Duffy, 1861).
12 Eglantina Remport, *Lady Gregory and Irish National Theatre: Art, drama, politics* (Basingstoke: Palgrave Macmillan, 2018), p. 59.
13 Ibid., pp. 57–60. Gregory's innovative concept and her reader-friendly style made her collections popular with Anglo-Irish writers, J.M. Synge famously calling *Cuchulain of Muirthemne* his 'daily bread' and W.B. Yeats remarking that 'this book is the best that has come out of Ireland in my time'. Synge qtd in Gregory, *Seventy Years*, p. 403; William Butler Yeats, 'Preface', in Gregory, *Cuchulain of Muirthemne*, p. 11.
14 See for instance, Long, *Assembling*, pp. 32–5, 42–3, and Mark Steven, 'Flann O'Brien's Aestho-Autogamy', in Julian Murphet, Rónán McDonald and Sascha Morrell (eds), *Flann O'Brien & Modernism* (New York: Bloomsbury, 2014), pp. 197, 200–1.
15 O'Nolan's literary forerunner, James Joyce, had written in a similar vein in the 'Cyclops' episode of *Ulysses*, which mocks the literary styles of Revival authors like Standish O'Grady and George Russell. James Joyce, *Ulysses* (London: Penguin, 1992), pp. 376–402.
16 Gregory, *Gods and Fighting Men*, p. 354.
17 Keith Hopper, '"Silent, so to speak": Flann O'Brien and the sense of an ending', in Michael McAteer (ed.), *Silence in Modern Irish Literature* (Leiden: Brill, 2016), p. 181.
18 Remport, *Lady Gregory*, p. 76.
19 Ibid.
20 Ibid., p. 78.
21 Jeffrey Richards, *The Ancient World on the Victorian and Edwardian Stage* (Basingstoke: Palgrave, 2009), pp. 61, 63.
22 Ibid., pp. 61–3.
23 Nicholas Daly, *The Demographic Imagination and the Nineteenth-Century City* (Cambridge: Cambridge University Press, 2015), p. 41.
24 Daly, *The Demographic Imagination*, p. 42.
25 Richards, *The Ancient World*, p. 63.
26 Edward Bulwer-Lytton, 'Preface', *The Last Days of Pompeii*, vol. 1 (London: Richard Bentley, 1834), p. viii. Bulwer-Lytton writes: 'Enough, if this book, whatever its imperfections, should be found a portrait – unskilful perhaps in colouring – faulty in drawing – but, not altogether an unfaithful likeness of the features and the costume of the age which I have attempted to paint: – may it be (what is far more important) a just representation of human passions and the human heart, whose elements in all ages are the same!' (ibid.).
27 William Guild Howard, ed. and trans., *Laokoon: Lessing, Herder and Goethe* (New York: Henry Holt, 1910), p. 41.
28 For the composition history, see William St Clair and Annika Bautz, 'The Making of the Myths: Edward Bulwer-Lytton's *The Last Days of Pompeii* (1834)', in Victoria C. Gardner Coates, Kenneth Lapatin and Jon L. Seydl (eds), *The Last Days of Pompeii: Decadence, apocalypse, resurrection* (Los Angeles: J. Paul Getty Museum and the Cleveland Museum of Art, 2012), pp. 52–9; and Judith Harris, *A Story of Rediscovery: Pompeii awakened* (London: Tauris, 2007), pp. 163, 165, 168.

29 Lionel Pilkington, *Theatre and the State in Twentieth-Century Ireland: Cultivating the people* (London: Routledge, 2001), p. 7.

30 Maria Tymoczko, 'Amateur Theatricals, *Tableaux Vivants* and Cathleen ni Houlihan', *Yeats Annual*, no. 10, 1993, pp. 33–64; and Catherine Morris, *Alice Milligan and the Irish Cultural Revival* (Dublin: Four Courts Press, 2012), pp. 246–7, 250, 253–7, 265–9.

31 Remport, *Lady Gregory*, pp. 122–4 and 127–32.

32 'Mr Yeats and Theatre Reform', *The Leader*, 28 May 1903.

33 Remport, *Lady Gregory*, pp. 28, 33.

34 Qtd in Anthony Cronin, *No Laughing Matter: The life and times of Flann O'Brien* (London: Grafton, 1989), p. 134.

35 Anthony Roche, 'Re-Working "The Workhouse Ward": McDonagh, Beckett and Gregory', *Irish University Review*, vol. 34, no. 1, 2004, pp. 171–84; and Emilie Morin, *Samuel Beckett and the Problem of Irishness* (Basingstoke: Palgrave Macmillan, 2009), pp. 103–4.

36 Janet Egleson Dunleavy and Gareth W. Dunleavy, *Douglas Hyde: A maker of modern Ireland* (Berkeley: University of California Press, 1991), p. 225.

37 Lady Augusta Gregory, *The Collected Plays of Lady Gregory, Volume One: Comedies*, Ann Saddlemyer (ed.) (New York: Oxford University Press, 1970), p. 105.

38 Ann Saddlemyer, 'Introduction', in ibid., p. x.

39 Ibid.

40 Ibid.

41 Jennika Baines, 'The Murders of Flann O'Brien: Death and creation in *At Swim-Two-Birds*, *The Third Policeman*, *An Béal Bocht*, and "Two in One"', in Ruben Borg, Paul Fagan and Werner Huber (eds), *Flann O'Brien: Contesting legacies* (Cork: Cork University Press, 2014), pp. 207–18.

42 Sinéad Garrigan Mattar, *Primitivism, Science and the Irish Revival* (Oxford: Clarendon, 2004), p. 220.

43 See, for instance, Jorge Luis Borges, 'When Fiction Lives in Fiction', in *Selected Non-Fictions*, Eliot Weinberger (ed.) (New York: Penguin, 1999), pp. 160–2, and Patricia Waugh, *Metafiction: The theory and practice of self-conscious fiction* (London: Routledge, 2002), p. 127.

44 Judith Hill, *Lady Gregory: An Irish life* (Stroud: Sutton, 2005), p. 19.

45 *Catalogue of Printed Books formerly in the Library at Coole, the Property of the Lady Gregory Estate – Sotheby Auction Catalogue for 20 and 21 March 1972* (London: Sotheby & Co., 1972), p. 18.

46 Ana María G. Laguna, *Cervantes and the Pictorial Imagination* (Lewisburg: Bucknell University Press, 2009), p. 30.

47 Ibid., pp. 26–7.

48 Ibid., pp. 27–9.

49 Ibid., pp. 29 and 26.

50 Ibid., p. 31.

51 Helena Percas de Ponseti, *Cervantes: The writer and painter of Don Quijote* (Columbia: University of Missouri Press, 1988); Frederick A. de Armas, *Quixotic Frescoes: Cervantes and Italian Renaissance art* (Toronto: University of Toronto Press, 2006); Alicia R. Zuese, *Baroque Spain and the Writing of Visual and Material Culture* (Cardiff: University of Wales Press, 2015).

52 Remport, *Lady Gregory*, pp. 22–3, 28–9, 33.

53 Helen H. Reed, 'Theatricality in the Picaresque of Cervantes', *Cervantes: Bulletin of the Cervantes Society of America*, vol. 7, no. 2, 1987, p. 75.

54 Ibid., p. 76.

55 Cory A. Reed, 'Cervantes and the Novelisation of Drama: Tradition and innovation in the *entremeses*', *Cervantes: Bulletin of the Cervantes Society of America*, vol. 11, no. 1, 1991, pp. 61–86; Melanie Henry, *The Signifying Self: Cervantine drama as counter-perspective aesthetic* (London: The Modern Humanities Research Association, 2013), p. 18.

56 M. [T.S. Munden], 'On the Less Celebrated Productions of the Author of *Don Quixote*', *New Monthly Magazine*, no. 1, 1821, p. 118.

57 Frederick A. de Armas, 'Cervantes and the Italian Renaissance', in Anthony J. Cascardi (ed.), *The Cambridge Companion to Cervantes* (Cambridge: Cambridge University Press, 2006), p. 34.

58 Margaret Wilson, *Spanish Drama of the Golden Age* (Oxford: Pergamon, 1969), p. 15.

59 Ibid., pp. 15, 22; for the painted scenery, see p. 178; for the Bosch-like quality, see p. 417.

60 Síghle Bhreathnach-Lynch, 'Twelve Irish Artists: A school of Irish painting?', *New Hibernia Review*, vol. 6, no. 2, p. 133.

61 Ibid., p. 134.

62 Ibid., p. 132.

63 M. Lluïsa Faxedas, 'Women Artists of Cercle et Carré: Abstraction, gender and modernity', *Woman's Art Journal*, vol. 36, no. 1, 2015, p. 46.

64 Ibid., p. 38. Faxedas does observe, however, that these exhibitions had little impact on the careers of these women artists (ibid., p. 42).

65 Mary Cosgrove, 'Ernie O'Malley: Art and modernism in Ireland', *Éire-Ireland*, vol. 40, nos 3–4, 2005, p. 96.

66 Ibid.

67 Remport, *Lady Gregory*, pp. 20–1.

68 Cosgrove, 'Ernie O'Malley', pp. 97–8.

69 *CL*, 1 June 1942, p. 2.

70 *CL*, 30 August 1944, p. 3; 31 August 1944, p. 3; 1 September 1944, p. 3; 4 September 1944, p. 3.

71 *CL*, 6 September 1944, p. 3.

72 Karen Brown, *The Yeats Circle: Verbal and visual relations in Ireland, 1880–1939* (Farnham: Ashgate, 2011), p. 109.

73 For the petition, see ibid.

74 *CL*, 31 August 1944, p. 3.

75 Clair Wills, *That Neutral Island: A cultural history of Ireland during the Second World War* (London: Faber & Faber, 2007), pp. 281–2.

76 Ibid., p. 282.

77 Ibid., p. 285.

78 *CL*, 31 August 1944, p. 3.

79 O'Keeffe, p. 54; Cronin, *No Laughing Matter*, pp. 86–90; Dieter Fuchs, 'The Dalkey Archive: A Menippean satire against authority', in Borg, Fagan and McCourt (eds), *Flann O'Brien: Problems with authority*, pp. 230–41; Stefan Solomon, '"The outward accidents of illusion": O'Brien and the theatrical', in Murphet, McDonald and Morrell (eds), *Flann O'Brien & Modernism*, p. 44; de Paor, '"a scholar manqué"?', pp. 189–203.

80 Kim McMullen, 'Culture as Colloquy: Flann O'Brien's postmodern dialogue with Irish tradition', *NOVEL: A forum on fiction*, vol. 28, no. 1, 1993, p. 63.

81 Gregory Dobbins, *Lazy Irish Schemers: Irish modernism and the cultural politics of idleness* (Dublin: Field Day, 2010), pp. 192–3, 197.

82 Bruce Arnold, *A Concise History of Irish Art* (London: Thames-Hudson, 1969), p. 174.

83 Niall Montgomery, qtd in Cronin, *No Laughing Matter*, p. 131.

15. *Cad é atá in ainm?*

1 For a recent comparative analysis of O'Nolan and Stephens, see R.W. Maslen, 'Fantastic Economies: Flann O'Brien and James Stephens', in Ruben Borg, Paul Fagan and John McCourt (eds), *Flann O'Brien: Problems with authority* (Cork: Cork University Press, 2017), pp. 136–51.

2   See Letter to The Director, Underwood Business Machines, 15 December 1964. O'Nolan writes that the roman type, though cheaper and more varied than available Gaelic typefaces, had 'the enormous drawback that the aspiration of a consonant, very frequent in Irish words, could be denoted only by putting an h after the consonant, given [*sic*] an unsightly and clumsy effect and even impairing legibility' (*L*, p. 440).

3   Brinsley MacNamara, *Margaret Gillan* (London: George Allen & Unwin, 1934), p. 21.

4   Ibid., p. 62.

5   Ibid., p. 73.

6   Quidnunc, 'Irishman's Diary', *The Irish Times*, 31 July 1933, p. 4.

7   Anon., 'Public Amusements', *The Irish Times*, 11 September 1933, p. 6.

8   Anon., 'Lean Year for Irish Drama', *The Irish Times*, 27 December 1933, p. 4.

9   Anon., 'Dublin Theatre Programmes', *The Irish Times*, 4 December 1934, p. 8.

10 Anon., 'University College Notes', *The Irish Times*, 10 December 1934, p. 9.

11 Anthony Cronin, *No Laughing Matter: The life and times of Flann O'Brien* (New York: Fromm, 1989), pp. 67–8.

12 Anon., 'The Dublin Stage', *The Irish Times*, 26 February 1935, p. 5.

13 Anon., 'Stage and Screen', *The Irish Times*, 15 February 1937, p. 8.

14 Quidnunc, 'Irishman's Diary', *The Irish Times*, 7 June 1937, p. 6.

15 Anon., 'Our Cartoonist sees *Margaret Gillan* at the Abbey Theatre', *The Irish Times*, 1 March 1937, p. 4.

16 While the original Irish-language script for the play *An Sgian* remains unpublished, Jack Fennell's English-language translation is available in *PT*, pp. 247–58.

17 Cronin, *No Laughing Matter*.

18 *CL*, 31 October 1953, p. 7.

19 Brian O'Nolan, *Maighréad Gilion*, manuscript, John J. Burns Library, Boston College, Flann O'Brien Papers, MS.1997.027, box 4 folder 9.

20 Anne Clissmann, *Flann O'Brien: A critical introduction to his writings* (Dublin: Gill & Macmillan, 1975), p. 263.

21 Padraic O'Farrell, *The Burning of Brinsley MacNamara* (Dublin: Lilliput, 1990), p. 95.

22 Ibid., p. 97.

23 I made requests to three archivists at RTÉ without success. I think we can infer that O'Nolan had given up the rights to it and was not consulted. I only speculate that his tetchiness about the 1943 manuscript may have held it up, although he was eager for the cash and probably would have sold out.

24 *CL*, 31 October 1953, p. 7.

25 MacNamara, *Margaret Gillan*, p. 15.

26 Brian Ó Nualláin, *Mairéad Gillan* (Baile Átha Cliath: Oifig an tSoláthair, 1953), p. 14.

27 Ibid., p. 12.

28 Niall Ó Dónaill, *Foclóir Gaeilge-Béarla*, Tomás De Bhaldraithe, Eagarthóir Comhairleach (Baile Átha Cliath: An Gum, 1992 [1977]), p. 230.

29 Ibid., p. 986.

30 Ibid., p. 1191. De Bhaldraithe lists '*taghdach*' as the second definition for 'impulsive'; '*ráscánta*' does not appear at all (p. 359).

31 MacNamara, *Margaret Gillan*, p. 15.

32 O'Nolan, *Maighréad Gilion*, p. 5.

33 Ó Nualláin, *Mairéad Gillan*, p. 14.

34 O'Nolan, *Maighréad Gilion*, p. 12.

35 Ó Nualláin, *Mairéad Gillan*, p. 23.

36 MacNamara, *Margaret Gillan*, p. 23.

37 O'Nolan, *Maighréad Gilion*, p. 11.

38 Ó Nualláin, *Mairéad Gillan*, p. 22.

39 MacNamara, *Margaret Gillan*, p. 11.

40 O'Nolan, *Maighréad Gilion*, p. 2.

41 Ó Nualláin, *Mairéad Gillan*, p. 9.

42 MacNamara, *Margaret Gillan*, p. 15.

43 O'Nolan, *Maighréad Gilion*, p. 7.

44 Ó Nualláin, *Mairéad Gillan*, p. 14.

45 MacNamara, *Margaret Gillan*, pp. 19, 18.

46 Ibid., p. 21 (quoting *Hamlet* 1.2.186).

47 Ó Nualláin, *Mairéad Gillan*, p. 20.

48 See Philip O'Leary, *The Prose Literature of the Gaelic Revival* (University Park, PA: Penn State University Press, 1994), p. 491.

49 MacNamara, *Margaret Gillan*, p. 26.

50 O'Nolan, *Maighréad Gilion*, p. 14.

51 Ó Dónaill, *Foclóir Gaeilge-Béarla*, p. 233.

52 O'Nolan, *Maighréad Gilion*, p. 12; Ó Nualláin, *Mairéad Gillan*, p. 13.

53 MacNamara, *Margaret Gillan*, p. 14.

54 Ibid., p. 26.

55 O'Nolan, *Maighréad Gilion*, p. 13; Ó Nualláin, *Mairéad Gillan*, p. 26.

56 MacNamara, *Margaret Gillan*, p. 44.

57 O'Nolan, *Maighréad Gilion*, p. 22.

58 Ibid., p. 47.

59 Ó Dónaill, *Foclóir Gaeilge-Béarla*.

60 *CL*, 31 October 1953, p. 7.

61 In fact, MacNamara's play has been compared to Ibsen's *Hedda Gabler* by Lennox Robinson and Robert Welch. See Robert Welch, *The Abbey Theatre, 1899–1999: Form and pressure* (Oxford: Oxford University Press, 2003), p. 115.

62 Henrik Ibsen, *Hedda Gabler: A play in four acts*, Edmund Gosse and William Archer (trans.) (New York: The Floating Press, 2009), p. 5.

63 MacNamara, *Margaret Gillan*.

64 O'Nolan, *Maighréad Gilion*, translator's note.

65 Qtd in O'Leary, *The Prose Literature of the Gaelic Revival*, p. 365.

66 Ibid., p. 363.

67 Maebh Long, *Assembling Flann O'Brien* (London: Bloomsbury, 2014), pp. 134–5.

68 Jacques Derrida, 'Who or What Is Compared? The concept of comparative literature and the theoretical problems of translation', Eric Prenowitz (trans.), *Discourse*, vol. 30, nos 1 & 2, 2008, p. 39.

69 Ibid., p. 36.

70 Ibid.

71 Long, *Assembling Flann O'Brien*, p. 133.

72 MacNamara, *Margaret Gillan*, p. 10.

73 O'Nolan, *Maighréad Gilion*, pp. 13, 14, 58, 60.

74 Ibid., pp. 50, 83, 96.

75 Ibid., pp. 24, 27.

76 Ibid., pp. 26, 27.

77 Ibid., p. 82.

78 Ibid., p. 21.

16. 'A play with two titles and several authors is a rather unusual event'

* I would like to thank Tobias W. Harris, Ondřej Pilný, Alana Gillespie, Paul Fagan, Ruben Borg and Dieter Fuchs for supplying me with materials and advice, and for their erudition and good humour. I recommend Pilný's extremely elucidating contribution to the field – 'The Brothers Čapek at The Gate: *R.U.R.* and *The Insect Play*', in Ondřej Pilný, R. van den Beuken and I.R. Walsh (eds), *Cultural Convergence: The Dublin Gate Theatre 1928–1960* (Cham: Palgrave Macmillan, 2021), pp. 141–73 – which, possibly due to an influx of black air, was written after this article, yet published before.

1 T.W., '*The Insect Play* at the Gaiety', *The Irish Press*, 23 March 1943, p. 3.

2 The play's name has been anglicised variously as *The Insect Play*; *Ad So Infinitum ...*; *From the Life of Insects*; *The Endless Swarm*; and *Pictures from the Insects' Life*. 'From the Life of Insects' is the literal translation.

3 See Anthony Cronin, *No Laughing Matter: The life and times of Flann O'Brien* (Dublin: New Island, 2003), pp. 135–6; and Robert Tracy, 'Introduction', in Flann O'Brien, *Rhapsody in Stephen's Green*, Robert Tracy (ed.) (Dublin: Lilliput, 1994), pp. 11–13, 15–17. For contemporary reviews not mentioned by Tracy, see especially C.C., *The Bell*, vol. 6, no. 2, May 1943, pp. 155–7; Maxwell Sweeney, 'Correspondent by Proxy', *The Irish Times*, 20 March 1943, p. 4; Maxwell Sweeney, 'Entomology in Eire', *The Irish Times*, 27 March 1943, p. 4 ('"Myles" is a master of burlesque, and he must have enjoyed doing this new script, turning his shafts against us here in Ireland'); L. Kiernan's letter in response to the review by 'T.W.' in *The Irish Press*, 25 March 1943, p. 3 ('the author was doing a national service'); The *Evening Herald*, 23 March 1943, p. 2 ('the play was well-received by a big audience last night'); *The Nationalist and Leinster Times*, 27 March 1943, p. 9 ('it is interesting and amusing [...] brilliantly acted and produced').

4 The controversy over the play is discussed in both Tracy's 'Introduction' and in C.C.'s review in *The Bell*, pp. 155–7.

5 See Anon., 'T.C.D. Notes', *The Irish Times*, 25 May 1942, p. 2; Anon., 'T.C.D. Notes', *The Irish Times*, 8 June 1942, p. 2.

6 Isaac Bickerstaff, Esq., *Stephen's-Green: A rhapsody exhibiting the characters of the belles, beaux, bucks, bloods, flashes, fribbles, jemmies, jesssamies, &c. of all ranks and professions, that frequent the beau-walk* (Dublin: 'Printed for and sold by the Booksellers', 1763), p. 7.

7 Ibid., p. 5 ('The Advertisement').

8 Ibid., p. 36: as 'metempsichosis'.

9 The Bowdlerised version of the play is unfortunately still in print: Josef and Karel Čapek, *R.U.R. and The Insect Play (And So Ad Infinitum)*, Paul Selver (trans.), Clifford Bax and Nigel Playfair (adaptation) (Oxford: Oxford University Press, 2002). However, a faithful, modern translation into English is finally available: Karel Čapek, *Four Plays: R.U.R., The Insect Play, The Makropulos Case, The White Plague*, Peter Majer and Cathy Porter (trans.) (London: Methuen, 1999).

10 Like the furore over the Myles na gCopaleen version, Karel Čapek also mentions in his introduction to the play that the play was criticised for vulgarity when it opened in New York, Sheffield and Berlin. See Bratří Čapkové, *Ze života hmyzu. Lidová knihovna Aventina Sv. 1* (Prague: Aventinum, 1924), p. 7.

11 Anon., 'Robot', *The Irish Times*, 27 December 1938, p. 6.

12 John Garvin, 'Sweetscented Manuscripts', in Timothy O'Keeffe (ed.), *Myles: Portraits of Brian O'Nolan* (London: Martin, Brian & O'Keeffe, 1973), p. 37.

13 Niall Sheridan, 'Brian, Flann and Myles', in O'Keeffe (ed.), *Myles*, p. 33.

14 See for example Josef's series of paintings titled *Touha* (Longing) or *Oheň* (Fire) where the main figure is a woman dressed in red, blue and white – the colours of the Czechoslovak flag.

15 Czechoslovak Authors' Association, Prague, 'To the Writers of the World', Letters to the Editor, *The Irish Times*, 23 September 1938, p. 13.

16 *The Irish Times*, 14 July 1939, p. 4.

17 *The Irish Times*, 10 April 1937, p. 7.

18 http://www.theatre-royal-workington.co.uk/1938-march-the-insect-play/.

19 Broadcast on 30 May, 7 June, 12 June 1939 (*Radio Times*, no. 817, 26 May 1939, pp. 14–15). There were an estimated 20,000 television sets in use in Britain at that time. See https://blog.scienceandmediamuseum.org.uk/chronology-british-television.

20 *The Irish Times*, 29 May 1944, p. 2.

21 Cronin, *No Laughing Matter*, p. 136.

22 The thematic effect of the play's structure was not understood by the *Spectator*'s theatre reviewer upon the London premiere of the play in 1923, who suggested Act I be rearranged between the 'two bitter acts' for comic relief. See Tarn., 'The Theatre', *Spectator*, 12 May 1923, pp. 800–1.

23 '*Toto území je historickým, životním, průmyslovým, svatým a vojenským zájmem našeho státu, tak že dle práva má mu náležeti*'. Čapkové, *Ze života hmyzu*, p. 56.

24 The superiority of O'Nolan's translations from *Buile Suibhne* is, however, mentioned in John Garvin's memoir of O'Nolan, in O'Keeffe (ed.), *Myles*, p. 55. In the same volume, Niall Sheridan states that he cut over a hundred manuscript pages from *At Swim-Two-Birds*, much of it translation from *Buile Suibhne*. Ibid., p. 47.

25 Josef and Karel Čapek, *The Life of the Insects*, Paul Selver (trans.), in Anthony Dent (ed.), *International Modern Plays* (London: J.M. Dent & Sons Ltd, 1950), pp. 91–151.

26 Josef and Karel Čapek, *The World We Live In*, Owen Davis (adaptation), in John Gassner (ed.), *Twenty Best European Plays on the American Stage* (New York: Crown Publishing, 1957), pp. 597–625. Stage scripts were published by William A. Brady (1922) and Samuel French (1933).

27 *The Irish Times*, 26 February 1929, p. 4.

28 Walter Moore, *Schrödinger, Life and Thought* (Cambridge: Cambridge University Press, 1992), p. 379. Moore provides no source for this information, so it cannot be discerned whether perhaps O'Nolan had a copy of the German translation he was consulting Schrödinger about or was simply consulting him as a friend and avid theatregoer. For more on Schrödinger and O'Nolan, see Ondřej Pilný, '"My kingdom for a pun": Myles na gCopaleen, Erwin Schrödinger and *The Third Policeman* in *Improbable Frequency*', *Irish Theatre International*, vol. 1, no. 1, 2008, pp. 38–52.

29 Quidnunc, 'An Irishman's Diary', *The Irish Times*, 30 May 1942, p. 2.

30 For more (though scanty) information on Hanuš Drechsler, see Gisela Holfter and Horst Dickel, *An Irish Sanctuary: German-speaking refugees in Ireland 1933–1945* (Berlin: Walter de Gruyter, 2017), pp. 72, 142, 214, 358.

31 'She came in the blue spring weather': Josef and Karel Čapek, *R.U.R. and The Insect Play*, p. 124. 'Say "ninety-nine"' (ibid., p. 125).

32 Apparently the first draft of Act I was about monkeys instead and written mostly by Niall Montgomery. O'Nolan writes that Edwards did not like it. See *L*, pp. 126, 126, n. 163, 127, n. 165.

33 Except for a fellow named Fagan, who managed to enter Queen Elizabeth II's bedroom in 1982, just to have a chat with Bess.

34 For analysis of O'Nolan's writing as Menippean satire, see Keith Hopper, *Flann O'Brien: A portrait of the artist as a young post-modernist*, 2nd edn, J. Hillis Miller (foreword) (Cork: Cork University Press, 2009), pp. 193–228; José Lanters, *Unauthorized Versions: Irish Menippean satire, 1919–1952* (Washington: Catholic University of America Press, 2000); Dieter Fuchs, '*The Dalkey Archive*: A Menippean satire against authority', in Ruben Borg, Paul Fagan and

John McCourt (eds), *Flann O'Brien: Problems with authority* (Cork: Cork University Press, 2017), pp. 230–41.

35 Čapek, *R.U.R. and The Insect Play*, p. 130.

36 'Mužský hlas (*za scénou*): *Jak to valíš? /* Ženský hlas: *Já? /* První hlas: *Ty! /*Druhý hlas: *Já?? /*První hlas: *Ty!! /*Druhý hlas: *Já??? /*První hlas: *Ty!!! Ty trdlo! /*Druhý hlas: *Hrubiáne! /* První hlas: *Nemehlo! /*Druhý hlas: *Mamlase! /*První hlas: *Cumplochu! Trajdo! /*Druhý hlas: *Hovnivale! /*První hlas: *Pozor na kuličku! Dej pozor! /*Druhý hlas: *Pomalu!'.* Čapkové, *Ze života hmyzu,* pp. 29–30. All the translations from the Czech herein are mine.

37 'TULÁK: *Do zbraně! Do zbraně! Vždyť cesta mezi stébly / je ohrožena! Slyšíte? Škvíra od stébla k stéblu, / píd' země od trávy k trávě, vaše svaté právo, / největší zájem státu, největší otázka světa, / všechno je ve hře! Mravenci, do zbraně! / Jak bylo by možno žít, jinému kdyby patřil / svět mezi dvěma plevami! Kdyby tam jiný nosil / mravenčí ranečky do cizího mraveniště! / Sto tisíc životů za ta dvě stébla trávy / je příliš málo! Já byl jsem ve válce, ó, / to přec je řemeslo pro hmyz! Kopejte zákopy, / ryjte se v hlíně, švarmlinie útočí, / laufšrit přes kupy mrtvol, bajonet auf, / padesát tisíc mrtvých, abyste dobyli / dvaceti kroků latrín! Hurá, do zbraně! / Vždyť jde o zájem celku, jde o odkaz vašich dějin, / ba víc, o svobodu vlasti, ba víc, o světovládu / ba víc, jde o dvě stébla! Takovou velkou věc / mohou jen mrtví vyřídit! Do zbraně! Do zbraně!'.* Čapkové, *Ze života hmyzu,* pp. 56–7.

38 Čapek, *R.U.R. and The Insect Play*, pp. 162–3.

39 Letter to Hilton Edwards, 20 October 1942.

40 Tracy, 'Introduction', p. 13.

41 Ibid., p. 10.

42 C.C.'s review in *The Bell*, p. 155.

43 Seventh impression reprinted in 1939 (London: Humphrey Milford).

44 William Blake, *The Poetry and Prose of William Blake*, Geoffrey Keynes (ed.) (London: Nonesuch Press, 1927).

17. Morphed into Myles

* This essay draws extensively from the conference paper 'Morphed into Myles', which I presented at *Metamorphoses: III international Flann O'Brien conference* in Prague, September 2015.

1 Note the choice of the pseudonym 'Flann O'Brien' while the society is concerned with all of Brian O'Nolan's writings and their context.

2 Maebh Long, *Assembling Flann O'Brien* (London: Bloomsbury, 2014), p. 7.

3 For the most recent examples, see *The Parish Review: Journal of Flann O'Brien studies*, vol. 5, no. 1, spring 2021.

4 Adrian Oțoiu, '"Compartmentation of personality for the purpose of literary utterance": Pseudonymity and heteronymity in the various lives of Flann O'Brien', *Word and Text: A journal of literary studies and linguistics*, vol. 1, no. 1, 2011, pp. 128–38.

5 Ibid., p. 138.

6 John Greaney, 'Resisting Representation: Flann O'Brien and Ireland', *Textual Practice*, vol. 34, no. 4, 2018, p. 588.

7 Scott Eric Hamilton, 'A Matter of Influence: Intersections of identity', *The Parish Review: Journal of Flann O'Brien studies*, vol. 5, no. 1, spring 2021, pp. 1–8. The editorial also contains an appraisal of past and current naming conventions in O'Nolan studies.

8 Ronan Crowley, 'Phwat's in a Nam? Brian O'Nolan as a late revivalist', in Ruben Borg, Paul Fagan and John McCourt (eds), *Flann O'Brien: Problems with authority* (Cork: Cork University Press, 2017), pp. 119–35.

9 Anne Clissmann, *Flann O'Brien: A critical introduction to his writings* (Dublin: Gill & Macmillan, 1975), pp. 1–37.

10 Jack White, 'Myles, Flann and Brian', in Timothy O'Keeffe (ed.), *Myles: Portraits of Brian O'Nolan* (London: Martin, Brian & O'Keeffe, 1973), pp. 62–76.

11 John Ryan, *Remembering How We Stood: Bohemian Dublin at the mid-century* (Dublin: Lilliput, 2008), pp. 127–43.

12 Tony Gray, 'Myles and Company', in *Mr Smyllie, Sir* (Dublin: Gill & Macmillan, 1991), pp. 162–82.

13 Ciarán Ó Nualláin, *Óige an Dearthár .i. Myles na gCopaleen* (Baile Átha Cliath: Foilseacháin Náisiúnta Teoranta, 1973).

14 Micheál Ó Nualláin, *The Brother (Myles)* (Dublin: Self-published, 2011).

15 Anthony Cronin, *Dead as Doornails: Bohemian Dublin in the fifties and sixties* (Oxford: Oxford University Press, 1976), p. 111.

16 Anthony Cronin, *No Laughing Matter: The life and times of Flann O'Brien* (London: Paladin, 1990).

17 Monique Gallagher, 'Flann O'Brien: Myles from Dublin', *The Princess Grace Irish Library Lectures: 7* (Gerrards Cross: Colin Smythe, 1991), p. 12.

18 For a discussion of Ciarán Ó Nualláin's *Óige an Dearthár* see Ian Ó Caoimh, 'The Ideal and the Ironic: Incongruous Irelands in *An Béal Bocht*, *No Laughing Matter* and Ciarán Ó Nualláin's *Óige an Dearthár*', in Borg, Fagan and McCourt (eds), *Flann O'Brien: Problems with authority*, pp. 152–68.

19 Rainer Emig, 'Right in the Margins: An eccentric view of culture', in Stefan Herbrechter and Ivan Callus (eds), *Post/Theory, Culture, Criticism* (Amsterdam: Rodopi, 2004), pp. 93–111. Note that Emig's work focuses on British culture. His diachronic survey of eccentricity *avant la lettre*, however, considers a wider European context and suggests more readily that the concept should be applied to a diversity of national contexts.

20 This assessment concerns O'Nolan's status in the field of cultural production, not in his capacity as a high-ranking civil servant, which would necessitate a consideration of the political field.

21 Emig, 'Right in the Margins', p. 93.

22 Pierre Bourdieu, *The Field of Cultural Production: Essays on art and literature* (Cambridge: Polity, 1993).

23 Ryan, *Remembering How We Stood*, p. 28.

24 Terence Brown, *The Irish Times: 150 years of influence* (London: Bloomsbury, 2015), pp. 111, 175.

25 Vivienne Knight, rev. of Tony Gray, *Mr Smyllie, Sir*, *Etudes irlandaises*, vol. 17, no. 2, 1992, pp. 262–3.

26 Ryan, *Remembering How We Stood*, pp. 27–8; Gray, *Mr Smyllie, Sir*, pp. 213–14.

27 Niall Sheridan, 'Brian, Flann and Myles', in O'Keeffe (ed.), pp. 49–51; White, 'Myles, Flann and Brian', pp. 62–3; Gray, *Mr Smyllie, Sir*, pp. 166–9.

28 While White keeps the details in his version to a minimum, Sheridan, a college friend and journalist with *The Irish Times*, recounts how O'Nolan had written for and run a student magazine as part of an illustrious generation of students at University College Dublin. Sheridan, 'Brian, Flann and Myles', p. 34.

29 Ibid., p. 50.

30 Gray, *Mr Smyllie, Sir*, p. 168.

31 Ibid., pp. 112–28.

32 Ibid., pp. 67–79.

33 Ibid., pp. 72–3.

34 Bourdieu, *The Field of Cultural Production*, p. 29.

35 Pierre Bourdieu, *Outline of a Theory of Practice* (Cambridge: Cambridge University Press, 1977), p. 86.

36 Gray, *Mr Smyllie, Sir*, p. 169.

37 Ibid., p. 171; Cronin, *Dead as Doornails*, p. 115; Johanna Marquardt, 'An Interview with the Brother', *The Parish Review: Journal of Flann O'Brien studies*, vol. 3, no. 1, fall 2014, p. 85.

38 Marquardt, 'An Interview with the Brother', p. 85.

39 Cronin, *Dead as Doornails*, p. 115.

40 John Wyse Jackson, 'Introduction', in Flann O'Brien, *Flann O'Brien at War: Myles na gCopaleen 1940–1945*, John Wyse Jackson (ed.) (London: Duckworth, 2000), pp. 10–11.

41 Terence Brown, *Ireland: A social and cultural history, 1922–2002* (London: Harper Perennial, 2004), p. 225.

42 For more on O'Nolan and Kavanagh's relationships in these different fields, see John Wyse Jackson, 'Profits in Their Own Land? Brian O'Nolan and Patrick Kavanagh', *The Parish Review: Journal of Flann O'Brien studies*, vol. 2, no. 2, spring 2014, pp. 4–14. For more on the eccentric public and personal performances of Behan and 'Myles', see Paul Fagan, 'Secret Scriptures: Brendan Behan in the *Cruiskeen Lawn*', in John McCourt (ed.), *Reading Brendan Behan* (Cork: Cork University Press, 2019), pp. 163–84.

43 Gray, *Mr Smyllie, Sir*, p. 162.

44 Ó Caoimh, 'The Ideal and the Ironic', pp. 152–68.

45 For more on these advertising campaigns which employed 'Myles na gCopaleen' as their spokesperson, see Cronin, *No Laughing Matter*, pp. 222–4; Carol Taaffe, *Ireland Through the Looking-Glass: Flann O'Brien, Myles na gCopaleen and Irish cultural debate* (Cork: Cork University Press, 2008), p. 9; and Amy Nejezchleb, 'The Myles Brand Franchise', *The Parish Review: Journal of Flann O'Brien studies*, vol. 1, no. 2, winter 2013, pp. 42–7.

46 Oṭoiu, '"Compartmentation of personality for the purpose of literary utterance"', p. 130.

47 White, 'Myles, Flann and Brian', p. 62.

48 Ibid., p. 67.

49 Ibid., p. 71.

50 Ryan, *Remembering How We Stood*, pp. 127–43.

51 Poet, actor and producer Valentin Iremonger edited the poetry section of *Envoy*. He himself constitutes a Mylesian theatrical interconnection, having appeared in Myles na gCopaleen's *Rhapsody in Stephen's Green*, an adaptation of Karel and Josef Čapek's *Ze života hmyzu* (The Insect Play) as part of the Gate Theatre Company ensemble at Dublin's Gaiety Theatre in 1943. His later career as a diplomat bespeaks connections between the cultural and the political field similar to but perhaps less troubled than O'Nolan's. A biographical note on Valentin Iremonger can be found in Anthony Bradley (ed.), *Contemporary Irish Poetry: An anthology* (Berkeley: University of California Press, 1980), p. 144.

52 Valentin Iremonger, 'Clear View in Summer', in *Reservations* (Dublin: Envoy, 1950); qtd in Ryan, *Remembering How We Stood*, p. vi.

53 Qtd in Ryan, *Remembering How We Stood*, p. 121.

54 Emig, 'Right in the Margins', p. 94.

55 Ryan, *Remembering How We Stood*, p. 127.

56 Ibid.

57 For a partial overview of the long critical tradition of comparing O'Nolan to Joyce, see John McCourt, 'Myles na gCopaleen: A portrait of the artist as a Joyce scholar', in Ruben Borg, Paul Fagan and Werner Huber (eds), *Flann O'Brien: Contesting legacies* (Cork: Cork University Press, 2014), pp. 110–11.

58 Ryan, *Remembering How We Stood*, pp. 127–8.

59 Ó Nualláin, *The Brother (Myles)*, pp. 15–16.

60 Ibid., p. 15.

61 Keith Hopper, *Flann O'Brien: A portrait of the artist as a young post-modernist*, 2nd edn, J. Hillis Miller (foreword) (Cork: Cork University Press, 2009), p. 16.

62 Cronin, *Dead as Doornails*, p. 111.

18. Sweeny Among the Moderns

* An earlier iteration of this essay's argument was published as S.E. Gontarski, 'Samuel Beckett and *Lace Curtain* Irish Modernisms', in *Revisioning Beckett: Samuel Beckett's decadent turn* (London: Bloomsbury, 2018), pp. 35–56.

1   Brian Coffey, 'Extracts from "Concerning Making"', *The Lace Curtain: A magazine of poetry and criticism*, no. 6, autumn 1973, p. 31.

2   Dennis Kennedy, 'Trinity Speech Oct 2010', speech at the Philosophical Society, Trinity College Dublin, 29 October 2010, supporting the motion 'that this house believes nationalism is a hangover from history', https://web.archive.org/web/20210518115537/ https://www.denniskennedy.eu/trinityspeechoct2010.htm.

3   See Terence Brown, 'Two Post-Modern Novelists: Beckett and O'Brien', in John Wilson Foster (ed.), *The Cambridge Companion to the Irish Novel* (Cambridge: Cambridge University Press, 2006), pp. 205–22; Rolf Breuer, 'Flann O'Brien and Samuel Beckett', *Irish University Review*, vol. 37, no. 2, 2007, pp. 340–51; Amanda Duncan, 'Communing with Machines: The bicycle as a figure of symbolic transgression in the posthumanist novels of Samuel Beckett and Flann O'Brien', in Jeremy Withers and Daniel P. Shea (eds), *Culture on Two Wheels: The bicycle in literature and film* (Lincoln: University of Nebraska Press, 2016), pp. 152–70; Yael Levin, 'Who Hobbles after the Subject: Parables of writing in *The Third Policeman* and *Molloy*', *Journal of Modern Literature*, vol. 40, no. 4, 2017, pp. 105–21; Dirk Van Hulle, '"widening out the mind": Flann O'Brien's "wide mind" between Joyce's "mental life" and Beckett's "deep within"', in Ruben Borg, Paul Fagan and John McCourt (eds), *Flann O'Brien: Problems with authority* (Cork: Cork University Press, 2017), pp. 105–18; Siobhán Purcell, 'Reading the Regional Body: Disability, prosthetics, and Irish literary tradition in *The Third Policeman* and *Molloy*', in Ruben Borg and Paul Fagan (eds), *Flann O'Brien: Gallows humour* (Cork: Cork University Press, 2020), pp. 181–96.

4   Andrew Belis [Samuel Beckett], 'Recent Irish Poetry', *The Bookman*, no. 86, August 1934, pp. 235–44. Reprinted in Samuel Beckett, *Disjecta: Miscellaneous writings and a dramatic fragment*, Ruby Cohn (ed.) (New York: Grove, 1984), pp. 70–6.

5   Terence Brown, 'Ireland, Modernism and the 1930s', in Patricia Coughlan and Alex Davis (eds), *Modernism and Ireland: The poetry of the 1930s* (Cork: Cork University Press, 1995), p. 25.

6   J.C.C. Mays, 'How is MacGreevy a Modernist?', in ibid., p. 104.

7   Deirdre Bair, *Samuel Beckett: A biography* (New York: Summit, 1990), p. 182. Bair's paraphrase here is already an anticipation of Beckett's generically entitled *Film* of 1963.

8   Beckett, *Disjecta*, p. 74.

9   One of Russell's epigraphs is from 'Proverbs' 20:27: 'The Spirit of man is the candle [or a lamp] of the Lord [searching all the inward parts of the belly]'. The book is dedicated to James Stephens, 'Best of companions'. George Russell, *The Candle of Vision* (London: Macmillan, 1918).

10 Samuel Beckett, *Murphy* (New York: Grove, 1957), pp. 102, 155.

11 Ibid., p. 6.

12 Trevor Joyce, 'New Writers' Press: The history of a project', in Coughlan and Davis (eds), *Modernism and Ireland*, p. 293.

13 Ibid.

14 *The Poems of Sweeney Peregrine* are reprinted in Trevor Joyce, *With the First Dream of Fire They Hunt the Cold: A body of work 1966–2000* (Dublin: New Writers' Press, 2001) and in the volume of translations, Trevor Joyce, *Courts of Air and Earth* (Exeter: Shearsman, 2008). In her 'Foreword' to *Courts of Air and Earth*, American poet Fanny Howe notes that Joyce's translations 'mediate between tradition and modernity', the former 'music [that] expresses a

single culture's necessity' and so develops community, the latter 'abandons the community in favour of a plurality of interpretations'. Seamus Heaney's version of the *Buile Suibhne* was published as *Sweeney Astray: A version from the Irish* (Derry: Field Day Publications, 1983).

15 Samuel Beckett, 'Recent Irish Poetry', *The Lace Curtain*, no. 4, summer 1971, pp. 58–63.

16 Michael Smith and Trevor Joyce, 'Editorial', *The Lace Curtain*, no. 2, spring 1970, p. 2.

17 Ibid.

18 Kavanagh had thirteen poems published in *The Lace Curtain*, no. 4, summer 1971, pp. 21–6, three of them nature poems under the general rubric of 'Four Birds'!

19 On Kavanagh and Ó Nualláin's falling out, over potatoes as it turns out, see Joseph Brooker, 'Ploughmen without Land: Flann O'Brien and Patrick Kavanagh', in Julian Murphet, Rónán McDonald and Sasha Morrell (eds), *Flann O'Brien & Modernism* (London: Bloomsbury, 2014), pp. 93–106. Brooker also deals with the issue at hand in this essay – sincerity vs. satire – via the relationship between poets of the land – early Kavanagh, at least – and their mockers – in this case Ó Nualláin, still treated as a University College Dublin cut-up.

20 On Ó Nualláin's role in that journal, see the memoir of John Ryan, editor of *Envoy* (something of a precursor to *The Lace Curtain*): 'In 1951, whilst I was editor of the Irish literary periodical *Envoy*, I decided that it would be a fitting thing to commemorate the tenth anniversary of the death of James Joyce by bringing out a special number dedicated to him which would reflect the attitudes and opinions of his fellow countrymen towards their illustrious compatriot. To this end I began by inviting Brian Nolan to act as honorary editor for this particular issue. His own genius closely matched, without in any way resembling or attempting to counterfeit, Joyce's. But if the mantle of Joyce (or should we say the waistcoat?) were ever to be passed on, nobody would be half so deserving of it as the man whom under his other guises as Flann O'Brien and Myles na gCopaleen, proved himself incontestably to be the most creative writer and mordant wit that Ireland had given us since Shem the Penman himself.' John Ryan, 'Introduction', *A Bash in the Tunnel: James Joyce by the Irish* (Brighton: Clifton, 1970), p. 13. *Envoy* also published 'An extract of *Watt*', the first sighting of *Watt*, in vol. 1, no. 2, 1950, pp. 11–19. Beckett was less than pleased with the results: 'An extract from *Watt*, massacred by the compositor, appeared in that filthy new Irish rag *Envoy*.' Samuel Beckett, *The Letters of Samuel Beckett, Volume II: 1941–1956*, George Craig *et al.* (eds) (Cambridge: Cambridge University Press, 2011), p. 202.

21 Smith and Joyce, 'Editorial', p. 2.

22 Joyce, 'New Writers' Press', p. 281. As a measure of its popularity, hence a gauge of its influence, the 1970 volume was reprinted in 1971, 1974, 1976, 1979, and a second edition appeared in 1981.

23 Coughlan and Davis, 'Introduction', p. 8.

24 Michael Smith, 'Irish Poetry and Penguin Verse', *The Lace Curtain*, no. 3, 1970, p. 4.

25 Brendan Kennelly, *The Penguin Book of Irish Verse* (London: Penguin, 1970), p. 20.

26 Ibid., p. 30.

27 A favourite with James Joyce, the poem is cited in 'Araby', and Joyce wrote two essays on Mangan, whose literary hoaxes and fake translations (dubbed 'reverse plagiarism') are occasionally cited as anticipations of Flann O'Brien. See James Clarence Mangan, *Poems*, David Wheatley (ed.) (Loughcrew: Gallery, 2004).

28 Smith, 'Irish Poetry and Penguin Verse', p. 8.

29 Samuel Beckett, '*Intercessions* by Denis Devlin', *The Lace Curtain*, no. 3, summer 1970, pp. 41–4. Beckett's review appeared originally in the Eurocentric *transition* magazine, no. 27, April–May 1938, pp. 289–94.

30 Beckett, '*Intercessions*', p. 41.

31 Michael Smith, 'Editorial', *The Lace Curtain*, no. 4, summer 1971, p. 3.

32 The Europa Press became something of a club for these new, urban Irish modernists, like New Writers' Press in the 1970s. Denis Devlin's poetry collection *Intercessions* (1934) and Brian Coffey's *Third Person* (1938) were also published by Europa Press, as was Beckett's translations of Paul Éluard's love poetry, *Thorns of Thunder* (1939).

33 *The Lace Curtain*, no. 4, summer 1971, pp. 5–7.

34 Samuel Beckett, 'Humanistic Quietism', *The Lace Curtain*, no. 4, summer 1971, pp. 70–1. Cited also in Stan Smith's assessment of MacGreevy, 'From a Great Distance: Thomas MacGreevy's "Frame of Reference"', *The Lace Curtain*, no. 6, autumn 1978, p. 50. This would be the journal's final issue.

35 Thomas MacGreevy, *Poems* (New York: Viking, 1934).

36 Beckett, 'Humanistic Quietism', p. 70.

37 Beckett, *Disjecta*, p. 74.

38 Mervyn Wall, 'Michael Smith Asks Mervyn Wall Some Questions about the Thirties', *The Lace Curtain*, no. 4, summer 1971, p. 85.

39 Samuel Beckett, *The Complete Dramatic Works* (London: Faber & Faber, 1986), p. 57.

40 Niall Montgomery, 'An Aristophanic Sorcerer', *The Irish Times*, 2 April 1966, p. 7.

41 Niall Montgomery, 'An Aristophanic Sorcerer', *The Lace Curtain*, no. 4, summer 1971, pp. 75–6.

42 Ibid., p. 76.

43 The journal had its share of typographical blunders over its six publications, including in issue 3, 'Then Icarus fell at out feet' in Gottfried Benn's poem, 'Icarus' (p. 38) and in issue 4, 'wnown' for known, as in 'not to have ever really wnown him', in Smith's interview with Mervyn Wall as Wall is speaking of meeting Beckett 'in the early thirties in his rooms at Trinity' (p. 85).

44 Montgomery, 'An Aristophanic Sorcerer', *The Lace Curtain*, p. 74.

45 Ibid.

46 Myles na gCopaleen, 'Three Poems from the Irish', *The Lace Curtain*, no. 4, summer 1971, pp. 46–7.

47 See full translation at https://www.poetrynook.com/poem/aoibhinn-leabhr%C3%A1in-do-thriall.

48 An alternate translation of the first stanza of these verses written by an Irish scribe in the margins of St Gall Priscian's *Institutiones Grammatice* [http://www.stgallpriscian.ie/]: 'Domfarcai fidbaidæ fál: / fomchain loíd luin, / lúad nad cél / huas mo lebrán ind línech fomchain trírech inna n-én'; 'A hedge of trees surrounds me: / a blackbird's song sings to me / praise which I will not hide / above my lined book, / the trilling of the birds sings to me.' Whitley Stokes and John Strachan (eds), *Thesaurus Palaeohibernicus: A collection of Old-Irish glosses, scholia, prose and verse*, 3 vols, vol. 2: Non-Biblical glosses and scholia; Old-Irish prose; names of persons and places; inscriptions; verse; indexes (Cambridge: Cambridge University Press, 1903), p. 290.

49 For Seamus Heaney's reading of 'Scél lem dúib' in Ó Nualláin's translation see https://www.youtube.com/watch?v=bNrfLdk_4Kg. Furthermore, in *The Irish Times* in 2012, Gabriel Rosenstock, who translated Beckett's playlet 'Come and Go' (among other works) into Irish, compares Beckett's style specifically to 'Scél lem dúib': 'Beckett is as strange and as familiar as the next job. But there's a sparseness in his writing that reminds me of the beginning of Irish literature. Look at these four lines from an Early Irish lyric. Scél lem dúib / dordaid dam, / snigid gaim / ró faith sam. [Kuno] Meyer [not Ó Nualláin] translates that stanza as: "My tidings for you / the stag bells / winter snows / summer is gone." There is a texture, terseness and tonality here that are Beckettian. In this regard, he sounds more

Irish to me than, say, Shaw.' Qtd in Caomhán Keane, 'Waiting for Beckett with Irish in Focus', *The Irish Times*, 10 April 2012, p. 10.

50 Myles's translation of 'Domfarcai fidbaidæ fál' is first published in *CL*, 9 January 1941, p. 6; 'Scél Lem Dúib' in *CL*, 20 March 1941, p. 6; 'Aoibhinn, A Leabhráin, Do Thriall' in *CL*, 7 June 1941, p. 6.

51 Donagh MacDonagh (ed.), *Poems from Ireland*, Donagh MacDonagh (introd.), R.M. Smyllie (preface) (Dublin: The Irish Times, 1944).

52 Flann O'Brien, *A Flann O'Brien Reader*, Stephen Jones (ed.) (New York: Viking, 1978), pp. 256–7. Donagh MacDonagh and Lennox Robinson (eds), *The Oxford Book of Irish Verse* (Oxford: Oxford University Press, 1958), poems 256 and 257, p. 315.

53 See John J. Burns Library, Boston College, Flann O'Brien Papers, MS.1997.027, box 8, folder 6.

54 J.C.C. Mays, 'Literalist of the Imagination', in Rüdiger Imhof (ed.), *Alive-Alive O! Flann O'Brien's At Swim-Two-Birds* (Dublin: Wolfhound, 1985), p. 85.

55 John Montague, *A Chosen Light* (London: MacGibbon & Kee, 1967), p. 65.

56 'All poetry, as discriminated from the various paradigms of prosody, is prayer.' Beckett, *Disjecta*, p. 68.

57 Kennedy, 'Trinity Speech Oct 2010'.

58 Ibid.

59 Ibid.

60 Fintan O'Toole, 'The Fantastic Flann O'Brien', *The Irish Times*, 1 October 2011, p. 53.

61 Samuel Beckett, *The Letters of Samuel Beckett, Volume I: 1929–1940*, George Craig *et al.* (eds) (Cambridge: Cambridge University Press, 2009), pp. 423–4.

62 John P. Harrington, *The Irish Beckett* (New York: Syracuse University Press, 1991), p. 105.

63 Ibid.

64 Wall, 'Michael Smith Asks Mervyn Wall Some Questions about the Thirties', p. 83. See Brian Fallon in *The Irish Times*: 'The death of Mervyn Wall a few years ago received less attention than it deserved, since he was a central figure in the Dublin literary world of the 1940s and '50s. *Fursey*, a medieval Irish monk tormented by the devil, has a place in the Irish comic pantheon along with Brian O'Nolan's Pooka MacPhellimey, or James Stephens's two Philosophers in *The Crock of Gold*. The book first appeared in 1946 (it is dedicated, incidentally, to Denis Devlin, one of Wall's many gifted contemporaries in University College Dublin) and Wall added a sequel, *The Return of Fursey*. Though the book is occasionally marred by the kind of garrulous whimsy which was a common fault of the period, it wears its age well and fully deserves resurrection. It might, incidentally, make an excellent film for TV, given an imaginative producer with flair.' Brian Fallon, review of *The Unfortunate Fursey* by Mervyn Wall, *The Irish Times*, 17 June 2000, p. 51.

65 Cited in Beckett, *Letters I*, p. 224, n. 2.

66 'Excerpts from Flann O'Brien's *The Poor Mouth*', *Antaeus: A quarterly magazine*, Daniel Halpern and Paul Bowles (eds), no. 16, Special Translation Issue, winter 1975. *Antaeus* also reprinted Ó Nualláin's short stories 'The Martyr's Crown' (no. 19, autumn 1975, pp. 42–6) and 'John Duffy's Brother' (no. 20, winter 1976, pp. 27–31) as well as his *Envoy* Joyce essay 'A Bash in the Tunnel' (nos 21–2, spring/summer 1976, pp. 119–24).

67 John Montague, 'A Few Drinks and a Hymn: My farewell to Samuel Beckett', *The New York Times*, 17 April 1994.

68 Samuel Beckett, *Watt* (New York: Grove, 1959), p. 248.

69 Samuel Beckett, *The Collected Shorter Plays of Samuel Beckett* (New York: Grove, 1984), p. 6.

70 Harrington, *The Irish Beckett*, p. 105.

71 Montgomery's essay on Beckett, 'No Symbols Where None Intended', appeared in *New World Writing: Fifth mentor selection* (New American Library, 1954), which billed itself as

'A New Adventure in Modern Reading'. The essay title derives from the very last words to the 'Addenda' of Beckett's novel *Watt*. Beckett recited the passage in a chatty letter to Montgomery of November 1955 as, apparently, an acknowledgement of, if not an homage to, Montgomery and the essay (Beckett, *Letters II*, p. 561), for which Montgomery had asked permission to write. Beckett approved and said: 'I learned a lot about myself I didn't know & hadn't suspected. I emerged more organized than I am' (Beckett, *Letters II*, pp. 426, 427, n. 1). 'Recent Irish Poetry' ends, however, as follows: 'of Mr Niall Montgomery's poetry [I know] nothing at all' (Beckett, *Disjecta*, p. 76). Further details on Montgomery's relationship with Beckett, Joyce and Ó Nualláin can be found in Frank McNally, 'An Irishman's Diary', *The Irish Times*, 13 November 2015, p. 15. See also Christine O'Neill, 'Niall Montgomery: An early champion of Joyce', *Dublin James Joyce Journal*, no. 1, 2008, pp. 1–16, a prelude to her 2015 anthology *Niall Montgomery, Dublinman: Selected writings* (Dublin: Ashfield, 2015), for which she wrote an 'Introduction' and to which McNally's 'Diary' entry alludes.

72 Montgomery, 'No Symbols Where None Intended', p. 326.

73 Beckett, *Murphy*, p. 46.

74 Ibid., p. 69.

75 Reprinted as Donal Ó Drisceoil, 'A Dark Chapter: Censorship and the Irish writer', in Clare Hutton and Patrick Walsh (eds), *The Oxford History of the Irish Book, Volume IV: The Irish Book in English 1891–2000* (Oxford: Oxford University Press, 2011), pp. 285, 303.

76 Beckett, *Disjecta*, p. 35.

77 Samuel Beckett, 'Dante ... Bruno . Vico . . Joyce', in *Disjecta*, p. 19.

78 See Ruben Borg, 'Reading Flann with Paul: Modernism and the trope of conversion', in Borg, Fagan and McCourt (eds), *Flann O'Brien: Problems with authority*, p. 219.

19. The Richness of the Mask

1 This essay builds on some preliminary suggestions on the pseudonym as it pertains to the O'Nolan *oeuvre* that I have made in 'Resisting Representation: Flann O'Brien and Ireland', *Textual Practice*, 2018, pp. 587–604.

2 Carol Taaffe, *Ireland Through the Looking-Glass: Flann O'Brien, Myles na gCopaleen and Irish cultural debate* (Cork: Cork University Press, 2008), p. 32.

3 Maebh Long, 'Plagiarism and the Politics of Friendship: Brian O'Nolan, Niall Sheridan and Niall Montgomery', in the present volume.

4 Adrian Oțoiu, '"Compartmentation of personality for the purpose of literary utterance": Pseudonymity and heteronymity in the various lives of Flann O'Brien', *Word and Text: A journal of literary studies and linguistics*, vol. 1, no. 1, 2011, p. 134.

5 Ibid.

6 Rónán McDonald and Julian Murphet, 'Introduction', in Julian Murphet, Rónán McDonald and Sascha Morell (eds), *Flann O'Brien & Modernism* (London: Bloomsbury, 2014), p. 2.

7 Ronan Crowley, 'Phwat's in a Nam? Brian O'Nolan as a late revivalist', in Ruben Borg, Paul Fagan and John McCourt, *Flann O'Brien: Problems with authority* (Cork: Cork University Press, 2017), pp. 119–35.

8 Walter Benjamin, 'The Destructive Character', in *Reflections: Essays, aphorisms, autobiographical writings* (New York: Random House, 1995), p. 301.

9 Niall Montgomery, 'An Aristophanic Sorcerer', *The Irish Times*, 2 April 1966, p. 7.

10 Ibid., p. 7.

11 Benjamin, 'The Destructive Character', p. 301.

12 Ibid.

13 Ibid., p. 303.

14 Walter Benjmain, 'The Work of Art in the Age of Mechanical Reproduction', in *Illuminations*, (London: Pimlico, 1999), p. 215.

15 Friedrich Nietzsche, *Beyond Good and Evil*, R.J. Holingdale (trans.) (London: Penguin, 2003), p. 69.

16 Ibid.

17 Ibid., pp. 69, 70.

18 W.B. Yeats, *Memoirs*, ed. Denis Donoghue (New York: Macmillan, 1972), p. 191.

19 Ibid.

20 W.B. Yeats, 'The Mask', in *The Poems*, Daniel Albright (ed.) (London: Everyman, 1994), p. 144.

21 See Louis MacNeice, *The Poetry of W.B. Yeats* (Oxford: Oxford University Press, 1948) and Richard Ellmann, *Yeats: The man and the masks* (New York: Macmillan, 1948).

22 Margaret Mills Harper and Warwick Gould (eds), *Yeats's Mask: Yeats Annual No. 19* (Cambridge: Open Book Publishers, 2013).

23 Daniel Keith Jernigan, '"Simulat Ergo Est": Brian O'Nolan's metaperformative simulations', *New Hibernia Review*, vol. 20, no. 1, 2016, p. 93.

24 Taaffe, *Ireland Through the Looking-Glass*, p. 32.

25 Heather Love, 'Close but Not Deep: Literary ethics and the descriptive turn', *New Literary History*, vol. 41, no. 2, 2010, p. 374.

26 Giordano Vintaloro, 'Brian O'Nolan, the Conspirator', *Studi Irlandesi*, no. 7, 2017, p. 262.

27 Ibid.

28 Flore Coulouma, 'Tall Tales and Short Stories: *Cruiskeen Lawn* and the dialogic imagination', *Review of Contemporary Fiction*, vol. 31, no. 3, 2011, p. 163.

29 Diarmaid Ferriter, *The Transformation of Ireland 1900–2000* (London: Profile, 2005), pp. 409, 468.

30 See Paul Fagan, '"Expert diagnosis has averted still another tragedy": Misreading and the paranoia of expertise in *The Third Policeman*', *The Parish Review: Journal of Flann O'Brien studies*, vol. 3, no. 1, fall 2014, pp. 12–41.

31 Taaffe, *Ireland Through the Looking-Glass*, p. 32.

32 Nietzsche, *Beyond Good and Evil*, p. 70.

33 Taaffe, *Ireland Through the Looking-Glass*, p. 32.

34 Nietzsche, *Beyond Good and Evil*, p. 69.

35 Yeats, 'The Mask', p. 144.

36 Taaffe, *Ireland Through the Looking-Glass*, p. 32.

37 Roland Barthes, 'From Work to Text', in *Image-Music-Text*, Stephen Heath (ed. and trans.) (London: Fontana, 1977), p. 161.

38 Ibid., pp. 159, 161.

39 Jean-Michel Rabaté, *The Pathos of Distance: Affects of the modern* (London: Bloomsbury, 2016), pp. 8, 9.

40 Ibid., p. 14.

41 Benjamin, 'Mechanical Reproduction', p. 225.

42 *CL*, 28 January 1956, p. 6.

43 Horace, *The Odes of Horace*, Jeremy H. Kaimowitz (trans.) (Baltimore: The Johns Hopkins University Press, 2008), p. 142.

44 Catherine Flynn, '"the half-said thing": *Cruiskeen Lawn,* Japan and the Second World War', in Borg, Fagan and McCourt (eds), *Flann O'Brien: Problems with authority*, p. 86.

45 Ibid., p. 74.

20. Productions and Adaptations of Brian O'Nolan's Works

* In compiling this overview of productions and adaptations of O'Nolan's work, I am grateful to the help of Ciaran Byrne, Peter Chrisp, Christian Dupont, James Hayes, Jon Haynes, Joseph LaBine, Gerard Lee, Paul Lee, Maebh Long, Pádraig Ó Méalóid, Kurt Palm, Ondřej Pilný, Matthew Sweney, Hugh Wilde, David Woods, as well as the RTÉ archives and the John J. Burns Library, Boston College.

1   Sabine Coelsch-Foisner, 'Das Paratheatrale, das Genetische und das Semiophorische – ein Forschungsprogramm zur wissenschaftlich-künstlerischen Erschließung theatraler Produktionen', in Sabine Coelsch-Foisner and Timo Heimerdinger (eds), *Theatralisierung* (Heidelberg: Universitätsverlag Winter, 2016), pp. 1–26.

2   See Vicki Mayer, Miranda J. Banks and John T Caldwell (eds), *Production Studies: Cultural studies of media industries* (New York: Routledge, 2009).

3   André Lefevere, 'On the Refraction of Texts', in Mihai Spariosu (ed.), *Mimesis in Contemporary Theory* (Amsterdam: John Benjamin, 1984), pp. 217–37.

4   See Alana Gillespie, 'Pipes Aloft: *After Hours* and "Shows and Showers"', *The Parish Review: Journal of Flann O'Brien studies*, vol. 5, no. 2, fall 2021, pp. 1–6.

5   John Finegan, 'Thirst', letter, *The Irish Times*, 23 November 1977, p. 9.

6   Anon., 'Defence Forces Entertained', *The Irish Times*, 31 March 1943.

7   Anon., 'Jack-in-the-Box', *The Irish Times*, 28 December 1942, p. 3.

8   Hilton Edwards, 'Thirst', letter, *The Irish Times*, 11 November 1977, p. 11.

9   The date of this production is uncertain. Seamus Kelly posits that to his recollection it pre-dated the Gate production, but this is debated and perhaps unlikely. See Quidnunc, 'An Irishman's Diary', *The Irish Times*, 23 January 1970, p. 9; Seamus Kelly, 'The Full of the Cruiskeen', *The Irish Times*, 1 April 1976, p. 10; Seamus Kelly, 'Thirst', letter, *The Irish Times*, 16 November 1977, p. 11; Arthur R. Bateman, 'Thirst', letter, *The Irish Times*, 21 November 1977, p. 9; Finegan, 'Thirst', p. 9.

10 Mark Hennessy, 'Lunchtime Treat at the Ivernia', *Cork Examiner*, clipping in John J. Burns Library, Boston College, Flann O'Brien Papers, MS.1997.027 (hereafter *Burns*), box 7, folder 7.

11 Gerry Colgan, '*Thirst* in TCD Theatre', *The Irish Times*, 11 September 1984, p. 10.

12 Seona Mac Reamoinn, '*Gibber* and *Thirst* at An Béal Bocht', *The Irish Times*, 2 October 1990, p. 8.

13 Gillespie, 'Pipes Aloft', p. 2.

14 The original production of *Faustus Kelly* was reviewed in the following publications: *Barrack Variety* (March 1943); *Dublin Evening Herald* (26 January 1943); *Dublin Evening Mail* (23 January 1943; 27 January 1943; 1 February 1943); *Dublin Opinion* (February 1943); *Dublin Sunday Independent* (1 November 1943); *Irish Independent* (27 January 1943); *Irish Press* (26 January 1943; 27 January 1943); *The Irish Times* (27 January 1943); *Nationalist and Leinster Times* (1 May 1954); *The Bell*, vol. 5, no. 6 (March 1943); *The Standard* (7 February 1943).

15 Frances O'Rourke, 'The Devil of a T.D.', *The Sunday Press*, 28 May 1978.

16 David Nowlan, '*Faustus Kelly* at the Peacock', *The Irish Times*, 23 May 1978, p. 8.

17 Ibid.; and Dermot Bolger (ed.), *Dudes and Beauty Queens: The changing face of Irish theatre* (Dublin: New Island Press, 2002), p. 159.

18 Owen Dudley Edwards, 'Macbeth and Flann O'Brien Revisited', *The Irish Times*, 22 August 1988, p. 12.

19 G.A. Olden, 'On the Air', *The Irish Times*, 4 February 1960, p. 8.

20 Dick Walsh, 'Small World of *Faustus Kelly*', *The Irish Times*, 20 December 1968, p. 12.

21 Ondřej Pilný, 'The Brothers Čapek at the Gate: *R.U.R.* and *The Insect Play*', in *Cultural Convergence: The Dublin Gate Theatre, 1928–1960*, Ondřej Pilný, Ruud van den Beuken, and Ian R. Walsh (eds) (Cham: Palgrave Macmillan, 2021), p. 156.

22 Walter Moore, *Schrödinger: Life and thought* (Cambridge: Cambridge University Press, 1989), p. 379.

23 Carol Taaffe, *Ireland Through the Looking-Glass: Flann O'Brien, Myles na gCopaleen and Irish cultural debate* (Cork: Cork University Press, 2008), p. 247, n. 27.

24 Pilný, 'The Brothers Čapek at the Gate', p. 157.

25 Ibid., p. 158.

26 Flann O'Brien, *Rhapsody in Stephen's Green*, Robert Tracy (ed.) (Dublin: Lilliput, 1994).

27 http://imperialfinch.nl/film/rhapsody-in-stephens-green.

28 Anon., 'Peacock', *The Irish Times*, 27 December 1944, p. 3.

29 Anon., 'Theatre, Film Reviews', *The Irish Press*, 29 January 1945, p. 2.

30 Louis de Paor, 'Twisting the Knife', *The Irish Times*, 29 March 2002, p. 12.

31 'A Letter from Dublin' is listed in the *Radio Times: Journal of the BBC*, 10–16 August 1952, p. 17, where it is described as a BBC recording and attributed to 'Myles na Gcopaleen' [*sic*].

32 See *PT*, p. vii, and Amy Nejezchleb, 'O'Brien's Your Man: Myles, modernity and Irish national television', in Jennika Baines (ed.), *'Is it about a bicycle?': Flann O'Brien in the twenty-first century* (Dublin: Four Courts Press, 2011), p. 111.

33 Evelyn O'Nolan, letter to Gunnar Rugheimer, 19 June 1966, *Burns* box 8, folder 6.

34 Nejezchleb, 'O'Brien's Your Man', p. 111. See Anthony Cronin, *No Laughing Matter: The life and times of Flann O'Brien* (New York: Fromm, 1989), pp. 233–4.

35 The following episodes are available to view in the RTÉ archives: 'The Language Question', 'Changed Times', 'Playing the Game', 'Is TV a Good Thing?', 'Th' Electric', 'The Horse Show', 'The Holliers', 'Hullabaloons'.

36 Programme Notes, *We're Joking of Course*, Gaiety Theatre, premiered 12 August 1963. It is unclear from the programme which episode was performed.

37 Eileen Battersby, 'Tickets Fly out for *At Swim-Two-Birds*', *The Irish Times*, 7 March 1998, p. 12.

38 Quidnunc, 'An Irishman's Diary', *The Irish Times*, 23 January 1970, p. 9.

39 Ibid.

40 Maeve Binchy, '*At Swim-Two-Birds* in London', *The Irish Times*, 3 May 1979, p. 10. The cast was rounded out by Michael Loughnan, Gerald McAllister, Tom McCabe, Luke Hayden, Moira Fitzgerald, Katy Feeney, Michael Spittal, Timothy O'Grady, Andrew Cox and Martin Kennedy.

41 Jon Haynes and David Woods, email to Paul Fagan, 10 March 2020.

42 See https://www.ridiculusmus.com/shows/past-shows/at-swim-two-birds-2/.

43 Jocelyn Clarke, 'Leaving Cert Girl Opts Out: Jocelyn Clarke at Kilkenny Arts Week', *The Tribune Magazine*, 27 August 1995, p. 16.

44 Gerry Colgan, 'Creative Lunacy Loses out on Stage', *The Irish Times*, 30 July 1998, p. 12.

45 Sara Keating, rev. of *At Swim-Two-Birds*, *The Irish Times*, 5 November 2009, p. 18.

46 Patrick Lonergan, 'Review of *At Swim Two Birds*', *Irish Theatre Magazine*, 6 November 2009, http://itmarchive.ie/web/Reviews/Current/At-Swim-Two-Birds.aspx.html.

47 Ibid.

48 Chris McCormack, 'Blue Raincoat, *At Swim: Two Birds*: Clown nose', *Musings in Intermissions*, 26 February 2011, http://musingsinintermissions.blogspot.com/2011/02/blue-raincoat-at-swim-two-birds-clown.html.

49 Joe Humphreys, 'Book Celebration Surprisingly Sober', *The Irish Times*, 4 October 1999, p. 3.

50 For more on the stage adaptation of *In Schwimmen-Zwei-Vögel* at the Sargfabrik, Vienna, see Manfred Eichel, 'Harry Rowohlt im Rampenlicht', in Anna Mikula and Peter Haag (eds), *Der Grosse Bär und seine Gestirne: Freunde und Weggefährten Grüssen, Dichten und Malen zum 60. Geburtstag von Harry Rowohlt* (Zürich: Kein & Aber, 2005) pp. 55–7; and the feature published in the Austrian magazine *Profil*, no. 22, 1991, pp. 78–9.

51 Humphreys, 'Book Celebration', p. 3.

52 Ray Comiskey, '"At Swim" on Radio' [interview with Ronald Mason], *The Irish Times*, 30 December 1981.

53 Ibid.

54 Gleeson announced at the 2011 Galway Film Fleadh that Parallel Pictures would produce the project with a budget of $11 million, but the film has been stuck in development hell ever since.

55 Eileen Battersby, in conversation with Kurt Palm, 'A Hilarious Slice of Flann', *The Irish Times*, 28 February 1998, p. 47.

56 Kurt Palm in discussion with Paul Fagan at a special screening of the film with a Q&A at *Acting Out: IV international Flann O'Brien conference* in Salzburg, 2017.

57 Battersby, 'A Hilarious Slice of Flann', p. 47.

58 See Gary Blake, 'In Dublin's Fair City: A theatre festival', *Performing Arts Review*, vol. 6, no. 1, 1975, pp. 29–31.

59 Desmond Rushe, 'Policeman's Lot Made a Most Happy One!', *Burns*, box 7, folder 7.

60 Gerald Colgan, 'A Cycle of Paradoxes', *Hibernia*, 11 October 1974.

61 John Boland, 'Enter a Strange "Policeman"', *Irish Independent*, *Burns*, box 7, folder 7.

62 Rushe, 'Policeman's Lot Made a Most Happy One!'.

63 Ibid.

64 Charles Lewsen, 'The Dublin Theatre Festival: Conversation before acting', *The Times*, 9 October 1974, p. 11.

65 Rushe, 'Policeman's Lot Made a Most Happy One!'.

66 Boland, 'Enter a Strange "Policeman"'.

67 Emmanuel Kehoe, 'Much of Novel Missing from Play', *Evening Press*, 1 October 1974.

68 Anon., 'Production News', *The Stage*, 28 February 1980, p. 2.

69 Anon., 'Campbell's Souse Theatre Strikes Again', *Marylebone Mercury*, 7 March 1980, p. 13.

70 James Nye, 'Ken Campbell: Furtive nudist', interview, *Gneurosis* 1, https://thefrogweb.wordpress.com/2009/12/11/ken-campbell-furtive-nudist.

71 Touring cast 1994 (three-hander): Andrew Ashenden/Barr (Yer Man), Woods (Divney/Pluck), Aidan McCann/Haynes (Macruiskeen/Finnucane/O'Corky). Highlands tour and the Black Box Galway 1997 cast (six-hander): Pete McCabe (Yer Man), Woods (Divney/Pluck), Sarah Wray (Pegeen), Simon Finch (Soul/de Selby), McCann (MacCruiskeen), Haynes (Mathers/Finnucane/ O'Corky). The Manor House, London 2001 (three-hander): McCabe (Yer Man), Woods (Divney/Pluck), McCann (Macruiskeen/Finnucane/O'Corky).

72 Haynes and Wood, email, 10 March 2020.

73 See https://www.ridiculusmus.com/shows/past-shows/the-third-policeman-2.

74 Haynes and Woods, email, 10 March 2020.

75 Peter Crawley, 'It's Wilful and Errant and Falls Apart', *The Irish Times*, 11 February 2009.

76 Sara Keating, rev. of *The Third Policeman*, *The Irish Times*, 19 October 2007, p. 14.

77 See 'Sandra O'Malley: *The Third Policeman* 2004', *Blue Raincoat Video Archives 1991–2021*, https://www.blueraincoat.com/video-archive-1.

78 *The Third Policeman*, Miracle Theatre, programme notes.

79 'Der dritte Polizist', *Deutschlandfunk*, 20 November 2002, https://www.deutschlandfunk.de/der-dritte-polizist.691.de.html?dram:article_id=46787.

80 Ergo Phizmiz, 'Colour, Noise, and Craniums: Adapting *The Third Policeman* as an electronic opera', *The Parish Review: Journal of Flann O'Brien studies*, vol. 1, no. 1, summer 2012, pp. 32–8.

81 Anon., 'Abbey Director Explains Why Gaelic Plays Fail', *The Irish Times*, 30 October 1944, p. 1.

82 Catriona Breathnach, Eoin De Faoite, Cormac Mac Coille, Nuala Ni Aodha, Caitlin Ni Bhradaigh, Caitriona Ni Bhriain, Nuala Ni Choille, Maire Ni Ghormain, Laslai Ni Leathlobhair, Brid Ni Suilleabhain, Emer Nic Ghiolla Choillin, Fidelma Nic Ghiolla Choillin, Maire Nic Ghuidhir, Seán Ó Briain, Seathrun Ó Goilidhe, Francesca Sydner.

83 Sean Page, 'Myles: From stoic jester to buffoon', *Sunday Press*, 30 July 1967, *Burns*, box 7, folder 7. For a more positive review, see R.O.C., 'Gaeltacht "Send-Up" Played with Gusto', *Irish Independent*, 27 July 1967, *Burns*, box 7, folder 7.

84 Anon., '*An Béal Bocht* Play Withdrawn', *The Irish Times*, 2 August 1967, p. 1.

85 Seán Ó Briain to Evelyn O'Nolan, letter, 4 December 1970, *Burns*, box 7, folder 1.

86 Programme notes.

87 Dominic Ó Riordan, '*An Béal Bocht* at the Peacock', *The Irish Times*, 8 January 1975, p. 11; see also M. de F., 'Fun and Pathos at Peacock', *Evening Press*, 8 January 1975, and Frances O'Rourke, 'Peacock: *An Béal Bocht*', *The Sunday Press*, 12 January 1975 (both in *Burns*, box 7, folder 7).

88 Francine Cunningham, rev. of '*The Poor Mouth* at An Béal Bocht', *The Irish Times*, 20 September 1989, p. 10.

89 My gratitude to Gerard Lee for this information about the production's revivals on stage and radio.

90 See Par Trina Mounier, 'Plongée dans l'Irlande mythique', *Les Trois Coups*, 21 March 2012. A five-minute trailer for the play is available at https://www.youtube.com/watch?v=vWDQ-qYTD1E.

91 Seona Mac Réamoinn, rev. of *The Poor Mouth*, *Irish Theatre Magazine*, 24 November 2012.

92 See *L*, pp. 419, 426–7, 430–2, 435–7, 470–1, 476–8, 503–7, 519–25, 528.

93 David Nowlan, '*The Saints Go Cycling In* at the Gate', *The Irish Times*, 15 February 1985, p. 10.

94 See https://archiv.ursulahuebner.com/buhne01.html.

95 Maev Kennedy, '*Dalkey Archive* at the Project', *The Irish Times*, 8 March 1979, p. 8.

96 Ibid.

97 R.B. Marriott, '*The Dalkey Archive*', *The Stage and Television Today*, 29 December 1978, p. 9.

98 Michael Coveney, 'Bush Theatre: *The Dalkey Archive*', *Financial Times*, 15 December 1978, *Burns* box 7, folder 7.

99 Ken Gray, '*The Hard Life* at the Peacock', *The Irish Times*, 8 October 1976, p. 11.

100 Con Houlihan, 'Good Moments But Scarce', *Burns* box 7, folder 7.

101 Tony Hennigan, 'Triple Ego of Myles No Problem for Layde', *Irish Independent*, 8 October 1976, *Burns* box 7, folder 7.

102 David Nowlan, '*The Hard Life* at the Abbey', *The Irish Times*, 7 February 1986, p. 10.

103 Terry Stoller, *Tales of the Tricycle Theatre* (London: Bloomsbury, 2013), pp. 96–9. Includes further descriptions of the set and an interview with lead actor Dermot Crowley. For more details see Christopher Edwards, 'Trials of an Irish Artist', rev. of *The Hard Life*, *The Spectator*, 5 October 1985, p. 44.

104 Stoller, *Tales of the Tricycle Theatre*, p. 99.

105 'Taste of Flann', *The Guardian*, 4 October 1985, *Burns* box 7, folder 7.

106 Maeve Binchy, '*Flann O'Brien's Hard Life* at Tricycle, Kilburn', *The Irish Times*, 7 February 1986, p. 10.

107 Ibid.

108 A trailer for the play is available online, https://www.youtube.com/watch?v=DXFHjCyjafM.

109 Harvey O'Brien, '*Slattery's Sago Saga*', *Irish Theatre Magazine*, 17 July 2010, http://itmarchive.ie/web/Reviews/Current/Slattery-s-Sago-Saga.aspx.html.

110 Quidnunc, 'An Irishman's Diary', *The Irish Times*, 24 December 1943, p. 3.

111 Shelley Scott, *Nightwood Theatre: A woman's work is always done* (Edmonton: AU Press, 2010), p. 226.

112 Andrew Sherlock, 'Adapting Flann O'Brien's "The Brother"', *The Parish Review: Journal of Flann O'Brien studies*, vol. 1, no. 2, 2013, pp. 53–9.

113 A recording of the musical version of the poem that closed the play is available on YouTube: Gerry McGowan [Smyth], 'A Pint O' Plain', 15 August 2011, https://www.youtube.com/watch?v=e3Yyhof5hho.

114 'A Stage Adaptation of Flann O'Brien's *The Dead Spit of Kelly*', https://www.youtube.com/watch?v=6UYx1RYycP8.

115 Maeve Binchy, 'Selling the Shamrock', *The Irish Times*, 16 March 1985, p. 13.

116 The full script of *Yer Man and the Brother* is held at *Burns*, box 5, folder 13.

117 Binchy, 'Selling the Shamrock', p. 13.

118 Quidnunc, 'An Irishman's Diary', *The Irish Times*, 5 September 1968, p. 9.

119 David Nowlan, '"The Brother" at the Peacock', *The Irish Times*, 19 February 1974.

120 Elgy Gillespie, '"The Brother" at the Eblana', *Burns* box 7, folder 7.

121 Val O'Donnell, 'Adapting the Journalism of Myles for the Stage', *The Parish Review: Journal of Flann O'Brien studies*, vol. 4, no. 2, spring 2020, pp. 1–7.

122 Reviewed by Robert Hanks in *The Independent*, 16 August 1997.

123 Aidan Higgins, 'Discords of Good Humour', in *Darkling Plain: Texts for the air*, Daniel Jernigan (ed.) (London: Dalkey Archive Press, 2010), p. 113.

124 Mick Heaney, 'Wheels Come Off as Breakfast Hosts Driven to Distraction', *The Irish Times*, 1 April 2017, p. 50.

Bibliography

Primary

na gCopaleen, Myles, 'Drink and Time in Dublin', *Irish Writing*, no. 1, 1946, pp. 71–7

na Gopaleen, Myles, 'Two in One', *The Bell*, vol. 19, no. 8, July 1954, pp. 30–4

—, 'The Fausticity of Kelly', *RTV Guide*, 25 January 1963, pp. 12–13

—, 'De Me', *New Ireland: Magazine of the New Ireland Society of the Queen's University of Belfast*, no. 2, March 1964, pp. 41–2.

Nolan, Brian, 'Editorial Note: A bash in the tunnel', *Envoy*, April 1951, pp. 5–11.

O'Brien, Flann, *A Flann O'Brien Reader*, Stephen Jones (ed.) (New York: Viking, 1978)

—, *Rhapsody in Stephen's Green: The Insect Play*, Robert Tracy (ed.) (Dublin: Lilliput, 1994)

—, *At Swim-Two-Birds*, William H. Gass (ed.) (Normal: Dalkey Archive Press, 1998)

Secondary

Adar, Einat, 'From Irish Philosophy to Irish Theatre: The blind (wo)man made to see', *Estudios Irlandeses*, no. 12, 2017, pp. 1–11

Adorno, Theodor W., *Notes to Literature*, 2 vols, Shierry Weber Nicholsen (trans.) (New York: Columbia University Press, 1991)

Agamben, Giorgio, *The Open: Man and animal*, Kevin Attell (trans.) (Stanford: Stanford University Press, 2004)

Ahearn, Catherine and Adam Winstanley, 'An Inventory of Brian O'Nolan's Library at Boston College', *The Parish Review: Journal of Flann O'Brien studies*, vol. 2, no. 1, fall 2013, pp. 46–64

Akin IV, Warren, '"I Just Riz the Loy": The Oedipal dimensions of *The Playboy of the Western World*', *South Atlantic Bulletin*, vol. 45, no. 4, 1980, pp. 55–65

Allen, Kieran, *Fianna Fáil and Irish Labour: 1926 to the present* (London: Pluto, 1997)

Anderson, Benedict, *Imagined Communities: Reflections on the origin and spread of nationalism* (London: Verso, 2006)

Arnold, Bruce, *A Concise History of Irish Art* (London: Thames-Hudson, 1969)

Asensio Peral, Germán, 'The Origins of Flann O'Brien's *At Swim-Two-Birds*', *ES Revista de Filología Inglesa*, no. 36, 2015, pp. 47–62

Austin, J.L., *How to Do Things with Words* (Oxford: Oxford University Press, 1962; Cambridge, Harvard University Press, 1975)

Ayling, Ronald (ed.), *J.M. Synge: Four plays – a casebook* (Basingstoke: Macmillan, 1992)

Bagocius, Benjamin, 'Queer Entomology: Virginia Woolf's butterflies', *Modernism/ modernity*, vol. 24, no. 4, 2017, pp. 723–50

Baines, Jennika, '"Un-Understandable Mystery": Catholic Faith and revelation in *The Third Policeman*', *The Review of Contemporary Fiction*, vol. 31, no. 3, fall 2011, pp. 78–90

— (ed.), *'Is it about a bicycle?' Flann O'Brien in the twenty-first century* (Dublin: Four Courts Press, 2011)

Bair, Deirdre, *Samuel Beckett: A biography* (New York: Summit, 1990)

Bakhtin, Mikhail, *Problems of Dostoevsky's Poetics*, trans. and ed. Caryl Emerson (Minneapolis: Minnesota University Press, 1984)

—, *Rabelais and His World*, trans. Hélène Iswolsky (Bloomington: Indiana University Press, 1984)

Balkin, Sarah, *Spectral Characters: Genre and materiality on the modern stage* (Ann Arbor: University of Michigan Press, 2019)

Bámgbóṣé, Gabriel Sunday, 'Naturalist Aesthetics in John Millington Synge's *Riders to the Sea* and *The Playboy of the Western World*', *Humanicus*, no. 8, 2013, pp. 1–20

Barthes, Roland, *Image-Music-Text*, Stephen Heath (ed. and trans.) (London: Fontana, 1977)

Beck, Harald (ed.), *James Joyce's 'Penelope': The last chapter of Ulysses* (Stuttgart: Reclam, 1989)

Beckett, Samuel, *Watt* (New York: Grove, 1959)

—, *Disjecta: Miscellaneous writings and a dramatic fragment*, Ruby Cohn (ed.) (New York: Grove, 1984)

—, *The Collected Shorter Plays of Samuel Beckett* (New York: Grove, 1984)

—, *The Complete Dramatic Works* (London: Faber & Faber, 1986)

—, *The Letters of Samuel Beckett, Volume I, 1929–1940*, George Craig *et al.* (eds) (Cambridge: Cambridge University Press 2009)

—, *The Letters of Samuel Beckett, Volume II, 1941–1956*, George Craig *et al.* (eds) (Cambridge: Cambridge University Press, 2011)

Bedos-Rezak, Brigitte, *When Ego Was Imago: Signs of identity in the Middle Ages* (Leiden: Brill, 2011)

Bell, Michael and Peter Poellner (eds), *Myth and the Making of Modernity: The problem of grounding in early twentieth-century literature* (Amsterdam: Rodopi, 1998)

Benjamin, Walter, *Reflections: Essays, aphorisms, autobiographical writings* (New York: Random House, 1995)

—, *Illuminations* (London: Pimlico, 1999)

Bhreathnach-Lynch, Síghle, 'Twelve Irish Artists: A school of Irish painting?', *New Hibernia Review*, vol. 6, no. 2, pp. 130–4

Bickerstaff, Esq., Isaac, *Stephen's-Green: A rhapsody exhibiting the characters of the belles, beaux, bucks, bloods, flashes, fribbles, jemmies, jesssamies, &c. of all ranks and professions, that frequent the beau-walk* (Dublin: 'Printed for and sold by the Booksellers', 1763)

Blake, William, *The Poetry and Prose of William Blake*, Geoffrey Keynes (ed.) (London: Nonesuch Press, 1927)

Bloom, Gina, *Voice in Motion: Staging gender, shaping sound in early modern England* (Philadelphia: University of Pennsylvania Press, 2007)

Bobotis, Andrea, 'Queering Knowledge in Flann O'Brien's *The Third Policeman*', *Irish University Review*, vol. 32, no. 2, autumn/winter 2002, pp. 242–58

Booker, M. Keith, *Flann O'Brien, Bakhtin and Menippean Satire* (New York: Syracuse University Press, 1995)

Booth, Wayne, *A Rhetoric of Irony* (Chicago: University of Chicago Press, 1974)

Borg, Ruben, *Fantasies of Self-Mourning: Modernism, the posthuman and the finite* (Leiden and Boston: Brill|Rodopi, 2019)

Borg, Ruben and Paul Fagan (eds), *Flann O'Brien: Gallows humour* (Cork: Cork University Press, 2020)

Borg, Ruben, Paul Fagan and Werner Huber (eds), *Flann O'Brien: Contesting legacies* (Cork: Cork University Press, 2014)

Borg, Ruben, Paul Fagan and John McCourt (eds), *Flann O'Brien: Problems with authority* (Cork: Cork University Press, 2017)

Borges, Jorge Luis, *Other Inquisitions, 1937–1952*, R. Simms (trans.) (Austin: University of Texas Press, 1964)

—, *Selected Non-Fictions*, Eliot Weinberger (ed.) (New York: Penguin, 1999)

Bourdieu, Pierre, *Outline of a Theory of Practice* (Cambridge: Cambridge University Press, 1977)

—, *The Field of Cultural Production: Essays on art and literature* (Cambridge: Polity, 1993)

Bourgeois, Maurice, *John Millington Synge and the Irish Theatre* (London: Constable & Company, 1913)

Bradley, Anthony (ed.), *Contemporary Irish Poetry: An anthology* (Berkeley: University of California Press, 1980)

Braidotti, Rosi, *The Posthuman* (Malden: Polity Press, 2013)

—, 'The Critical Posthumanities; or, Is Medianatures to Naturecultures as Zoe is to Bios?', *Cultural Politics*, vol. 12, no. 3, 2016, pp. 380–90

Brecht, Bertolt, 'The Fourth Wall of China: An essay on the effect of disillusion in the Chinese theatre', Eric Walter White (trans.), *Life and Letters*, vol. 15, no. 6, winter 1936, pp. 116–23

—, *Brecht on Theatre: The development of an aesthetic*, John Willett (ed. and trans.) (New York: Farrar, Straus & Giroux, 2001)

Breuer, Rolf, 'Flann O'Brien and Samuel Beckett', *Irish University Review*, vol. 37, no. 2, 2007, pp. 340–51

Brooker, Joseph, *Flann O'Brien* (Tavistock: Northcote House, 2005)

—, 'Do Bicycles Dream of Atomic Sheep? Forms of the fantastic in Flann O'Brien and Philip K. Dick', *The Parish Review: Journal of Flann O'Brien studies*, vol. 4, no. 2, spring 2020, pp. 1–23

Brown, Karen, *The Yeats Circle: Verbal and visual relations in Ireland, 1880–1939* (Farnham: Ashgate, 2011)

Brown, Terence, *Ireland: A social and cultural history, 1922–2002* (London: Harper Perennial, 2004)

—, *The Irish Times: 150 years of influence* (London: Bloomsbury, 2015)

Buchanan, Bradley W., *Oedipus Against Freud: Myth and the end(s) of humanism in twentieth-century British literature* (Toronto: University of Toronto Press, 2010)

Budgen, Frank, *James Joyce and the Making of 'Ulysses' and Other Writings* (Oxford: Oxford University Press, 1972)

Bulwer-Lytton, Edward, *The Last Days of Pompeii*, vol. 1 (London: Richard Bentley, 1834)

Burian, Jarka M., 'K.H. Hilar and the Early Twentieth-Century Czech Theatre', *Theatre Journal*, vol. 34, no. 1, 1982, pp. 55–76

Butler, Judith, *Gender Trouble: Feminism and the subversion of identity* (London: Routledge, 1990)

—, *Bodies That Matter: On the discursive limits of 'sex'* (London: Routledge, 1993)

Butsch, Richard and Sonia Livingstone (eds), *Meanings of Audiences: Comparative discourses* (London: Routledge, 2014)

Cammack, Zan, *Ireland's Gramophones: Material culture, memory and trauma in Irish modernism* (Clemson: Clemson University Press, 2021)

Campana, Joseph, 'The Bee and the Sovereign: Political entomology and the problem of scale', *Shakespeare Studies*, no. 41, 2013, pp. 94–113

Čapek, Karel, *Four Plays: R.U.R., The Insect Play, The Makropulos Case, The White Plague*, Peter Majer and Cathy Porter (trans.) (London: Methuen, 1999)

Čapek, Karel and Josef, *R.U.R. and The Insect Play (And So Ad Finitum)*, Paul Selver (trans.), Nigel Playfair and Clifford Bax (adapt.) (Oxford: Oxford University Press, 1961; 2002)

Čapkové, Bratří, *Ze života hmyzu. Lidová knihovna Aventina Sv. 1* (Prague: Aventinum, 1924)

Cascardi, Anthony J. (ed.), *The Cambridge Companion to Cervantes* (Cambridge: Cambridge University Press, 2006)

Casebier, Allan, *Film and Phenomenology: Towards a realist theory of cinematic representation* (Cambridge: Cambridge University Press, 1991)

Catalogue of Printed Books formerly in the Library at Coole, the Property of the Lady Gregory Estate – Sotheby Auction Catalogue for 20 and 21 March 1972 (London: Sotheby & Co., 1972)

Chamberlain, Houston Stewart, *Goethe*, 3rd edn (Munich: F. Bruckmann, 1921)

Chion, Michael, *The Voice in Cinema*, trans. Claudia Gorbman (New York: Columbia University Press, 1999)

Clare, David, Des Lally and Patrick Lonergan (eds), *The Gate Theatre, Dublin: Inspiration and craft* (Oxford: Peter Lang, 2018)

Clissmann, Anne, *Flann O'Brien: A critical introduction to his writings* (Dublin: Gill & Macmillan, 1975; New York: Barnes & Noble Books, 1975)

Coates, Victoria C. Gardner, Kenneth Lapatin and Jon L. Seydl (eds), *The Last Days of Pompeii: Decadence, apocalypse, resurrection* (Los Angeles: J. Paul Getty Museum and the Cleveland Museum of Art, 2012)

Coelsch-Foisner, Sabine and Timo Heimerdinger (eds), *Theatralisierung* (Heidelberg: Universitätsverlag Winter, 2016)

Coleman, Deirdre, 'Entertaining Entomology: Insects and insect performers in the eighteenth century', *Eighteenth-Century Life*, no. 30, 2006, pp. 107–34

Conrad, Kathryn, Cóilín Parsons and Julie McCormick Weng (eds), *Science, Technology and Irish Modernism* (New York: Syracuse University Press, 2019)

Corporaal, Marguérite and Ruud van den Beuken (eds), *A Stage of Emancipation: Change and progress at the Dublin Gate Theatre* (Oxford: Oxford University Press, 2021)

Cosgrove, Mary, 'Ernie O'Malley: Art and modernism in Ireland', *Éire-Ireland*, vol. 40, nos 3–4, 2005, pp. 85–103

Costello, Peter and Peter van de Kamp, *Flann O'Brien: An illustrated biography* (London: Bloomsbury, 1987)

Coughlan, Patricia and Alex Davis (eds), *Modernism and Ireland: The poetry of the 1930s* (Cork: Cork University Press, 1995)

Coulouma, Flore, 'Tall Tales and Short Stories: *Cruiskeen Lawn* and the dialogic imagination', *Review of Contemporary Fiction*, vol. 31, no. 3, 2011, pp. 162–77

Cronin, Anthony, *Dead as Doornails: Bohemian Dublin in the fifties and sixties* (Oxford: Oxford University Press, 1976)

—, *No Laughing Matter: The life and times of Flann O'Brien* (London: Grafton, 1989; London: Paladin, 1990; New York: Fromm International, 1998; Dublin: New Island, 2003)

Cullingford, Elizabeth Butler, 'National Identities in Performance: The stage Englishman of Boucicault's Irish drama', *Theatre Journal*, vol. 49, no. 3, October 1997, pp. 287–300

Daly, Nicholas, 'The Many Lives of the Colleen Bawn: Pastoral suspense', *Journal of Victorian Culture*, vol. 12, no. 1, spring 2007, pp. 1–25

—, *The Demographic Imagination and the Nineteenth-Century City* (Cambridge: Cambridge University Press, 2015)

de Armas, Frederick A., *Quixotic Frescoes: Cervantes and Italian Renaissance art* (Toronto: University of Toronto Press, 2006)

De Chiara, Marilena, 'Life is a Succession of Habits: Pirandello's *Umorismo* and Beckett's *Proust*', *Pirandello Studies*, no. 29, 2009, pp. 38–45

Deák, František, 'Théâtre du Grand Guignol', *The Drama Review*, vol. 18, no. 1, March 1974, pp. 34–43

Dean, Joan FitzPatrick and José Lanters (eds), *Beyond Realism: Experimental and unconventional Irish drama since the Revival* (Leiden: Brill, 2014)

Deane, Seamus, *Strange Country: Modernity and nationhood in Irish writing since 1790* (Oxford: Clarendon, 1997)

—, *et al.* (eds), *The Field Day Anthology of Irish Writing, Volume II* (Derry: Field Day Publications, 1991)

Deleuze, Gilles and Felix Guattari, *A Thousand Plateaus: Capitalism and schizophrenia*, Brian Massumi (trans.) (London: Continuum, 2004)

Dent, Anthony (ed.), *International Modern Plays* (London: J.M. Dent & Sons Ltd, 1950)

Derrida, Jacques, *The Animal That Therefore I Am (More to Follow)*, David Wills (trans.), *Critical Inquiry*, vol. 28, no. 2, winter 2002, pp. 369–418

—, 'Who or What Is Compared? The concept of comparative literature and the theoretical problems of translation', Eric Prenowitz (trans.), *Discourse*, vol. 30, no. 1/2, 2008, pp. 22–53

Diamond, Elin (ed.), *Performance and Cultural Politics* (New York: Routledge, 1996)

Doane, Mary Ann, 'The Voice in the Cinema: The articulation of body and space', *Yale French Studies*, no. 60, *Cinema/Sound*, 1980, pp. 33–50

Dobbins, Gregory, *Lazy Irish Schemers: Irish modernism and the cultural politics of idleness* (Dublin: Field Day, 2010)

Dobrin, S.I. and S. Morey (eds), *Ecosee: Image, rhetoric, nature* (Albany: Suny Press, 2009)

Donohue, Keith, *The Irish Anatomist: A study of Flann O'Brien* (Dublin: Maunsel, 2002)

Douglas, R.M., 'Ailtiri na hAiséirghe: Ireland's fascist new order', *History Ireland*, vol. 17, no. 5, September–October 2009, p. 44.

Doyle, Rob, *The Other Irish Tradition: An anthology* (McLean: Dalkey Archive Press, 2018)

Dunleavy, Janet Egleson and Gareth W. Dunleavy, *Douglas Hyde: A maker of modern Ireland* (Berkeley: University of California Press, 1991)

Eagleton, Terry, *Heathcliff and the Great Hunger: Studies in Irish culture* (London: Verso, 1995)

—, *Figures of Dissent* (London: Verso, 2003)

Edelman, Lee, 'The Future Is Kid Stuff: Queer theory, disidentification and the death drive', *Narrative*, vol. 6, no. 1, January 1998, pp. 18–30

Elam, Keir, *The Semiotics of Theatre and Drama* (London: Methuen, 1980)

Eliot, T.S., *Selected Prose*, Frank Kermode (ed.) (London: Faber, 1975)

Ellmann, Maud, '*Ulysses*: Changing into an animal', *Field Day Review*, no. 2, 2006, pp. 74–93

Ellmann, Richard, *Yeats: The man and the masks* (New York: Macmillan, 1948)

Engel, Adam J., 'Talking Heads: Bodiless voices in *Heart of Darkness*, "The Hollow Men" and the First World War', *Conradiana*, vol. 45, no. 3, fall 2013, pp. 21–46

Fabre, Jean-Henri, *The Sacred Beetle and Others*, Alexander Teixeira de Mattos (trans.) (New York: Dodd, Mead & Company, 1918)

Fagan, Paul, '"Expert diagnosis has averted still another tragedy": Misreading and the paranoia of expertise in *The Third Policeman*', *The Parish Review: Journal of Flann O'Brien studies*, vol. 3, no. 1, fall 2014, pp. 12–41

Fagan, Paul, Dieter Fuchs and Tamara Radak (eds), *Stage Irish: Performance, identity, cultural circulation*, *Irish Studies in Europe*, vol. 10 (Trier: Wissenschaftlicher Verlag Trier, 2021)

Fallon, Gabriel, 'The Future of the Irish Theatre', *Studies: An Irish quarterly review*, vol. 44, no. 173, 1955, pp. 93–100

Faxedas, M. Lluïsa, 'Women Artists of Cercle et Carré: Abstraction, gender and modernity', *Woman's Art Journal*, vol. 36, no. 1, 2015, pp. 37–46

Feldman, Matthew, Erik Tönning and Henry Mead (eds), *Broadcasting in the Modernist Era* (London: Bloomsbury, 2014)

Fennell, Jack, 'Myles in Space: Science fiction and *Cruiskeen Lawn*', *The Parish Review: Journal of Flann O'Brien studies*, vol. 3, no. 1, fall 2014, pp. 64–77

—, 'The Case for John Shamus O'Donnell', *Journey Planet*, no. 43, 2018, pp. 28–38

Ferriter, Diarmaid, *The Transformation of Ireland 1900–2000* (London: Profile, 2005)

Flanders, Judith, *The Invention of Murder: How the Victorians revelled in death and detection* (London: Harper Press, 2011)

Foley, John, 'The Historical Origins of Flann O'Brien's Jem Casey', *Notes and Queries*, vol. 52, no. 1, March 2005, pp. 97–9

Foley, Martha, *The Story of STORY Magazine* (New York: W.W. Norton & Company, 1980)

Forster, Chris, *Modernism and Its Media* (London: Bloomsbury, 2021)

Foster, Halsey Edward, *William Saroyan* (Boise: Boise State University, 1984)

Foster, John Wilson (ed.), *The Cambridge Companion to the Irish Novel* (Cambridge: Cambridge University Press, 2006)

Foster, R.F., *W.B. Yeats: A Life. I: The Apprentice Mage 1865–1914* (Oxford: Oxford University Press, 1997)

Freshwater, Helen, *Theatre and Audience* (London: Palgrave Macmillan, 2009)

Freud, Sigmund, *The Interpretation of Dreams*, 3rd edn, A.A. Brill (trans.) (New York: The Macmillan Company, 1913)

Fricke, Gerhard, Franz Koch and Lemens Lugowski (eds), *Von Deutscher Art in Sprache und Dichtung*, vol. 4 (Stuttgart: W. Kohlhammer Verlag, 1941)

Gabler, Hans Walter, 'The Christmas Dinner Scene, Parnell's Death and the Genesis of *A Portrait of the Artist as a Young Man*', *James Joyce Quarterly*, vol. 13, no. 1, 1975, pp. 27–39

Gallagher, Monique, 'Flann O'Brien: Myles From Dublin', *The Princess Grace Irish Library Lectures: 7* (Gerrards Cross: Colin Smythe, 1991), pp. 7–24

Garrigan Mattar, Sinéad, *Primitivism, Science, and the Irish Revival* (Oxford: Clarendon, 2004)

Gassner, John (ed.), *Twenty Best European Plays on the American Stage* (New York: Crown Publishing, 1957)

Genet, Jacqueline and Richard Allen Cave (eds), *Perspectives of Irish Drama and Theatre: Irish literary studies*, no. 33 (Gerrards Cross: Colin Smythe, 1991)

Genette, Gérard, *Narrative Discourse: An essay in method*, Jane E. Lewin (trans.) (Ithaca: Cornell University Press, 1980)

Gewitz, Arthur and James J. Kolb (eds), *Art, Glitter and Glitz: Mainstream playwrights and popular theatre in 1920s America* (Westport: Praeger, 2004)

Gillespie, Alana, review of *Flann O'Brien: Plays and teleplays*, Daniel Keith Jernigan (ed.), *The Parish Review: Journal of Flann O'Brien studies*, vol. 2, no. 2, spring 2014, pp. 31–6

—, 'Pipes Aloft: *After Hours* and "Shows and Showers"', *The Parish Review: Journal of Flann O'Brien studies*, vol. 5, no. 2, fall 2021, pp. 1–6

Goethe, Johann Wolfgang von, *Goethe's Faust: Translated into English verse*, 2nd edn, George Lefevre (trans.) (London: D. Nutt, 1843)

—, *Faust: A Norton critical edition*, 2nd edn, Walter Arndt (trans.), Cyrus Hamlin (ed.) (New York: Norton, 2001)

Goldhill, Simon, *The Buried Life of Things: How objects made history in nineteenth-century Britain* (Cambridge: Cambridge University Press, 2015)

Gontarski, S.E., *Revisioning Beckett: Samuel Beckett's decadent turn* (London: Bloomsbury, 2018)

Goodall, Jane, 'Transferred Agencies: Performance and the fear of automatism', *Theatre Journal*, vol. 49, no. 4, 1997, pp. 441–53

Gordon, Mel, *Theatre of Fear and Horror: The grisly spectacle of the Grand Guignol of Paris, 1898–1962* (Port Townsend: Feral House, 2016)

Gray, Ronald, *Goethe: A critical introduction* (Cambridge: Cambridge University Press, 1967)

Gray, Tony, *Mr Smyllie, Sir* (Dublin: Gill & Macmillan, 1991)

Greaney, John, 'Resisting Representation: Flann O'Brien and Ireland', *Textual Practice*, vol. 34, no. 4, 2018, pp. 587–604

Gregory, Lady Augusta, *Gods and Fighting Men* (Gerrards Cross: Colin Smythe, 1970)

—, *The Collected Plays of Lady Gregory, Volume One: Comedies*, Ann Saddlemyer (ed.) (New York: Oxford University Press, 1970)

—, *Our Irish Theatre* (Gerrards Cross: Colin Smythe, 1972)

—, *Cuchulain of Muirthemne: The story of the men of the red branch of Ulster* (Gerrards Cross: Colin Smythe, 1975)

—, *Seventy Years: Being the autobiography of Lady Gregory* (Gerrards Cross: Colin Smythe, 1974)

Grene, Nicholas, *Synge: A critical study of the plays* (London: Macmillan, 1975)

Grene, Nicholas and Chris Morash (eds), *The Oxford Handbook of Modern Irish Theatre* (Oxford: Oxford University Press, 2016)

Griffin, Gerald, *The Collegians* (London: Atlantic, 2008)

Grimm, Reinhold and Jost Hermand (eds), *Our Faust? Roots and ramifications of a modern German myth* (Madison: University of Wisconsin Press, 1987)

Guild Howard, William (ed. and trans.), *Laokoon: Lessing, Herder and Goethe* (New York: Henry Holt, 1910)

Hamilton, Scott Eric, 'A Matter of Influence: Intersections of identity', *The Parish Review: Journal of Flann O'Brien studies* 5, no. 1, spring 2021, pp. 1–8

Haraway, Donna, *When Species Meet* (Minneapolis: University of Minnesota Press, 2008)

Harmon, Maurice (ed.), *The Celtic Master: Being contributions to the first James Joyce symposium in Dublin* (Dublin: Dolmen Press, 1969)

Harrington, John P., *The Irish Beckett* (New York: Syracuse University Press, 1991)

— (ed.), *Modern and Contemporary Irish Drama: Backgrounds and criticism*, 2nd edn (New York: W.W. Norton & Company, 2008)

Harris, Judith, *A Story of Rediscovery: Pompeii awakened* (London: Tauris, 2007)

Harris, Tobias W. and Joseph LaBine, 'John Garvin and Brian O'Nolan in Civil Service: Bureaucratic, Joycean modernism', *The Parish Review: Journal of Flann O'Brien studies*, vol. 6, no. 1, spring 2022, 1–17.

Hassan, Ihab, *The Literature of Silence: Henry Miller and Samuel Beckett* (New York: Alfred A. Knopf, 1967)

Hauskeller, Michael, Curtis D. Carbonell and Thomas D. Philbeck (eds), *The Palgrave Handbook of Posthumanism in Film and Television* (New York: Palgrave Macmillan, 2015)

Hawkes, Terence, *Structuralism and Semiotics* (London: Methuen, 1977)

Hayles, N. Katherine, *How We Became Posthuman: Virtual bodies in cybernetics, literature and informatics* (Chicago: The University of Chicago Press, 1999)

Heaney, Seamus, *Sweeney Astray: A version from the Irish* (Derry: Field Day Publications, 1983)

Hedges, Inez, *Framing Faust: Twentieth-century cultural struggles* (Carbondale: Southern Illinois University Press, 2005)

Heininge, Kathleen, *Buffoonery in Irish Drama: Staging twentieth-century post-colonial stereotypes* (New York: Peter Lang)

Henry, Melanie, *The Signifying Self: Cervantine drama as counter-perspective aesthetic* (London: The Modern Humanities Research Association, 2013)

Herbrechter, Stefan and Ivan Callus (eds), *Post/Theory, Culture, Criticism* (Amsterdam: Rodopi, 2004)

Higgins, Aidan, *Darkling Plain: Texts for the air*, Daniel Jernigan (ed.) (London: Dalkey Archive Press, 2010)

Hill, Judith, *Lady Gregory: An Irish life* (Stroud: Sutton, 2005)

Hogan, Robert, *After the Irish Renaissance* (Minneapolis: University of Minnesota Press, 1967)

Holfter, Gisela and Horst Dickel, *An Irish Sanctuary: German-speaking refugees in Ireland 1933–1945* (Berlin: Walter de Gruyter, 2017)

Holloway, Joseph, *Joseph Holloway's Irish Theatre*, 3 vols, Robert Hogan and Michael J. O'Neill (eds) (Dixon: Proscenium, 1999)

Hopper, Keith, *Flann O'Brien: A portrait of the artist as a young post-modernist* (Cork: Cork University Press, 1995)

—, *Flann O'Brien: A portrait of the artist as a young post-modernist*, 2nd edn, J. Hillis Miller (foreword) (Cork: Cork University Press, 2009)

Horace, *The Odes of Horace*, Jeremy H. Kaimowitz (trans.) (Baltimore: The Johns Hopkins University Press, 2008)

Houen, Alex (ed.), *Affect and Literature* (Cambridge: Cambridge University Press, 2019)

Hutton, Clare and Patrick Walsh (eds), *The Oxford History of the Irish Book, Volume IV: The Irish Book in English 1891–2000* (Oxford: Oxford University Press, 2011)

Ibsen, Henrik, *Hedda Gabler: A play in four acts*, Edmund Gosse and William Archer (trans.) (New York: The Floating Press, 2009)

Imhof, Rüdiger, 'How it is on the Fringes of Irish Fiction', *Irish University Review*, vol. 22, no. 1, spring/summer 1992, pp. 151–67

— (ed.), *Alive-Alive O! Flann O'Brien's At Swim-Two-Birds* (Dublin: Wolfhound, 1985)

Iremonger, Valentin, *Reservations* (Dublin: Envoy, 1950)

Irving, Washington, *The Legend of Sleepy Hollow and Other Stories* (New York: Penguin, 1978)

Jackson, John Wyse, 'Profits in Their Own Land? Brian O'Nolan and Patrick Kavanagh', *The Parish Review: Journal of Flann O'Brien studies*, vol. 2, no. 2, spring 2014, pp. 4–14

James, Richard S., 'Avant-Garde Sound-on-Film Techniques and Their Relationship to Electro-Acoustic Music', *The Musical Quarterly*, vol. 72, no. 1, 1986, pp. 74–89

Jameson, Fredric, *Postmodernism, or, the Cultural Logic of Late Capitalism* (Durham: Duke University Press, 1991)

Jernigan, Daniel Keith, '"Simulat Ergo Est": Brian O'Nolan's metaperformative simulations', *New Hibernia Review*, vol. 20, no. 1, spring/earrach 2016, pp. 87–104

— (ed.), *Drama and the Postmodern: Assessing the limits of metatheatre* (Amherst: Cambria Press, 2008)

Johnson, Stephen, 'The Integration of Theatre History and Theatre Practice in the University: A case study using *Ze života hmyzu* (*From the Life of Insects*) by Karel and Josef Capek', *Theatre Topics*, vol. 4, no. 2, 1994, pp. 189–204

Johnston, Kirsty, *Disability Theatre and Modern Drama: Recasting modernism* (London: Bloomsbury Methuen Drama, 2016)

Jones, Ernest, 'The Oedipus-Complex as an Explanation of Hamlet's Mystery: A study in motive', *American Journal of Psychology*, no. 21, 1910, pp. 72–113

Joyce, James, *A Portrait of the Artist as a Young Man: Text, criticism and notes*, ed. Chester G. Anderson (New York: Penguin Books, 1968)

—, *Ulysses*, Hans Walter Gabler (ed.) (New York: Vintage, 1986)

—, *Ulysses* (London: Penguin, 1992; 2000)

—, *Dubliners*, Hans Walter Gabler and Walter Hettche (eds) (New York: Garland, 1993)

—, *Ulysses*, Oxford World's Classics, Jeri Johnson (introd. and ed.) (Oxford: Oxford University Press, 1998)

—, *James Joyce: Occasional, critical and political writing*, Kevin Barry (ed.) (Oxford: Oxford University Press, 2002)

Joyce, Trevor, *With the First Dream of Fire They Hunt the Cold: A body of work 1966–2000* (Dublin: New Writers' Press, 2001)

—, *Courts of Air and Earth* (Exeter: Shearsman, 2008)

Kaganovsky, Lilya, *The Voice of Technology: Soviet cinema's transition to sound, 1928–1935* (Bloomington: Indiana University Press, 2018)

Kaiser, Birgit Mara (ed.), *Singularity and Transnational Poetics* (London: Routledge, 2015)

Kearney, Richard, *Transitions: Narratives in Irish culture* (Dublin: Wolfhound Press, 1988)

Kennelly, Brendan, *The Penguin Book of Irish Verse* (London: Penguin, 1970)

Kenner, Hugh, *A Colder Eye: The modern Irish writers* (New York: Knopf, 1983)

Keown, Edwina and Carol Taaffe (eds), *Irish Modernism: Origins, contexts, publics* (Bern: Peter Lang, 2010)

Kiberd, Declan, *Inventing Ireland: The literature of a modern nation* (London: Vintage, 1996)

—, *Irish Classics* (Cambridge: Harvard University Press, 2001)

Kirkpatrick, Kathryn J. and Borbála Faragó (eds), *Animals in Irish Literature and Culture* (Basingstoke: Palgrave Macmillan, 2015)

Klibansky, Raymond, Erwin Panofsky and Fritz Saxl, *Saturn und Melancholie: Studien zur Geschichte der Naturphilosophie und Medizin, der Religion und der Kunst*, 3rd edn (Frankfurt: Suhrkamp, 1998)

Kristeva, Julia, *Desire in Language: A semiotic approach to literature and art*, Leon S. Roudiez (ed.), Thomas Gora, Alice Jardine and Leon S. Roudiez (trans.) (New York: Columbia University Press, 1980)

Kundera, Milan, *The Art of the Novel*, Linda Asher (trans.) (New York: Perennial Classics, 2003)

Laguna, Ana María G., *Cervantes and the Pictorial Imagination* (Lewisburg: Bucknell University Press, 2009)

Lanters, José, *Unauthorized Versions: Irish Menippean satire, 1919–1952* (Washington: Catholic University of America Press, 2000)

Levin, Yael, 'Who Hobbles after the Subject: Parables of writing in *The Third Policeman* and *Molloy*', *Journal of Modern Literature*, vol. 40, no. 4, 2017, pp. 105–21

Levitt, Paul Michael, 'Fathers and Sons in Synge's *The Playboy of the Western World*', *The Explicator*, vol. 66, no. 1, 2007, pp. 18–21

Lloyd, Michael, 'Playboy of the Ancient World? Synge and the classics', *Classics Ireland*, no. 18, 2011, pp. 52–68

Long, Maebh, *Assembling Flann O'Brien* (London: Bloomsbury, 2014)

—, 'Is It About a Typewriter? Brian O'Nolan and technologies of inscription', *The Parish Review: Journal of Flann O'Brien studies*, vol. 4, no. 2, spring 2020, pp. 1–16

Love, Heather, 'Close but Not Deep: Literary ethics and the descriptive turn', *New Literary History*, vol. 41, no. 2, 2010, pp. 371–91

Luppi, Fabio, *Fathers and Sons at the Abbey Theatre (1904–1938): A new perspective on the study of Irish drama* (Irvine: Brown Walker, 2018)

Lyttle, Charles H., 'Historical Bases of Rome's Conflict with Freemasonry', *Church History*, vol. 9, no. 1, 1940, pp. 3–23

M. [T.S. Munden], 'On the Less Celebrated Productions of the Author of *Don Quixote*', *New Monthly Magazine*, no. 1, 1821, pp. 113–21

MacDonagh, Donagh (ed.), *Poems from Ireland*, Donagh MacDonagh (introd.), R.M. Smyllie (preface) (Dublin: The Irish Times, 1944)

MacDonagh, Donagh and Lennox Robinson (eds), *The Oxford Book of Irish Verse* (Oxford: Oxford University Press, 1958)

MacGreevy, Thomas, *Poems* (New York: Viking, 1934)

MacKenzie, Scott (ed.), *Film Manifestos and Global Cinema Cultures: A critical anthology* (Berkeley: University of California Press, 2014)

MacLean, Hugh H., 'The Hero as Playboy', *University of Kansas City Review*, no. 21, 1954, pp. 9–19

MacNamara, Brinsley, *Margaret Gillan* (London: George Allen & Unwin, 1934)

MacNeice, Louis, *The Poetry of W.B. Yeats* (Oxford: Oxford University Press, 1948)

Mannion, Elizabeth, *The Urban Plays of the Early Abbey Theatre: Beyond O'Casey* (New York: Syracuse University Press, 2014)

Marlowe, Christopher, *Dr Faustus*, 2nd edn, Roma Gill (ed.) (London: Methuen, 1989)

Marquardt, Johanna, 'An Interview with the Brother', *The Parish Review: Journal of Flann O'Brien studies*, vol. 3, no. 1, fall 2014, pp. 78–89

Maslen, R.W., 'Flann O'Brien's Bombshells: *At Swim-Two-Birds* and *The Third Policeman*', *New Hibernia Review*, vol. 10, no. 4, 2006, pp. 84–104

Mathewes, Jeffrey, 'The Manichaean Body in *The Third Policeman*: or Why Joe's Skin Is Scaly', *The Scriptorium: Flann O'Brien* (2005)

Mayer, Vicki, Miranda J. Banks and John T. Caldwell (eds), *Production Studies: Cultural studies of media industries* (New York: Routledge, 2009)

Mazzeo, Tilar J., *Plagiarism and Literary Property in the Romantic Period* (Philadelphia: University of Pennsylvania Press, 2004)

McAteer, Michael (ed.), *Silence in Modern Irish Literature* (Leiden: Brill, 2016)

McCaw, Dick, *Bakhtin and Theatre: Dialogues with Stanislavsky, Meyerhold and Grotowski* (London: Routledge, 2016)

McCourt, John (ed.), *Reading Brendan Behan* (Cork: Cork University Press, 2019)

McFeely, Deirdre, *Dion Boucicault: Irish identity on stage* (Cambridge: Cambridge University Press, 2012)

McHale, Brian, *Postmodernist Fiction* (London: Routledge 2001)

McLoughlin, Michael, 'At Swim Six Characters or Two Birds in Search of an Author: Fiction, metafiction and reality in Pirandello and Flann O'Brien', *Yearbook of the Society for Pirandello Studies*, no. 12, 1992, pp. 24–31

McMullen, Kim, 'Culture as Colloquy: Flann O'Brien's postmodern dialogue with Irish tradition', *NOVEL: A forum on fiction*, vol. 28, no. 1, 1993, pp. 62–84

McNulty, Eugene, 'The Cultural Afterlife of the Colleen Bawn Murder: From crime scene to law scene', *New Hibernia Review*, vol. 20, no. 2, summer 2016, pp. 98–114

Mikula, Anna and Peter Haag (eds), *Der Grosse Bär und seine Gestirne: Freunde und Weggefährten Grüssen, Dichten und Malen zum 60. Geburtstag von Harry Rowohlt* (Zürich: Kein & Aber, 2005)

Mills Harper, Margaret and Warwick Gould (eds), *Yeats's Mask: Yeats Annual No. 19* (Cambridge: Open Book Publishers, 2013)

Modleski, Tania (ed.), *Studies in Entertainment: Critical approaches to mass culture* (Bloomington: Indiana University Press, 1986)

Montague, John, *A Chosen Light* (London: MacGibbon & Kee, 1967)

Montgomery, Niall, *Niall Montgomery: Dublinman – Selected writings*, Christine O'Neil (ed.) (Dublin: Ashfield Press, 2015)

Moore, Steven, *The Novel: An alternative history – beginnings to 1600* (New York: Continuum, 2010)

—, *The Novel: An alternative history – 1600–1800* (London: Bloomsbury, 2013)

Moore, Walter, *Schrödinger: Life and thought* (Cambridge: Cambridge University Press, 1992)

Morash, Christopher, *A History of Irish Theatre, 1601–2000* (Cambridge: Cambridge University Press, 2002)

Morash, Chris and Shawn Richards, *Mapping Irish Theatre: Theories of space and place* (London: Cambridge University Press, 2013)

Morin, Emilie, *Samuel Beckett and the Problem of Irishness* (Basingstoke: Palgrave Macmillan, 2009)

—, 'W.B. Yeats and Broadcasting, 1924–1965', *Historical Journal of Film, Radio and Television*, vol. 35, no. 1, 2015, pp. 145–75

Morra, Linda M. (ed.), *Moving Archives* (Waterloo, ON: Wilfrid Laurier University Press, 2020)

Morris, Catherine, *Alice Milligan and the Irish Cultural Revival* (Dublin: Four Courts Press, 2012)

Murphet, Julian, Rónán McDonald and Sascha Morrell (eds), *Flann O'Brien & Modernism* (London: Bloomsbury, 2014)

Murphy, Brenda, '*The Iceman Cometh* in Context: An American Saloon Trilogy', *The Eugene O'Neill Review*, no. 26, 2004, pp. 215–25

Murray, Rachel, 'Beelines: Joyce's apian aesthetics', *Humanities*, vol. 6, no. 2, 2017, https://doi.org/10.3390/h6020042

Nejezchleb, Amy, 'The Myles Brand Franchise', *The Parish Review: Journal of Flann O'Brien studies*, vol. 1, no. 2, winter 2013, pp. 42–7

Nietzsche, Friedrich, *Beyond Good and Evil*, R.J. Holingdale (trans.) (London: Penguin, 2003)

—, *The Birth of Tragedy*, Shaun Whiteside (trans.) (London: Penguin, 2003)

O'Connell, Daragh, 'Pirandello and Joyce Say Yes! in Denis Johnston's *The Old Lady Says No!*', *Pirandello Studies*, no. 27, 2007, pp. 75–92

O'Curry, Eugene, *Lectures on the Manuscript Material of Ancient Irish History* (Dublin: Duffy, 1861)

Ó Dónaill, Niall, *Foclóir Gaeilge-Béarla*, Tomás De Bhaldraithe, Eagarthóir Comhairleach (Baile Átha Cliath: An Gum, 1992 [1977])

O'Donnell, Val, 'Adapting the Journalism of Myles for the Stage', *The Parish Review: Journal of Flann O'Brien studies*, vol. 4, no. 2, spring 2020, pp. 1–7

O'Farrell, Padraic, *The Burning of Brinsley MacNamara* (Dublin: Lilliput, 1990)

Ó hÁinle, Cathal G., 'Fionn and Suibhne in *At Swim-Two-Birds*', *Hermathena*, no. 142, 1987, pp. 11–49

O'Keeffe, Timothy (ed.), *Myles: Portraits of Brian O'Nolan* (London: Martin, Brian & O'Keeffe, 1973)

O'Leary, Peter, *Shiana* (Dublin: The Irish Book Company, 1916)

O'Leary, Philip, *The Prose Literature of the Gaelic Revival* (University Park, PA: Penn State University Press, 1994)

O'Neill, Patrick, 'The Reception of German Literature in Ireland 1750–1850: Part 2', *Studia Hibernica*, no. 17/18, 1977/8, pp. 91–106

Ó Nualláin, Ciarán, Óige an Dearthár .i. Myles na gCopaleen (Baile Átha Cliath: Foilseacháin Náisiúnta Teoranta, 1973)

Ó Nualláin, Ciarán, The Early Years of Brian O'Nolan (Dublin: Lilliput, 1998)

Ó Nualláin, Micheál, The Brother (Myles) (Dublin: Self-published, 2011)

Oțoiu, Adrian, '"Compartmentation of personality for the purpose of literary utterance": Pseudonymity and heteronymity in the various lives of Flann O'Brien', Word and Text: A journal of literary studies and linguistics, vol. 1, no. 1, 2011, pp. 128–38

Parikka, Jussi, Insect Media: An archaeology of animals and technology (Minneapolis: University of Minnesota Press, 2010)

Parker, Patricia and Geoffrey Hartmann (eds), Shakespeare and the Question of Theory (New York: Methuen, 1985)

Pavis, Patrice, Dictionary of the Theatre: Terms, concepts and analysis, Christine Shantz (trans.) (Toronto: University of Toronto Press, 1998)

Pelias, Ronald J., Performance Studies: The interpretation of aesthetic texts (New York: St Martin's Press, 1992)

Percas de Ponseti, Helena, Cervantes: The writer and painter of Don Quijote (Columbia: University of Missouri Press, 1988)

Phelan, Peggy, Mourning Sex: Performing public memories (London: Routledge, 1997)

Phizmiz, Ergo, 'Colour, Noise, and Craniums: Adapting The Third Policeman as an electronic opera', The Parish Review: Journal of Flann O'Brien studies, vol. 1, no. 1 (summer 2012), pp. 32–8

Pilkington, Lionel, Theatre and the State in Twentieth-Century Ireland: Cultivating the people (London: Routledge, 2001)

—, Theatre & Ireland (Basingstoke: Palgrave Macmillan, 2010)

Pilný, Ondřej, '"My kingdom for a pun": Myles na gCopaleen, Erwin Schrödinger and The Third Policeman in Improbable Frequency', Irish Theatre International, vol. 1, no. 1, 2008, pp. 38–52

Pilný, Ondřej, Ruud van den Beuken and Ian R. Walsh (eds), Cultural Convergence: The Dublin Gate Theatre, 1928–1960 (London: Palgrave 2020)

Pirandello, Luigi, Three Plays (New York: Dutton, 1922)

—, Better Think Twice About It! (London: John Lane, 1933)

—, Quattro Novelle (London: Harrap, 1939)

—, Luigi Pirandello: Short stories, Frederick May (ed. and trans.) (London: Oxford University Press, 1965)

—, Tales of Madness: A selection from Luigi Pirandello's short stories for a year (Brookline Village: Dante University of America Press, 1984)

—, Three Plays, Robert Rietty, Noel Creegan, John Linstrum and Julian Mitchell (trans.) (London: Methuen, 1993)

—, Sei Personaggi in cerca d'autore, Einaudi Tascabili, Classici 118 (Torino: Einaudi, 1993)

—, Eleven Short Stories, Stanley Applebaum (ed. and trans.) (New York: Dover Publications, 1994)

Poovey, Mary, 'Creative Criticism: Adaptation, performative writing and the problem of objectivity', Narrative, vol. 8, no. 2, May 2000, pp. 109–33

Puchner, Martin, *Stage Fright: Modernism, anti-theatricality and drama* (Baltimore: Johns Hopkins University Press, 2002)

Quintelli-Neary, Marguerite, *Folklore and the Fantastic in Twelve Modern Irish Novels* (Westport: Greenwood, 1997)

Rabaté, Jean-Michel, *The Pathos of Distance: Affects of the modern* (London: Bloomsbury, 2016)

Reed, Cory A., 'Cervantes and the Novelisation of Drama: Tradition and innovation in the *entremeses*', *Cervantes: Bulletin of the Cervantes Society of America*, vol. 11, no. 1, 1991, pp. 61–86

Reed, Helen H., 'Theatricality in the Picaresque of Cervantes', *Cervantes: Bulletin of the Cervantes Society of America*, vol. 7, no. 2, 1987, pp. 71–84

Remport, Eglantina, *Lady Gregory and Irish National Theatre: Art, drama, politics* (Basingstoke: Palgrave Macmillan, 2018)

Richards, Jeffrey, *The Ancient World on the Victorian and Edwardian Stage* (Basingstoke: Palgrave, 2009)

Richards, Shaun (ed.), *The Cambridge Companion to Twentieth-Century Irish Drama* (Cambridge: Cambridge University Press, 2004)

Robin, Thierry, 'Representation as a Hollow Form, or the Paradoxical Magic of Idiocy and Skepticism in Flann O'Brien's Works', *The Review of Contemporary Fiction*, vol. 31, no. 3, fall 2011, pp. 33–48

Robinson, Douglas, *Estrangement and the Somatics of Literature: Tolstoy, Shklovsky, Brecht* (Baltimore: Johns Hopkins University Press, 2008)

Robinson, Lennox (ed.), *The Irish Theatre: Lectures delivered during the Abbey Theatre Festival held in Dublin in August 1938* (New York: Haskell House, 1971 [1939])

Roche, Anthony, 'Oedipus at the Abbey', *Classic Ireland*, no. 8, 2001, pp. 102–10

—, 'Re-Working "The Workhouse Ward": McDonagh, Beckett, and Gregory', *Irish University Review*, vol. 34, no. 1, 2004, pp. 171–84

Rodger, Ian, *Radio Drama* (London: Macmillan, 1982)

Rowell, George (ed.), *Nineteenth-Century Plays* (London: Oxford University Press, 1953)

Russell, George, *The Candle of Vision* (London: Macmillan, 1918)

Ryan, John, *Remembering How We Stood: Bohemian Dublin at the mid-century* (Dublin: Lilliput, 2008)

Ryan, John (ed.), *A Bash in the Tunnel: James Joyce by the Irish* (Brighton: Clifton, 1970)

Saguaro, Shelley (ed.), *Psychoanalysis and Woman: A reader* (New York: New York University Press, 2000)

Saroyan, William, *The Daring Young Man on the Flying Trapeze and Other Stories* (New York: Harcourt Brace, 1934)

—, *Peace: It's wonderful* (New York: Modern Age Books, 1939)

—, *Razzle Dazzle* (New York: Harcourt Brace & Company, 1942)

—, *Three Plays: The Beautiful People, Sweeney in the Trees, and Across the Board on To-morrow Morning* (London: Faber & Faber, 1943)

—, *The Human Comedy* (New York: Harcourt Brace, 1943)

Schechner, Richard, *Performance Studies: An introduction* (London: Routledge, 2002)

Schnapp, Jeffrey and Mathew Tiews (eds), *Crowds* (Stanford: Stanford University Press, 2006)

Schott, Georg, *Goethes Faust in heutiger Schau* (Stuttgart: Tazzelwurm Verlag, 1940)

Scott, Shelley, *Nightwood Theatre: A woman's work is always done* (Edmonton: AU Press, 2010)

Shakespeare, William, *The Complete Works of William Shakespeare*, John Dover Wilson (ed.) (London: Octopus Books, 1984)

Shea, Thomas F., *Flann O'Brien's Exorbitant Novels* (Lewisburg: Bucknell University Press, 1992)

—, 'Patrick McGinley's Impressions of Flann O'Brien: *The Devil's Diary* and *At Swim-Two-Birds*', *Twentieth-Century Literature*, vol. 40, no. 2, summer 1994, pp. 272–81

Sheppard, Jennifer, 'How the "Vixen" Lost Its Mores: Gesture and music in Janáček's animal opera', *Cambridge Opera Journal*, vol. 22, no. 2, 2010, pp. 147–74

Sheridan, Niall, 'Matter of Life and Death', *Esquire*, October 1939, p. 110

—, 'Brian O'Nolan: A postscript', *Meanjin*, vol. 30, no. 2, 1971, p. 240

Sherlock, Andrew, 'Adapting Flann O'Brien's "The Brother"', *The Parish Review: Journal of Flann O'Brien studies*, vol. 1, no. 2, 2013, pp. 53–9

Shin, Hyewon, 'Voice and Vision in Oshii Mamoru's *Ghost in the Shell*: Beyond Cartesian optics', *Animation*, vol. 6, no. 7, 2011, pp. 7–23

Spariosu, Mihai (ed.), *Mimesis in Contemporary Theory* (Amsterdam: John Benjamin, 1984)

Squiers, Anthony, *An Introduction to the Social and Political Philosophy of Bertolt Brecht: Revolution and aesthetics* (Amsterdam: Rodopi, 2014)

Staley, Gregory A., *Seneca and the Idea of Tragedy* (Oxford: Oxford University Press, 2010)

Steiner, George, *Language and Silence: Essays on language, literature and the inhuman* (New York: Atheneum, 1967)

Stewart, Susan, *Nonsense: Aspects of intertextuality in folklore and literature* (Baltimore: Johns Hopkins University Press, 1979)

Stoller, Terry, *Tales of the Tricycle Theatre* (London: Bloomsbury, 2013)

Sturgeon, Sinéad, *Essays on James Clarence Mangan: The man in the cloak* (Basingstoke: Palgrave Macmillan, 2014)

Sullivan, Alvin (ed.), *British Literary Magazines: The modern age, 1914–1984* (New York: Greenwood Press, 1986)

Sullivan, Mary Rose, 'Synge, Sophocles and the Un-Making of Myth', *Modern Drama*, vol. 12, no. 3, 1969, pp. 242–53

Synge, J.M., *Collected Works, Vol. 4: Plays, Book 2*, Ann Saddlemyer (ed.) (London: Oxford University Press, 1968)

—, *The Playboy of the Western World and Other Plays*, Ann Saddlemyer (ed.) (Oxford: Oxford University Press, 1995)

Taaffe, Carol, *Ireland Through the Looking-Glass: Flann O'Brien, Myles na gCopaleen and Irish cultural debate* (Cork: Cork University Press, 2008)

—, rev. of *The Short Fiction of Flann O'Brien*, *The Parish Review: Journal of Flann O'Brien studies*, vol. 2, no. 1, fall 2013, pp. 65–8

Thomson, Peter and Glendyr Sacks (eds), *The Cambridge Companion to Brecht* (New York: Cambridge University Press, 1994)

Timms, Edward, *Karl Kraus: Apocalyptic Satirist, Vol. II: The post-war crisis and the rise of the swastika* (New Haven: Yale University Press, 2005)

Tymoczko, Maria, 'Amateur Theatricals, *Tableaux Vivants* and Cathleen ni Houlihan', *Yeats Annual*, no. 10, 1993, pp. 33–64

Van den Beuken, Ruud, *Avant-Garde Nationalism at the Dublin Gate Theatre, 1928–1940* (New York: Syracuse University Press, 2021)

Van Hulle, Dirk, 'Samuel Beckett's "Faust" Notes', *Samuel Beckett Today/Aujourd'hui*, no. 16, 2006, pp. 283–97

Vinnai, Gerhard, *Jesus und Oedipus: Zur Psychoanalyse der Religion* (Fischer: Frankfurt am Main, 1999)

Vintaloro, Giordano, 'Brian O'Nolan, the Conspirator', *Studi Irlandesi*, no. 7, 2017, pp. 261–82

Walker, Jarrett, 'Voiceless Bodies and Bodiless Voices: The drama of human perception in *Coriolanus*', *Shakespeare Quarterly*, vol. 43, no. 2, summer 1992, pp. 170–85

Watson, Nick and Simo Vehmaas (eds), *The Routledge Handbook of Disability Studies* (New York: Routledge, 2019)

Waugh, Patricia, *Metafiction: The theory and practice of self-conscious fiction* (London: Routledge, 2002)

Welch, Robert, *The Abbey Theatre 1899–1999: Form and pressure* (Oxford: Oxford University Press, 1999)

— (ed.), *The Oxford Companion to Irish Literature* (Oxford: Oxford University Press, 2001)

—, *The Abbey Theatre, 1899–1999: Form and pressure* (Oxford: Oxford University Press, 2003)

White, John J., *Bertolt Brecht's Dramatic Theory* (Rochester: Camden House, 2004)

Whitehead, Kate, *The Third Programme: A literary history* (Oxford: Clarendon Press, 1989)

Whitty, Michael James, *Tales of Irish Life: Illustrative of the manners, customs and condition of the people* (London: J. Robins & Co., 1824)

Wills, Clair, *That Neutral Island: A cultural history of Ireland during the Second World War* (London: Faber & Faber, 2007)

Wilson, Margaret, *Spanish Drama of the Golden Age* (Oxford: Pergamon, 1969)

Withers, Jeremy and Daniel P. Shea (eds), *Culture on Two Wheels: The bicycle in literature and film* (Lincoln: University of Nebraska Press, 2016)

Wright, Julia M. (ed.), *Irish Literature 1750–1900* (New York: Blackwell, 2008)

Yeats, W.B., *The Collected Plays of W.B. Yeats* (London: Macmillan, 1952)

—, *The Autobiography of William Butler Yeats* (New York: Collier, 1965)

—, *Uncollected Prose of W.B. Yeats, Vol. 2: Reviews, articles and other miscellaneous prose*, J.P. Frayne and C. Johnson (eds) (London: Macmillan, 1975)

—, *Collected Poems*, Augustine Martin (ed.) (London: Vintage, 1990)

—, *The Poems*, Daniel Albright (ed.) (London: Everyman, 1992; 1994)

Younger, Kelly, 'Irish Antigones: Burying the colonial symptom', *Colloquy: Text, theory, critique*, no. 11, 2006, pp. 148–62

Zuese, Alicia R., *Baroque Spain and the Writing of Visual and Material Culture* (Cardiff: University of Wales Press, 2015)

Index

NOTE: Page locators in **bold** refer to pictures/illustrations.